THE
INVENTIONS
OF
MARK TWAIN

Also by John Lauber

THE MAKING OF MARK TWAIN: A Biography

THE
INVENTIONS
OF
MARK TWAIN

JOHN LAUBER

HILL AND WANG — New York

A division of Farrar, Straus and Giroux

All but two of the photographs in this volume are reproduced through the courtesy of the Mark Twain Memorial
in Hartford, Connecticut.

Mark Twain, 1868, and the family portrait of Mark Twain,
Olivia, and their three daughters are reproduced courtesy
the Mark Twain Papers, Bancroft Library, University of California, Berkeley, California.

Copyright © 1990 by John Lauber

All rights reserved

Published simultaneously in Canada by Harper & Collins, Toronto

Printed in the United States of America

First edition, 1990

Designed by Design Oasis

Library of Congress Cataloging-in-Publication Data
Lauber, John.
  The inventions of Mark Twain.
  Includes indexes.
  Bibliography: p.
  1. Authors, American—19th century—Biography.
2. Humorists, American—19th century—Biography.
I. Title.
PS1331.L377 1989   818'.409 [B]   89-11055

For Jean, as always

ACKNOWLEDGMENTS

I wish first to thank my own university, the University of Alberta, for providing me with time—through leaves of absence and reduced teaching loads—for the preparation of this book. I am grateful as well to the staff of the Stowe-Day Foundation, in Hartford, Connecticut, for their courtesy and helpfulness in showing me relevant documents and photographs. Finally, I must acknowledge a deep debt to the staff of the Mark Twain Papers at the University of California at Berkeley for their unfailing helpfulness in aiding me to find my way through their holdings of unpublished correspondence, manuscripts, and documents of every sort.

CONTENTS

Preface xi

1. Apprentice 3
2. Author 21
3. Return to the River 54
4. The Dimensions of Success 72
5. *Huckleberry Finn* 103
6. Colonel Sellers 124
7. Mugwump 150
8. Twins of Genius 167
9. "The Best Book Ever Written" 196
10. Publisher to a Hero 208
11. Standing Outside the Door of Plenty 234
12. "Immortal Hopefulness" 260
13. "Shall We Ever Laugh Again?" 292
    Sources 309
    Notes 315
    Index 327

Photographs follow page 180.

PREFACE

Mark Twain was fascinated by the inventions of his century, which seemed to him to prove its immense superiority over all earlier periods. The inventors were "poets in steel," as he called James Paige, creator of an incredibly complex automatic typesetting machine. Mark Twain himself was an inventor in a small way, patenting a self-pasting scrapbook and a self-adjusting vest strap, copyrighting a game to teach historical facts, even imagining microprint. He invested heavily in other men's inventions, a "steam generator" and an engraving process (both failures), and between 1886 and 1890 he spent and lost a fortune in developing the Paige typesetter. To the end of his life he could not resist a novelty, whether a carpet-weaving machine, a health food made from dried milk, or a spiral hairpin.

As an inventor himself, Twain was no more than a gadgeteer, and in backing other men's inventions, he invariably chose badly. But invention is not limited to technology or to gadgetry. A successful writer, by definition, is a creator, a true inventor, making that which had never existed before. *Huckleberry Finn*, that profoundly innovative work, was an invention, at least as original as Edison's phonograph, and Mark Twain's other major fictions—*Tom Sawyer, A Connecticut Yankee in King Arthur's Court, Pudd'nhead Wilson*—were inventions, too. So even were such apparently factual and autobiographical writings as the early chapters of *Life on the Mississippi*, describing Sam Clemens's apprenticeship as a steamboat pilot, or *Roughing It*, supposedly recounting the actual experiences of Mark Twain in the West. But the "Mark Twain" of those books is at least a semifictional character, often far different from the Sam Clemens of biographical reality, and a good many of his experiences either did not happen or happened to other people.

And "Mark Twain," the authorial self that first appeared in February of 1863, when the earliest pieces signed with that name were printed in the Virginia City *Territorial Enterprise*, and that would in time create *Huckleberry Finn*, was likewise an invention—to be refined and elaborated over the next forty-seven years.

But if "Mark Twain" was an invention, so in a sense was "Samuel Clemens, Esq.," of 351 Farmington Avenue, Hartford, Connecticut—businessman, citizen, husband, and father—and so were his way of life, his home and his family and his marriage, all at least half-consciously designed according to the highest ideals of the age. One might say that there was the self that created, "Mark Twain," and the self that lived, "Samuel Clemens," but that would be to oversimplify—the artist lives most keenly in his moments of creation. There was no crude dichotomy, with the artist Mark Twain stifled by the Victorian gentility of Clemens. Those two selves were not at war with each other; rather, they were mutually dependent. But while "Samuel Clemens" was known to his family, his friends and neighbors, his business associates, "Mark Twain" made himself known to the American people and then to the English-speaking world, and finally to the world in general.

The Inventions of Mark Twain covers Twain's entire life and career, but it differs from other biographies in its detailed attention to the writing, publication, and reception of *Huckleberry Finn*, Twain's most important and most innovative work, the book by which he is principally remembered, and in its emphasis on his life in the early and mid-1880s. This was the time of his greatest literary success and personal happiness, which yet foreshadowed disasters to come. But the picture of those final decades is far from one of unrelieved gloom. They contained their satisfactions and accomplishments, and Mark Twain continued to create almost until the end.

THE
INVENTIONS
OF
MARK TWAIN

ONE

Apprentice

M an of letters, man of business, humorist, lecturer, international celebrity, householder, husband and father, leading citizen of Hartford, and owner of a mansion that had become a landmark in its own right—it was a long journey Mark Twain made, from the two-room shanty in a Missouri village where he had been born on November 30, 1835, the sixth child of Jane Lampton Clemens and John Marshall Clemens. Of course, John Clemens had always believed that the Clemenses were gentry and someday, somehow, would take their rightful place in the world. But he could never have foreseen the career that his third son would follow, or the fame that he would win.

John Clemens had been a failure. Proud of his Virginia ancestry, trained in the law, self-consciously a gentleman, yet never able to earn a gentleman's income, he failed embarrassingly to live up to the status he coveted. After a brief success in the remotest backwoods of Tennessee, where he had been Squire Clemens and where he and his wife had owned seven slaves, his career had been a succession of defeats. Success, then failure, then a move—that was the pattern of John Clemens's life. The decline of the Clemenses could be traced in the steadily diminishing number of their slaves, from the original seven to the single slave girl of Sam's early childhood, and then to none at all. Farming, keeping store, practicing law when he could, moving often and growing poorer with each move, he had failed in Tennessee and moved to the almost invisible village of Florida, Missouri, where a brother-in-law offered help. (Almost forty years later, Mark Twain would recount that move, drawing on family tradition, in the opening chapters of *The Gilded*

Age.) Again a short success, again failure, and again the family moved, this time to nearby Hannibal, on the Mississippi River. And there young Sam Clemens lived the childhood that would become the most famous in American literature.

But he did not record everything in his books, and not all that he recorded happened. The fights, the pranks, boating and fishing and swimming, the escapes to Jackson's Island, the alternating boredom and terror of school and church (fear of the master's stick or the wrath of God)—all that would appear in the book, along with much that was invented. Young Sam Clemens did not discover a treasure or attend his own funeral or witness murder in a graveyard at midnight. But he did see murder done on the street, at midday, when William Owsley, a prosperous merchant, shot a defenseless man to avenge an insult. John Clemens, then justice of the peace, recorded the testimony of twenty-eight witnesses. That would be remembered and, almost forty years later, in *Huckleberry Finn*, would be transformed into the killing of Boggs by Colonel Sherburn. Another memory was more painful. Only in his autobiography, dictated in old age, did Mark Twain tell the story of his abandonment, as it seemed, by his father. John Clemens, alone in Hannibal with his son while the rest of the family was visiting at his brother-in-law's farm, had ridden off early in the morning to join them, absentmindedly leaving the seven-year-old boy behind. The father realized that he had forgotten his son only when he arrived at the farm, several hours later. Hungry, crying, and frightened, young Sam was finally rescued that night.

Neither would Mark Twain tell of the humiliations of poverty, of bankruptcy and sheriffs' sales, of seeing his mother forced to cook for another family to provide lodging for her own, while his father was apparently helpless to provide. And he would never mention John Clemens's fantastic projects—his perpetual motion machine, or his hopes for rebuilding the family fortunes with silkworm culture. But he would write, in *The Gilded Age*, of the Tennessee Land—75,000 acres supposedly rich in coal, copper, timber, waterpower, and arable land, bought by his father for a penny an acre to create the Clemens estate and eventually bring wealth to the family. In fact, it brought only disappointment. "It kept us hoping and hoping during forty years," Twain would recall in his *Autobiography*, "and forsook us at last. It put our energies to sleep and made visionaries of us . . . It is good to begin life poor . . . but to begin it poor and *prospectively* rich! The man who has not experienced it cannot imagine the curse of it."

In the spring of 1847, when young Sam was eleven, John Clemens died of pneumonia, leaving his wife and surviving four children nothing but hopes for the Tennessee Land. An honorable man, struggling to the best of his ability against continuous misfortune, he had yet failed both as a breadwinner and as a father. Mark Twain would remember the deathbed scene, with the father drawing his daughter, Pamela, toward him and kissing her. That kiss was unique, Mark Twain would recollect. His father had been "stern, unsmiling," a man who "never demonstrated affection for wife or child." John Clemens never punished his children, or needed to: "a look was enough, and more than enough." His marriage had been a marriage of opposites, correct, not loving, between the cold and distant husband and the spontaneous, impulsive wife. Jane Lampton Clemens took an intense and continuous interest in everything and everyone about her.

With the father's death, the Clemens family broke up. Orion, the oldest, was already working as a printer in St. Louis; Pamela left home to earn her way by teaching music. Henry was still a child, but Sam, at thirteen, was apprenticed to Joseph Ament, publisher of the weekly Hannibal *Courier*, to learn the printer's trade—the first in what he would later call the miserable succession of apprenticeships that made up his early life. That was the end of Sam's schooling—a more important education began in Ament's shop.

Working first for Ament, then for Orion, when his brother came back to publish the Hannibal *Journal*, Sam learned the craft of typesetting, picking the separate letters out of their cases, assembling them in a metal frame, justifying the lines by putting spacers between the words. He became a good workman, proud of his ability to set a clean sheet. His literary education he owed to the newspaper office more than to school. The papers of the day filled out their columns with poems, stories, and humorous sketches, by local contributors and by established authors. Young Sam set them in type, and before long began to imitate them, no doubt setting his own words as fast as they came to mind.

He was following a long-established American tradition. More than a century earlier, young Ben Franklin, learning the printer's craft in Boston, had inserted his own compositions in his brother's paper. Sam wrote poetry, humor, satire, farce—crude stuff, but good enough for Hannibal. Once he was more ambitious. At sixteen he published a brief, humorous story, "The Dandy Frightening the Squatter," in *The Carpet Bag*, a nationally circulated humor magazine. He did not sign his name to it—only his initials—or to anything else that he wrote. He used instead a variety of pen names—Grumbler, Rambler, Peter Pencilcase's Son, John Snooks, W. Epaminondas Adrastus Blabb. Again he followed tradition; since the *Spectator* papers of Addison and Steele almost a century and a half before, newspaper essayists and humorists had written under pen names, often grotesque.

But working on a country weekly offered no future. At seventeen, Sam had mastered his trade and exhausted the possibilities of Hannibal and the *Journal*. He quarreled with Orion, but he would have left in any case. The *Journal* was about to fail, as all of Orion's enterprises would, and Sam's adolescence was over. Sam was a grown man by the standards of his time, he had learned his trade, and it was time for him to prove his independence. Leaving home in the summer of 1853, he commenced the traditional *Wanderjahr* of the journeyman—after taking an equally traditional oath to his mother that he would not drink or gamble until she released him from his pledge.

He would never live in Hannibal again, but it had shaped him for life. He had learned his trade there, and much more. He had learned of murder and violence; he had learned to fear God—the wrathful, all-knowing Calvinist God of the Presbyterian Church who created man hopelessly depraved, then punished him mercilessly for his sins. And he learned that a man was responsible for *all* the consequences of his actions, whether foreseeable or not. Once young Sam gave matches to a drunken tramp who begged for them. The tramp was arrested and put in the Hannibal jail. That night his mattress caught fire from the ashes of his pipe, the key to his cell could not be found, and the whole town, including Sam Clemens, awoke and watched in horror as the man died. Sam had meant no evil, but it was he who had given matches to the tramp and he was responsible—therefore guilty. He would always be ready to assume guilt, or to invent it.

Young Sam Clemens had learned the realities of race as well, in a community where slavery was considered the basis of society, not to be apologized for as a necessary evil but to be praised as a blessing for both slave and master. He saw realities that might have shattered that illusion: slave gangs waiting in chains for shipment down the river, casual, even fatal, brutality from whites toward blacks (yet Hannibal whites were good Christian people); he saw the insurmountable barrier fixed between the races from earliest childhood. Of course he did not question these things—that was how the world worked.

His wanderings took him first to nearby St. Louis, then East, to New York and Philadelphia, to find work in both cities. He attended the theater and was deeply impressed by the famed tragedian Edwin Booth; he saw America's first world's fair, the great Exposition of 1853 in New York. He visited Washington, where he watched the Senate in session but took more interest in Franklin's original printing press at the Smithsonian. He wrote home about his travels, long letters for Orion to print and more intimate letters to his sister, Pamela, not meant for publication. Writing to Pamela, he proudly asserted his independence: "If you have a brother nearly eighteen years of age, who is not able to take care of himself a few miles from home, such a brother is not worth one's thoughts." He proved that he could support himself anywhere, but he was homesick. To a young Southerner the North seemed strange and cold, full of "abominable foreigners," abolitionists, and "God-despising heathens." Twenty years later, looking back on that youthful self, Mark Twain would see in him "ignorance, intolerance, egotism, self-assertion . . . dense & pitiful chuckleheadedness—& an almost pathetic unconsciousness of it all." That, he added, "is what the average Southerner is at 60 today."

In the late summer of 1854, he went home—now the thriving river town of Keokuk, Iowa, where he worked at the Ben Franklin Book and Job Office, a printing shop Orion had set up after selling the Hannibal *Journal*. There Sam began keeping a journal, a practice that he would follow for most of his life. He used it partly for self-analysis, copying long extracts from a textbook of phrenology, then widely accepted as a science. He found his own character described in the author's account of the "sanguine" personality. (Phrenologists often supplemented their charting of the bumps and hollows of the skull with a theory of basic "temperaments.")

The sanguine type, according to this doctrine, was "the burning, flaming, flashing temperament," elastic and buoyant, fond of change, impulsive and hasty, loving excitement, sensitive and easily hurt, quick to anger. Its feelings were sudden and intense—"great warmth of both anger and love." That description exactly fitted both the young Sam Clemens and the adult Mark Twain. His capacities for suffering and for enjoyment were greater than those of most men. The textbook classification seemed surprisingly accurate, then, but it gave more than self-knowledge—it provided justification. In his childhood, Sam had absorbed the Calvinist doctrine of predestination, that at the instant of its creation every soul was doomed or saved by God's decree; now he replaced it with a psychological determinism, which he would hold till the end of his life. The sanguine temperament was his nature, and he must fulfill it.

"Shall I ever be cheerful again, happy again?" he would write fifty-five years later, after the sudden death of his daughter Jean. "Yes. And soon . . . A man's temperament is born in him, & no circumstances can ever change it. My temperament has never allowed my spirits to be depressed long at a time."

Always a hopelessly incompetent businessman, Orion could not pay his brother the five dollars a week he had promised; the Ben Franklin Book and Job Office was plainly doomed. Restless and discontented, Sam left for Cincinnati, working there through the late fall and winter of 1855–56. He began to write for publication again; signing himself Thomas Jefferson Snodgrass and taking the age-old role of the bumpkin in the city, he sent humorously misspelled letters back to the Keokuk *Post*. The *Post* gave him five dollars a letter, the first time anyone had paid him for his writing. But he soon grew restless again. While in Keokuk, he had read an enthusiastic account of the healthful climate and untapped resources of the Amazon Basin, awaiting development by American enterprise, had believed everything, and instantly decided that he must go to the Amazon at the first opportunity. That was his temperament. After a few months' delay, probably to earn money, in April of 1857 he boarded the *Paul Jones*, a steamboat bound for New Orleans, hoping there to find passage to Brazil and make a fortune growing coca. But he would never reach the Amazon. Before the *Paul Jones* reached New Orleans, Horace Bixby, one of its two pilots, had agreed to teach Sam Clemens the craft of piloting, on the "lower river," between St. Louis and New Orleans. Sam had entered a new and more demanding apprenticeship.

There were no aids to navigation on the Mississippi in the 1850s, no reliable charts. A "cub pilot" had to "learn the river"—to commit innumerable facts to memory. He had to learn the shape of the river, and the location of safe channels, to be able to steer by moonlight and starlight or in fog; he had to learn the location of every snag and sandbar and sunken wreck on a thousand miles of the Mississippi, for any one of them could rip out the bottom of a boat. And he had to learn these things over and over again, for the river was always changing. To a careless, impatient man—a man with a sanguine temperament—the task must have seemed nearly impossible.

But the rewards were high. In those last great years of steamboating, the pilot was the aristocrat of the river, better paid even than a captain and carrying a greater responsibility. Compared to wages on land, his salary was princely, often two hundred dollars a month or more. Sam would soon be earning far more than his father ever had. And once at the wheel, the pilot was master; the safety of boat, cargo, and passengers depended largely on him. There were intangible rewards as well: the beauty of the river from the pilothouse, by moonlight or sunrise; the sense of power that came from handling the great wheel that guided the gaudy, gilded boats; the pleasure of being accepted as an equal by the masters of his craft.

While still an apprentice, he fell in love for the first time, with Laura Wright, a Missouri girl of fifteen. But Laura's family opposed Sam's courtship and intercepted his letters, and somehow the two were separated. When they parted on May 26, 1858, the romantic Laura said, "We shall meet again 30 years from now." In fact, they never saw each other again, but Sam did not forget that brief romance. No other girl or woman would seriously attract him until he met Olivia Langdon, ten years later. His adolescence and young manhood seem curiously innocent—records tell only of Laura Wright and of boyish wanderings with an earlier sweetheart, Laura Hawkins, on the bluffs above the Mississippi near Hannibal, gathering wildflowers. It's impossible to know when he first experienced sex—on the river, or later in the brothels of Virginia City or San Francisco, or on his wedding night.

Steamboating was dangerous. Boats could sink, they could run aground, they could burn or blow up. Sam's younger brother, Henry, had followed him, becoming a clerk on the *Pennsylvania*, a boat on which Sam served for a few months as a cub. One of the two pilots, William Brown, was a tyrant who took an instant dislike of his new apprentice. Sam had forced himself to bear the man's continuous insults and curses, but when Brown attacked Henry, without provocation, it was too much. Instantly Sam knocked Brown to the deck with a heavy stool, then battered him with his fists until the pilot broke free and sprang to the unattended wheel. Striking the pilot on duty was a serious breach of discipline, but Brown was universally disliked, and Sam suffered no punishment. Instead, that fight probably saved his life.

Brown refused to serve on the same boat with him, and so Sam Clemens was not on board when the *Pennsylvania* made its last voyage. But Henry stayed. Near Memphis, the boilers exploded, setting the boat on fire and instantly killing hundreds of passengers and crew. Others, like Henry, were fatally burned by scalding steam. His case was hopeless; but Sam reached the Memphis hospital in time to watch his brother's lingering death, and to blame himself— after all, Henry had followed him onto the river. In his old age, he would make his own guilt more direct, inventing a complicated story that made him responsible for Henry's being given a fatal overdose of morphine just as he was beginning to recover.

In the early spring of 1859, after a grueling, sometimes humiliating two-year apprenticeship, Sam Clemens passed the examination for his pilot's license. For two more years he practiced his craft as a master pilot, enjoying the prestige and the pay of his new profession. He was competent and cautious, and he could always find work. He found time for writing, publishing two short pieces. One of them, in the New Orleans *Crescent*, parodied the style of Isaiah Sellers, the oldest pilot on the river, a pompous veteran who paraded his knowledge and experience in semiliterate communications to the newspapers. But Sam was writing simply to amuse himself and his fellow pilots. He had succeeded in his new vocation, and it was only the outbreak of civil war that drove him off the river in the late spring of 1861.

Yet his career as a pilot would surely have ended soon in any case; steamboating was doomed by the new railroads, and the psychological demands of his profession were greater than Sam Clemens would have been willing to meet for long. He was an anxious pilot as well as a safe one, noting in his journal all the risks he did not take, and long after he left the river he would wake from nightmares in which he stood at the wheel in deep darkness, steering his boat through some dangerous passage. By the time he quit piloting, he had gotten all that he could from the craft. Thirteen years later, he would recount his two-year stint as a cub pilot in "Old Times on the Mississippi," a series of articles published in the *Atlantic Monthly*. Those pieces would eventually make up the first third of *Life on the Mississippi*. And he would find other uses for his experience. If Sam Clemens had never become a pilot, had never gained his knowledge of the river and of the life along its shores, he might still have written *Tom Sawyer*, but not *Huckleberry Finn*.

In the late spring of 1861, traveling as a passenger, he went upriver to St. Louis on the last boat to pass the Union blockade. Civil war was reaching the Mississippi, and it was time to choose sides. He was no fire-eating secessionist, but he was born and bred a Southerner, accustomed to slavery. When the governor of Missouri, a Confederate sympathizer, called out the militia to repel Union "invaders," Sam and a few Hannibal friends formed the Marion Rangers, an improvised home guard. (Hannibal was located in Marion County.) The Rangers elected officers, choosing Sam Clemens as lieutenant, and spent a few days in the field, quarreling with one another and panicking at every rumor, and finally breaking up without ever seeing an enemy. Sam Clemens may have been the only casualty; he developed saddle boils while riding a mule and sprained his ankle leaping out of a barn, when the hay on which the Rangers were sleeping caught fire. (He would use that brief, inglorious experience, twenty-four years later, in "The Private History of a Campaign That Failed.")

Plainly, he felt no great enthusiasm for the Confederate cause, and none at all for war. But in wartime a healthy young man of twenty-five, with no dependents, must do something. Several of his companions in the Rangers enlisted in one army or the other and served through the war; one or two were killed in battle. Sam made a separate peace. Believing, like many others, that the war would be over in a few months, he decided to wait it out in the West. Orion had campaigned for Lincoln—for once choosing the winning side—and had been rewarded with appointment as territorial secretary to the new territory of Nevada. Sam went with him, for a Western holiday—a "holiday" that would last five and a half years. His second apprenticeship had ended, and it would be more than twenty years before he would return to the South.

On a two-week journey west by stagecoach, Sam and Orion saw buffalo, Indians, mountains, deserts, and badmen for the first time (all to be recorded in picturesque detail ten years later, in the opening chapters of *Roughing It*). Sam clerked for a month in his brother's office in Carson City, the tiny Nevada capital. But mining fever raged through the territory, and Sam Clemens, young and sanguine, could not sit for long at a desk for eight dollars a day while the nearby mountains were stuffed with gold and silver, and men were becoming millionaires almost overnight—at least, so the newspapers said. The brothers began to speculate, buying and trading shares in mining stocks, but that distant involvement was not enough. Sam went into the field himself, staking out claims, sometimes even working them. His letters to his mother and his sister show his fanatical resolve to strike it rich: "I go to work tomorrow with pick and shovel. Something's got to come, by G——, before I let go here." He would never go back to Missouri, he declared, unless he could return as a rich man. In moments of sanity, he might realize that he was mastered by his "uncongealable sanguine temperament," but such moments were few.

He soon learned that determination was not enough, that mining meant digging holes in stony mountainsides, enduring cold and dirt and discomfort, living on coffee and beans. By August of 1862, money had run out and Sam was desperate. His piloting career had ended through no fault of his own, but this apprenticeship to mining had been a humiliating failure. Still his luck held. He had begun writing again, sending humorous letters under the name of "Josh" to the Virginia City *Territorial Enterprise*, the leading newspaper of the territory. The editors recognized his talent and offered him a reporter's job at twenty-five dollars a week. That must have seemed a niggardly figure, compared to the fortune Sam had expected to make in the mines, but he accepted the offer at once—he had no choice. His most important apprenticeship had begun.

Reckless, violent, extravagant—the biggest and richest mining camp in the West, built over an apparently inexhaustible lode of silver, in the flush times of its first great boom—Virginia City was the right place for him. Sam learned his new trade quickly. There was always plenty of news, of fights and killings, of rich strikes and rumors of strikes, and Sam Clemens could be a competent reporter when he had to. But he quickly realized that accurate reporting was not enough. *Enterprise* readers wanted personal journalism, they wanted humor and color, even fantasy. Within a few months, Sam Clemens proved that he could meet those demands better than any other newspaperman in Nevada, or, for that matter, on the Pacific Coast. He invented hoaxes, he wrote travel letters full of free-ranging comment and humorous exaggeration, he individualized even routine reporting.

But to make a name for himself, he knew, he must sign his work, and in early February of 1863 he first used the name Mark Twain. His earlier pen names had been commonplace, like Josh, or grotesque, like Thomas Jefferson Snodgrass, but Mark Twain was distinctive, memorable, appropriate to an ex-pilot. (On the river, when the leadsman took soundings, "by the mark twain" meant "two fathoms deep"—safe water for a steamboat.) Best of all, the name did not stereotype him; Josh could only be funny, but Mark Twain could be humorous, satirical, angry, pathetic, nostalgic—just as he chose.

The new name was an instant success. Within weeks, he was "Mark" to everyone but his relatives and his oldest friends. California papers began picking up "Mark Twain" pieces and reprinting them, and soon his work was nearly as well known in San Francisco as in Virginia City. Within a year, he had made his reputation—he was the Wild Humorist of the Sagebrush Hills, soon to become the Wild Humorist of the Pacific Slope. And his salary had been raised to forty dollars a week.

Then, for a moment, he seemed to risk losing everything he had gained. In October of 1863 the *Enterprise* printed an unsigned story, headlined "A Bloody Massacre Near Carson" (Carson City). The story reported in gory detail how a deranged speculator armed with ax, knife, and club had murdered his wife and children. To all appearances, it was an ordinary news item; in fact, it was pure invention. The next day, he admitted the truth, and a storm of denunciation raged about him, from editors and readers who had been taken in by the hoax. Rival newspapers denounced that fountain of lies the *Enterprise* and that lunatic Mark Twain. For a moment, he considered resignation, believing that he had destroyed his paper's credibility and ruined his career. But the anger soon died, the affair became a joke, and in the end it served only to increase Mark Twain's reputation as a man who might say *anything*.

That winter the most popular humorist in America, Artemus Ward (born Charles Farrar Browne), came to Virginia City on a lecture tour and singled out Twain for attention—dining and drinking with him, praising his work and his talent. Such recognition was deeply flattering and in time would advance Mark Twain's career, when Ward placed "Jim Smiley and His Jumping Frog" (later to be known as "The Celebrated Jumping Frog of Calaveras County") in an Eastern journal. At the moment, though, it simply increased his restlessness. Mark Twain had had enough of sagebrush and desert; the *Enterprise* could teach him nothing more. He had completed this new apprenticeship, he had made himself a capable reporter and a popular humorist as well, and it was time to move on. He insulted a variety of people in print and became involved in a bitter feud with James Laird, editor of the Virginia City *Union*— challenging him to a duel, denouncing him as a contemptible poltroon. Laird answered in kind, and their letters, full of brag and bluster, were printed in the *Enterprise*. In the end, there was no duel, but Mark Twain left Virginia City, to escape ridicule and perhaps prosecution. He had made a fool of himself conspicuously, and by issuing a public challenge he had broken Nevada law. Words, not revolvers, were his weapons. The earlier fight with Brown the pilot is the only time in his adult life when Twain is known to have used physical violence.

Sam Clemens had acquired a new name in Nevada, and with it a new identity. His Confederate sympathies had quickly disappeared. In this new setting he began to think of himself as a Westerner and an American, not as a Southerner. His letters show the change: within a few months after his arrival in Nevada, he had become an ironic observer of the war—a few months more, and he was a Union man, rejoicing in Northern victories, mourning defeats. Long afterward his intimate friend the novelist and critic William Dean Howells would remark that Mark Twain had been the most de-Southernized Southerner that he had ever known. By the spring of 1864, that process was well under way.

Twain arrived in San Francisco in the first week of June 1864 with a suitcase full of mining stocks, expecting to make a modest fortune by selling them and then to go home in style. While he waited for the time to sell, he took a job as local reporter, *the* local reporter, with the San Francisco *Morning Call*. He soon discovered that working for a metropolitan daily, trying to cover a city with more than a hundred thousand people, was unhappily different from Virginia City journalism. The *Call* seemed to have no need for Mark Twain's unique abilities; it simply wanted a pair of legs.

It censored his work as well, refusing to print a story about the brutal beating of a Chinese by white men for fear of offending its readers. Mark Twain still shared the racism of nearly all white Americans of the time, but brutality revolted him. Overworked and resentful, he lost all interest in his job, and within three months he was no longer working for the paper. Probably he had been fired. Freedom might be welcome, but Twain knew that his brief employment with the *Call* had been a humiliating failure. There was to be no quick fortune from mining stocks; the market had crashed. Instead, for the next two years, Twain supported himself precariously with freelance journalism.

He began contributing regularly to the *Californian*, a new journal with literary pretensions. The pay was only twelve dollars a week, but it released him from the drudgery of daily reporting. Now he could experiment freely with language and develop his talents for humor and satire. He burlesqued popular modes of fiction such as sentimental romances and moral tales for children, and he parodied the jargons of fashion and sports reporting and of the stock market. He made friends among the little circle of San Francisco writers—notably Bret Harte, generally regarded as the most promising young writer in California—and for two years lived the uncertain life of a literary bohemian. Seventeen years later, Twain would recall that he had been "dead broke for several months & served up bursted grain sacks on the San Francisco wharves for a starvation living" when he "was already sufficiently famous to be welcome in the best society of the city & state."

He was barely making a living and deeply in debt. There was a promising offer for the Tennessee Land, an offer that would have made the Clemenses comfortably wealthy, but Orion had become a temperance man and refused the offer on learning that the prospective owner might plant grapes and debauch America with wine. It was a time of disappointment and of deep discouragement, a time when, so Mark Twain would recall in his old age, he once put a pistol to his head, but couldn't pull the trigger. In October of 1865, he confided his feelings and his intentions to Orion in a crucial letter. "I have a religion, but you will call it blasphemy," he begins. "It is that there is a God for the rich man but none for the poor." He threatens suicide: "If I do not get out of debt in three months—pistols or poison for one—exit *me*." But he has a plan to offer. Let each of them accept his calling, in the strong Puritan sense of the role in life for which a man is uniquely fitted and to which he is summoned by God. Let Orion think of "the glory of snatching an immortal soul in mercy from the jaws of hell!" and become a preacher. As for himself, he had had only two strong ambitions: "One was to be a pilot, & the other a preacher of the gospel." But he had lacked "the necessary stock in trade—*i.e.* religion."

Yet he has discovered his own vocation: "a 'call' to literature, of a low order—*i.e.* humorous." It might be nothing to be proud of, he adds, but it is his "strongest suit," and so he must give up affairs for which he is "by nature unfitted" (stock speculation?) and set himself to "seriously scribbling to excite the *laughter* of God's creatures. Poor, pitiful business!" He would accept his destiny, "drop all trifling, & sighing after vain impossibilities, & strive for a fame— unworthy & evanescent though it must of necessity be." As a first step he would set to work at once, to write his way out of debt.

Did Mark Twain become a humorist against his will, compelled by the rough, semibarbarous environment in which he found himself? That suggestion was made by Van Wyck Brooks in 1920 in his influential *The Ordeal of Mark Twain*, and this letter, with its contemptuous reference to "literature, of a low order—*i.e.* humorous," appears to support Brooks's theory. Certainly the emotion of the letter seems genuine, although the language is melodramatic, as Twain's language would often be when he was sincerely expressing conventional sentiments. He could feel agonizing despair, as he could feel guilt. Both would pass, and both would return. Yet from the time he first began writing for publication, he had written humorous pieces, and whenever possible his reporting had been touched with humor. As for how a man who entirely lacked religion could have felt an ambition to preach the gospel, that Tom Saw-yerish image of the preacher melodramatically snatching sinners from the jaws of hell suggests an answer. In his own way, Mark Twain would soon satisfy his ambition to preach by going on the lecture platform—winning laughter rather than saving souls.

By the end of the letter, he had written himself back into hope-fulness. (Mobility, after all, was the characteristic quality of his temperament.) The humorous talent, he admits, "is a mighty engine when supplied with the steam of *education*"—and he would labor all his life to supply that missing power. And he already anticipates lasting fame, even in this poor calling. A postscript advises Orion to "shove this in the stove . . . I don't want any absurd 'literary remains' & 'unpublished letters of Mark Twain' published after I am planted."

The deep depression of that letter, or at least of its opening, quickly passed. Signs of success in his calling had become unmistakable. On the Pacific Coast he had no rival, *Californian* pieces had been reprinted in Eastern papers, and Eastern readers were becoming aware of Mark Twain. And when the New York *Saturday Press* printed "Jim Smiley and His Jumping Frog" in November, it was recognized immediately as a classic of American humor. "James Russell Lowell . . . says the Jumping Frog is the finest piece of humorous writing ever produced in America," Twain proudly reported to his mother. That success must have settled his doubts— proving him a master of his craft, raising him at once above the scores of other newspaper humorists in America.

With his new reputation, new possibilities opened. He persuaded the Sacramento *Union* to send him to the Sandwich Islands, as the Hawaiian Islands were then called, as a traveling correspondent. He would go, and see, and write—an assignment that suited him perfectly. For the next four months, he scoured the islands for copy. He wrote about sugar and whaling, he condescendingly described the history, traditions, and superstitions of the natives, and he commented satirically on the omnipresent influence of the missionaries. He mixed statistics of coffee and sugar with grandiloquent descriptions of tropical scenery. Intensely personal journalism, the letters to the *Union* were reprinted in other Western papers and were widely read.

Californians wanted to hear more from Mark Twain about the Sandwich Islands, and he obliged them. Back in San Francisco, he hired a hall and announced a lecture. Promotion was raucous: "The trouble to begin at 8" announced a poster, and audiences were promised "A SPLENDID ORCHESTRA, A DEN OF FEROCIOUS WILD BEASTS, MAGNIFICENT FIREWORKS, A GRAND TORCHLIGHT PROCESSION." "In fact," said the small print below, "the public are privileged to expect whatever they please." He had spoken in public before, but never to such a crowd, and never had so much depended on it. He found himself tongue-tied for a paralyzing moment as he faced a full house, but recovered before the audience could sense his fear. The lecture was a hit, an artful mingling of the humorous and the serious—even the sublime, in his descriptions of Hawaiian scenery. At his first attempt, Mark Twain had mastered another trade.

It would be a resource for the rest of his career. More lectures followed, in the mining camps of the Sierra foothills, in Virginia City—which welcomed him back, forgetting the absurd quarrel with Laird—and again in San Francisco. Within a few months he had made a stake, and in December of 1866 he sailed for the East, crossing the continent through Nicaragua, as correspondent for the leading San Francisco paper, the *Alta California*. To be a California celebrity was not enough; he wanted to build on the national reputation that he had begun to win with the "Jumping Frog." He lectured in New York, and he arranged for publication of his first book, *The Celebrated Jumping Frog of Calaveras County and Other Sketches*, issued in May by C. H. Webb of New York City. Besides the title piece, it contained about three dozen short pieces, many of them selected from his contributions to the *Californian*.

In the spring, he found his chance and took it. A cruise from New York through the Mediterranean on the steamer *Quaker City* was advertised. Pleasure cruises were a novelty in 1867, and Twain persuaded his paper to send him along as a correspondent. He would see the world, educating himself by travel. He saw a great deal. He visited Gibraltar and Morocco, took a side trip to Paris—viewing Notre Dame, Versailles, the Champs-Elysées, the Louvre, and the Paris Exposition of 1867 in four days. He toured Italy, from Milan to Naples; in Greece he rowed ashore for a midnight visit to the Parthenon (the ship was quarantined and the passengers forbidden to land). The *Quaker City* stopped at Istanbul (then Constantinople) and went on to the Crimea, where its passengers met Czar Alexander II at his summer palace and presented him with an address composed by Twain. Then came the Holy Land, Egypt, a few days in Spain, and the return, after months of tireless sightseeing and of constant writing, of confrontation with the Old World, its art and its religion, its past and its present, from the glittering Paris of the Second Empire to the wretched mud villages of Syria and Palestine.

Out of this chaos of new experiences, Mark Twain sent back his letters—brash, irreverent, prejudiced. They were often satirical, at the expense of the Old Masters in Italy, or of the Catholic Church, or of the Holy Land with its "miraculous" history, or of pious fellow passengers, they often revealed his ignorance, but they were free from the religion of culture with its automatic reverence for Europe and the past. Twain spoke for a self-confident America, exhilarated by victory over disunion, assured that the future belonged to it. Shrewdly, he had arranged to send several letters to be published in the New York *Tribune*, the most influential American newspaper of the day, earning that "New York stamp" for his work.

One of the readers of those letters was Elisha Bliss, manager of the American Publishing Company in Hartford, Connecticut. Two weeks after his return, Mark Twain received a letter from Bliss, inviting him to write a book about his travels, to be sold by subscription, through door-to-door canvassers who began soliciting orders months before publication. The offer excited him; he visited Hartford and was impressed by the prospects of a mass audience and lucrative returns that Bliss held out. The *Jumping Frog* book had sold well, for a collection of short pieces, but it had brought him no money. In January, he signed a contract with the American Publishing Company, calling for a book of five or six hundred pages—subscription buyers expected value for their money—and giving him a 5 percent royalty. That contract determined his future as a writer. Without subscription publishing, Mark Twain's literary career would have been unimaginably different—if he had written books at all. Conventional publishing might have had no place for a Mark Twain who was still no more than an obscure humorist from the West.

Newspaper commitments remained, but by spring he was free of them. Learning that the *Alta California* planned to copyright his letters and publish them as a book, which would prevent him from using them, he sailed for California at once to win his rights. The *Alta* publishers obligingly gave up their plan, and after Twain earned money for his keep with a few lectures, he settled down to work in his San Francisco hotel room, using his letters as the backbone of the book. With several weeks of steady writing, the job was done; he had added a substantial amount of new material and had thoroughly revised his letters. Taking Bret Harte as mentor and carefully following Harte's advice, Twain removed Western slang and corrected his grammar ("he don't" disappears from his published writing with *The Innocents Abroad*) and modified or deleted possibly offensive passages, such as a too graphic description of seasickness. But he kept the humorous freshness of thought and expression that had delighted and scandalized newspaper readers. He had also completed his first real book. His apprenticeships were nearly over—he had found his trade at last.

Author

B ack in the East, awaiting publication of his book, Mark Twain solved that recurring problem of what to do next by arranging a lecture tour and by falling in love. In New York City, he had met Olivia Langdon, sister of young Charley Langdon, a shipmate on the *Quaker City*. Visiting the Langdons at their home in Elmira a few months later, Twain fell instantly in love with Olivia, a frail, gentle woman ten years younger than himself. An accident at sixteen had left Olivia mysteriously paralyzed for two years, until a faith healer, through prayer and laying on of hands, enabled her to walk. One can only guess at the nature of that paralysis. If curable through faith healing, it must have been at least in part psychosomatic. Such cases, though usually less extreme, were not uncommon, serving to delay a girl's departure from home, her marriage, and her sexual initiation. Olivia would marry, although late, would bear four children, manage a busy household, travel widely, and live to be almost sixty, yet she would never be robust. Female "delicacy," both physical and spiritual, appealed strongly to many Victorian males—the first quality seemed proof of the second. Certainly Mark Twain was attracted, and before his visit ended, he had proposed to Olivia.

She rejected him, of course. The proposal was too sudden, and the barriers between them were obvious: he was a freelance journalist, living from hand to mouth, with only the uncertain prospects of a forthcoming book, while Jervis Langdon, Olivia's father, had made a fortune of nearly a million dollars in the coal business. Mark Twain was a humorist, and neither Olivia nor any other member of the family displayed a sense of humor. "Anybody who could convince her that I was not a humorist would secure her eternal gratitude!" Mark Twain confessed to a friend. "She thinks a humorist is something perfectly awful." The Langdons not only lacked humor, they were devout and highly proper Christians, while Mark Twain smoked and drank and swore picturesquely and had no visible religion. His manners were questionable and his morals were unknown; he was a stranger from the West—and that alone could arouse suspicion in conservative Elmira.

But Olivia's rejection had not been total. She allowed him to write to her as to a sister. While he prepared his lecture on "The American Vandal Abroad," and delivered it through the Northeast and Middle West, incidentally publicizing his forthcoming book, he wooed her by mail in pious, passionate letters. He committed himself to becoming whatever she might want; he would stop swearing, he would keep his hands out of his pockets, he would accept Christ, he would begin a new life. Olivia could not resist such devotion. When his tour brought him back to Elmira, he proposed again, and she accepted. A rapturous Mark Twain reported his success to a friend in a letter headed "Paradise, November," and signed "Yrs in ecstasy."

Olivia was a dutiful daughter, and her acceptance had been conditional, subject to her parents' approval. They were doubtful, they inquired into Mark Twain's background, they even asked for references, but they could no more hold out against his impassioned campaign than Olivia could. In early February of 1869 the two lovers became formally engaged: "On bended knees, in the presence of God only, we devoted our lives to each other & to the service of God," Mark Twain wrote to Joe Twichell, a Hartford minister who had become his friend. Only the first half of that pledge would be fulfilled, but Twain genuinely believed that he could make himself into whatever Olivia wanted him to be.

Visiting the Langdon home at the end of winter, with his lecture tour ended, he could work on his book in company with Olivia. While they read proof together, they came to know each other. He could call her "Livy" now, and he began to teach her to laugh. She found a name for him as well. She might speak of him as "Mr. Clemens" in public, but in private, although he was ten years older, he would always be "Youth" to her for his quick enthusiasms, his hopefulness, his readiness for play, his unpredictable behavior, his flares of temper and abrupt swings of mood.

To marry, Mark Twain needed a regular position and a permanent location. He could not support Olivia on a reporter's salary or expect her to share the kind of life he had lived in the West, but he still thought of himself as a newspaperman, not a writer of books. He would become an editor, and part owner, of a newspaper, and after a long search, he borrowed money from his future father-in-law to buy a one-third interest in the Buffalo *Express*—a thriving paper, he said, that he proposed to make more thriving. He took up his new position in mid-August 1869.

His new book appeared at almost exactly the same time, meeting a success that more than fulfilled his hopes. At the last moment, Mark Twain had found the perfect title, *The Innocents Abroad*. Instantly understandable, that title summed up the national self-image. *Innocents* would sell almost seventy thousand copies in its first year, and even with a meager 5 percent royalty brought in twelve to fifteen hundred dollars a month—more money than he had ever made before. Twain had begun his career as an author with a runaway success that had to be followed up. His Western experience seemed to offer an ideal subject—his life was his material. But he was restless, waiting impatiently for his marriage, and he wanted cash quickly. Instead of beginning another book, or settling down to his work on the *Express*, he went on the lecture circuit again. He wrote constantly to Livy, but about his successes and failures on the lecture platform now, not his struggles to become a Christian.

He finished the tour at the end of January, and on February 2, 1870, he and Olivia were married in the Langdon home. It was a wedding with two ministers—the Reverend Thomas K. Beecher of Elmira, the Langdon family minister, and Joe Twichell of Hartford, both Congregationalists. The newlyweds left at once for Buffalo and a splendid surprise (for Mark Twain, not for Livy). Determined that his daughter would live in the style she was accustomed to, Jervis Langdon had bought the new couple an expensive house as a wedding present, fully furnished, complete with horse and carriage and servants. That gift had lasting consequences: it pitched their standard of living at a level far above anything Mark Twain had ever experienced, but which he felt bound to maintain.

The next months were happy ones; the young couple felt sometimes like two children playing house. Each was influencing the other, Livy quietly domesticating her husband (as far as that could be done) while he taught her that smoking, drinking, and swearing might not be deadly sins. She taught him to love, as well; she kissed and caressed him with an openness and a profusion that astonished him—he had grown up in a reserved, undemonstrative community, and the relationship between his father and mother had never been more than polite. Then the idyll was broken. Jervis Langdon's health had been failing, his illness was finally diagnosed as cancer of the stomach, and he died after a month of devoted nursing by all his family, leaving three quarters of a million dollars to be divided equally among his wife, son, and daughter. Before Livy could fully recover from her father's death and from the strain of nursing, a visiting friend fell sick with typhoid fever and died after weeks of illness. Livy cared for her friend throughout, then collapsed from exhaustion. In early November she gave birth prematurely to a son, named Langdon for her father, and for many weeks it seemed that neither Livy nor her son would live.

The honeymoon idyll had turned into a nightmare, and the Buffalo house became hateful to both husband and wife. Mark Twain had lost interest in his work on the *Express* as well. In April 1871, he sold his interest in the paper for $10,000 less than he had paid, and the Clemenses moved to Quarry Farm, a Langdon property on a hill overlooking Elmira. There Twain wrote while Livy and her child gained strength. Mark Twain had written nothing during those desperate months of Livy's collapse, but now, with his anxieties relieved, he could work again. In July he finished *Roughing It*, as he entitled his new book. He would never be a newspaperman again.

He and Livy had already decided where they would live. In early October, they moved to Hartford, renting a house in the pleasant subdivision of Nook Farm, occupied by the intellectual and professional elite of the town, including Harriet Beecher Stowe, world-famous author of *Uncle Tom's Cabin*. It might have seemed incongruous for the onetime Wild Humorist to settle in sedate, Puritan Hartford, already the insurance capital of America, but it had been Livy's first choice when her husband was searching for a newspaper to edit, and he had tried unsuccessfully to buy an interest in the Hartford *Courant*. The Langdons had friends in the city, and it seemed beautiful to Mark Twain. The burnt brown hills of California could not match the summer greenery or the autumn colors of Connecticut. It was a convenient location as well, for Twain was almost next door to his publisher and only a few hours' train ride from New York City and Boston. Most important of all, Hartford and New England stood for morality, culture, tradition, stability— qualities that Mark and Livy desired for themselves and their children.

Within a few weeks of the move, he was on the lecture trail again, trying out and discarding one topic after another, until he found the obvious solution: to draw a lecture from his forthcoming book, promoting it while entertaining his audiences with fresh material. So he went on, speaking in towns large and small, enduring slow trains and bad hotels, winter cold and the loneliness of travel. But the tour was a success; halls were crowded and audiences enthusiastic. Other humorists lectured, but Mark Twain's style was his own, with his intensely slow speech (125 words a minute, or fewer, he once calculated), which he had learned from his mother, his deeply serious face and apparent unawareness that he was saying anything funny, his air of surprise when the audience laughed, and the variety—the serious relief—that he offered. He had learned the psychology of audiences, and he was a master of the pause, knowing exactly how long to maintain it for maximum response. Audiences found his performances unique, unclassifiable; in New York, said the *Times*, his lecture had been "meteorological, historical, topographical, geological, zoological, and comical."

Although a humorist, he realized that his hearers could be sated with laughter. "Any lecture of mine," he wrote to Livy, "ought to be a running narrative-plank, with square holes in it, six inches apart, all the length of it, and then in my mental shop I ought to have plugs (half marked 'serious' & the other marked 'humorous') to select from & jam into these holes according to the temper of the audience." He knew instinctively that instant response to the changing moods of an audience was essential. The metaphor of the "narrative-plank" could apply to writing as well; *The Innocents Abroad* had been just such a plank, with humorous and serious plugs inserted at calculated intervals, and *Roughing It* would be another.

It appeared in January of 1872, a typical subscription book, over six hundred pages long, illustrated with hundreds of crude black-and-white cuts. An English edition, from Routledge & Sons, followed, and a pirated edition from Toronto (international copyright did not yet exist). The new book was autobiographical—that gave it authority—but fictional as well. Mark Twain treated himself as a representative character, freely inventing experiences, such as the story of the "blind lead," a rich strike that he claimed would have made him a millionaire, if he hadn't thrown away his chance through carelessness. As *The Innocents Abroad* had recorded an American's first encounter with the Old World, *Roughing It* became in part a story of initiation into the ways of the West. Again the public bought—65,000 copies by the end of July, although total sales would not equal the sale of *Innocents*. It was already clear that Mark Twain's first success had not been the result of some unrepeatable freak of public taste. And even with a smaller sale, *Roughing It* earned almost as much for its author as *Innocents* had done. On the strength of his first success, Twain was now getting a 7½ percent royalty. That 7½ percent equaled half profits, said Elisha Bliss.

On March 19, 1872, Livy gave birth to a daughter, Olivia Susan Clemens, invariably called Susy. The birth was normal, the baby was healthy. But while Susy flourished, Langdon, the firstborn, failed. He had never been strong or active, he had developed slowly, and in early June of 1872 he died of diphtheria. The parents grieved, but the odds had been against Langdon from birth, and a healthy daughter gave some comfort. Late in life, feeling that someone must have been to blame for Langdon's early death, Mark Twain blamed himself—but the story he tells, of giving his child pneumonia by carelessly exposing him to the winter cold, seems pure invention.

In late August that year, with wife and daughter well, Mark Twain sailed for England alone, to gather material for a sequel to *The Innocents Abroad*. He fell passionately in love with the English countryside ("too absolutely beautiful to be left out of doors") and with London, metropolis of the world. English titles, English antiquities, English pageantry and ritual gripped his imagination. He wrote to Livy that he "would rather live in England than America—which is treason." His work, he found, seemed to be nearly as well known there as at home. Cheap paperback editions of his sketches could be bought at every railway bookstall, while *The Innocents Abroad*, retitled *The New Pilgrim's Progress*, had sold more than forty thousand copies.

The doors of London opened for him; he met Browning, Meredith, Trollope, Herbert Spencer, he walked arm in arm with "the nation's honored favorite, the Lord High Chancellor, in his vast wig and gown," and the chancellor confided that he could forget the affairs of state by reading Twain's books. Even the great Darwin knew his work, keeping the *Jumping Frog* volume by his bedside for midnight relaxation. Twain joined the Savage Club, meeting and establishing friendships with Stanley the explorer, newly returned from Africa after discovering Dr. Livingstone, and with Henry Irving, the greatest tragedian of the day. He came home a complete Anglophile.

He had meant to work on the English book that winter, but other interests distracted him. The Clemenses bought land in Nook Farm and commissioned an architect, Edward T. Potter, better known for his churches than for his houses. Work would begin in the spring, and soon they would have a home of their own, appropriate to Livy's wealth (her money would pay for both house and land) and to her husband's success. And in collaboration with his friend and neighbor Charles Dudley Warner, Mark Twain began a novel, *The Gilded Age: A Tale of To-day*. Writing almost independently of each other, Warner and Twain finished the book within three months. Amateur novelists both, they realized too late that in effect they had written separate books, each with its own plot and characters, with only a tenuous connection between the two stories. Warner's half, a conventional romance, was inoffensive; Twain's was bitingly satirical. Deeply impressed by the order and decorum of Victorian England at the height of its power and prestige, he had come home prepared to be critical, and he found much to condemn. The newspapers that winter were full of political scandals, the trial of Boss Tweed in New York, bribery of congressmen by the Union Pacific Railroad, investigation of a Kansas senator for buying the votes of state legislators to win reelection.

Mark Twain's part of *The Gilded Age* was written out of headlines, truly *A Tale of To-day*. Bringing his characters to Washington, he portrayed blackmail, bribery, and intrigue in the capital against a background of public and private dishonesty at every level, of reckless speculation, a mania for instant riches, and blind adoration of wealth, however gained—presented so powerfully that the book has given its name to the era that it describes. His readers could easily recognize that Senator Pomeroy of Kansas must have served as the model for Senator Dilworthy, self-proclaimed "Christian Statesman," or that the "Indigent Congressman's Retroactive Bill" caricatured an actual bill that would have raised congressional salaries by 50 percent, retroactive for two years. And in his Colonel Sellers, with his cry "There's millions in it!," dreamer and confidence man who always deceives himself first, Twain had presented an American type, as the public instantly recognized. Sellers "was" his cousin Jim Lampton, Twain would insist, but with his visionary optimism, his capacity to overlook all obstacles, he was also Mark Twain. And for a decade, Sellers seemed almost to be every American.

By May of 1873, with *The Gilded Age* finished and construction beginning on his new house, Twain was free to make a return visit to England, this time with Livy and Susy, as well as a lifelong friend of Livy's, Clara Spaulding. This was purely a pleasure trip—he would never write that book on England. American readers would expect satire from Mark Twain, and with his admiration for England, he was in no mood to be critical. There was more than enough to satirize in his own country.

He was lionized in London as before; then the party visited the North of England, Scotland, and Ireland, and finished with two weeks in Paris for sightseeing and shopping—a necessity for the female American tourist. With that, Livy had had enough of Europe and was more than ready to go home. But first Mark Twain would lecture in London on "Our Fellow Savages of the Sandwich Islands." He appeared under the best auspices, managed by George Dolby (who had handled Dickens's reading tours), in the Queen's Concert Rooms, the most fashionable hall in London. There were full houses, and the reviews were favorable. In late October, Twain escorted his party back to America, but barely a month after sailing from Liverpool, he was back in London, to lecture there through December on "Roughing It on the Silver Frontier."

It was the most continuously satisfying of all his lecture series. In spite of choking fog that often seemed to fill the hall with blue smoke, making the audience "vague & dim & ghostly," the house was full night after night. He hired a private secretary, mostly for company—Charley Stoddard, a young San Francisco writer who happened to be in London then. They would rise at noon, take breakfast, read the newspapers and enjoy their cigars in their suite, and perhaps go for an afternoon walk in the fog. Back at their hotel, Stoddard would deal with invitations or fill a scrapbook with clippings concerning the notorious trial of the Tichborne Claimant, who had impersonated the long-lost heir to a title and estate. Throughout his life, Mark Twain would be fascinated by claimants and impostors. (His mother's family, the Lamptons, believed that they were related to the English Lambtons, Earls of Durham, and Jesse Leathers, a distant cousin, wasted his life in pursuing a shadowy claim to the earldom and a fortune that might be worth 150 million pounds.) While Stoddard worked, Twain might sing spirituals or sea chanteys, accompanying himself on the piano. Once he picked up a Bible and read the Book of Ruth "perfectly," "beautifully," "thrillingly," hardly needing to look at the pages.

After dinner, with Mark Twain in faultless evening dress, they would stroll through the foggy streets to the Queen's Concert Rooms in Hanover Square. There they would wait in the anteroom, with Mark Twain pacing restlessly while Stoddard counted the carriages rolling up. Back at their hotel, after the performance, they would relax with hot scotch. Late at night, Twain might grow homesick and tearful, foreseeing that a time would come when he could no longer write or lecture, and then " 'What would he and his family do for a living? There was nothing for it'—tears—'but the poorhouse.' " A half-comic performance, yet serious, too. He could never forget the fear of poverty in the Hannibal years, never quite convince himself that the poorhouse did not threaten.

He was enjoying a triumph that he could not have imagined a few years before, but the nightly applause could not compensate for his separation from Livy at the Christmas season. He needed her, both emotionally and physically. "If I'm not homesick to see you, no other lover ever *was* homesick to see his sweetheart. And when I get there, remember, 'Expedition's the word,' " he wrote before going to the lecture hall. Back from his lecture, dating his letter at 2 a.m., he wrote again: "I *do* love you, Livy darling, & my last word is when I come 'Expedition's the word.' " In another letter he pictures his return, at midnight: "ever so many kisses," then his "cock-tail" and undressing, while Livy stood by, and finally "to bed, and—everything happy & jolly as it should be." "Expedition," then, must mean speeding to bed and to lovemaking. (Recognizing that implication, some prudish guardian of Mark Twain's papers has crossed out both occurrences of the suggestive phrase, once so heavily that the pen went through the paper.) Frail as Livy might be, those letters suggest a full and sexually satisfying relationship between husband and wife.

He returned to Hartford in late January of 1874, to find all well at home, with Livy and Susy in good health, the new house progressing, and *The Gilded Age* in print and selling well—fifty thousand copies by the end of March. At about this time, he observed with comfortable self-satisfaction that "anything but subscription publication is printing for private circulation." Trade publishers might resent the competition of the subscription house, critics commonly ignored their books, genteel readers might scorn the crude and bulky volumes, while genteel authors envied the sales, but subscription publishing gave Mark Twain his audience.

Those sales figures, which trade publishers never approached, gripped his imagination. Each book might be a bonanza. And Twain needed that money—not for survival, of course, but to live in the style that he admired, to match his wife's wealth, to maintain his self-respect. Writers like William Dean Howells or Henry James, who published in the "trade," could hardly live on their royalties—certainly could not live well. Their solution was to serialize their novels in the magazines, before issuing them in book form, thus getting a double return that was still much less than Twain's. But Mark Twain could never plan his work in advance, and he hated writing to a schedule. Deadlines turned writing into agony—he had had enough of them as a reporter. He preferred to begin writing when an idea attracted him, stop when he lost interest, pick up the manuscript again when interest returned—if it ever did. He was totally incapable of the disciplined labor that would enable his friend William Dean Howells to produce eighteen novels and two volumes of criticism in the twenty years between 1880 and 1900.

His life was falling into a pattern. In that spring and summer of 1874, the Clemenses escaped to Quarry Farm, as they would almost every summer for sixteen years, sharing a farmhouse with Susan Crane, Livy's foster sister, and her husband, Theodore. There, free from social and business distractions, Mark Twain dramatized his half of *The Gilded Age*, leaving out most of the plot to give room to Colonel Sellers. With a popular comedian, John Raymond, in the leading role, the play would tour the country for years, earning the author royalties of at least $70,000 and making Sellers's exclamation "There's millions in it!" a byword. (Warner claimed no share in the returns because *Colonel Sellers*, as the play was called, was based entirely on Twain's half of *The Gilded Age*.) "The play is a singularly emphatic success," Twain observed to a friend. "It ran 115 nights in New York"—an extraordinary success for a play with "no scenic effects & no bare legs." Inevitably, he would try to repeat that success.

In that same summer, he began work on *Tom Sawyer*, writing until the book suddenly stopped itself at the beginning of September. As long as the writing came easily and spontaneously, he could work with enormous energy, producing as many as four thousand, even five thousand words a day. But he would not force himself to write unless facing an imminent deadline. As usual, he worked almost without plan: "Since there is no plot to the thing [*Tom Sawyer*], it is likely to follow its own drift." When he found that he had nothing more to say—when his tank ran dry, to use a favorite metaphor—there was nothing to do but wait, and occupy himself with other things while a process of "unconscious but profitable cerebration" went on and the tank filled up again. That might take years, or it might never happen, but writing could not be forced.

That fall, he found an irresistible subject. Howells, editor of the *Atlantic*, had urged him to contribute to the magazine. Howells was a close friend (he had reviewed *The Innocents Abroad* enthusiastically, and he and Twain had taken to each other instantly when they met, commencing a lifelong friendship), and that invitation was an honor that could not be refused, for the *Atlantic*'s prestige was enormous. Howells had already accepted Twain's "A True Story," an account of a black woman's separation from her son during slavery days, and their reunion after emancipation, narrated by the mother herself. He had praised the piece for its dialect— "the best and reallest kind of black talk"—had paid the unprecedented rate (for the *Atlantic*) of twenty dollars a page, and wanted more. After a little thought, Mark Twain had found a subject that would be completely new to literature. He would do a series of articles on "the old Mississippi days of steamboating glory & grandeur" as seen from the pilothouse. In *Roughing It*, he had drawn on his four years in the West; now he would narrate an earlier apprenticeship, writing of his life as a cub pilot under the stern tutelage of Horace Bixby. Beginning with the January 1875 issue, "Old Times on the Mississippi" ran for seven months. It was a success, and it gave Mark Twain a new status, far more important than the twenty dollars a page that the *Atlantic* paid him. Status mattered—humorists ranked low on the literary scale, and so did writers of subscription books.

"Old Times" won much admiration, but of all the praise he received, Twain probably enjoyed most the comment of John Hay, future biographer of Lincoln and Secretary of State for President Theodore Roosevelt, but then best known as the author of *Pike County Ballads*, poems in Missouri dialect dealing with Southwestern life: "It is perfect—no more nor less. I don't see how you do it . . . You have the two greatest gifts of the writer, memory and imagination."

It was a happy and prosperous time. Mark Twain's reputation was steadily growing, whatever he attempted appeared to succeed, and the Clemenses had their own home at last. In September of 1874, they had moved into the new house at 351 Farmington Avenue, occupying only one floor at first, for the builders were still at work. Twain was delighted with their new residence. From the beginning, it had been much more than simply bricks and mortar to him. "It is a quiet, murmurous, enchanting poem done in the solid elements of nature," he had written to Olivia while it was building. "The house and lawn do not seem to have been set up on the grassy slopes & levels by laws & plans & specifications—it seems as if they *grew* up out of the ground & were part & parcel of Nature's handiwork."

The Clemens mansion quickly became one of the sights of the town, not simply because it was clearly the home of a wealthy and successful man—there were a good many such men in prosperous Hartford—but because it was the intensely personal home of Mark Twain, Hartford's most celebrated citizen. Its building had been an architectural event; it became a landmark almost before its completion in 1874. "The palace of the King of humorists," *The New York Times* had called it. Travelers who were not lucky enough to have a letter of introduction to its owner might still go out of their way to see his house.

> This is the house that Mark built.
> These are the bricks of various hue
> And shape and position, straight and askew,
> With the nooks and angles and gables too,
> Which make up the house presented to view,
> The curious house that Mark built.

So Twain himself described his house in verses published in the January 1877 issue of *The Travelers Record*. That it was unique, intensely individual, all visitors agreed: it seemed "a gradual and organic outgrowth of the owner's mind," wrote an English journalist. Howells put it more simply: "As Mark Twain was unlike any other man that ever lived, so his house was unlike any other house ever built." The architect had set out to build a "real poet's house," and had conferred constantly with his clients. It was the product of a true collaboration.

Its size alone could impress: 103 feet long and three stories high, up to sixty-three feet wide, with an octagonal tower sixty-two feet high on the west side, five baths, nineteen "large rooms," and a hundred windows. Its red brick, decorated with horizontal lines, geometric patterns, and rays shooting out from windows, caught the eye at once, sharply contrasting with the sober dark brown of its neighbors. Gabled, chimneyed, and turreted, it was at the furthest extreme from the large and small boxes typical of Hartford architecture. Balconies sprouted from the upper floors, the largest of them a kind of observatory that visitors inevitably compared to the pilothouse of a Mississippi steamboat. At one end, a huge shaded porch, the "Ombra," offered a private place for warm-weather lounging and casual suppers. The house seems an architectural cakewalk, as Mark Twain defined that term: a competition of elegance in dress and manners held among Southern blacks. To Howells, it was "the stately mansion in which Clemens satisfied his love of magnificence"—a passion that had been starved for most of his life. The design was unconventional, expenses had vastly exceeded estimates, but the Clemenses could afford it.

The exterior testified to the wealth and social position of its owners, as well as to their unconventionality; the interior, rich, dark, and ornate, demonstrated their taste. Money and taste—Livy's taste, according to Twain—had combined to create that atmosphere. There were Oriental rugs on the floor, there were paintings and statues, hand-carved tables and beds, the loot of Europe. For the well-to-do American of the 1870s and '80s, it was not enough merely to travel abroad. He must demonstrate his affluence and his culture, or his wife's, with the spoils he brought home. Not even Mark Twain, who had ridiculed the superstition of Europe in *The Innocents Abroad*, could escape that cultural command.

The visitor would be immediately impressed by the great entrance hall, rich with carved beams and paneling and an elaborate Tudor staircase. Depending on the occasion and degree of friendship that existed, he or she might be taken to the elegant, silvery drawing room, or to the spacious library where the family actually lived, stuffed with books and bric-a-brac, dominated by a massive oak mantel brought from a Scottish castle that the Clemenses had visited. In winter, one could enjoy the contrast between the falling snow outside and the blazing logs in the fireplace, or momentarily forget ice and snow while gazing at the greenery and splashing water of a conservatory that opened off one end of the library. On a brass plaque attached to the mantel was inscribed Emerson's saying "The ornament of a house is the friends who frequent it." Twain accepted the sentiment—the Clemens house was abundantly frequented by friends—although he ridiculed the awkward correctness of its grammar.

Guests were lodged in the mahogany room on the ground floor, with private bath and dressing room, and in two smaller rooms on the second and third floors. The second floor held the servants' wing and bedrooms for the parents—also with dressing room and bath—and the children. Here, too, was Mark Twain's study, a spacious, many-windowed room, with an enormous divan copied from one he had seen in a Syrian monastery. On the third floor was the billiard room, opening onto a hexagonal balcony.

Livy's money had paid for it all. (When Mark Twain's publishing firm went bankrupt in 1894, the house would be saved from the wreck because it was considered to be her property.) The cost had been frighteningly high—well over a hundred thousand dollars. Husband and wife had insisted on the best of everything, every detail must be individual, plans were constantly changed. Mark Twain was not a man to haggle with contractors over bids, or argue the details of their bills, and despite his fears of poverty, he did not worry over the cost of maintaining such a home. He earned money easily and spent it freely. He had grown up in the slaveholding South, where a mark of the gentleman was to have money and spend it easily, and that lesson had been reinforced by the lavish spending of the new millionaires on the Pacific Coast. "He did not care much for money in itself," his friend Howells would comment long after, "but he luxuriated in the lavish use of it." And even after paying for the house from her inheritance, Livy still owned stocks and mortgages and received a substantial income from her share of the Langdon family business.

Like most Americans of his day, Mark Twain was devoted to progress, and his home was thoroughly up-to-date, with five complete bathrooms. There would soon be a telephone as well, installed in 1878 and connected by a private wire to the office of the Hartford

Courant, later to the telegraph office. It was the first home telephone anywhere in the world, he believed. A year later, with the earliest transcontinental telephone line almost forty years in the future, he published "The Loves of Alonzo Fitz Clarence and Rosannannah Ethelton," a story in which the hero and heroine meet, fall in love, quarrel, and finally marry—all by telephone. "Great *is* the telephone," Twain would exuberantly pronounce in 1880, adding that "we *do* live in an age compared to which all other ages are dull & eventless."

The site of the house was charming, near the western edge of the city, yet only a mile or so from the railroad station, with a horse-drawn streetcar passing every fifteen minutes. (Driver and passengers nearly froze in the winter.) To the west, below the Clemens land, lay a wide meadow. Through it ran the north branch of the Park River—actually a creek—sometimes known as the Meandering Swine or, more poetically, as the Riveret. "Lovely woods, a river, and silence," his daughter Clara would recall. When snow fell, the slope down to the meadow might be used for sledding, while the river itself offered skating. In the other direction, toward town, lay the spacious homes of their neighbors. There were no hedges or fences to separate them; Nook Farm was a sort of residential park, where neighbors were friends. A few blocks away, the 230-foot-high Gothic steeple of Joe Twichell's handsome brownstone church testified to the prosperity of its congregation. Although the religious fervor that Mark Twain had shown during his courtship of Livy had cooled—he no longer considered himself a Christian in any sense—he kept a pew and the Clemenses sometimes attended.

Houseguests were treated with a charming informal courtesy. "You must know that yours is one of the few *restful* homes in which intelligence, culture, luxury and company combine," wrote one appreciative visitor, the Reverend Thomas K. Beecher of Elmira. The diary of another visitor, Mrs. James Fields, offers a sympathetic view of the Hartford household as it was in the mid-seventies. She was impressed by her host: "He is forty years old," she wrote, "with some color in his cheeks and a heavy light-colored moustache, and overhanging light eyebrows," small ("his mass of hair seems the one rugged-looking thing about him"), careless yet "exquisitely neat." He was eccentric, she added, seemed disturbed by every noise, and could not be an easy man to take care of. To her surprise, she found that "he reads everything." As for Livy, "she looked like an exquisite lily . . . So white and delicate and tender!" It was "a very loving household," Mrs. Fields concluded, with "two beautiful baby girls" (a second daughter, Clara, had been born in June of 1874).

Twain spoke of the autobiography he intended to write "as fully and simply as possible, and to leave behind him," and to compose it by a unique method, disregarding chronological order, dealing at any point with any moment of his life that happened to interest him. (He would finally try to carry out that plan forty years later, with his autobiographical dictations.) When Livy "laughingly said she should look it over and leave out objectionable parts," he replied, "almost sternly," that she was not to edit it, that it must appear as written, "with the whole tale told as truly as I can." Livy had begun editing her husband's work, at his invitation, during their engagement, and she would go on doing so until her death. He seldom showed any resentment, probably seldom felt any.

She tried to edit his behavior as well, with limited success—she had already give up her efforts to make him stop swearing, smoking, and drinking. (Twain was a moderate drinker throughout his life.) He must have been irked at times, and a late fragment, "Indiantown," satirically presents his own imperfections and his wife's continuous effort to improve him while simultaneously doing her best to believe him perfect as he was. Susan Gridley, like Olivia "utterly refined," high-principled, religious—"she had none but high ideals"—sets herself to work remodeling her husband, "an easy-going, lazy, soft character," and succeeds—outwardly. She creates a "humbug," a "sham," a husband who generally dresses, talks, and behaves like a gentleman, while inwardly loathing "society and its irksome polish and restraints." The wife worships her self-created idol, while the husband wonders at her blindness. But David Gridley, like Mark Twain, takes for granted this characteristic folly of women.

But "Indiantown" must be read as a caricature of the Clemens marriage, rather than a literal account (just as Mark Twain's jokes in his letters to Howells about Livy's "ferocity" were funny only because her gentleness was so evident). Certainly Twain found her "editing" of himself irksome at times, but without Livy he would surely have done his best to satisfy Eastern standards of gentility— during his courtship, he had heavily edited his natural self to become acceptable to her—and throughout his life he needed and searched for guides and mentors. (Howells was his literary mentor, and in later years the millionaire Henry H. Rogers would guide him in all matters of finance.) And to Victorians it was the role of Woman to refine and spiritualize the crude male.

By early July of 1875, Mark Twain had finished *Tom Sawyer*, although the book would not be published until December of the following year. Sales were disappointing by Twain's standard— fewer than twenty-four thousand copies in the first year, largely because of competition from a cheap, unauthorized Canadian edition—and reviewers generally ignored the book, but within a few years it began to establish itself as a classic of its kind. Twain had meant to lead Tom through "the Battle of life in many lands," but decided not to take him beyond boyhood, realizing too late that he should have written the book "autobiographically, using the first person." Readers also wanted to follow Tom out of boyhood. Within a year after publishing *Tom Sawyer*, Twain had received so many requests for a sequel that he composed a form letter to answer them: "Dear ———, It is my purpose to write a continuation of Tom Sawyer's history, but I am not able at this time to determine when I shall begin the work." *Tom Sawyer*, then, remains the story of a boy, although Tom is developing toward maturity as the book nears its end. The boy who overcomes his fear of the murderous Injun Joe to testify at Muff Potter's trial is not quite the boy who had whitewashed the fence or given painkiller to the cat. Whether he had written a "boy's book" or a book about boys for grownups was a question that the author could never quite decide. In either case, he had created an enduring myth of American boyhood, embodied in mischievous, good-hearted Tom.

Mark Twain had become an *Atlantic* author, and Howells wanted more of his work. In the October 1875 issue "The Curious Republic of Gondour" appeared, a sort of appendix to *The Gilded Age*, presenting a conservative Utopia that perhaps reflected an idealized Victorian England. In Gondour, women could vote and hold even the highest office, the spoils system was replaced by civil service examinations, and the evils of excessive democracy were cured by allowing multiple votes to persons of property or education. "The Facts Concerning the Recent Carnival of Crime in Connecticut" (June 1876) was more deeply personal, with a narrator strongly resembling the author who encounters his taunting, sadistic conscience and gleefully tears it to bloody shreds, so freeing himself from its tortures. But Mark Twain could quiet his conscience only in fantasy.

His next project would surely have startled genteel visitors such as Mrs. Fields. He had been studying "ancient English books" in order to imitate their style, and at Quarry Farm, in the summer of 1876, he wrote *1601; or Conversation as It Was by the Social Fireside in the Time of the Tudors*, an eight-page sketch in which Queen Elizabeth, Raleigh, Shakespeare, Francis Bacon, Ben Jonson, and various members of the court talk freely of farts, maidenheads, and other unmentionable subjects. "Delicacy—a sad, sad, false delicacy," wrote Twain jocularly, "robs literature of the best things among its belongings: Family-circle narratives & obscene stories." *1601* was a joyful breaking down of barriers, a romp among forbidden words, written to be read by masculine friends and the friends of friends. Circulating at first in handwritten copies, then in surreptitious printings, it soon became an underground classic.

A man of sudden enthusiasms, quickly bored, Mark Twain needed to have a variety of projects on hand, allowing him to move from one to another as his interest shifted—sometimes returning and completing the abandoned work, sometimes losing interest permanently, leaving behind a trail of unpublished, often unfinished manuscripts. He wrote for his own pleasure at least as much as for money. He began *Huckleberry Finn* at Quarry Farm, in the summer of 1876, writing four hundred manuscript pages (about forty thousand words) by early August, but he had no suspicion of its importance. He had given up a mysterious "double-barreled novel," never referred to again, and begun "another boy's book—more to be at work than anything else," he reported to Howells, adding that he might "pigeonhole or burn the MS when it is done." But although he might not have realized its significance, he had made the crucial decision, instantly distinguishing his new story from *Tom Sawyer*, in the opening sentence—"You don't know about me without you have read a book by the name of 'The Adventures of Tom Sawyer.'" He would write *Huckleberry Finn* in the first person, as he wished he had written *Tom Sawyer*.

By late August, Mark Twain had launched the central action of *Huckleberry Finn*, as a white boy and a black man on a raft float down the Mississippi River together in search of freedom, and had established the essential difference between Tom and Huck: one is in society, the other is outside it. But as Huck and Jim drift down the river toward Cairo, where they plan to sell their raft and buy steamboat passage up the Ohio into the free states, Mark Twain must have realized that he had been writing himself into an impasse. He did not want to take his characters up the Ohio; he knew almost nothing of it. He did know the Mississippi, intimately, from his piloting days. But why should an escaping slave go farther south, deeper into slave territory?

He wrote a pair of ferocious letters that may have grown out of his frustration—to his brother Orion, denouncing one of Orion's impossible schemes, and to Will Bowen, a boyhood friend, accusing Bowen, in words that would have applied equally to Twain himself, of "mental and moral masturbation" in his sentimental musings over the past. Then, in his anger, Twain finished his summer's work with the terrifying scene in which the raft is struck by a monstrous steamboat: "all of a sudden she bulged out, big and scary, with a long row of wide-open furnace doors shining like red-hot teeth, and her monstrous bows and guards hanging right over us . . . and as Jim went overboard on one side and I on the other, she come smashing straight through the raft." And with that, *Huckleberry Finn* was put aside until the tank filled up again. Mark Twain would not return to it for three years, and would not finish it for seven.

With the completion of *Huckleberry Finn* indefinitely postponed, Twain turned to playwriting. His old California friend Bret Harte approached him in October, proposing that they write a play together "& divide the swag," and Twain promptly agreed. He was in a mood to be enthusiastic; he had just received a check for sixteen hundred dollars, royalties from the first week's run of *Colonel Sellers* in Philadelphia. Success seemed certain. Five years after Mark Twain came East, Harte had followed, winning instant fame with his poems and stories of gold-rush days in California. His work provided a combination of humor, melodrama, and local color that suited the public taste exactly. By 1876, the formula was becoming obvious, and he apparently had nothing else to offer, but his name still carried weight. A Twain-Harte collaboration seemed a guarantee of success.

Disappointment was correspondingly bitter, but the project had been doomed from the outset. The collaboration was as loose as that of *The Gilded Age*, with each man to provide a comic character and to draw up a plot; then, as Twain explained to Howells, "we shall use the best of the two, or gouge from both and build a third." Their friendship broke down under the strain of collaboration and forced intimacy (Harte was a houseguest of the Clemenses for weeks). As for the play, entitled *Ah Sin*, after a comic Chinese contributed by Harte, it failed when it was produced in the spring of 1877. Mark Twain blamed Harte for that failure, feeling that he was lazy and had not done his share of revision. Worse, he had spoken insultingly to Livy, and that could never be forgiven—Twain's hate was passionate and enduring. But he had lost only his time. Harte suffered more deeply, as the failure of *Ah Sin* accelerated his long slide into obscurity—incidentally removing Twain's most serious competitor.

The possibilities for comedy offered by his older brother's personality and career increasingly interested Mark Twain. In March of 1877 he set to work on a novel featuring Orion as its central character (Twain misleadingly called his manuscript "Orion's Autobiography"). "Bolivar," the central character, is an Orion figure, a young printer's apprentice, "soft & sappy, full of fine intentions . . . & not aware that he is an ass," an intellectual weathervane at the mercy of every argument or theory he encounters, regularly changing his religion, his diet, his way of life. Unstable in everything, endlessly reforming himself, he is a Methodist, then an "infidel," then a Methodist again; he rises at 3 a.m. for a cold plunge in a neighboring creek; he lives on bread and water, until he is persuaded that a vegetarian diet is healthier. But Twain wrote only a few farcical chapters, omitting the pathos of Orion's failures. He might have sensed that in ridiculing Orion he was attacking himself. With his inventions, his projects, his surging, short-lived enthusiasms, his perpetual optimism and instant forgetting of previous failure, Orion often seems almost indistinguishable from his younger brother. By his incessant ridicule of Orion's instability, Mark Twain may have unconsciously desired to exorcise the same quality in himself. It was essential to his genius, that freshness of vision and openness to new ideas and new experience, but it could also be dangerous.

Undiscouraged by the failure of *Ah Sin* and still hoping for a new success on the stage, Twain wrote another play at Quarry Farm in the summer of 1877: *Cap'n Simon Wheeler, the Amateur Detective*, a four-act farce, with Wheeler as a nineteenth-century Quixote who has read detective stories until he takes them as fact and tries to practice detection himself. *Simon Wheeler* was the product of a creative euphoria—"conceived, plotted out, written & completed in 6½ working days of 6½ hours each," he boasted to Howells. That almost incredible outflow of words, which could never have resulted from conscious effort, appeared to demonstrate that *Simon Wheeler* must have been the product of true inspiration. But inspiration was no guarantee of quality, as Twain admitted a year and a half later, when he found the play "dreadfully witless and flat." It remains unproduced.

Reports of a mysterious prowler at the Hartford house offered Mark Twain the chance to play detective himself, with more satisfying results. He traveled from Quarry Farm to investigate, and quickly found that the "housebreaker" had been a lover of Lizzie, a housemaid. She had been "betrayed," she said, and Mark Twain laid a trap to save her honor. Inviting the lovers for an interview, he coaxed, argued, pleaded with the man to marry, "made him choke & cry a little," wearing down his resistance until "he said hesitatingly, 'I—I believe I'll do it—yes, I am willing, though—'" (if he had refused, a detective was waiting in the library to arrest him on a charge of unlawful entry). Instantly Twain rang a bell and the butler and the cook entered, to serve as witnesses; he threw open the bathroom door, and Joe Twichell emerged, holding a marriage license. The marriage was performed, with the groom muttering, "But it was a put-up job." Then the butler brought champagne, "whereat, general jollity." In conclusion, Twain gave husband and wife a hundred dollars each. Morality was satisfied, Lizzie was made an honest woman, and Twain spent the evening reading *Simon Wheeler* to the Twichells. He had directed and starred in his own script, and the production had been a complete success. As for the marriage, it apparently worked out as well as most.

Back in Hartford in the fall, Mark Twain did not forget *Simon Wheeler*. Finding no producer for his play, he set to work novelizing it, bringing it closer to his own experience by shifting the scene from upstate New York to a remote Missouri village. A new character, Judge Griswold—cold, intellectual, intensely conscious of his status as a gentleman—bears an unmistakable resemblance to John Clemens. There is a feud between two families, Griswolds and Burnsides, its origin so ancient that no one remembers it, and so implacable that members of the rival clans kill one another on sight. Twain left the manuscript half-finished, after beginning a love story between a man and a girl on the opposite sides, but his time had not been wasted. When he went back to *Huckleberry Finn*, sometime between the fall of 1879 and late spring of 1880, he would make Huck a spectator of the murderous Grangerford-Shepherdson feud, the climax of which was a massacre after Sophia Grangerford eloped with Harney Shepherdson.

He had another project in mind. He had been considering a story in which two boys, a prince and a pauper, exchange identities, at first planning to set the story in Victorian London, with the future Edward VII as the Prince. But the action seemed unbelievable in his own world, and he decided to set the scene in Tudor England (while composing *1601*, he had found that he enjoyed imitating sixteenth-century English). His prince became the young son of Henry VIII, the future Edward VI. He summed up his plan in a journal entry, dated November 23, 1877: "Edward VI & a little Pauper exchange places by accident a day or so before Henry VIII's death. The prince wanders in rags & hardships & the pauper suffers the (to him) horrible miseries of princedom, up to the moment of crowning, in Westminster Abbey, when proof is brought & the mistake rectified." He had already been reading Tudor history, and now he began writing—for love, not for money. He would publish anonymously, he resolved, "such grave & stately work being considered by the world to be above my proper level." It was a resolution he would not keep.

Life seemed tranquil enough in the fall of 1877, with Mark Twain free to enjoy his work and his fame and his family, until his peace was destroyed by the unlucky Whittier dinner. On December 17, the *Atlantic Monthly* simultaneously celebrated its twentieth anniversary and the seventieth birthday of the poet John Greenleaf Whittier. The dinner was an occasion for self-congratulation: on the good fortune of the participants in having such a magazine as the *Atlantic* and such poets as Whittier and the other guests of honor (Emerson, Holmes, and Longfellow), in being New Englanders or, best of all, Bostonians. The atmosphere was deeply self-satisfied, intensely provincial; the company, said the Boston *Advertiser*, was "the most notable that has ever been seen in this country within four walls."

The guests of honor were more than mere writers, they were priests of Culture; their presence, according to one Boston paper, "gave a reverend, almost holy air to the place." The speakers paid them fulsome compliments in prose and verse; such occasions and such men, it was said, helped to "save the American nation from the total wreck and destruction of the sentiment of reverence." That term "reverence" carried powerful social and political implications in a society and a culture being transformed by immigration, by the mushroom growth of cities, by the rise of modern journalism and the yellow press. The "high" culture was associated with the "higher" classes, whose supremacy seemed increasingly threatened by the "lower." But the sentiment of reverence appeared safe for that night at least—until Mark Twain spoke.

Recalling his Western years, he offered an imaginary reminiscence, set in a lonely miner's cabin in the Sierras. Knocking at the door, "Twain" asks for a meal and a bed. After feeding him a miner's supper of beans and bacon, followed by whiskey, the owner tells him that he is "the fourth littery man that's been here in twenty-four hours"—Longfellow, Emerson, and Holmes having all stopped by the night before. Emerson had been "a seedy little bit of a chap—red-headed"; Holmes "as fat as a balloon," with "double chins all the way down to his stomach"; Longfellow was "built like a prizefighter" with the "cropped and bristly head" of a convict. They quoted or misquoted from each other's poems, bragged, played cards and cheated, and drank their host's whiskey. "Between drinks they'd swell around the cabin and strike attitudes and spout"—as the king and the duke would do in *Huckleberry Finn*. The next morning they left, "Longfellow" taking the miner's boots, explaining that he was "going to make tracks with 'em," because, in one of the most quoted verses of the century,

> Lives of great men all remind us
> We can make our lives sublime,
> And, departing, leave behind us
> Footprints on the sands of time.

"Why, my dear sir," exclaims "Twain," in a speech exactly mimicking the adulation of the evening, "*these* were not the gracious singers to whom we and the world pay loving reverence and homage; these were impostors." With the miner's reply, Twain finished by turning the joke on himself: "Ah! impostors, were they?—are *you?*"

As Mark Twain told the story to his first biographer, Albert Bigelow Paine, almost thirty years later, the diners "became petrified with amazement and horror" as his speech went on. The speaker who followed Twain was totally demoralized—"he began to hesitate and break, and lose his grip, and totter and wobble"—and collapsed without finishing; the next could not even rise, and the banquet broke up. Howells gives supporting details in *My Mark Twain*: as soon as Twain began to speak, "the amazing mistake, the bewildering blunder," was clear to all. Silence deepened, "broken only by the hysterical and bloodcurdling laughter of a single guest." Back in his hotel room, Howells would recall, Twain "tossed in despair," convinced that he had grossly insulted Emerson, Longfellow, and Holmes. Later, returned to Hartford, he wrote to Howells, offering an abject apology—"It seems as if I must have been insane when I wrote that speech"—and offering to withdraw a piece that the *Atlantic* had accepted. His reputation had been injured "all over the country" and it would be best for him to "retire from before the public at present."

Yet the speech had not been the disaster that Twain and Howells believed it to be. Newspaper stories prove that the ceremonies went on to their conclusion as scheduled. One Boston paper reported that Twain had "set the table in a roar" with "a characteristic series of parodies on Longfellow, Emerson, and Holmes," and two days later another punningly complimented him: "It would have been hard to make a Whittier speech than Mark Twain's." The Boston *Transcript* and a few out-of-town papers were severe, but at worst Twain had committed an embarrassing gaffe; there had been no instant and universal condemnation, no reverberating scandal. Very likely the timid Howells, himself an outsider from Ohio and never quite sure of his own standing in the New England literary establishment, convinced his friend that the speech had been a frightful blunder. And Mark Twain, trusting Howells's judgment and prone to self-blame, was always ready to flagellate himself for real or imagined misdeeds, to turn blunders into crimes, embarrassments into catastrophes. The Whittier dinner, he foresaw, "is going to add itself to my list of permanencies—a list of humiliations that extends back to when I was seven years old, & which keep on persecuting me regardless of my repentances."

Luckily he could soon put aside his embarrassment in the distractions of travel. He had planned to take his family to Europe, and in April of 1878 they sailed for Hamburg. It was not meant to be entirely a pleasure trip; he had signed a contract with the American Publishing Company to produce a book about his travels. He would make a book in his old way, taking a journey and writing about it as he went. For a year and a half the Clemenses—a party of six with their two children, the children's nurse, and an unmarried friend of Livy's—toured Europe, moving their mountains of baggage from one grand hotel to another, in Germany, Italy, Switzerland, and France. They visited galleries and attended operas; they went sightseeing; they shopped everywhere, for clothes, plates, glassware, mirrors, tapestries, paintings, bric-a-brac, an elaborate and expensive Swiss music box, even an antique bed—"a massive regal affair with serpentine columns surmounted by . . . graceful cupids . . . with other cupids sporting on the headboard." Mark and Livy would share that bed as long as they lived in Hartford.

There were pleasurable times: three months in the old university town of Heidelberg, where Mark Twain delighted in the spectacular views of the picturesque town and the beautiful valley of the Neckar, as seen from the glass-enclosed balconies—"great glass bird-cages"—of their enormous hotel suite, or a walking tour through the Swiss Alps with his Hartford friend Joe Twichell. Tall, handsome, and outgoing, unconcerned with theological subtleties, Twichell was "Joe" to all his congregation. He had served as a military chaplain for three years with the Army of the Potomac and had seen human nature at its best and its worst. He enjoyed earthy humor (including Mark Twain's *1601*), and he liked to travel incognito, so that people around him could talk and behave naturally. Genial, tolerant, optimistic, a tireless walker and conversationalist, Twichell made an ideal companion. He and Mark Twain were constantly together in Hartford and took long walks into the countryside, endlessly talking, arguing, reminiscing, sharing their enthusiasms and interests. (That walk through the Alps was not their first joint excursion. In 1874, they had set out to walk the 130 miles from Hartford to Boston, doing thirty-four miles on foot before taking the train, and in May of 1877, Twain had taken Twichell to Bermuda for a few pleasant days.) For Mark Twain, their joint tour through the Alps was without comparison the most deeply enjoyable experience of his sixteen months in Europe. For

Twichell—a minister supporting a large family on a small income—
that freedom, that setting, and that companionship made their out-
ing the unsurpassable vacation of his life.

Twain admired Bismarck's Germany, with its cleanliness and order and its combination (as he saw it) of "great freedom and superb
government." At Bayreuth, he even tried to enjoy Wagner, and
predictably failed, but his description of the sound—"the banging
and slamming and booming and crashing . . . The racking and
pitiless pain . . . the howlings and wailings and shriekings of the
singers, and the ragings and roarings and explosions of the vast
orchestra"—brilliantly reproduces the effect of Wagnerian opera on
the untrained ear. He puzzled over the unmistakable enthusiasm of
the audience: "whenever the curtain fell, they rose to their feet
. . . and the air was snowed thick with waving handkerchiefs, and
hurricanes of applause swept the place." He would have liked to
share that emotion, but he was excluded. Nothing in his background
had prepared him for such an experience.

Meanwhile, the book he had contracted to write went badly and
his exasperation mounted; he was exasperated by hotel life and the
discomforts of travel, by the operas and paintings that he was expected to admire and could not—a crescendo of exasperation, reaching a climax as the Clemens family spent the spring and early summer
of 1879 in Paris. He found that the Continent, and France in
particular, lacked the moral purity of Anglo-Saxon civilization. In
Paris, he read Carlyle's *French Revolution* and visited revolutionary
sites, but he was simultaneously entering impassioned denunciations
of everything French in his notebook until it became a compendium
of Anglo-Saxon prejudices.

He summed up a thousand years of history with "France has
usually been governed by prostitutes." Frenchmen were trivial,
fickle, cruel, and treacherous; the language itself was appropriate
only for "lying compliments" and "illicit love." Every married
woman had a lover. Every French girl, even if she remained tech-
nically chaste until marriage, must be "nasty-minded" because she
had been "reared in an atmosphere which is suffocating with nas-
tiness"—unlike English and American girls, who were "clean &
sweet & wholesome," because "their minds are not acquainted with
unclean thoughts." America was the most civilized of all nations,
he declared, because in it "pure-minded women are the rule."

That prudery is unexpected in the man who had written *1601*, and who delivered a humorous talk, "Some Thoughts on the Science of Onanism," to a club of male expatriates in Paris. "Make a collection of my profane works, to be privately printed," Twain suggested to himself in his journal at about this time; whether he is referring to works now lost, or works intended but never written, is uncertain. Yet he was no hypocrite. Unquestioningly, he accepted the double standard. Men could read books that women could not safely read, they could laugh at jokes that women should not even understand. In 1869, during his engagement to Livy, Twain had cautioned her against reading *Don Quixote*, even though it was "one of the most exquisite books that was ever written." "Neither it nor Shakespeare," he declared, "are proper books for virgins to read until some hand has culled them of their grossness." In the same letter he offered to "mark" and "tear" *Gulliver's Travels* until it was fit for her eyes. French culture, as Mark Twain understood it, sullied the sanctity and purity of womanhood—a woman's most precious possession—thereby undermining the family and civilization itself. It seemed to threaten his own family, the family that gave meaning to his success.

The Clemenses sailed for home in late August of 1879, not to go abroad again for twelve years. Twain's Americanism, already intensified by the experience of Europe, was heightened still more by an invitation to speak at the grand reunion of the Army of the Tennessee (the Union army in the West, commanded first by Grant, then Sherman), held in Chicago in November. For Mark Twain, ex–Confederate militiaman, who had made his own peace after two weeks, then sat out the duration of the war in Nevada and California, the invitation to attend that reunion must have seemed highly ironic. But the Sam Clemens of 1861 had become Mark Twain. He was a national figure, and this was a national event.

After nearly a week of parades, orations, and music, the climax for Mark Twain came on the final night, with his own speech at the great banquet for Grant. Mark Twain was deeply sensitive to oratory, and as he wrote to Howells, four of the speeches "carried away all my wits and made me drunk with enthusiasm." The audience had gone wild at seeing "a bullet-shredded old battle-flag reverently unfolded"—then Grant had stepped into view "and someone struck up 'Marching through Georgia'—you should have heard the thousand voices lift that chorus & seen the tears stream down."

As the evening wore on, with "the army songs, the military music, the crashing applause," the "tremendous and ceaseless bombardment of praise and gratulation," he wondered at Grant's incredible self-command. Apparently he never moved a muscle.

Mark Twain's turn came last, after hours of flag-waving oratory and responses to endless toasts. Declining the hackneyed "To Woman," he had written his own toast: "The Babies. As they comfort us in our sorrows, let us not forget them in our festivities." At 2 a.m., he climbed onto a table and began to speak, winning the audience almost at once with "We haven't all had the good fortune to be ladies; we haven't all been generals, or poets, or statesmen; but when the toast works down to the babies, we stand on common ground." After imagining future Presidents, generals, and admirals lying in their cradles at that moment, he pictured Grant, as a baby, "giving his whole strategic mind . . . to trying to find out some way to get his own big toe into his mouth."

He paused while suspense built. Would he go too far? Would he insult the guest of honor? Abruptly, he turned, facing Grant, and concluded: "And if the child is but a prophecy of the man, there are mighty few who will doubt that he *succeeded*." That brought down the house, even Grant, famed for his imperturbability; "he had sat through fourteen speeches like a graven image, but I fetched him! I broke him up, utterly!" Twain boasted in a letter to Livy. He had "measured this unconquerable conqueror," had won his own kind of victory by triumphing over the stubbornest audience in America: Grant. He had both challenged and asserted the hero's greatness by submitting it to the test of laughter, as he had disastrously failed to do, he believed, at the Whittier dinner.

It was a season of successes. Mark Twain had finally decided that he was finished with the book on his European travels, and it was published in March of 1880. *A Tramp Abroad*, as he punningly entitled it—the walking tour with Twichell filled many chapters—sold 62,000 copies and earned him $32,000, more than any of his earlier books, because he had held out for half profits instead of a royalty. That success surprised him. The *Tramp* had been the hardest of his books to write; he had slaved at it endlessly and hopelessly during the European tour. He had never really finished it; he had simply thrown up his hands and refused to write any more. To the end, the details had refused to cohere, and the exhilarating freshness of observation and comment that had marked *The Innocents Abroad* was gone. The dominant mood was exasperation, and the humor often depended on a kind of mechanical exaggeration and burlesque; as an English reviewer observed, "the process of manufacturing the jocularity was so obvious that it spoilt the reader's enjoyment."

His third daughter, Jane Lampton Clemens—named after Mark Twain's mother, but always known as Jean—was born in July of 1880, and with her the family was complete. Mark Twain showed no sign of discontent at the birth of another daughter; he enjoyed the company of women, and he was devoted to the Victorian ideals of feminine purity and girlish innocence—more complete than any possible masculine purity and innocence. This pregnancy, too, had gone well; Livy quickly recovered her strength, the new baby was healthy, and her father could write without feeling anxiety for wife or child.

After completing *A Tramp Abroad*, Mark Twain had turned to more congenial work, taking up *The Prince and the Pauper* again, alternating between the picaresque adventures of the true prince among tramps and outlaws, while "the small bogus king [Henry VIII has died and the false Edward has succeeded him] has a gilded & worshiped & restrained & cussed time of it on the throne." He wrote on through the summer, taking so much pleasure in the work that he did not want to finish. Mark Twain wrote *The Prince and the Pauper* for his family and families like his own, and as the story progressed, he read aloud from it to Livy and to Clara and Susy, now six and eight years old, and to selected friends. That reading of work in progress to his wife and daughters soon became a family custom. It was the most carefully plotted of his books, the most refined and genteel, the most "serious"—for those readers to whom absence of humor equaled seriousness. It was the sort of book that his wife, and Nook Farm, wanted from him, a work that would have "a sober character & a solid worth & a permanent value," as the Reverend Edwin Parker, a Hartford friend, observed. It was the kind of book that, in certain moods, Mark Twain wanted to write. There were times when being considered "merely" a humorist could not satisfy him. He knew he was more than a joker.

Yet *The Prince and the Pauper* was not simply a concession to gentility. Tom Canty, the pauper who becomes a prince, seems almost a sixteenth-century Tom Sawyer, with his reading and his fantasies, and a Huck Finn in his distress at the complicated discomforts of royalty. (Mark Twain had taken up the unfinished *Huckleberry Finn* as well, alternating between it and *The Prince and the Pauper* through the summer of 1880.) The main action of the book, the Prince's journey through England as a commoner, often in the company of thieves and beggars, resembles Huck's experience of Southern "civilization" as he and Jim floated down the Mississippi. And for all of Mark Twain's admiration of nineteenth-century progress, the "romance" of history—pageantry and show, quaint customs, picturesque language, even barbarous laws, the contrast between the colorful past and the utilitarian present—fascinated Mark Twain. *The Prince and the Pauper* satisfied deep imaginative longings, starved in Victorian America.

The Prince and the Pauper was published in mid-December 1881—by subscription as usual, but this time by James R. Osgood and Company of Boston. Shrewd and unscrupulous, knowing his public and his author, old Elisha Bliss of the American Publishing Company had helped to make Mark Twain the best-known American writer of his time and had earned him a substantial fortune as well. (The American Publishing Company sold 337,902 copies of his books between 1869 and 1879.) But Mark Twain believed that Bliss had lied to him in claiming that a 7½ percent royalty equaled half profits, and that lie could not be forgiven. Even though Bliss was now dead, his company would get no more of Twain's work. (Mark Twain was always ready to see himself as a victim, the helpless prey of sharpers—although he never learned caution. And he never forgave those who had taken advantage of him.) Now he would protect himself by reversing the normal relationship of author and publisher. The author would fix the selling price and get the profits, the publisher would receive a royalty on every copy sold, the amount depending on the total sale. Osgood would pay the cost of advertising and marketing, and he would arrange for printing and binding but would send the bills to Mark Twain.

Dedicated to "those good-mannered and agreeable children Susy and Clara Clemens," *The Prince and the Pauper* was clearly meant for all such children. "Good-mannered and amiable"—those adjectives fit the book itself. One old friend called it "your masterpiece in fineness." Harriet Beecher Stowe declared that it was "the best book for young folks that ever was written." Susy would consider it "perfect." Reviewers were generally kind; Mark Twain had finally lived up to his promise, they felt. He had "fulfilled the earnest hope of many of his best friends," said the Hartford *Courant*, "in writing a book which has other and higher merits than can possibly belong to the most artistic expression of mere humor." (Always "mere"!) The Clemens children, as they grew older, agreed; Susy would believe that it was her father's best work, showing "something of his kind, sympathetic nature" and proving that he was not only "a humorist joking at everything."

Howells found a deeper meaning, reading the book as a satire on monarchy and calling it "a manual of republicanism" when he reviewed it in the New York *Tribune*. Only Joe Goodman, old friend and ex-editor of the Virginia City *Territorial Enterprise*, dissented: "What could have sent you groping among the driftwood of the deluge for a topic?" he had asked in a private letter to Twain on first hearing of the book. The public seemed to agree; *The Prince and the Pauper* sold only seventeen thousand copies. That would have been a great success for most American writers of the day, but not for Mark Twain. Yet there were readers who would return to it again and again, thinking of it as the one work in which Twain had shown his true abilities.

While *The Prince and the Pauper* had not been written primarily for money, that sale was disappointing. The Clemenses lived extravagantly, and money would have been welcome. Consequently Mark Twain was irritable, ready to listen, when, in January of 1882, he was warned by a friend that the New York *Tribune*, the most influential newspaper of the time, had been regularly printing unprovoked slurs and attacks on him. Instantly, he planned revenge; he would print a slanderous "biography" of Whitelaw Reid, editor of the *Tribune*, and he filled pages of his notebook with insults: Reid had "the aspect of a derrick without its dignity"; he "had chased after all the rich girls in California" before marrying one of them; he was a moral and political eunuch; he lied, slandered, and betrayed; he was an assassin without the courage to kill. Then, at Livy's suggestion, he decided to see whether the alleged insults justified his intended revenge. Investigation found four remarks, all harmless, in two months of the *Tribune*. Mark Twain had wasted three weeks; he "could have earned ten thousand dollars with infinitely less trouble," he observed. But he felt no regret; he had simply acted in character. To feel unreasoning, unforgiving anger, anger that fed on itself, and to express it instantly and ferociously—

that was his temperament, and temperament was unchangeable. He could never quite forgive Reid, not so much for the imagined injury, but because so much hate had been wasted.

But in early February, a new interest, a real-life "romance," helped to put Whitelaw Reid out of Mark Twain's mind. One morning, while Livy and Mark were still sitting at a late breakfast, George Griffin, the black butler, entered to announce that "a lady in the drawing room wants to see you." Twain felt savage at this disturbance from an unknown caller, but her youth and beauty softened him. Her husband, a machinist with Pratt & Whitney, had "made a statue in clay," she said. Would Mark Twain view it, and tell him if it had promise? Twain denied any expertise in art, but she insisted, and he agreed.

Making his promised visit, he found her alone, her husband at work. She took him to the kitchen, snatched off the rags covering an object in the corner, and revealed the statue, a girl interrupted as she was about to bathe, "nude to the waist . . . the expression attempted being a modified scare." She put herself beside the statue, explaining that she had been the model, and then she and Twain turned the statue around to view it from all sides. Twain was charmed, he confided to Howells, by the girl's "innocence & purity—exhibiting her naked self, as it were, to a stranger & alone, & never once dreaming that there was the slightest indelicacy about the matter." As they talked, Twain learned that Karl Gerhardt, the husband, passionately desired to become an artist but had never been able to afford a lesson. Then Karl arrived, and lived up to expectations, possessing "a marvelous head & a noble eye."

The next day Livy visited the Gerhardt house and came away enchanted. A sculptor was brought from New York, who found promise in Gerhardt's work and said that "Hartford must send him to Paris." But the Clemenses did not wait to call on Hartford for help, but sent the Gerhardts to Paris at their own cost, with money enough for two years. (In 1883, they would finance a third year of study.) The money was to be regarded as an interest-free loan, to be repaid when convenient. Gerhardt was not the first promising beginner that Mark Twain had helped. A few years earlier, he had aided young Will Gillette, a Hartford neighbor, to go on the stage in spite of his parents' opposition, had found a part for him in *Colonel Sellers*, and had advanced $3,000 to cover the production of a play he had written. Gillette, still remembered for his performance as Sherlock Holmes, went on to a long and successful career in the theater. Clearly, Mark Twain had not forgotten those dismal months in San Francisco in 1864 and 1865, when he had been penniless and in debt, when his ambitions had seemed unattainable and the future utterly hopeless, when he had even considered suicide. If he had finally succeeded without help, that was no reason for withholding aid from others who might be just as deserving, but not so tough, or so lucky.

By spring, Mark Twain had a consuming new interest. He would make a book out of the "Old Times on the Mississippi" pieces. He would go back to the river, traveling by steamboat from St. Louis to New Orleans and then back upriver all the way to St. Paul, to gather material.

THREE

Return to the River

"T he Romance of boating is gone now . . . the steamboatman is no longer a god." The past was irrecoverable. So Mark Twain would learn on his nostalgic return to the river in the spring of 1882. Twain began his Mississippi journey on the eighteenth of April, traveling by train to St. Louis, where he would catch a steamboat for New Orleans. With him were James Osgood, his new publisher, and Roswell Phelps, a shorthand reporter—Osgood, a genial man, for companionship, and young Phelps to take down Twain's dictation. For this was a business trip, and he would be taking notes constantly. He was traveling to make a book, just as he had traveled to Europe in 1878–79 to produce *A Tramp Abroad*. But he was also returning to his past. In the spring of 1861, after four years of piloting, he had left the river when the outbreak of civil war had cut off all traffic except for the movement of gunboats and troop transports. Now he would go back to discover the inevitable changes, becoming the latest in a line of travelers dating back to La Salle, who had descended the great river to the Gulf just two hundred years before.

As early as the winter of 1866, Mark Twain had considered making a book of his river experiences, but fortunately had dropped the plan. He was not yet ready. Five years later, he had returned to the idea: "When I come to write the Mississippi book, *then* look out! I will spend 2 months on the river & take notes, & I bet you I will make a standard work." In 1874, he had finally taken up the subject in his *Atlantic* series, "Old Times on the Mississippi," a humorously heightened account of his two years as a cub pilot. The "Old Times" pieces had won high praise, both for their literary quality and for their value in documenting a vanished phase of American life, but they were too brief to make a book. For years, he had planned to go back to the river with a companion—preferably Howells, but Howells seemed always to be at work—and gather material enough for a full-length book. He would note the changes brought by twenty years, contrast the past and the present, assess the much discussed New South.

To pick up impressions more freely, he had planned to travel incognito, under the name of "C. L. Samuels," but that soon proved to be impossible. Mark Twain was probably the most photographed and the most widely recognized man in America. That mass of densely curling reddish hair (now rapidly graying), the beetling eyebrows, the heavy mustache, would give him away wherever he went. His anonymity broke down at once in St. Louis, he confessed to Livy; he had met too many old acquaintances. (But hotel clerks and even passersby on the street would have known him.) "We swore them to secrecy, & left by the first boat," the nine-hundred-ton *Gold Dust*—destination Vicksburg, where the party could transfer to a New Orleans boat. He had planned to work his way slowly downriver, taking local boats and lying over at every sizable town, but there were no more local boats. The railroads had seized the traffic.

On board the *Gold Dust*, his anonymity lasted no longer than it had on land; again he was promptly recognized, this time not as Mark Twain, humorist, but as Sam Clemens, ex-pilot. When he entered the pilothouse, Lem Gray, the pilot, treated him at first like any other visitor, telling him the usual lies in answer to the usual questions, then suddenly turned, saying, "I want to get a cup of coffee. You hold her, will you, till I come back?" And he was out of the pilothouse, without waiting for an answer. Mark Twain could still steer a boat, he found, but he had forgotten nearly all the details of the river, recalling only that they were in the Grand Chain, "a succession of hidden rocks, one of the most dangerous places on the river." At one point there were two rocks no more than seventy feet apart, and a pilot had to steer his boat exactly down the middle. Twain was in a panic, "about ready to drop dead," when the pilot casually reentered and took the wheel, introducing himself as a former cub who had been examined for his license by Sam Clemens. Gray had known him at once by his drawl and his habit of running his hands through his hair.

At least, that is the story as it appears in Paine's biography, where it is given in Mark Twain's own words, taken down twenty-five years or so after the event. What actually happened, as Twain reported to Livy in a letter written the next day, was less dramatic. He came into the pilothouse to get warm, began talking with another passenger, "& presently felt the pilot's eye on me. He had recognized my voice, after 21 years . . . He waited a while for confirmation of his suspicions; & presently when I raised my hat & passed my fingers up through my hair, he had no further doubts, & just called me by name."

Life on the Mississippi offers a third version, closer to the first: the pilot on duty recognizes Twain with his first words, but pretends to take him for a tourist, spinning fantastic lies, then suddenly offers him the wheel. Mark Twain's imagination needed facts to work on—we find them, no doubt, in that letter to his wife—but facts were infinitely malleable. His fiction is autobiographical, his autobiography is fictional. His reminiscences are vivid, circumstantial, appropriate to the time, the place, the situation—but often made so by invention, presenting what could or should have happened, or what did happen, to someone else. And as time passed, Mark Twain himself might forget that they were fiction.

South of Cairo, where the Ohio joined the Mississippi, the river was full, the channel wide, and Twain could be trusted at the wheel, often steering for long stretches while the pilot slept. Holding the boat on course, in midstream, he could "dream that the years had not slipped away; that there had been no war, no mining days, no literary adventures," that he was still a pilot and still young (although sighting the *Mark Twain*, an eighty-ton stern-wheeler, reminded him of new realities). Spring was far advanced, the generous Southern spring, not the reluctant New England season. He had himself called at four one morning to watch the sunrise, and in writing to Livy he lyrically described how the rim of the sun pushed itself above the trees, lighting "the luxurious green walls of forest . . . the jutting leafy capes . . . & the remote, shadowy, vanishing distances away down the glistening highway under the horizon! *and* the riot of singing birds!"

The sunrises were the same, and so, too, were the storms, with their crashes of thunder and deluges of rain. He described one "rattling nice storm" for Livy: "strong wind, blue-black sky, crawly white waves, vast sheets of driving rain, superb bursts of lightning,

& a most inspiring cannonade of big thunder." Thirty miles south of Memphis, the *Gold Dust* tied up to the bank to "let a hurricane, thunder & hail storm pass over. The wind snapped off several forest trees . . . making sounds like reports of a rifle." That, too, was familiar; he had sheltered his boat from a storm in just that way.

From the deck, it was easy to imagine that nothing had changed in the twenty-one years since he had left the river. The sunrise and the storms, the forest lining the riverbank for mile after mile, with the monotony broken only by the occasional miserable cabin in its clearing—those were the same. Yet that sameness was deceptive: the river itself had changed, whole islands had been washed away ("At 5 PM got to where Hat Island *was*. It is now gone, every vestige of it") or been joined to the mainland, bends had been cut off, old channels filled and new ones opened. Most of the knowledge he had gained so laboriously was forgotten now, and what remained was obsolete. His training, he found, had left him with nothing but the ability to remember street names and numbers!

Steamboating, too, had changed: its "romance" had faded as buoys, searchlights, and charts had eased the pilot's work and re-duced the danger. Making a landing at night, young Sam Clemens had groped his way in the darkness, when shadows could hardly be distinguished from shore; now "a blinding glory of white electric light burst suddenly from our forecastle." (Not all the dangers were gone, though; three months later, the *Gold Dust* blew up, and seventeen persons were killed, as well as forty-seven injured by scalding steam. One of the latter was Lem Gray, the pilot who had recognized Mark Twain. He died of his injuries.) There were no more stops at woodyards—the boats burned coal now. There was even steam heat in the pilothouse, and the pilot communicated with the engine room by a speaking tube instead of pulling clumsy bell cords.

While the pilot's craft had grown easier, its status had fallen. No longer could the pilot be considered the one truly independent gentleman in the world; now he was outranked by the captain. Steamboating had been modernized. The officers wore uniforms, boats ran on schedule, they no longer raced each other, the old devil-take-the-hindmost individualism had vanished. But modern-ization came too late. Railroads had taken the passenger traffic—steamboats could be incredibly slow; once the *Gold Dust* took six hours to go twenty-three miles—and a tug with a string of barges could handle more freight than any steamboat at a fraction of the cost. In comparison to the old days, the river was empty; two boats in sight at the same time were worth an entry and an exclamation mark in Twain's journal. In Hannibal, on the return trip, he would note that steamboating had lost its fascination and glamour had passed to the railroads. Instead of talking "river slang," boys now prided themselves on casually referring to railroad lines by their initials, rolling them "as a sweet morsel under the tongue."

Everywhere were memories: here he had run a boat aground, there he had struck a snag, at a third place he had "tried to snag another boat." At Cairo, when a cub pilot, he had obeyed the orders of his master as a cub was expected to do, consequently "mashing" his own boat when he drove it into another. There was news of old companions—of adventures in the war, of accidents, of who was alive and who was dead. And he heard again the old cry that had given him his pen name: "Apr. 25 p.m. Off Hilliard's took soundings and found *mark twain* for the first time."

He changed boats in Vicksburg, before moving into the deepest South. But steamboats were no longer the floating palaces of the old days, glorious in gilt and fresh paint, that had "tallied with the citizen's dream of what magnificence was, and satisfied it." The new boat, the *Charles Morgan*, was caked in "ancient and obdurate dirt." (In his notebook he was blunter, calling it a "gilt-&-filth sty.") But onshore he found happier signs of change. The notorious Natchez-under-the-hill, once wickedly famous for drinking, gambling, whoring, and murder, had become a workaday factory town, producing cotton yarn. And one ancient custom had been weakened, if not destroyed, by the emancipation of the slaves: "Was told that South they don't keep negro mistresses as much as befo' the waw," Twain observed in his journal. (That comment would not make its way into his book.)

Some things had stayed the same, of course. Arkansas City, he observed, still offered the traveler impassable mud and nineteen separate stinks. "Below Natchez now and then a reposeful alligator," just as he might have seen them from the pilothouse nearly twenty-five years before. And Southern speech remained the same, still soft, gentle, caressing, yet formal. The old-fashioned "sir," by which gentlemen once addressed one another, had disappeared from the North but survived in the South. "*R*'s" seemed to disappear as he went downriver, with the universal "sir" becoming "suh," and final "*g*'s" likewise vanished. And after eleven years in New England, Mark Twain found Southern speech deplorably lax: "college-bred men use the most atrocious grammar—doubling up their negatives &c."

He recorded the racy talk of a pair of black laundresses—a kind of talk that he had not heard for two decades. Speaking about "low down houses," one commented: "I jest tell you this: Some women takes up with everybody and anybody that comes along. But I jest tell you if I was a girl I wouldn't sleep with no stranger, don't care what he'd pay." The same woman joked suggestively with a young black waiter, "who went off saying 'I was pretty close to it.' She said, 'Couldn't get much closer,' " then commented, after he had gone, "I don't want anything to do with *boys*. If I want anybody I want a *man*." Mark Twain would have been deeply shocked to hear a white woman speak so freely, but the rules of propriety applied to ladies, and in the America of 1882, a black laundress could not possibly be considered a lady.

Hearing black talk might make him feel that he had come home again, but white conversation, with its constant references to the happy days befo' the Waw, and endless reminiscences of the war, constantly reminded him that he had become a stranger, almost a foreigner. No matter what subject might be started, it was sure to remind somebody, man or woman, of some wartime experience. But he had no recollections to offer—he had missed, by his own choice, the universal Southern experience of war, invasion, and conquest.

He was well aware of Southern violence—he had already written the feud chapters of *Huckleberry Finn*—and he meant to feature it in his book, to make it a part of his criticism of the traditional South. He collected gory examples. Two shopkeepers quarreled. One of them reached into a hip pocket for some papers; the other, thinking he was going for a gun, "drew his pistol and began shooting. The first called out 'I'm not armed; don't kill an unarmed man.' But the other kept on firing and killed him." A pair of farmers argued over the ownership of some fence rails that had been carried from one farm to another by floodwaters. They fought, one first pulling a revolver and then slashing the other's throat with a knife, and while they struggled, the man whose throat was cut seized the revolver and shot the other dead.

He recalled the long-standing Darnell-Watson vendetta, from his own days on the river: "The old man Darnell & his 2 sons came to the conclusion to leave that part of the country. They started to take steamboat . . . The Watsons got wind of it and as the young Darnells were walking up the companion way stairs with their wives on their arms they shot them in the back." Once a boy of twelve belonging to one family was riding on the wrong side of the river (one family lived in Kentucky, the other in Missouri): "He was overtaken by a full grown man and he shot that boy dead." Both families attended the same church, "armed with shot guns." Twain himself had narrowly missed seeing murder done in that feud, when a boy of nineteen was cornered in a woodpile by a half-dozen of the enemy. "He dodged among the wood piles & answered their shots. Presently he jumped into the river & they followed on after & peppered him & he had to make for the shore. By that time he was about dead—did shortly die." Here was the murderous counterpart of the Grangerford-Shepherdson feud in Chapters 17 and 18 of the still-unfinished *Huckleberry Finn*.

Hot-tempered, litigious, often vengeful, Mark Twain nevertheless disliked physical violence. Reading of a quarrel and a shoot-out between police detectives in New Orleans, he commonsensically observed, "I think I could wipe out a dishonor by crippling the other man, but I don't see how I could do it by letting him cripple *me*," and added advice to himself: "insert my duel with Laird." But the story of that absurd affair in Virginia City, with its bombastic challenges and insults, did more than demonstrate the absurdity of dueling; it also showed the young Mark Twain as a hot-tempered fool. It would not appear in *Life on the Mississippi*.

Ten days after leaving St. Louis, he reached New Orleans on a Friday morning for a week's stay. There were the inevitable marks of change to be noted: the city's Confederate cemetery, holding twelve thousand dead, offered a somber reminder of war, while the glare of electric lights for miles along the waterfront gave proof of progress. But sewage still ran down the gutters, and the smells were still "the liveliest things in N. Orleans and the most variegated." The cool porch of his hotel, the sawdust-covered floor of the barroom, and the mint juleps and their drinkers were also just what they had been more than twenty years before.

He had meant to look up old steamboatmen in the city and reminisce with them, to get book material. But celebrity interfered. "We are in the midst of a whirlpool of hospitality, breakfasts, dinners, lunches, cock-fights, Sunday schools, mule-races, lake-excursions . . . & all sorts of things," he explained to Livy. Three days later, "we are still booming along in the sociabilities, & find it a pretty energetic business & rather taxing." There was a cruise down the river below New Orleans in a fast steam tug, with Mark Twain steering; churchgoing, including an evening at a black church that turned out to be unsuitable for literary—that is, humorous—purposes because the service was performed in such excellent order; a performance of the balcony scene from *Romeo and Juliet* by a boy of six and a girl of four. Intensely susceptible to childish innocence, Twain was deeply moved at seeing the two children play their parts "in the quaintest most captivating way, with . . . perfect simplicity & unconsciousness."

Pursuing local color, he attended a Sunday cockfight and carefully noted the bloody details: "At the end of each round the pitters would blow water on their heads & legs, & lick off the blood. After 3 rounds one chicken had both eyes gouged out; the other had one eye left but couldn't see out of it . . . on account of blood." One of his companions left in the middle of the fight, disgusted by its brutality and shocked by the violation of the Sabbath. (In his journal, Mark Twain mentioned the day without comment, but in *Life on the Mississippi* he would transfer that fight to a Saturday afternoon. Buyers of subscription books were likely to be Sabbath keepers.) At the French Market, "the sights here are bad, but the smells heartrending." Cattle waiting for slaughter were "so poor & discouraged that a man holds them up on their legs while the butcher goes thro' the form of knocking them down with his axe."

He noted the flamboyant rhetoric of Southern journalism— "They have not got rid of flowery and fulsome speech in the newspapers . . . high-wrought rhetoric & eloquence"—and mocked its clichés. "The beauty and the chivalry of New Orleans" meant simply "ladies and gentlemen." A Southern reporter covering the Sermon on the Mount, Twain commented in *Life on the Mississippi*, would certainly have observed that "the beauty and the chivalry of Galilee" were in attendance. Journalistic prose might be straightforward until Woman was mentioned, then it became "flowery and idiotic." "South still in the sophomoric (gush) period," he noted in his journal. "All speech there is flowery & gushy—pulpit, law, literature." His own theory and practice were exactly opposite. "When you catch an adjective, kill it," he had advised a schoolboy in 1880, then modified that command to "kill the most of them—then the rest of them will be valuable." The "modern way, & the best way" to write English was to use "plain, simple language, short words, & brief sentences," and to shun "fluff & flowers & verbosity."

He had arranged to meet George Washington Cable, novelist and local colorist, and Joel Chandler Harris, author of the Uncle Remus tales, in New Orleans. Cable and Harris were the only contemporary Southern writers whose work he admired; they had freed themselves from the tyranny of an obsolete rhetoric. They were Southern without being provincial. As Harris put it (and Mark Twain would surely have agreed), "The spice and principle of all literature is localism," but paradoxically, "Whatever is truly Southern is truly American." Nothing could have seemed more Southern than the Uncle Remus stories, supposedly told by an old black man to a young white boy, and Mark Twain delighted in them.

Harris's presentation of black character and black speech seemed entirely authentic; he was "the only master the country has produced" in the writing of black dialect. And Mark Twain could judge; he had listened to such tales once, told by old Uncle Dan'l in a slave cabin at his uncle's farm, and he, too, was working with black speech, in *Huckleberry Finn*. (Modern readers are likely to prefer Twain's rendering to the dense and difficult dialect of Uncle Remus: "Brer Rabbit come prancin' 'long twel he spy de Tar-Baby, en den he fotch up on his behime legs like he wus 'stonished . . . 'Mawnin'!' sez Brer Rabbit, sezee—'nice wedder dis mawnin', sezee.") He read the Uncle Remus tales to his daughters, and when Harris later visited the Clemenses in Hartford, Twain's casual account offers a startling insight into race relations during the 1880s, even in relatively enlightened New England. Susy and Clara had eagerly looked forward to meeting "Uncle Remus," and they were deeply disturbed to see that his skin was white—until their father explained that Uncle Remus had whitewashed himself so that he could enter people's houses through the front door!

George Washington Cable was a more serious writer. Specializing in the history and folkways of New Orleans and the characterization of Louisiana Creoles, he had won a national reputation with *Old Creole Days*, a collection of short stories first published individually in *Scribner's Magazine*, and *The Grandissimes*, a novel set in the years following the Louisiana Purchase, when New Orleans was still principally French, offering picturesque contrasts between the traditional Creole culture and the go-ahead spirit of the American newcomers. But Cable was primarily concerned with race. In narrating the tragic destiny of the mulatto Honoré Grandissime, f.m.c. (free man of color), he became the first Southern writer to explore seriously the problem of miscegenation.

Cable, like Harris, owed much of his popularity to his exploitation of "local color," especially of speech. It was a time when American writers seemed to be mapping the literary geography of the country and staking out claims, and when the reading public delighted in quaint customs and speech, faithfully recorded. The work of the local colorists seemed to disprove the charge of monotonous sameness that foreign visitors regularly leveled at American society, and to demonstrate that American life and American scenes could provide literary diversity equal to anything Europe might offer. Cable had fascinated magazine readers with the picturesque broken English of his Creoles. (" 'Ah!' retorted Aurore, *'par exemple!* Non? Eee thing we is ridge, eh? Ligue his oncle, eh? Eee thing so, too, eh? You wan' to tague the pard of do Grandissimes?' ") Howells and Twain had been so impressed by *The Grandissimes*, and so charmed with the speech of its Creole characters, particularly the ladies, that they had once gone about all day "talking Creole" to each other.

Twain and Cable had met before, when Cable visited Hartford in the summer of 1881, and had taken to each other at once, in spite of their differences—Cable was a devout Presbyterian, painfully scrupulous, a rigid keeper of the Sabbath. After their meeting, he had sent Twain a copy of his latest work, *Madame Delphine*, a novelette in which a self-sacrificing quadroon mother denies her relationship to her octoroon daughter, thus allowing the girl to marry her white suitor. The mother dies while confessing her perjury, as the priest exclaims, "Lord, lay not this sin to her charge." That melodramatic sentimentality was very much to the taste of the time, and Twain responded enthusiastically: "I read it last night, & the charm of it, & the pain of it, & the deep music of it are still pulsing through me."

By 1882, Cable was recognized as one of the most important writers of his generation, a spokesman for the New South. "The South's finest literary genius," Mark Twain would call him; "a masterly delineator of its interior life and history," and for a modern biographer, Cable's first novel, *The Grandissimes*, ranks as "the first

modern Southern novel"—that is, the first "uncompromising attempt to deal honestly with the complexity of Southern experience"
and, above all, with the social effects of slavery and racism. Cable
was an uncompromising man. He devoted his life to the service of
God, and his piety expressed itself not only by churchgoing and
Sabbath-keeping, but in a strong social conscience, leading him to
consider the relations of black and white more seriously than any
Southern writer before him. Yet he had impeccable Southern cre-
dentials; born into a slaveholding family, he had served as a Confederate cavalryman in the last desperate years of the war and had
been seriously wounded. For a time, that record protected him in
a society that seldom tolerated dissent.

This second meeting with Cable would have consequences. Mark
Twain had not made a lecture tour since the season of 1871–72,
for he hated the loneliness of it. Yet he delighted in his power to
move an audience to laughter and applause, and the money was
welcome as well. Finally he had invented a solution: he would
appear, he hoped, on the stage—the "platform," he always called
it—in company with three or four other writers, personal friends.
They would travel in a private railroad car with their own cook,
performances would last no longer than an hour and a half, and
instead of lecturing, each writer would read from his own work.
Twain would be their impresario, making all the arrangements and
paying them seventy-five dollars a day apiece. Cable seemed willing and congenial; Mark Twain invited him to join the "menagerie" and make a tour that fall or winter. He hoped to have Howells,
and another friend, the poet and essayist Thomas Bailey Aldrich,
and Harris as well. The scheme failed, for the time; "the 'menagerie'
has to be given up for a year," he wrote to Cable a few weeks after
returning to Hartford. Howells and Aldrich would be traveling in
Europe, and Harris could not conquer his shyness—he would not
even test himself by reading in an empty hall. But in the fall of
1884, as a menagerie of two, Twain and Cable would finally make
that tour.

In New Orleans, Twain spent as much time as he could in the
company of his fellow writers, even attending Presbyterian service
with Cable. But while he enjoyed their company, he neglected his
work. Mark Twain had nothing to learn from the Uncle Remus
tales, or from Cable either. His own mastery of dialect already
surpassed their labored "authenticity," and while he might admire

Cable's sentiment, he could not imitate it. Suddenly it was time for him to leave, with his real work still undone. Hoping "to hunt up and talk with a hundred steamboatmen," Twain had let himself become so involved in social life that he "got nothing more than mere five-minute talks with a couple of dozen of the craft." He might have talked to his steamboatmen while Osgood accepted the invitations, but Mark Twain enjoyed society and found it hard to turn away admirers. He would pay for that pleasure when he came to write the book, filling the later chapters with guidebook detail instead of the living talk he had hoped to record.

He started upriver to St. Louis on May 6, for a five-day voyage— a reasonably fast passage—on the *Baton Rouge*, commanded by Horace Bixby, who had taught young Sam Clemens the river twenty-five years before. Weighing 2,300 tons, with six bridal chambers, and electric landing lights controlled from the spacious, steam-heated pilothouse, the *Baton Rouge* was one of the finest boats on the Mississippi. Here at least some of the glamour of steamboating survived, with modern conveniences added. Again, Twain spent hours in the pilothouse, sometimes taking the wheel. Again, it was easy to forget that years had passed. Bixby at fifty-six was still slender, erect, decisive, just as he had been at thirty, when he began teaching young Sam Clemens the river—"not an inch gained or lost in girth, not an ounce gained or lost in weight, not a hair turned."

Bixby also had stories of the war to tell; his record (unlike Mark Twain's) had been distinguished. Serving on the Union side, he had been responsible for the capture of an enemy troop transport and tug, and as chief pilot of the Union river fleet, he had taken part in the Battle of Memphis, when the Confederate fleet had been wiped out in forty minutes, and Memphis had been forced to surrender. Listening to those stories of the war he had missed, Mark Twain realized once again that the world of his young manhood had disappeared, that he was no longer a Southerner.

Reporters caught him again in St. Louis, and as always he let himself be interviewed. They noted his appearance: his hair was "slightly gray," his head was "massive" and "well-formed," his mustache "rakish," giving him a "devil-may-care" look. He was "fabulously wealthy and living in great splendor in Hartford," said one. This was not literally true, but in comparison to any newspaper reporter, and to most newspaper readers, Mark Twain was rich and did indeed live in splendor. But the reporters were not envious;

without any advantages of birth or fortune, he had earned his fame with his talent, in the American way. And Twain sometimes comforted them in their own obscurity by confiding that celebrity had its drawbacks, that because he had won a reputation as a humorist at the outset of his career, he was expected to play the jester, to appear always in cap and bells.

He said goodbye to his Mississippi, the lower river between St. Louis and New Orleans (he would never return to it), and went north on the *Gem City*, a fast boat of the St. Louis & St. Paul Packet Company. There were still familiar sights for the first day. Passing the village of Louisiana, Missouri, Twain would observe in *Life on the Mississippi* that "when I retired from the rebel army in '61 I retired upon Louisiana in good order . . . for a first attempt at a retreat it was not badly done." But stopping at Hannibal, he found that the drowsy village of his childhood had become a busy little city, "a thriving and energetic place" of fifteen thousand people, "with a Mayor, and a council, and water-works, and probably a debt." Only the mud in the streets had not changed.

But he was not concerned with the Hannibal of the present. Instead, he lost himself in nostalgia: "That world which I knew in its blossoming youth is old and bowed and melancholy, now. It will be dust and ashes when I come again." The past overwhelmed him; asked to address the Sunday school, he talked nonsense to hide the depth of his feelings as he recalled the vanished friends and enemies of his childhood. He saw Bear Creek, "hidden out of sight now, under islands and continents of piled lumber," remembering that "I used to get drowned in it every summer regularly, and be drained out, and inflated and set going again by some chance enemy." (Mark Twain liked to declare that youth, the time of romance and illusions, was the only part of life worth reliving.) Memories of fear and of guilt came back to him. He recalled the death of Lem Hackett, drowned by the wrath of God—so the boys believed—for playing in an empty boat on a Sunday; the drowning of Dutchy, in a practical joke played by other boys; the death of that drunken tramp in his cell, in a fire he had accidentally set with matches borrowed from young Sam Clemens.

Then north again, finding, as he would report in *Life on the Mississippi*, "all the enlivening signs of the presence of active, energetic, intelligent, prosperous, practical nineteenth-century populations," with well-kept farms between the towns, instead of the solitudes of the lower river. Quincy, Keokuk, Burlington, Davenport, Rock Island, La Crosse—one "fine and flourishing city" after another, each with its factories, its opera house, and its go-ahead spirit. Not everyone could be prosperous, though, even in this thriving new West. On his boat, Twain saw "a wretched poor family . . . going to the frontier." While the father stayed on deck all night with his wagon, the mother and five small children were "allowed into the cabin for charity's sake. They slept on sofas & floor in glare of lamps & without covering. Must have frozen last night." He gave them money and told the steamboat clerk to feed them at the second table and charge their meals to him.

Those bustling towns seem indistinguishable, as Twain would present them in the final chapters of *Life on the Mississippi*. There was nothing in their commonplace prosperity that could stir his imagination. On the upper Mississippi, romance had disappeared even more completely than from the lower river. Everywhere, from St. Louis to St. Paul, the railroad was in sight, the trains "ripping the sacred solitude to rags and tatters" with their "devil's warwhoop." (Like many Americans of his generation, and later, Mark Twain felt a deep ambivalence toward "progress." He would have preferred to have both the locomotive and the solitude, but if forced to choose, he would take the locomotive.) Lumber rafts still came downriver, as they had done in Sam Clemens's childhood, "but not floating leisurely along, in the old-fashioned way, manned with joyous and reckless crews of fiddling, song-singing, whisky-drinking, breakdown-dancing rapscallions." Instead, they would be "shoved swiftly along by a powerful sternwheeler," and carry small crews of "quiet, orderly men, of a sedate business aspect." "Rapscallions and deadbeats is the kind the widow and good people takes the most interest in," Huck Finn remarks, and so did Mark Twain. As a writer, he could make nothing of those quiet, businesslike men.

He found St. Paul "cold as the very devil," but shivered through a few hours of sightseeing. Then it was time to take the train for Hartford. Mark Twain's travels were over, and he was thoroughly tired of them even before he reached St. Paul, but there was still a book to be written.

There was also a book to be published. In early June, Osgood would issue *The Stolen White Elephant*, a collection of short pieces, written over the past few years and notable mainly for including Twain's allegory of conscience "The Facts Concerning the Recent

Carnival of Crime in Connecticut." The title piece again burlesqued the detective story. A white elephant (named Hassan Ali Ben Selim Abdallah Mohammed Moise Alhammal Jamsetjejeebhoy Dhuleep Sultan Ebu Bhudpoor, but commonly called "Jumbo") disappears from its quarters in Jersey City. In a blaze of publicity, an army of detectives tracks the elephant across New York State, constantly losing the trail, never quite catching up—until after three weeks its rotting carcass is discovered in the basement of the police station. (The story seems to have been inspired by a widely reported case in which the corpse of a New York millionaire was kidnapped from its mausoleum and held for ransom.)

The Stolen White Elephant was not likely to increase either Mark Twain's reputation or his fortune, yet it was exactly the sort of book that some readers expected from him. "There is a kind of monstrosity about them [Mark Twain's comic inventions]," said the *Nation* in what might have been the *White Elephant*'s only review, "which we remember in no other writer—a wild extravagance which is not simply that of exaggeration." In "The Invalid's Story," another piece from *The Stolen White Elephant*, the smell of ripe Limburger cheese in a railway express car is mistaken for the stench of a decaying corpse being carried in its coffin for burial. Mark Twain's readers had recognized that extravagance from the time he had begun to write for the Virginia City *Territorial Enterprise*; that was why they had named him the Wild Humorist of the Pacific Slope. At times he seemed possessed by it—an uncontrollable, manic energy. By definition, it was excessive, always in bad taste—at times Livy or Howells had to protect Mark Twain from its excesses. Yet without this wild comic energy, he would have been a lesser writer. The books in which it is most conspicuously absent are his least individual, and therefore least interesting. Good taste, after all, is essentially a negative quality.

Almost before Twain could begin to settle back into his busy Hartford life, it was time for the annual migration of the Clemens tribe to Quarry Farm. There, on a hill above Elmira, they could escape the summer heat and malaria of Hartford, and the children could play in the sun, with the animals on the farm or with their Langdon cousins, children of Livy's brother, Charley, who managed the family business. There Livy could relax, free at last from the cares of entertaining and of managing the Hartford household, and Mark Twain could write, spending the days in his isolated study.

It was a time to look forward to, his best working time—the best time of the year. Twain expected to write the new section of his Mississippi book at Quarry Farm. But this year, the family's summer escape would be drastically shortened by unforeseen, frightening delays.

Ordinarily, the packing was completed by mid-June (the Clemenses did not travel light) and the house secured for the summer—all this overseen by Livy, since her husband had no organizing ability. "After infinite labor and fatigue," Livy had gotten what her husband liked to call "the menagerie" ready to move, and a special railroad car—an impressive mark of status in Victorian America—had been engaged, when Jean, not quite two, was struck down with scarlet fever. "A horrible rash appears upon the body of the baby!" Twain wrote in a frantic letter to Cable. "We are . . . unspeakably alarmed. The doctor cannot tell, yet, whether this rash is only heat or the other dreadful thing."

The house was quarantined, Susy showed symptoms, and her father believed that she, too, was "stricken—& savagely—with this dire scarlet fever." His panic was understandable, since the disease was terrifying, sometimes ushered in by convulsions, and bringing high fever and a rash of minute red spots covering the body, then peeling of the skin. It was often fatal, and there could be dire aftereffects: arthritis, rheumatic fever, permanent deafness. As with the other childhood diseases of the time—mumps, measles, diphtheria, whooping cough, "membranous croup"—doctors could do little more than diagnose, quarantine, and prescribe useless remedies, while parents waited and hoped. Now that danger threatened Mark Twain's own children. Jean's disease really was the "dreadful thing" (she made a complete recovery), but Susy, it developed, had never had scarlet fever; Mark Twain was a nervous, excitable parent, exaggerating symptoms, always expecting the worst—with some reason, for he and Livy had lost their only son. Finishing *Huckleberry Finn* the next summer, remembering his own terror, Twain would create the pathetic scene in which Jim recalls how, when about to punish his four-year-old daughter for disobedience, he discovered that she'd been left "plumb deef en dumb" by "de sk'yarlet fever."

By mid-July, Jean, though not yet fully recovered, was able to travel, and the Clemenses finally moved to Quarry Farm. There Mark Twain set to work, but he had lost nearly four weeks, he had been distracted just when he was ready to write and while the impressions of his trip were still fresh, and he had been shaken by his children's sickness. Worst of all, he found that his new book simply did not interest him. Without the obligation of the contract he might never have finished it, but that contract itself turned the work into drudgery. He already expected to fill out his book by contrasting the present-day South with impressions of earlier travelers. In late July, Osgood shipped him twenty-five volumes to draw on, mostly written by English visitors to America in the first half of the century.

In spite of his late start, in spite of suffering from what he believed were intermittent attacks of malaria, leaving his brain "stuffy and cloudy nearly all the time," Mark Twain managed to produce fifty thousand words of manuscript. He had it copied by a typist in Elmira and was well satisfied with the result; the impersonality of the typescript pleased him, as he disliked reading his own work in someone else's hand. The technology of writing and of printing fascinated Mark Twain. He searched endlessly for the perfect pen, and in 1874 he had bought one of the earliest typewriters and had written a few pages of *Tom Sawyer* on it, becoming probably the first American author to compose on the machine. He had soon given it up, exasperated by the machine's clumsiness and his own mistakes. But he could recognize its value for producing readable copy, when operated by someone else.

In the grip of inspiration, Twain would forget the outside world, but this summer he welcomed distractions. The monthly installments of Howells's latest novel, *A Modern Instance*, in *Century* magazine seemed more interesting than anything he himself was doing. The novel focuses on the moral decline of Bartley Hubbard, an agreeable and unprincipled young reporter, and on the breakup of his marriage. After reading a scene in which Bartley gets drunk for the first time and barely escapes being thrown in jail, Twain enthusiastically complimented Howells on his realism: "That's the best drunk scene—because the truest—that I ever read. There are touches in it which I never saw any writer take note of before. And they are set before the reader with amazing accuracy. How very drunk, & how recently drunk, & how altogether admirably drunk you must have been to enable you to contrive that masterpiece!"

Twain's response to Howells's story was deeply personal; he identified with Bartley Hubbard. It's not likely that Howells—scrupulous and conscientious, self-controlled and self-disciplined, incredibly industrious—had ever been drunk, but in his bachelor days Mark Twain surely had been. And he had been more than merely threatened with jail, as Bartley Hubbard was; in San Francisco, in 1865, a hostile reporter charged that Twain had once been jailed for drunkenness. The accusation might have been only a slander, but in the winter of 1866 he had spent a night in jail in New York and had unabashedly described his experience for the readers of the *Alta California*. While he and a friend tried to break up a drunken brawl, he claimed, they had been arrested along with the brawlers.

After reading Howells's next installment, he had to express his enthusiasm again: "You didn't intend Bartley for me, but he *is* me just the same, & I enjoy him to the utmost uttermost without a pang . . . Mrs. Clemens indignantly says he doesn't resemble me— which is all she knows about it." In a sense, Livy was right; there was little resemblance between her devoted husband and the "false scoundrel Hubbard," as Howells called his own character. But her husband knew better; Hubbard represented not what Mark Twain was but what he just possibly might have become—if he had never met Olivia Langdon, never written *The Innocents Abroad*, but stayed in California, a frustrated and unhappy bohemian.

Suddenly it was late September, with *Life on the Mississippi* still unfinished. "The weather turned cold, and we had to rush home, while I still lacked thirty thousand words," Twain confessed to Howells. Writing those words would be hard.

FOUR

The Dimensions of Success

"H e has everything a man could have," wrote a Texas schoolboy in 1880, explaining why he would like to be Mark Twain. In Mark Twain's eyes, his home would have made an essential part of that "everything." An architectural freak it might appear to some viewers, but Mark and Livy treasured it. In 1881, they bought a strip of land bordering theirs for $12,000 (an outrageous price, but the neighbor had begun digging a cellar and threatened to build a house there, "right in our faces," as Mark Twain put it). Then they relandscaped the property, moving the driveway and leveling the ground to bring the house more fully into view from the street— it was, after all, built to be seen.

They renovated the interior at great expense, enlarging the kitchen, tearing out the reception room "to make our front hall bigger," engaging Louis Tiffany's Associated Artists, the outstanding decorators in the country, to redecorate the walls and ceilings of the entire lower floor. The house now seemed perfect to them. "How ugly, tasteless, repulsive" were the interiors of European homes, Twain would exclaim on revisiting Hartford in 1895 after a four-year absence, when "compared with the perfect taste of this ground floor, with its delicious dream of harmonious color, & its all-pervading spirit of peace & serenity & deep contentment."

One important change had already been made inside. Mark Twain had soon abandoned the luxurious study designed for him on the second floor. It had been too luxurious—he could not work in it. He moved instead to the billiard room above, with the former study becoming a schoolroom for the children. "Where do I write? In the billiard room—the very most satisfactory study that ever was," though on cold winter days, even with a fire in the fireplace, it could be heated barely above the freezing point. In a household of women, it was a masculine sanctum. Here Twain could invite a favored guest for conversation or a game (often played according to the host's improvised rules), play solitary billiards for hours at a stretch, or bring his cronies in the evening for beer and cigars and talk.

Designs of billiard cues, meerschaum pipes, and wine bottles and glasses on the walls and ceiling announced the social purposes of the room. But there was a desk where Twain could work, while smoking his endless cigars till the room was filled with an impenetrable haze. A true addict, he preferred his cigars cheap and strong. "He smoked as much as a man could," was Howells's comment, "for he smoked incessantly." (Three hundred cigars a month was Twain's own figure, probably an underestimate.) In his effort to reform, at the outset of his marriage, he had cut down his smoking time to one afternoon a week, but under the pressure of completing *Roughing It* he had found that he could not work without cigars, "the best of all inspirations for the pen." On "vacation" at Quarry Farm, he ordinarily allowed himself fifteen cigars during a five-hour working session, "and if my interest reaches the enthusiastic point . . . I smoke with all my might, and allow no intervals." The habit was perfectly harmless, he insisted, and his health was perfect.

It was not simply a home, the Clemens place, it was an establishment, with a governess for the children and a staff of servants—cook and housemaids, besides butler and gardener and coachman. There were horses in the stable and cats in the house. Always there were cats, whether at Hartford or at Quarry Farm, with names like Sin, Satan, Sourmash, Beelzebub, and Blatherskite. Mark Twain was "a lover & believer in cats," as his daughter Jean would describe him. He could admire the beauty of a fine dog, but he preferred the grace, the cleanliness, and above all the self-possession and independence of the cat, in contrast to the servility of the dog—or the human. The contented cat became a symbol of domesticity for him: "A house without a cat—a well-fed, petted and properly revered cat—may be a home, but how can it prove its title?" he would write in *Pudd'nhead Wilson*.

The relationship of the Clemenses to their servants was almost feudal. Patrick McAleer, the coachman, had been with them since their marriage in 1870, when he was twenty-five. He would work for them until they left Hartford in 1891, never to live there again. Prompt and alert, always to be found when he was needed, he had once saved the lives of Susy, Clara, and a neighbor's girl who had been exploring the oat bin at the stable when the heavy lid sprang shut. Patrick discovered them there, terrified and close to suffocation. Katy Leary, a maid, stayed with the family for thirty years, until her master's death in 1910. (Later, helped by a ghostwriter, she would make a book out of her memories: *A Lifetime with Mark Twain*.) George Griffin, the black butler, came to wash the windows, as Twain would recall, and stayed for eighteen years.

George was a man who knew the world—he had been the body servant of a Union general during the Civil War—and he was a leader in the black community of Hartford, with a keen interest in politics. A steady churchgoer, George did not drink or smoke or swear, but he was an inveterate and usually successful gambler on elections and horse races. He and his employer delighted in each other's eccentricities. George might talk politics to a visitor while taking off his coat, or stand behind a guest's chair at dinner to laugh at Mark Twain's jokes. He could be "serenely and dispassionately slow . . . phenomenally forgetful," but he was utterly honest and reliable. He was a ready playmate for the children, and he could lie convincingly when the need required. That might shock the truthful Livy, but her husband was more tolerant—his occupation was writing fictions—and he found George's lies indispensable in warding off unwelcome visitors. George was an institution; he seemed a part of the family. That relationship of master and servant, black and white, seemed to embody the Southern myth, but with the difference that George had chosen his role.

Breakfast was Mark Twain's favorite meal, Howells would recall; "he sat longer at his steak and coffee than at the courses of his dinner." Clara confirms that recollection: no one but her father seemed to find "any real joy in life so early in the morning." "Of course," she adds, "he didn't *find* it, he created it." After breakfast, if there were no guests to entertain, he would retreat to his study, to read or to write, or to deal with correspondence and business, or to play a solitary game of billiards. As a rule he would eat no lunch, not wishing to interrupt his work or his game.

Full of vigor, he would finally descend for dinner, the day's main social occasion. Whether the family dined alone or with guests,

Twain would dominate the talk. "With no more inspiration than a 'yes' or 'no' from one of us . . . Father could lead, fill, and finish the conversation all by himself," Clara would recall. "He was never more fascinating than when giving the entire entertainment." Dining with Kaiser Wilhelm II in 1891, he would notice that the rules of conversation at the imperial table were just what they had been at Hartford: guests spoke when they were spoken to. Sometimes he forgot to eat. Talk mattered more. "I could talk when I was not ten seconds old," Mark Twain would observe in his old age, "and the moment I cease to be able to talk I shall die."

One owned such a house to display it, and the Clemenses did. There were perpetual visitors from out of town. Some of them were welcome. Cable came to Hartford briefly in that fall of 1882 and, with his "limpid innocence" and "blemishless piety," made a profound impression. In comparison, "the apostles were mere policemen," Twain observed. But the hordes of strangers, curiosity seekers, were a continual nuisance. Mark Twain himself was the outstanding tourist attraction of Hartford, with his home taking second place. If unknown callers had letters of introduction, he would usually see them; if not, he tried to avoid them—they were likely to be seeking his autograph, or collecting contributions for some Western college, or canvassing for subscription books. Still, they often managed to make their way in.

And there were always the casual calls by neighbors, who could not be turned away, and the calls to be made on them. (Years before, Howells had noted the charming informality of Nook Farm, observing that its "delightful people" went "in and out of each other's houses without ringing, and nobody gets more than the first syllable of his first name—they call their minister *Joe* Twichell.") In the evenings, the Clemenses were always ready to receive friends. The consequence was obvious; as Mark Twain explained in an interview, twelve years later, "for many years while at home, I have written little or nothing on account of social calls upon my time." Only at Quarry Farm, while he was supposed to be "holiday-making," did he find time to work, adding, with mild regret: "I seemed to think then that I was never going to grow old."

Probably no other major American writer has enjoyed a standard of living equal to Mark Twain's—a standard dangerously high, because Twain could not retreat from it. He was no Scott Fitzgerald, unbalanced by early success. He had been a man of thirty-three, with a wide experience of the world, when *The Innocents Abroad* brought him fame. But standards of living, once established, are not easily lowered; luxuries become necessities—self-esteem requires them. To retrench would have been to admit that he could not provide for his wife and daughters, according to the expectations of upper-middle-class America. In his own eyes, he would have been repeating his father's failure. In any case, Mark Twain had always been careless, impulsive, impatient with details. That was his temperament, and it was also the way of the South. No doubt he was regularly cheated, as he often complained. The household expenses were enormous, of course—thirty thousand dollars a year, Twain confided to a visitor, this at a time when a factory worker could think himself well paid at two dollars a day, and a Harvard professor might draw a salary of two thousand a year.

"To live in this style," Mark Twain had observed enviously on his first visit to Nook Farm, while he was still a roving newspaperman, "one must have his bank account, of course." The Clemenses had their bank account. Livy was a wealthy woman; her money had paid for the house and land. Livy never presumed on that; she had far more practical sense and organizing ability than her husband, but she left all their financial affairs to him, as a dutiful wife was expected to do, never objecting to his foolhardy speculations, never complaining about their disastrous outcome. As for Mark Twain, he had brought principally his talent to their marriage—a fact that he had been sensitive about—but he had proved his earning power, with more than a hundred thousand dollars in book royalties between 1869 and 1882. No other American writer of the period could have approached that figure, or the seventy thousand dollars that Twain made from the *Colonel Sellers* play. *The Prince and the Pauper*, one of his least successful books, sold seventeen thousand copies—three thousand more than *Daisy Miller*, Henry James's most popular novel. And he could earn money at will by taking to the lecture platform, although he avoided it for years.

Twain's literary status did not equal his celebrity or his sales, as he well knew. He was, without question, the most popular American humorist. The early death of Artemus Ward, the most successful humorist of the 1860s, and the self-exile of Bret Harte in the late '70s had removed the only possible rivals. To some readers he would never be anything more than "America's Greatest Funnyman," as the reporters called him—a newspaper clown. There were critics who apparently considered laughter to be vulgar, who preferred the polite humor, offering "truth and wholesomeness . . . and a power to amuse without conspicuous effort," that they found in the work of Washington Irving or Oliver Wendell Holmes or in the essays of Twain's neighbor Charles Dudley Warner (his collaborator in *The Gilded Age*), to the "rude and clownish 'merriment' " provided by Mark Twain.

Yet his reputation steadily grew, and his humor was already proving more durable than that of his competitors—"Josh Billings," the "Danbury *News* Man," "Petroleum V. Nasby," and dozens of other now almost forgotten figures. He offered more than deliberate incoherence or laborious misspellings, puns or folksy aphorisms. He could build a book; he could create character; his work had content. He had made himself a national celebrity, as Dickens had done in England but as no other American writer had yet become, and he figured continuously in the newspapers and the magazines of his day. He gave himself generously to the world. Interviewers sought him out in Hartford and pursued him wherever he went, expecting quaint or spicy comments, and he obliged them, even when he had come to believe that interviews were invariably "twaddle," no matter how accurately reported, simply because the "soul" of talk disappeared when it was put into print. "Color, play of feature, the varying modulations of voice, the laugh, the smile, the informing inflections"—all vanished.

Since the late 1860s, when his sketches had first appeared in cheap English editions, he had been nearly as well known in England as in America, a fact that pleased him, for he had been a confirmed Anglophile since his first visit to England in 1872. Fame was supplemented by substantial royalty checks from his English publisher, Chatto & Windus, who had replaced Routledge & Sons. His work was becoming known outside the English-speaking world. His writings had been translated into Dutch and Swedish, even Russian. He was popular in Germany and Austria—*Tom Sawyer* had been translated into German in the year of its American publication and read by Friedrich Nietzsche, among others, and other books would follow it. By the time of his death in 1910, he would surely be the most famous writer in the world—perhaps the most widely known private citizen.

Throughout the United States, his name and his face would be instantly recognized. "Sometimes," Howells had written to him prophetically, "I think we others shall be remembered merely as your friends and correspondents." His sister, Pamela, noted that "people make a great deal of me if they find out who I am. If they cannot know Mark Twain, the next best thing is to know a near relation." He was even worth impersonating. In 1882, he read in the Irish *Times* of June 9 "that a bogus Mark Twain is fooling people in Belfast."

No doubt he would have preferred to be a celebrity on his own terms, but that was impossible. At times he felt harassed almost to a frenzy by the demands of newspapermen and of his correspondents. But at least he could guard his private life. "I hate all public mention of my private history," he confided to Orion, "it is none of the public's business." Inquiring interviewers would never get more than a bare outline of his life. In old age he would appoint an official biographer, Albert Bigelow Paine, supply him with materials, and shape his point of view, but that biography could not be published until after Twain's death. Twain would allow no biography while he lived: "A man's history *is his own property* until the grave extinguishes his ownership in it," he told a distant cousin who hoped to produce a book about his famous relative. To the limit of his ability, Mark Twain would control his own public image.

His children knew very well that their father was not like the fathers of their friends. He read his manuscripts to them; they saw his many callers and his mail. When their governess asked the two older girls to make lists of famous men and women, Susy's list of men included "Longfellow, Papa (Mark Twain), Columbus, Teneson [Tennyson], Ferdinad [*sic*]," while Clara's were "Columbus, Mr. Clemens, Mr. Millet [an artist and family friend], Henry Hudson, Mr. Dickens." Susy was the more perceptive; she knew that it was Mark Twain, not Mr. Clemens, who was famous. It would not be long before she would sense something dubious about that fame, compared with the fame of a Tennyson. Humor, after all, seemed frivolous at best, vulgar and degrading at worst. Her father's humor made her laugh, but she could not help wishing that he would write something more worthy of himself.

So did others. By Mark Twain's standards, sales of *The Prince and the Pauper* had been disappointing—the public stubbornly preferred humor—but to some reviewers and some readers (including Livy) its pathos and drama revealed a truer and deeper Mark Twain than his more popular books had shown. Occasionally, he believed that himself. But he could not forget for long where his true audience lay—an audience that recognized and valued his distinctive qualities rather than wishing he were a quite different kind of writer, as genteel readers and critics sometimes did. To the public at large, and to the buyers of subscription books, Mark Twain was the author of books and sketches that were all humorous, in part or in whole, from "The Celebrated Jumping Frog of Calaveras County," in 1866, to *A Tramp Abroad* in 1880. With *The Prince and the Pauper* he had partially lost that audience; with *Huckleberry Finn* he would recapture it.

Yet in an unruly democracy, in which corrosive irreverence constantly seemed to threaten the foundations of all established traditions and even of the social order itself, humor could seem to be cultural sacrilege, subverting respect for authority of every sort. And not only in America. No other living writer, said an English critic, had done so much "to lower the literary tone of English speaking people." Those genteel critics were right: a reverent humor seems an impossibility, and certainly Twain had been noted for his irreverence from the beginning. As he well knew, it was precisely its jokes and its irreverence in the face of Old World culture and traditions, his mockery of the Old Masters and the alleged beauties of the Holy Land, that had made *The Innocents Abroad* a smashing success. Yet he was a virtuoso in prose, who could produce sublime or pathetic effects at will—but was more likely to burlesque them. An unclassifiable oddity, then, unless one simplified matters by assuming that he was only a newspaper funnyman enjoying an unaccountable run of good luck.

Some English reviewers took him more seriously: "He shares with Walt Whitman the honour of being the most strictly American writer of what is called American literature," observed a critic in the *Athenaeum*. Like Whitman, he owed nothing to Europe or to England except "the rudiments . . . already archaic to him, of the speech he has to write." "Of what is called American literature"— that phrase could have been a sneer, but more likely it indicated the difficulty, for a British reviewer, of coming to terms with a literature in English that could not be considered English literature.

(If that reviewer could have seen the manuscript of *Huckleberry Finn*, he might have decided that Americans had abandoned even the "rudiments" of English.)

Mark Twain had expected to finish *Life on the Mississippi* at Quarry Farm, but his summer had been brief and the writing came hard. Clearly, there was no hope of meeting the October 1 deadline set in his contract with Osgood. The problem was to find something to say that interested him. "Old Times" had dealt only with his apprenticeship to the pilot's craft, covering two of his four years on the river, and he might have expanded it with reminiscences of his career as a licensed pilot. Certainly there should have been material enough in those two final years. He had thought of that, noting the possibility in his journal. But it was the apprenticeship itself, with its comic blunders and its freshness of perception, that attracted him. His first great success, *The Innocents Abroad*, had humorously recorded an American's initiation into the cultural mysteries of the Old World. *Roughing It*, his third book, had been the record of an apprenticeship to a region, showing how the young Clemens-Twain, with his youth and his naïveté much exaggerated, had learned the ways of the West while failing as a silver miner and succeeding as a reporter.

He had not quite completed the story of his two years as a cub pilot in "Old Times on the Mississippi," and now he filled out the record with five new chapters, the two most important dealing with his fight with the pilot Brown on the *Pennsylvania* and the death of his brother Henry when the *Pennsylvania* blew up. This was deeply painful material; without reason, he blamed himself for Henry's death. When he wrote "Old Times on the Mississippi," those memories might still have been too sensitive to deal with. Now he was ready. In his notebook, he had instructed himself to write the full story. By narrating those events, he might find at least temporary relief—for him, guilt could never be finally erased—while giving a fuller picture of steamboating in the 1850s.

Then he summed up his two years as a licensed pilot in a single paragraph and turned to the Mississippi of the present, narrating his visit that past spring, with a good many digressions. In doing so, he gave the final two thirds of *Life on the Mississippi* the pattern of a journey, the basic form of at least half his books. He stretched out his firsthand material with facts from histories and guidebooks, whether strictly relevant or not. "Get statistics of width, length, & volume of Misspi," he advised himself in his journal, "and something about La Salle's trip out of Parkman." To illustrate the life of the Mississippi raftsmen who had once ruled the river, and to fill out his book, he borrowed a chapter from the still-unfinished manuscript of *Huckleberry Finn*, in which Huck, naked, swims at night to a log raft, hoping to find out whether he and Jim have drifted past the junction of the Ohio and the Mississippi, and watches the raftsmen sing and dance and brag and fight, until he is discovered.

He inserted irrelevant stories—"The Professor's Yarn," the story of a confidence trick played by a gambler on other gamblers; "A Thumb-Print and What Came of It," a Gothic tale of murder and atrocious revenge; "A Burning Brand," a twelve-page account of an ingenious convict's effort to win sympathy and pardon through a forged letter. To make time, he even freed himself from his correspondence, reading letters only one day a week and dictating his replies to a typist. He must have laughed sardonically at Osgood's proposal, on October 14, that he should take a month off to advertise his forthcoming book by giving twenty lectures in twenty cities. In a spurt of desperation, as he reported to Howells on October 30, Twain "wrote" 9,500 words in a single day—"mainly stolen from books, tho' credit given," he confessed. But that still left him twenty thousand words short. Meanwhile, letters from Osgood advised him to cut and condense, doubted the relevance of long passages, proposed omitting unpleasant details.

He copied four pages recounting the bloody deeds of the notorious river bandit Murrell, and he borrowed freely from Francis Parkman's *LaSalle and the Discovery of the Great West* for historical background. He stole a five-thousand-word account of a Mississippi flood from the New Orleans *Times-Democrat*. Intoxicated with inspiration, Mark Twain could write prodigiously—day after day, even week after week—but the set task bored him, wearied him, and soon infuriated him. Both writing *A Tramp Abroad* and completing *Life on the Mississippi* were agonizing ordeals; he might have seen much, but he had experienced very little. It would be fourteen years before he would manufacture another book, *Following the Equator*, in that way, and then it would be done out of necessity, to finish paying off debts incurred by the bankruptcy of his publishing company.

So he went on, tearing up one day what he had written the day before, announcing one week that he was nearly done, gloomily observing the next that his book was "unfinished and nearly unfinishable." Bad luck dogged him. Scarlet fever had delayed the writing that past summer and now complicated the book's completion. Going to his typist at the end of December to pick up copy, Twain found her sick with scarlet fever. The typescript had to be disinfected with carbolic acid before shipping, and again before Osgood could read it. But the work was almost done. By mid-January, Osgood had applied for copyright and a week later Mark Twain could report that he had read all of the proofs and Livy nearly all.

With the recollection of that grinding labor still fresh, he wished for a moment that he could "write all books for the mere pleasure of writing them, & with no prospective audience before me & no intent to publish." But that was an illusion. Every author imagines an audience, no matter how small, or how remote. Certainly Mark Twain always did. Only in his old age would he write pieces that he had no intention of making public in his lifetime, believing that they would shock too many readers. Even then he expected them to be published eventually, perhaps after a hundred years. With his overflowing energy, his continuous and vivid self-expression in every aspect, every detail of his life, he communicated continuously with his world. When he counted sales, it was the audience, not the money, that mattered most.

As far as that new section of *Life on the Mississippi* had a coherent theme, it became a comprehensive attack on whatever seemed most Southern about the South. After twenty years of absence, Mark Twain saw his native region as culturally, socially, economically, and politically backward, hardly belonging to the nineteenth century at all. Southern violence, Southern "culture," Southern literature all came under attack. Slavery at least was gone—"that horror," he called it, in a passage omitted from the book—but whites were not yet free. The "solid South" rested on a rigid conformity, with the white dissenter likely to be forced into exile, as Cable would soon discover.

In a chapter ultimately omitted, "The South and Slavery," Twain denounced the cowardice of Southerners, as shown by the failure of juries to convict murderers and by the total absence of dissent. In "Doses for Adults" (also dropped, at Osgood's suggestion), he catalogued Southern faults—not only slavery, but "rowdyism, 'chiv-

alrous' assassinations, sham godliness," and "other devilishnesses"—
and then widened his condemnation to cover the "civilization" of
that earlier America: "Everybody bragged, everybody blustered,"
and "all over the land, two things could count upon reverence and
championship—religion and slavery." Mark Twain did not make
those cuts simply from fear of losing sales. The criticism that he
left is harsh enough. As he probably came to realize, those chapters
were simply a blast of bad temper—violent, confused, and repetitious. But the time spent in writing them had not been lost. That
denunciation of moral cowardice, widened to include all humanity,
would be more powerfully expressed when he went back to *Huckleberry Finn*, in Colonel Sherburn's denunciation of the mob that
comes to lynch him.

The culture of the South was a sham, Mark Twain decided. In
"The House Beautiful" (Chapter 38 of *Life on the Mississippi*) an
enormous, five-page paragraph catalogues the interior of a fashionable Southern home before the war, covering every detail from the
"Corinthian" columns in front, made of painted wood, to the stiff
daguerreotype portraits on the walls, mercilessly satirizing the cultural crudity and falsehood revealed. As he wrote, he was surely
contrasting those cultural atrocities with his own beautiful home.
Twain borrowed heavily, in "The House Beautiful," from his still-
unpublished description of the Grangerford home in Chapter 17
of *Huckleberry Finn*, but extended it. And his critique went beyond
interior decoration. The South suffered from a sham romanticism
that debased every aspect of its culture—"Walter Scottism," he
called it.

It was a writer's judgment that Mark Twain made—the South
was backward because Southerners had read the wrong books—
but his complaint was more than simply aesthetic. Literature shapes
attitudes and behavior and therefore can shape history. Scott's books
had helped to bring on the Civil War by infecting the region with
a pernicious cult of "chivalry" that kept it backward in its economy
and politics as well as in its literature and had led Southerners to
despise the industrial North and to think themselves able to beat
any odds. *Don Quixote*—one of Twain's favorite works—had destroyed "the mediaeval chivalry-silliness," until Scott, with his immensely popular novels, *Ivanhoe* in particular, "sets the world in
love with dreams and phantoms; . . . with decayed and degraded

systems of government; with the sillinesses and emptinesses, sham grandeurs, sham gauds, and sham chivalries of a brainless and worthless . . . society."

The Confederacy had been defeated, but "Walter Scottism" survived. A love of pretentious, flowery diction, learned from Scott, still deprived Southerners of what the region most needed, a modern literature. Using that obsolete language, Twain argued, writers could not deal with the realities of their own time and place, could not bring their region out of its self-imposed isolation, could not bring Southern readers into their own century. Of the South's contemporary writers, only Harris and Cable, in Twain's view, had escaped the blight. Cable made a similar point in a commencement address at the University of Mississippi: the Old South, in concentrating its intellect on the defense of slavery, "broke with the world's thought."

It was time for the South to enter the modern age. And so Mark Twain noted signs of modernity wherever he found them, of factories, electricity, machinery, commerce, of everything that suggested that the region might at last be entering "the genuine and wholesome civilization of the nineteenth century." So he praised the prosperous towns along the upper Mississippi, offering them as models for the South. But there was not very much he could say on those subjects beyond citing statistics—cotton mills in this town or that had so many thousand spindles and so many hundred "hands." And while he might admire the bustling towns along the upper river, he gives that practical, prosperous region fewer than forty pages in a five-hundred-page book.

He could not wholly welcome this modernity. Like many Americans, of his own time and later, he seems deeply ambivalent toward it. A chapter describing the Natchez mills is entitled "Manufactures and Miscreants" and concludes with his report of a conversation overheard between two traveling salesmen, one Northern and one Southern, one selling margarine that hotels and restaurants could pass off to their customers as butter, the other selling cottonseed oil labeled olive oil. Progress and fraud—were they inseparable, as the chapter title implies? But even if they were, might not this new world, with its "wholesome and practical smell of cotton factories and locomotives," still be preferable to the feuding, lynching, slaveholding Old South that *Huckleberry Finn* portrays? The question is never answered. Huck and Jim float down the Mississippi on a raft, which is smashed by a terrifying steamboat—but Sam Clemens had piloted steamboats. Fascinated by inventions, Mark Twain was too deeply involved in the technology of his time to reject it. In his old age he would come to believe that the innocent America of his childhood had been fatally corrupted, yet he would blame, not industrialization and "progress," but the accident of California gold.

Even while the work on his manuscript dragged on toward completion, Mark Twain was planning the subscription campaign for *Life on the Mississippi*. Unluckily, Osgood was a trade publisher, who had to learn the techniques of door-to-door bookselling. Consequently, there would be a divided authority, between Osgood and Charley Webster, a young engineer who had married Twain's niece, Annie Moffett, and had forced a gang of swindlers to refund a few thousand dollars that Mark Twain had invested in a worthless watch company. Twain needed a man to develop Kaolatype, an engraving process in which he held a controlling interest, and in April of 1881 had brought Webster to New York to take command. Webster had become in effect Twain's business agent, and now his responsibilities expanded. He would be general manager for the New York City region, setting the subscription machinery in motion. Osgood, in turn, must supply "all the thunder-and-lightning circulars" needed to promote sales. As for the author, "I will not interest myself in *any*thing connected with this wretched God-damned book." (That was a pledge that he could not keep.)

Much depended on the success of *Life on the Mississippi*. Mark Twain wanted to recapture his audience, after the disappointing sales of *The Prince and the Pauper*. And of course he wanted the money—that was the proof of success, one of the prizes in the game of authorship, together with the celebrity that he cursed but enjoyed and the intense pleasure that he often found in the act of writing. This time he wanted money urgently, for besides the expenses of buying land and renovating his home, he had suffered heavy losses in unsuccessful "investments" over the past few years. In the late 1870s, at the urging of an optimistic friend, Mark Twain had spent several thousand dollars on a "steam generator" which unaccountably produced "no more steam and no cheaper steam" than standard boilers. Finally the device had to be sold as scrap, and that would be Mark Twain's only compensation.

He learned nothing from that experience. "I must speculate in something, such being my nature," he once confessed to Howells, and most of his "investments" were in fact speculations, long chances. Mark Twain was a gambler—although he would have angrily rejected that name—and the thrill of gambling became necessary to him. He wanted the coup, the sudden killing, the chance for profits on what he liked to call a "princely" scale. And like most gamblers, he believed in his luck. The slow accumulation of money would never interest him. Inventions fascinated him, particularly when they promised to supersede instantly some existing machine or process.

The Kaolatype process for making the stereotype plates used in printing illustrations seemed to offer that kind of chance. (The process involved coating a steel sheet with kaolin, or china clay; a picture would be engraved through the kaolin, and molten metal would be poured into the clay matrix to make the plate.) Twain bought four fifths of the Kaolatype patent, for "several thousand dollars," in February of 1880. Ten days later, he enthusiastically reported to Orion, he had thought of an application that would "utterly annihilate & sweep out of existence one of the minor industries of civilization, & take its place—an industry which has existed for 300 years." The possibility had occurred to him of using the Kaolatype process in molding the brass plates used for stamping book covers, instead of engraving them.

A young German mechanic named Sneider was hired to work out the details, at $150 a month and the promise of a $5,000 bonus "when he is able to put patents into my hands." By March of 1881, Sneider claimed to have discovered a method and had produced plates. On the strength of that evidence, Twain immediately paid the $12,000 his neighbor had demanded for that strip of land next to the Clemenses'. He had decided that "if the utility of our invention was *doubtful*," he would let his neighbor put up a house there, but now he was sure of success. The price was outrageous, but as Twain explained, the neighbor "had me where the hair was short." Confident that Kaolatype would pay for everything, he not only bought land at an inflated price, but committed himself to a costly renovation of his home.

Two weeks later, Twain was writing to Dan Slote, an old friend who was supposed to manage Kaolatype affairs, that before April was over, he hoped to see "palpable & demonstrable . . . reasons for going on." His hopes had been dashed, and he felt "sore &

humiliated" by the events of the last few months. At the end of April, he put Webster in charge of Kaolatype. Webster's responsibilities had continuously increased since then, until he was in the process of becoming Mark Twain's publisher. It was an unlucky choice, although the consequences would not be plain for years. Webster was honest, intensely hardworking (he would die at forty, mentally and physically broken), self-pitying, ignorant, and arrogant, sure that there was only one side to every question and that side was his own.

A week later, Twain had proposed arresting Sneider "on a charge of obtaining money under false pretenses." He had invented nothing at all, had used established methods, had not even produced what he claimed to have produced. The affairs of Kaolatype dragged on, with Twain devising new techniques that might make the brass-casting process work, and Webster consulting experts and hiring workmen to try out his employer's ideas. Mark Twain was not an easy man to work for. "MY BRASS PATIENCE IS RUNNING LOW," he telegraphed Webster on November 22, 1881. "PUT A HUNDRED MEN ON IT AND TELEGRAPH A RESULT OF SOME SORT OR OTHER IN TWENTY-FOUR HOURS." Webster replied with spirit: "SO IS MINE. IT'S HARD TO GET 100 SKILLED MEN IN TWENTY-FOUR HOURS," and grudgingly, Twain admitted that Kaolatype could not do what he wanted it to. By 1886, when it had cost him several times more than the steam generator, he was ready to sell the process to anyone who would make an offer, "whether he is good or not."

Surely an unreasoning fear of "the poorhouse" and the shame of poverty—a fear rooted in the anxieties of his childhood—partly motivated Mark Twain's involvement in business. But there was more than that. The business of America in the 1880s was business, and the businessman was the representative American. Howells knew this, wryly commenting that the writer in America was "a kind of mental and moral woman to whom a real man, a business man, could have nothing to say after the preliminary politenesses." Some American writers—Crane, London, Hemingway—have desperately feared that identification of writing and "culture" with femininity, demonstrating with self-destructive displays of masculine toughness that they were men as well as writers. There is no evidence that Mark Twain ever doubted his manhood because he was a writer, any more than he felt himself, as an artist, at war with a crudely materialistic culture. But the struggle to master and exploit a continent, to build a great industrial nation, was the national enterprise and he wanted to share in it—he "craved a participatory role in his age," as one modern scholar has written. And what else was he to do while he waited for inspiration?

He also had a more exciting invention than Kaolatype to sponsor. In 1880, he had bought $5,000 worth of stock in an automatic typesetter, invented by James Paige, a Hartford mechanic. It was, he remarked to Webster, the best investment he had ever made. Paige's machine would absorb a steadily increasing share of his time, attention, and money over the next fourteen years. In the early 1880s, the human typesetter still sorted and set the individual letters, cast in metal, just as Gutenberg's workmen had done more than four hundred years before. That ancient method seemed hopelessly inefficient in an age of mass-circulation periodicals and daily newspapers, and of great steam presses that could throw off thousands of sheets an hour. For decades, inventors had been trying to produce a mechanical typesetter. The problem would surely be solved, and solved soon. But by whose machine? Mark Twain was sure that he knew the answer.

In the fall of 1881, the stockholders met and decided to give a contract for developing the typesetter "to somebody with $300,000 in his pocket, who can clear $2,000,000 on said contract in four or five years." Always sanguine, Twain felt sure that finding that somebody could easily be managed. Experts went to Hartford to examine the machine and were impressed, but men with $300,000 in their pockets proved disappointingly scarce. Yet Mark Twain was not disturbed. A onetime printer and newspaperman, he saw the scale of the opportunity. In words that his own Colonel Sellers might have used, "I reckon it will take about a hundred thousand machines to supply the world, & I judge the world has got to buy them."

The nineteenth century was the age of invention, of Morse, Bell, Westinghouse, Edison. Next to the capitalist, the inventor was the American hero—every village had its inspired tinkerer. Inventing ran in the Clemens family: his father had imagined a perpetual motion machine; Orion had worked on, or at least conceived of, a power saw, a solar helmet, a steam-powered railway brake, a drilling machine, a paddle wheel that would enable a steamer to cross the Atlantic in twenty-four hours, even a flying machine (for a time, Mark Twain, too, had believed in that flying machine). Twain himself had not only been one of the first to try the telephone and the typewriter, but in the early 1870s he had actually patented two inventions: an elastic strap with buttonholes at each end, usable on vests, corsets, and trousers, and a self-pasting scrapbook (the pages covered with strips of glue, ready to be moistened) that actually earned a few thousand dollars when put on the market. But while Mark Twain could devise gadgets himself, his real hope was to find a promising invention still under development, finance its completion, and ride it to a fortune. In the words of his own Colonel Sellers, there might be millions in it—or tens of millions!

Yet financing and marketing inventions involved business, and Mark Twain hated the inevitable complications and technicalities. "Complexities annoy me; they irritate me . . . I cannot get far in the reading of the simplest contract—with its 'parties of the first part' and 'parties of the second part' and 'parties of the third part'— before my temper is all gone." Or more simply, "I wish I could understand *some* details of business." He was lazy, he insisted, forgetful, impatient "of everything like business-detail." His daughter Susy would put it more generally: "He has the mind of an author exactly, some of the simplest things he can't understand." Surely this was a stubbornness, a necessary defense, at least in part. He lived, deeply, in his imagination, and business could distract him at crucial moments—"Remember," he would complain to his Hartford agent in 1887, "I am deep in a book [*A Connecticut Yankee in King Arthur's Court*], & when I am snatched suddenly back into this world, everything seems confused & I can't get my bearings."

As the holiday season of 1882 approached, with Kaolatype shut down, and completion of *Life on the Mississippi* in sight, Mark Twain could give attention to his family and to his social life. Celebrations crowded each other in the late fall—Livy's birthday on November 27, Mark's on November 30 (he turned forty-seven in 1882; she was ten years younger). Photographs of Livy from the early years of their marriage show a delicately beautiful face, seeming to be made for cameo portraits, but by 1882 she had firmly accepted middle age, as Victorian women were likely to do. Her husband might be ten years older, but he was still "Youth" to her, as he would always be. He seemed young to others as well, with his restless movements, his rapidly varying, instantly expressed emotions, his quick enthusiasms ("I never saw a man with so much variety of feeling as papa has," Susy would observe), and his end-lessly multiplying projects. "He has life enough in him for ten generations," a wearied Howells had remarked after a visit to Hart-ford that spring, when, before going to bed, the two men "had planned a play, a lecturing tour, a book of travel and a library of humor."

It is not easy to form an impression of Olivia Clemens; her contemporaries praised her in a vocabulary now obsolete. "Never have I known a lady possessing every quality that the word implies, to compare with Mrs. Clemens," said Major Pond, Twain's lecture agent. She was "the flower and perfume of ladylikeness," wrote Howells; that is, she was delicate (both morally and physically), refined, cultured, invariably polite and considerate. Nobody would have said that Mark Twain was the quintessence of gentlemanliness, although few would have denied that he was a gentleman—that would have been a serious insult.

Husband and wife complemented each other; their marriage was close. Mark's love for Livy, said Howells, "was a greater part of him than the loves of most men for their wives." He idealized, he idolized her; "I am notorious, but you are great—that is the dif-ference between us," he once observed. Writing to a friend about to marry, Twain offered one piece of advice—"a nugget": "There isn't *time*—so brief is life—for bickerings, apologies, heartburnings, calling to account. There is only time for loving—& but an instant, so to speak, for that." Yet he loved to shock the proper Livy, to startle her into exclaiming "Youth!" with "a half-terrified expression in the tone." Once, Clara would remember, while Livy had been reading aloud a description of some devout clergyman, "Father sprang to his feet and danced a kind of hornpipe while he sang, 'By the humping, jumping Jesus, what the hell is that to you?' "

From the time he had left Hannibal at seventeen, to begin his year of wandering in the East, until his wedding in 1870, Mark Twain had never experienced a true home. But the Victorian ideal of home, of a close-knit family at the center of a man's existence, was his own, and he had realized it. To him, that great house was the scene of his family idyll, unthinkable without its setting. His marriage, his children, his house—all these, even more than money and fame, constituted success.

He was likely to be available for play, when his children were not in the schoolroom. His own father, John Clemens, had been cold and remote, had died and left his wife and children in poverty—had failed both as father and provider. Mark Twain's daughters would enjoy the security and the love that his own childhood had lacked. Much of his time, energy, and imaginative power went into entertaining them—inventing games, playing "jungle" when they were small (with the library as the jungle, Mark Twain as the elephant carrying the hunters, and George as lion or tiger), or sledding and skating as they grew older. He read to them, during family evenings in the library, or told fantastic stories, inspired by the paintings and bric-a-brac figures around the room, with every one of them appearing in the story in its proper order.

He would entertain at the frequent children's parties as well—often, as one girl would remember, with "his fear-compelling story of the *Golden Arm*, in which a ghost returns to ask in a wailing voice 'Who-o-o-s got my golden arm?,' repeated and gradually increasing to a high crescendo, and ending with almost a shriek, 'You!,' " as he pointed toward some one of the audience, at which "we all jumped, terrified but delighted." He delighted in that story, performing it on his tours, even telling it at dinner parties. "The company always said the shivers went straight down their spines—they felt like they was freezing to death!" So at least Katy Leary testified.

Music played a central part in family life. Clara had already shown her interest in the piano (fifteen years later, in Vienna, she would study under Leschetizky, the greatest teacher of the day). Her father, Clara would remember, liked to perform what he called "darky songs" while accompanying himself on the piano, first clearing his throat, then singing vigorously "with his head thrown back and his eyes fixed on the ceiling . . . He interrupted himself constantly to correct wrong chords, but usually in vain, for he could not find the right ones." Then, irritably, he would begin another song. "Swing Low, Sweet Chariot," and "Go Chain the Lion Down" were special favorites, and he could sing "Rise and Shine and Give God the Glory, Glory," with unforgettable fervor.

Jean was hardly more than a baby, but Clara (eight) and Susy (ten) already differed sharply from each other. Even three years earlier, Livy had noted that Susy "is an old, thoughtful little thing" when compared to Clara, "who is as sweet as possible, but appears to have no mind." When a favorite cat died, Susy speculated about its chances for an afterlife; Clara arranged the funeral. Susy "was all contemplation and nerves; Bay serene and practical." ("Bay" was one of Clara's various nicknames; she later became "Ben," then "the Ash-Cat.") Susy was nearsighted and timid, Clara adventurous—she had been the leader in that nearly fatal exploration of the oat bin. Their father agreed with the mother's judgment: Susy was "reflective, dreamy, spiritual"; Clara, "alert, enterprising, business-like, earthy, orderly, practical." Mother and father would surely have claimed that they loved all of their children equally, but Susy was closest to them both. On May 24, 1883, a delighted Livy would report Susy's words to her husband, then off in Canada: "Today . . . she [Susy] alluded again to mothers & daughters not getting on smoothly together, and I said 'Susy I hope we shall always agree,' she said 'Mamma we can never disagree we think just alike about things, why Mamma we seem like *one* person.' "

With birthdays past, it was time to make ready for Christmas, a holiday observed strenuously by the Clemenses and their neighbors. December was filled with preparations. For weeks, Livy would be occupied, first in "writing lists of names and trying to determine the needs or wishes of each individual," both family and relatives, then in shopping and in wrapping presents. Every gift must be appropriate. Her husband might grumble that she endangered her health with "that infernal Christmas-suicide," but Livy always did what she considered her duty. There were social responsibilities to be met as well—presents for servants, for the poor, the sick, the insane. Baskets would be packed, each containing a turkey and a bottle of wine, with other good things of the season; and on the day before Christmas, Patrick would load them into a sleigh for delivery. Wrapped in mufflers and furs, the children would ride with him, learning their duty to the unfortunate.

On Christmas Eve, they would ceremoniously hang their stockings in the "schoolroom" next to the nursery, and Livy would recite " 'Twas the night before Christmas." "Father sometimes dressed up as Santa Claus," Clara would recall, and after running about the room to warm himself, he would tell of his adventures that day. Then the girls would go to bed, but not to sleep. "Launched on a long night of wakefulness," they listened for sounds of movement and noises of rustling paper as presents were brought into their schoolroom, next door to the nursery. Once, peeking in through the door, they saw a "huge black thing" that seemed to fill the room.

But they must wait until six in the morning, when their nurse would come to build a fire and help them dress. Then the schoolroom door would open and the presents be revealed: games, toys, books, dolls. The "black thing" proved to be an upright piano. Six-year-old Clara had exclaimed, "How wonderful it must be to be able to play on the piano!" and then had asked plaintively, "Do girls ever play?"

On Christmas morning, the parents would rest from their labors of the night before, rising late to open their own presents, and then to receive visitors. Hospitality, often with games and charades and impromptu dancing, would go on through the holiday season, for Nook Farm was a close-knit, gregarious community. The exchange of visits would not be limited to neighbors. The Clemenses were known throughout Hartford, and there would be other callers, many of them. Too many, Mark Twain occasionally felt—particularly of the "mentally dead people" who "brought their corpses with them." The holiday season might be enjoyable, on the whole, but it could not be called restful.

With the holidays over and *Life on the Mississippi* finally written, Twain's life could return to its normal course. He could attend to his mail again, that never-ending, exasperating, yet necessary stream of letters from admirers, autograph hunters, aspiring writers, editors seeking contributions, from unknown relatives announcing themselves, from beggars, cranks, fanatics, and occasionally from lunatics, that testified on six days a week to his success. He had his admirers in England, in Ireland, in Germany, in the Netherlands and Sweden, in Australia, even in India. His books were read in the shadow of the Himalayas, as Donald Grant, a surgeon with the Sixth Bengal Cavalry, wrote to him—read so eagerly that they were worn out with handling.

Social life consumed much time and energy, sometimes for serious purposes. Like most New England towns, Hartford had its discussion groups, combining sociability with intellectual activity. There was the Saturday Morning Club, a group of girls in their late teens, which had been organized by Mark Twain in about 1875—"I've been a member of it from the start; I'm the only young girl of my sex that *is*," he remarked. Clearly, Mark Twain basked in the company of intelligent and sympathetic girls and women. The members composed and read brief essays, on topics ranging from current fashions to the American Revolution, then talked—

"talking is the thing." Sometimes Twain would read from his un-published work, or bring notable visitors, like Howells or Harte or Cable, to read or speak. (Harte, Twain liked to recall, had sat up all night with a quart of whiskey to finish a story, "Thankful Blossom," then read it in the morning to the club. Nobody but Twain had realized his condition.)

More important to him, probably, was the Monday Evening Club, a group of men belonging to Hartford's business and professional elite, who met regularly in one another's homes to drink beer, listen to papers, and comment on them, with each member in turn being called on for his opinion. Twain had been taken into the club on his arrival in Hartford, and he regularly contributed papers. In the winter of 1883, his topic was "What Is Happiness?" He argued that every human action, no matter how self-sacrificing it might seem, is fundamentally selfish, performed to increase the self-esteem or self-content of the doer. He shocked the club, as he had intended—self-denial and self-sacrifice were at the heart of the Victorian ethos, glorified in sermons, novels, plays, and poems—but no one could answer his arguments. He liked to provoke; he enjoyed scandalizing the members and answering their indignant replies. He had already written "The Facts Concerning the Recent Carnival of Crime in Connecticut," with its indictment of conscience as a sadistic destroyer of human happiness, for delivery to the club.

But he did not write those papers merely to shock—they had grown out of experience and deep belief. With "What Is Happiness?" he began the "studies," as he called them, that would finally result in *What Is Man?*, a set of philosophical dialogues that he would publish privately in 1906. *What Is Man?* not only refutes the ideal of altruism, it argues for a rigid psychological determinism, based on a concept of inborn and unchangeable temperaments. That concept, a sort of secular Calvinism or psychological predestination, had been part of Mark Twain's thought since he had studied phrenology at nineteen, and he had been prepared for it by the sermons and Sunday school lessons of his Hannibal childhood.

Mark and Livy entertained often, in a variety of styles. There were carefully arranged parties for the children and their friends, evenings of beer and male conversation in the billiard room, and formal dinners with a stately procession of courses from soup to dessert, each accompanied by its appropriate wine. The arrangements for one dinner provide an example of the elaborate hospitality of the day. First, each gentleman was given a sealed envelope containing the name of the lady he would escort to dinner. There was a printed menu at every place, listing a dozen separate dishes in their order: clams on the half shell, clear soup with sherry, soft-shell crabs, shad roe balls with shad cream sauce, asparagus with cream sauce, roast lamb with cream curry sauce, creamed sweetbreads, Roman punch, broiled squab on toast, tomato aspic and lettuce with mayonnaise, ice cream (in the shape of flowers), and finally coffee for the ladies in the drawing room while the gentlemen enjoyed their cigars and brandy. Livy, of course, had planned every detail. But formality often broke down. Between courses, Mark Twain would sometimes rise from the table and pace the floor of the dining room while he delivered a monologue, or George, the butler, might burst out laughing at his employer's jokes. Susy and Clara, eavesdropping from the stairs, could often tell what stage the dinner had reached from the story their father was telling.

Neighbors liked to pay unannounced calls, and a writer, with no office to go to and no fixed hours to keep, must have seemed always available. Friends could not simply be turned away. Often Mark Twain would feel "persecuted to the verge of lunacy by strangers"— by reporters seeking interviews, by celebrity hunters armed with letters of introduction, by fellow writers, foreign tourists, famous actors stopping off between New York and Boston. That, too, it seemed, could not be prevented. And business offered a constant distraction. For a writer, the cost of these interruptions was high. "Work? One *can't*, you know, to any purpose," he had complained to a friend in 1881, adding that "I keep three or four books on the stocks all the time, but I seldom add a satisfactory chapter to one of them at home."

When the spur and burden of a contract became unbearable, Mark Twain could work from nine in the morning to midnight. But he could not bring himself to ban those incessant interruptions or schedule his life to avoid distraction and provide regular quiet periods for writing. Solitary imprisonment, he once remarked, offered "the one perfect condition for perfect performance." But since prison was unavailable, he could only escape "clear out of the world on top of the mountain at Elmira"—like a man with an unbearably cluttered desk who suddenly sweeps everything onto the floor.

Writing to Howells in March—Howells was then living in Italy

and complaining that his time was consumed with social triviali-
ties—Twain told of hearing a lecturer who had "described how
retired tradesmen and farmers in Holland load a lazy scow with the
family and the household effects, and then loaf along the waterways of the Low Countries all the summer long, paying no visits,
receiving none . . . and doing their literary work, if they have any,
wholly uninterrupted." If he had been living on such a boat, he
added, he might have had a book ready for the press bearing "no
visible marks of interruption and weariness." But while he might
sometimes long for Huck's raft, or its equivalent, he could approach
that happy freedom only at Quarry Farm. His way of life was the
price of success, as he sometimes recognized, but it was also the
reward, the visible proof of success. He had invested too much in
the Hartford home and Hartford life to change, even if he had truly
wished to. And on quiet family evenings, in the library by gaslight,
he and Livy wanted to keep house forever.

If winter was the season of hospitality, it was also a dangerous
season, a time of sickness, when death seemed close. Neither rich
nor poor could escape, and the sick suffered at home. "This is a
deadly winter . . . Pneumonia is slaughtering people right and left,"
Twain would observe in March. Fears for the children's health were
constant, summer or winter, and for the parents' as well. False alarms
were common. Everyone in the Clemens family was in the doctor's
hands in January, but "the scare is over," Twain confessed to a
friend, soon after: "Clara's membranous croup is not that; Susie's
scarlet fever is *not* that." The Clemens children may have been no
more prone to the usual range of childhood diseases than others,
but their parents worried continuously and intensely, magnifying
every symptom. In his old age, Mark Twain would declare that "no
writer should ever marry," adding that "if writers *would* marry, they
should have no children . . . he & Livy should not have had children;
they could have had no idea of what the combination of their highly
strung natures could produce in a child."

Both parents feared for their children, and Mark Twain feared
for Livy. "Intense," in the manner of many American women, and
girls, of her time and class (Susy, too, was intense), she took her
responsibilities with total seriousness, fully accepting the various
roles of the upper-class Victorian woman. Frail as she seemed, Livy
successfully played her various roles as wife, mother, and Angel in
the House. (Mark and Livy had read Coventry Patmore's then

famous poem of that title during their courtship, and admired it greatly.)

Writing to her mother, after the family's return from Europe in 1879, Livy had outlined the demands made upon her in a unique complaint: "I have felt rebellious about it [housekeeping] ever since I came home. I told Mr. Clemens [even to her mother he was "Mr. Clemens"] the other day that in this day women must be every-thing—they must keep up with all the current literature, they must help in one or two benevolent societies, they must be perfect moth-ers, they must be perfect housekeepers & graceful gracious hostesses, they must know how to give perfect dinners, they must go and visit all the people in the town where they live [all the people of their own class, of course, but Livy also visited the poor], they must always be ready to receive their acquaintances, they must dress themselves & their children becomingly, and above all they must make their houses 'charming' & so on without end—then if they are not studying something their case is a hopeless one." She could grumble, then, but rarely—and she never rebelled.

The cost of this life of cultured affluence was higher for the wife than for the husband. While Livy had recovered from the mysterious paralysis of her adolescence, she never became strong, and period-ically she paid a price for her way of life in physical collapse, often with debilitating back pains, followed by agonizingly slow recovery. In May of 1883, her husband would write that "Livy has been sick abed for a month or two, with a procession of diseases passing through her"—including, by his surely exaggerated report, diph-theria, fever, quinsy, and "several minor things." A professional nurse had been brought in, he explained to a friend, "but I am the *main* nurse." He could never forget for long the fragility of his happiness. "Success" without Livy would have seemed a cruel joke.

Three or four months later, she was still frighteningly thin—"I could shave with her shoulder blades . . . I never have seen so emaciated a person." (That humorous exaggeration shows that his anxiety was passing, but it could never entirely disappear.) Mark Twain sensed the relationship between Livy's duties and her ill-nesses. "I think my wife would be twice as strong as she is, but for this wearing and wearying slavery of house-keeping," he complained to a friend. "However, she thinks she must submit to it for the sake of the children."

Frail Livy played all her roles and played them well. To delegate her responsibilities to another woman would have been to confess failure. There was no solution, then, unless, as Twain once jokingly suggested, "some true friend" might set their house on fire. Accepting the need of an establishment with half a dozen servants and of continuous entertainment of neighbors and visitors as essential to their social status and her husband's fame, and believing it her wifely duty to take the burden of household management entirely on herself, Livy regularly worked to the limits of her strength, and beyond. "Sometimes," she wrote, "it seems as if the very sight of people would drive me *mad*," adding, "This is my work, and I know that I do very wrong when I feel chafed by it." She did not ask if that work was necessary. Neither did her husband, except as a joke.

In the late winter of 1882/83, Mark Twain somehow freed himself for a few weeks from the chains of society, correspondence, and business. "Of course the highest pleasure to be got out of freedom," he commented in a letter to Howells, ". . . is labor." Writing, when there was no deadline to meet, provided some of the highest pleasures of his life. Consequently, he wrote—"one hour or four, as happens to suit my mind." What he labored on, he did not say. It might have been *Captain Stormfield's Visit to Heaven*, a manuscript he had worked on intermittently for years, and would publish only at the end of his life, burlesquing the paradise of wings and harps and endless hymn-singing imagined by naïve Protestants. It might also have been at least a chapter of *Huckleberry Finn*—probably Chapter 21, which begins with the king and the duke rehearsing the balcony scene from *Romeo and Juliet* and a burlesqued version of Hamlet's soliloquy ("But soft you, the fair Ophelia: / Ope not thy ponderous and marble jaws, / But get thee to a nunnery—go!") and ends with a mob on its way to lynch Colonel Sherburn after he has killed the harmless, drunken Boggs.

Cable came in early April, at Mark Twain's urging. He was considering a national tour, reading from his own works, and would try his wings at Hartford, with a favorable audience, and with Twain to make all arrangements and ensure "the right sort of newspaper attention." A hall was found, and Twain prepared an invitation, signed by eminent citizens of Hartford. But Cable's first appearance was almost his last. Twain introduced him to a crowded house, there was deafening applause, then Cable rose and stared speechless at the audience. "He stood motionless for what seemed an eternity," an eyewitness reports, "and would have been there yet if Mark

Twain had not risen, seized one of Cable's books . . . opened it, found a place, thrust it into Cable's hand and told him to read." Twain knew that sudden terror—he had gone through just such a moment of helpless panic at his first lecture in San Francisco—and he liked to help beginners.

Life on the Mississippi finally appeared in the middle of May 1883, after much cutting—including the expensive, last-minute removal of two illustrations, one of the author being cremated and another showing a staring corpse, from the fifty thousand copies that Osgood had printed. Both illustrations had been approved, and probably suggested, by Mark Twain, but Livy, reading proof as she habitually did, had insisted that they should go. Her husband could play the Wild Humorist still, but Livy did not enjoy the performance. Nothing was lost by this concession to gentility—the illustrations were crude and quite unnecessary.

Twain had never forgotten that in 1876 the American sale of *Tom Sawyer* had been badly hurt by a pirated Canadian edition brought over the border. International copyright did not yet exist, and American law gave him no protection. He bitterly resented the unauthorized publication of his work—barefaced theft, he considered it. In 1882, he had tried to protect himself through trademark law, claiming that his pen name was his property because it constituted a trademark—exactly like the name of the Singer Sewing Machine. J. S. Ogilvie & Company, an American publisher issuing a collection of humor that included Mark Twain pieces (and one piece falsely attributed to Twain), was sued for violation of trademark by Alexander & Green, Twain's New York lawyers. The outcome was thoroughly satisfying. Before the case could go to court, Webster reported, the repentant Ogilvie "came with *literal* tears in his eyes," pleading ignorance of the law and his need to support a large family and aged mother, offering to withdraw the book and pay all legal costs.

When a case was actually tried, the outcome would be different. In the middle of 1882, Belford, Clark & Co. of Chicago—clearly affiliated with Belford Brothers of Toronto, who had pirated *Tom Sawyer*—had issued a collection of Twain's pieces without permission or payment, even including a false preface signed "Mark Twain." Twain promptly launched suit for violation of copyright. But in January of 1883, the Circuit Court of the United States,

Northern District, ruled against him, deciding that laws for the protection of trademarks did not apply to authors' pen names. He might have considered that piracy was a nuisance that could no more be avoided than his correspondence and, like his correspondence, was a tribute to his success. But Mark Twain was not a man to accept thievery with equanimity.

At least he had found a method for guarding his new book against Canadian piracy. English publication must precede American, and he must be on Canadian soil on the day that *Life on the Mississippi* was issued by Chatto & Windus in London, in order to secure copyright for his authorized Canadian publisher, Dawson of Montreal, and so to prevent the piratical Belford Brothers from flooding the American market with a cheap, unauthorized edition. A quick visit to Montreal in mid-May met the legal requirements, but Mark Twain had barely had time to get home when he had to return in late May, to answer what was almost a royal summons. It came from the Governor-General, the Marquess of Lorne (who was married to the Princess Louise, a daughter of Queen Victoria), inviting him to attend the annual meeting of the Royal Literary & Scientific Society of Canada at Ottawa. He would be a guest of Lorne and his wife at Rideau Hall, their official residence. Mark Twain's role was to entertain the society with an after-dinner speech. He took Adam as his subject, in place of the standard topics: "Who ever talks about Adam at a banquet? . . . who ever says a good word for Adam?," the benefactor of the human race, "for to him we owe the two things which are most precious—life, and death."

Otherwise he was simply an honored guest. Ottawa, hardly more than a village lost in forests, offered little to a visitor, but his hosts were cordial and human and life at Rideau Hall proved delightfully simple and relaxed. A visitor could pass a Sunday morning at billiards in sinful pleasure, while the Marquess and the Princess did their duty by going to church. On Sunday afternoon, there was a long walk in the woods with the Governor-General, a dog, and a young lady, and later Mark Twain could try the new and fashionable game of lawn tennis. He had a great stroke of luck at dinner. Sitting beside the Princess, he noticed a portrait hanging on the opposite wall and began to praise it enthusiastically, then discovered that Louise had painted it. "God was very good to me in this instance," he observed in a letter to Livy.

A thoroughly satisfying visit, apparently, yet a month later Twain was confessing to his Canadian publisher that "it makes my heart ache . . . to remember how miraculously dull, stupid, silent & unentertaining I was . . . However, I played it for an eccentricity of genius & let it go at that." No doubt his heart had truly ached, although there need not have been any cause that others could observe. Mark Twain could feel deep guilt for behavior that no one else was aware of. He had soon abandoned those frantic efforts during his courtship to make himself a Christian—Livy had lost her faith instead. The God of the Old Testament—"irascible, vindictive, fierce . . . fickle and changeful"—who was to read each man's conscience on the Day of Judgment and pronounce sentence, seemed to him an outworn concept, belonging to a primitive age. But he had gained no freedom by his disbelief. That "trained Presbyterian conscience" of his, as he called it, was always ready "to hunt and harry its slave upon all pretexts and on all occasions." Only in fantasy could he destroy it, as in "The Facts Concerning the Recent Carnival of Crime in Connecticut." Yet Mark Twain could never be permanently depressed by guilt, no matter how intense—his temperament, his "natural buoyancy of spirit," prevented that.

The Clemenses would be summering at Quarry Farm as usual, but in the final days before leaving Hartford, Mark Twain found time to embroil himself in a threatened suit for libel by Captain Charles Duncan, who had organized and commanded the cruise of the *Quaker City* in 1867. Duncan's strenuous, noisy piety seemed to Twain to be sanctimonious hypocrisy, a Victorian vice that he, like Dickens, detested. He and Duncan had quarreled publicly in 1877, with Duncan remarking in a lecture that Twain had seemed drunk when he signed on for the *Quaker City* voyage and Twain answering with a sulfurous newspaper attack. There had been threats of a libel suit from Duncan, and apparently a settlement out of court.

But Mark Twain did not forget injuries, real or imagined. He may have drawn on his recollections of Duncan when he created the king of *Huckleberry Finn*, all "soul-butter and hogwash," and he had returned to the attack in early June, with an interview, headed "Mr. Mark Twain Gets Excited," in *The New York Times*. In it, he had denounced Duncan's corruption and nepotism as shipping commissioner of New York, had called him a "canting hypocrite, filled to the chin with sham godliness and forever oozing and dripping false piety and pharisaical prayers," and observed that Judas Iscariot could be considered respectable in comparison. Duncan replied with a libel suit against the *Times* for $100,000, and Twain unheroically sheltered himself by claiming that "the interviewer has invented both the ideas & the language." Men of a sanguine temperament were likely to speak first, think of the consequences later.

The case was settled in March of 1884, when a New York jury found that Duncan's character had indeed been libeled by the *Times*'s story, then showed its evaluation of that character by awarding damages of twelve cents. That verdict must have chagrined Mark Twain—he could have afforded to be brave after all.

FIVE

Huckleberry Finn

"For thirty-five years," Mark Twain recalled in 1907, "I exercised my pen . . . in the summer-time and in the summertime only. I worked three months in the year and amused myself in other ways during the other nine . . . my life for the past thirty-five years and more had really been nothing more than one long holiday, with three months' scribbling in each year . . . which to me was not work at all, but only play, delicious play." An old man's nostalgia, perhaps—but almost true for the summer of 1883.

Leaving their house to the servants, with the reliable George in command, the Clemenses traveled to Elmira in mid-June, in a private railroad car, as usual. Their first duty was to visit Livy's mother in the great, gloomy Langdon mansion in town, a house that fascinated the children with its "mysterious staircases and unexpected hallways." Then they would go up to Quarry Farm, high above the town, with its panoramic view of Elmira, the winding Chemung River, and the surrounding hills, sharing the farmhouse with Susan Crane, Livy's deeply religious foster sister, and her husband, Theodore. Susan was a special favorite of Twain's—"Saint Sue" and "Holy Samuel" they nicknamed each other—while Theodore provided male companionship for Twain.

In the kitchen was the majestic "Auntie Cord"—"six feet high and nearly twice as black," Mark Twain would recall—who filled the children's heads with her lore of ghosts and witches and omens. "A True Story," Mark Twain's first contribution to the *Atlantic*, had been Auntie Cord's story, retold. Occasional callers would arrive from Elmira, and the children might go by wagon down the steep, curving road to visit their grandmother or their Langdon cousins, but essentially Quarry Farm became the family's world for the summer. At Quarry Farm, Livy could rest, occasionally attending to the education of her daughters but freed at last from the burdens of entertaining and of managing the Hartford establishment. Mark Twain was also free, with no visitors, no interruptions or distractions of any kind, except those that he invented for himself.

"The highest pleasure to be got out of freedom . . . is labor," he had told Howells a few months before. At Quarry Farm, then, he labored. His vacation was his working season—even though that work might often seem play. "Labor" meant writing, and within a week, he was "grinding out manuscript by the acre" all day long, even forgetting his eternal correspondence, "allowing myself only time to scratch off two or three brief letters *after* they yell for me to come down to supper." He enjoyed the perfect workplace, a study presented to him by Susan Crane. Perched on a knoll a hundred yards above the farmhouse, "with just room in it for a sofa and a table and three or four chairs," it was about the size of the pilothouse on a steamboat and looked a good deal like one too, with windows on all sides, commanding a view of the valley and the town and range after range of blue hills.

From it, Mark Twain could watch the lightning flashes of summer storms and listen to the rain driving on his roof, or on hot days he could open windows and door to the wind, anchoring his papers with bricks, "and write in the midst of the hurricane." He would stroll off to the study after breakfast, in the white linen suit that he wore in the summer. He disliked the somber colors allowed to men by Victorian fashion, and in his old age, he would defy convention by wearing white the year round. Once in the study, he would work all day long when the writing was going well, smoking furiously, undisturbed by family or visitors. In the evenings, Livy might read aloud while Twain played chess or cards with Theodore Crane, still catching enough of the reading to throw out comments on the author's style. Or Twain might read his day's work to Livy and the Cranes—for him, reading aloud was always the ultimate test of his own work or of any writer's.

If he had no consuming new interest, there were always projects on hand to take up. Unless burdened with a contract, Mark Twain would begin writing when an idea seized him, and go on as long as his interest held out, then toss the manuscript aside until his interest returned, or the tank filled up, in his favorite metaphor. There were manuscripts that he tinkered with year after year: a diary, supposedly written by one of Noah's sons, giving the inside story of the Ark, or *Captain Stormfield's Visit to Heaven*, finally published in 1907. Often the tank never did fill up again; Twain's literary career is strewn with abandoned projects.

He had possibilities enough to choose from that summer, whether actually begun or only imagined: the *Library of Humor*, which he was collaborating on with Howells, a work that would drag along for years; a burlesque etiquette book—even a burlesque *Hamlet*, introducing a new character into the play, a subscription book agent who deflates the high-flown language of Shakespeare's characters with ironic comments in nineteenth-century slang, foreshadowing the Connecticut Yankee in King Arthur's court. There were unfinished manuscripts that might have surprised both disparaging critics and the faithful subscription public. He might have continued "The Mysterious Chamber," a sixty-eight-page manuscript—the scenario for a novel of which he had actually written only the introduction. After considering Defoe's story of Robinson Crusoe and his own plan for "the diary of a solitary prisoner in the Bastille," he invented a situation that would offer an agony of solitude more intense than either of those. He imagined a bridegroom accidentally imprisoned whose "life must be as miserably solitary as the Bastiler's [*sic*], and as deliciously and busily solitary as Crusoe's," with an extra refinement of suffering—"*he must know what is going on around him* without being able to make anybody understand that he is still alive."

Twain's hero, a young Italian nobleman of the early eighteenth century, finds himself trapped on his wedding day in a maze of tunnels and secret passages beneath a castle—able to hear the world outside but unable to communicate with it—where he will be imprisoned for twenty years. His suffering is increased when he learns that the search for him has been abandoned, that his bride-to-be has married a former suitor, and, finally, that she has borne children. Borrowing from both *Robinson Crusoe* and Dumas's *The Count of Monte Cristo*, the story relates in detail the expedients by which the narrator survives and keeps his sanity. He discovers a mysterious chamber containing old documents and books (including a Bible), a chest of jewels, a pair of skeletons. He studies the books, making himself a scholar (paralleling Mark Twain's self-education), and "becomes learned and religious"—like the prisoner Edmond Dantès in *The Count of Monte Cristo*.

Like Crusoe, Twain's prisoner is endlessly resourceful. He lives principally on scraps of food washed down the kitchen drain, he finds flint to light fires, he captures wild goats that fall into an ancient tunnel connected to the castle and makes clothes from their hides and candles from their fat, he tames mice for company, he manufactures ink and keeps a diary. When the chamber is finally opened, decades later, "there sits a calm savage, clad in Robinson Crusoe skins . . . smoking his wood or clay pipe, having a mighty good time, and translating a Greek or Hebrew work."

Or he might have concluded a tale that seems modeled on Poe, in its plot and its narrator, though not in its language. The story is told by a man who murders his devoted wife (she is rich and sickly) in order to marry a younger and more beautiful woman, who does not know of his previous marriage. He has apparently committed the perfect crime, for it is not possible that anyone can suspect him. Yet someone knows his secret, follows him wherever he goes, leaves obscure warnings—no matter how ingeniously he tries to hide himself. The story seems near completion, breaking off on the morning of the wedding day, when the murderer's guilt will surely be revealed, together with the identity of his pursuer. The reader is left to guess who the mysterious pursuer might be and how he could have found out the murder, and to wonder if Mark Twain suddenly broke off his story because he sensed a ghastly parallel to his own marriage. His wife, too, was wealthy, her health was frail, and she loved him deeply.

He might have finished another story, "The Coward's Revenge," in which the narrator finds that he simply does not have the physical courage to take a violent revenge on the man who has "ruined" his innocent young sister and caused her mother to die of grief. Instead of killing the seducer, the coward insinuates himself, in disguise, into the man's household, intending to kidnap the young daughter to whom the scoundrel is devoted and to rear her himself, while letting her father know from time to time that his daughter lives and longs for him—apparently the cruelest revenge that Mark Twain could imagine.

Or he could have worked from notes in his journal, developing a fantasy concerning "Life in the interior of an iceberg," which had been settled by survivors of a shipwreck. "Courtings, quarrels; feuds; masaccers [*sic*]" follow, and children are born and grow up, knowing only the iceberg. The berg drifts endlessly, in a great circle. Finally, "all found dead & frozen"—the story reconstructed from a diary. Mark Twain would never write that story, but elements of it can be found in unfinished work of his later years. "The Great Dark" describes a fantastic voyage through darkness in a ship whose passengers can remember no other world, while "The Enchanted Sea-Wilderness" presents a gruesome image of ships manned by frozen corpses, drifting eternally in the "Everlasting Sunday," a region of the Antarctic Ocean where no wind ever blows. Twain's imagination naturally tended toward fantasy, violence, and melodrama—the everyday realism of a writer like Howells was impossible for him.

"I cannot answer letters; I can ill spare the time to read them," Mark Twain wrote angrily at the end of June, when a letter from Webster demanded his attention. "I am writing a book; my time is brief . . . I *won't* talk business—I will perish first. I hate the very idea of business, in all its forms." Business could not match the excitement offered by writing, when the writing went well. In that summer of 1883, Twain chose to resume work on the manuscript concerning the adventures of Huckleberry Finn that he had casually begun at Quarry Farm seven years before and had turned to from time to time since. (He had never carried out his threat to burn the manuscript; he saved everything.) This summer he would take it straight through to completion, swept on by an irresistible flood of creative energy—writing freely, from memory and imagination, rather than working from notes and casual observation, to fill five hundred pages, as he had done with *Life on the Mississippi*. By the end of the summer, *Huckleberry Finn* would be completed, except for light revision.

Before breaking off in late August of 1876, he had launched the central action of his book: a white boy and a black man floating down the Mississippi together on a raft, in search of freedom. In the character of Jim, he had created probably the most convincing black figure in American fiction up to that time—neither saintly martyr, faithful servant, rapist, nor clown. Jim is intelligent, winning his arguments with Huck, but he is also illiterate, ignorant, superstitious, and submissive—exactly what slavery would have made him. When he considered what he had done, Twain should have been well satisfied with his characterizations and his handling of dialect, both in conversation and in Huck's narrative.

Huckleberry Finn had been started simply as a continuation of *Tom Sawyer*; its opening, dealing with Huck's rebellion against being "sivilized" by the Widow Douglas and Miss Watson, and Tom's instruction on the etiquette of robber gangs, overlaps the conclusion of the earlier story. Mark Twain needed a few chapters before the story could shake itself free from the childish games of Tom Sawyer's gang—playing robbers, attacking a Sunday school picnic. Huck grows older after those opening chapters. The boys of Tom Sawyer's gang—and he is one of them—cannot be much more than ten.

But from its opening words, *Huckleberry Finn* moved beyond the "boy book" tradition. "You don't know about me without you have read a book by the name of 'The Adventures of Tom Sawyer,' but that ain't no matter": from that sentence everything follows, not only Huck's grammar but his character, his social position, his relationship to the reader, the things that can happen to him and his response to them—there would be no puppy love, no tricks on schoolmasters, in this book. Huck's complaints against "sivilization," by which he means having to wear shoes or go to school or say his prayers, imply an attitude basically different from Tom Sawyer's. Tom, no matter how mischievous, was inside his society, acknowledging its authority even while breaking its rules to assert his independence or draw attention to himself, always coming back to school and home and Aunt Polly. Huck is outside Tom's world; he simply does what he wants. If his freedom is interfered with, he lights out. (In fact, Huck is mischievous only twice, when he plays pranks on Jim with disastrous results—once causing him to be bitten by a rattlesnake, once deeply humiliating him. In both cases, he has in a sense become part of a society that allows whites to play brutal jokes on blacks, without considering the consequences.)

"That book was made by Mr. Mark Twain," says Huck in the opening paragraph, "and he told the truth, mainly. There was things which he stretched, but mainly he told the truth. That is nothing. I never seen anybody but lied one time or another, without it was Aunt Polly, or the widow, or maybe Mary." With their implication that telling the truth "mainly" is the most that can be expected from imperfect human beings, or at least from imperfect men and boys, those sentences defy the absolute morality of sermons and Sunday schools. Huck lies often, always harmlessly and generally in a good cause, although sometimes he appears to take a creative pleasure in elaborating his "stretchers." Humorless critics would denounce the book for the bad example that it set for young readers.

But while *Huckleberry Finn* has been enjoyed by generations of boys, and girls, it was not written primarily for them. Children would not have appreciated the satire on racism and the sovereign democratic voter implied in the angry monologue of drunken, illiterate Pap Finn about the free negro from Ohio, who is "a p'fessor in a college, and could talk all kinds of languages, and knowed everything," and who can vote when he's at home. "Thinks I, what is the country a-coming to? It was 'lection day, and I was just about to go and vote myself if I warn't too drunk to get there; but when they told me there was a State in this country where they'd let that nigger vote, I drawed out. I says I'll never vote agin."

Only adults could fully understand Huck's conclusion, after he struggles with his conscience over whether to return Jim to slavery, suffers from guilt after deciding not to betray his friend, and finally realizes that he would feel equally guilty with either decision: "Well, then, says I, what's the use you learning to do right when it's troublesome to do right and ain't no trouble to do wrong, and the wages is just the same? I was stuck . . . So I reckoned I wouldn't bother no more about it, but after this always do whichever come handiest at the time." That indictment of a senselessly tormenting conscience derives not from *Tom Sawyer* but from "The Facts Concerning the Recent Carnival of Crime in Connecticut," this time presented realistically rather than as grotesque farce. A decade after publishing *Huckleberry Finn*, Twain would characterize it in a journal entry as "a book of mine where a sound heart & a deformed conscience come into collision & conscience suffers defeat."

Pap Finn dominates the early chapters, from the moment that Huck sees his footprints in the snow outside the Widow Douglas's house. (So powerful is the impression he creates that readers coming back to *Huckleberry Finn* are likely to be surprised to find that Pap actually appears in only three chapters.) Comic yet terrifying, the definitive portrayal in American literature of the degraded poor white, Pap is presented with a realism unprecedented in American literature. "There warn't no color in his face . . . it was white; not like another man's white, but a white to make a body sick, a white to make a body's flesh crawl"—whiteness itself becomes repellent, in contrast to the rich darkness of Jim.

Just as he had said that Colonel Sellers was "really" cousin Jim Lampton, Mark Twain would insist that Huck was modeled on, or rather *was*, Tom Blankenship, a Hannibal boy that young Sam Clemens had known. But surely that is too simple. Tom Blankenship might have avoided school and gone barefoot the year round while other boys envied his freedom, he might even have slept in a sugar barrel, but it's not likely that he ever battled with his conscience and humbled himself to a "nigger," or that he possessed Huck's deep sensitivity to the natural world, or his pity for all the unnecessary suffering that human beings inflict on one another. (Another Blankenship, an older brother of Tom, befriended an escaping slave, bringing him food while he lay in hiding—an act for which he risked imprisonment, even lynching. He, too, might have served as a model for Huck.) And surely Huck "was" as much the adult Mark Twain as the Tom Blankenship of the 1840s. But Twain liked to suggest real-life originals for his characters; such claims seemed to prove the authenticity of his work.

He had broken off his story in 1876 with the destruction of the raft, very likely without knowing what would happen next. He did not, probably could not, carefully plan his work, constructing elaborate scenarios in the manner of Henry James. He let the writing carry him as the river carried Huck and Jim. (When he did write a scenario, about the solitary prisoner, he did not bother to write the story.) Only *The Prince and the Pauper*, with its complicated exchange of identities and working out of the consequences, must have been plotted in advance. "I can't write a novel—haven't the faculty," he once confessed to Howells, by which he might have meant either that he could not write a love story, or that he could not construct the dense, multilayered Victorian novel—Dickens's *Bleak House*, George Eliot's *Middlemarch*, Trollope's *Barchester Towers*—with its interlocking plots and sets of characters. For *Huckleberry Finn* he chose an older form, the picaresque journey, infinitely extendable and variable at will.

He probably took up the story of *Huckleberry Finn* again after his return from Europe, at some time between the late fall of 1879 and the summer of 1880, writing Chapters 17 and 18, dealing with the Grangerford-Shepherdson feud (based on the Darnell-Watson feud that had reached a bloody climax during his piloting years).

He worked at *Huckleberry Finn* intermittently over the next three years, introducing the king and the duke, who take control of the raft. Now Huck and Jim go on down the Mississippi for a good reason: they have no choice. Probably, then, in that summer of 1883, he took up his story with the shooting of Boggs by Colonel Sherburn, not quite halfway through the completed book. That episode also is based on fact, the killing of Sam Smarr by William Owsley at noon on the main street of Hannibal in January of 1845— an event that impressed itself unforgettably on the mind of the nine-year-old Sam Clemens.

Yet Mark Twain did not simply reproduce history—Owsley gave no warning, Smarr had no daughter to witness her father's death, and no lynch mob came after the murderer. (Undramatically, Owsley was brought to trial a year later and acquitted.) The narrative mask slips briefly with Colonel Sherburn's scornful speech to the mob, unrealistically reported in Sherburn's correct English rather than creatively paraphrased by Huck as he sometimes paraphrases the king's speeches. Here, for a moment, we seem close to those denunciations of the damned human race that Twain would repeat so often in his old age. But the narrative instantly recovers with Huck's naïve delight in the traveling circus. Juxtaposition, contrast—these are the principles by which *Huckleberry Finn* is constructed.

When Mark Twain took up *Huckleberry Finn* in that summer of 1883, it seems likely that he went back to the early part of his story, inserting Huck and Jim's visit to a wrecked steamboat, the *Walter Scott*—that name ironically echoing his denunciation in *Life on the Mississippi* of Scott's cult of chivalry and its baneful influence on the South, leading to the shipwreck of civil war and defeat. Then the work moved straight ahead, from the Royal Nonesuch (the phallic show staged by the king and the duke) to Tom's revelation that Jim's owner, Miss Watson, has freed him in her will, and concluding with Huck's plan to light out for the Territory. The intervening chapters seem a complicated game of impersonations. The king and the duke impersonate the missing heirs of Peter Wilks, before they betray Jim by selling him back into slavery; Huck impersonates Tom Sawyer at the Phelps farm, and when Tom arrives, he impersonates his brother Sid—all this written by Mark Twain, impersonating Huckleberry Finn. And "Mark Twain" was of course legally Samuel Clemens.

Biographers have argued that Mark Twain's apparently obsessive interest in impersonators and false claimants arose from his own sense of playing a role, false to his true nature, as "Mr. Clemens, Esq.," the respectable gentleman of 351 Farmington Avenue, Hartford, Connecticut. But impersonations, false claimants, have been the stuff of comedy from its beginnings. Humor—and not only Mark Twain's—continuously provokes laughter by revealing the gulf between pretense and reality, exposing the hypocrite, the braggart, the impostor.

The writing went well, week after week. On July 20, Twain confided in a letter to Howells that "it's like old times, to step straight into the study, damp from the breakfast table, & sail right in & sail right on, the whole day long, without thought of running short of stuff or words. I wrote 4000 words to-day & I touch 3000 & upwards pretty often, & don't fall below 2600 on any working day." For week after week he enjoyed his paradoxical freedom—the freedom to ride his "inspiration" wherever it might carry him. But even at three thousand or more words a day, he was not writing carelessly. Mark Twain's manuscript, the part of *Huckleberry Finn* that he wrote that summer, survives. It is remarkably clean—at least a third of the pages have no corrections or revisions at all, and on many others only a word or two has been changed. He would make more revisions later, but after he had a publishable text.

By late August, he could boast that "I've done two seasons' work in one." The work had hardly been work at all—it had seemed pure play when compared to the labor of grinding out chapters to fill *Life on the Mississippi*. This time there was no lack of material— Mark Twain could easily have made *Huckleberry Finn* longer than it is. He had prepared a set of working notes for himself, and he left many ideas in them undeveloped. Scenes representing the culture of the Mississippi Valley in that early day—"A house-raising . . . The country cotillion. The horse-trade. Country quilting. Candy pulling . . . Dinner manners at the tavern with a crowd." Broad farce, probably suggested by "The Stolen White Elephant"— "Farmer has bought an elephant at auction. Gives him to Tom Huck & Jim & they go about the country on him & make no end of trouble." And, after a note on "The Circus"—"Can't he escape somewhere on that elephant?" A dramatic scene remained unwritten—"in a close place," Huck offers to sell Jim, who "dasn't speak—

secretly is supported . . . by firm belief that Huck is incapable of betraying him." "Ruffian burnt up in calaboose"—Mark Twain might have tried to exorcise that ancient guilt as he had tried to purge himself of guilt for Henry's death by writing of it in *Life on the Mississippi*. A good many of those episodes could have become links in the chain of happenings that make up *Huckleberry Finn*.

Almost from its beginning, *Huckleberry Finn* was a darker book than *Tom Sawyer*. *Tom Sawyer* had its villain, Injun Joe, but unlike Pap Finn or the king and the duke, Joe is a stereotype—the murderous half-breed. The killing of Dr. Robinson may shock, but it is not likely to move the reader, as the killing of Buck Grangerford and his cousin, with Huck's understated horror and grief, does. The king and the duke seem a pair of harmless tricksters at first, but their true viciousness appears as they impersonate the heirs of Peter Wilks, while the funeral scene turns into an orgy of credulous sentimentality that almost proves the king's boast: "Hain't we got all the fools in town on our side? And ain't that a big enough majority in any town?" The humor of the two frauds vanishes when, Judas-like, they sell Jim for forty dollars—which the king gambles away.

The narrative comes full circle with their final appearance, as they suffer the fate they had been running from when they first encountered Huck and Jim. Huck sees a "raging rush of people with torches . . . whooping and yelling . . . and they had the king and the duke astraddle of a rail—that is, I knowed it *was* the king and the duke, though they was all over tar and feathers, and didn't look like nothing in the world that was human." Their betrayal of Jim brings about their punishment when Jim informs on them and they, the victimizers, become victims. For their punishment bears no relation to their crimes; it is inflicted for sadistic pleasure by men who have never been injured by "them poor pitiful rascals." "Human beings *can* be awful cruel to one another"—the fact is demonstrated, although Huck's comment suggests that it's not a complete or final truth.

The story concludes with a startling surprise, almost a necessary miracle, when Tom Sawyer reveals that Jim had been freed months before by his owner's will. A modern author, John Seelye, has written a tongue-in-cheek version of *Huckleberry Finn* (*The True Adventures of Huckleberry Finn*, 1970), to satisfy the expectations of present-day readers and critics. Besides providing the obscenity and profanity that Mark Twain omitted, Seelye offers a "realistic" ending, simply cutting out the last twelve chapters. Instead, as Huck paddles a canoe toward the shore, on his way to the Phelps farm, he sees Jim emerge from the woods, bloody and in chains, and plunge into the Mississippi to escape a pursuing crowd of men with guns and dogs, led by Silas Phelps. While Huck watches in horror, powerless to help, Jim goes under, dragged down by the weight of his chains. "Jim was gone forever, down deep in that old muddy river." And a despairing Huck is ready to head for the Territory, alone. That conclusion is powerful, yet unsatisfying—though preferable to a televised version of *Huckleberry Finn* in which Huck exclaims, "That's enough of your booky foolishness, Tom Sawyer!" when Tom starts to explain his plans, then picks up an ax and breaks down the door of Jim's prison.

Jim *must* be freed—the whole novel points toward that outcome; given the time, the place, the circumstances, no probable way to free him exists. Twain escapes from his dilemma by turning to burlesque, but at this point in the book, the absurdity of burlesque may be appropriate. It is absurd for Tom to "liberate" a slave who is already free, but slavery itself is absurd, a monstrous imposition. Huck's conclusion—"I reckon I got to light out for the Territory ahead of the rest, because Aunt Sally she's going to adopt me and sivilize me, and I can't stand it. I been there before"—seems entirely appropriate, promising new adventures while leaving each reader free to decide just how seriously to take Huck's rejection of "sivilization."

On September 1, Mark Twain could proudly claim that "I've just finished writing a book; & modesty compels me to say it's a rattling good one, too—'Adventures of Huckleberry Finn.' (Tom Sawyer's Comrade.)" He knew his book was good, but he never quite realized how good—at most, he would rank it with the later *Personal Recollections of Joan of Arc*, his favorite among his works. But it can never be easy for a writer to admit even to himself that he has already done his best work, and Mark Twain was always likely to overvalue his current project. His total absorption in its creation seemed to guarantee the value of the finished product. "Inspiration"—that sudden, unaccountable influx of energy and continuous upwelling of ideas—was the same, whatever the result might be.

Twain surely had a right to exult, even though to say that he had "finished" was not strictly accurate. Revision remained and would go on intermittently during the following months. The book was "rattling good" already, he felt, but he meant to make it better, to please himself at least as much as to ensure success. His revisions are largely matters of detail, detail that mattered to a writer intensely concerned with the sound of speech. In his opening "Explanatory" note, he had claimed that "a number of dialects" were used: "the Missouri negro dialect; the extremest form of the backwoods South-western dialect; the ordinary 'Pike County' dialect; and four mod-ified varieties of this last." The "shadings" that distinguished them from one another, he added, had been done "painstakingly," based on "personal familiarity with these several forms of speech." A good deal of those "shadings" were done in this final revision.

For several generations, readers have been content either to be-lieve without question that there really were seven different dialects or subdialects in *Huckleberry Finn*, or to suppose that the claim was just another of Mark Twain's jokes, as the conclusion to his opening explanatory note suggested: "I make this explanation for the reason that without it many readers would suppose that all these characters were trying to talk alike and not succeeding." But a modern scholar has demonstrated that there are at least seven distinct varieties of speech, regional or social, in the book. If Huck says "I know," while Jim says "I knows," that difference does not result from the author's carelessness. "Missouri negro" is spoken by all the black characters in the book, "backwoods Southwestern" by Sister Hotchkiss and the other gossiping neighbors at the Phelps farm: "That's my opinion, take it or leave it, it mayn't be no 'count, s'I, but sich as 't is, it's my opinion, s'I, 'n' if any body k'n start a better one, s'I, let him *do* it, s'I, that's all."

The "ordinary 'Pike County' " is used by Huck, Tom, and Pap, among others; the four varieties of "modified Pike County" by the robbers on the *Walter Scott*, the king, the loafers in Bricksville, and Aunt Sally and Uncle Silas. There actually seem to be seven, not four, varieties. The differences are often subtle, but to Mark Twain they were important, satisfying his own standard for linguistic re-alism. He had proved that he could beat the local colorists at re-producing dialect, without making a futile and self-defeating attempt at exact accuracy.

Twain worked continuously to make his language more expres-sive—he was always more concerned with words and sentences than with structure. Originally, Huck commented on the king's "humbug and hogwash," but "humbug" is vague and conventional. Twain replaced it with the more original and appropriate "soul-butter and hogwash." When the mob comes to lynch Colonel Sherburn, its members tear down his fence and "roll in like a wave"; when he faces them with his shotgun, "the crowd fell back," says the manuscript. But in the book itself, "the racket stopped, and the wave sucked back," brilliantly completing the original image.

Huck's language is individualized. In the typescript, Huck tries to persuade Jim to board the wreck of the *Walter Scott* by telling him that "steamboat captains is always rich, and have everything they want, you know." In the book, he specifies what they might find, revealing exactly what "rich" means to him: "Seegars, *I* bet you—and cost five cents apiece, solid cash." Literary clichés are pruned from standard speeches, such as Sherburn's when he defies the mob, or Dr. Robinson's when he warns the mourners at the Wilks funeral against accepting the king as Peter Wilks's heir. "Cast this paltry villain out," he had originally begged them, speaking like a character in melodrama.

"Ever since papa and mama were married," Susy would write in her "biography" of her father, "papa has written his books and then taken them to mama in manuscript, and she has expergated [*sic*] them Papa read *Huckleberry Finn* to us in manuscript, and sometimes Clara and I would be sitting with mama while she was looking the manuscript over, and I remember so well, with what pangs of regret we used to see her turn down the leaves of the pages, which meant that some delightfully terrible part must be left out." Did Mark Twain sacrifice his book and his literary integrity to Victorian gentility by making his wife, with her narrow, conventional taste, his censor? That accusation was made long ago by Van Wyck Brooks in his *Ordeal of Mark Twain* (1920), and has often been repeated, but the evidence disproves it.

The description of the Royal Nonesuch, the "play" that the king performs for the yokels of Bricksville, was the most daring scene in *Huckleberry Finn*: "the king come a-prancing out on all fours, naked; and he was painted all over, ring-streaked-and-striped, all sorts of colors, as splendid as a rainbow. And—but never mind the rest of his outfit; it was just wild . . . Well, it would make a cow laugh to see the shines that old idiot cut." "LADIES AND CHILDREN NOT ADMITTED," read the handbills for the show. "If that line don't fetch them," says the duke, "I don't know Arkansaw!" After that, adult readers will understand that the "shines" cut by the naked king must be indecent, that his performance is a phallic show.

Certainly Livy saw those implications when she wrote "scandalous" in the margin of the manuscript beside this passage. To reduce its power of scandalizing, Twain altered the name of the "play" from "The Burning Shame" to "The Royal Nonesuch." The king becomes merely "naked" instead of "stark naked." One sentence is cut: the king's remark that he "judged he could caper to their base instincts." Other changes are purely stylistic: the conventional, and uncharacteristic, "I won't describe the rest of his outfit because it was outrageous" is turned into Huckspeech as "but never mind the rest of his outfit; it was just wild," while the vague "Everybody rose up mad" becomes concrete as "Everybody sings out, 'Sold!' " The scene remains as scandalous as Livy had called it.

But if Mark Twain allowed Livy and Howells to take the trouble of expurgating his manuscripts, he would have done the job for himself if they had not. When both of them somehow overlooked Huck's complaint in *Tom Sawyer* about life at the Widow Douglas's—"They comb me all to hell"—Twain himself made the necessary change to "They comb me all to thunder." By the standards of his time, "hell" was unprintable, and it never occurred to him to defy those standards, or even to question them. Illustrations, of course, also had to be examined carefully. A scene involving the king—"the lecherous old rascal kissing the girl at the campmeeting"—was "powerful good," but just for that reason it had to go. "The subject won't *bear* illustrating," he commented; "pictures are sure to tell the truth about it too plainly." But Mark Twain had already "told the truth about it" in his prose.

Other changes reflect Livy's personal objections to particular words: Huck's "it was too rancid for me" (describing the garbage brought by the audience to the final performance of the Royal Nonesuch) becomes a tamer "it was too various for me," and the description of Jim disguised as a sick Arab—"he didn't only look like he was dead, he looked considerable more than that"—had first been a more telling "he looked like he was mortified." But all of those changes together, in a book of more than three hundred pages, seem insignificant. *Huckleberry Finn* was published as Mark Twain intended it. His intentions were conditioned by his culture. It would never have occurred to him that he should reproduce the profanity and obscenity that a real Huck would have constantly heard and spoken. Yet more than a century later, the illusion holds: that this is *Huck* speaking.

After seven years, Mark Twain had brought his book almost to its end. He could finish at his leisure, revising intermittently through the coming months at Hartford, getting the dialects right, and reading proof in the summer of 1884. With delays caused by his decision to set up his own publishing house to issue his own books, *Huckleberry Finn* would not be published until February of 1885.

Of course, he had not spent the entire summer finishing *Huckleberry Finn.* When he got "fagged out," he would "lie abed a couple of days & read & smoke, & then go it again for 6 or 7 days." Quarry Farm gave him freedom to read, as well as to write, without the distractions of Hartford. "He reads everything," a surprised visitor had once noted, and he read in French and German as well as English. Reading German, he observed, gave him "the solid enjoyment which one gets out of almost understanding what he is reading," when the mind is left "in a state of enthusiastic confusion." The humorous talent, he had told Orion almost twenty years before, "is a mighty engine when supplied with the steam of *education*," and though schooling had ended for him at thirteen, he went on educating himself through reading for the rest of his life. (But like a good many other Americans of his time whose schooling had been cut short, he had acquired the basis of a literary education almost without knowing it. He knew the Bible intimately, and Shakespeare nearly as well.)

He read the magazines of the day, *Atlantic, Harper's,* and *Century.* They were dense, demanding, packed with solid content, serializing such writers as James and Howells and Cable, educating their readers in science, history, literature, art, nature, and politics. He read the major novelists—forming his own judgment, taking nothing on faith. His prejudices were strong; he detested Scott and Cooper, while reading Jane Austen made him "feel like a barkeeper entering the kingdom of heaven." He disliked both her characters and their society—so complacent, so constricting. Howells, he said, was his only author—meaning his only novelist. That was an exaggeration, though nearly true as far as contemporary American writers were concerned. Like everyone else in his day, Twain read Dickens, but he had little interest in the other major Victorians. He disliked

George Eliot and Henry James for their laborious analyzing of motives and feelings. Most of all he despised artificial sentiment and formulaic writing, ridiculing Bret Harte's "saintly wh's and self-sacrificing sons of b's." There are no whores in Mark Twain's books, but the sons of bitches behave like sons of bitches.

The Wild Humorist of the Sagebrush Hills had become a careful stylist, concerned with the rhythm of the sentence and choice of the exact word. "I amend dialect stuff by talking & *talking* it till it sounds right," he once told Howells. There were no synonyms in the English language, he held; no two words had exactly the same meaning. As a critic, whether of his own writing or the writing of others, he looked at the text with microscopic attention. His criticism of Scott had been largely an attack on Scott's language and its disastrous effect on the language of his Southern imitators. In the only critical essay he ever wrote, "Fenimore Cooper's Literary Offenses," Twain would list eighteen separate offenses in the work of Sir Walter's leading American disciple. Nine of them are linguistic. Most of all, he disliked the inappropriateness of Cooper's dialogue to its speakers, particularly the illiterate Leatherstocking. The "rules governing literary art in the domain of romantic fiction," he held, ". . . require that when a personage talks like an illustrated, gilt-edged, tree-calf, hand-tooled, seven-dollar Friendship's Offering in the beginning of a paragraph, he shall not talk like a negro minstrel in the end of it. But this rule is flung down and danced upon in the *Deerslayer* tale."

On the whole, he preferred fact to fiction, delighting in books that seemed to reveal human nature in the raw—collections of famous trials, histories, autobiographies, diaries, and memoirs. Any life, recorded honestly by the subject in his own words, seemed worth reading. There were a few works that he constantly reread— Carlyle's *French Revolution*, Pepys's *Diary*, Suetonius's gossipy, scandalmongering *Lives of the Caesars*, the Duc de Saint-Simon's unsparing memoirs of the court of Louis XIV, which he read in both French and English, Dana's *Two Years Before the Mast*, revealing the hell that a common sailor's life could be, in contrast to "the lying story-books that make boys fall in love with the sea." Those were books that seemed to present humanity as it actually was— unflatteringly, as a rule, but Mark Twain relished their realism. His wife and daughters preferred more elevating works. (Clara would try to read Saint-Simon and give up in disgust—his memoirs were only "a series of vulgar anecdotes about people so low and meaningless that all one can do is blush and regret.")

Carlyle's descriptions of men acting in times of crisis fascinated Mark Twain—Huck's description of the mob coming to lynch Colonel Sherburn seems to owe something to Carlyle's descriptions of revolutionary crowds—and even a theoretical work like W. E. H. Lecky's *History of European Morals* interested him deeply in its presentation of the moral and psychological laws governing human behavior. (He dramatized an ethical dilemma in *Huckleberry Finn*, when Huck's socially conditioned, or "deformed," conscience almost persuades him to return Jim to slavery, but at the last moment his sound heart saves Huck from that betrayal.) As Twain grew older, searching for truths, the determinism of Victorian science influenced him powerfully, appearing to echo, in secular terms, the Calvinist teaching of his childhood.

In 1888, asked to name his twelve favorite authors, Twain would cite nine authors or works—Shakespeare, Browning, Carlyle ("French Revolution only"), Malory (*Le Morte d'Arthur*), *The Arabian Nights*, "Parkman's Histories" (Francis Parkman's many-volumed account of the struggle between England and France for possession of North America), Boswell's *Life of Johnson* "because I like to see that complacent gasometer listen to himself talk," Jowett's translations of Plato (an unlikely choice, it might seem, but in his sixties, Mark Twain himself would take to writing Socratic dialogues), and " 'B. B.' (a book which I wrote some years ago, not for publication but just for my own private reading)." "B. B." is a mystery: there is no other known reference to it, and no manuscript with that title survives. That description, a book written "not for publication but just for my own private reading," suggests *1601*, but the initials will match only if we suppose that "B. B." is an abbreviation of some alternative title that Twain had given to it.

But he did not often get fagged out that summer, and he did not often take to his bed or his hammock for reading. In that letter to Howells in which he told of the enormous quantity of manuscript he had been producing, he boasted that he was "boiling with energy." Finishing *Huckleberry Finn* was not enough: he alternated between it and a second, smaller book, which he called "The 1002d Night." It was a burlesque of *The Arabian Nights*, a work that Twain knew intimately, retelling its stories to his children, apparently fascinated by its variety and its narrative power. (The impulse to burlesque was irresistible for Mark Twain, and the works that he admired were often its target, as if to demonstrate that they could survive the test of ridicule.) "The 1002d Night" is a fantastic tale involving mistaken sexes, when newborn babies—the Vizier's daughter and the Sultan's son—are secretly exchanged through the machinations of a malicious witch.

The inevitable complications follow as the changelings enter adolescence and each begins to assume the stereotyped role of his or her true sex. As he had done in "The Stolen White Elephant," Twain makes play with enormous, pseudo-Arabic names: "Suleyman-Mohammed-Akbar-ben-Selim-ben-Ali-ibn-Noormahal-ben-Saladin-Badoorah-el-Shazaman-Aladdin-ben-Yusef-ibn-Kismet-el-Emir-Abdallah-ben." Howells's verdict was kindly but firm: "on the whole it was not your best or your second-best." Mark Twain eventually accepted that judgment, leaving "The 1002d Night" in manuscript. But he had been well paid for his time and effort by the sheer pleasure of writing, of being swept along by an irresistible flood of creative energy when words seemed to come faster than they could be written down. Mark Twain would finally come to distrust that energy—"One should never write under an inspiration; for at such a time one is mentally drunk"—but he could hardly write, or at least write well, without it. "Inspiration" might result in laborious farce—"The 1002d Night," *Cap'n Simon Wheeler*, "The Stolen White Elephant"—but it also produced *Huckleberry Finn*.

But writing alone, even on two manuscripts, could not exhaust him that summer. One day in July, "feeling not in condition for writing," Twain left his study, but he was bursting with energy—he must do something. Clara and Susy had been painfully trying to master the dates of English history. Suddenly a method for turning study into play struck their father. Choosing "a great granite flower-vase overflowing with a cataract of bright-yellow flowers" on the farmhouse porch to represent William the Conqueror, Mark Twain staked out the reigns of the kings and queens of England along the carriage road leading to the house at the rate of one foot to the year, driving a three-foot stake into the turf beside the road to mark the beginning of each reign. "Kings & battles are the great landmarks of history," he declared, although he knew better. *The*

Prince and the Pauper had been concerned not with battles but with individual lives, and with the institutions, laws, and customs that shaped those lives.

As Clara remembered, "the game consisted in racing past the stakes and calling out names and dates of the numerous kings and their reigns." Mark Twain joined in enthusiastically, racing around the course, his curly hair waving in the breeze. "He was picturesque in all circumstances," Clara remarks—as he well knew. A day of play with his daughters in the summer sun, and that might have been all. But again inspiration possessed him. Before going to sleep that night, he had devised a way to play the game with cards and a cribbage board. With that change, it could be copyrighted.

He saw unlimited possibilities. Players might score points for giving the dates of individual reigns, and for listing major events during that reign or (for advanced players) in particular years. Orion was set to work, preparing booklets of events. And the principle seemed infinitely expandable. Why not a "Game of Napoleon I," or a "Game, in months, of French Revolution," or "Games of all Histories & Countries, ancient & modern"? Why not geography ("Games of each of the states? & Canada?"), literature ("Game of Authors & their books of each country"), technology ("names & nationalities of inventors")—all to be playable on the same board? He promptly sent an enthusiastic account of the game to Joe Twichell, whose response nearly ended a valued friendship. Twichell passed the letter on to the Hartford *Courant*, which immediately printed it—as Twichell expected. "The History game made a mighty nice little piece in this morning's Courant," he wrote complacently. Other papers reprinted the letter; any reader could have stolen the idea.

Mark Twain was furious at this well-meaning betrayal of his confidence. (The feelings of the sanguine person, young Sam Clemens had written in his journal twenty-eight years before, are sudden and intense; he is sensitive, deeply hurt by any slight; "the next emotion is violent rage.") Worst of all, for weeks Twichell failed to respond to his upbraidings, and when he at last replied, he refused to apologize for his offense or even to admit that it had been an offense. He had expected the letter to make the rounds of the newspapers, and "what a creditable and amiable Mark Twain it is, who shines forth in it." Twain could not quite forgive this breach of confidence, even in an intimate friend: "I think I shall never thoroughly trust him again." (The sanguine temperament, he had once noted, "never entirely forgets an injury.") In reality, there had been no injury. No one tried to steal the game, Twain would patent it, and a few years later it would be briefly put on sale by his own publishing company in the form of a pegboard with a booklet of names, dates, and facts.

By mid-September, it was time to leave Quarry Farm. The summer had been well spent. With *Huckleberry Finn*, Mark Twain's way of writing had been justified, had served him superbly. The boundary between work and play had been erased—the composition of *Huckleberry Finn* was play at the highest level, creative, all-engrossing, deeply enjoyable, with its total immersion of the author in his imagined world. The history game and "The 1002d Night" had been necessary diversions, expending the surplus energies, the excitement, the arousal, created by the writing of *Huckleberry Finn*. Mark Twain's writing depended on impulse and inspiration, and while inspiration sometimes misled him, without it he could produce only hack work. That summer, it had not misled him. Although it would be a generation before any critic would dare say so, he had produced a classic book—surely one of the unlikeliest of all classics!

SIX

Colonel Sellers

T he family returned to Hartford, to the life of business and society which Mark Twain had created, which he periodically denounced, but could not forsake—and never truly wished to. The children went back to their lessons, Livy to her household, and Twain to his speculations and investments, to his engrossing social life, to his inescapable correspondence, to making a leisurely revision of *Huckleberry Finn* (he would finally send the manuscript to the printer in late April), and to watching and worrying over the disappointing sale of *Life on the Mississippi*.

Becoming in effect his own publisher had multiplied the complications of his life, without bringing the profit he had expected. Of course, the disappointingly small sale of *The Prince and the Pauper* could be explained. The book had been written for a select audience—the Clemens family, and families like the Clemenses. The public did not expect a serious historical novel from the author of *Tom Sawyer* and *The Innocents Abroad*. Besides, profits had been smaller than might have been expected, even for the actual sale, because *The Prince and the Pauper* had been expensively produced, with paper, binding, and illustrations of a quality rarely found in subscription publishing. Osgood loved fine books.

But with *Life on the Mississippi*, Mark Twain had tried to go back to his old manner, and he wanted a big success—a sale of a hundred thousand copies. Webster had taken over the New York agency, the largest in the country, along with wide authority "in the matter of running the book," while Twain supplied advice. That direct involvement would make failure all the more bitter, yet by December, after a sale of only thirty thousand copies since its publication in mid-May, Twain believed that *Life on the Mississippi* had indeed failed, thanks to Osgood's blunders. The prospectus had been badly prepared, excerpting too many pages from the "Old Times on the Mississippi" sketches, and leading the public to suspect that the new book merely reprinted old material. The preliminary canvass had been short, beginning only a few weeks before publication, and Twain insisted, against the evidence, that the American Publishing Company had never issued any of his books until an enormous sale had been guaranteed by advance orders—"*The orders that come in after the ISSUE of a subscription book don't amount to a damn.*" Bitterly, he charged that "the publisher who sells less than 50,000 copies of a book for me has merely injured me, he has not benefitted me," adding that he "had no experience of that kind, and never once thought of it." Osgood had learned the subscription business at Mark Twain's expense—and had been paid for doing so.

As often happened, Mark Twain's imagination had revised the past. Not only *The Prince and the Pauper*, but *Tom Sawyer* and *Sketches: New and Old* (1875) had sold fewer than thirty thousand copies each. With *Tom Sawyer*, delays in publication and the competition of a pirated Canadian edition might have caused the failure, but with *The Prince and the Pauper* and *Life on the Mississippi*, the blame could be laid on the books themselves. The public sensed that the vitality of *Life on the Mississippi* was largely in its first third, already familiar as "Old Times on the Mississippi," and available in a cheap Canadian paperback. Most readers would probably have agreed with the British reviewer who found Mark Twain the pilot "fresh, vigorous, irresistibly interesting," but Mark Twain the tourist simply dull, and concluded that what was good in the book dealt with the past—"the rest is mere reporting." And the failure, after all, was only relative. For any other American writer of the time, a sale of thirty thousand copies would have been a sensational success.

Osgood denied responsibility, insisted that "we have worked harder over it [*Life on the Mississippi*] and had more trouble and anxiety in connection with it than any book we ever had to do with"—very likely true. But Mark Twain's expenses had been enormous over the past two or three years, he had counted on a vast sale, and his disappointment was too bitter to allow for any admission that the "failure" might have been due to the book itself. His connection with Osgood had been a mistake, as he saw it, and Osgood would handle no more of his books. Briefly he considered withdrawing from the business of bookselling, turning *Huck* over to the American Publishing Company—then reached the inevitable solution. He would have no more intermediaries; for *Huckleberry Finn* he would set up his own publishing house.

But Mark Twain could do nothing to increase the sale of *Life on the Mississippi*; he could only worry. Luckily, he had the final revision of *Huckleberry Finn* to occupy himself with, and new projects multiplied in his notebook. He planned a story, to be narrated by Huck Finn, about "Tom Sawyer's far-western cousin," a "Montana belle," who "hunts bears . . . breaks horses, etc." Or he would "gravely write a story in which at intervals, hero saves his girl from ruffians, drowning, burning, & all the other stock accidents, & she persistently refuses to marry him, to his great astonishment, he never having heard of such a thing in the books." Mark Twain could never resist burlesquing the clichés of "the books"—sentimental, melodramatic popular fiction. He jotted down notes for a story set in the Missouri of his childhood, with "a candy-pulling, a singing party, skating & swimming adventures," a steamboat wreck, "paterrollers & slavery" ("pater-rollers": patrols supervising the behavior of both slaves and free blacks in the Old South). He would take up that theme, "pater-rollers & slavery," fourteen years later in "Tom Sawyer's Conspiracy," an abortive sequel to *Huckleberry Finn*.

Another plan would surely have surprised his readers: "America in 1985. The Pope here & an Inquisition." (The flood of Irish immigration before the Civil War had brought nightmares of Popish domination to Protestant Americans.) "The age of Darkness back again . . . Europe is *republican*—& full of science and invention—none allowed here." From early in his career until its end, Twain was concerned with the future of America, and his imaginings usually involved replacement of the republic by "monarchy" in some form. In November of 1874, in a letter meant to amuse Howells and other friends, he had written a fantasy describing the America of 1935, an empire ruled by the O'Mulligan dynasty, with an established church (Twichell is Archbishop of Dublin, formerly New York) and a hereditary aristocracy (Mark Twain, aged one hundred, is the Earl of Hartford). Later, he would treat the Church more seriously. In *A Connecticut Yankee in King Arthur's Court*, the unrelenting hostility of the Catholic Church defeats the Yankee's effort to bring freedom and progress to Arthurian England, and in "The

Secret History of Eddypus, the World-Empire," written in 1901 or 1902, Twain would imagine a world returned to the Dark Ages of superstition and tyranny, controlled by a sort of religious trust— a combination of Christian Science and Catholicism.

These were projects, most of them, never to be carried out. But Mark Twain's most engrossing project that fall was a new play, *Colonel Sellers as a Scientist*, a grotesque farce that he wrote in collaboration with Howells. The theater was a true popular art in nineteenth-century America, continuously demanding new material. A play that provided a vehicle for a favorite actor might earn a fortune for its author as well. (Even Henry James would be tempted by the lure of the theater, and fail humiliatingly.) Mark Twain had succeeded once, with *Colonel Sellers*, loosely based on his section of *The Gilded Age*, and he intended to repeat that success.

At the peak of *Colonel Sellers*'s popularity, postcards arrived daily, notifying Twain of his share in the receipts for the previous night. The cards came late in the afternoon, Howells would recall, and Twain might read them aloud, "in wild triumph," as he came in to dinner. "One hundred and fifty dollars—two hundred dollars— three hundred dollars were the gay figures which they bore, and which he flaunted in the air before he sat down." He had written other plays, of course. *Ah Sin* had failed, and he had finally decided that *Cap'n Simon Wheeler* was unplayable. But surely a new Sellers play, with Raymond playing the lead again, would succeed.

It was not only the box-office returns that lured him. The theater fascinated him, as it had fascinated Dickens. He delighted in charades—a favorite family entertainment for the Clemenses, the more absurd the better—he was also a highly successful performer on the lecture platform, and he had actually appeared on stage in Hartford, in a benefit performance of an old comedy, *The Loan of a Lover*. Rewriting the character's lines until he could speak them, he had made such a hit in his part that the producer Augustin Daly had invited him to play the part in New York, "not for one night but for many." And he was a role player in life as well. "Mark Twain" had been in part a conscious construction, composed of qualities already present, of course, but selected, heightened, dramatized. Samuel Clemens, Esq., was equally a construct, but a more limited and less interesting one.

Thinking of possible subjects for a play, Twain naturally considered his brother. Orion still seemed to offer rich comic material, with his continual veering in politics and religion and his impossible projects. He had begun writing a science fiction novel about a journey to the center of the earth—a plagiarism of Jules Verne. He had considered selling everything he owned and prospecting for silver in the Colorado Rockies, emigrating to Germany to teach English (Orion knew no German), writing a burlesque of *Paradise Lost*, and writing short stories for *The New York Times*, hoping to earn a hundred dollars a column, as Bret Harte did. Orion had been an inventor, too, until his mother, no doubt fearing for her son's life if he ever built his flying machine, had forced him to swear that he would give up inventing. He not only seemed a real-life Sellers, he was almost a parody of his brother—as Twain must have realized at times. That realization might account for his recurring, intense exasperation with Orion.

Twain believed that he need only put an Orion figure on stage to guarantee success. He had invited Howells to collaborate, but Howells hesitated, not wanting to cause pain to Orion, and the plan was changed. They would work out a second Sellers play instead—but the visionary Sellers had much in common with Orion, and with Mark Twain as well. They had been thinking of such a project for years, and in the spring of 1883 the Mallory brothers, owners of the Madison Square Theatre in New York, had shown interest. "Next October you will come here and roost with me," Twain wrote exuberantly to Howells, "and we will lock ourselves up . . . and put the great American comedy through." Howells came, at the beginning of November, and the two men had a "jubilant fortnight" together, hammering out their play, with Twain providing the characters and Howells outlining the plot.

In that collaboration, Howells could escape from the sober realism and the moral concerns of his novels and from the constant discipline of his life. His father had been a "visionary," a publisher of short-lived periodicals, an enthusiast for Utopian causes, incompetent and impractical. Predictably, the son had reacted against the father's failings, carefully directing his own life, regularly producing a novel a year, controlling his expenses, making himself intensely respectable and responsible, and continuously self-conscious. "I am cursed with consciousness to the core," he would tell Mark Twain, while "you are dramatic and unconscious." (Ten years later, at a garden party in Paris, Howells would warn a young American friend to live life to the full, adding that he himself had never done so.

That advice would be reported to Henry James and provide him with the germ of *The Ambassadors*. "Live all you can; it's a mistake not to . . . I haven't done so—and now I'm old"—so Lambert Strether, James's protagonist, warns a young artist.) But under the liberating influence of his friend, Howells could drop his usual reserve, forget his anxieties and responsibilities, free himself from that disastrous self-consciousness, laugh till he was red in the face. He could, almost, become Mark Twain.

As they worked, they outdid each other in flights of fantasy. Borrowing from Jane Clemens's family history, they would make Sellers believe himself the rightful heir to an English earldom. He would be a mad inventor as well. He would appear on stage with an enormous fire extinguisher of his own invention strapped to his back, ready to prove its value whenever a fire broke out; he would wear homemade wings throughout one act and try to fly from the kitchen table; he would believe that he could materialize the dead and make a fortune by supplying cities with materialized policemen who would last forever (and be as active as the living ones), by filling Congress with dead statesmen in place of living mediocrities, and by furnishing Europe with kings and emperors whom no terrorist could kill.

The Colonel Sellers of *The Gilded Age*, and of the play taken from it, had been a recognizable American type, living in a familiar American world—and that recognition, together with the affectionate satire with which he was drawn, had accounted for his success with the public. But this new, exaggerated figure seems to be Mark Twain's attempt to exorcise the qualities that he shared with his character: the same irresistible obsession with his current project, the refusal to admit any obstacle or impossibility, or to submit his enthusiasm to the test of reality. But while Mark Twain's failures could be expensive, not only in money but also in energy expended, and in the humiliation of failure, Sellers's failures cost him nothing. No matter how often he is knocked down, he bounces up again, unhurt.

Howells, a skilled professional, could easily imitate Twain's style, and they "took the play scene and scene about," as he would recall, working separately all day, then meeting before dinner to read over the day's work. Exhilarated by their own creation, vying with each other in comic invention, swept irresistibly on by a common inspiration, the two friends did not realize that in trying to write a comedy, they had in fact written a wild, unplayable farce. They would earn nothing from it, but for Howells, at least, the liberating joy of those days of intellectual intoxication might have been payment enough.

With *Colonel Sellers as a Scientist* completed and put aside until the authors could find an actor—preferably Raymond—to play the leading role and a theater to stage the play in, Howells went back to his labors in Boston, and Mark Twain could take up his normal routine again. He could attend, for example, to his mail. Some fifteen thousand letters are on file today in the Mark Twain Papers at the University of California at Berkeley, many of them with brief comments by Twain scrawled on the envelopes. And those are only a fraction of the total that he received. Family mail could not be avoided, for he was the unquestioned head of the Clemens tribe, supporting his mother and older brother (Orion received a pension of a hundred dollars a month for himself and his wife, besides fifty dollars to care for his mother), dispensing favors and advice. Jane Clemens, Twain's sister, Pamela, and his nephew Sam Moffett, Pamela's child (an intelligent boy with a taste for books, who became a kind of surrogate son for Mark Twain), distant, sometimes unknown, relatives—all wrote to ask for help or advice, or simply to complain.

Most of all Mark Twain dreaded Orion's plodding, interminable letters, listing the number of pages of Blackstone he had read in his endless study of the law—he had "practiced" for years, renting an office and waiting for clients who never came—offering unwanted advice on his brother's affairs, describing his latest enthusiasm, hopefully submitting hopeless manuscripts for criticism. One twenty-five-page letter concerned the electric light business in Keokuk, with Orion's hopes for organizing "an energetic, powerful company . . . an anti-monopoly electric light"—if Mark Twain chose to invest, Orion generously offered to manage the business free of charge—besides arguments for free trade, against Western Union, and in favor of a postal telegraph.

Finally, provoked beyond endurance, Twain had demanded that Orion "solemnly swear" that during 1883 and 1884 he would "make no proposition of a business or literary nature to my brother, in writing, by telegraph, or other vehicle," would not lecture, would "submit any piece of writing to him for judgment or criticism"—

Orion could not expect to "achieve even a respectable mediocrity" in either lecturing or writing. And Twain's failure to reply to any proposal should not be taken for agreement, "for it always means *dissent* [double underline]." Orion had intended, on the advice of a Keokuk doctor, to lecture on religion to a stag audience—his remarks might have been too daring for female ears. The lecture was wickedly clever, he felt, and he offered to send Mark Twain the fifty-one-page manuscript.

That lecture was never given, but it would not have been Orion's first attempt to pronounce on religious matters. In 1879, he had been formally excommunicated from the Presbyterian church of Keokuk for a lecture on "Man, the Architect of Our Religion," in which, among other heresies, he had denied the divinity of Christ. Believers had been warned to avoid contaminating themselves through unnecessary communication with the infidel.

Orion dutifully signed the oath his brother proposed, "keeping a copy to read over once a week," and humbly apologized for the "worry and loss of valuable time" that he had caused, adding that he meant to turn his attention to the law and "study it diligently." Eight years before, Mark Twain had commented that the two things Orion was constant to were "his literary and legal aspirations"— naturally enough, since he was "wholly & preposterously unfitted" for both. But while Orion might take that oath, he could not keep it, as Mark Twain should have realized. Temperament, after all, was unchangeable.

Always there were letters from his public—and not only from his readers, for Mark Twain was known to millions of Americans who had never read his books. Again and again he was thanked for the pleasure his work had given, sometimes to hopeless invalids. A cheerful variation on this theme cited his work as an aid to romance. A young man had been nursed back to health in a Colorado home after an injury, and the daughter of the family had amused him by reading *Tom Sawyer* aloud. During the readings, they fell in love, and in due course married. There were requests and suggestions, most commonly for a sequel to *Tom Sawyer*. There was hate mail, asking him to stop writing, to give the public a rest. There were letters from cranks and lunatics, from religious fanatics, urging him to turn away from his vanities and seek salvation. Sometimes the mail seemed to offer examples of telepathy: on the envelope of a letter offering to dramatize *Tom Sawyer*, Twain jotted: "Mental Telegraphy. I was finishing the fourth & last act of my drama of Tom Sawyer yesterday, Jan. 29, while he was writing this letter."

Letters from foreign admirers were frequent. In spite of Mark Twain's prejudice against most things French, it must have been pleasant to hear that one H. Gauthier had first discovered Mark Twain's work one night in a hotel in Darmstadt, Germany ("petite ville formidablement ennuyeuse"), when he was alarmed by sounds from the next room. Investigating, he found his neighbor, a young American, "twisted like an eel on his bed, biting his handkerchief," to control his explosions of laughter. In explanation, he simply handed Gauthier a volume of Mark Twain.

Would-be writers regularly asked for his opinion of their work, or his influence with editors; they invited him to collaborate with them, or simply to put his name on their manuscripts to make them salable. Often he would patiently read their work, advising them on the need to write from experience and to serve a laborious apprenticeship, as he had done. Rarely, the mail brought work that showed talent. In early February, Twain received a privately printed novel, *The Story of a Country Town*, by E. W. Howe, an unknown writer from Kansas. Howe had sent his book to Mark Twain, he explained, because "I regard you as the foremost American writer & the book is a 'Missouri' story."

The Story of a Country Town, at times crudely melodramatic, was memorable for its portrayal of the narrator's father, the Reverend John Westlock, a prairie patriarch ruling not only his submissive wife and frightened son but the entire community, preaching a joyless religion of work and duty. Twain promptly read the book and wrote enthusiastically to Howe, praising his style, "so simple, sincere, direct, & at the same time so clear & so strong," and his "pictures of that arid village life . . . I know, for I have seen it all, lived it all." "That arid village life"—Howe's description must have reminded him not only of the Hannibal of the 1840s but of the mean and shabby river towns in *Huckleberry Finn*. He offered detailed criticism and gave Howe, a newspaper editor, permission to print parts of the letter. Like Mark Twain, Howe had admired the realism of *A Modern Instance*, and he sent a copy of his book to Howells as well. He, too, was enthusiastic, finding that the work's "simple, naked humanness" outweighed its faults. When *The Story of a Country Town* was published in a trade edition, a few months later, their praise helped to make it a success. Although Howe proved to be a one-book writer, *The Story of a Country Town* stands as an early classic, or at least semiclassic, of prairie realism.

Worst of all were the beggars. There is often a disarming simplicity in their requests: Mark Twain was rich, and if they asked, he might give. A Presbyterian congregation in Alabama needs help in building their church: " 'Who knows,' said the pastor, 'what he [Mark Twain] might do. He is rich in purse, let us try his generosity.' " "A race of beggars. No answer," Twain scrawled on the envelope. A brother and sister plan to travel around the world and write a book about their journey; they ask Mark Twain for help, offering to repay him out of their royalties. Vashti Garwood wishes to move to Ann Arbor, Michigan, so that her daughter can attend medical school there. She asks for money to buy a house, offering, as security, to make Twain the beneficiary of her life insurance, a frequent ploy. A man writes from Chicago asking for help; he is lame and destitute, he says, and among strangers, but he has a valuable, but unspecified, invention.

The requests could be deeply pathetic: Sarah Griswold writes on behalf of a lifelong cripple who supports himself by making cigars: "He is quite a genius—a great reader and no man ever had a better heart or head." ("Order sent for one box of cigars," Twain notes on the envelope.) Myra Fuller is a teacher in Northampton, Massachusetts, with a salary of $350 a year. She asks for six hundred dollars to help pay for a house she has bought for her aged parents. She is "almost crushed with care," she writes. "You cannot know the sufferings of the poor." But there was usually no way to distinguish the fraudulent from the needy, and only a Vanderbilt or a Carnegie could have helped them all.

They wrote because Mark Twain was famous. Whatever he did was news—if he fell off his bicycle, the story might be worth half a column. Journalists sought him out in Hartford and interviewed him wherever he went. (Twain was a good subject. He felt no Jamesian revulsion toward the vulgarity of the press, and he knew from experience the reporter's need for copy.) The papers regularly exaggerated his wealth: they made him a millionaire, and the public believed. But those pleading letters did not arrive merely because he was richer than Howells or James or Cable. He seemed approachable, as they did not. His readers saw him as one of themselves but luckier, someone who could understand them, to whom they could appeal. And Mark Twain, in spite of his complaints, found reassurance in those letters, for they proved that he still held his public, and they relieved the essential loneliness of a writer's life. Even the begging letters testified to his success.

He complained endlessly about the burden of his correspondence—"My entire day has gone to the devil with answering letters"—but like the Hartford home and the Hartford life, it was both the reward and the price of fame. He could have hired a secretary to sort through his mail, answer most of what needed answering, and throw out the rest, but he would not cut himself off from his public. He might complain about violations of his privacy or his trust when personal letters somehow made their way into print, as his letter to Twichell about the history game had done, but often he wrote letters that he knew would get into the papers.

Seeing an advertisement by the Magnetic Rock Spring Company of Colfax, Iowa, claiming that its bottled water would cure "Rheumatism, Dyspepsia, Constipation, Dropsy, Paralysis, St. Vitus' Dance, Delirium Tremens, Diabetes, Stone in the Bladder, Scrofula, Ulcers, Female Weakness and General Debility," Twain promptly answered, remarking that the list of ailments "reads just like my symptoms," and inquiring whether the water "would go with temperance beverages," such as lemonade, whiskey, or soda water. The manager advised him to take one part of the water to ninety-nine parts of whiskey, and had the letters printed in an Iowa paper, as Twain must have expected. Exchanges like that combined pleasure with publicity, reinforcing the public image of "Mark Twain."

Often Twain's mail concerned business. Royalty checks were always welcome—$773.20 from a self-pasting scrapbook (his own invention), £900 from Chatto & Windus for *Life on the Mississippi*. A check for $1,081.32 from the American Publishing Company proved the continuing popularity of his earlier books, particularly *The Innocents Abroad*. Humor might be the most ephemeral of literary forms, but Mark Twain's already seemed more durable than most. Always there were family and household affairs, the furnace or the burglar alarm to be repaired, bills to be paid, contracts to be made with tradesmen, gifts to be bought in New York. But much of Mark Twain's business was self-created. There were lawsuits to be threatened or prosecuted—Twain's correspondence with Alexander & Green, his New York law firm, was regular and voluminous. There were stocks to be bought and sold, generally at a loss; there were inventions to be imagined, or even developed and marketed, and profits to be calculated.

In bringing Charley Webster to New York—first to manage Kaolatype, then to "run" *Life on the Mississippi*, as well as to do errands of all sorts and deal with fraudulent contractors—Mark Twain had hoped to reduce his own business cares and distractions. In fact, he had increased them. He might write in exasperation that he did not want to be involved in details, he wanted only to make decisions, but he could not make decisions without details and he demanded continuous information. Webster would respond with closely written letters eight or ten pages long, explaining how intensely busy he was for twelve hours a day.

It was no use for Mark Twain to complain that "you are there to take care of my business, not make business *for* me to take care of." It was no use even to print cards referring correspondents to "my agent, Mr. C. L. Webster." Business produced business, and Webster liked to exaggerate problems in order to magnify his own importance. Making Webster his agent had simply increased Mark Twain's involvement and anxieties: "Try to remember that I fly off the handle altogether too easily, and that you want to think twice before you send me irritating news," he complained, but he complained just as bitterly when he did not receive news often enough.

Society offered a more pleasurable distraction. Besides the incessant congeniality of Nook Farm, there were notable visitors to be met by the Clemenses and often to be entertained. Matthew Arnold, the apostle of Culture and scourge of philistines, lectured in Hartford in November, on his way from New York to Boston. Arnold's favorite topic on his American tour was "Numbers, or the Saving Remnant." He denounced the barren materialism of American life, lamented the "absence of the discipline of respect," the "want of soul and delicacy," reading from Howells's novels to illustrate the "life of hideousness and immense ennui" that Anglo-Saxons could produce, with its fatal lack of "elevation and beauty." He looked for hope to the enlightened few, the "saving remnant"—who in a nation of fifty million might be numerous enough to civilize their society.

That was not a doctrine that Mark Twain was likely to sympathize with, although his meeting with Arnold was cordial enough. Arnold was entertained at a reception before his lecture, Mark Twain was present, and Arnold, noticing his dramatic crest of red hair and the laughter that seemed to surround him, demanded an introduction. With his wife and daughter, he was entertained by the Clemenses the next day and proved unexpectedly approachable—"gentler and more sympathetic" than might have been expected from his writings, Twichell noted in his journal.

But friendship with this visitor was impossible. Twain could be an elitist at times, but only in politics; he could never have been at ease with Arnold's role as defender of Culture, or accepted his supercilious dismissal of the public that bought Mark Twain's books, and therefore of the books themselves. And he resented Arnold's contempt for newspapers, to the point of composing a thirteen-page manuscript on "The American Press," defending it against Arnold's charge that the press threatened to destroy the "discipline of respect." On the contrary, argued Twain, an active and discriminating irreverence was essential to the preservation of human freedom. Irreverence, whether discriminating or not, was essential to the humorist as well.

Mark Twain observed his forty-eighth birthday on November 30 and reacted to his age with a maxim: "The man who is a pessimist before he is forty-eight knows too much; the man who is an optimist after he is forty-eight knows too little." A few weeks later he wrote a curious letter to his mother and sister: "Merry Christmas from this household. Let us be unusually merry, for we are all one year nearer to 'finding out.' —Not that I am strongly interested in the matter, but I judge by the multitude of churches in the world that most people are." He would have denied indignantly and sincerely that he was unhappy or dissatisfied—he had everything a man could wish for, as he knew. His success was real, and he took great pleasure in it, yet somehow it was not enough. He was aware that his moods swung widely and he was likely to pay for happiness with depression—although he also knew that the depression would not endure. But more was involved than the chemistry of mood swings. Mark Twain had learned in his childhood that earthly happiness must be fleeting, and he had long since lost the compensating illusion of heaven. He did not feel that he had compromised or sold himself; he regretted something more fundamental: the inevitable loss, with maturity, of some glamour, some innocence, some hope. He was continually nostalgic, looking back to a happier past, his piloting days, his Hannibal childhood. "The birthday is Nov. 30," he would write to an English inquirer, "& I do wish it had been a hundred years earlier or 30 years later—either would serve."

Celebrity might be a poor substitute for lost youth, might often be a bore and a nuisance, yet it had its compensations, which Mark Twain enjoyed. He kept himself in the public eye. On December 4, the *Times* printed a letter from Twain to the Bartholdi Pedestal Fund, then raising money to provide a pedestal for the Statue of Liberty. Twain suggested a statue to Adam instead: "What do we care for a statue of liberty when we've got the thing itself in its wildest sublimity? What you want of a monument is to keep you in mind of something . . . you've lost." Adam was about to be lost; evolution was "steadily and surely abolishing him." Readers must have taken that letter as a typical Mark Twain joke, but it was something more as well. In the theology which his intellect had rejected, but which gripped his imagination still, Adam's fall, the loss of innocence, had cost us paradise, had brought us death. But to Mark Twain as he grew older, death seemed deeply ambiguous; in a fallen world, with paradise unattainable, it might provide the only salvation to be had, the one sure escape from suffering.

Somehow, during the weeks after Christmas, in spite of business, correspondence, and society, Twain found time for writing—even though Livy had invited Thomas Bailey Aldrich—poet, editor, and wit—and his wife for a four-day visit, hoping to bring the Howellses also, and to ask fifty or so Hartford friends and acquaintances to meet them. He planned new plays; he dramatized his own works; he commenced a novel, set in the Sandwich Islands. Mark Twain had not gone back to the islands after his four-month visit in 1866, but he never forgot them. They had left in his mind an image of perfect beauty and peace, the ideal refuge, not only from personal vexations but from what, in some moods, he called the "cyclones, & earthquakes, & deluges, moral, political, financial, & physical," of late-nineteenth-century America, adding that his idea of heaven was a place where all the issues were dead ones, "& no man cares a damn." His billiard table was piled with books on the islands, he wrote to Howells on January 7, and "the walls are upholstered with scraps of paper pencilled with notes drawn from them."

He had been saturating himself "with knowledge of that un-imaginably beautiful land & that most strange & fascinating people," and he had begun a story dealing with the life of Bill Ragsdale, a half-white interpreter (a historical figure). The story would open with "Ragsdale at 12 years of age, & the heroine at 4, in the midst of the ancient idolatrous system, with its picturesque & amazing customs & superstitions, 3 months before the arrival of the missionaries & the erection of a shallow Christianity upon the ruins of the old paganism." The two characters would "become educated Christians, & highly civilized." Then the story would jump ahead to the tragic ending of Ragsdale's life—engaged to be married, he discovers that he has leprosy. He might have hidden the disease for years, but he would not inflict such a marriage on his betrothed. Instead, he sails for the leper colony on Molokai, to suffer "the loathsome and lingering death that all lepers die."

That conclusion was intensely pathetic, but the tale had a "hidden motive" as well, to demonstrate "that the religious folly you are born in you will *die* in, no matter what apparently reasonabler [*sic*] religious folly may seem to have taken its place meanwhile." (How the two principal characters return to their original "religious follies" is unknown.) On January 24, in a letter to Mrs. Fairbanks, Twain reported that "I finished a book last week, & am shirking all other duties in order to give the whole remnant of my mind to a most painstaking revision of it—for this book is not a humorous but a serious work, & may damn me, tho' Livy says *No*."

That letter is puzzling. The book could only have been the Hawaiian story, yet it seems impossible for him to have written a book-length manuscript in the time available, especially since that January he was also at work dramatizing *Tom Sawyer*. But everything concerning the Ragsdale story is mysterious. He did not publish it, and there is no other mention of it in his letters. Only a few fragments of the manuscript survive—descriptions of Hawaiian scenery. As for why it should have damned him, if published, the only possible cause seems to be the heretical religious or antireligious opinions that he meant to imply. The loss may not be great—given Twain's plot, the temptation to sentimentality or melodrama might have been irresistible. Yet curiosity remains.

It was playwriting that dominated that winter. Twain had hoped to dramatize his Hawaiian story, perhaps in collaboration with Howells, and Webster was negotiating with Raymond, the actor who had first created the role of Sellers, over the new Sellers play. Nothing came of those negotiations—Twain demanded too much,

$400 a week as long as the play was running. But he believed that he had been cheated out of his fair share of the returns from the earlier Sellers play, and was determined to get his rights. If Raymond refused, they could find some other actor to take the part. His hopes, and Howells's, were still high. They planned exuberantly; they would write half a dozen more plays, Howells confided to a friend, "with always the same character for protagonist." Sellers would become "*the* American character," a stock figure for the American theater, like the Harlequin and Pantaloon of the Italian commedia dell'arte.

But Mark Twain also wanted to be serious. "*Now* let's write a tragedy," he suggested. He had found a situation in Carlyle's life of Oliver Cromwell, when Cromwell, sentencing three rebels, decided that one of them must die, and that the victim should be chosen by lot. They refused to draw for themselves, saying that to do so would be suicidal for the loser, and therefore sinful. Finally, wrote Carlyle, a child drew the lots. Twain enclosed his draft of a final scene, heightening the melodrama by making the child the daughter of one of the condemned rebels. Predictably, she dooms her father. Howells, surprisingly, found the plot "touching and effective." Almost two decades later, Twain would write his play, *The Death Disk*, alone. It has never been published or produced.

Meanwhile, he was busily dramatizing his own work. Even the Ragsdale book seems to have been started partly to provide material out of which Twain and Howells could build a play. And on February 13, Twain reported to Howells that in the past month he had written a four-act dramatization of *Tom Sawyer* (applying for copyright at the end of February) as well as beginning another two and one-half acts of another, dramatizing *The Prince and the Pauper*. He meant to use adult actors to play Tom and his friends, but put the script aside when Augustin Daly rejected the *Tom Sawyer* play, remarking that while Tom might be played successfully "by a clever comedian," the other parts "would seem ridiculous in grown peoples [*sic*] hands." A few months later, Howells condemned Twain's dramatization of *The Prince and the Pauper*—it was "altogether too thin and slight," really no more than "a good outline."

There seemed no chance for an immediate production of *Colonel Sellers as a Scientist*. Raymond offered only $250 a week, on condition of his approving the script after reading it, and in any case he already had a successful play running. Webster attended the New

York theaters, searching for other comedians who might be able and willing to take the role, but one by one they refused, or insisted that at least the title of the play and the name of the central character should be changed. To the public, "Sellers" meant "Raymond." But Mark Twain would not accept that demand. Only by using the old name for its protagonist could the new play build on the success of the earlier one.

One comedian, Nat Goodwin, showed interest, but Howells—squeamish, intensely moralistic, and possessing, in his own words, a "temperamental love of backing out of any undertaking"—developed qualms at the last moment, even beyond the last moment, and refused to have his name associated with such a production. Goodwin had performed in "low flung burlesques," Howells objected, "and his family appear before the public habitually in nothing but stockings" (bodystockings) and in Montreal the Howellses had seen him in a play so indecent that they were forced to leave the theater. Twain sarcastically demolished that "infantile objection," pointing out that since Goodwin was unknown, his reputation could not affect the play, and that in any case the names of Howells and Twain should be enough to make any actor or play respectable. Howells surrendered—but Goodwin, too, required that the protagonist's name be changed, and that demand could not be accepted.

With his writing, his projects, and his social life, it was an intensely busy winter for Mark Twain. There were the usual distinguished visitors: Henry Irving, the English tragedian, recognized as the greatest actor of his time; Augustus Saint-Gaudens, the outstanding American sculptor; and George Washington Cable. Irving dined with the Clemenses and friends, including Twichell, who was pleased to find that their visitor did not look, sound, or behave like an actor. At least half an actor himself, Mark Twain surely got along a good deal more easily with Irving than with Matthew Arnold.

As for Cable—rigidly pious, a nonsmoker, nondrinker, nonswearer, a scrupulous keeper of the Sabbath—he seemed as different from Mark Twain as a man could be. Yet their friendship had intensified, and they sometimes called each other "Uncle" and "Nephew" in their letters. (Twain was "Uncle." He was both older and far better known.) Cable, too, was a Southerner in the process of freeing himself from the prejudices of his region, though he had been doing it not in Connecticut but in Louisiana, which was a good deal riskier. He had begun to question not only slavery—a dead issue—but the injustices still inflicted on the Negro, in spite of the nominal freedom won by the Civil War. That was a dangerous stand, in a region that tolerated no criticism of white supremacy and the methods by which it was enforced. But Cable would not be deterred; to speak the truth was his God-given duty. (Mark Twain also felt the needs of blacks, but responded to the individual case—he was financing the studies of Charles Porter, a young black painter, in Paris, and helping him obtain commissions.)

The visit began badly. Cable came to Hartford in late January and promptly fell sick, apparently suffering from a "bilious attack, and a swollen neuralgic face." He was given a stiff dose of calomel and put to bed "in the mahogany bedroom—such a little man for so big a bed!" one neighbor commented. After Mark Twain stayed up most of the night with him, a nurse was brought in. In fact, Cable had mumps, as his swollen face should have indicated. After a few days of pain and high fever, he began to recover. Letters to his wife, written during his convalescence, provide an intimate view of Mark Twain at home: there was a long, impassioned talk with Mark Twain, when "each seemed to kindle the other's mind . . . By and by we were both on our feet, he walking up and down the drawing room and I back and forth across it. Our talk was generally earnest—about our great Century and the vast advantages of living in it." The talk turned to publishers, and Twain "got ferocious and funny." Then, going to the piano, he sang "O Tannenbaum"—he would have learned the song during his stay in Germany in 1878–79—with Cable taking the tenor part.

They moved to the library. There "Mark proposed a little literary scheme for him and me and three or four others, and when Mrs. Clemens came in at 1 P.M. we were still talking." They had interrupted themselves only once, "consulting Audubon to identify a strange and beautiful bird that we had seen at breakfast-time." Cable noticed the father's storytelling, a regular part of family life, observing that little Jean had "a magnificent mental digestion," requiring a tiger in every story. Or Livy would read aloud "to Mark and the children" from Howard Pyle's "beautiful new version of Robin Hood." In spite of sickness and temperamental differences, the visit had been a success. Cable experienced the exuberant, multifarious personality of Mark Twain, so different from his own, with shocked fascination. "God bless you!" he wrote a few days after

leaving. "May something—*something* that isn't affliction or distress—cure you of swearing & so make you *perfectly* lovely!"

Cable had brought with him a copy of *The Enemy Conquered, or
Love Triumphant*, by G. Ragsdale McClintock, a forgotten Southern
novel of the 1840s, notable only for the continual absurdity of its
style. "Oh! thou exalted spirit of inspiration—" exclaims Mc-
Clintock's hero, clasping hands with a young stranger whom he
has just met on the road and who has given him directions, "thou
flame of burning prosperity, may the Heaven-directed blaze be the
glare of thy soul, and battle down every rampart that seems to
impede your progress!" That overblown rhetoric delighted Mark
Twain, seeming to support his attack, in *Life on the Mississippi*, on
the preposterous pseudo-chivalry of the Old South and its disastrous
effect on Southern writing.

But while they got on surprisingly well, Mark Twain never became a wholehearted admirer of Cable. There was a streak of stin-
giness in the man; he made no offer to pay the doctor who had
attended him, and Twain finally settled the bill with a gift of books,
in Cable's name. And Cable had not suffered in silence. Writing to
an old friend crippled by gout, Twain summed up: "He's a bright
good fellow—*but*—Why, man, he made 280 times more fuss over
his little pains than you did over your big ones." Mark Twain deeply
respected Cable's intelligence and much of his work—but . . . There
would always be a "but."

For the time, though, they seemed to have consolidated their
friendship. They had even planned a joint literary project, that little
scheme which Cable had mentioned to his wife. It was a revival of
a plan that Twain had contemplated for years: a collection of stories
by well-known writers, each one handling the same situation in his
own style. In its original version, the plan included a plot supplied
by Twain, involving "a murder, a mystery and a marriage." This
time, the starting point for each writer was to be a "personal"
advertisement, supposedly from the notorious New York *Herald*.
Cable submitted the plan to *Century*, and with R. W. Gilder, the
editor, who was delighted by the scheme, a list of possible authors
was drawn up, including such unlikely participants as Henry James
and Joel Chandler Harris, creator of "Uncle Remus." But like so
many of Mark Twain's literary plans, this one would never be carried
out.

The new friendship inspired Cable to commit a totally uncharacteristic act. He played an elaborate April fool's joke on Mark Twain, based on Twain's hatred of autograph hunters, mailing a printed circular marked "private and confidential," to a hundred and fifty writers, reporters, and editors—all friends or acquaintances of Mark Twain—inviting their participation. Each one was to write to Twain, asking for his autograph and the customary "sentiments," timing the letters for delivery on April 1. They were not to include stamps or return envelopes. More than a hundred letters came in, the writers making their letters as impertinent and their demands as outrageous as possible.

Cable worried intensely—suppose there should be some sudden, serious illness in the Clemens family—but the joke was a great success. The letters, more than a hundred of them, were delivered exactly on time (an unctuous letter signed "Captain Duncan," and dated March 31, offering to forgive all past injuries and differences and asking for autographs for himself and his two sons, must have been part of the joke), and papers around the country picked up the story. Indeed, the Kern County *Californian* still found it newsworthy in mid-July, three and a half months later. "Mark Twain in a Rage, The Ghastly Victim of a Great April Fool Joke," read one headline. In fact, he had enjoyed the joke, and his opinion of Cable rose. (But he would reject a proposed subscription for bringing Cable and his family to New England, declaring that it was "simply a crime against Cable's manliness," and asking "if a man should . . . pass the hat around on your behalf, would you ever forgive him for it?")

There was another, less enjoyable, consequence of Cable's visit. One by one, the Clemens children contracted mumps—six weeks of doctors and sleepless nights, with no interval of rest for the parents between the recovery of one and the sickness of the next. On March 5, Twain reported to Howells on "the hellfiredest days and nights" that Susy had endured, suffering "13 times more than Cable," shedding "whole barrels of noiseless tears. She staid in our room last night . . . I think she & her mother spent the night praying. But I didn't."

From the archives of the Mark Twain Papers, we can reconstruct still more of Mark Twain's interests, activities, and anxieties that winter. There were winter pleasures with his daughters and their friends: "in the afternoon Mr. Clemens took Susy and Clara and myself on the river [skating] and it was perfectly lovely," a neighbor girl reported. There were also the usual fears for the children's health—Livy was terrified of diphtheria, and their family doctor frightened her with it whenever Susy had a sore throat. And Mark Twain found time to read, or at least to look into, a surprising variety of books; writing to an invalid friend in mid-January, he mentions that, among other books, he has been reading in English, "the middle portion of the Breadwinners [a contemporary American novel, violently attacking organized labor]; all of Clarissa Harlowe" (a voluminous, sentimental, eighteenth-century novel by Samuel Richardson, *Clarissa Harlowe* seems an unlikely book for Mark Twain to have been reading), a volume of Pepys, and "the second volume of The Autobiography of a Whore" (possibly *Fanny Hill*). In French, a volume each of the memoirs of Saint-Simon, an old favorite, and of Casanova, and in German, the poems of Schiller. "I seldom or never read anything that is new," he concludes, "& *never* read anything through."

He developed a new plan for persuading Congress to allow foreign authors to copyright their work in the United States, thus protecting American writers from the competition offered by cheap reprints of British authors, who received no American royalties, and possibly shaming other nations into following the example of the United States in protecting foreign writers. On grounds of both principle and profit, Mark Twain was a lifelong advocate of international copyright. He believed devoutly in the rights of the author—copyright should be international and eternal. But since moral appeals had failed, he decided, it was time for more practical methods.

Drawing on his experience as a Washington reporter in the winter of 1867–68, he developed a new strategy. Authors would pledge themselves to monthly contributions to finance the campaign, a bill would be introduced by a favorable congressman, and two full-time lobbyists would be hired to stay through a whole session of Congress, canvassing the members one by one and pledging them to support a copyright bill, until a majority was obtained. Mark Twain knew the power of lobbying—he had shown lobbyists at work in *The Gilded Age*. Ideally, such methods should be unnecessary, since an honest publisher would always refuse to steal, by printing a foreign book without payment to its author. Unfortunately, there seemed to be only one honest publisher in the world: Baron von

Tauchnitz of Germany, with his international series of paperback reprints. On March 31, 1884, von Tauchnitz offered eighty-five pounds for the rights to *Life on the Mississippi*—an unimpressive figure, by Mark Twain's standards, but then, Tauchnitz need not have paid anything at all.

Mark Twain had invested in the stock market that spring—disastrously, as might have been expected. A friend advised him that Oregon Transcontinental, a railroad stock, was due for a rise, and Twain bought 300 shares at $73 each. The stock did rise briefly, but the friend had fallen sick when the price peaked at $98, and could not give advice to sell. Then the value collapsed. On April 25, Twain instructed Webster to sell his shares, "now worth 15 or 16" dollars. By the time Webster arranged for the sale, the price had fallen to $12—representing a loss of $18,300. On May 4, Twain wrote to the Gerhardts in Paris to explain why the Clemenses would not be visiting Europe that summer: "We have made but few investments [that "we" is misleading; Livy had made no investments] in the last few years which have not turned out badly. Our losses during the past three years have been prodigious. Three or four more of such years would make it necessary for us to move out of our house & hunt for cheaper quarters . . . I must settle down to work & restore things to the old condition."

He had already begun. *Huckleberry Finn* was finally ready for the publisher, and he was determined not to let himself be swindled by a trickster like Elisha Bliss or to allow an incompetent like Osgood to botch the sale. He would set up his own publishing company to issue his own books. He would take all the profits and avoid Osgood's blunders. For a writer who distrusted the competence or the honesty of all established publishers, it seemed the only alternative. That decision would lead at first to brilliant success, and finally to disaster.

On April 11, 1884, he signed a contract with Webster, establishing a publishing house in New York under the name of Charles L. Webster and Company, binding himself to supply the necessary funds and pay all expenses. It was a decision that would lead to spectacular success, and to ultimate disaster. Webster's partnership was nominal: he was paid a salary of $2,500 to manage the business, he received no share of the profits and could not be held liable for debts, he could not make any expenditure of more than $1,000 without written permission. Those terms guaranteed Twain's own deep involvement; most problems would be referred to him, he would be called on to make decisions, he would be continuously asking for information. Webster and Company, as everyone knew, was in fact Mark Twain. His proprietorship was never meant to be secret; his name would be as substantial a part of the firm's capital as the $15,000 he provided to cover the printing and binding and marketing of *Huckleberry Finn*. Inevitably, the new firm would soon outgrow its original purpose, publishing other men's books, scoring an enormous, unrepeatable opening success with the *Memoirs* of General Grant.

He felt that he had to make up for the "failures" of his last two books. And, with some justification, he believed that he understood the mechanics of subscription publishing and the psychology of the subscription audience better than Webster, or any trade publisher. He would be no sleeping partner. *Huckleberry Finn* would be copyrighted in December 1884 (although delivery to subscribers would not begin for another two months), and in the meantime, Twain regularly complicated Webster's life with anxieties and demands for reassurance, with inquiries and suggestions. Why not dispose of those useless copies of his earlier books, now filling up warehouses, by offering *Tom Sawyer* and *Huckleberry Finn* together, at a bargain price of $4.50 (*Huckleberry Finn* alone would sell for $3.50), or a package of *Tom Sawyer, Huckleberry Finn*, and *The Prince and the Pauper* at a reduced price? The American Publishing Company held the rights to *Tom Sawyer* and finally refused to cooperate. But that frustrated plan had its consequence—the chapter recounting Huck's swim to a log raft and his capture by the raftsmen, inserted as a filler in *Life on the Mississippi*, was not restored to *Huckleberry Finn* because it might have made the book too long to seem a companion piece to *Tom Sawyer*.

As publisher, Twain could choose his own illustrator. He picked E. W. Kemble, a virtually unknown young artist—only twenty-three—whose cartoons he had admired in the comic magazine *Life*, and in so doing launched Kemble on a long and successful career. From his first publisher, Elisha Bliss, Twain had learned the value of illustrations, regardless of their quality, in marketing a book to the unsophisticated subscription audience, which was likely to measure value by the number of pages and pictures. But Twain knew also that illustrations could shape the attitude of readers toward characters and events. Consequently he meant to guide the artist at every stage; he must examine and approve each of the 174 drawings that would go into *Huckleberry Finn*, although Kemble would choose the subjects. Kemble's work is often crude, with heads out of proportion, gaping, expressionless faces, and unnatural gestures, but it pleased Mark Twain, once the artist's initial "violence" had been softened, and it pleased readers as well. The book has had other illustrators, but Kemble's frontispiece—a smiling boy in straw hat and jeans held up by one suspender, with a dead rabbit in one hand and a long-barreled gun in the other—has created the image of Huck Finn for a century and more.

Kemble often diverges from Mark Twain's text. His Huck in general looks younger than the story indicates, sometimes no more than eight or nine years old. The effect, whether intended or not, is to move the book closer toward the "boy book" tradition, to make it appear to be a sequel to *Tom Sawyer*. Proprieties had to be respected; the text might say that Huck and Jim spent most of their time on the raft naked, but in the illustrations they are clothed. Jim is invariably presented as a comic "darky"; instead of following the text, the artist simply used a popular stereotype.

The Royal Nonesuch presented a special problem. Twain had described an unmistakably phallic show—the white-bearded king prances on stage, naked, "painted all over, ring-streaked-and-striped, all sorts of colors," and performs indescribable antics. The scene could only be illustrated with careful modification; there are no phallic implications in Kemble's drawing. The king appears to be wearing a sort of striped union suit, although close examination shows that he is naked. The effect is grotesquely comic, but in no way sexual. Kemble could have avoided that scene entirely, but perhaps the text needed that saving ambiguity, to prevent squeamish readers from realizing quite what it was that Huck was describing.

Violence is softened as well, and often ignored. There is no illustration for the most shocking scene in the book, the death of fourteen-year-old Buck Grangerford and an older cousin: "The boys jumped for the river—both of them hurt—and as they swum down the current the men run along the bank shooting at them and singing out, 'Kill them, kill them!' It made me so sick I most fell out of the tree." An illustration might have seemed too harrowing; those killings had to be left to the reader's imagination. So, apparently, did another powerfully dramatic scene, when the drunken Pap, knife in hand, chases Huck around the cabin, believing him to be the Angel of Death.

Meanwhile, life went on as usual. Letters, personal and business, poured in as always. There was more news of Orion—"Ma [Jane Clemens] and Orion find time for further experiments," wrote Mollie Clemens to her brother-in-law. "Orion is living on bread and water." That was hardly news—Orion was always changing, and always the same. More interesting was a letter from Charles A. Dana, editor of the New York *Sun*, demanding two or three short stories of ten to twenty thousand words each: "As for pay . . . you shall have more than you ever got." Dana had a scheme for publishing American short stories "in a few great American newspapers. I have got Henry James and Bret Harte [a highly unlikely combination] and I must have you." Mark Twain showed interest—he felt poor just then—but he could not find time or ideas.

No one could have seemed younger at forty-eight than Mark Twain, with his profusion of interests and activities and projects, but in his own mind he "confessed to age" in May by wearing glasses for the first time. "In the same hour," as he described his experience in a speech to a Banquet of Wheelmen a few months later, "I renewed my youth, to outward appearance, by mounting a bicycle for the first time." "The spectacles stayed on," he added. He might have been moved to assert his youthfulness, after submitting to the indignity of spectacles, but in any case he could not resist a new invention. He had bought one of the earliest typewriters, he had been one of the first to install a telephone in his home, and now, in company with Twichell, he set out to master the high-wheeled, solid-rubber-tired bicycle of the 1880s. Unstable and hard to steer, likely to pitch the rider headfirst over the handlebars at any sizable bump, it was a dangerous machine even for the expert. Simply learning to mount and dismount required instruction, and to turn was a hazardous adventure. Every stone in the street, every dog, every passing wagon could terrify a beginner.

But he hired an instructor, taking a daily lesson of an hour and a half for eight days, then practiced with Twichell on Farmington Avenue, enduring the inevitable falls. "I must have been rather young for my age then," Twain would remark more than twenty years later, recalling the experience in one of his autobiographical dictations. (He would always be young for his age.) No matter what happened, he seemed to fall. "Every time I tried to steal a look at a pretty girl or any other kind of scenery, that single moment of inattention gave the bicycle the chance it had been waiting for, and I went over the front of it and struck the ground on my head or my back." And no matter how he fell, the result was always the same—"the bicycle skinned my leg and leaped up into the air and came down on top of me."

"We have fought the creature a couple of weeks . . . & we have honorable wounds to show for it," he wrote to a friend on May 23. Eventually they mastered the machine well enough to ride a few miles into the countryside, and Twain began writing a comic article on his misadventures, but was dissatisfied with it and put it aside. The sense of renewing his youth might, however, have been compensation enough for his bruises.

Mugwump

M ark Twain's "vacations" at Quarry Farm were meant to be
his working times, and work meant writing. But that summer
of 1884, something else always interfered. He found other ways to
occupy himself: sitting for a portrait bust by Gerhardt; planning a
reading tour with Cable for the late fall and winter; observing and
finally involving himself in a hard-fought, intensely controversial
Presidential campaign; trying to market the Sellers play; preparing
the sales campaign for *Huck*. And for weeks he went down to Elmira,
two or three days a week, to have his teeth scraped and "one or
two gouged out & stuffed," spending two hours or more in the
chair each time, listening to the dentist's chatter while he gouged
and dug. (That dentist, Twain noted, "had the calm, possessed,
surgical look of a man who could endure pain in another person.")
He tried to make literary capital of his experience, beginning
"Happy Memories of the Dental Chair," then abandoning it after
a few pages. Otherwise, the only writing that Mark Twain would
have to show for his summer would be an abortive sequel to *Huckleberry Finn*.

For his wife and daughters, in contrast, the idyll of Quarry Farm
would be repeated; a photograph shows a serene mother standing
beneath a tree with her children around her, Clara in front with
Livy's hand on her shoulder, a chubby Jean nestling close to her
mother, and a thoughtful Susy alone on the other side. Jean, at
four, was becoming an individual. While Susy cared for books and
theater and Clara for music, Jean was devoted to animals. Her father
noted in his journal that she would go to the barn every evening
"to look at the cows—which she adores." When the milking was

done and the three cows turned into their lot, "we have to set Jean on a shed in that lot, and stay by her" while she watched them. The cows did nothing, but the mere sight of them was enough. To the end of her short life—she died at twenty-nine—Jean Clemens would be passionately fond of animals.

She had begun to develop a will of her own, and a temper to match. On an evening walk with her father, she wanted to go on, to view more cows in a nearby field. He did not, and they argued, Jean "using English for light skirmishing and German for 'business.'" (All the Clemens children were bilingual in English and German.) Her father answered all her arguments, and Jean was clearly getting the worst of it, until suddenly she exclaimed sharply, "Wir werden nichts mehr darüber sprechen!" [We won't talk about it anymore!"]. "I suppose I ought to have been outraged," Mark Twain observed, "but I wasn't. I was charmed."

He meant to work seriously (those losses in the market had to be made right). He laid aside the bicycle piece; he would make no commitments to newspapers or magazines, declaring that he needed all his time "for regular work." But distractions promptly appeared—Karl Gerhardt, for one. Gerhardt had decided to come home and begin his artistic career, leaving his wife and child in Paris for the time. He brought with him a sketch for a proposed work—*Indian on Horseback Fighting a Panther*—and hoped to get commissions for Civil War monuments. Gerhardt's imagination was literary, not sculptural. He planned another work showing Oedipus and his daughter Antigone, where Oedipus, old, blind, and outcast, curses himself while Antigone tries to comfort him, emphasizing the contrast between "passionate old man and the loving, caressing daughter." It seems ironic that Mark Twain, who was about to publish one of the most radically innovative works in American literature, should have paid for the education of an artist who would conceive this sentimental banality. But Mark Twain's own taste in painting and sculpture was rudimentary, requiring the most literal realism.

Gerhardt had studied at Paris during the development of Impressionism, an artistic revolution that he angrily rejected. In a letter to Twain he had enclosed an announcement of the "Exposition Manet" at the Ecole Nationale des Beaux-Arts; he had avoided it on principle, protesting angrily against Manet's "horrid daubs" being exhibited in the Salon and receiving a prize, when Manet could not even draw—what an example for aspiring students! His own career would be obscure and undistinguished; he was a fairly competent technician, able to make a reasonable likeness in a portrait bust, but unimaginative and thoroughly conventional.

No commissions were forthcoming, so Gerhardt came to Elmira to make a bust of his patron, hoping to sell copies. He worked for several weeks, but he was inexperienced and ruined the bust while trying to make a cast. Doggedly he began over and this time succeeded. The bust was completed, and the family was delighted with the likeness; Twain himself was so pleased that he decided to use it in the forthcoming edition of *Huckleberry Finn*. The first edition would have two frontispieces: Kemble's drawing of Huck as a carefree ragamuffin, and on the opposite page, Gerhardt's classic bust of the author, shown in profile, giving the book a dignity that subscription books did not usually possess. Gerhardt had not only presented a likeness, said the Hartford *Courant*, he had revealed a character, handling his material "with perfect freedom and boldness"; the bust was "massive and solid in treatment," possessing "a noble dignity and repose."

Mark Twain was ready to advance his protégé's career in less orthodox ways as well. Gerhardt applied for the commission to do a memorial statue of the Revolutionary War hero Nathan Hale, remembered for his declaration, before being hanged as a spy, that he regretted having but one life to lose for his country. The committee awarding the commission was split; almost twenty years later, Mark Twain recorded the outcome in his notebook: "Nathan Hale '$150 will secure the vote' [*sic*]. It was furnished." A bribe was required, and he paid it.

Twain was already making plans for the fall and winter; he would recoup his losses with a lecture tour, the surest way of raising money quickly. In the years just before and after his marriage, he had lectured all through the East and Middle West, appearing at least once in almost every good-sized town north of the Mason-Dixon line and east of the Mississippi—the South had never acquired the lecture-going habit, while the West, except for California, was too sparsely settled to make a tour profitable. Mark Twain had earned money and reputation on the lecture circuit and had developed a masterful technique, which seemed to be no technique at all but utterly natural.

He enjoyed his hours on the platform, but lecturing was hard work, and as a season progressed, he would grow to hate the strain of constant travel, most often in the winter, of grueling train journeys, bad food, and lonely hotel rooms, of testing and revising his lectures, even of scrapping them and writing new ones if audiences failed to respond. At times, he would proclaim his loathing of the lecture platform, withdraw "forever"—then return, when he wanted money or applause. He would go on talking in public almost until the end of his life. Letters from readers could never equal that direct communion with an audience.

But this tour would be different. He was famous now, he would be earning far more than on those early tours, he would read from his own books instead of lecturing, and he would not travel alone. ("A man can start out alone and rob the public, but it's dreary work," he would confess to a Minneapolis reporter.) At last he would carry out his plan for the "menagerie" of touring lecturers, or the "circus," as he called it now. It would be a circus of two, with Cable as his partner, while Major James B. Pond, a professional agent and manager, would accompany them "as boss & head ringmaster." Pond would arrange their schedule, fix their routes, hire halls, print circulars, make hotel reservations, and "attend to everything which comes under the head of *business*," taking 10 percent of the profits. Twain and Cable had gotten on well together, and Cable had experience now; reading before a private audience in Hartford, he had been so warmly received that he left "perfectly convinced that my future is open to me & that great success is in store," adding characteristically, "May God's cause be advanced thereby."

Mark Twain was of the same opinion. After hearing that Hartford performance, he had called Cable "just a rattling reader, the best amateur I ever heard," adding that "with 2 seasons of practice," he would be "the best professional reader alive." After strengthening his voice with elocution lessons, Cable had made a great hit in Boston: the *Transcript* declared that his prose style could be compared to Hawthorne's and his performance only to those of "the actors of the Shakespearean era." Then he had gone on the circuit, touring the North and West.

At first Pond was doubtful about the collaboration. "Everybody says 'Mark Twain' would do better alone," he wrote on July 3, "as he would be the one everybody wants to hear." A note on the letter, in Twain's hand, reads: "Have already told him no, will not go alone." Three days later, Pond offered an alternative, "a scheme that has an immense amount of money in it," a joint tour with Thomas Nast, the cartoonist, whose savage caricatures had helped smash the notorious Tweed Ring in New York. Twain would talk for half the program while Nast would illustrate his lecture on a blackboard, then Nast would draw while Twain commented. Again Twain refused, scrawling a "No" on the envelope.

Mark Twain would not tour alone, and he would have Cable as his partner. Cable hesitated over an offer of $350 a week, with all expenses paid; it was raised to $450, and he accepted, after considering "on every side the advisability of accepting your offer," as Major Pond explained. He would also get sixty dollars for each matinee beyond the first two per week. A man of piety and principle, Cable refused to perform or even to travel on Sundays; that stipulation was written into the contract. There could be no doubt about who was in charge, but there is no evidence that Cable resented being a hired employee. As Mark Twain's companion, he would publicize himself and his work and earn a good deal more than he could have made in the same length of time by writing or by touring alone.

The tour would commence on November 5, 1884, with a half-dozen or more tryouts in smaller towns. They would read almost every night. Pond "must make the journeys as short, and easy, as circumstances will permit," because, Twain jokingly explained, "I am old & shaky, & a breakdown would be expensive." There would be a ten-day break at Christmas, and they would close at the end of February, concluding sixteen weeks on the road. (That contract seemed to cover every possibility but one—differences between the two performers.) In his enthusiasm, forgetting that he had claimed to be "old & shaky," Twain wanted the tour to run longer: "Goodness knows *I* would gladly run 20 weeks, & I did my best to persuade the madam, but did not succeed," he confided to Pond. But even with sixteen weeks, it was a demanding schedule. Whatever the contract might say, there was no way to make the daily journeys "short" or "easy"—especially in winter.

* * *

Work on *Huckleberry Finn* was not quite finished; there were still proofs to read, and Mark Twain cursed and read them. He made a few last revisions, he jealously guarded his punctuation (punctuation must be individual, Twain held, because its purpose was to reproduce the infinitely variable rhythms of actual speech). And then he was done. Webster could write the chapter titles of *Huckleberry Finn* and the summaries in the table of contents, together with the running heads for the book. All of that must have seemed a mechanical process, which need not concern the author.

Mark Twain's major project that summer was intended to be the sequel to *Huckleberry Finn* that its final chapter promised, as Tom proposes that he and Huck and Jim should "go for howling adventures amongst the Injuns, over in the Territory." On July 6, Mark Twain wrote to Webster, asking for books—"*personal* narratives of life and adventure out yonder in the plains & in the mountains; I mean to take Huck Finn out there." By the fifteenth, he could report to Howells that "on my off days I work at a new story (Huck Finn & Tom Sawyer among the Indians 40 or 50 years ago)." But writing on "off days" between his ordeals in the dentist's chair, distracted by pain or anticipation of pain, he could not hope to achieve that intense concentration, that total forgetfulness of self and the world, that he had experienced in finishing *Huckleberry Finn* the summer before.

On August 6, declining a very cordial invitation to visit from Charles Eliot Norton, a Harvard professor who enjoyed Twain's humor, he explained that "the summer is my only effective working-season, and as I have been hindered a great deal since we arrived here, I am so much behind-hand that I dare not venture to spend a day out of the few weeks that are left me." He must hold his grip on his work and stick to it steadfastly. He added a self-deprecating postscript: "I seem to enlarge upon my work as if it were something important. Indeed it is not; but I do it just as if it were—*that's* the heroism of the thing."

That modesty was justified; "Huck and Tom Among the Indians" was indeed not important, as Mark Twain soon recognized, putting it permanently aside after writing about twenty thousand words. The story is a formula Western. Huck and Jim and Tom join a family crossing the plains by wagon. They meet a small group of Indian braves, who pretend to be friendly until the whites are off guard, then slaughter the parents and their grown sons and kidnap the two daughters. One of them, Polly, is a beautiful girl of seventeen, the other a child. Jim is also taken; only Huck and Tom escape. When Brace Johnson, Polly's lover and an experienced frontiersman, rides up a few days later, they join him in pursuing the Indians. (Brace Johnson seems a dime-novel hero: "a beautiful man . . . more than six foot tall, broad shoulders . . . straight as a jack-staff . . . built as thin as a race-horse," dressed always in spotless buckskin.) The three are lost in a fog, they barely escape drowning by a "water-spout" (cloudburst), and as the story breaks off, they have found evidence at a campsite that a woman has been raped: "four stakes drove in the ground," to which a woman who resisted must have been tied.

Rape by a dark-skinned "savage"—the ultimate horror, in Victorian America. Mark Twain had set out to satirize the Indian of James Fenimore Cooper's novels, the "noble savage" that Tom Sawyer of course believes in, by contrasting him with the "real" Indian, treacherous, cowardly, murderous. He had replaced one stereotype with another, while believing that he was simply being realistic. (In *Huckleberry Finn*, Mark Twain had undermined various myths of the Old South by letting Huck report the realities of brutality, violence, and murder behind the façade of chivalry and honor; but in "Huck and Tom Among the Indians," author and character are both taken in by the mythology of the West.) To complete his indictment, Mark Twain had made his Indians guilty of the worst crime he could imagine, and in doing so, had written himself into an impasse. He could not deal with rape, he could not even report his characters' words when they talk about the possibility, although Huck and Tom and the reader must understand why Brace Johnson so desperately hopes that Polly had a knife with which to kill herself if necessary.

(Surprisingly, Mark Twain finds the religion of these treacherous, murderous Indians to be more sensible and civilized than the white man's. They believe in two gods—one good, one bad—and give all their attention to propitiating the bad one. The good god, by his nature, will do everything he can to help them. "We have to keep our God placated with prayers," Twain noted, "and even then we are never sure of him—how much higher and finer is the Indian's God.")

Mark Twain could deflate the illusions of the Old South in *Huckleberry Finn* and *Life on the Mississippi* because he knew, from experience, the reality behind them. He had no such knowledge of the West. All that he knew of the Great Plains was what he might have picked up from crossing them by stagecoach in the summer of 1861. He knew the Pacific slope, but his experiences in the Nevada silver mines or the California mother lode had no relation to the story he chose to tell. Most of his plainscraft, his knowledge of Indian ways, and key episodes of the story—the fog, the cloud-burst—came from two books by Colonel Richard Dodge: *Our Wild Indians* and *The Plains of the Great West and Their Inhabitants.*

That lack of firsthand experience accounts for the story's vagueness; the texture is thin, the sharp detail of *Huckleberry Finn* lacking. Huck narrates again, but his language is less individual, used for objective description as a rule, making no implied comments. And it was not enough simply to let Huck speak—Twain finds nothing for him to do, he is only a sightseer. The scenes, the characters, the action of *Huckleberry Finn* in large part grew out of experience and memory. "Huck and Tom Among the Indians" is the product of a few weeks of hasty reading.

"I haven't a paragraph to show for my summer," Twain confessed to Twichell in September. Nothing had worked out as he intended. Even the bicycle had failed him. He had had it shipped to Quarry Farm, then mounted it once, took a bad fall, and gave it up. More seriously, negotiations with Raymond over the new Sellers play had finally collapsed. When he was at last given the manuscript to read, Raymond found fault with it. As Webster reported to Mark Twain, he objected to making Sellers the claimant to an English earldom and disliked even more the proposed materialization of dead bodies—"he [Raymond] said Sellers while a very sanguine man was not a lunatic; no one but a lunatic could . . . imagine that he had done such a work." He wanted the piece lengthened, and he proposed that one of Sellers's projects should succeed, so that he could be shown squandering his money. With the euphoria of composition worn off, the discouraged authors had no interest in rewriting their play, and Raymond rejected it, sure that it would fail. "Never mind about the play," Howells wrote consolingly to Mark Twain. "We had fun writing it, anyway."

Four years later, *Colonel Sellers as a Scientist* would finally be staged at Mark Twain's expense, with the leading role played by an elocutionist. Stage properties included a "shocking machine" and other devices supplied by Edison, as well as "old patent models of queer machines," to represent the Colonel's inventions. It was withdrawn after a brief tryout in New York City and a few smaller towns. It was not a play but a "laughable monologue," commented one reviewer, that ought to have run for one hour instead of two. But Mark Twain eventually found another use for the Colonel and his projects, working them into a novel, *The American Claimant*, in 1892.

Back in Hartford after the summer at Quarry Farm, Twain could forget the disappointments and frustrations of the summer in preparation for his reading tour with Cable and in the excitement of politics. There was a bitterly fought Presidential campaign to become involved in—a campaign totally focused on the character of the two major candidates, James G. Blaine and Grover Cleveland, since no major issues divided the country. Party loyalists would vote the straight ticket as usual, while independent-minded voters wanted simply to turn the rascals out, replacing them with honest men, and to do away with the spoils system, making appointments to office through competitive examination.

For the reformers, as well as for the party regulars, the role of government in society was minimal. "Nearly all the machinery of Congress," a laissez-faire philosopher of the time wrote approvingly, "is an elaborate mechanism for preventing anything from being done." The distinction between parties was geographic (with Southern blacks intimidated and disenfranchised, the South was solidly Democratic) and social (the Republican Party was the party of respectable people, while Democrats were likely to be unreconstructed rebels in the South or Irish Catholics in the North). And the entire Democratic Party seemed tainted by association with Tammany Hall, the symbol of corruption and boss rule.

Mark Twain, like his Nook Farm neighbors, had been automatically Republican. The reelection of Grant in 1872 had seemed to him a triumph for progress and civilization. A Twain speech on civil service reform, given during the campaign of 1876, had been reprinted in *The New York Times*, and when the election returns had begun to swing toward Hayes, the Republican, he had dispatched a triumphant telegram to Howells: "Praise God from whom all blessings flow praise him all creatures here below praise him above ye heavenly host praise Father Son & Holy Ghost, The congregation will rise & sing." Four years later, in the closing days of the 1880 contest between Garfield and Hancock, he had even delivered a campaign speech, satirically outlining the "benefits" to be expected from the Democratic low-tariff platform: no more factory smoke, permanent vacations for all factory hands, with prosperity for the South, which could buy cheap manufactured goods from abroad, and wealth for England, which would supply them. But he, like many other loyal Republicans, had been outraged by the candidate chosen at the Republican national convention, in early June of 1884.

The self-designated party of intelligence and virtue had nominated Senator James G. Blaine of Maine (the Plumed Knight, to his supporters) as its Presidential candidate, and everyone knew, or suspected, that the Plumed Knight was corrupt. Somehow, Blaine had become a wealthy man on his congressional salary. Damning letters from him—one of them warning the receiver to "burn this letter"—had been printed in the newspapers. Those letters clearly suggested that in 1869 Blaine had used his position as Speaker of the House to favor a railroad company, even reminding it of his latest services and asking for a reward, while acknowledging its "unbounded liberality" toward him in the past.

Blaine was the candidate of the practical politicians; independent-minded Republicans were scandalized by his nomination. The Democrats, seeing their chance, nominated Grover Cleveland, governor of New York, a man known for his impeccable honesty and stubborn resistance to political pressures. Republicans such as Twain and Howells faced a dilemma: should they follow their party or their principles, support the bribe taker or the honest man? For Twain, even before Cleveland's nomination, the choice was clear. While the final balloting was going on at the Republican convention in Chicago, Mark Twain and a group of friends had gathered in his billiard room to await the results, relayed through the latest technology. George, the butler, was at the telephone downstairs, in contact with Republican headquarters in Hartford, and reported the balloting as fast as results were received by telegraph from Chicago. Through the speaking tube came George's announcement that Blaine had been picked, and as Paine reports the scene in the official biography:

"Then Henry Robinson said: 'It's hard to have to vote for that man.'

"Clemens looked at him under his heavy brows.

" 'But—we don't—*have* to vote for him,' he said.

" 'Do you mean to say that you're *not* going to vote for him?'

" 'Yes, that is what I mean to say. I am not going to vote for him.' " (Mark Twain must have deeply enjoyed that confrontation.)

Argument followed, with party loyalists insisting that the party's choice must be accepted, regardless of personal opinions, and Twain replying that "no party holds the privilege of dictating to me how I shall vote." In the end, "most of those present remained loyal to Blaine"—although they had denounced him before. The Hartford *Courant*, edited by Charles Dudley Warner, a close neighbor, who had collaborated with Twain on *The Gilded Age*, supported the ticket. Only Twichell stood with his friend, against Blaine.

The Republican platform advocated protectionism and a "vigorous" foreign policy, whereas the Democrats traditionally favored low tariffs, but there was only one real issue: the personal character of the two candidates. The *Nation* loftily declared that the Independents, the anti-Blaine Republicans, "were determined to support no candidate who was not upright, able, and clean." Cleveland was the man for all those voters "who long for a better era in politics." Then came the great shock of the campaign: the revelation that Cleveland, a bachelor, had fathered a bastard child. The mother, a widow, had had other lovers and paternity was uncertain, but Cleveland had accepted responsibility.

It was an age when "virtue" was commonly a euphemism for "chastity." Protestant ministers denounced Cleveland; the morally squeamish began to desert his cause. Chastity or honesty, private or public virtue—which mattered more in a President? Should the public "choose the trickster and the jobster because he is chaste?" asked the *Nation*. One editor jocularly proposed that since Cleveland admittedly possessed the public virtues of honesty and courage, while nobody questioned Blaine's qualities as a husband and father, each man should be sent to the sphere for which he seemed best qualified: Cleveland to the White House and Blaine to his family fireside. But not all readers would have laughed. In 1884, chastity did seem, to many Americans, to be the highest of all virtues.

Passions rose, and the campaign became the most rancorous in a generation. The country was filled with oratory and mass meetings; crowds marched through the cities, chanting their taunts to their opposition: "Blaine, Blaine, James G. Blaine! / The continental liar from the state of Maine!" or "Ma, Ma, where's my pa? / Gone to the White House, ha, ha, ha!" "Isn't it the damndest canvass you ever saw?" a cynical friend wrote to Mark Twain in late August. "Finagling on both sides, and the parsons taking a hand! The properest symbol of virtue is an empty scrotum." Mark Twain's view was the same; nothing could be more absurd than for grown men to argue "against a bachelor's fitness for President because he has private intercourse with a consenting widow!" They knew his alternative, to resort to prostitutes, "& tacitly they seem to prefer that to the widow. *Isn't* human nature the most consummate sham & lie that was ever invented?" He put the issue more succinctly in his notebook: "10 Commandments. Cleveland violated 1— Blaine 9."

The race was close, the outcome unpredictable until the very last. The votes and the influence of the independent Republicans— "Mugwumps," "dudes," and "pharisees," party regulars contemptuously named them—could decide the election. Mark Twain was no dude or pharisee, but proudly claimed the title of "Mugwump"— "I am a mugwump," he told Susy, "and a mugwump is pure from the marrow out." (The term seems to come from an Indian word meaning "great man," used ironically to describe a fence-sitter.) Twain's politics were simple: honesty and efficiency were all that mattered in government, and both could be assured by putting the best men in office. Blaine was clearly the worst man, and before the campaign ended, Twain became convinced that Cleveland was the best. Above all, he would not be a slave to a pack of politicians, letting them dictate his vote.

As the election neared, he began to take an active part in the campaign. He presided at meetings, introduced speakers, and of course was quoted in papers on both sides. He could laugh at the moral tone of the campaign; introducing a noted Mugwump at a mass meeting in late October, he briefly stated the cause of his own political conversion (the things that Republican papers had said about Blaine before his nomination), then added that he himself had just been nominated for President by "the ablest newspaper in Colorado—the ablest newspaper in the world," and that he had one great qualification: "the crimes that can be imputed and proved against me can be told on the fingers of your hands. This cannot be said of any other Presidential candidate in the field."

He ridiculed the politicians and the party stalwarts, some of them his friends, who had once denounced Blaine and now compared him to Gladstone and Bismarck, calling him "the first statesman of the age." He reversed the charge of "turncoat"; the Mugwumps consistently stood for honesty in government, it was the party that had turned its coat, after rejecting Blaine for the nomination in 1876 for precisely the reasons that the Mugwumps rejected him eight years later. And the honorable men who had despised Blaine until his nomination, and then supported him—they had turned their coats.

He did his best to convert Howells: "I don't ask you to vote *at all*—I only urge you to not soil yourself by voting for Blaine." Not parties but individuals made the greatness of a nation: "a man's first duty is to his own honor; not to his country & not to his party." His sister, Pamela, disagreed; for her, private virtue was more important than public. Because a few voters insisted on "principle," she wrote to her son after the election, the country must "be ruled by a libertine and a drinking man." Howells's position was more complex. He had strong ties to the Republican Party—his wife was related to ex-President Hayes; he had written campaign biographies of two Republican candidates, Lincoln and Hayes; he had been appointed American consul in Venice as a reward for his Lincoln book—and he had convinced himself that the Republican Party represented not only the wealth of America but its morality and intelligence. "A great cycle has come to a close; the rule of the best in politics for a quarter of a century is ended," he observed gloomily after Cleveland's victory. "Now we shall have the worst again."

That remark showed the triumph of faith over fact; the "rule of the best" had produced unparalleled corruption in the national government. But Howells was plainly uncomfortable with his candidate. When Twain had challenged him, urging him simply to refrain from sullying himself by voting for Blaine, he defended himself with painfully contorted arguments. The charges against Blaine were not proved, Cleveland had a "hangman's face," and, finally, Howells would vote against Cleveland as a protest against the double standard—"that contemptible, hypocritical, lopsided morality which says a woman shall suffer all the shame of unchastity and a man none. I want to see him destroyed politically by his past."

Twichell was braver. Although he had a large family to support, he risked angering his wealthy and Republican congregation by signing an open letter offering evidence of Blaine's corruption and denouncing him as morally unfit for the Presidency. But he, too, could not bring himself to vote for a Democrat. In the end, he cast his vote for the candidate of the Prohibition Party. Like Howells, he accepted what the *Nation* would call the "malignant superstition" that only the Republican Party was fit to govern, that people who voted the Democratic ticket were somehow not real Americans and could safely be allowed to vote only as long as they were in a minority. As the election neared, with the outcome too close to call, Mark Twain proposed nominating a Republican senator known for his integrity as an independent candidate, with or without his consent, thus defeating Blaine and saving "the country's honor" by allowing an escape for honorable Republicans who could not bring themselves to vote for a Democrat; but the idea came to nothing.

The campaign reached a climax of frenzy in its final days. In New York City six thousand businessmen marched down Broadway, all wearing black derbies and carrying white canes, sometimes shouting "Burn—burn—burn this letter!" and demonstrating that respectable men could support a Democrat. A few days later, an estimated thirty thousand Cleveland supporters paraded by a reviewing stand in Madison Square where the candidate stood, taking three hours to pass. Cleveland won a narrow victory, carrying New York State by only 1,149 votes. History credits a foolish speech by a minister supporting Blaine, who denounced the Democratic Party as the party of "Rum, Romanism, and Rebellion," with giving Cleveland his victory. But surely the revolt of the independents was at least as important in bringing about the fall of James G. Blaine.

The Mugwumps rejoiced. "It seems too good to be true that, having got all the rascality and clap-trap of politics together in one heap, we have really swept it out of existence," declared the *Nation*. "Since the fall of Richmond there has been no such triumph in this country." And shortly after the election, Mark Twain wrote a "Mock Oration on the Dead Partisan"—"a meek and docile, cringing and fawning, dirt-eating and dirt-preferring slave; and Party was his lord and master"—who practiced what today we would call Orwellian doublethink, teaching that "the only true freedom of thought is to think as the party thinks . . . the only true freedom of speech is to speak as the party dictates; that the only righteous toleration is toleration of what the party approves." Two months later, a friend would suggest that in recognition for his services during the campaign, Twain should arrange to get himself appointed minister to Japan. Twain made no response—he preferred

Hartford, and in any case, he had no interest in the spoils of office.

In a paper on "Consistency," read to the Monday Evening Club, most of whose members would have voted for Blaine, more or less reluctantly, he generalized the lessons of the campaign in an Emersonian diatribe against consistency. To be inconsistent was to obey "the most rigorous moral law of our being," the law of "Growth." He ridiculed the doctrine of "Once a Presbyterian, always a Presbyterian," or "Once a Democrat, always a Democrat." For a man to take pride in his consistency meant that he was proud to be "unchanging, immovable, fossilized." As for becoming a "traitor" to a party, the only real treason was to disobey one's changed convictions. He would widen that position later; a man should no more give automatic loyalty to his country, even in wartime, than to a party. But he would also doubt whether human beings could resist the pressure toward conformity any more than sheep could resist the movement of the herd.

Mark Twain did not give all his attention to politics that fall. There was the publication of *Huckleberry Finn* to concern himself with. Webster had set up an office on Broadway, and throughout October he had been touring the country, recruiting general agents, filling a fat notebook with comments on their offices, their experience, their reputations. The agents would recruit the canvassers, so they had to be men of standing in their communities; they should also possess push and a thorough knowledge of their territories, and be financially sound—they would be taken on, as Webster commented in his notebook, only "if they could give me a guarantee that would make me safe." (Webster sometimes convinced himself that *he* was Webster and Company.) His terms were stiff—agents must pay the publisher 55 percent of list price on every copy they ordered—but he offered free copies when their sales reached a certain figure: "They swear they will not take the book at 55% at first . . . but when I show them the book they itch for it, and the rebate fixes them."

Canvassers, the field troops in the campaign, were recruited by aggressive advertising, promising sure sales and profits. "EVERY LINE FRESH AND NEW . . . WRITTEN IN MARK TWAIN'S OLD STYLE," reads a typical circular. "A BOOK FOR THE YOUNG AND THE OLD, THE RICH AND THE POOR . . . A MINE OF HUMOR," it proclaimed, boasting that 525,000 copies of his books had been sold in the United States alone, "to say nothing of THE IMMENSE SALES IN

ENGLAND, GERMANY AND OTHER PARTS OF THE WORLD." Not only did *Huckleberry Finn* offer Twain's brightest humor, as well as a gripping story, but—the clinching argument—"MARK TWAIN'S BOOKS ARE THE QUICKEST SELLING IN THE WORLD."

Then the canvassers—men and women, clergymen, teachers, war veterans—set to work. Armed with prospectuses and with sample bindings, from cheap cloth to full morocco, they went to villages and farms across the East and the Middle West. They were not exactly missionaries of culture; profit came first, and they practiced the hard sell. But they reached thousands of prospects who never went near a bookstore and would never have bought a book otherwise. Sales could be enormous, for the right book—although Howells, who did not publish by subscription, remarked that he had never known any work of literary value, except Mark Twain's, to be moved by subscription selling. The subscription audience was Mark Twain's audience; he had captured it in 1869 with *The Innocents Abroad*. His hold on it seemed to have slipped with *The Prince and the Pauper* and *Life on the Mississippi*—with *Huckleberry Finn* he meant to regain it.

But Webster was not allowed to give all his energy to publishing. At any moment, he might be distracted by instructions to arrange for furnace repairs at the Hartford home, to look into tradesmen's bills, or to inquire at Tiffany's about the price of "small *chime* traveling clocks." And he was apparently expected to read his employer's mind—to know when Mark Twain had lost interest in a project, or when some new speculation required priority over everything else, including the publishing of Twain's books. With Kaolatype abandoned, Mark Twain had found another invention to sponsor: a "bed clamp" designed to prevent infants from kicking off their blankets or rolling out of bed. Its only fault had been that it was too cheap, but Twain himself had corrected that, inventing "a more expensive & more convenient one."

Webster, then, not only had to direct the sale of *Huckleberry Finn*, but must test the bed clamp (on his own child), find a way to market it, hire an agent and negotiate his salary and expense account, and answer anxious inquiries from his employer. When the clamp failed its test, tearing the sheets, Twain decided the test must have been at fault. The bed clamp appears in letter after letter, distracting Webster from his real work, until finally he offered his own, unasked opinion: "I have no doubt it will prove a failure. It is so entirely foreign to our business that I think it unwise to go into it." Mark Twain reluctantly accepted that verdict.

Meanwhile, new possibilities had opened for *Huckleberry Finn*. In October, R. W. Gilder, editor of *Century*, urged Twain to delay publication in order to allow the magazine to print half or two thirds of it—with a reservation: "There are some few expressions not adapted to our audience that we would wish the liberty of expunging." Surprisingly, Gilder seems to have considered the educated readership of *Century*, a highly literate magazine, to be more squeamish than the subscription public. "In naming a price," Gilder adds, Twain is not to forget that he has "the largest audience of any English writer above ground." He telegraphed acceptance at once, but only for three or four excerpts. A few installments appearing in *Century* would do more for the book than any advertising, but half or two thirds of the book could dull the public's appetite. In spite of Gilder's exuberant offer, the pay seems to have been only thirty dollars a page, good but not spectacular. But there were reasons for publishing in the *Century* beyond the price per page. America's most successful magazine, and its most successful writer, needed each other.

EIGHT

Twins of Genius

S uddenly, during the final days of the campaign, it was time for the tour with Cable to begin. Too late, Mark Twain regretted his decision: "I am leaving home, now, to infest the platform for 4 months," he wrote to a friend on October 31. "Think of the insanity of it! I wish I hadn't promised; but it is too late, now, to cry about it." He had committed himself to a four-month tour with 104 performances in sixteen states and the District of Columbia, as well as Toronto, Montreal, and other Canadian cities. That schedule, as a rule, meant performing six evenings a week, with matinees as well in the largest cities. No wonder that on the day of their first performance, he pledged that "this trip's my *last*—forever & forever." He would keep his pledge for eleven years.

But regret was useless. Everything had been arranged, even to the programs to be handed out at the door; they were to be printed on cards instead of paper, Twain insisted, so that they would not rustle. He had carefully considered the offerings—he knew the limits of an audience's endurance. A program requiring two full hours of reading was too much; there would be applause and "a dozen other little eaters-up of valuable seconds & minutes." Audiences should "go away hungry, not surfeited . . . to a well-tired crowd, the next-to-the-last minute weighs upward of a ton."

The two authors tested themselves in a half-dozen smaller towns in early November, beginning with New Haven. "An emphatic success," said Cable, although to Mark Twain the audience seemed cool. By Twain's own admission, they (or rather he) suffered a defeat at Springfield, "the forever accursed town," as he called it. He dramatized both victories and defeats; Cable, writing to his wife, reported that in spite of the difficulties, "I did well & so did Mark, though not his very best." They had performed against impossible odds—with the election close at hand, a political rally was going on, with crowds in the streets, "brass music & fire-works in front of the hall . . . and cannon firing directly in the rear of the house." But Livy had been in the audience, and her husband would have wanted a brilliant success.

By the time they reached Boston, everything seemed to be well in hand; Cable sang Creole songs and read from his current novel, *Dr. Sevier*, while Twain, according to the Boston *Transcript*, read from the still-unpublished *Huckleberry Finn*, "narrated his struggles with the German language and its unreasonable genders" ("The Awful German Language," from *A Tramp Abroad*), and "gave other samples of his odd humor." Howells attended and was a good deal more enthusiastic than the *Transcript* reporter: "You were as much yourself before those thousands as if you stood by my chimney-corner . . . You *are* a great artist, and you do this public thing so wonderfully well that I don't see how you could ever bear to give it up." He read "King Sollermun" and "How come a Frenchman doan talk like a man?"—dialogues in which by common sense and logic Jim outargues Huck—the killing of Boggs by Colonel Sherburn, the attempted lynching of Sherburn, and Pap Finn's diatribe against the "govment" for allowing a "free nigger" to vote. Reading from *Huckleberry Finn* was sound strategy; audiences were flattered at being taken into the author's confidence when he offered them passages from an unpublished work, and it sharpened their appetites for the forthcoming book.

At first he simply read the written text, as he had seen Dickens do on his American tour almost twenty years before, but the result was "ghastly." Dickens had been deliberately theatrical, but Mark Twain could not be. In his lectures, he had always appeared completely unconcerned with the effect that he might be making, to be quite unaware that he was saying anything funny, and to be surprised by the audience's laughter. So he set himself to work, making his readings as apparently spontaneous and "natural" as he could—preparing his selections carefully before delivery, marking words in his selections for emphasis and revising when needed, condensing, simplifying, eliminating "all their obstructing preciseness and formalities"—all to the end that his selections should seem like "flexible talk."

Later, he would memorize his pieces, leaving his text behind when he came onstage—unlike Cable—thus allowing himself to keep his eyes on the audience. And his work did not end there. His notebook for the trip contains page after page of possible programs, with the selections often timed, even indicating the time to be allowed for encores. Twain "has worked & worked incessantly," Cable noted; each piece was to be more entertaining than the one before it, creating "a gradual growth of interest & humor." "I don't want them to get tired out laughing before we get to the end," he explained. Cable, in contrast, seems to have performed the same pieces in the same way from the beginning to the end of the tour. "Self-complacency, sham feeling & labored artificiality"—so Mark Twain would sum up his partner's style, a few weeks after their tour had ended. That was not the audience's impression of Cable, as a rule, but they heard him only once.

"Twins of Genius," Pond called Twain and Cable in his advertising, but that was a joke. The happiness of the pairing lay in its unexpectedness—they were exact opposites, in appearance and in temperament. Mark Twain was not a large man, only five feet eight and comparatively slender, but he towered over the diminutive Cable, who weighed less than a hundred pounds. Cable would sometimes open their program by walking onstage and announcing, "I'm not Mark Twain." Laughter always followed. Everyone knew what Mark Twain looked like. Often they would walk onstage together, both in evening dress, but otherwise totally different— Twain careless and shambling, with his apparently unkempt, densely curling hair, the color of "bleached brick-dust"; Cable small and neat and proper, his hair black and smooth and glossy, compensating for his minute size with a long, pointed mustache and a heavy beard.

That contrast alone could arouse laughter. Twain had left the South almost twenty-five years before, yet he still fitted the popular image of the Southerner a good deal better than the Bible-reading, Sabbath-keeping Cable, "exact as to habits, neat, prim," and miserly. Under the strain of a four-month tour, their differences might lead to conflict, as Livy foresaw. "Don't allow yourself to get awry with Mr. Cable; he is good & your friend," she warned her husband,

and three days later, "Be careful how you refer to Mr. Cable in public—even in fun."

They would offer "the intelligent public," said one of Pond's circulars, "the double force of exquisite pathos and genuine humor," with Cable providing the pathos. As to which Twin was the major attraction, Mark Twain could have no doubt: he was by far the best-known writer in America, if not in the English-speaking world, and the whole enterprise was his, with Cable only a salaried employee. To the general public, Cable must have been nearly unknown. But for the cultivated, including those to whom Mark Twain was "merely" a humorist, publication of *The Grandissimes* in 1880 had made Cable the most promising new writer of the day. His second novel, *Dr. Sevier*, had just finished its run in *Century*; he had begun to make a name for himself as a reformer with a controversial speech, later printed in *Century*, condemning the convict leasing system practiced in the South, by which black prisoners were in effect enslaved to private contractors. To conservative Southerners, he was "a Quixotic moral reformer," riding "against the immovable windmills of fixed institutions."

Even Mark Twain's admirers might have wondered if he had finally written himself out—he had not published a book that had made a real impact since *Tom Sawyer* in 1876. In fact, Twain was about to publish his masterpiece, *Huckleberry Finn*, while *The Grandissimes* had marked the end of Cable's career as a significant writer. But in November of 1884, that was unknowable; the inevitable competition between the two men for applause and recognition was not so one-sided as it might have seemed.

As the tour went on, the Twins learned how to deal with annoyances and interruptions, even turning them to advantage: when "a man with creaking shoes stalked out of the hall in the midst of one of Mark's numbers," Cable reported to his wife, "Mark calls out in the most benevolent & persuasive tone, 'take your shoes off, please; take your shoes off'—to the great delight of the applauding audience." In Cincinnati, while Cable was still in his opening number, somewhere in the building a piano began to play loudly. He stopped and stood listening, then suggested that since the audience "cannot listen with intent appreciation to the reading and the piano at the same time," they should sit quietly and listen to the music. "This simple gag brought long continued laughter."

Twain's readings were nearly always humorous; a Hartford friend, Lilly Warner, had suggested that he read from *The Prince and the Pauper*—"I think he can make people cry just as much as he can make them laugh"—but he left the tears to Cable. He wanted a different kind of approval. From Washington: "Splendid times, Livy dear! A Congregational church packed with people . . . We did make them shout, from the first word to the last. I say 'we,' for the honors were exactly equal . . . I worked the ghost-story right this time, & made them jump out of their skins."

Cable's almost daily letters to his wife, often written backstage while his partner was performing, provide a running diary of the tour. They went south after New England, working back and forth between Philadelphia, New York, Washington, and Baltimore. In Philadelphia: "Mark is on the stage" reciting his "Desperate Encounter with an Interviewer," and the roars of laughter "fall as regularly as a surf." (Twain's own comment to Livy was more modest: "a most noble big audience, & a most prodigious good time.") In Washington, President Chester A. Arthur attended (Cleveland would not be sworn in until March) and paid a visit to the performers afterward. Frederick Douglass, escaped slave, famed orator, and black marshal of the District of Columbia, arrived soon afterward, and he and the President greeted each other: "They met as acquaintances. Think of it! a runaway slave!" Cable exclaimed. In Baltimore, "Mark is making the house roar as only a Southern audience can." Clearly, Twain's humor had not staled during his long absence from the platform. Two months later, writing from Ann Arbor, Michigan, Cable would note that "it is astonishing how much like the steady tumble of the surf the laughter was when Mark was reading." And from Toronto, "Such roars of British applause."

With Twain, manner and content were brilliantly combined. A Washington reporter noted that "the aggrieved way in which he gazes with tilted chin over the convulsed faces of his audience, as much as to say 'Why are you laughing?' is irresistible . . . He jerks out a sentence or two and follows it with a silence that is more suggestive than words." Audiences came with expectations that Twain satisfied: "These characteristics agree so well with his description of himself in his books—Innocence victimized by the world, flesh, and Devil," as one reporter put it, that no one could miss the resemblance or fail to "laugh at this grotesque image."

Both men promoted their latest works, with Cable reading most often from *Dr. Sevier*, and Mark Twain from *Huckleberry Finn*, but audiences wanted the familiar as well as the new. "Jim Baker's Bluejay Yarn," a fable of talking birds from *A Tramp Abroad*, often appeared on Twain's programs, and so did "The Awful German Language" (again from *A Tramp Abroad*). Occasionally he would read from his still-unproduced Colonel Sellers play—the play might be new, but the Colonel was an old favorite with audiences. "The Man with the Golden Arm," also called "The Ghost Story," often provided a change of pace. Done exactly right, the climax—with Twain leaping into the air and shouting "You've got it!" as he pointed straight at one member of the audience, usually some impressionable girl—could make the whole house jump. And then, before the audience could recover, he might bow and leave the stage. Timing was everything. Delayed a second too long, his shout would produce only mild laughter. (Once two or three people walked out at the crucial moment and the effect was ruined.)

Cable would sometimes read from his earlier books, *The Grandissimes* and *Old Creole Days*, delighting audiences with Creole "English"—Raoul Innerarity describing his "pigshoe" (picture) of "Louisiana riffusing to hanter de h'union" was a favorite—although he could make passages in Irish and German dialect almost unintelligible by straining for phonetic accuracy: "You know, Mr. Richlin' he told me fnfty dtimes, 'Misses Reisen, doant kif up te pissness!'" His favorite selection, "Mary's Night Ride," from *Dr. Sevier*, offered a melodramatic account of the heroine's ride with her young daughter through Union and Confederate lines to reach her dying husband in New Orleans. ("'Hush, darling!—mama's here. Don't be frightened, darling baby! O God, spare my child!' and away she sped.") Audiences were deeply moved. The "Night Ride" "took the house by storm," reported the Dayton (Ohio) *Democrat*. Sometimes Cable would open by singing—occasionally Confederate army songs, but most often songs of "Place Congo" in New Orleans, songs of Louisiana slaves in a French dialect, with "strong, pulsing wild melodies," as one hearer described them. He disliked singing in public, feeling it undignified, but audiences demanded it.

The Twins came to New York in late November, giving three performances, at prices of seventy-five cents and one dollar, reading to "huge audiences," in spite of competition: Beethoven's *Fidelio* at the Metropolitan, *Twelfth Night*, *Nell Gwynne* (a comic opera), Sardou's *Fedora* and Pinero's *Lords and Commons* and even the "thrilling sensational drama" *Jesse James*. Reviews were mixed, with the *Times* hostile and the *Sun* favorable. The *Times* reviewer decided that Cable had both the genius and the versatility, found Twain's world-famous wit inferior to his partner's exquisite humor and pathos, added superciliously that "Mr. Clemens confined his efforts to the ridicule of such ridiculous matters as aged colored gentlemen, the German language, and himself," and threw in a sneer at the "earthy" *Huckleberry Finn*—the first installment had just appeared in *Century*. (The *Times* might have borne a grudge against Mark Twain, for his separation of himself from the Duncan libel suit in the summer of 1883 by disavowing remarks he had made to a *Times* reporter.)

The *Sun* was more encouraging, giving most of a long review to a description of Twain's performance. "The Ghost Story" had been a clear hit, and reporters enthusiastically described its effect: "In the night of tempest that followed a low steamwhistle whisper chased the man around inquiring: 'Who-o-o-o's got my go-o-o-olden arm?' " The husband locks himself in his room and hides in his bed, but still "the soft steamwhistle whispersighed in his ear; 'Who-o-o-o's got my go-o-o-o-lden arm?' " This time there was a variation in the climax: "Mr. Twain at this point jumped up two feet in the air and came down with a bang shouting 'Nobody!' Everybody else jumped, too."

Probably while he was in New York, Twain learned that during the printing of *Huckleberry Finn*, one of Kemble's "cuts," at the end of Chapter 32, had been altered, making it clearly obscene. Huck has just arrived at the Phelps farm. With his back to the reader, he faces Uncle Silas and a smiling Aunt Sally. Silas stands with pelvis thrust forward, and someone, never identified, had made a small alteration to the plate: Silas's fly is open, with an erect penis jutting out. Huck seems to be staring at it, and in this context, Aunt Sally's smile becomes a leer. If copies containing that plate had been delivered to buyers, a reverberating scandal would have instantly resulted—a scandal that might have ruined the sale of *Huckleberry Finn* as subscribers canceled their orders or returned their books, and that could have permanently damaged Mark Twain's reputation.

Luckily, that cut had been included in the prospectus issued to canvassers, and an alert salesman discovered the change. Luckily again, no copies of *Huck* had left the printing house. All canvassers were required to tear the offending page out of their prospectuses and return it immediately, or face dismissal. Then the plate had to be corrected and the page reprinted, and the offending page replaced, in both bound and unbound copies. The job was done, and the first edition was saved. But the news could not be kept from the papers, and on November 27 the New York *World* broke the story, putting it on the front page and headlining it, with a cruel pun, "MARK TWAIN IN A DILEMA [*sic*]—A Victim of a Joke He Thinks the Most Unkindest Cut of All." Mark Twain was beginning to learn that publishing had its problems.

The Twins moved on to upstate New York. Governor Cleveland, the President-elect, could not attend their Albany reading—his presence was required at a banquet for the Presidential electors of New York, after they had officially cast their ballots for him—but at his request, they paid him a visit at the Capitol. In spite of his rigid morality, Cable was deeply impressed. Cleveland's countenance was strong and commanding, and its strength seemed "mainly moral," while "his manner and speech are those of a man to whom great things are easy." Mark Twain, very much at ease himself, leaned back comfortably, half sitting on a corner of the Governor's desk. Suddenly four young men, official pages, appeared through various doors and stood waiting. There was a moment of silence, then the Governor spoke: "You are dismissed, young gentlemen. Your services are not required. Mr. Clemens is sitting on the bells."

"An Adventure of Huckleberry Finn: With an Account of the Famous Grangerford-Shepherdson Feud" had just appeared in the December *Century*, in company with the third installment of *The Rise of Silas Lapham* (Howells's latest novel), as well as a romance ("The Knight of the Black Forest") and articles on nature, art, poetry, solar energy, and house drainage, besides the inevitable Civil War pieces. The most successful magazine in America—"the best magazine that ever was," Mark Twain called it—*Century* gave its readers solid content, aiming to educate them as well as to entertain them, making demands on their attention that no general magazine today would risk.

That December selection from *Huckleberry Finn* brought a flattering response. On January 7, 1885, Edmund Clarence Stedman, editor of *A Library of American Literature* ("a scholarly and standard collection") asked permission to use Twain's account of the feud in his multivolumed anthology, explaining that he considered it not only "the most finished and condensed" passage that Mark Twain had ever written, "but as dramatic and powerful an episode" as could be found in modern literature. More selections would follow in *Century*—"Jim's Investments" and "King Sollermun" in the January issue, and "Royalty on the Mississippi: The Duke and Dauphin Come Aboard" in February. That issue included another installment of Howells's *Silas Lapham* and commenced the serializing of Henry James's *The Bostonians*, as well as Grant's account of the intensely controversial battle of Shiloh, the first section of his memoirs to be printed. With Twain, Howells, and James all represented by major work, the quality of that February issue of *Century* has probably never been surpassed in the history of American magazines. (Not that the participants recognized its importance—James took no notice of *Huckleberry Finn*, and Twain confessed to Livy that he "tried to read the Bostonians," but found it "unspeakably dreary.") Meanwhile, the enthusiasm of his audiences encouraged Twain to prepare new passages from *Huckleberry Finn* for performance.

Century's selections from *Huckleberry Finn* were not quite the versions that buyers of the book would receive and that modern readers know; the text had occasionally been altered, sometimes expurgated. What was permitted in a book might not be allowable in a family magazine. Huck's grammar and spelling were occasionally corrected, and he was not allowed to be "in a sweat," or to exclaim "dern your skin." His description of life on the raft with Jim—"we was always naked, day and night, whenever the mosquitoes would let us"—had to go. So did "LADIES AND CHILDREN NOT ADMITTED" on the playbill for the performance of the Royal Nonesuch, and the duke's comment: "if that line don't fetch them, I don't know Arkansaw!" "Coarseness" had to be eliminated; Huck could no longer say, "He didn't only look like he was dead, he looked considerable more than that" (already softened from "he looked like he was mortified"). Gilder, the editor of *Century*, seems to have been a prude even by the standards of his time, but Twain made those concessions without complaint; an experienced journalist, he knew and accepted the current limits on expression, generally without even thinking of them as limits.

Life on the road had quickly settled into a pattern: by day, the grueling train rides, with Twain generally in the smoking car and Cable, a nonsmoker, joining him there for as long as he could stand the atmosphere, then (if their train was on schedule) time for dinner and a short rest at their next stop, before performing—but often they had to go direct from the station to the lecture hall. After the performance, there might be a reception, or talk between Twain and Cable in one or the other's hotel room. Major Pond, a jovial man with endless stories from his experience of lecturers and lecturing, made an ideal traveling companion: "He is good company, cheery & hearty, & his mill is never idle," Twain summed up long after. After years of domesticity, Mark Twain reverted happily to bachelor habits; his hotel room would be a chaos of opened luggage, of letters, books, and clothing scattered across the floor.

Sunday was a compulsory day of rest, since Cable reasoned that not only was Sunday work forbidden to a Christian, but also traveling on Sunday in order to work on Monday. Mark Twain might lounge in bed for half the day or more, sometimes embarrassing reporters by receiving them there, still in his nightgown. Cable's Sundays were different; he would attend morning and evening church services, and Sunday school as well, where he would often be recognized and invited to speak. After a week passed in entertaining audiences, he welcomed the chance to teach. "What a happy Sabbath I have spent," he wrote to his wife after one such day. He felt sure that Mark Twain's Sunday had not been happier than his, he added. "Oh, how I wish he were a man of prayer and worship."

Cable seems to have looked at his companion with a kind of awed admiration, as a unique specimen of humanity, untamed and unpredictable, whom nevertheless he would have liked to tame. At the beginning of the tour, he tried conversion. When Twain "was comfortably settled in bed with a relaxing book," according to Albert Bigelow Paine in his official biography, Cable appeared, Bible in hand, to read a chapter aloud. Mark Twain said nothing that night, or the next; then he had had enough, and firmly declared that Cable could read the Bible as much as he liked, but not to him.

They performed at Troy, Syracuse, Utica, and Rochester, where Twain viewed the Salvation Army in action for the first time and described it for Livy: "four very military young men in military costume grouped upon the broad sidewalk . . . swaying this way & that, about a gaudy banner, & making violent & absurd gestures with their hands, & singing unhymn-like hymns in loud voices." Then it was north to Toronto (*Huckleberry Finn* was to be published in London on December 10, and Twain must be on Canadian soil on that day to obtain imperial copyright, good throughout the

British Empire), back to Buffalo, and west to Michigan. They scored a great success at the university town of Ann Arbor, where the audience "combined discrimination & enthusiasm," giving "Mary's Night Ride" a double encore, and keeping the lecturers on stage thirty minutes longer than usual.

Toledo, Detroit, Cleveland, Elmira remained, before their Christmas holiday. Travel was long and hard—"eight, ten, twelve hours in the cars every day or night, & a talk on the platform at the end"—but Mark Twain thrived on it; "we prance out onto the platform half asleep . . . but it isn't any matter, we could do our work & do it well if we *were* asleep, we are so pat & posted in it." They had learned how to thaw out a "frightened & frozen audience," to "rouse them up & make them shout." Exhilarated by their success, he wrote to his English publisher, Andrew Chatto, about the prospects of reading in London. Should he come? Would he draw?

Even eight-hour railroad journeys could not tire him. He had learned to sleep in the daytime, he wrote to Livy: "the roar of wagons in the street even seems to lull me to sleep. This trip's a great thing for my health—haven't felt so robust in years." He could make a joke of the reporters' hackneyed questions. How did he like Detroit? "Considering that I arrived after dark . . . and was driven direct to the theater and then direct to the hotel, my impression was favorable; I think you have a very good quality of nights"—pause—"indeed, fully equal to the nights I have encountered elsewhere." "Twain was as Twain always is, quaint, queer, and quirky," said the Detroit *Journal*—and not only onstage.

He had not been on the road since the early 1870s, and he noted the changes for the better that twelve years had brought. The telephone had replaced "the petrified messenger boy"; hotel rooms offered dry towels and electric push buttons to call for service. The height of luxury on the tour seems to have been a hotel suite in New York City with two open fireplaces and a private water closet—a rarity that Twain considered worth an entry in his notebook. Most spectacular of all these signs of progress were the new electric lights; on the streets of Detroit, they seemed "clusters of coruscating electric suns . . . casting a mellow radiance upon the snow covered spires & domes & far stretching thoroughfares." Not everything had changed, of course. "The usual new bride" boarded the train "& began as usual her furtive love-pattings & pawings of her lovey-dove," finally cushioning her head on his shoulder and falling asleep.

But this time there was a difference: the bride began to snore: "It was an immense improvement . . . because it demonstrated that the sleep was honest, & not gotten up for effect."

In Toledo the Twins encountered David Locke, editor of the Toledo *Blade*, but better known by his pen name, Petroleum V. Nasby. During the Civil War, Locke-Nasby had made himself famous by his newspaper letters ridiculing Confederate sympathizers, and he had become a highly successful lecturer as well. A reformed alcoholic, he bragged of his success in curing himself and of his feats as a drunkard during his lecturing days. He had given one lecture 480 times: "I've given that lecture when I was so drunk that the audience was *invisible*; and I knew it was going right only by the laughter and applause coming up out of that rayless gulf at the proper intervals."

Cable described him vividly: "A big man with disheveled hair, knotted forehead, a heavy middle and dowdy dress. An easy talker, a coarse man of the harder world, successful and unsatisfied." Nasby came back to their hotel after the reading and talked until his cigar was out. He gloried in his crude materialism: "I'll tell you, Clemens, I've settled down upon the belief that there is but one thing in this world better than a dollar, and that's a dollar-and-a-half." Cable was outraged: "I'm glad he's gone. He's a bad dream." Such a figure could not be comprehended in his view of the world.

The Christmas break was short, only ten days. For Cable, it was a time for sober thought: he would use his receipts from the tour to pay off debts and mortgage, he decided, and then would go back to his desk. Writing might not be as profitable as reading, but, he reminded his wife, their lives were not to be guided by the pursuit of profit—"We are just as completely dedicated to God's service as though we were Chinese missionaries." Mark Twain used his holiday differently. "Make not one single engagement outside the house," he had warned Livy; he would meet "particular friends" at his own dinner table, but that was all. He would spend his time working and studying ("all day long & every day") in the billiard room, and pass the evenings with his family. While Cable thought about his duty to God, Mark Twain considered his responsibility toward his audiences. He was not satisfied with his program for second nights, in towns where they gave two performances. Before leaving home, he meant to "be letter-perfect" in a new program, perhaps two—a task that meant selecting new pieces, choosing the most effective order for them, revising them to give that essential impression of "flexible talk," and finally learning them by heart, so that he could speak without book.

Then it was back to the road, opening the second half of the tour in Pittsburgh on December 29—but without Major Pond, who had been replaced by his frail brother Ozias. For the first time, Twain read from the final section of *Huckleberry Finn*, "the episode where Huck & Tom stock Jim's cabin with reptiles, & then set him free, in the night, with the crowd of farmers after them with guns." It was "the biggest card" in his repertory, he wrote enthusiastically to Livy, after the performance. "It went a-booming; & Cable's praises are not merely loud, they are boisterous. Says its literary quality is high & fine . . . its truth to boy nature unchallengeable; its humor constant & delightful & its dramatic close full of stir, & boom, & go." The piece lasted forty-five minutes, with a break in the middle for a few songs by Cable, and he had given it without a text or even notes. "Ah, if it goes like that in its crude rude state, how *won't* it go when I get it well in hand?"

Twain and Cable had their amusements offstage. Writing to Livy, Twain praises a virtuoso banjoist who played for them one evening at their hotel, inventing "as many & as complex & brilliant variations to Sweet Home [*sic*] and other tunes as you would hear on the piano—some of them stirring & triumphant, many of them soft, & rich, & full of poetry & sentiment . . . his Way Down Upon the Swanee River, with soft, fine variations was singularly tender & beautiful." That music and that instrument—the "glory-booming banjo," he had called it once—were part of his heritage. Once he rewrote a passage from *Life on the Mississippi*, "speeches of a couple of bragging, loud-mouthed raftsmen" (the passage transferred to *Life on the Mississippi* from the manuscript of *Huckleberry Finn*), for private performance. "I cut it up into single-sentence speeches— these sentences to be spoken alternately (a lively running-fire of brag & boast) by Cable & me, for Pond's amusement, nights, in our room." When he and Cable visited a bookstore together, Cable persuaded him to buy a copy of Sir Thomas Malory's *Morte d'Arthur*. Malory's language, the "absolute English" of the fifteenth century, fascinated him. The eulogy on Sir Launcelot, beginning "Ah, Launcelot, thou wert head of all Christian knights," could be equaled only by the Gettysburg Address, he believed, "for tender eloquence & simplicity." Twain and Cable promptly nicknamed Ozias Pond "Sir Sagramour le Desirous," and soon the three of them were speaking Arthurian English to one another on the trains and in the hotels.

That reading of Malory had lasting consequences. As Twain recalled later, "I began to make notes in my head for a book." Some of those notes went into his journal: "Dream of being Knight errant in armor in the middle ages," and "Have a battle between a modern army, with gatling guns . . . torpedos, balloons, 100-ton cannon, ironclad fleet &c & Prince de Joinville's Middle Age Crusaders." Those entries contain the germ of *A Connecticut Yankee in King Arthur's Court*, which would be published late in 1889, and foreshadow its final episode—a "battle" in which the Yankee and a few dozen of his disciples use land mines, Gatling guns, and electrified wire to exterminate the massed chivalry of England.

And, as always, there was business—long, closely written letters from Webster reporting the progress of *Huckleberry Finn*, or of the bed clamp, stocks to be bought, lawsuits to be threatened. Mark Twain insisted on receiving weekly reports, complaining sharply when they failed to come, even though they were usually discouraging: "Perpetual Calendar:—nothing. Historical Game: I haven't been able to get a competent man to perfect it yet . . . Bed clamps: nothing. Am. Ex. in Europe [American Express in Europe, a speculative stock] is in brokers' hands but he reports he can not sell it." The American Publishing Company's annual report of sales for the preceding year offered more cheering news: *The Innocents Abroad*, 1,178 copies; *Tom Sawyer*, 1,243; *Roughing It*, 791; *A Tramp Abroad*, 580; *The Gilded Age*, 435; *Sketches: New and Old*, 311. Humor might be the most short-lived of literary forms, but Mark Twain's humor already seemed more durable than most.

Then west and farther west. Twain had arranged at the last moment for readings in Hannibal, Missouri ("where I spent my entire boyhood, in company with Huck Finn & Tom Sawyer," he explained to Major Pond), and Keokuk, where he had worked in Orion's printing shop in 1855–56, and where Orion now lived with his wife and his mother. (It was a more adventurous trip than he had bargained for. The engine and baggage car of their train jumped the track just before reaching the bridge across the Mississippi, "the cars were wrenched terribly," Ozias Pond recorded in his diary, and crashed violently into each other, "and for a moment it looked as though we were all going to be smashed up." But there was no smashup, and the passengers walked over the bridge to St. Louis. Installed in a hotel, Twain spent his Sunday reading the manuscript of a novel submitted by an unknown young woman who had asked him to recommend it to a publisher.

It was of "no account," he remarked to Cable, like all such manuscripts, yet he criticized it, humorously and searchingly, explaining that the author had written an essay rather than a story, and pointing out improbabilities. If the writer had had experience on the stage, he observed, she would not have made her inexperienced heroine ask for a star part and immediately get it. "And after you yourself shall have tried to descend a rainwater pipe, once, unencumbered, you will always know better . . . than to let your hero descend one with a woman in his arms." Experience was the writer's capital: "Whatever you have lived, you can write," he summed up, "& by hard work & a genuine apprenticeship, you can learn to write well; but what you have not lived . . . you can only pretend to write." He had served a strenuous, sometimes painful apprenticeship himself, and he resented amateurs who thought they could dispense with it.

The return to Hannibal was profoundly moving—"such worlds of talk, & such deep enjoyment of it," he confided to Livy. "You can never imagine the infinite great deeps of pathos that have rolled their tides over me." At Keokuk there was a reunion with Orion and with Jane Clemens, now eighty-one. Her memory had been failing, but on that evening "she was her old beautiful self . . . The unconsciously pathetic is her talent—& how richly she is endowed with it—& how naturally eloquent she is when it is to the fore! What books she could have written!" The Keokuk performance was a great success, with the audience fighting its way to the reading through a bitter snowstorm. The local paper had gushed over the event, paying "Mr. Clemens" the highest compliments it could imagine: not only was he "the foremost living humorous writer in the world," surpassed only by "Cervantes and but one or two others," but he was "the only American who can make a hundred thousand dollars a year by his literary work."

The town was excited over a miraculous windowpane that had just been discovered in a local schoolhouse. It contained a discolored patch in which various viewers found a portrait of Martha Washington, or a portrait of "some distinguished man or other," or the face of a pretty girl, or even (to spiritualists) a "spirit face" sent "to confound the disbeliever." Mark Twain saw only a splash of purple, resembling "a ragged big bath sponge," but he was not disturbed by this example of human folly: "If all the fools in this world should die, lord God how lonely I should be."

The lecturers moved into deep winter then, blizzards and polar cold, with temperatures of ten and twenty degrees below zero day after day. But the performances went on. Audiences might be thinned by the cold, they might need to be thawed before they could laugh, but Twain and Cable could always fetch them. At Burlington, Iowa, Twain arrived an hour and a half late—he had stayed behind in Keokuk to have more time with his mother, and his train had been delayed by a blizzard. But Cable went onstage and held the audience until his partner arrived. They had good houses in Chicago in spite of "a raging snowstorm" one night, and a packed house in La Crosse, Wisconsin, at a temperature of minus forty-two degrees. Only Ozias suffered, finding himself "so overcome by the cold" that he could hardly breathe, and at the end of January he gave up, fearing pneumonia, to be replaced by the Major. Reviewing his brief experience with the Twins, Ozias decided that Cable was "the most perfect man" he had ever met. As for Mark Twain, "he dreads to look upon suffering"—including perhaps Ozias's suffering.

In Quincy, Illinois, Twain met with more reminders of his past. "An old man with bush gray whiskers down to his breast" proved to be "Pet" McMurry, once a journeyman printer in the office of the Hannibal *Courier*, where young Sam Clemens had learned the printer's trade. McMurry had been a dandy then, "with plug hat tipped far forward & resting almost on his very nose; dark red, greasy hair, long & rolled under at the bottom, down on his neck; red goatee; a most mincing, self-conceited gait . . . possible nowhere on earth but in our South & in that old day . . . But now—well, see O W Holmes's 'The Last Leaf' for what he is now." (Twain was probably thinking of the best-known stanza from Holmes's immensely popular poem:

> And if I should live to be
> The last leaf upon the tree

In the spring,
Let them smile, as I do now,
At the old forsaken bough
Where I cling.)

In Quincy, too, he met Wales McCormick, a fellow apprentice in the old days. McCormick had been a hero to young Sam Clemens, a "reckless, hilarious, admirable creature." Now he, too, was poor and old, and Mark Twain sent him money. But Twain would prefer to remember McCormick as he had been: in "No. 44, the Mysterious Stranger," a fragment written toward the end of his life, a dashing young printer named "Doangivadam," after McCormick's favorite exclamation, plays a major part.

Mark Twain might be only a few years younger than McMurry and McCormick, but Holmes's pathos did not apply to him; he was not and would never be a "last leaf." No doubt they were worn out by poverty, disappointment, and hard work—prosperity and success can be great preservers of youth. (Mark Twain occasionally boasted, with some exaggeration, that he had never done a day's work in his life—defining work as anything he did not want to do.) But there was more than that to his perennial youthfulness. At the core of his personality was an enthusiastic and unquenchable interest in the world around him (no matter how he might damn it!), a love of novelty, a mobility of temperament that would always make him younger than his years.

If Cable's testimony can be believed, Mark Twain at least once rebelled against his role of mere entertainer. Twenty-five years later, after Twain's death, Cable recalled that during one performance he had been sitting in the wings, waiting for his turn to go on and listening to "the tides of laughter gather and roll forward and break against the footlights, time and time again," believing his partner "to be glorying in that triumph." But in their carriage, returning to their hotel, Twain confessed: "Oh, Cable, I am demeaning myself. I am allowing myself to be a mere buffoon. It's ghastly. I can't endure it any longer." And "all that night and the next day," adds Paine in his biography, "Mark Twain devoted himself to the study and rehearsal of selections which were justified not only as humor, but as literature and art." Even for Mark Twain's official biographer, humor could not be literature or art.

The story is dramatic, and appears to prove that Mark Twain agreed with the various friends and readers, as well as later critics and scholars, who wished that he had been something other than he was, but Cable's unsupported account, twenty-five years after the event, is dubious evidence. Letter after letter from Mark Twain contradicts it, and at no time did he make any such change in his programs. On January 14, in Chicago, he reported that he and Cable had enjoyed "the greatest triumph we have ever made." He read the "Jumping Frog," condensed to thirteen minutes, and "Tom & Huck setting Jim free from prison—25 minutes—but it just went with a long roll of artillery-laughter, interspersed with Congreve rockets & bomb shell explosions, from the first word to the last," and there was "a thrice-repeated crash of encores." The "Jumping Frog" had "swept the place like a conflagration. Nothing in this world can beat that yarn when one is feeling good & has the right audience in front of him."

On February 1, he boasted to Livy that "we carried that Rockland house by storm." And at Davenport, he had been "old & seedy & wretched from travelling all night & getting no sleep," changing trains twice and crossing the frozen Mississippi by sleigh, but a cup of black coffee restored him, and "we made a great triumph before a great audience." Twain boasted that he had answered three encores: "I guess we sent that multitude home feeling jolly." On February 4: "Livy, dear, we hit them again last night, & hit them hard. We have now appeared four times before big audiences here [Chicago] & made a ten-strike every time. The ghost story was simply immense. I made those 1600 people jump as one individual." (That performance was the greatest "artistic and pecuniary success of our season," Cable reported to his wife.) A letter to Livy on February 8 sums up Twain's view of his platform success: "I have learned my trade at last: I know to read my stuff . . . I did make 'em shout last night. The blue-jays & the other stuff went booming." If Twain had been reading alone, he might have chosen more serious selections as well. He knew that audiences should not be sated with laughter, but Cable was there to provide contrast.

On those nights when everything went well, he exulted in his mastery over the audience. Those tidal waves and "bomb shells" of laughter proved his success, they rewarded his preparation, his study, his experimenting, repaid him for the constant discomforts of winter travel—the all-night journeys and the early risings, the "dingy, dirty platforms & auditoriums," the "fiendish stove heat, & dirty hacks and drafty railway cars smelling of coal furnaces and human-kind," as Cable described their hardships. Once, when exasperated at being forced out of bed to catch an early train, Mark Twain "vented his anger by squaring off with the window shutter & knocking it completely out in one round" while Cable and Ozias Pond "looked on with bated breath." Applause and laughter were the true reward, not the box-office receipts, which Twain almost never mentions in his letters to Livy. The money provided a useful rationalization, justifying—even to himself—a four-month absence from his wife and daughters.

When Mark Twain altered his programs, it was always to arouse more laughter, not less. There might have been times in Hartford when he would have preferred to be thought of as "serious"—but not on the road. Perhaps Cable exaggerated and dramatized some momentary complaint. Perhaps he invented; he was not a saint, after all, only a staunch Presbyterian, and there surely were times when he envied his partner's applause.

That dubious recollection of Cable's might have had another source: a growing tension between the two men, frankly acknowledged in Twain's letters to Livy, but never mentioned by Cable, although he could not have helped realizing it. Under the strain of continuous association, of constant travel and daily performances, their differences loomed larger and larger—at least to Mark Twain. Cable's rigid keeping of the Sabbath became a constant annoyance; Twain could accept his partner's refusal to read on Sundays, but his unconditional refusal to travel, even though that, too, had been written into their contract, seemed infuriatingly unreasonable. The most harmless conventions of society had to give way to Cable's "idiotic Sunday superstition." On one Saturday night, he abruptly left a reception, in the midst of conversation and storytelling, in order to reach his hotel room before midnight—like Cinderella running for her coach. And no matter how long a journey they might have to make before reading on a Monday night, they could not board the train until Monday morning. "Cable wouldn't even go to heaven on Sunday," Twain commented sourly.

Cable displayed a grotesque miserliness: he "never bought one single sheet of paper or an envelop [*sic*] in all these 3½ months— sponges all his stationery . . . from the hotels," Mark Twain confided to Livy. He starved himself when he paid for his own meals, gorged when his expenses were paid. Most absurd of all, after their Christmas holidays, "when we came to do our washing . . . in Cincinnati," Cable "piled out a whole trunkful—all saved up since we were on the road last"—in order to have his laundry done at Twain's expense. He rejected appeals for charitable performances, he would do nothing for nothing: "I don't believe he 'lays over' Sundays gratis: I believe he keeps an account against God." Even that did not end the catalogue of complaints. Cable was "insulting & insolent" to servants. And Twain summed up with a blast of invective: "His body is small, but it is much too large for his soul. He is the pitifulest human louse I have ever known."

There were grievances on the platform, too, and as early as December 22, Twain poured out his complaints to his manager. Pond had been right in saying that he would draw better alone: Cable had "been *every*where" and was "a novelty nowhere." ("Especially," he explained to Livy, "as he offers his same old stuff all the time.") Twain would have liked to offer him two hundred dollars a week to withdraw from the tour and hire a musician to take his place. But since that could not be done, Cable must be "curtailed." "He invariably does two-thirds of the reading. I cannot stand that any more." And Twain proposed a revised schedule, allotting each man three appearances, but giving Cable only thirty-eight minutes against his own fifty-two. The tactful Pond promised that he would require Cable to "epitomize his part," reassured Twain that they were drawing well and that spectators universally agreed "that it is the most charming & pleasing entertainment ever offered." Cable was an attraction himself, said Pond, but more important, he whetted the audience's appetite for Mark Twain.

Professional jealousy, a clash of egos? In part, certainly. Mark Twain, too, extended his time, and he might have resented sharing the platform and the audience, *his* audience, with any man—no matter that he had made the arrangement himself. Early in the tour, he might be pleased to see ladies undisguisedly wiping their eyes after hearing "Mary's Night Ride," might even have envied Cable his power of drawing those tears. But Cable's reading had lost the naturalness that had once delighted Twain. "Cover the C H I L D !" shouts Mary's guide as they ride past Union pickets, who fire on them. Cable's melodramatic rendering of that line became a standing joke in the Clemens family. And Cable appears to have been a lazy performer, relying on a few stock pieces and stock effects; he did not take the trouble to learn his selections, or to revise them for oral delivery; he seldom varied his programs, even for repeat performances in a town.

But Mark Twain still admired Cable's earlier books, if not *Dr. Sevier*, and Cable was doing other work that he could not help praising—work requiring exactly the principled stubbornness that could make him an uncomfortable traveling companion. If ever a man had a New England conscience, it was George Washington Cable, Southerner though he was. On his first journey north, he recognized his spiritual home. In "The Freedman's Case in Equity," published in the January *Century*, he outraged the white South, defying its racial attitudes and condemning its institutions and practices.

Southerners had thought of him as one of their own, taking pride in his accomplishment as a writer. They were shocked when, in *Dr. Sevier*, the author interrupted a description of Union troops marching down Broadway, singing "John Brown's Body" as they go, to advance his own opinion: " 'Go marching on,' saviors of the Union, your cause is just." The white Southerner might accept the outcome of the Civil War but could never admit that he had fought for an unjust cause. It could easily be thought that Cable had become a traitor to the South, seeking applause and profits from the North.

But the war was history, and so was slavery. To question the peculiar institutions of the postwar South, through which whites still controlled blacks, was more dangerous. Cable took that step when he exposed the system of leasing convict labor to white contractors. In an address given in Louisville, Kentucky, later published in *Century*, he had demonstrated that the number of blacks in prison was grossly out of proportion to the number of whites, that blacks regularly received more severe sentences for the same offenses, and that the death rate in the convict work camps was appalling. Yet Cable found Southern supporters. Offering irrefutable evidence, he had appealed to simple decency and justice, without challenging the basis of Southern society. White supremacy did not depend on the use of convict labor.

In "The Freedman's Case in Equity," he crossed the line from the barely acceptable to the forbidden by attacking legally enforced segregation. He could frankly call blacks "an inferior race" and see their mere presence as a "problem" confronting the "American people"—a group that apparently did not include blacks. Yet he in-

furiated white Southerners by demonstrating just how far the
emancipated slave, the "freedman," was from being in fact a free
man. In practice, he pointed out, separation by race invariably meant
giving the black "the most uncomfortable, uncleanest, and unsafest
place." Barring the way to "every public privilege and place—
steamer landing, railway platform, theater, concert-hall, art display,
public library, public school, courthouse, church, everything," stood
a white man "flourishing the hot branding-iron of ignominious
distinctions." Blacks might be "an inferior race," Cable argued, but
that did not prevent individual blacks from being superior to individual whites. Logically, then, he condemned every device used
"to maintain a purely arbitrary superiority of all whites over all
blacks."

Cable believed deeply in the moral power of literature and the
responsibility of the writer to instruct his age, to correct wrongs,
even if that required him to shake the foundations of society, and
he paid for his courage. He believed that he wrote for his country,
as well as for his region, but the country was not listening. The
time was wrong; Northern whites no longer wanted to hear about
black rights, but preferred to believe, against all the evidence, that
problems would solve themselves. Cable was still more mistaken in
imagining that he spoke for a "Silent South" of intelligent and well-
meaning whites. Indignant letters deluged the *Century*'s office;
throughout the old Confederacy, newspapers denounced him, and
he found no Southern supporters. He was denounced as a "negro-
philist," charged with advocating "the social intermingling of the
races." As Mark Twain, less principled and less naïve, had pointed
out in *Life on the Mississippi*, the South was a closed society, with
no room for dissent.

Admiring Cable's courageous "fight for the negro," Twain could
forget his "Sunday superstition" and his miserliness, could declare
to Livy that "he is a *great* man" and predict that "his greatness will
come to be recognized—& it will be greatness of a kind & size that
will overshadow his merits as a novelist." And into his notebook
went the germ of a story: "America in 1985. (Negro supremacy—
the whites under foot.") He imagined laws forbidding miscegenation, enforced by blacks, with whites terrorized by a black equivalent of the Ku Klux Klan, their houses burned, their wives and
daughters driven out naked. He never wrote such a piece, but in a
long fragment from the late 1890s, "Which Was It?," he would

reverse the traditional relationship of white and black when Jasper, a revengeful mulatto, blackmails a white man, Harrison, forcing him to play the role of slave and to suffer every humiliation and cruelty that Jasper had endured.

Mark Twain himself admitted a moral function in literature, although he liked to ridicule the obvious moral. He did not yet write polemics, but his sympathies found expression in *Huckleberry Finn* through the characterization of Jim, through Huck's painful decision to humble himself by apologizing to a "nigger," through the ridicule of white supremacy, as expressed by Pap Finn. He had already taken concrete action as well, aiding individual blacks—Charles Porter, the black painter in Paris, and several students at Lincoln University, a segregated college in Pennsylvania. In 1885–87 he would pay the board of one of those students, Warner McGuinn, while he attended Yale Law School. He did not know the man personally, but that made no difference; as he explained to Howells, he "was doing it as part of the reparation due from every white to every black man." (Warner McGuinn would graduate and practice law in Baltimore, winning a major civil rights case in 1917, when a federal court declared a Baltimore ordinance requiring segregated housing to be unconstitutional.)

The tour went on. February 10, Columbus, Ohio: "Livy darling, rode all day in a smoking car, yesterday, stopping every 30 yards, arrived here in a rain storm . . . jumped into evening dress in a desperate hurry & came before a full Opera House . . . & made them shout, & tore them all to pieces till half past 10 . . . I have been 3 months learning my trade, but I have *learned* it at last." After the performance, and supper, Twain played billiards with Pond until 2 a.m., read and smoked for another hour, and rose at nine-thirty, feeling perfectly refreshed: "Not for many years have I been in such splendid condition physically." Success made everything worthwhile: constant changing of trains, temperatures far below zero, long waits in overheated stations, endless delays—often reaching the destination just in time to rush from the station to the lecture hall. But all that could be forgotten when he made his hearers shout. In such moments of triumph, he admitted, he "would rather be on the platform than anywhere in the world."

Including Hartford, Livy might have commented. But at least her husband was constantly in touch with home. He wrote to his daughters often, in both English and German (even to four-year-old Jean), and Susy reported on family affairs. Livy handled correspondence and business matters in Twain's absence, no doubt at least as competently as he would have done, and much more calmly. In late December, Twain had discovered that Estes & Lauriat, Boston booksellers, were advertising *Huckleberry Finn* in their catalogue of forthcoming books as "now ready" (they were not authorized to sell the book) and were offering a fifty-cent discount from the subscription price of $2.75. Always combative, Twain promptly tore the page from the catalogue and scrawled a message to Webster on it: "let Alexander & Green sue them for damages instantly. And if we have no chance at them in law, tell me at once & I will publish them as thieves and swindlers."

Receiving a courteous protest from Estes & Lauriat, Livy for once remonstrated strongly: "How I wish you were less ready to fight, & more ready to see other people's side of things . . . if you write, write civilly." Twain did write civilly, at least for him—he never ignored Livy's requests—although in the end the case went to court. But it was seldom that she could overcome her husband's combativeness, his fear that he was being exploited, that his prosperity and his family's happiness were threatened. He was fighting for her and for his children, he believed. (A Boston court would deny Webster and Company an injunction to prohibit Estes & Lauriat from advertising and selling *Huckleberry Finn*, but eventually peace was made.)

The long tour neared its end. In mid-February, the Twins swung north again, for an exhilarating finish in the depths of the Canadian winter. They performed successfully in Toronto and visited a "Female College" outside the city, traveling by sleigh over deep snow in bright sunshine, at a temperature of minus twelve degrees. Tobogganing followed, an exciting novelty: "You sit in the midst of a row of girls on a long broad board with its front end curled up, & away you go, like lightning."

Montreal delighted them both; "one of the brightest, liveliest and most charming cities—at least in winter—that can be," wrote Cable. They saw an ice palace and ice statuary, left over from a winter carnival. They marveled at the sleighs, the furs, the brilliantly colored clothes of snowshoers and tobogganers, both male and female, with their "sashes & belts & hoods & moccasins." Cable, the Southerner, was amazed: "The people have simply turned the bitter months of the year into days so full of exhilaration that there is hardly left time for sleep," he exclaimed in a letter to his wife.

The visit to Montreal was a triumph. The Athenaeum Club, a literary society, gave them a grand reception, with five hundred notables of the town invited—"the most elaborate affair," wrote Cable, that he had ever taken part in. He had "shaken no less than two hundred and fifty hands." Advertisements had invited the "intelligent public" to enjoy "Mark Twain's Wit, Mr. Cable's Exquisite Humor and Pathos," for a price of only fifty cents (general admission) or seventy-five cents or one dollar (reserved seats), and the intelligent public had responded. The local papers were enthusiastic. "There is only one Mark Twain in the world who can write such genuine fun," said the *Gazette*, praising Cable, too, and concluding with the ultimate compliment: Montreal had seen no event of such interest since "the immortal Charles Dickens delighted the English speaking people of the old and new world" in his reading tour, almost twenty years before.

After the reading, the performers and their manager were wrapped in furs, bundled into a sleigh, and driven out of the city by starlight over the "creaking, groaning snow" to the headquarters of the Tuque Bleue Snowshoe Club, where all three were initiated. Husky young men seized them, tossed them again and again to the ceiling, and caught them in their hands. (Afterward, Twain commented that he would remember that gathering as long as he lived, and the initiation after he was dead.) Then Cable sang, Twain told a story, the evening finished with "God Save the Queen," and they were driven back to their hotel at a gallop. They performed again the next night and then took the train back to the United States, riding through a superb winter landscape, with the frozen, snow-covered Lake Champlain glistening in the sunlight and snowy hills beyond. They read at Saratoga, then worked their way south.

With the end in sight, Twain took a more balanced view of his partner. Writing to Howells from Philadelphia, he summed up his impressions: Cable's "gifts of mind," he had found, were "greater and higher" than he had suspected. He had seen also "how loathsome a thing the Christian religion can be made," and had learned "to abhor & detest the Sabbath-day & hunt up new & troublesome ways to dishonor it." But while his partner's religion might be detestable, personally "he is pleasant company; I rage & swear at him sometimes, but we do not quarrel." (For Mark Twain, there was no necessary contradiction in that remark.) As for Cable, he promptly went on another tour, but it was not the same. "It comes hard reading alone, without Mark, I mean," he wrote forlornly to his wife. Those four months had been the high point of his career, with the excitement of the tour, the constant companionship of Mark Twain and the apparent equality between them, and the sense that with the controversy over "The Freedman's Case in Equity," he himself had become a national figure. He would go on more reading tours—he badly needed the money—and he would publish a book on *The Negro Question* (1888) as well as half a dozen more novels, but his significant work was done.

A matinee and an evening performance in Washington, and the long campaign was over. Mark Twain went home, to be welcomed with a splendid surprise: a carefully staged performance of scenes from *The Prince and the Pauper* at a neighbor's house before an audience of friends, with scenery painted by Gerhardt, costumes produced by everyone concerned, dramatized and directed by Livy, and performed by the children of Nook Farm. He actually arrived too soon, before preparations were quite complete, but as he sat in the library with his family, Livy withdrew to finish packing the costumes, then Susy and Clara followed. "Papa was left all alone," Susy recorded, "except that one of us every once in a while would slipp in and stay with him a little while." Anyone else "would have wondered at mammas unwonted absence," but her father was too absentminded—"he very seldom notices things as accurately as other people do."

The next night, without explanation, a reluctant Twain was dragged out to the Warners' house, where he found the drawing room transformed into a theater with a crowd of people facing the curtain and a vacant seat in the front row for himself. Then the curtain was drawn, and he saw a neighbor girl in the Pauper's rags and Susy, in silk and satin, as the Prince, and the play began. The performance was a success, and the dramatic illusion was broken only once. During that first scene with the Pauper, Susy spoke the line "Fathers be alike mayhap; mine hath not a doll's temper," someone giggled, and the audience burst into laughter. A return engagement seemed called for, and the play was repeated on April 23, this time with Mark Twain himself in the role of Miles Hendon, the swaggering soldier who befriends the Prince. Twain had written in parts for Katy Leary and George Griffin, as well as exciting new lines and action for himself: "(Confusion without—Hendon's voice heard) I *will* enter! Out of my way! Or I'll spit a dozen of ye as I would gizzards on a *skewer*! (Plunge in with drawn sword.)" "He was inexpressibly funny," Susy noted, "with his great slouch hat and gait—such a gait! . . . He certainly could have been an actor as well as an author."

The play would be performed two more times in the next twelve months. Mark Twain delighted in private theatricals, improvised dramas, charades for adults and children. Comedy was his strong point; Clara would never forget her father's marvelous absurdity when, costumed in a bathing suit and a straw hat ("tied under his chin with a big bow"), and with a hot water bottle slung across his chest, he played Leander swimming the Hellespont.

And the tour: had it been worth the effort? The gate receipts, as recorded in Major Pond's cashbook, had never been more than a thousand dollars in the largest cities, and under two hundred dollars in a few of the smaller towns. (Admission was usually seventy-five cents or a dollar.) But Cable had certainly done well. He had earned his $450 a week, much more than he could have gained from four months of writing, and all his expenses on the road had been paid. Mark Twain's profit is not so easy to calculate, but after deducting the costs of advertising, rental of halls, railroad fares, hotels, meals, Cable's salary, and Pond's commission, there might have been fifteen thousand dollars or so left for him. (That return needs to be balanced against the level of prices in the 1880s—a dollar for dinner, two to four dollars a night for a hotel room, except in New York City, where the price rose to $6.40.)

"I ought to have staid at home and written another book," Twain had complained to Webster in January. "It pays better than the platform." But books did not always pay so well, and he would probably not have written a book if he had stayed at home; as a rule, he wrote books in Hartford only under compulsion. The return from the tour was substantial, and the cash was not all he had gained; he had renewed his reputation as a performer, he had advertised *Huckleberry Finn* throughout the East and Middle West, and night after night he had triumphed on the platform, exulting in his mastery over his audience.

There was an unpleasant aftermath. Mark Twain always talked freely with reporters, and apparently he, and Major Pond as well, had said too much about their dissatisfaction with Cable. Exaggerated stories about their differences, of Cable's parsimony and puritanism, began to appear in the papers. Those stories, based on gossip and no doubt often on second- or thirdhand reports of casual remarks, must have seemed worth printing because of the notoriety, and hostility, Cable had aroused by his stand on civil rights for blacks. In May, the Boston *Herald* ran a story on "Personal Peculiarities of a Well Known Author." Cable, the article claimed, had ordered five-dollar breakfasts while his expenses were being paid, he had charged "so highly luxurious a thing as champagne" to his account (an absurd accusation—Cable was a rigid abstainer) as well as "so lowly a one as the blacking of his boots" (quite probable). "The bills rendered by Cable," Pond was quoted as saying, were "greater curiosities of literature than the best of his Creole dialect." As reported by the papers, Cable's unwillingness to travel on Sunday became not a matter of principle but a stubborn refusal to consider the convenience of others.

When Cable protested that the story was slanderous, the *Herald* retracted and apologized. Cable appealed to Twain by telegram: "All intimations that you and Pond are not my Beloved Friends are false and if you can say the same of me do so as privately or as publicly as you like." There was no response. Cable wrote assuring Twain of his own continued esteem and his regret "if scandal mongers were to make an estrangement between us." Twain answered with a note: Cable must not be made uncomfortable by "the slander of a professional newspaper liar—we can*not* escape such things . . . Why, my dear friend, flirt it out of your mind, straight off." He casually dismissed charges that must have originated with himself—treating them lightly, perhaps, to avoid admitting his own responsibility. In any case, intimacy ended; their relationship would never again be more than distantly cordial.

That seems a sad outcome for the tour, a shabby performance by Mark Twain—but highly characteristic. Other men might have been irritated by Cable's exaggerated piety and his absurd scruples; in months of close and continuous association, that was inevitable. But Twain—quick to anger and quick to express his anger—had expressed his irritation freely, unthinkingly, exaggerating his companion's foibles. At such times, his own grievance, whatever it was, would seem so overwhelming that he must declare it, instantly, without stopping to weigh the consequences or the provocation.

Ten years later, writing to Cable, he could make a more balanced judgment, maintaining his own objections while indirectly apologizing: "Yes, *sir*! I liked you in spite of your religion; & I always said to myself that a man that could be good & kindly with that kind of load on him was entitled to homage," adding that as a companion, Cable had been ideal—"the only railroad-comrade in the world that a man of moods & frets & uncertainties of disposition could travel with, a third of a year, and never weary of his company."

NINE

"The Best Book Ever Written"

D elayed for weeks by removal of the indecent plate, losing Christmas sales as a result, *Huckleberry Finn* had finally appeared in February of 1885. It *must* be a success, Mark Twain felt. It had been eight years in the writing, and it followed two successive "failures"—at least by Twain's standards. *Huckleberry Finn* was intended to regain the readers he had lost with *The Prince and the Pauper* and *Life on the Mississippi*. This time there could be no excuse for failure. The book seemed to mark a return to his old style—it was a sequel to *Tom Sawyer*—and it was issued by Twain's own publishing company. A poor reception would have been deeply discouraging, would have suggested that Mark Twain was only another "funnyman" and that his fun had worn out its welcome at last.

Nobody, including its author, suspected that a classic had been born. Outwardly, *Huckleberry Finn* seemed just another crudely made subscription book—almost square, a violent blue, bulked out by thick bindings, heavy paper, and wide margins, although offering an unexpected novelty with its second frontispiece, Gerhardt's bust of Mark Twain. That dignified image sharply distinguished the author from his creation, and incidentally might annoy conservative reviewers who suspected that Mark Twain, a mere humorist, was getting above himself.

A magazine poll published that spring indicates Mark Twain's status among intellectually inclined readers. *The Critic* had asked its subscribers to nominate "Forty Immortals," men of letters suitable for membership in an American Academy, to be modeled on the Académie Française. Mark Twain was chosen, but he was fourteenth on the list, which was headed by Oliver Wendell Holmes and James Russell Lowell. Howells was there, in fifth place, and James (thirteenth), and even Bret Harte (eighth), although for a decade he had been industriously repeating the early stories that had won his reputation. That fourteenth place is not really surprising; the more one enjoyed Mark Twain's humor, the harder it would have been to think of him as a man of letters, still less as an academician, or an "Immortal."

Not that Mark Twain was likely to feel any deep interest in a hypothetical Academy. He had more pressing concerns: his tour with Cable, and the reception of *Huckleberry Finn*. He had convinced himself that *Huck* was sure to fail, but by the end of winter all the signs were reassuring. On March 14, Webster jubilantly reported that "Huck Finn is a success." Thirty-nine thousand copies had been sold—already more than doubling the sale of *The Prince and the Pauper*—and ten thousand more were printing, with orders for nine thousand of them in hand. Final sales would reach only 51,000. *Huck* had found its market. Those figures might not equal the sensational success of *The Innocents Abroad* and *Roughing It*, but after the disappointment of *Life on the Mississippi*, they gave comforting reassurance to Mark Twain that he had not lost his audience.

Of course, that sale meant a handsome profit as well; a year later, Webster would present the author with a check for $54,500. Fifteen thousand was for repayment of the capital that Twain had advanced to cover publication costs. The rest was profit—more than twice as much as he could have earned with the highest royalty he had ever received. Webster and Company's first venture had succeeded; Mark Twain's decision to become his own publisher had been vindicated.

Huckleberry Finn was widely reviewed and commented on in the newspapers, although American magazines said little about it. That neglect might have been due to the low status of subscription books, but it was also the fault of Twain and Webster, who had failed to send out review copies in time. *Huck* had been published first in England, in early December (prior publication there was necessary to obtain British copyright), and the earliest reviews had appeared in English journals. They were surprisingly favorable. "For some time past," said the *Athenaeum*, "Mr. Clemens has been carried away by the ambition of seriousness and fine writing," but with *Huckleberry Finn*, "he returns to his right mind, and is again the Mark Twain of old." Clearly, the reviewer had been thinking of *The Prince and the Pauper* when he wrote that sentence.

The Hartford neighbors who had urged Twain to write such a book as *The Prince and the Pauper*, and Livy and Susy, who considered it his best work, would surely have been surprised by that remark from the citadel of culture, but some English critics preferred American writers to be American, to offer something their own literature could not give them. Comparison with *Tom Sawyer* was obligatory, and here, to the modern reader, the reviewer showed himself less discriminating: to say that Jim and Huck "are real creations, and the worthy peers of the illustrious Tom Sawyer," is not only to rate a major book with a lesser one, but to make a serious misjudgment in classifying *Huckleberry Finn* as a book for boys. (Kemble's illustrations probably encouraged that misreading.)

A London journal, the *Saturday Review*, likewise saw *Huck* as a companion to *Tom Sawyer*, written for boys and men who had been boys (not all had been), but the reviewer made the essential distinction between the two books: "the skill with which the character of Huck Finn is maintained is marvellous. We see everything through his eyes—and they are his eyes and not a pair of Mark Twain's spectacles." He praised the consequence: "the sober self-restraint" with which Huck presents, without comment, "scenes which would have afforded the ordinary writer matter for endless moral and political and sociological disquisition." And he recognized fundamental differences between Tom and Huck—Huck is a "walking repository" of folklore, he has a "feeling for nature . . . caught during his numberless days and nights in the open air."

American criticism was moral. Literature existed not simply to amuse, but to teach, and that meant to offer moral instruction. The doctrine of "Art for Art's sake," a reviewer for the *Nation* declared in its issue of March 12, 1885, commenting on Henry James's novelette *The Author of Beltraffio*, was alien to "the English race" and to that "strong puritanism" which had shaped it. In the "English race," he added complacently, "the individual conscience plays a prominent part." The consequence was the remarkable purity of Anglo-American literature—in contrast to the notorious impurity of the French. Most literate Americans would have agreed.

Seeing *Huck* as a "boy's book," reviewers asked a simple question: Would reading it make a boy better or worse? The moral standard was strictly enforced on children's books; it was the young who most needed moral indoctrination. And morality had to be explicit, to teach, among other things, that boys should not lie, swear, or steal. Such reviewers were not likely to recognize the significance of Huck's decision to aid Jim or to humble himself by apologizing to a "nigger," or of Twain's satirical presentation of the psychology of racism in Pap's angry monologue about the prosperous and educated "free nigger" from Ohio.

The real question was, what kind of example did Huck offer, both as narrator and as character? Plainly, not a very elevating one. "A wretchedly low, vulgar, sneaking and lying Southern country boy," the New York *World* called him—transparent hypocrisy, from a paper notorious for its yellow journalism. Enraged, Twain filled pages of his journal with a list of stories of murder, suicide, seduction, and abortion taken from a single issue of the *World*, concluding with an ironic "Moral: If you want to rear a family just right for sweet & pure society here & Paradise hereafter, banish Huck Finn from the home circle & introduce the N. Y. World in his place."

Huckleberry Finn was praised for its realism, but for many readers, realism offered no defense. They expected literature to be unrealistic and "beautiful," to offer "inspiration" by presenting the ideal, not the real. Polite readers and reviewers condemned Huck's speech— ungrammatical, a crude dialect, full of "inelegant" expressions—and objected even more to his behavior. Not only did Huck regularly lie, steal, and exhibit disrespect toward family, school, church, law, and society in general, but he felt no guilt and suffered no punishment. The book was "low," it was "vulgar," in its language, its characters, its incidents. "Low," "vulgar": those adjectives recur regularly; it was easy to confuse social, moral, and literary standards—to suppose that a book dealing with "low" characters and written in a "low" language must be "low" itself, and therefore worthless.

For conservative reviewers, the book had no redeeming literary value—if literary value could have redeemed its faults. (Clearly, those reviewers did not know the humor of the Old South and Southwest in the 1840s and '50s, the source for much of Mark Twain's work—a humor of brawling and bragging and brutal practical jokes.) All the objections were summed up in the verdict of the Concord library committee. The library had bought a copy of *Huckleberry Finn*, but in mid-March the library committee examined the book and decided to withdraw it from circulation, and to make its reasons public.

One member found it "trash," not "absolutely immoral," but "coarse," and lacking even humor! Another stated his objections systematically: *Huck* "deals with a series of adventures of a very low grade of morality; it is couched in the language of a rough, ignorant dialect, and all through its pages there is a systematic use of bad grammar and an employment of rough, coarse, inelegant expressions." Moralism and a sense of humor are usually not found together; this committee member saw nothing absurd in solemnly noting that Huck uses "bad grammar."

Worse still, it was "very irreverent." Undeniably, the book was irreverent toward the doctrine of white supremacy, toward Southern "chivalry" and the code of honor, toward parental authority as embodied in Pap, toward human nature as displayed by lynching or tar-and-feathering mobs, toward the frenzy of revival audiences, toward sentimentality, humbug, and hogwash in general. But the reviewer did not specify; reverence—in itself, regardless of its object—was a favorite virtue of the genteel, a virtue constantly threatened by an unruly democracy. By cultivating "irreverence," then, Mark Twain seemed to have betrayed his literary calling. *Huckleberry Finn* dealt "with a series of experiences that are certainly not elevating." In short, it was "trash," fit for the slums, not for respectable homes.

That condemnation carried weight; Mark Twain might exclaim that "those idiots in Concord are not a court of last resort," but to many readers, especially in New England, they were exactly that. The confrontation was dramatic: Concord, the home of Emerson and synonymous with Culture, versus Mark Twain, who in his personality, his career, symbolized the crude vitality of American life. Twain might protest that he was "not disturbed by their moral gymnastics" and justify himself with the claim that "no other book of mine has sold so many copies within 2 months after issue as this book has done," but in fact he was hurt and angry, and he surely knew that pointing to sales figures did not answer the indictment. On March 17 and 18, newspapers in Boston, New York, and St. Louis printed the library committee's condemnation of *Huck*, and within two days, the story reached the Pacific Coast, arousing special interest there, because of Mark Twain's four years as a newspaper-man in the West.

Everywhere, editors and reviewers felt called on to comment, ridiculing or supporting the committee's decision and arguments. The strongest denunciation of Mark Twain and his book came from the influential and highly conservative Springfield (Massachusetts) *Republican*, a longtime enemy. It was time, said the *Republican*, that the power of "Mr. Clemens's" pen name "should cease to carry into homes and libraries unworthy productions." Admitting that Mark Twain was a true humorist and a powerful satirist, the *Republican* promptly qualified its praise. His "vein of satire" often "degenerates into a gross trifling with every fine feeling. The trouble with Mr. Clemens is that he has no reliable sense of propriety." (Undeniably true!) The editor had not read the book he condemned, but he had no need to; the "advertising samples," as he called them, that had appeared in *Century* were enough. Simply reading them, said the *Republican, must* be harmful.

Huck had his defenders, vigorous ones. The San Francisco *Chronicle* pointed out that *Huckleberry Finn* was in no sense a boy's book— "the more general knowledge one has, the better he is fitted to appreciate this book." The *Chronicle* praised its humor, its characterization, its satire, and its realism (particularly in the Grangerford-Shepherdson feud), adding that the "large class of people impervious to a joke" might find it "dreary, flat, stale and unprofitable." A Georgia paper saw the episode as one battle in a cultural war; Mark Twain was condemned because he "refused to worship Longfellow, Emerson and Whittier."

But essentially the quarrel over *Huckleberry Finn* was a clash of attitudes, and perhaps of generations, not of regions. In late May, Thomas and Anna Fitch, old friends from Nevada days, wrote to Mark Twain that they had just finished *Huckleberry Finn* and had then reread *The Prince and the Pauper*, for the third time. Twain had money enough, urged Fitch; let him stop producing "potboilers" like *Huckleberry Finn* and write another *Prince and the Pauper* instead. That was the kind of book Mark Twain should write— genteel, instructive, more often pathetic than humorous.

Mark Twain always knew what the papers were saying about him, and he was not in the habit of letting attacks pass in silence. When the Concord Free Trade Club offered him honorary membership (perhaps trying to make amends for the action of the library committee), he saw his chance. He replied with a satirical letter of thanks to the "great commonwealth of Massachusetts" for the "kindnesses" it had bestowed on him (referring to the decision against him in the suit to prevent Estes & Lauriat from offering *Huckleberry Finn* for sale at a discount), thanked the committee of the Concord library for increasing sales—anyone in Concord who wanted to read *Huckleberry Finn* would now have to buy it—and for causing buyers to read it "instead of merely intending to do so after the usual way of the world." Reading it, they would discover, to "their own indignant disappointment, that there was nothing objectionable in the book, after all." Finally, he thanked the Free Trade Club itself for endorsing him as fit to associate with men "whom even the moral icebergs of the Concord library committee are bound to respect."

That letter had been carefully composed; it had gone to Howells for his suggestions, then Twain had made revisions of his own—the climactic phrase, "moral icebergs," had gone through "moral glaciers" and "moral icicles." ("The difference between the *almost right* word and the *right* word is really a large matter," he once observed; it was "the difference between the lightning bug and the lightning.") He signed the letter "S. L. Clemens," then added a postscript: "(Known to the Concord Winter School of Philosophy as 'Mark Twain.')" As almost every paper noted, Concord was the home of an annual Summer School of Philosophy.

That letter had been written for the newspapers, not for the Free Trade Club, and it was quickly printed in full in Boston and New York. Other papers picked it up, to make their readers laugh. Twain's opponents were infuriated: he had shown no repentance, no respect for the moral and critical authority of Concord and New England; he had even boasted that his sales might be increased by the library's condemnation. In a long editorial, the Boston *Advertiser* saw the affair not merely as a matter of one objectionable book, but as a cultural battle. Noting the "eagerness and unanimity" with which libraries throughout the country had followed Concord's example—a deliberate lie; they had not—and the "general condemnation" of *Huckleberry Finn*, the *Advertiser* found evidence of improving public taste. "The old school of coarse, flippant and irreverent joke makers," represented by Mark Twain, the most successful of them all, had lost favor.

Worst of all, for the *Advertiser*, was the fondness of these "joke

makers" for "the corroding element of burlesque." Nothing was
sacred to them; "over subjects dignified by age, tragedy and romance" they laid "the slimy trail of the vulgar humorist." Now that
Twain's latest effort had "ignominiously failed"—it had not—the
Advertiser charitably hoped that he would employ his talents and
industry "in some manner more creditable and more beneficent to
his country." It seems a classic example of cultural provincialism,
to assume that New England's denunciation (specifically, the judgment of the Concord library committee and the attacks of a few
newspapers) had ensured the failure of *Huckleberry Finn*.

Twain might have considered that the violence of his critics demonstrated the originality of his work, but he was not likely to be
philosophical about such denunciations. Instead, furious at what
seemed to be personal attacks carried out by the *Advertiser* and the
Springfield *Republican*, he planned a vituperative reply, just as he
had done four years earlier for the supposed insults of Whitelaw
Reid in the New York *Tribune*. On April 4, he sent Webster a
"Prefatory Remark," to be given to the press immediately and to
be inserted in all future editions of *Huckleberry Finn*. Huck, said
the note, "is not an imaginary character" but had been modeled on
the editors of the *Advertiser* and the *Republican*. "In character, language, clothing, education, instinct, & origin, he is the painstakingly
& truthfully drawn photograph of these two gentlemen as they
were in the time of their boyhood," although his language had been
"softened, here & there, in deference to the taste of a more modern
& fastidious day."

Then he, or Livy, thought better, and the note was never released.
After all, it seemed to concede the case, to admit that Huck was as
coarse and vulgar as genteel reviewers had claimed. Instead, writing
in the privacy of his notebook, perhaps for circulation to selected
friends, Twain fantasized retribution for his enemies. The editor of
the Boston *Advertiser*, he declared, was "taking . . . revenge upon
me" for an unlucky accident. Twain had "had the misfortune to
catch him in a situation which will not bear describing." But he
described it: "the accident in a sitz-bath with a steel-trap to the
editor of the Springfield Republican." The two enemies had fused
in his mind. A year later, still smarting: "Tell Smith how the Boston
Ad man got his ——— caught in the steel trap." And later still, he
was explicit at last: "How the editor of the Springfield Republican
got his Nüsse [nuts] caught in the steel trap." Castration seemed

to him to be the fitting punishment for that pair of moral eunuchs.

With every new book, Mark Twain hoped for a favorable and definitive review, by an authoritative critic in a major journal, a review that would "set the sheep jumping," as he liked to put it, that would set the tone and establish the issues for lesser critics and give them some catchwords to repeat. When Howells had edited the *Atlantic*, he had always been willing to provide such a review— Howells believed deeply in the genius of Mark Twain—but he had left the magazine to gain more time for his own writing. The review of *Huckleberry Finn* in the May issue of *Century*, written by Thomas Sergeant Perry, was finally what Twain must have hoped for. Making the inevitable comparison with *Tom Sawyer*, Perry firmly stated the superiority of *Huck*. Its first-person narrative added vivid immediacy to its episodes and made it, unlike *Tom Sawyer*, "for the most part, a consistent whole."

Like other reviewers, Perry singled out the episode of the Grangerford-Shepherdson feud for praise, but he found its highest excellence in just the quality that conservative critics deplored: the total absence of moralizing, of "signposts and directions" telling the reader how he was to understand it. For Huck to express either condemnation or surprise "would be bad art." That comment would have baffled the reviewers who demanded morality—by which they meant moralizing.

Like other readers again, Perry found documentary value in Twain's record of the "hideous fringe of civilization" bordering the Mississippi in the 1830s and '40s. As for Huck himself, he represented "the better side of the ruffianism" of American life. And Perry recognized a deeper significance in Mark Twain's work, and in the tradition from which it sprang. Two years before, writing as "An American on American Humor," Perry had seen American humor as the inevitable outgrowth of American democracy. And the spirit of American democracy was destructive, "at war with all the literary conventions we have inherited" from Greece and Rome. (Whitman, he added, was a collaborator in that work of destruction.) Those conventions were weak and vulnerable in America, depending for survival on the "thin varnish of European culture" along the Atlantic coast.

In his review, Perry stated clearly a point suggested but never directly expressed in some of the newspaper comments—the falling interest of the final section—and located its source: "the caricature of books of adventure [through Tom's fantastically elaborate schemes for rescuing Jim] leaves us cold." That burlesque had no place in *Huckleberry Finn*. There was a review that might have set the sheep jumping, as Twain hoped, or might even have guided reviewers and editors to a more searching examination of the book itself, instead of arguing for or against the Concord library committee's decision, but it came too late. Instead of setting the tone or defining the issues, it finished the critical discussion.

But of all the contemporary comments, only two seemed to recognize the full value of his book. "I have just read Huck through . . . It is the best book ever written," wrote one admirer, William Alden, to Mark Twain on March 15, 1885. And on June 1, when the critical controversy had ended, Joel Chandler Harris observed, also in a letter to Twain, that *Huckleberry Finn* was "the most original contribution that has yet been made to American literature."

Huckleberry Finn had the reception that might have been expected, considering the official morality and the literary conventions of the 1880s. Faced with a truly innovative work, the reviewers, like reviewers at most times and places, were at a loss. Dimly recognizing the book's originality, they lacked a vocabulary to describe its techniques and effects. In the end, they were likely to fall back on a single word, "grotesque," to sum up its unconventionalities in characters, episodes, language, and humor. They failed also to recognize *Huck*'s literary ancestry—its clear affinities with the centuries-old tradition of the picaresque romance, dealing with the adventures of a boy or young man not particularly troubled with moral scruples, as he views the underside of his society in the company of rogues and criminals. Probably it never occurred to them to consider the influence of tradition on a work by Mark Twain.

In the end, the battle of cultures, or at least of attitudes, had been neither won nor lost. Gentility had had its say, had won support across the country, but had not succeeded in getting *Huckleberry Finn* banned from most libraries and had not interfered with its sale. For a time, old-fashioned readers and reviewers would go on dismissing the book as rubbish, occasionally regretting that its author had wasted his talent. "It is only when as 'Mark Twain' he writes some such trash as *The Adventures of Huckleberry Finn*," as one of them remarked in 1894, "that this really capable writer can make sure of an appreciative hearing." But *Huck* had found its public, regardless of what some library committees and editors might say. With its final sale of 51,000 copies, it was a solid success.

Writing to Webster on March 18, just when the story of the Concord library's action had broken, Twain had exultingly predicted that the news "will sell 25,000 copies." It did not; Webster's report on March 14—39,000 copies sold, 10,000 more printing—almost equaled the final, quite satisfactory sale. By mid-April, Webster no longer mentions *Huck* in his letters to Twain. Did the Concord committee or the Boston *Advertiser* and Springfield *Republican*, then, prevent *Huckleberry Finn* from becoming a runaway success? Probably not; the sale was normal, close to the figure for *A Tramp Abroad*; the book was bought by readers who knew what to expect from its author and were not likely to be put off by warnings of "irreverence" and "coarseness." That was what they read him for—although not only that.

A few months later, the librarian of the Buffalo YMCA would write to Mark Twain, asking him to contribute to a collection of manuscripts by American authors. Mark Twain seldom threw away an unfinished manuscript, but he never showed much reverence for manuscripts of published works. Fortunately, he had something on hand. "Sent what was left of Huck Finn," he noted on the envelope. The manuscript is now in the Buffalo Public Library.

Huck's audience would steadily grow, both at home and abroad. Three years later, Robert Louis Stevenson would write of his admiration for "a book which I have read four times and am quite ready to begin again," and in 1890, an English critic, Andrew Lang, would announce that the great American novel had been written—it was *Huckleberry Finn*. And William Morris—socialist, poet, and designer—became "an incurable Huckfinnomaniac," or at least so Bernard Shaw would assure Mark Twain. Kipling would show his admiration in *Kim*, in which a resourceful English boy traverses India on the Great North Road and encounters its immensely varied life, as Huck had encountered the South while he journeyed down the Mississippi. Since then, translated into dozens of languages, *Huckleberry Finn* has traveled around the world. Huck and Jim on their raft have joined Don Quixote charging his windmills and Ahab pursuing the white whale—images that seem to lead an independent life, known to millions who have never read the books from which they are derived.

Simultaneously, *Huck* began to work its influence on American literature, as an early and essential part of the literary experience of generation after generation of American writers. (Twenty-five years or so later, the young Ernest Hemingway, aged ten or eleven, would have himself photographed in the role of Huck Finn, wearing overalls and a straw hat, barefoot, holding a string of fish in place of Huck's rabbit.) Twenty years after that, in *The Green Hills of Africa*, he would make his famous declaration that "all modern American literature comes from one book"—*Huckleberry Finn*. T. S. Eliot would echo that judgment in 1950, declaring that in *Huckleberry Finn*, Mark Twain had joined the company of those rare authors "who have discovered a new way of writing, valid not only for themselves, but for others." (Not that Huck's language can be literally taken over by other writers; its equivalent must be invented, as Saul Bellow did in *The Adventures of Augie March*, or J. D. Salinger in *The Catcher in the Rye*.) *Huckleberry Finn* has become the unlikeliest of all classics. Literary gentility and official morality had lost the battle after all. But not completely, for that cultural war was also fought within Mark Twain himself; he never quite recognized the superiority of *Huck* to his other books. In 1896, he published *The Personal Recollections of Joan of Arc*, an undistinguished historical romance reverent enough to find a place in the Concord public library, and ten years later, he would rank *Huckleberry Finn* and *Joan of Arc* equally, as his own favorites among his books. At times he would even put *Joan* first.

The sales of *Huck* encouraged him to consider, once again, a sequel, or at least another story of old times on the Mississippi: "Write the story of a cub and pilot," he suggested to himself in his notebook, "and of a jour [journeyman] printer"—that seems a more promising situation than Huck and Tom among the Indians. Yet that story was never written, probably never begun. Apparently, Mark Twain had said all that he had to say about old times along the Mississippi, and he had another, all-consuming interest: Webster and Company was preparing to publish the memoirs of General Ulysses S. Grant.

TEN

Publisher to a Hero

"O ne of the highest satisfactions of Mark Twain's often su-
premely satisfactory life was his relation to Grant," Howells
would observe twenty-five years later, in *My Mark Twain*, and
Twain himself would have agreed wholeheartedly. Grant had been
important in his life since the fall of 1879, when Twain spoke in
Chicago at the grand reunion of the Army of the Tennessee, presided over by its old commander, just returned from a world tour.
Twain would remember that evening—he had made Grant laugh—
and his interest in the general had been kept alive through occasional
contacts ever since. (The interest had been one-sided; Grant was
barely aware of Mark Twain's existence, and probably had read
none of Twain's books—he was not a reading man.) When the ex-
President visited Hartford in the fall of 1880, Twain was called on
to make the introductory speech. Learning with surprise and in-
dignation that the general "had not even income enough to enable
him to live as respectably as a third-rate physician," he decided to
make that national ingratitude his text.

After listing Grant's accomplishments, both as soldier and as
President, and mentioning England's reward to Wellington after
Waterloo—a dukedom and a fortune—Twain concluded with a
fervent peroration, expressing America's gratitude, then collapsing
into anticlimax: "Your country loves you, your country is proud of
you, your country is grateful to you . . . Your country stands ready,
from this day forth, to testify her measureless love and pride and
gratitude toward you, in every conceivable—inexpensive way."

He visited Grant with Twichell not long after, asking him to urge
the Chinese government to keep its students in America (a hundred

of them had been sent, and most of them were being educated in Hartford). Twichell had come primed with a speech to explain the case, but Grant, who had visited China on his world tour, soon showed that he "was master of the whole matter and needed no information from anybody," that he was deeply interested, and that "as always," he "was not only ready to do what we asked of him, but a hundred times more." He wrote to the imperial government, and for a time, the program was saved.

Twain and Howells together sought Grant's help in March of 1882, calling on him in his Wall Street office (Grant had bought a partnership in a brokerage firm) and asking him to use his influence to prevent Howells's father from being ousted from his position as American consul in Toronto. Without hesitation, Grant agreed to intervene and invited them to lunch—nothing more than baked beans and coffee, Howells would remember, "but eating them with Grant was like sitting down to baked beans and coffee with Julius Caesar." Twain urged the General to write his memoirs, suggested publishing them by subscription, and promised an enormous sale. But Grant no longer felt any need for money; he doubted his ability to write, was sure that his memoirs would not sell, and promised only that he would make full notes, which his children could turn into a book, if they chose. Twain went a third time to Grant in the winter of 1884, with Yung Wing, the Chinese minister to the United States, to ask for aid in selling bonds for building railroads in China. Grant was offered a generous commission, which he declined absolutely, promising his help simply for "the pleasure he would derive from being useful to China."

Then, after a reading in New York near the beginning of his tour with Cable, as Twain came out of the lecture hall one evening into the darkness and rain, he recognized the voice of Richard Watson Gilder, editor of *Century*, speaking to a companion: "Do you know General Grant has actually determined to write his memoirs and publish them? He has said so today, in so many words." Twain's interest was aroused at once. He overtook Gilder, went home with him, and learned that Grant was in serious financial difficulties and had agreed to write three pieces for *Century's* monumental "Battles and Leaders of the Civil War" series—a history of the war written by participants on both sides—for a payment of $500 each. Having once started, Grant had decided to complete his memoirs.

Mark Twain was a publisher himself, and instantly he saw a

tremendous opportunity. He paid a call on the Grants the next day and learned that much of the book had been written and a contract with *Century* had been drawn up, but not yet signed. Grant read the contract aloud, and as he listened, Twain realized that the *Century* people had no idea of the book's potential. They offered the General a choice between half profits ("after subtracting *every sort of expense connected with it*, including *office rent, clerk hire, advertising*, and *everything else* [italics Twain's]") and a 10 percent royalty, just what they would have given any unknown writer. The magazine had offered Grant $1,500 for three long articles—a grotesque underpayment—yet he was grateful for it. That money had saved him from "the grip of poverty." Twain could do nothing then, as he had to leave New York almost at once, but he did not forget.

For the past year and a half, everything had gone badly for Grant. His bid for the Republican Presidential nomination in 1880 had failed. (War was his trade, politics a poor substitute, but he needed the income of the Presidency.) Abandoning politics, he had turned to business, for which he had even less aptitude. One of his sons, Ulysses Jr., had gone into partnership with Ferdinand Ward, a bold speculator who was generally considered the most promising young man on the Street. His father bought into the business, risking his total savings.

Grant & Ward seemed to flourish, with Ward, the young Napoleon of Finance, as the newspapers liked to call him, apparently earning incredible profits for investors and for the firm. Like Mark Twain's Colonel Sellers, Ward talked in millions, but unlike Sellers, he seemed to make them. In three years, the firm's capital grew from $400,000 to $15 million, and Grant believed that he, personally, was worth a million. For the first time in his life, he had a bank account on which he could draw freely. He could buy a town house on New York's Upper East Side; he could spend as much as he liked on horses and cigars, his two luxuries. His future, and his wife's, appeared safe.

Century first proposed that Grant write an account of one or two of his battles in December of 1883, but Grant, vigorous and apparently prosperous at sixty-one, showed no interest. Then his luck began to turn. On Christmas Eve, he fell on an icy pavement, badly straining a thigh muscle and causing intense pain. For weeks he was confined to bed, during which time he suffered through a severe attack of pleurisy. By spring, prospects seemed brighter, he could at least hobble about on crutches and drive his own carriage once more, he was even being talked about again for the Presidency—and Grant & Ward still flourished.

But the spectacular profits that Ward had seemed to make did not exist. The young Napoleon was a confidence man, receiving money to invest but investing it for himself, paying his victims imaginary "profits" from the principal to persuade them to invest still more, making loans for the firm and accepting stocks as security, then using those stocks as collateral for his own borrowing, sometimes pledging the same stocks for several different loans, and keeping two sets of books, one for himself and one for the Grants. While the General enjoyed his dignified and seemingly profitable position, Ward speculated wildly.

On a Sunday in early May of 1884, he suddenly announced that the firm needed to raise $150,000 immediately, to meet a temporary difficulty. Grant went to William H. Vanderbilt, the richest American of the day, who at once gave him the loan he asked for, without security. Ward took the money and disappeared. The locked safe in which securities were supposed to be kept was found empty. Grant & Ward collapsed, its assets no longer existed, and Grant himself was left penniless. Worse, he might have lost his reputation as well. It was hard to believe that he had not been a partner in the fraud, or at least that he had had no suspicion of what was going on. Where did he think those incredible profits had come from? How could he have been so ignorant of his partner's actions? He had gone to his office regularly, but what had he been doing there? The best that could be said was that he had been almost criminally negligent, letting his name be used by a swindler without taking the most routine financial precautions, meanwhile enjoying the prestige and profits that he had done nothing to earn.

The hero disgraced—Grant's situation would grip the imagination of Mark Twain, and thirteen years later, in a fragment entitled "Which Was the Dream?," he would imaginatively combine his own financial disaster of 1894, when Webster and Company failed, with the collapse of Grant & Ward. The brilliant young Major General X, idol of the nation for his services in the Mexican War, already a senator and destined for the Presidency, seems a composite of Grant and Twain. His exploits are Grant's; his wife and daughters are Twain's. His ruin and disgrace represent them both. He is crushed by a relentless succession of disasters, beginning on his daughter's birthday (his mansion burns and everything is lost, the insurance has not been paid, his bank accounts are empty, the California gold mine in which he has invested proves to be non-existent, he is charged with forgery). The General's only defense is an unbelievable, almost criminal, credulity: he had utterly trusted his man of business (as Grant trusted Ward), who had lied to him, betrayed him, even forged his signature.

With the disgraceful failure of his firm, Grant had hardly enough money left to pay his household bills. When *Century* renewed its offer, he had no choice but to accept. Small as it was, the first payment came as a godsend. And as he wrote the articles, Grant discovered in himself a gift for clear and exact narration. Writing came easily, almost naturally, to him. That might have been ex-pected; during the war, he had been able to absorb and comprehend the most complicated military situations and to write the appro-priate orders, instantly and with such clarity that they could not be misunderstood. What could not have been expected were the telling anecdotes, the memorable thumbnail characterizations of both Union and Confederate commanders, the quiet, ironic asides, and the absence of self-promotion and apology. Both magazine and author began to consider the possibility of a book.

But even as he wrote, Grant's health continued to fail. He smoked endless cigars, rank, black, and poisonous—"the most appalling smoker of his time," an early biographer called him. (The *Nation*, a year later, would mention "the suspicion suggested by General Grant's death . . . that tobacco is to some extent responsible for the alarming increase of cancer.") Swallowing had become painful in the summer of 1884; he had consulted doctors, but by the time that cancer of the throat had been positively diagnosed, the cancer had grown until it could not be excised. No other treatment existed.

When Mark Twain had seen him in November of 1884, Grant still looked in reasonable health. But on Twain's next visit, near the end of the reading tour, he "was astonished to see how thin and weak" Grant looked. The papers had reported that all of Grant's symptoms had disappeared, and Twain remarked that he had been glad to hear that news. Grant "smiled & said, 'Yes—if it had only been true.'" A physician who was present startled Twain "by saying that the General's condition was the opposite of encouraging." Euphemisms were not needed; Grant knew the truth. As Twain was leaving, Fred, the oldest of Grant's sons, followed him to the

Albert Bigelow Paine's *Mark Twain: A Biography* referred to this photograph as "Mark Twain at 50"

Mark Twain, 1868

Olivia Clemens in the early 1870s

Mark Twain with Olivia and their daughters

The Clemens home in Hartford, Connecticut

Susy at thirteen, 1885

Joseph Twichell

William Dean Howells

Mark Twain and George Washington Cable, 1884

Henry Huttleston Rogers

door, to "stun" him by confiding that the doctors considered his father "to be under sentence of death," and not likely to live more than two or three weeks longer.

As he worked on the articles for *Century*, Grant realized that after all, he could write his memoirs. By doing so, he might pay off his $150,000 debt to Vanderbilt, he might provide for his wife and his children and grandchildren, and he could rehabilitate himself before the American people. Once he began, the writing engrossed him; except for his family, it became his only interest. By the time of Mark Twain's second visit, he had already been at work for several months, five or six hours a day. His life story, up to Appomattox, seemed a national epic. The book was dedicated "to the American soldier and sailor," and the opening sentence established Grant's credentials as a national hero: "My family is American, and has been for generations, in all its branches, direct and collateral."

He began his story at the beginning, with his childhood and his years at West Point, then provided lively and detailed recollections of the Mexican War as seen by a young lieutenant, and briefly summed up the discouraging years after his resignation from the army in 1854, until he had been rescued from failure by the Civil War. By the end of the winter, he had almost reached his appointment as supreme commander of the Union armies in the winter of 1864, and it was clear that the book would run to two volumes, if the author lived to finish it.

Mark Twain had had to go back on the road almost as soon as he learned of Grant's intention, but through the winter, while Cable and Twain were barnstorming the Northern states and Canada, Webster had been negotiating with Grant, reporting regularly to Twain. Finally, he made a dramatic, irresistible offer: in view of the sales of the issue of *Century* containing Grant's first article (200,000 instead of the usual 135,000), Webster and Company would pay 70 percent of net profits, defined as all proceeds beyond the cost of printing, binding, and advertising. Other publishers, including *Century*, might have matched that offer, but they could not match Webster and Company's facilities for subscription publishing, demonstrated by the success of *Huckleberry Finn*. Grant agreed to supply material enough to make two 500-page volumes, to submit the manuscript for the first volume by August 1, 1885, and for the second by August 1, 1886. (He would not live to see even that first deadline.)

On March 2, 1885, Fred Grant wrote to rival publishers to announce his father's choice of Webster and Company, which at once advanced $10,000 to its new author, relieving him of immediate financial anxieties. The publicity value of that announcement was enormous. Webster and Company instantly became, as Paine writes, "the most conspicuous publisher in the world," or at least in America. But as Mark Twain said, and as everybody except Webster knew, "I am Webster & Co., myself, substantially." For the next five months, the lives of Grant and his publisher would be inseparably intertwined. (Twain even began to imagine that Grant had nearly captured him in the opening days of the Civil War—an impossibility, since Grant did not campaign in that corner of Missouri until weeks after Sam Clemens had taken a stagecoach for Nevada.) Mark Twain had become a central figure in a great national event, at once a celebration and a tragedy. Grant might have saved the Union, but now Mark Twain would save him, and his family as well.

Outwardly, nothing could be more different from the dour reserve of Grant (a man who said little and never showed feeling) than Mark Twain's lively and continuous self-expression, yet the two men had much in common. Each of them knew the bitterness of failure—Twain in his years of debt and discouragement in San Francisco between 1864 and 1866 (when he had once threatened suicide if he could not get out of debt within three months), Grant with his miserable resignation from the army in 1854, under threat of dismissal for drunkenness. Both had walked the streets of San Francisco, penniless and in debt.

Each man had served a variety of apprenticeships, each had seized his chance when it finally came, and succeeded spectacularly—Mark Twain at thirty-three, with publication of *The Innocents Abroad*; Grant at thirty-nine, with the capture of Fort Henry and Fort Donelson. Both came out of middle America, spoke its language, and shared its ambitions, particularly the ambition for quick, easy money, and admiration for those who could gain it. They could understand each other. (The bafflement of Henry Adams, a New England intellectual, at the phenomenon of Grant would have puzzled Mark Twain.) Grant's generalship, like Twain's writing, seemed uniquely American. Mark Twain was not an author like other authors; Grant was not a general like other generals. The public recognized that and gave them a status of their own. To most Americans, nothing could have seemed more fitting than that Mark

Twain, America's most popular writer, should publish the memoirs of Grant, America's greatest living hero.

On learning that Grant planned to write his memoirs, Twain instantly foresaw a sale of 300,000 copies. He could recognize that possibility because Grant's potential audience was the audience that he himself had always written for. As for the magazine's offer of a 10 percent royalty for the *Memoirs*, Mark Twain commented in his notebook that it was "the most colossal bit of cheek the 19th century can show," a "cold-blooded attempt to rob a trusting & inexperienced man." Almost twenty years later, his friend Henry H. Rogers, a Standard Oil millionaire who helped Twain pull himself out of bankruptcy, would remark that "Clemens has a very remarkable business head for large things, but absolutely none for small . . . To see his mind go to wreck and ruin over a poor little complexity that wouldn't puzzle a child—why it's pathetic!" For Grant's *Memoirs*, the vision was enough. Webster could handle the details.

Century had been mean-spirited and shortsighted, in about equal proportions, throughout its dealings with Grant. Although his three articles already published had sharply increased circulation and were far longer than the magazine's average, the magazine offered no bonus to supplement the meager payment stipulated in the contract and insisted on its right to include any or all of his articles in its *Battles and Leaders* collection without further payment. Roswell Smith, the publisher of *Century*, had refused to guarantee a sale of at least 25,000 copies of the *Memoirs*, exclaiming that he "wouldn't risk such a guaranty on any book that ever was published." Grant was under no legal or moral obligation to *Century*; there was no reason why Twain should not intervene, to save him from a disastrous commitment. There was another consequence; with this contract, Webster and Company became a true publishing house.

Webster and Company had its contract, but no one could predict whether its new author would live to finish his book. Grant could write with surprising speed, but he revised carefully, constantly checking the accuracy of his facts. It seemed more important to him that the work should be perfect, as far as it went, than that it should be complete. At first, doubting his own abilities, he had invited Adam Badeau, one of his staff officers in the last campaigns and author of *A Military History of Ulysses S. Grant*, to assist him. But little help was needed; his son Fred could gather materials, and Grant proved more than able to do his own writing. There was nothing for Badeau to do but read the manuscript from time to time and comment on it, and even that role was lost when Mark Twain appeared. Badeau left in anger.

Only once during those weeks was Grant distracted by an outside interest. Twain was with him when "a telegram arrived that the last act of the expiring congress late this morning retired him with full General's rank and accompanying emoluments [a pension]." (Grant had received no pension because he had resigned his commission before taking the oath of office as President in 1869.) That restoration of his military rank brought a much needed income, but its symbolism meant more: his rehabilitation in the eyes of the country. Grant showed his pleasure—his famed "imperturbability" had broken down under the impact of good news, as it never did under bad. He rigidly suppressed all signs of anxiety and all evidence of suffering, as far as that was physically possible. ("He is the most suppressive man I ever knew," said one of his doctors.)

While Grant wrote, his publisher prepared. Webster and Company moved to spacious quarters on Union Square, in New York City. The business had outgrown Twain's original intention simply to publish his own work, and a new contract was drawn up, recognizing Charley Webster's increased responsibilities and allowing him one third of the firm's profits until he had received $20,000, and one tenth after that. The company would continue to publish Mark Twain's books and give him the same terms as Grant, 70 percent of net profits. Then came the immediate, practical requirements: paper to be ordered, in enormous amounts; press time to be contracted for; binderies to pledge themselves to work exclusively on the book; general agents to be found and canvassers to be hired; and prospectuses to be prepared for the canvassers. Meanwhile, the *Memoirs* had still to be completed, and Grant was dying of cancer.

Webster began to exhibit signs of megalomania. The success of the *Memoirs*, he boasted, "will be largely due to my personal efforts," and he calculated that "my own *personal* profits on General Grant's book within the coming two years will not fall below $30,000." He saw himself as a Napoleon of publishers, but there was no need for a Napoleon. To sell the *Memoirs*, all that was needed was to place them before the public—a job requiring nothing more than hard work and a moderate amount of organizing ability. Mark Twain, not self-effacing as a rule, recognized that Grant's book was now the firm's most valuable property and proposed that Webster

and Company should have new envelopes printed, announcing itself
as publishers of "Mark Twain's Books & the forthcoming *Personal
Memoirs of General Grant*," adding that the italicized words should
be printed "in just a *shade* larger type, & in RED INK."

Promotion stressed both the historical and the personal significance of Grant's work. The publisher's announcement asked what
the demand might have been for the memoirs of Napoleon, or
Wellington, or Washington, then declared that Grant—"THE
GREATEST CAPTAIN OF MODERN TIMES" it called him, in boldface
type—had written his account of "THE GREATEST AND MOST
BLOODY REBELLION in the history of the world," and assured the
public that "the great bulk of the profits on this book go to General
Grant himself [last three words boldface], and it is the only one
which he has ever written or in which he has any interest whatever
[last eight words boldface]." That final statement was needed; there
were unscrupulous publishers ready to supply their own hack-
written Grant books and even to hint that the General or his family
might share in the proceeds.

Peace was made with *Century*; neither side could afford a quarrel.
A contract drawn up in mid-April provided that Webster and Company would allow the magazine to print the remaining Grant articles
that it had bought. To provide time for the articles to appear first
in the magazine, publication of the first volume would not take
place before December 1, 1885—hardly a concession, since the
books could not have been printed and bound before then—with
the second volume to follow three months later. *Century* invited
Twain to contribute a piece on his own experiences in the Civil
War, and he eagerly accepted: "I would like mighty well to be in
the Century War Series . . . the War Series is the greatest thing of
these modern times, & nobody who is anybody can well afford to
be unrepresented in it." Mark Twain knew he was somebody, and
admitted it freely.

Webster set to work, preparing for publication of the *Memoirs*
and organizing the sales campaign. By April 22, he could report to
Mark Twain that he was at work on the prospectus, and when that
was done, would appoint the general agents. Better still, "I have
obtained the first 313 pages of manuscript which brings us up to
Shiloh & some of Vicksburg." The prospectus offered a novelty, a
full-page daguerreotype of Grant as a young second lieutenant at
the time of his Mexican service (everyone knew what he had done

in the Civil War; hardly anyone knew of his record in Mexico). It reproduced Grant's dedication, "to the American soldier and sailor," stressing the national significance of the work, and the title page and table of contents. Sample pages presented unfamiliar material: Grant's boyhood, the Mexican War, the opening days of the Civil War. (Newspapers promptly began to reprint the excerpts, but that was expected—and it made good advertising.) There was even a facsimile of a letter by Grant, asserting that the book was entirely his own work. Sales strategy had been determined; the appeal would be above all to patriotism and sentiment, stating the work's literary and historical value, but stressing the fact "that it was the work of a soldier who had saved the country written in his last hours to pay debts of honor and to leave a provision for his family."

The two-volume set was priced at seven dollars in the standard cloth binding. That made it a major purchase, in a time when a farmer's cash income for a year would usually amount to only a few hundred dollars, when a workman would have to labor for three or four ten-hour days to earn seven dollars. However, no payment was required until the first volume was delivered, in December. Buy now, pay later was the rule in subscription publishing. In any case, the high price must have seemed only fitting for this book, the last word of the man who, next to Lincoln, had done most to save the nation. Publication of the *Memoirs* would be a national event; one could not expect to participate at a bargain price.

"Furnish canvassers a list of truthful & sensible things to say— not rot," Mark Twain had suggested, and Webster prepared a thirty- seven-page pamphlet combining hucksterism and moral uplift, thor- oughly in the spirit of the time. The canvasser should keep his prospectus out of sight until he was admitted into the house, then introduce himself by name and shake hands, saying, "I called to give you an opportunity to see General Grant's book, of which so much has been said in the papers." He should be "rapid and en- thusiastic," leaving no time for objections, although the instructions warned that "brass and cheekiness" were "disgusting" and should be avoided, and he should accept no excuses of "hard times," point- ing out that "the cost of a cigar a day" would pay for the book by delivery time. Customers would be released from their orders only in case of sickness or death in the family or loss of house, barn, or store by fire.

The instructions contained a direct lie—which it is not likely that

Mark Twain approved—stating that Grant owned the book and would receive all profits. The contract had been unprecedentedly generous, but Webster and Company was not a charitable enterprise. Neither was there any mention of the fact that Webster and Company had awarded itself the lucrative general agency for the New York region, thus saving the agent's commission on about 15,000 sets. That, too, was simply good business, in no way lessening the author's earnings, yet mention of it might have tarnished the enterprise. The canvasser must not be daunted by cold or stormy weather; people were more likely to be at home, and they would admire his pluck.

Prices were not to be mentioned until the prospect's interest had been thoroughly aroused. "One of the strongest arguments that can be used to get a man's order is by telling him of his influence"— or that all his neighbors had ordered the book and would wonder why he hadn't. But the salesman must not forget his mission as an agent of civilization, "causing dark ignorance to recede before the light of truth." With "a little real earnestness," success was assured. Certainly Mark Twain was in earnest. He was as much concerned with sales as Webster, but he also believed deeply in the literary and historical value of the *Memoirs*.

The excerpts in the prospectus and the *Century* articles that had already appeared proved that Grant could write a terse narrative prose and marshal complex masses of detail, while enlivening his account with occasional vivid details and telling personal comments on men he had fought with, or against. The Mexican experiences, taking up a substantial part of the first volume, offered picturesque novelty as well, and incidentally provided the best account of the war by any participant on the American side. It was also a surprisingly unbiased account, for Grant viewed that war as an unprovoked act of aggression. Knowledgeable readers might question Grant's narrative here and there; they might see that he never acknowledged that his army had been surprised at Shiloh, or that he skimped on his account of the useless slaughter at Cold Harbor. But to the general public, the *Memoirs* gave an impression of transparent honesty and absolute candor. Here, it seemed, was a book written by a man who would not, almost could not, conceal or distort the truth.

But success did not depend on Grant's unexpected literary skill. To the North, with Lincoln gone, Grant symbolized the war, the victory, the reunion. And he was now suffering and in need, racing against death to record his actions and, in doing so, to provide for his family. The appeal was irresistible. By April 8, when Webster and Company had not yet even received all the manuscript for the first volume, or appointed all the general agents, Mark Twain could report exultantly to Livy that twenty thousand sets had been ordered from two states alone, Michigan and Iowa—"wait till you hear from the other 37!" Livy had been "a little afraid to have me venture on the book & take all the risks" for only 30 percent of the profits, but now she could be secure. That first report, from two states out of thirty-seven, afforded "a clear profit to *us* of $13,000—& over $26,000 to Mrs. Grant." "To Mrs. Grant"—the author, as everyone knew, would never live to share in those profits.

The appearance of the *Memoirs* would be the most important publishing event of the decade, culminating and concluding a kind of national catharsis as the nation relived its great crisis. Along with Grant, Mark Twain was the center. For the next nine months, he would attempt almost no writing of his own except for his own war memoir, "The Private History of a Campaign That Failed." Nothing that he might do himself would have seemed as important as the sale and publication of the *Memoirs*. Wishing to document his own involvement, in May, Twain hired a shorthand reporter and dictated an account of his relationship to Grant and Grant's book. With the contract signed, he spent much of his time in New York, regularly visiting Grant, both as publisher and as friend, observing and participating in that national rite of passage. He even read proof—the manuscript was being set in type as fast as Grant wrote it—and he hated proofreading. But his real function was to encourage and divert. "It is curious & dreadful," he noted after one visit, "to sit up this way & talk cheerful nonsense to Gen. Grant & he under sentence of death with that cancer." Cheerful nonsense was just what the situation required, and nobody could have supplied it better. Sentence of death might have been pronounced, but Grant was still a living man, and he could not always be writing the *Memoirs*.

Well before the end of the winter, news of Grant's illness had become public knowledge. The doctors issued regular bulletins on his condition, the newspapers set up a deathwatch, churches held days of prayer. Death seemed imminent. Grant showed the "limp whiteness of a suffering invalid," observed one reporter; all his teeth were gone, and his hair and whiskers had been allowed to grow. He could barely eat and had lost nearly a third of his weight, he slept fitfully, he was in almost constant pain. The anxiety was not over whether Grant would die, but whether he would live to finish his memoirs. He had tried dictating, but even whispering pained his throat and forced him back to the pen. As Grant's publisher, Mark Twain considered the possibilities, if the second volume were left unfinished. Subscribers were promised two volumes; two volumes must be delivered. What Grant had written, including his articles, could be printed; the gaps could be filled by Fred, formerly a colonel in the U.S. Army, or even by Adam Badeau. An unsatisfactory solution, but seemingly the only one possible.

On April 4, Mark Twain wrote in his notebook: "General Grant is still alive to-day & the nation holds its breath & awaits the blow." All other news took second place. *Harper's Illustrated Weekly* devoted its April 11 issue to Grant, with a cover picture showing him, while still in health, driving his carriage through Central Park. "Night Scene in Front of General Grant's House," another full-page illustration, showed reporters keeping the deathwatch, and "Our Ulysses," a double-page spread by Thomas Nast, presented the apotheosis of Grant as the heroic savior of his country: wearing a Grecian tunic, with sword and shield, he faced a scaly monster in the sea. Beside him was a kneeling slave, behind him a woman (Liberty or Columbia), and in the background the dome of the Capitol, seemingly detached from the earth, rose into the sunlight. Elaborate preparations had been made to observe the expected death—across the nation, as the news was received by telegraph, fire bells would ring—sixty-three strokes, one for each year of his age. It would be "the first time in the world's history that the bells of a nation have tolled in unison," Mark Twain noted in his journal. But the blow did not come. Miraculously, to devout and patriotic Americans, Grant experienced a remission. He could eat, walk, talk, and work.

Karl Gerhardt had made a small portrait bust of Grant, working from photographs, and showed it to his patron. Twain instantly decided it was the best image of the General that he had ever seen, and the next day he set off for New York with the artist to show the work to the Grants. Mrs. Grant and two daughters-in-law were at home and admired the bust also, but argued over whether the sculptor had gotten the nose and the forehead quite right. To settle the matter, they invited him to go into the next room, where Grant was resting, and look at the subject for himself. "Stretched out in a reclining chair . . . muffled up in dressing gowns and afghans, with his black woolen skull-cap on his head," Grant submitted uncomplainingly to inspection, just as he submitted to whatever his doctors might order. Then Mrs. Grant suggested that Gerhardt should work there, and for two hours he worked quietly at his bust while his subject relaxed, then slept peacefully, "the serenity of his face disturbed only at intervals by a passing wave of pain." Consequently, Twain believed, that bust revealed the suffering which Grant hid during his waking hours.

Gerhardt's eye was always on the main chance; he used his entry to gain permission to make the death mask of the General when the time came (after warning the family against a rival, "a cheeky, unprincipled sort of man," who might have the impudence to force his way in). A month later, he sent Mark Twain a circular containing a reproduction of the bust, a facsimile of a letter by Fred Grant praising it as "an excellent likeness," and a statement by a dealer that he was offering for sale "in Terra Cotta the bust of General Grant . . . sculptured from life at the private residence of the General . . . by Karl Gerhardt."

Gerhardt could dream almost as expansively as his patron. He wanted to carve a full-size statue of Grant, seated (modeled on a statue of Napoleon). He expected a great sale of the bust and offered to sell his rights in it to Twain for $10,000 and cancellation of his debt. (Twain had already observed in his journal that Gerhardt's principal trait was thanklessness.) Twain refused that offer, but did take a share in the bust, without allowing his name to be used—for Grant's publisher, that might have smacked too much of hucksterism.

With his strength partly restored, Grant used the time given to him. Finding himself able to talk with less pain, he wished to dictate to a shorthand reporter. Webster made the arrangements, taking extraordinary precautions. He was present himself during every dictation, and oversaw the making of a longhand copy after each session. (The transcription was then given to the author for review and correction.) All this would allow him to testify, if required, that "I heard him utter to my stenographer every word in the last volume."

Grant dictated prodigiously (up to 10,000 words in a single

session, said the newspapers; the figure seems vastly exaggerated, but half of that would have been remarkable). All that was left for him now was the recording of his life—or rather, of its best part—and to that work he gave himself to the limits of his strength, regardless of pain. The *Memoirs*, if completed, would not only provide for his wife and children, but could erase the scandalous, ignominous failure of Grant & Ward. By May 6, the second volume was nearly done, and knowing that he might die at any moment, Grant had already dictated its conclusion, Lee's surrender at Appomattox. What was more, his dictation was in almost finished form; only minor revisions were needed.

Inevitably, there were rumors that Grant was too sick to finish the *Memoirs* himself; no precautions that Webster might take could stop the gossipmongers. On April 29, the New York *World* had stated that "another false idea of General Grant is given out by some of his friends, and that is that he is a writer. He is not a writer . . . The work upon his new book about which so much has been said is the work of General Adam Badeau." That slanderous report infuriated Twain, particularly because he knew that Grant was indeed a "writer" in the fullest sense. He already bore a grudge against the *World*, for its sanctimonious condemnation of *Huckleberry Finn*, and his impulse was to sue at once, to ask for crippling damages of $250,000 or $300,000, and to accept no apology or compromise.

But his lawyers advised against it: such a suit "would be long, expensive, and annoying, not only to us, but to Genl. Grant." Instead, Grant himself wrote a dignified remonstrance, asserting his own authorship of the entire work. The *World* printed it, and the matter ended there, without lawsuits—the lie had done no harm. The guilty went unpunished, and Mark Twain reluctantly accepted that outcome: "I recognize the fact that for General Grant to sue the World would be an enormously valuable advertisement for that daily issue of unmedicated closet-paper."

The source of that story must have been Badeau himself, who had hoped to share in the profits and the glory. He seems to have considered the *Memoirs* his own literary property, on which Grant himself had no right to encroach, still less Mark Twain. (In an article on Grant's last days, published in *Century* in its October issue, Badeau would not even mention Twain's name.) There would be an unpleasant scene a few days later, when Badeau made a final appearance, forcing himself upon Grant with a letter demanding a thousand dollars per month to finish the book and 10 percent of the profits. Grant's refusal finally ended the long association between the two.

Badeau could not threaten the success of the *Memoirs*; nothing could—if only Grant could finish his work. Mark Twain believed that Grant's book "must take rank with the best purely narrative literature in the language." As for Webster and Company's part, he wrote confidently to Orion that "Charley has tackled the vastest book-enterprise the world has ever seen, with a cool head & capable hand, & is carrying it alone in a serene unhalting fashion which is fine to see." By the first of May, 60,000 sets had been ordered "by a region comprising one-fourth of the territory between Canada & Mason & Dixon's line, & the Mississippi river & the Atlantic Ocean." The sale was sure to reach 300,000 sets, and Grant's royalties would amount to at least $420,000—if those royalties were paid in silver dollars, Twain calculated, the total would weigh more than seventeen tons.

He had read that Lord Macaulay had received the largest single royalty payment ever recorded, a check for twenty thousand pounds, for the third and fourth volumes of his *History of England*; Webster and Company would break that record. "Macaulay's grand edition weighed 45 tons; our first issue (Dec. 1) ought to weigh 300 tons." All his life, Mark Twain delighted in making such calculations; this time, and only this time, they proved almost exactly correct. "He liked the game of business," writes Paine, "especially when it was pretentious and showily prosperous." For once, the prosperity was real.

He might simply have waited for the triumphant success that was now clearly inevitable, but that was not Mark Twain's nature. He worried about French and German translations, and the importance of having them under the firm's control. Exuberantly, he planned special editions: "100 editions de luxe at auction"—or 300—each one containing five pages of Grant's manuscript—at a "knockdown price" of $100. Why not include twenty pages of manuscript, and arrange an opening bid of $500, or "get Mackay to make a great bid for the 1st copy"? (John Mackay, "bonanza king" and multi-millionaire, was an old acquaintance from Twain's Virginia City days.) Or two thousand copies of a "special edition" might be sold at fifty dollars apiece. In the end, nothing came of those plans, but the regular edition offered reward enough.

On April 23, an anonymous correspondent, moved to write by "the unrelenting hatred of hypocrisy and oppression" that ran through all of Mark Twain's work, urged him to follow the example of Voltaire: as Voltaire had "ridiculed the dogmatic superstition of the 18th century out of existence . . . why should not Mark Twain imitate his noble example and wield his mighty pen for the abolition of wage-slavery—the curse of the 19th century!" The letter is signed "Socialist." That letter was mistimed, with Twain about to make a fortune for the Grants and himself through the capitalistic device of subscription publishing. But in any case, "Socialist" had mistaken his man; Mark Twain indeed hated hypocrisy and oppression, or rather hated hypocrites and oppressive acts, but no collectivist philosophy could ever attract him. He might denounce individual wrongdoers, but he accepted the system that produced them. He belonged to it, he profited from it, from childhood he defined success in its terms. For him, civilization had reached its climax with the capitalistic, democratic nineteenth century. Even in old age, when he foretold the disappearance of the American republic and projected future histories of ignorance and tyranny, he saw his own century as a unique epoch of enlightenment and progress.

Mark Twain found no time for his own writing that spring, putting off even the article on his wartime experiences that he had agreed to write for *Century*. The completion and publication of Grant's work, which meant the completion and fulfillment of Grant's life, must have seemed vastly more significant than giving an account of his farcical experiences as an amateur soldier. Even the success or failure of *Huckleberry Finn* might have seemed unimportant when compared to the completion and publication of Grant's *Memoirs*, the national drama in which Twain had given himself a major supporting role.

With his appetite for business sharpened by the enormous success that now appeared certain for the *Memoirs*, Mark Twain's interest in Paige's automatic typesetter revived. He had invested $5,000 five years before, but had done little since—unusual behavior for him. Five years should have been more than enough to complete the machine and build a reliable working model, but Paige was a perfectionist, never ready to believe that his work was actually done, always tinkering with some new refinement or improvement. He failed to meet his own deadlines, and the machine was never quite ready for demonstration. Prospective buyers, coming to Hartford to observe the typesetter in action, were likely to find it in pieces on the floor, disassembled to correct some flaw or add some feature. But by April of 1885, Mark Twain had decided that at last the machine was "in perfect working order . . . & stands ready & willing to submit itself to any test an expert chooses to apply." With his confidence in his own judgment inflated by success, he began to concern himself more deeply with its prospects.

He made elaborate calculations, comparing the amount of work that a human typesetter could do, in a twelve-hour day, with the machine's performance. Three average workmen could set 20,000 ems in ten hours, then distribute (sort and store) the type for the next day's work in another two and a quarter hours. The machine, with its operator at the keyboard and another man for justifying each line (spacing between words, to make the lines even) could do nearly twice as much work in the same time. A single metropolitan paper might save $50,000 a year. Figures like those seemed to guarantee success, making even the profits from the *Memoirs* appear trivial in comparison. In his notebook, Twain jotted down other advantages:

> This typesetter does not get drunk.
> He does not join the Printers' Union.
> A woman can operate him.

Each typesetter would cost $1,000 to manufacture, but it would sell for $5,000. A factory could be built for $800,000, to produce the first 400 machines. Paige would get a royalty on every typesetter produced, and a cash payment of $350,000 as well. In all, $1,750,000 should be enough, Twain estimated. It was time for Webster to "sail in . . . with the experts & capitalists" and arrange everything.

His lawyer, Daniel Whitford, warned that Paige's delays had killed all interest among newspaper and book publishers, but concerning the typesetter, Mark Twain would take no advice. He felt himself the expert; he knew the need for such a machine (and he was right) and he was equally sure that only the Paige compositor, as it was officially called, could satisfy the need. Printing had been mechanized; in newspaper pressrooms in New York and London, thousands of copies an hour rolled off the great steam presses. It was intolerable that the craft of typesetting had not advanced in four hundred years. Every major newspaper in America and Europe, every book and magazine publisher, would require Paige machines. Like his own Colonel Sellers, Twain saw millions in it. But he would have angrily rejected that comparison. The typesetter was real, and he was no dreamer. He saw an opportunity—as he had done with the Grant memoirs—saw it more clearly than other men. Success seemed just as sure. And nowhere else could he find a success that would be even more spectacular than his success with the *Memoirs*.

If he needed escape from the excitements and the concerns of business, family life could provide it, during the intervals between journeys to New York. The Clemenses were close, as a Victorian family was expected to be, but as Mark Twain's own had not been—with a stern and distant father, with the threat of poverty, with constant moves. He gave his daughters everything that he had not known as a child, above all, a father's attention and love. Susy, now thirteen and "perhaps the busiest bee in the household hive, by reason of the manifold studies, health exercises, and recreations she had to attend to," had become her father's favorite companion. Precocious, serious beyond her age, "she was *intense*," Mark Twain would recall, "a magazine of feelings . . . her waking hours were a crowding and hurrying procession of enthusiasms . . . Joy, sorrow, anger, remorse, storm, sunshine, rain, darkness . . . her approval was passionate, her disapproval the same, and both were prompt." Much of that description, of course, applied equally to himself. She read with the same intensity, living in poetry—Shelley, Swinburne, Tennyson, Rossetti—for weeks at a time. And she wrote as well: bloody tragedies, full of melodramatic stage directions: "Shrieks and faints," "Falls and dies," "Shrieks, falls and dies." Susy, at thirteen, was almost dangerously *intense*, like many American girls and women (and fictional heroines, too) of her background and class—an intensity that could find no use or outlet in their society.

Almost every day, Mark Twain would recall, he and Susy would " 'promonade' [Susy's spelling] . . . up and down the library," their arms around each other's waists, conversing on "affairs of State, or the deep questions of human life, or our small personal affairs."

Susy knew very well that her father was not like the fathers of her friends. Later, in her early twenties, she would discover the drawbacks of her status as a celebrity's daughter and of her own belief that she must not simply be a girl like other girls. She must write, or act, or sing—she must, somehow, excel, she must be an artist herself. But at thirteen, no one could expect her to match her father's accomplishment. Apparently, she felt no rivalry with him, unless the act of writing itself constituted rivalry. She had begun to compose his "biography," writing at night in her bedroom and hiding the work. But the closeness of the Victorian family left no room for privacy and secrets. Her parents discovered the work, they complimented her, and she continued it.

Mark Twain was flattered. He would talk for his "biographer," posing for her, just as he would do more than twenty years later for Albert Bigelow Paine, his secretary and official biographer. Susy expected to have no trouble in finding things to say about "Papa," since he was "a *very* striking character." She found him "an extrodinarily [*sic*] fine looking man," with "beautiful gray hair" and "a Roman nose, which greatly improves the beauty of his features . . . a wonderfully shaped head, and profile," and "a very good figure." "He *has* got a temper," she added, "but we all of us have in this family." In short, he was "the loveliest man I ever saw or ever hope to see—and oh, so absent-minded."

Susy observed shrewdly and objectively. She had wondered why her father did not like to go to church, until he explained that "he couldn't bear to hear any one talk but himself." "Of course he said this in joke," she adds, "but I've no dought [*sic*] it was founded on truth." There were, of course, other reasons why Mark Twain did not attend church. He found Christian doctrine incredible: "If God is what people say" (infinitely loving and compassionate), he noted in his journal, "there can be none in the universe so unhappy as he; for he sees, unceasingly, myriads of his creatures suffering unspeakable miseries"—a comment that might refer to both the unavoidable sufferings of human life and the sufferings of the damned in hell, according to the Presbyterian faith he had been brought up in. A year or two before, he had written to a friend who had become a Catholic convert that "I look back with shuddering horror upon the days when I believed, as you do upon the days when you were afraid you did not believe."

In late April, Susy's parents took her to New York, Susy recording everything in the biography. With her father, she visited Grant—"a man I shall be glad all my life that I have seen," she noted. While mother and daughter were occupied in shopping, Mark Twain took part, with other authors, in two afternoon readings at the Madison Square Theatre for the benefit of the American Copyright League. He was at his best. Howells was there, too, and noted Twain's easy mastery over his audience: "You simply straddled down to the footlights, and took that house up in the hollow of your hand and *tickled* it."

Susy was now old enough to travel without her mother's care. The next morning, Livy went back to Hartford, while father and daughter caught a train to Poughkeepsie, as Mark Twain had scheduled a reading at Vassar for that night. The drive from the station to the college was long, and "papa and I had a nice long time to discuss and laugh over German profanity," Susy noted, adding that her father's favorite example was "O heilige Maria Mutter Jesus!" Mark Twain, an irascible man, considered himself an authority on profanity, as well as being an expert practitioner. He probably chose that weak example as suitable for the ears of a thirteen-year-old girl. They reached the college in the rain and were left alone, in the guest parlor, in their wet clothes, for half an hour, while Twain's temper rose. He was not used to that kind of reception. Probably Mark and Livy had been considering Vassar as a college for Susy; if so, that cool reception discouraged them. Five years later, she would spend an unhappy year at Bryn Mawr—college could not compare with home. In the evening, Susy attended her father's reading, the first time she had seen him perform in public. When he gave his favorite "Man with the Golden Arm," she observed, the whole roomful of girls "jumped as one man."

The Clemenses would spend the summer of 1885 at Quarry Farm as usual, but before they left, the daughters had to be examined by their governess on their year's work. It was an important occasion, and the girls had decorated the schoolroom with wildflowers, ferns, and grasses. Susy, the genius of the family, distinguished herself, telling the story of Cupid and Psyche in Latin and summing up ancient history in an hour-long discussion, defining history, describing the various races of man, and assessing the contributions of Egypt, Assyria, Babylonia, and Phoenicia to civilization. She did more than parrot her lessons, as Livy proudly noted: "Occasionally she would say, well Miss Foote, the book says so and so, but it seems to me . . ." and then she would state her own opinion.

Mark Twain was ready for Quarry Farm. Momentarily, he revolted against fame, hospitality, business, and correspondence, pronouncing a definitive curse on letter writing in a letter to Pamela. "My correspondence is the despair of my life. Suppose *you* had to have 15 teeth pulled every day; & every time you lost 3 days—a thing that happens once a fortnight on an average—must have 45 pulled at one sitting? . . . I count only those people my friends who release me from the sense that I must some time or other write them." As for Livy, "she keeps hotel, & the business is beyond her strength, the days have but 24 hours, while her mere unavoidable duties require 48." He has spent three days in New York "on imperative business" and as a consequence must spend an entire day at his table, answering letters, "adding a deep, strong, heartfelt curse to each & every one of them except this one." He concludes philosophically: "Am I in a bad temper? Indeed I am not. I accept my destiny & keep my temper." ("Don't imagine that I have lost my temper," he had written to Orion on May 22, "I am merely preparing to lose it.") Becoming Grant's publisher had multiplied those demands, not only giving him constant business to attend to, but bringing him into the public eye still more frequently. The exasperation seems real, but the destiny, after all, had been self-chosen. Given a choice, it is not likely that he would have retired into a contented obscurity.

On June 14, Grant moved to Mount McGregor, twelve miles north of Saratoga Springs, to escape the summer heat. There, in a gimcrack "cottage," with his wife, a son, and a daughter, besides nurse, doctor, valet, and maid, he would spend the few weeks left to him. Reporters, photographers, sightseers flocked to the cottage. Doing his duty as he saw it, Grant exhausted himself by receiving them all, writing notes when he could not speak. He knew that his end was near. On June 17, he wrote with grim wit to his doctor that he expected to die of "hemorage [*sic*], strangulation or exhaustion," but was ready to be examined by another physician "if you are unwilling to have me go without consultation"—even though he feared "more Drs. & more treatments & more suffering." Yet in spite of his suffering, he worked on, determined to make his book complete and perfect before he died.

The first volume of the *Memoirs* was already in press; Grant was reading proof for the second, revising carefully and still adding material. A photograph shows him, serious and preoccupied, sitting on the porch in a wicker chair, with proofs and a pencil in his hand. He did an astonishing amount of work in those last few weeks, revising his account of the whole final year of the war, and adding a new section on the Wilderness Campaign. On July 20, Webster and Company could announce that "THE BOOK IS FINISHED" and that it contained more text than subscribers had been promised. Pious Americans saw the hand of God at work: "When all the circumstances . . . of their [the *Memoirs'*] origin and preparation are considered, they afford a striking illustration of Providential interposition," remarked the *Lutheran Observer*.

Mark Twain paid a final visit to Grant at the end of June. What he saw increased his admiration. Death was imminent—only Julia Grant still denied the inevitable—"yet the General is as placid, serene, & self-possessed as ever, & his eye has the same old humorous twinkle in it, & his frequent smile is still the smile of pleasantness & peace. Manifestly, dying is nothing to a really great & brave man." A *Times* reporter commented that "he did not see, since death was certain, why it should not be talked of." Grant would have been pleased by that; whatever human fears might lie behind the mask of his famed "imperturbability" could never be known. Appearances were kept up until the end; the last photograph, taken on July 21, only two days before his death, shows him in shiny top hat and black suit, a cane beside him, sitting on the porch of his cottage and reading a paper. He is visibly drawn and sick, but the slippers on his feet mark his only concession to illness.

In front-page, full-column stories, the newspapers reported every detail of Grant's dying: the medication he was given, the naps that he snatched, his temperature almost from hour to hour. All the details of his illness were given to the public: the huge swelling under his ear, twice as big as a man's fist, the frightfully emaciated body, the "accumulations from his throat" that filled his mouth, until he could not sleep lying down, for fear of choking to death. Grant himself made the definitive statement on his condition: "The fact is I think I am a verb instead of a personal pronoun. A verb is anything that signifies to be; to do; or to suffer. I signify all three." He was receiving brandy, morphine, and cocaine in those final days, at his own request—perhaps to hurry the end, and perhaps because with his work done or nearly done, he could see no reason why he should die in pain. "There is nothing more I should do to it [the *Memoirs*] now," he wrote on July 14, "and therefore I am not likely to be more ready to go than at this moment." Nine days later, he died. A maudlin newspaper story lamented that Grant's suffering was increased by the strain of his writing—"we regret to see the short tale of comfortable days reduced by such exhausting demands"—but Mark Twain knew better. As he wrote to Livy from New York City, the day after Grant's death, "General Grant having not another interest in this world to live for, died. He would have died three months ago if his book had been completed."

A tragic drama had been staged before a national audience fascinated by deathbed scenes. While the nation watched, the hero endured his ordeal, and his heroism survived the test. Grant's last days were exemplary, in his patient, uncomplaining endurance and his determination to complete his task and redeem his honor by paying his debts (particularly that debt of $150,000 to Vanderbilt), but above all in his devotion to his children and his wife, thus demonstrating that he possessed the domestic virtues that his age considered as important as his public qualities. As every report noted, he died in the bosom of his family.

The public forgot Grant's disappointing Presidency and remembered only his victories, placing him in the American pantheon just beneath Washington (who had awaited death with equal dignity) and Lincoln. Twain had prepared a eulogy for the Hartford *Courant*, quoting his favorite passage from the *Morte d'Arthur*, Sir Ector de Maris's lament for Launcelot: "Ah, Launcelot, thou wert head of all Christian knights." In his notebook he recorded a briefer verdict on the General: "He was a very great man—& superlatively good."

Twichell, who had seen the bloodiest battles of the war as an army chaplain, felt his own inadequacy in responding to the news, but found nothing in that outpouring of print that could relieve, or even express, his emotion. He could not put out of his mind the image of "the General lying cold and still, under the flag, yonder at Mt. McGregor, with the soldiers guarding him. There's a lump in my throat half the time." He needed to see Mark Twain. Nothing that he might say to himself or to anyone else could relieve him, but "between us we could get ourselves expressed."

Grant would be buried in New York, with all pomp and ceremony, fitting the death of a symbol as well as a man. Mark Twain
was there, of course; it was unthinkable that he would not have
been. To see Grant's body consigned to the tomb was almost as
much a duty as to see Grant's book put into the hands of subscribers.
He described the funereal draping of the city in a letter to Livy:
swathes of black covering the stone and brick fronts of the business
and public buildings—black drapery on white marble made the most
dramatic effect. Where there were stone porticos and columns, the
columns were solid black. He saw "a thousand big portraits of the
General set in the centre of a desert of black." It was not only official
grief; private homes were draped in black as well. The next day he
watched the procession taking Grant's body to City Hall, there to
lie in state while an estimated 250,000 people viewed what one
reporter called "the white, hollow hand and the milky, fading face."
And on August 8, from the office windows of Webster and Company, Twain "witnessed the imposing funeral pageant of Gen.
Grant," five hours long, as the coffin moved to the temporary tomb
in Riverside Park, with Sherman and Sheridan and two Confederate
generals, Joseph Johnston and Simon Buckner, marching in the
procession.

ELEVEN

Standing Outside the Door of Plenty

"**Y**ou are exhilaratingly rich as an author and sodden with wealth as a publisher," a friend had written to Mark Twain in April. The sale of *Huckleberry Finn* had been more than satisfying, but had not really produced a fortune, and while Grant's book promised much more, it would bring only expenses for many months, until the first volume could be released. The success of the *Memoirs* had been guaranteed when Grant finished the second volume and put down his pen a few days before his death. Yet anxieties and alarms continued—Webster was an inveterate anxiety-monger, and simply to wait quietly for publication and profit was not in Mark Twain's nature. From distant Keokuk, Orion watched and worried as well, and at the end of August wrote in panic to his brother, foreseeing imminent disaster from defaulting general agents with resulting ruin for all the Clemenses. With surprising patience, Twain assured him that "books are not delivered to General Agents till we get the money," adding with a touch of asperity that "*live* General Agents will have no trouble about selling all the books they have contracted to sell . . . None but a *dead* General Agent would have difficulty fulfilling his contract."

On August 20, Webster forwarded to his employer a copy of a circular "which is being broadcast over the country, and which is causing us a vast amount of harm." Signed "Appomattox," it charged that the Grant family would receive only 12½ percent of the profits from the *Memoirs*—"less than is usually paid to authors by first-class houses"; that by the time the book was published, interest would have abated and more than half the subscribers would refuse to accept it; that "there are twenty other Grant books in the field . . . the country will be overrun with canvassers for Grant books . . . and the public become thoroughly nauseated." Certainly the public was in danger of nausea, from the newspaper coverage alone of Grant's sickness, death, and burial. Alexander & Green, Mark Twain's law firm, hired a detective, who discovered that a subscription house in Philadelphia had issued the circular, on finding that "all the best book people were engaged on the Grant book," just as it was about to publish a new book of its own, *Wonders of the World*. But for all of Webster's alarm, there is no evidence that "Appomattox" did any harm at all.

Inevitably, there were damaging rumors, some of them spread by *Century* people, Twain suspected, although there was no proof. In any case, he could not afford a public quarrel with *Century*; neither could he answer the rumors and slander that might appear in the papers or circulate in talk. The commonest report, one that no denials could entirely squelch, was that Grant had left his work unfinished, that there was not enough material to fill the promised two volumes. (In fact, Grant had done enough before going to Mount McGregor, and he went on writing there for another month.) Such lies might exasperate, but they could be ignored. It was harder to ignore the General's oldest son. On August 10, the *World* published an interview with Fred Grant which quoted him as saying that "we do not yet know exactly what or how much manuscript there is. The last pages my father wrote have not been looked over, and there is a large amount of matter not in form for publication . . . I am not yet sure whether there will be enough matter for two volumes."

That there was "a large amount of matter not in form for publication" was simply untrue, but Fred Grant's claim might do more harm than the lies spread by a hundred anonymous rumormongers. The *World* was notoriously unreliable, but Whitford, Twain's personal lawyer at Alexander & Green, admitted that to increase his own importance, Grant might have said what he was quoted as saying. Whitford prepared a statement refuting all rumors that the manuscript was incomplete, to be sent to leading newspapers with a request that they publish nothing contrary to it, whether in the form of interviews or news stories.

But Whitford counseled silence. As he explained, advance orders for the *Memoirs* were coming in at a rate of 12,000–15,000 copies a week, even faster than had been expected. "The position is as good as it can be," and silence was the best policy for "all parties on our side"; any incautious word might be twisted to Webster and Company's disadvantage. Sound advice, but hard to follow, especially for a man like Mark Twain, always ready to believe that he was being victimized and eager to attack his enemies, real or supposed. But not even Grant's son could destroy the public's image of the General struggling against constant pain to finish his book and record his life, and dying when the work was done. That image, after all, was true.

Mark Twain could joke that a reputation for sharp dealing might be the best asset a publisher could have, but in fact he was intensely sensitive to criticism. He would not dignify accusations of sharp practice, whether against the Century Company, or General Grant, or the public, or Webster and Company's agents, with a public reply, but in his notebook he ironically defended himself against newspaper charges that he had done a shameful thing "in persuading the plundered & impoverished old soldier" to "burn a contract which promised him a pittance & a publisher a fortune." His only crime had been to point this out to Grant, a crime committed "without a qualm of conscience."

The competing Grant books were exasperating, if not dangerous, often misrepresented as "the genuine Memoirs or 'companions' to the genuine Memoirs." Worse, those rival publishers impudently charged Webster and Company with profiteering at Grant's expense, while their own books paid nothing at all to him or his family. Undeniably, Webster and Company, too, had capitalized on the public emotion at Grant's death: on July 25, a story given to the New York *Morning Journal* announced "PEN WORK OF THE HERO—HIS BOOK WILL PLACE MRS. GRANT BEYOND WANT." But seventy cents of every dollar of profit from the *Memoirs*, after all, would go to Grant's heirs. A good many other people wanted to enrich or advance themselves, without benefit to the Grants. One of them was Gerhardt. He hoped to market his bust of the General and had found a promoter, a Colonel W. N. Woodruff, to manage the enterprise. The colonel wrote enthusiastically to Twain on July 21 that he would soon have a prospectus ready for canvassers and that "nothing short of a sale of 100,000 will satisfy me." But no such figure was approached—there seems to have been a touch of Sellers in Colonel Woodruff. The public wanted Grant's book, not his bust.

Gerhardt hoped to do more than make a bust. By exploiting his connection with Mark Twain, he planned to get a commission for a "colossal" memorial statue, a work that might draw national attention and make his career. Twain was helpful, proposing to "get some rich men to join in," and offering to pay one tenth of the cost himself and to see that Gerhardt should have access to Grant, to study him. "You've got a big chance . . . & I'm just determined you shan't lose it." Nothing came of that plan, finally, or of Gerhardt's scheme for a subscription, headed by Mrs. Jesse Grant, wife of the general's youngest son, to raise money for a statue of Grant, seated, in a room at the Capitol where his captured battle flags would be displayed. But Twain had done his best for his protégé, encouraging Gerhardt with his richest rhetoric: "the features which you are modelling are those of a man whose name will still be familiar in the mouths of men in so remote a future that the very constellations in the skies . . . will have visibly changed their places." Mesmerized by his own prose, he surely believed that as he wrote it.

Mark Twain of course traveled to New York for the General's funeral, but otherwise life at Quarry Farm followed its usual course. Grant's death could hardly be a matter for deep grief—it brought him a long-delayed release from pain—and in any case, the farm was a world in itself. Susy recorded the family's daily occupations in her biography: "Papa rises about ½ past 7 in the morning, breakfasts at eight, writes, plays tennis with Clara and me and tries to make the donkey go, in the morning [Mark Twain had bought a donkey for his girls and had it shipped to Quarry Farm]; does various things in P.M., and in the evening plays tennis with Clara and me and amuses Jean and the donkey." (While finishing *Huckleberry Finn*, two summers before, he had stayed in his study all day long.) As for "Mama," after breakfast she spent an hour with Jean, teaching her German, then read German for another hour with Susy, then read to Clara and Susy about "things connected with English history (for we hope to go to England next summer)" while they sewed. After lunch, Livy would "studdy," or read to her daughters again, "then studdies writes reads and rests till supper time," and after dinner, husband and wife might play whist till bedtime.

As for the children, "Clara and I do most everything from prac-ticing to donkey riding and playing tag," wrote Susy, "while Jean's time is spent in asking mama what she can have to eat." Passionately fond of all animals, Jean also studied natural history with her mother, collecting insects in the nearby fields. They were careful to examine the captives without injuring them, since Livy feared that it might "blunt a child's sensibility . . . to kill the little creatures." As usual, there were cats at Quarry Farm: Stray Kit, Cleveland, Abner, Motley, Fraulein, Lazy, Buffalo Bill, Soapy Sal, Pestilence, and Famine. Clearly, Mark Twain had named them.

The girls had their special place, a "vine-covered nook" near their father's study, and Susan Crane had a playhouse (named "Ellerslie" by Susy, from a novel she had been reading) built for them, complete with a working kitchen. There, Mark Twain would recall, "they spent a great deal of time . . . cooking dishes that were not in the cook-book and giving me a chance to suspend work and eat them." Susie read aloud Schiller's tragedy on Joan of Arc, *Die Jungfrau von Orleans*, to her mother—"she reads it very well, and it is delightful to read it with her," Livy found. A precocious critic, Susy had been reading Scott's *The Betrothed* as well, and commented to her mother on Scott's "cool way of writing . . . even when the event is exciting he writes of it coolly."

Quarry Farm was an ideal place for reading. After he had "bored through" George Eliot's *Middlemarch* (George Eliot was a favorite author of Livy's), Twain turned to the second installment of How-ells's latest novel, *Indian Summer*, in *Harper's*. Howells seemed end-lessly productive. His contract with Harper and Brothers called for a novel a year, and *The Rise of Silas Lapham* had not yet finished its run in *Century*—Twain had been reading the installments aloud to Livy—when the serializing of *Indian Summer* commenced. *Indian Summer* brings a middle-aged man, who suspects that he has wasted his life, back to Florence, the scene of an unhappy love affair in his youth. There he allows a passionate girl to fall in love with him, to his own deep embarrassment, before finally deciding to propose to his former sweetheart—now widowed—and make the best of mid-dle-aged love. Mark Twain, the novelist of boyhood and himself a man approaching fifty, responded deeply to the irony and pathos of Howells's story, and wrote enthusiastically to his friend.

"You are really my only author," he began—a compliment to

delight any writer, even if not literally true. He had read that installment three times, he wrote, and had found not a single line
that could be improved. He composed his own prose poem to re-
create its effect. *Indian Summer* "makes a body laugh all the time,
& cry inside, & feel so old & so forlorn; & gives him gracious
glimpses of his lost youth that fill him with a measureless regret,
& build up in him a cloudy sense of his having been a prince, once,
in some enchanted far-off land . . . & lord, no chance to ever get
back there again!" (He deeply admired Omar Khayyám's "perfect"
poem, the *Rubáiyát*, with its plangent laments for the ravages of
time, for the same reasons.) Best of all, Howells had made "all the
motives & feelings perfectly clear without analyzing the guts out
of them," as George Eliot did, or Henry James.

Twain liked to insist on the authenticity of his own work, claiming
that it was taken direct from life, but except for Howells's novels,
he showed little interest in "realism." Realistic characters were likely
to seem "paltry and tiresome" and realistic stories "unexciting &
uninteresting." He was always uneasy with "high" culture, whether
the music of Wagner or the novels of Eliot and James, uncomfortable with its social and intellectual pretensions, unsure of
whether he could meet its demands. Often he ridiculed it, yet he
could never quite make a simple, philistine dismissal. But generally
he preferred the popular culture of his day ("low" by definition);
with it, he could relax and simply enjoy himself. His own books
were a part of that culture.

It is not easy to imagine James or Howells attending a performance of Buffalo Bill's Wild West Show, but when Cody brought
his spectacle to Elmira that summer, he of course sent complimen-
tary tickets to Mark Twain. (The note accompanying the tickets is
written on business stationery; half the page is filled with Indians,
frontiersmen, and wagons on a landscape of desert and mountains.)
Twain went twice, and wrote enthusiastic thanks: "it brought back
to me the breezy, wild life of the Rocky mountains, and stirred me
like a war song. The show is genuine, cowboys, vaqueros, Indians,
stage-coach, costumes, the same as I saw on the frontier years ago."
His West had been the mining West, he had no firsthand knowledge
of cowboys, vaqueros, Indians, and buffalo, but he liked to believe
that he had been a Wild Westerner himself—that he had shared in
that part of the national experience.

* * *

Summer was Mark Twain's usual time for work, and his study the place, but he spent little time in it, as Susy's schedule indicates. Even with his visit to Grant and his attendance at Grant's burial, besides the vastly increased business of Webster and Company, he could easily have found time to write. But with his deep concern for Grant and for Grant's book, with his worries, his fears, his angers, his exultations, Twain could not hope to enter that state of total concentration in which he had finished *Huckleberry Finn*. Instead of writing a book of his own, he planned one for his nephew Sam Moffett to write: *Picturesque Incidents in History & Tradition*, to be published by Webster and Company. It would be drawn "from the history & traditions of *all* countries & epochs," and if "ingeniously contrived" and "captivatingly written," would "sell handsomely" and "*keep on* selling, permanently." Enthusiastically, Twain jotted down ideas and sources in his notebook: "Describe what England was like during the 6 years wherein no church bell was heard—John & his whole realm being under papal curse & interdict." Sam should describe the fire of London and the plague (to be cribbed from Pepys's *Diary*), the Children's Crusade, King Canute commanding the ocean, the discovery of the microscope, the origin of the Order of the Garter, the coronation of George III, when "the biggest jewel in his crown dropped out," foretelling the loss of America. Mark Twain delighted in picturesque history. Sam Moffett never wrote that book, but his uncle must have enjoyed planning it.

He considered lecturing on humor to the Nineteenth Century Club, a New York society for the discussion of social, literary, artistic, theological, and scientific issues, and made entries in his notebook: "I have no sense of humor," he begins, and ironically "proves" it by confessing that he had never been able to find a humorous passage in Dickens's *Pickwick Papers*. He qualified that heretical judgment later by remarking that except in *Pickwick*, almost all of Dickens's humorous characters were truly humorous. Humor should never seem to be aware of itself; the humor of *The Pickwick Papers* was "the kind the clown makes in the circus . . . Every line in the book says: 'Look at me—ain't I funny!'" American humor, like his own platform manner, was "ostensibly unconscious." He freshened the traditional distinction between wit and humor with an up-to-date metaphor: "if any difference, it is in *duration*—lightning and electric light. Same material, apparently; but one is vivid, brief, & can do damage—tother [*sic*] fools along & enjoys elaboration." Surprise was essential. *Punch*'s advice to persons considering marriage—"Don't"—failed because it was old "before Punch was born."

Yet the summer was not quite lost for writing. Mark Twain had been carefully revising that reminiscence of his own Civil War experience for *Century*. The editors were urging him to hurry, to have his piece ready for the December issue, which was intended to be less military and more literary than the preceding ones. To sharpen the contrast with bloodier memoirs, Twain's recollections would be illustrated by Kemble, in the style of his work for *Huckleberry Finn*. By mid-August, Twain could assure *Century* that while his "Campaign" might still not be good enough, "it is better than it was before, anyway," adding that "Mrs. Clemens will edit it tonight; I will re-edit tomorrow." He had made so many changes, he added, that it must be read as if it were completely new. He was not always so painstaking, but he felt a "restraint" in writing for *Century*: "It is not intemperate to say that is the best magazine that was ever printed." That was no empty compliment; Mark Twain had proved his sincerity by investing nearly five thousand dollars in the company's stock.

He still had his doubts about the "Campaign." Livy did not like it, and he proposed putting it into *Century*'s planned collection, *Battles and Leaders of the Civil War*, where "its defects might be lost in the smoke and thunder of the big guns all around it," rather than into the magazine, where it "will look like mighty poor weak stuff." He underestimated his work. Readers who do not care for smoke and thunder are likely to find the "Campaign That Failed" one of Twain's best shorter pieces, mingling farce with terror; that painstaking revision had been worthwhile. Livy might have disliked it for personal reasons, fearing that the story of her husband's brief and inglorious part in the war might shame him as a slacker and a coward, or might seem to mock the sufferings of braver men. But *Century* had no such fears. On September 11, C. C. Buel, one of the magazine's editors, wrote that the "Campaign" had gone to press. "It is a great advance on the first draft," he added, predicting that it would succeed "with warriors as well as with the Peace Congress."

In late August, as the summer neared its end, Mark and Livy paid a week's visit to friends who were summering in the Catskills. "It was the perfection of a visit," wrote Twain exuberantly in his thank-you letter, with "just enough rain, just enough sunshine . . . just enough exercise, just enough lazying around; just enough of everything desirable." Then a week or two back at Quarry Farm, and it was time for packing. Livy became saddened at the prospect of leaving her mother and her foster sister, then scolded herself in her diary for her weakness. It is not likely that her husband felt any regrets. He did not want to escape from business for long. The game had never been showier or more pretentious, and it could be played more effectively in Hartford or New York than at Quarry Hill. The *Memoirs* could not satisfy his appetite; that success was assured, it could already be measured.

Twain needed to speculate, and Paige's inventions were ready. He had developed a telegraphic printer, and he had been working on a dynamo, with backing from Twain. In July, he had confessed failure; the dynamo ought to have worked, being "in accordance with the laws laid down by the best writers on the subject," but it did not. Nothing ever came of the printer either, but those failures could not shake Twain's faith in the typesetter. And now Paige had a new improvement that promised to overcome a fatal flaw in other mechanical typesetters: a device for testing type and removing defective letters that might jam the machine. That fault, Twain remarked in his journal, had been "the rock upon which all former typesetters have jammed." Now the machine seemed perfect. It would set a cleaner proof than a human printer, Mark Twain believed. It could do everything but justify—" 'Justifying' will become an expert trade," Twain believed, "& this person will be the only expert left . . . in type setting and distributing."

For a moment, the game of business seemed to extend itself all the way to Baghdad. When Leland Stanford, one of the builders of the Central Pacific, had visited Turkey a year or two earlier, the Sultan had offered him a franchise to build a railroad from Istanbul to Baghdad. Stanford had passed on the chance to Jesse Grant. Seeing vast possibilities (there might be millions in it!), and needing money to go to Turkey and investigate, Jesse turned to Mark Twain, the patron of the Grant family, for help. Webster advised against the scheme, but Baghdad and the romance of the East seemed irresistible to Twain, who casually advanced five thousand dollars. He had the golden touch, why shouldn't he be as successful in railroading as in publishing? In the end, hearing of revolutions in

Turkey, Jesse Grant got no farther than London. Nothing more is heard of the scheme, or of Mark Twain's money. Begging letters multiplied, as newspapers exaggerated the riches that Mark Twain could expect from the *Memoirs*. "Sir, what will you think of me a perfect stranger writing to beg you to give me a hundred dollars I have just seen an article which tells me you are worth a million," wrote Lucia Booth, on August 5. Everything he touched turned to gold, they knew—the papers told them so. But one letter—also, no doubt, a response to newspaper publicity—was unique. A. P. Fulkerson of New Orleans, addressing himself to

"Col. S. L. Clements
Mark Twain
Hartford,"

demanded to know whether Twain had been referring to him in an article entitled "Yaller Dog," published in the New Orleans *Picayune* in 1870. He had been told "forty millions of times since . . . that you had reference to me . . . You said that any body could curse the yaller dog with impunity. It has done me a great deal of injury." If the article did refer to him, he offered Twain the chance to "test my courage with anything that will shoot a ball, at any number of paces," adding that no one "had ever cursed me, that did not get d——d badly hurt, or get more cursing than he gave." If Twain had really been referring to him, and refused to fight, he would publicly denounce "Samuel L. Clements."

Of course, Mark Twain had published no such article. He had not visited New Orleans between 1861 and 1882, had never contributed to the New Orleans *Picayune*, and probably did not know of A. P. Fulkerson's existence before receiving that letter. He made no comment, merely scribbling "yaller dog" on the envelope. But with its brag and brutality, the letter must have seemed to confirm everything he had written concerning Southern "chivalry" in *Life on the Mississippi* and *Huckleberry Finn*. Fulkerson showed himself a ruffian and a bully in every line, while ceremoniously addressing his opponent as "Col." He might have been a lunatic, or he might simply have wanted to boast to his cronies that he had challenged the famous Mark Twain, who had been afraid to answer him.

On the twenty-eighth of September, Webster reported orders for 217,885 sets of the *Memoirs*, including 76,312 in Sheep, 15,065 in Half Morocco, 1,152 in Full Morocco, and ninety-two in Tree Calf. Statements given to Twain reveal the economics of subscription publishing. Prices ranged from $3.50 per volume for the standard cloth binding to "Tree Calf" at $12.50. The cost of production for each volume, with the cheapest binding, was less than fifty cents; the cost of selling (general agent's and canvasser's commissions) totaled about $1.92, leaving a profit of $1.10, of which the firm received 30 percent, or thirty-three cents (that, of course, was an extraordinary arrangement).

The sale of those luxury bindings was good news; the more expensive the binding, the greater the profit margin for agent, author, and publisher. A volume bound in calf cost $1.59 more to produce—but the buyer paid nine dollars extra. The canvasser had reason to aim high, since on a cloth set his commission was $1.43; on the most expensive binding, about $6.65. One phenomenally successful canvasser, who reported selling 240 sets, only thirty-five of them in the basic cloth binding, described his technique to Webster's assistant: "He says he always strikes first for the highest style of binding, and then works down. He says that some parties would never think of taking a book, if you struck them for the cloth at first . . . they think that by the time they get down to seven dollars, they are getting the book very cheaply." Many customers must have been willing to pay those high prices because they regarded the *Memoirs* as a book to be cherished and preserved.

It was clear that the Grants would receive a fortune, but Fred, the General's oldest son, wanted more. Success (his father's, not his own) had gone to his head. Being the son of a national hero might have its advantages, but there were drawbacks as well. Fred Grant could not have believed that he had been promoted on his merits from second lieutenant to lieutenant colonel within two years after graduating from West Point. He must have realized that whatever he had achieved, he owed to his father's fame, not to his own abilities. At thirty-six, Fred craved recognition, yet he could think of no way to win it except by trading on his family name. He would show that he, too, could write a book, but it would be a book about his father.

He planned to supplement the *Memoirs* with a biography of Grant from Appomattox to his death and claimed that he was besieged by publishers, but preferred to consult Mark Twain first. As Whitford, Twain's attorney, reported, Fred had "swaggered around" the offices of Webster and Company, "saying he had the same rights there that Mr. Webster had," talking about his own book and how much it was sought after by other publishers. Whitford suspected as well that Fred had made his statements to the *World* "with the idea that it would help his own book." Mistaking his father's celebrity for his own, Fred rejected Webster's offer of half profits on a sale of up to 50,000 copies, and 60 percent thereafter, demanding the same terms General Grant had received. Not all of the manuscript for the second volume had been delivered to the printer yet, and Fred threatened to delay publication of the second volume by holding back those sections.

Normally, such behavior would have enraged Mark Twain, but perhaps his reverence for the General protected the General's son. Perhaps, also, he forced himself to hold his peace until the book was published. As Whitford advised, with lawyerlike coolness, "The fortune is too great to have any feelings one way or the other until the book is sold and the money pocketed." The manuscript would be forthcoming; if there were any difficulties, it would only be necessary to inform Mrs. Grant that if the manuscript was not delivered, publication of the first volume, and with it her royalties, would be delayed. "They are very hungry for the money."

For once, Mark Twain seems to have practiced diplomacy. His answer to the warnings concerning Fred Grant was "worthy of Talleyrand," according to Mr. Alexander of Alexander & Green. Diplomacy succeeded. Threats and injunctions were not required, there was no trouble about the manuscript, and a public quarrel between Grant's publisher and Grant's oldest son was avoided. No doubt the Grants were indeed hungry for the money, and after all, Fred Grant might not have been intending to blackmail Webster and Company into better terms either for his father's book or for his own, might not have been intending anything at all. He might simply have been swaggering for his own satisfaction.

But Fred still seemed hungry for something, and not only money. Somehow he must assert himself—even if he could think only of ways to exploit his father's name. A month later, Webster learned that Fred planned to publish General Grant's diary of his journey around the world in 1877–79—first in the *North American Review*, then through a rival subscription house that had hired away Webster's bookkeeper (raising his salary from five hundred to twelve hundred dollars a year) in order to steal Webster and Company's list of general agents.

A week later, Webster warned that the same publisher planned to issue "Anecdotes of President Lincoln by General Grant" and others, including material rejected from the *Memoirs*, supplied by Fred Grant. The public must not be "nauseated" with Grant books until the selling campaign for the *Memoirs* was finished, and Webster would stop publication by injunction if necessary, on the grounds that those publications would violate Webster and Company's contract with Grant. (In fact, none of Fred's projects materialized; no doubt writing, or even editing, a book proved harder work than he had expected.)

Webster and Company had competitors, hoping to exploit the public's grief. The American Publishing Company of Hartford—Twain's old publisher—offered a complete life of Grant, over seven hundred pages long, in one volume for only two dollars. Referring satirically to Mark Twain as "Innocents Abroad," its advertising inquired "how many dollars on each copy we must pay Innocents Abroad for carrying the cents to Mrs. Grant." But no money at all went to the Grants from the American Publishing Company. A Philadelphia subscription firm offered the *Military and Civil Life of General U. S. Grant*, cheaply bound, abundantly illustrated with bad engravings, including portraits of all the Presidents from Washington to Grant, and written in a purple prose very different from Grant's: "Day by day he fought his losing battle with the dread monster" (from a chapter entitled "The Dying Hero"). Even children were provided for, with *Our Hero, General Grant: When, Where, and How He Fought, in Words of One Syllable*. And Adam Badeau published a lengthy, reverential article on Grant's bankruptcy and illness in the October *Century*. Badeau might have quarreled with Grant, but he knew what the public wanted to hear.

With an enormous success now assured for Grant's *Memoirs*, Webster and Company began to receive other military memoirs. McClellan's were offered by his widow and accepted. In spite of his doubts about the quality of the manuscript and the character of its author, Mark Twain had high hopes—"another hundred-thousand dollar book," he called it, probably expecting that every soldier who had served in the Army of the Potomac under McClellan would buy. The book earned a satisfactory profit for Webster and Company, but Grant's success could not be repeated—there could be only one savior of the Union. Adam Badeau planned a book on Grant's career after Appomattox and offered it to the firm, but Twain refused it, for "two very good reasons: 1. If it be cleanly, decent, and respectful, it will have but a poor sale. 2. If it be malicious and try to undermine the General's character and reputation, it may be expected to have a great sale, but we can't touch it." That forecast was correct; when Badeau published his book, it was "decent," and the sale was small.

A proposal from General Sherman, a hero in the North although a ruthless conqueror in the eyes of Southerners, offered Mark Twain a problem in diplomacy. He had struck up a friendship with Sherman at the grand reunion of the Army of the Tennessee in Chicago in 1879. The two men had little enough in common, but they recognized each other's stature and they shared a concern for Grant's welfare and reputation. Sherman had successfully published his own memoirs through the normal channels of the trade; now, retired from the army and with the example of Grant's success, he considered another book. In a letter addressed to "My dear friend," he asked if Twain would give him an *honest* opinion" on a 300-page manuscript of travel notes from a European tour made in 1871– 72. "Answer today," reads Mark Twain's note on the envelope.

Twain promised to examine Sherman's manuscript—he could hardly have refused—to give "as square and honest an opinion" as he could, and to advise on the disposal of it. Sherman promptly dispatched his manuscript, by express. "If you have the patience, read," he requested, "and let me know your conclusion, *honest*, or as you used to say 'honor bright.'" Ten days later, Twain gave his verdict: "*Do not publish it*; & do not allow affection-blinded friends to persuade you that I am wrong." That judgment was truly "square and honest," expressed clearly yet tactfully. Mark Twain demonstrated the inferiority of the new work by comparing it to Sherman's own earlier book. His memoirs had been "rich in incident, anecdote, fact, history," but this new manuscript was the skeleton of a book rather than the book itself.

Sherman accepted that verdict with dignity, remarking that it agreed with his own judgment. He had "plenty of leisure to read the current literature, even the sensational novels," he added with a touch of pathos, "so that if you come across anything extra-fine let me have it." Instead of a sensational novel, Twain recommended one of his own favorites, a condensed English version of the *Memoirs* of the Duc de Saint-Simon. There was a book that might amuse a soldier with a taste for fact: "It furnishes all of St. Simon's rich & racy gossip & his incomparable pictures of Louis's absurd court," while leaving out his "interminable rot . . . about ducal 'preeminence.' " The correspondence closed four days later, when Sherman acknowledged the return of his manuscript, to be tied up, marked, "and deposited in the boneyard along with other original papers."

In mid-November, Mark Twain became a published author again, when "The Private History of a Campaign That Failed" appeared in the December issue of *Century*, securing him his small place in the great war series. But the "Private History" mocked that series, and the war itself. No important facts are revealed, and the "campaign" is a farce, a succession of quarrels, of groundless rumors, and panicky retreats from imaginary enemies, while the "Battle maps" ("First Position of Dogs," "Second Position of Dogs" at "Engagement at Mason's Farm") in the "Private History" are a burlesque of sober military histories. The twenty-five-year-old Sam Clemens of June 1861 and his comrades in the Marion Rangers seem to revert to adolescence in the "Campaign That Failed," almost to become Tom Sawyer's gang at war (Kemble's illustrations show them as boys, physically smaller than the adults they meet).

That farcical tone may have been true to fact; amateur soldiers often hold absurd illusions, and part of their disillusionment is to learn that war can mean not only heroic death in battle, but hunger, rain, and fatigue, and that it takes place in a fog of confusion, of unfounded rumor and senseless fear. Of course, it also excused his own participation on what, to himself as well as to Livy and his Hartford neighbors, was clearly the wrong side. And in a sense it exonerated him; if he had sat out the war in the safety of Virginia City and San Francisco, that was at least better than fighting for the Confederacy. Southern fire-eaters might denounce him for cowardice, but he could ignore them. ("If you have a boy, I hope he has not read this shameful story of cowardice & folly," wrote one. "*23* years old! & man enough to have been a river pilot." "Anonymous ass," Twain scrawled on the envelope.) But the "Campaign" had more than a personal significance, more than a limited documentary accuracy; it quietly subverted the basic concept of the

Century series—of war, no matter how terrible, as somehow a *rational* activity.

While he waited for the first volume of the *Memoirs* to be delivered to subscribers, and for the door of plenty to open, Twain distracted himself with calculating profits and planning future publications for Webster and Company. On November 11, he wrote to Webster concerning a book of Hawaiian legends put together by Rollin M. Daggett, a friend from Nevada days who had later served as American minister in Honolulu. The islands were still an independent monarchy, and the King, David Kalakaua, had collaborated with Daggett on the book. Webster was to offer 15 percent profits to Daggett if his name only was used, but 40 percent "with mention of the King as collaborator in the introduction," or 60 percent "with *both names in the title page* as authors." It was eventually published by Webster and Company (in 1888) as Twain had wished, "By his Hawaiian Majesty Kalakaua," but the sale was insignificant. Daggett and his wife had paid a twenty-four-hour visit to the Clemenses earlier in the fall of 1885, and no doubt he had talked about his intended book. Mark Twain could never quite realize that personal relationships, whether friendly or hostile, had no place in business.

There was a book of Grant's letters to his wife, edited by her, that Webster and Company must secure immediately (it never materialized), in order to "get it out a year in advance of the pope's book [a biography of Pope Leo XIII by Father Bernard O'Reilly]." The revival of interest in the war had reached its climax with Grant's death, and the great public that bought his book did not want his letters to his wife or the memoirs of lesser generals. But Twain and Webster would not admit that the success of Grant's book could not be repeated.

Between imagined crises and mundane problems, Mark Twain found time for invention, or at least for imagining needed inventions. The urbanizing of America offered an opportunity: "Could not a full line of creatures be made of paper pulp cast in moulds?" he asked himself in his journal—these to be used in city schools whose pupils "can't go insect-&-snake hunting to get their own specimens for study." On October 3, he casually imagined microprint: "I think I've struck a good idea. It is to reduce a series of big maps to mere photographic fly-specks & sell them together with a microscope." Either of those ideas would have been a good deal more practical than the history game or the bed clamp, but he made no effort to follow them up. The proceeds could not have compared with the profit he was guaranteed from the *Memoirs*, much less the millions he expected from the Paige typesetter.

High living, public service, and family occasions all helped to keep Mark Twain occupied. Writing to Livy from New York, he described in loving detail a dinner given by his friend William Laffan, publisher of the New York *Sun*, attended by Twain, Osgood, and "two young Harpers." Instead of the inexorable procession of courses that made up the usual Victorian dinner, there were only three, each one superb. First "very small raw oysters—just that moment opened, & swimming in their own sea-water. Delicious," then "terrapin stew, in dainty little covered pots, with curious little gold & silver terrapin spoons from Tiffany's. Sublime," and finally, the climax: "an entire canvass-back duck, red hot from the oven," for every guest. At each place "stood a quart of champagne, in a silver cooler," with an extra quart on the sideboard for emergencies. "No coffee, desert [*sic*], cheese"—but nothing more was needed. "Not a scrap of the 3 courses was left. Five skeletons represented the ducks; 6 empty bottles represented the champagne. A memorable dinner."

The next morning, November 18, he left for Washington to "talk international copyright" with President Cleveland that afternoon. A conference on the subject had been held in Bern in 1885, which two years later would result in a treaty signed by most of the major European nations. But the United States had not participated. "One must not refuse an office of that kind," he explained to Livy. "A man who prides himself on his citizenship *can't* refuse." It was a simple moral issue—American publishers should not be allowed to steal foreign works by issuing them without payment to the author—but the cause also directly concerned American writers. Such piracy depressed the value of their works. Mark Twain gave a prepared speech and urged the President "to make I.C. the child of his administration, & nurse it, & raise it." Cleveland was encouraging, and Twain returned to Washington in late January to testify before a Senate committee, but it would be another five years before the United States granted copyright to foreign authors.

November birthdays were observed appropriately. Both Livy and Mark were entering new decades; she her fifth, he his sixth. The

preliminaries for Livy were joyful: on the night before, neighborhood friends and children were invited in, to play charades and
dance the Virginia Reel—"a most merry time," Livy observed in
her diary. At her birthday dinner, on November 27, the Clemenses
entertained the actor Joseph Jefferson, nationally famous for his
portrayal of Rip Van Winkle, along with the Warners, the Twichells,
and a son of John Bright, the English Liberal politician. "Had a
riotous time," wrote Mark to Orion the next day. Presents were
simple that year: "Mr. Clemens gave me a most beautiful copper
vase," Livy recorded. Afterward, they took Susy and Clara to see
Jefferson perform; it was the first time Clara had ever gone out in
the evening to any place of public amusement, and only the second
time for Susy. The Clemenses were careful parents, even for their
day.

"Our faces are toward the sunset, now," Twain had written to
Livy in a birthday note, "but these [their children] are with us,
now, to hold our hands, & stay our feet, & while they abide, &
our old love grows & never diminishes, our march shall still be
through flowers & green fields." Far from the language of *Huckleberry Finn*, but no doubt sincere, and what Livy would have expected. "Huckspeech" was unthinkable for such an occasion, and
this rhetoric, the language of the age for the sublime, the beautiful,
or the pathetic, was the only alternative Mark Twain had, although
nothing in his life suggests that he had turned his face toward the
sunset. Livy left no record of her feelings, but in a photograph of
the time, her face is severe, that of a woman who disclaims any
pretense of youthfulness. Ten years later, she would look no older.

Two days after Livy's birthday, Mark Twain turned fifty. One
magazine, *The Critic*, gave a page to the event, printing a tribute
in verse from Oliver Wendell Holmes, at seventy-six the most widely
admired humorous writer in America, and according to *Harper's
Weekly* the most successful writer of occasional verse "in the whole
range of English literature," author of such stock anthology pieces
as "Old Ironsides" (on the frigate *Constitution*), "The Deacon's
Masterpiece" (on the wonderful one-hoss shay), and "The Chambered Nautilus" ("Build thee more stately mansions, O my soul").
His easy humor and gentle moralizing had made him a universal
favorite with cultivated readers. "Ah, Clemens, when I saw thee
last, / We both of us were younger," Holmes began, going on for
eight stanzas.

The Clemenses were delighted; recognition by the revered Dr. Holmes was a high compliment. (Mark and Livy had read his *Autocrat of the Breakfast Table* together, during their engagement.) Twain sent appropriate thanks, in florid prose: the delight of his family on seeing *The Critic* had made him "feel as the victor feels when the shouting hosts march by," it had raised him up "to remote and shining heights in their eyes [not necessarily in his own, it appears]," to "fellowship with the chambered Nautilus itself." There was a transatlantic tribute in a letter from Andrew Lang, a British critic:

> "We turn his pages and we see
> The Mississippi flowing free;
>   We turn again and grin
> O'er all Tom Sawyer did and planned
> With him of the ensanguined hand,
>   With Huckleberry Finn!"

That would have been welcome, for Twain valued his English reputation. The amateurs were heard from as well, in verses not very much worse than Lang's or Dr. Holmes's.

Such poems were conventional compliments, to be responded to conventionally; probably he took more pleasure from Charles Dudley Warner's remark that while it was easy enough to be fifty, he would not find it so easy to stay there, or Joel Chandler Harris's answer, in that issue of *The Critic*, to the moralizers who had condemned *Huckleberry Finn*: "there is not in our fictive literature a more wholesome book . . . we are taught the lesson of honesty, justice, and mercy." Twain wrote his thanks, "particularly for the good word about Huck, that abused child of mine who has had so much unfair mud flung at him." Most of all, he might have enjoyed the summing up of his blessings in a letter from Rollin Daggett: "Famous, wealthy, and the center of a charming household, and d——d if my wife don't even think you are handsome. If your luck continues, you will reach the bosom of Buddha in a single translation."

"When a man reaches fifty," Twain would note twenty-one long years later, "age seems to descend upon him like a black cloud." And he recalled that at fifty, he thought he had written himself out, "for everybody who has ever written has been smitten with that superstition at about that age." But, he added, even at seventy-one, he had not yet written himself out. Like many men, Twain no doubt felt a certain gloom at entering a new decade. But nothing in his behavior suggests any serious or long-lasting depression. He had too much to do, too much to look forward to: his close-knit family life, the popularity that he might curse but had no desire to lose, and the ever-engrossing game of business. The first volume of the *Memoirs* had still to be delivered to subscribers, and the largest royalty check in the history of the world was yet to be made out. And to a sanguine man, that seemed only the beginning. "The pope's book," the biography of Leo XIII, would surely outsell even the *Memoirs*—there were more Catholics than veterans—while the typesetter promised even greater riches.

The first volume of the *Memoirs* was finally delivered to subscribers in December. The printers and the binderies had been at work for months, with twenty presses going day and night. (Twain remarked longingly that "if we could get 37, we could print a complete volume every second." But that was Colonel Sellers speaking—printing a volume every second, "night and day," would have meant printing more than 86,000 volumes a day, an impossible figure.) Twain was nervous, he feared the work was going too slowly, he panicked when Webster failed to send a weekly report on the progress of the printers: "here is the hellish result—asleep over a volcano." His fears might be unreasonable, but in October he had borrowed a hundred thousand dollars to cover costs of printing and binding.

There could be no money until the books were delivered to subscribers, and the wait until publication of the first volume in December must have seemed interminable. "A starving beggar," Mark Twain called himself, "standing outside the door of plenty." Forgetting his praise of Webster's generalship, it seemed to him that the whole weight of responsibility fell on his shoulders. "Since last March," he confided to Howells, "you know I am carrying a mighty load, solitary & alone." Webster—endlessly busy—might have been surprised to hear that Twain carried his load alone, but while Webster could attend to the mechanics of publishing, he could not share Twain's conviction that Grant's work was not simply a book like other books.

"I've got the first volume launched safely," Twain announced to Howells on December 2. "Half of the suspense is over . . . We've bound & shipped 200,000 books, & by the tenth shall finish & ship the remaining 125,000." (In that moment of exhilaration he could forget Webster's part.) Simply as a feat of publishing, it had been phenomenal. Mark Twain collected the statistics later: producing both volumes had required 906 tons of paper, along with 35,261 skins of sheep, goats, and calves for the bindings, besides "25¼ miles of cloth a yard wide" and 276 barrels of paste. Forty-one steam presses had finally been employed, working day and night.

Soon he would set another record; on February 27, Webster and Company would write a check to Julia Grant for $200,000, her royalty on the first volume. Webster promptly released the story to the newspapers—to make it better, he had overpaid Mrs. Grant by several thousand dollars, to bring the figure to an even $200,000. That was double the twenty thousand pounds that Macaulay had received. (The canceled check can still be seen, framed and hanging on a basement wall of the Twain home in Hartford.) That first payment would be followed by a second, for $150,000, on October 11, 1886. The Lynchburg *Virginian*, apparently edited by an unreconstructed Confederate, grumbled that if Grant's book was worth a quarter of a million (the amount of that check had no doubt been exaggerated), then *Hamlet* should be worth enough to pay off the national debt of England; but to the Northern public the success of the *Memoirs* seemed entirely natural and appropriate.

Mark Twain had seen the opportunity, seen it in all its magnitude, as *Century* had not—and seized it; he had been right, because in his unquestioning reverence for Grant and for the Union cause he *was* the average American, or at least the average Northerner and Westerner. (No sale could be expected in the old Confederacy.) He had carried the publication to success because it was in his own realm of expertise, because he had a reasonably competent agent to attend to details, and because there was a clear and limited project to complete within a specified time. None of those conditions would apply to his other ventures.

Publication of the *Memoirs* was a solemn national event. Copies bound in full morocco had been sent to Sherman and Sheridan, with their names printed in gilt. This was no cheap and gaudy book, filled with crude woodcuts, of the kind that brought subscription publishing into contempt. No thick paper was needed to add bulk; Grant had provided all the content required. When Webster and

Company issued Sheridan's memoirs a few years later, the cover displayed a flamboyant Sheridan on a galloping horse, in gilt, waving his hat, but there had been nothing colorful about Grant's personality or achievement. His book expressed, and required, a dignified reticence.

Howells was thoroughly pleased: "I'm reading Grant's book with a delight I've failed to find in novels," he wrote on December 11; "I think he is one of the most natural—that is, *best*, writers I ever read." Mark Twain eagerly recorded that praise in his notebook. For him, Howells would always be the critical court of last resort. Sherman, speaking with the experience of a man who had written his own memoirs, felt that Grant had "been very fortunate in his choice of materials, omitting surplusage, & occasionally warming up the narration by a quiet piece of wit, an illustrative story, or a side fling at some party he did not like." The book was admirable, everyone agreed, not only as history, but as a composition.

The newspapers applauded, printed excerpts, marveled at the sale. Reviews were uniformly reverential in dealing with the work of the "dead hero." *The Critic* predicted that of all the actors in the war, only Grant would be remembered, eclipsing even Lincoln. The *Nation* observed that the work "has the basic element of thoroughly good writing, since we are made to feel that the writer's only thought . . . is how to express most directly and simply the thing he has to say." The style was the man. The clarity of Grant's prose proceeded from and guaranteed the honesty of the narrator. But Mark Twain needed no reassurance from reviewers to confirm his opinion of the *Memoirs*. Howells's comment and the public verdict were enough. A few years later, annoyed by Matthew Arnold's schoolmasterish criticism of Grant's use of the verb "to conscript" and his alleged misuse of "shall," "will," "should," and "would," Twain would compose a reply, "General Grant's Grammar," declaring that Grant had "linked words together with an art surpassing that of the schools, and put into them a something which will still bring to American ears, as long as America shall last, the roll of his vanished drums and the tread of his marching hosts." But Arnold had died, and that answer remains unpublished, at the Mark Twain Papers.

The second volume of the *Memoirs* was received with the same enthusiasm as the first. The dean of the Yale Law School wrote to Mark Twain that he and his wife were reading the *Memoirs* aloud to each other, treating themselves with the book as if it had been candy, sorry to reach the end. "THE GREATEST BOOK OF THE AGE!" screamed a Webster and Company circular. Grant had "died like a soldier facing victory. His tongue is silent forever, *but his thoughts live in these speaking pages*." But hard selling was not needed. The book had found its audience, and there was nothing for Webster and Company to do but wait for the money to come in. (Webster and Company's share of the profits should have reached about $150,000. Mark Twain would never benefit from that money; he left it in the business as operating capital, and it had disappeared well before the firm went bankrupt in 1894.) Webster received a share, as he had been made a partner in recognition of his increased responsibilities. The hopes, the anticipation, the constant excitement and suspense, were over, but Mark Twain could not quietly draw his profits and go back to his writing. He had immensely enjoyed his business success and the attention that his connection with Grant had brought him—his own imagination could not have created a more dramatic role for himself to play. But after living at such a level, ordinary existence could not satisfy him. Only "the pope's book" and the typesetter could save him from a descent into everyday reality.

Occupying himself continuously with business, his mind filled with anxieties from his position as General Grant's publisher, and increasingly dazzled with hopes of fortune from the typesetter, Twain almost believed that his career as a writer was over. One evening, Susy records, "as papa and I were promonading up and down the library he told me that he didn't expect to write but one more book . . . he had written more than he had ever expected to, and the only book [*Captain Stormfield's Visit to Heaven*] that he had been particularly anxious to write was . . . locked up in the safe down stairs, not yet published." Mark Twain explained his intentions more fully to a friend, several months later: he would write "three chapters a year [of the *Connecticut Yankee*] for thirty years . . . for posterity only; my great grandchildren." He would amuse himself with it for six days every summer, as long as he lived, and did not expect to publish it.

He planned two more books, one of them probably the *Visit to Heaven*, the other his autobiography—"if one's autobiography may be called a book." He would actually compose an autobiography of a sort in his old age, leaving most of it unpublished, and he would complete *A Connecticut Yankee in King Arthur's Court* over the next few years, publishing it in the fall of 1889, when he badly needed the money. His wife and daughter knew him better than he knew himself: "Mama says that she sometimes feels, and I do too, that she would rather have papa depend on his writing for a living than to have him think of giving it up," wrote Susy in her biography. But Susy was confident that she and her mother could persuade "papa" to go on writing—"when mama realy desires anything and says that it must be, papa allways gives up his plans." But Livy never had to give such an order, and it probably would not have been given even if Mark Twain had made the millions that he dreamed of with the typesetter. He would write *A Connecticut Yankee*, and he would go on writing until he died.

The *Yankee* was already under way. On February 13, Twain confided to Webster that he was at work on a story "whose scene is laid far back in the twilight of tradition: I have saturated myself with the atmosphere of the day & the subject, & got myself into the swing of the work. If I peg away for some weeks without a break, I am safe; if I stop now for a day, I am unsafe, & may never get started right again." He gave himself directions in his notebook. The story was to be published as a holiday book, under the title "The Lost Land." "First part written on ancient yellow parchment (palimpsest), the last chapter on fresh new paper . . . with watermark, British arms & '1885.' In palimpsest one catches remnants of monkish legends." And he advises himself, "Get them from Wm of Huntingdon."

Within two weeks, he was able to test the work in his usual way: "Yesterday evening papa read to us the beginning of his new book, in manuscript," Susy recorded, "and we enjoyed it very much, it was founded on a New Englanders visit to England in the time of King Arthur and his Round Table." His plan had already moved beyond the burlesque of chivalry that he had first conceived. The theme, as he now imagined it, would be his favorite: a lament for lost youth. "He [the 19th-century narrator] mourns his lost land— had come to England & revisited it, but it is all changed & become old, so old!—& it was so fresh & new, so virgin before . . . Has lost all interest in life—is found dead next morning—suicide He is also grieving to see his sweetheart, so suddenly lost to him." The pathos of the opening and the close of *A Connecticut Yankee in*

King Arthur's Court, so strongly contrasting with its uproarious farce and vehement protest, is foreshadowed in that note.

The contract for "the pope's book" was finally signed in May of 1886. From New York, Mark Twain passed on the news at once to Livy. She had worried when she bought an expensive sofa, but now, he told her, she could order a thousand sofas: "the future book will foot the bill & never miss it . . . we'll sell a fleetload of copies." Webster was equally optimistic, and equally wrong: "If we get all that is promised" (official approval by the Church, an autographed letter from the Pope that could be reproduced in facsimile), "we will beat the record on Grant by a great distance." (Both Webster and Twain seemed to believe that every Catholic in America would buy the book as an act of faith on learning that the Pope had approved it.) From New York, Twain shared his hopes with the faithful Twichell, who recorded the brilliant prospects in his journal: "The issue of this book will be the greatest event in the way of book publishing that ever occurred; and it seems certain M.T. will make a vast amount of money." A later note adds a melancholy correction: "P.S. Proved quite otherwise in the event."

Publication and sale of Grant's *Memoirs* had been completed by the spring of 1886, but Mark Twain's interest in them was abruptly revived in late spring, when John Wanamaker, founder of Wanamaker's Department Store in Philadelphia, advertised copies for sale. Wanamaker had acquired about five hundred copies and offered them at $5.50 per set, well under the basic subscription price of $7.00. Worse, he had said in his advertisement that the price had been set "unreasonably high because of the unfortunate method of publication" and offered the *Memoirs* at a discount as a public service to whoever could not afford to pay $7.00, or did not wish to be harassed by a book agent. "The publishers meant to keep these books, in which the American people take so deep an interest, out of the bookstores. They intended you should open your door to whatever book-peddler happened to pull your bell, or go without the Personal Memoirs of U. S. Grant."

Finally, the advertisement summed up all the prejudices against subscription publishing: "Big, thick books; big letters far apart; thick paper; pictures; plenty of gilt on the cover; the subject—no matter; the author—no matter." A library of such books "would be a library of ignorance, vulgarly bound." While those criticisms did not apply to the *Memoirs*, Wanamaker was right on the whole—subscription publishing lacked dignity. All that could be said in its favor was that it placed books in the homes of a multitude of readers who never went near a bookstore. If the memoirs of a national hero should be marketed with due reverence, then subscription publishing was inappropriate. But if the best acknowledgment of the nation's debt to Grant was to place his book in the hands of as many readers as possible, while providing the highest possible return to the author's family, then Webster and Company was truly performing a public service.

It was not in Mark Twain's nature to let such an attack go unanswered; it embarrassed him not only as Grant's publisher but as a heavy contributor himself to that "library of ignorance." Insulted and injured (he believed), he responded furiously, ordering Webster to "go for Wanamaker" at once: "Otherwise I will go down there & rise up in his Sunday School and give him hell, in front of his whole 3,000 pupils" (conspicuous piety was an essential part of Wanamaker's public image). War was carried on in the newspapers and in the courts. Webster and Company would lose its suit to enjoin Wanamaker from selling the book, and Mark Twain would never forgive that "unco-pious butter-mouthed Sunday school-slobbering sneak-thief John Wannemaker [*sic*], now of Philadelphia, presently of hell," but no real harm had been done—the *Memoirs* had already reached their audience.

TWELVE

"Immortal Hopefulness"

W ith publication of the first volume in early December 1885, the sale of the Grant *Memoirs* was virtually completed. Webster and his clerks could handle the job of getting the second volume to subscribers. Mark Twain could never expect to repeat the unique experience of his role in the publication of the *Memoirs* and of his personal association with Grant. "The pope's book" could not match that, even if it sold as well as the *Memoirs*. But the Paige typesetter, Twain believed, offered the chance of a business success on an even larger scale. If it succeeded, it could offer profits not in the hundreds of thousands but in the millions. And it was, he imagined, *his* enterprise; greatly as he admired Paige ("a poet in steel"), at times he seemed almost to forget Paige's contribution. The typesetter became Mark Twain's machine, and more than a machine.

On January 18, 1886, Twain addressed the annual meeting of the Typothetae, an association of master printers in New York City. He used the occasion to promote the Paige typesetter. His speech was an affectionate reminiscence, full of printer's jargon, humor-ously recalling the trade as he had known it in a Missouri village thirty-five years before. But the humor seems forced, and in distant San Francisco, Ambrose Bierce, reading that speech, sensed a change: "foremost among the desecrators of the tomb of Mark the jester is Mark the Money-worm." His speech to the Typothetae was "an epitaph . . . the indisputable proof that Samuel Clemens, Es-quire, of Hartford, Connecticut, was masquerading in the motley of Mark Twain." So Bierce anticipated by more than thirty years the accusation of Van Wyck Brooks, in his *Ordeal of Mark Twain*, that Twain had sold out, sacrificing the artist—or "jester," in Bierce's term—in himself to the respectable citizen and business-man, the "Money-worm."

"Meeting of Hamersley, Paige & Clemens in my billiard-room," Twain noted in his journal on January 26, 1886. "Paige says 'Every expense connected with making the model machine *cannot* reach $30,000' . . . This includes every possible cost of wages, drawings, building the machine, taking out *all* patents, etc." With its latest improvement, an automatic justifier, the entire process of typeset-ting had been automated. Twain had made a last effort, in the late fall of 1885, to raise money to build a new model of the typesetter, approaching John Mackay, a Nevada silver king whom Twain had known in his Virginia City days, but Mackay showed no interest.

If the capitalists were blind to their opportunity, why shouldn't Mark Twain finance the new machine himself? Then the capitalists would come, and pay his price. He was sure of success, but in any case, he could afford to risk $30,000. On February 6, he signed a contract committing himself to pay the expenses of building and testing one new machine, then of exhibiting and demonstrating it in New York. Paige agreed in return to transfer $9/20$ of net profits to Twain and $1/20$ to William Hamersley, a Hartford lawyer who would provide professional services in lieu of cash. When the ma-chine had been completed and tested, more capital would be needed to build a factory, and Twain agreed to pay the cost of finding it. He also agreed to pay a salary of $7,000 a year to Paige, until Paige's profits should equal that amount. On March 15, Pratt & Whitney, in Hartford, agreed to manufacture one "typesetting, dis-tributing and justifying machine" for cost plus 10 percent, mean-while submitting monthly bills for Mark Twain to pay.

Mark Twain had made himself entirely responsible for the cost of the new typesetter; Hamersley and Paige risked nothing. Even in case of total failure, Paige would have been well paid for his time, spent in doing what he liked best—endlessly correcting faults and refining his machine, increasing its cost and complication—with no incentive to hurry or to control expenses. (That $30,000 limit would be passed within the first year.) As for Hamersley, he had committed himself to nothing more than a vague promise of legal services—"Of Yamersley [*sic*]. About $2/3$ of him is knave & the other $9/10$ is fool," Twain would sourly observe after disillusionment had set in. But at the time, a sanguine Mark Twain would hardly have noticed those risks, certainly would not have considered them significant. It is even possible that he had not read the contract through; figures bewildered and legal language infuriated him.

And the reward must have seemed so great that details hardly mattered. Yet for decades, inventors had struggled to develop a mechanical typesetter and had failed, producing scores of clumsy, unworkable machines. In 1886, the human typesetter, or "compositor," still picked out the letters he needed from their cases, put them in the "composing stick" (a metal frame), and inserted spaces where needed to justify the lines (making them even). The best compositor, working a ten-hour shift, could hardly set more than two thousand words. And when the printing was done, the type had to be distributed—another two hours' work. Now, with the addition of the justifier, a single operator at the keyboard of a Paige typesetter could do the work of half a dozen men, and do it more accurately. According to a circular prepared by Twain, Paige, and Hamersley, thirty thousand newspapers in Europe and North America would require Paige compositors (Paige's awkward name for his invention), at a cost of $300 million, and thousands of book-publishing and job-printing establishments would follow. (There was a hint of Colonel Sellers in those calculations.) The *Memoirs* had earned what would have seemed a fortune to most Americans, but here was an opportunity that offered millions, even tens of millions—and it would be money gained by foresight and risk-taking, not by stock swindles, bribery, and theft, or the ruthless crushing of competitors.

The prize was great, and inevitably there were rival machines. The most dangerous of them was the Linotype, invented by Ottmar Mergenthaler and financed by a syndicate of newspapers headed by Whitelaw Reid of the New York *Tribune*. It was Reid who gave Mergenthaler's machine its apt and easily remembered name. "Linotype" was an exact description; the Mergenthaler was a typecasting rather than a typesetting machine, also operated by a single man at a keyboard, but casting (and justifying) a whole line of type in one operation. Everything was simplified; there were no individual letters to be set or distributed. Instead of duplicating the actions of the human compositor with exquisite precision and incredible complexity of design, as the Paige compositor did, the Linotype machine eliminated them.

It was a dangerous competitor—if it worked, its backing guaranteed success, and it was a real machine, not under interminable development in distant Hartford but already in use in New York pressrooms. And Mark Twain could never hope to match the resources available to Mergenthaler. He was aware of the Linotype machine, of course. Two weeks before signing the contract with Paige, he had been warned by his friend William M. Laffan, publisher of the New York *Sun*, that "every daily in this town will be set up by that machine [the Linotype] within twelve months. The *Tribune* will have 12 of them ready by Feb. 15th and I have . . . secured second place on the list . . . you'd better haul in your lente and festina like hell." (*Festina lente:* "Make haste slowly.") But the Linotype machine had its problems, and two months later, Twain scribbled a triumphant comment on the envelope of Laffan's letter: "O lame & ineffectual prophet. About 2½ months are sped and none of those machines are visible yet—& I, unaffrighted, am still at work building my machine." As he would be, for another three years.

Mark Twain saw the problem, but his own experience as a typesetter blinded him to the answer and prevented him from recognizing Linotype as a dangerous rival. The fact that Whitelaw Reid, a man he disliked, was Mergenthaler's most important backer might have influenced him as well—to defeat Reid would have been deeply satisfying. Twain shared the unquestioning confidence of his partner Hamersley "that no machine can be invented to take the place of moveable type." The only method of mechanizing the typesetter's work seemed to be to do what Paige had done, to create a kind of automaton that would repeat every human action involved. In its final form, it would have more than eighteen thousand parts, making it probably the most complicated machine of its century. But the precision and the complexity required fascinated Mark Twain; the typesetter seemed almost to possess human intelligence. It summed up the progress of the nineteenth century. Twain had succeeded with the *Memoirs*; how could he fail here, where the opportunity was so much greater?

As for the money, the millions that he dreamed of were literally incomprehensible—"vague, splendid ungraspable dollars," like the treasure that Tom Sawyer hunted—and it might have been of no more use to him than the buried gold that Tom and Huck discovered had been to them. Success would have multiplied the distractions of business, with the confusions and irritations of contracts and balance sheets, lawyers and lawsuits. Mark Twain would surely have been bored by the company of his fellow millionaires, and when "inspiration" came, he would have written again, as he had always done. It's not easy to see what he might have bought that he did not already have. But he could not admit even to himself that the reward from the game of business was in the playing, that he found his satisfaction in simply associating himself with this marvelous machine, which seemed to express the spirit of its age, and in displaying again the foresight, the grasp of possibilities over-looked by other men, that had led to his triumph with the *Memoirs*. Yet he needed the dollars. Without them, how could he have known that he had succeeded?

Month after month, year after year—long past the promised limits of time and money—construction of the machine went on, financed by monthly checks from Twain. The contract had committed him to a maximum of $30,000, but that limit was soon passed. He would ultimately spend at least $190,000. Paige was a perfec-tionist—his machine had to do everything before he would release it—and he had no incentive to hurry. Inevitably, he and his crew fell into the habit of "going right along as if there was to be no end of time or money," as Twain's business agent in Hartford remarked. The anxieties, as one deadline after another was missed, were all Mark Twain's. Months turned into years: 1886, 1887, 1888—the work went on. Expenses continually exceeded estimates, unexpected faults appeared—notably a tendency to break types (the separate letters), in spite of its automatic type tester—each requiring a delay of weeks while the machine was taken apart and reassembled. Paige devised ingenious refinements, each again requiring the ma-chine to be taken down, often just before prospective buyers would arrive to see the machine, only to find it scattered in pieces on the floor. And while Paige slowly built and rebuilt his machine, the Linotype was proving itself in the pressroom of the New York *Tribune*, and its inventor was developing an improved model that would soon be ready. But Mark Twain refused to see that "his" typesetter had been superseded before it had been completed.

Mark Twain was spending much more than he could afford; he knew that. But success seemed so sure, and so close, and the pros-pects so brilliant! He could not even think of withdrawing, of cutting his losses, when just a little more time, a little more money, would surely bring success. He had invested too much, not only in money but in time, in hopes, in anxiety. To withdraw would be to admit that he had been a reckless fool, that he had squandered his own fortune and his wife's.

By the end of 1888, the ordeal seemed nearly over. On October 3, Twain confided to Orion, "Today I pay Pratt & Whitney $10,000 . . . That outgo is done." Now his role would truly outshine Paige's: "I shall be in supreme command; it will not be necessary for the capitalist to arrive at terms with anybody but me." "The capitalist"— he delighted in that term. But the capitalists did not come.

Meanwhile, newspapers regularly carried stories praising his business ability and exaggerating his wealth and success. "Mark Twain is now said to be worth something like $1,500,000," reported the Atlanta *Constitution* in the late fall of 1886. How Mark Twain must have wished that those stories were true! Even Webster and Company began to disappoint him. The success of Grant's book had been unique, and Webster was breaking down under his self-imposed burden of work. He mismanaged affairs, the business was carelessly run, statements were irregular and incomplete, supervision was lax, a general agent defaulted, and in 1887 it was discovered that a bookkeeper had been embezzling ever since he had been hired two years before. Webster and Company had lost about $25,000, and only a fraction of that could be recovered. Twain himself did not help matters when, over Webster's objection, he insisted on publishing a volume of sermons by a Hartford minister who happened to be a friend. Sermons did not sell.

Webster's behavior and judgment became increasingly erratic. Signs of megalomania increased. ("Don't you worry about business, I have never yet made a business mistake that I am aware of," he had assured Mark Twain in October of 1885.) He had made an expensive journey to Rome, to get the Pope's endorsement of the biography, traveling in grand style, "in keeping with the millions we are supposed to have made," distributing luxurious editions of Grant's *Memoirs* to the Pope and cardinals, describing the papal interview in a thirteen-page letter to Mark Twain. He was knighted by the Pope, receiving the Order of the Golden Spur, with a gorgeous uniform (white cashmere trousers, blue coat with gold epaulettes, "sword with gilded hilt . . . pointed hat embroidered with gold"), and for the rest of his life his hometown paper, the Fredonia *Censor*, would refer to him as "Sir Charles Webster." "All this cost money like smoke but it *paid*," he assured his partner. Just when it no longer needed extra space, with work on the *Memoirs* done, Webster moved the firm into splendid new quarters, with storage room for a hundred thousand books, a freight elevator able to carry six hundred books at a time, a general office three times as large as the old one and a private office, "conversation tight," and space to carry on a retail trade.

Webster and Company became the nation's publisher of war books, issuing the memoirs of one general after another—Mc-Clellan, Sheridan, Hancock—Mrs. Custer's biography of her husband, a collection entitled *Yanks and Rebs*, and a new edition of Sherman's memoirs as well. But the public was soon sated with war. Each book sold less well than the one before, and unsold copies accumulated. As young Fred Hall, Webster's assistant, reported in 1888: *"war literature of any kind and no matter by whom written is played out."* Finally, hoping to dispose of the "immense quantity of poor stock that we have on hand," the firm put all its war books into a package: "Can you afford Eight Cents a Day—FOR THE GREAT WAR LIBRARY?" shouted the circulars.

Webster was often incapacitated by punishing headaches. He lost a valuable book by his delay—in spite of Twain's repeated urgings—in making an offer for the autobiography of Joseph Jefferson, the immensely popular actor. Jefferson's book was published by Century and went through several editions. But Webster would admit no mistakes, would not even admit that he could make a mistake.

He retired in 1888, dying at forty, only two years later. But his retirement made no difference. Fred Hall, eager and enthusiastic but with no more knowledge of books than Webster and even less business experience, replaced him, and the decline continued. In a disastrous blunder, the firm had taken over in 1887 E. C. Stedman's eleven-volume *Library of American Literature*. Such a work had to be sold on the installment plan, and every set delivered cost the publisher ten dollars more than the customer's down payment, while subsequent payments would often be delayed. Within a few years, the continuing drain of capital would ruin Webster and Company. There would be a profit in the long run, but the long run was never reached. By the middle of 1890, $70,000 had been sunk into the *Library*. It absorbed all profits from other books; even Twain's royalties could not be paid. The firm's indebtedness grew that year from $13,000 to $39,000. The cycle leading to bankruptcy had commenced, with Webster and Company regularly borrowing from the banks to meet immediate obligations, such as printers' bills and binding charges, and renewing old loans instead of paying them off.

In spite of steadily increasing losses and anxieties, life went on for the Clemenses with no outward change. Distinguished visitors to Hartford were still welcomed. Of them all, Henry M. Stanley, the explorer who "discovered" Dr. Livingstone, was the most impressive. Lecturing in Hartford on December 8, 1886, on "Through the Dark Continent," he was invited to dinner before his lecture by Mark Twain, and to a late supper with friends afterward, followed by a long talk. He lived up to all expectations. Twichell found him "modest, intelligent, strong, honest," and a thrilling storyteller, and decided that he had never seen a more satisfactory hero. For years, Mark Twain tried unsuccessfully to persuade Stanley to write his autobiography for Webster and Company.

Family festivities remained important; Susy's fifteenth birthday was elaborately and expensively celebrated. Ten girls were invited for supper; at each place were a bunch of flowers, a dish of candy, tied with ribbons, and a "Japanese card" with the guest's name. There were vases of roses, a "pyramid of nasturtiums," and tall silver candlesticks on the table. The dinner closed with strawberries and ice cream—a rare luxury in March, in the 1880s.

Family ties did not loosen as the children grew; the intimacy of Susy and her father, in particular, remained as close as ever—dangerously close, for the happiness of them both. When Susy reached eighteen, she would be sent to Bryn Mawr, no doubt in part to wean her from her home. But the experiment proved a failure—college could not compare with home. Her parents accompanied her, staying on for weeks, and when they finally went back to Hartford, the parting was hard. In a letter to Pamela, Mark Twain described the last view of his daughter: "Our train was moving away, & she was drifting collegeward afoot, her figure blurred & dim in the rain & fog, & she was crying." Susy stayed out her year at Bryn Mawr, homesick and unhappy. She did not return.

The intense social life of Nook Farm, and Hartford, went on. It was a small community, upper-middle-class Hartford, and Mark Twain was deeply involved in everything that happened: the public events, the dinners and receptions, the continuous round of visiting at Nook Farm. And there were always the clubs, the Monday Evening Club, the Saturday Morning Club, even a Browning class that Mark Twain organized and taught, with great success. Membership was entirely female (men would be at their various businesses), and the teaching consisted of Twain's carefully prepared readings. At first he had tried to explain the poetry, but soon gave that up; properly read, he found, it explained itself. He took the class seriously, studying the poems and carefully marking them for reading aloud just as he had marked a copy of *Huckleberry Finn* during his tour with Cable. Mark Twain normally took little interest in poetry, and Browning's verse was notorious for its obscurity, but Browning was a poet of the spoken word, and his dramatic monologues, with their endless variety of voices, offered splendid opportunities to a skilled reader.

In spite of typesetter costs, Twain was still involved in charities and philanthropies. He had paid board for Warner T. McGuinn, a black student attending Yale Law School, in 1885–86 and renewed his support in 1886–87, after receiving a favorable report from the dean. Twain did not know McGuinn, but that did not matter. In giving this help, he felt that he was simply paying a small part of the debt that every white man in America owed to every black man. He leased a farm in Connecticut, offering it as a free residence for life to Prudence Crandall, who had "made the great fight for the negro" in Connecticut long before the Civil War, having her school wrecked by a mob when she tried to admit black girls. In 1887 he gave a "generous donation" to a fund to buy a summer cottage for Walt Whitman, remarking that by comforting Whitman in his old age, Americans could pay part of their debt to him. Whether Mark Twain had read, or read in, *Leaves of Grass* is not known, but his admiration for Whitman as a literary figure was undeniable. He had attended Whitman's lecture at Madison Square Garden in the spring of 1885, and he had contributed to another fund to buy a horse and buggy for the half-paralyzed poet, commenting that he felt "a great veneration for the old man."

When Yale awarded Mark Twain an honorary M.A. in 1889, the highest recognition he had yet received from the American cultural establishment, he was grateful, especially since the award came not long after, as he wrote in accepting the award, "the late Matthew Arnold" had "rather sharply rebuked the guild of American 'funny men' in his latest literary delivery." Arnold had condemned the American taste for a crude and primitive humor, singling out

Twain's work as an example, and that criticism had stung. Mark Twain might cast himself as a philistine, writing to Howells that "high and fine literature is wine, & mine is only water; but everybody likes water," but the charge of philistinism amused him only when he made it himself. In his letter of thanks to the president of Yale, he admitted that "a friendly word was needed in our [humorists'] defense," and argued that it was deserved, for by exposing shams and falsities, by laughing at superstitions, the humorist inevitably became the enemy of rank and privilege and the "friend of human rights and liberties." As evidence for that claim, he might have offered his own *Connecticut Yankee in King Arthur's Court*.

Twain had read in public from the manuscript of *A Connecticut Yankee* in November of 1886, and at Quarry Farm the next summer he resumed work on it, producing hundreds of pages of manuscript. As he wrote, the book moved in a new direction. The opening chapters combined an elegiac lament for the lost land from which the Yankee, returned to the modern world, is separated by thirteen centuries, with a farcical burlesque of "chivalry," as presented in Malory's *Morte d'Arthur*, and of the discomforts of medieval life as experienced by a late-nineteenth-century American. Now his book became increasingly an indictment of the injustices and sufferings inflicted on the English people by Church, aristocracy, and king, and of the servility and credulity that made oppression possible. Since writing *The Gilded Age* and "The Curious Republic of Gondour" more than ten years before, he had unconsciously radicalized himself. Rereading Carlyle's *French Revolution*, Twain found, to his surprise, that he no longer sympathized with the moderate Girondins, as Carlyle did, but with the revolutionary extremists, the sansculottes.

For all his dislike of the French, their Revolution now seemed to him the "noblest" and "holiest" event in history, next to the American Revolution, and its work was not yet done. Twain's old Anglophilia had weakened, and he began to ridicule English class-consciousness. As he wrote, he deepened the significance of *A Connecticut Yankee*, while creating great inconsistencies. At times his Yankee seems a confidence man, exploiting the rubes of the dark ages while laughing at their stupidity; at times, a grown-up Tom Sawyer, ready to run any risk or sacrifice any purpose for a spectacular display with himself at the center; and at times, a democratic reformer, bringing liberty and enlightenment to feudal England, as liberty and enlightenment were understood in the America of the 1880s.

He finished *A Connecticut Yankee* in the spring of 1889, in spite of all his business anxieties and distractions, again expressing the democratic populism of the summer before, but less confidently now. The goal remained, but human weakness prevented its achievement. The Yankee's effort fails, defeated not by the strength of English knighthood (which he annihilates with nineteenth-century technology) but by the stupidity and cowardice of the English people, breaking their chains for a moment, then rallying to the support of their oppressors, unable to overcome their superstitious fear of the Church and their deep-rooted reverence for rank.

A Connecticut Yankee was published by Webster and Company in December of 1889. Howells, who had been converted to socialism by reading Tolstoy, reviewed it enthusiastically in *Harper's*, finding in it "a force of right clear feeling and thinking . . . that never got into fun before." Another admirer saw it as a sequel to *Don Quixote*, a satire on the "fallacies which made chivalry possible once, and servility and flunkeyism and tyranny possible now." Twain agreed, and his illustrator, Dan Beard, had dramatized the contemporary relevance of the work by showing Jay Gould, the notorious speculator, as a slave driver with a whip, and had symbolized aristocratic pride by portraying the young Kaiser Wilhelm II, in a dramatic full-page illustration, as a knight on horseback, in full armor. Predictably, English reviewers denounced the book; it simply offered "a coarse pandering to that passion for irreverence which is at the basis of a great deal of Yankee wit," said the *Daily Telegraph*. Mark Twain had risked his English popularity for principle, hoping to teach the British a useful lesson, and he paid the price. *A Connecticut Yankee* hurt the sales of his books in England for years. In America, the *Yankee* had only a modest success, selling 32,000 copies compared with *Huckleberry Finn*'s 51,000, but the author was pleased with his book and its effect, even though Webster and Company could not afford to pay him his royalties.

With *A Connecticut Yankee* in print, Mark Twain could give full attention to the typesetter. Disillusionment had set in, not with the machine but with the inventor, who had broken all his promises, continually delaying completion and calling for more and more money. Writing to Pamela, in December of 1887, to explain why

Christmas gifts would be inexpensive that year, Twain had explained that "the typesetter goes on forever—at $3,000 a month." But the end was in sight at last, he added. Only three or four months of work, "& then the strain will let up and we can breathe freely once more." He was wrong. In January, Paige promised that the machine would be ready in April or May—it was not. Then it would be completed by September, then by January or February of 1889. The financial strain became increasingly severe—even the children understood that spending must be postponed until the machine was finished. Then there would be abundance. "How strange it will seem," Livy wrote to a friend, "to have unlimited means, to be able to do whatever you want to do, to give whatever you want to give without counting the cost."

But not even Paige could delay forever. On January 5, 1889, Twain wrote a memorandum, headed "EUREKA!," marking the apparent completion of the typesetter: "*Saturday, January 5, 1889*— 12:20 p.m. At this moment I have seen a line of movable type *spaced and justified by machinery!*" Exuberant letters carried the good news to friends and relations. "All other wonderful inventions of the human brain sink . . . into commonplaces contrasted with this awful mechanical miracle," he exclaimed in a letter to Orion. Soon the miraculous machine began to break type and had to be taken apart. In a month or two it was up again, operating with amazing speed and precision. Then Paige decided that an "air-blast" was required, with another delay. By this time, the Clemenses' stocks and savings had disappeared. And the machine grew steadily more complex. Paige had decided earlier that it should be electrically powered, and had taken time to develop a dynamo and electric motor. The motor did not work, but Mark Twain would decide that Paige had nearly anticipated Nikola Tesla's revolutionary invention of the alternating current motor—but he had had tried only direct current.

On July 2, Paige telegraphed to Quarry Hill: "The machine is finished; come & see it work." By mid-August, it had broken down again, but by mid-September, it was running, and Twain had forgotten all previous failures. Nothing, apparently, could disillusion him—he had fallen in love with a machine. "Our dream," he called it in a letter to a friend: "Our dream is a mechanical miracle; when a body sees it work, he says 'it's poetry.' " And that was before the justifier had been added. "There are two times in a man's life when he should not speculate," Twain wrote in his journal sometime between July of 1888 and May of 1889: "when he can afford it, & when he can't." But he would have furiously denied that his investment in the typesetter was a speculation.

The typesetter finally seemed to be ready, but it could not be marketed until it could be manufactured in quantity, for which $2 million would be needed. Mark Twain had already acquired a right to a $500 royalty on every machine sold and had sold shares in his royalty to friends, to raise immediate cash. Then, in August of 1890, he made a new contract with Paige. For the sum of $250,000, to be paid within six months, Paige transferred all rights to his machine to Mark Twain, reserving only one quarter of gross receipts for himself. The stakes had been raised, and everything depended on Twain; he must find that two million, at once. Recruiting Joe Goodman, his onetime employer on the Virginia City *Territorial Enterprise*, as an assistant, he turned to old Western friends, to John P. Jones, a millionaire senator from Nevada, and once more to John Mackay. (Both Paige and Twain seem to have been living in a world of fantasy. A year earlier, Twain noted in his journal that Paige "expressed his hearty willingness" to let Twain "raise the capital by selling the English patents for $10,000,000"—while perhaps keeping "4/10 of the English stock.")

Mackay dismissed the proposal at once; the typesetter should be handled by a syndicate of newspaper owners, he declared. Jones showed interest, gave assurances, raised hopes, then delayed, and finally, in a humiliating scene, allowed Mark Twain two minutes to make his case, then said he could do nothing. There were reasons for that refusal, although Twain would not acknowledge them: Jones had approached other capitalists and found that some of them had already invested in the Linotype machine; the first time he planned a visit to Hartford to see the typesetter in operation, he was told that it had been taken to pieces again; when he finally came, the demonstration ended abruptly when a lever broke.

Jones's decision was final, and Twain could only rage uselessly against his betrayal by "this penny-worshipping humbug & shuffler," this "sage-brush imitation of the Deity." He had failed to raise $250,000, and he could no longer meet ongoing expenses. Nothing depended on him now, everything was in Paige's hands. He had spent $190,000 and had nothing to show for it. Yet he did not lose faith; he had been betrayed, by Jones, by Paige, he thought, but not by the machine. The machine was not dead, but Paige was in command now, and Mark Twain could only hope that Paige could raise money where he had failed. Then he might at least collect a royalty on every machine sold. Meanwhile, he could only wait.

On June 6, 1891, the Clemenses, accompanied by Katy Leary, sailed for Europe. None of them could have suspected that it would be more than ten years before the family would live in America again, that their rich and satisfying life in Nook Farm had ended. For Mark Twain, that way of life, more than anything else, had constituted success. Economy seemed essential now, but the Clemenses could not reduce their scale of living, Livy felt, as long as they stayed in the Hartford house. (That move offered another advantage to Mark Twain: escape from the scene of his bitter disappointment, his humiliating failure to raise money for manufacturing the typesetter.) The Clemenses were searching for health, as well as for economy. Susy seemed frail, Livy showed alarming symptoms that might mean heart disease, while Twain himself had begun to contract bouts of bronchitis, which would afflict him for the rest of his life (probably caused by his incessant smoking, although he would not admit that tobacco could damage his health), and he suffered acutely from rheumatism in his right arm and shoulder, making it nearly impossible to write. That was a serious problem, when he badly needed money and could earn it only with his pen. He had tried dictating to a phonograph, filled four dozen cylinders (unfortunately lost or destroyed), then stopped. He could not talk to a machine; it was "compressive, unornamental & as grave & unsmiling as the devil."

The Clemenses were hardly poor, although they felt so. They traveled widely, they stayed in grand hotels, they visited expensive spas, they went to Bayreuth for the opera. In September, defying his rheumatic pains (he could not even dress himself without help), he floated down the Rhône, not quite on a raft, as Huck Finn would have done, but at least in a flat-bottomed boat, with one boatman, and going ashore every night. It was an idyllic experience, a "mild adventure," and if the excursion produced no publishable writing, it offered something at least as valuable: a happy "extinction from the world and newspapers, & a conscience."

The family wintered in Berlin, entering into society. Mark Twain's work was widely known in German-speaking countries—Nietzsche had admired *Tom Sawyer*, Freud would use examples from Mark

Twain's sketches in his analysis of humor—and he was welcome everywhere. He was even invited to dine with the Kaiser, Wilhelm II. When Wilhelm observed that *Life on the Mississippi* was Mark Twain's best book, Twain recalled that the hotel porter had said the same thing and decided that he had received the verdict of the German nation.

The dinner was not a success. The atmosphere was constrained, and Twain felt that he had violated etiquette by venturing a remark when he hadn't been asked, and by disagreeing with an imperial opinion. But he had already had his reward. On seeing the invitation, Jean had exclaimed, in awe, "Why, papa, if it keeps on like this, pretty soon there won't be anybody for you to get acquainted with but God." He might be a theoretical democrat, but it was not easy to be indifferent to the attention of an emperor. (In fact, the Kaiser was Mark Twain's second emperor—he had met Czar Alexander II in the Crimea in 1867, during the voyage of the *Quaker City*.)

The spring of 1892 was spent in touring northern Italy, followed by a flying visit to America on typesetter business—Paige, now in complete control, had persuaded some Chicago capitalists to form a company to manufacture the machine, and Twain felt that he must be on the scene. Summer was spent in Germany, at Bad Nauheim, where Twain worked on *Tom Sawyer Abroad*, and "Those Extraordinary Twins" (later to be transformed into *Pudd'nhead Wilson*.) "A howling farce," he called it. It was a happier time—Twain's arm was better and he could write more easily, and Livy's condition, doctors assured them, was less dangerous than they had feared: "She had no heart disease, but only weakness of the heart-muscles."

The family passed the fall and winter at the Villa Viviani, set on a hill with a glorious view, a few miles outside Florence—but without one daughter. Clara stayed in Berlin, taking piano lessons, attending a school for American girls, and enjoying her comparative freedom. Life in the little Anglo-American colony of Florence, with reading for her only diversion, was dull for Susy; she felt herself "lonely and anxious for a taste of the 'rage of living,' " as she complained in a letter to Clara. (Susy's letters occasionally remind the reader of a Jamesian heroine.) Her existence seemed purposeless. She was of marriageable age, but she did not marry. Intelligent, attractive, somehow she could not draw men to her. And if she had succeeded, she probably would have felt the immense inferiority of any young man to her incomparable father. (Clara could attract men, if she liked, but even Clara did not marry until she was thirty-five and her father was near death.) As for Susy's writing, she had composed plays and stories, but no more: "I should love to, but I can't now anyway and I don't ever expect to be able to."

As Clara recalled long after, she and Susy enjoyed the stares and the remarks when the family entered a dining room; they "confessed to each other that it must be queer to belong to a family in which no one was distinguished or famous." But they knew that they were singled out and welcomed not for their own sake but because they were Mark Twain's daughters. They longed to distinguish them-selves, but how? Susy had been deeply interested in the theater from childhood, writing, directing, and acting in her own plays, but a theatrical career for Mark Twain's daughter must have seemed im-possible. She had given up writing—she could not hope to match her father. Clara chose music, where there could be no competition.

Mark Twain went on writing. Dining with William James, also living in Florence at the time, he would remark that he had "written more in the past four months than he could have done in two years at Hartford." He had no choice; the family depended entirely on his earnings now. No profits came from Webster and Company, only cheerful letters from young Fred Hall, explaining why the last season had been a bad one for books and why the next one would be better. Twain had already produced *The American Claimant*, a potboiling novelization of the Sellers play, and *Tom Sawyer Abroad*, in which Huck and Jim and Tom travel across the Atlantic and over Africa in a balloon—probably the best of the abortive sequels to *Huckleberry Finn*, even though it owes an obvious debt to Jules Verne. Unfinished as it was, Twain published it in *St. Nicholas*, a popular children's magazine. He produced unclassifiable oddities— "The £1,000,000 Bank Note," a short story in which a beggar is given the use of a million-pound note for a month; "Adam's Diary," a comic retelling of the Creation story; "Those Extraordinary Twins," a wild farce in which a pair of Siamese twins appear in a Southern town in slavery days. Physically identical, they are moral opposites: Luigi is a drinker, Angelo a teetotaler; Luigi is a fighter, Angelo a coward. Pressed for money, Twain lowered his standards, as Livy noted regretfully, publishing in *Cosmopolitan* as well as *Harper's* and *Century*.

In the peace of the Villa Viviani, he could undertake more sub-

stantial work. He began a long-considered book on Joan of Arc—
one of the greatest figures of history, in his judgment—doing substantial research, consulting the published records of Joan's trial as
well as modern works in English and French. Deeply reverential,
almost worshipful, *The Personal Recollections of Joan of Arc* was not
done for money, much as he needed it. (Twain planned at first to
publish the book anonymously, to ensure that it would be taken
seriously.) Together with *Huckleberry Finn*, *The Personal Recollections*
would become his favorite among his books.

And at Livy's prompting, he drastically revised "Those Extraordinary Twins," turning it into *Pudd'nhead Wilson*, and adding
"Pudd'nhead Wilson's Calendar," a set of maxims, one or two of
them preceding each chapter. ("April 1. This is the day upon which
we are reminded of what we are on the other three hundred and
sixty-four.") Livy had shown him that he had in fact written two
books, a wild farce and a tragedy. The Siamese twins became ordinary twins, with their part reduced to the minimum required by
the plot, and the book centered on the story of Roxy, a "black"
slave (in fact, she is fifteen-sixteenths white) and her son, fathered
by an aristocratic planter living in the town. Disastrous consequences result when she exchanges her infant for the son of her
own master. Each child grows up irrevocably conditioned to his
role, until the exchange is finally discovered and the master becomes
a slave, the slave a master. Twain goes more deeply into the psychology and sociology of racism than he had ever done before;
"blackness" becomes, at times, not a color but a state of mind, a
product of "training," to use his own term. And Tom Driscoll's
despairing cry, on learning that he, the white man and the master,
is in law a "nigger" and a slave, might have been written by Faulkner:
"What crime did the uncreated first nigger commit, that the curse
of birth was decreed for him?"

Pudd'nhead Wilson would be serialized in *Century* before being
issued in the fall by the American Publishing Company. It had
never been Mark Twain's custom to serialize his books, but Webster
and Company had now gone bankrupt, and he needed to make his
writing pay in all possible ways. Through 1892 and 1893, Fred
Hall had written encouraging letters, saying over and over that
Webster and Company simply required more capital, that things
were looking up and the ship was nearing port, but, in fact, the

firm was going down and nothing could save it. The country had entered a deep recession (a "panic" in the blunt language of the day), there was no capital to be had, and Webster and Company's load of debt grew steadily. Twain admitted that he was "terribly tired of business," acknowledging at last that he was "by nature and disposition unfit for it."

He was helpless, desperate, "in a strange land," seeing his resources "melt down to a two months' supply," without "any sure daylight beyond." "The billows of hell have been rolling over me," he confessed to Livy in September. He wanted to sell out, but there were no buyers for subscription book companies. Desperately he shuttled back and forth between Europe and New York, simply needing to be on the scene. To an impatient man, any action was better than passively waiting for disaster. And typesetter affairs must be investigated—report now had it that fifty machines were to be built in Chicago. That had to be looked into, his rights protected.

He felt no fears about leaving his wife and daughters. "With your grit & intelligence & unapproachable good sense," he told Livy, "you are better off than if you had two or three husbands to help you & confuse you & make your efforts abortive." Two years later, Twain would decide that for all practical purposes, such as government, war, "building the homes & cities of the commonwealth, tending the family," only the female was required. All these affairs could be carried on "harmoniously & successfully without help or advice from the overestimated male." But while he might sardonically reproach himself, Livy never did.

That fall, while in America, he met Henry Huttleston Rogers, a vice-president and director of the Standard Oil Company. Rogers had heard Mark Twain lecture on the Sandwich Islands, twenty or so years before, had admired him ever since, and had asked for an introduction. "The best new acquaintance I've ever seen," Twain called him in a letter to Clara. He had "helped us over Monday's bridge" (a demand for money that Webster and Company could not meet), after Twain had suffered the humiliation of being refused by various Hartford friends. A self-made man, Rogers was worth several tens of millions. Aided by a clear head and a ruthless competitive drive, he had made himself a power in the Pennsylvania oil fields while still in his twenties. For him, business was war. He had fought the Rockefellers, then joined them, becoming a dominant figure in Standard Oil, though he avoided all publicity. His interests spread throughout the economy; he was in copper, in railroads and streetcar and ferry lines, in banks and insurance companies. Tall, handsome, and dignified, with his great fortune and his dominating presence, Rogers was the embodiment of American capitalism.

He had his charities, although they were little known; he endowed the town of Fairhaven, Massachusetts, where he had grown up, with paved streets, an inn, a library, schools, churches, a Masonic hall, a town hall, a park. He could be generous, and not only with money. He took Mark Twain's affairs into his own hands, becoming in effect his business manager and literary agent, giving days of his precious time to the affairs of his new friend. He had enough to do: to salvage Webster and Company, if that could be done, while guarding Twain's interests in the typesetter.

Paige's backers, of course, had less money than reported; on investigation, the fifty machines supposed to be under production had dwindled to ten, then to one. Rogers set out to establish a workable company and ensure completion of that one machine, and to arrange a decisive test for it, as well as to increase the value of Twain's royalties by gaining him the right to exchange them for cash or stock. Paige and his supporters were opposed, but Rogers was too much for them—always cool, dividing the opposition, outbluffing or outwitting them. Traveling to Chicago with Rogers in his private railroad car, attending those meetings, Mark Twain could watch the game of business played by a master.

Twain spent the rest of his time in New York. As prospects brightened, he seemed rejuvenated, his energy inexhaustible. "The belle of New York," a friend christened him, as he plunged into social activities—dinners, suppers, balls, prizefights. He dined on raw oysters and corned beef and cabbage with John Mackay, eating "without fear or stint," and escaping indigestion. He saw James J. Corbett fight, and visited him in his dressing room, finding him "the most perfectly and beautifully constructed human animal in the world." Then he went to a musical evening, at the home of a friend. It ended with dancing; by 4:30 a.m., he had "danced all those people down," and went home, untired. After four hours' sleep, he was up, refreshed, for a busy day of letter writing, visiting, and talking. He recorded all that for Livy in a long letter, brimming with high spirits. Writing to Clara, he listed his "health-restoring irregularities": "meals at no particular hour; bed at no particular hour; eat when hungry only; sleep only when you can't keep awake any longer . . . eat *all* the forbidden things. And *confidence*—confidence that they won't hurt you."

Rogers finally forced a satisfactory arrangement for the typesetter on the reluctant Paige, found capital (supplying some of it himself), and arranged for the manufacture of a working model, to be tested in the printing room of a Chicago newspaper that fall. Twain had no fears for the outcome. "Our ship is safe in port," he joyfully cabled to Livy on their wedding anniversary. And when he was saved, farewell to business! "I will live in literature, I will wallow in it, revel in it; I will swim in ink!" Rogers, who had done all this, became "the only man I would give a *damn* for." When Webster and Company was offered a muckraking book, exposing Standard Oil and its executives, Twain refused it unhesitatingly: "the only man who is lavishing his sweat & blood to save me & mine from starvation is a Standard Oil magnate." Friendship came first—and in any case, Mark Twain had no objection to riches. For nearly ten years, he had been expecting to become a millionaire himself.

Did Rogers himself believe in the typesetter? Enough, at least, to invest some thousands of dollars that he could safely risk, and to arrange a test that would settle the question. It *was* a marvelous machine, and Paige was a highly persuasive talker. As for Rogers's association with Mark Twain, there is no reason to doubt that their friendship was deep and genuine (it would last until Rogers's death in 1909). Certainly, association with America's best-loved humorist might have public relations value for a director of the hated Standard Oil trust, but Rogers was never a man to concern himself about public opinion. His reward was the companionship and admiration of Mark Twain—no doubt a welcome contrast to the company of his fellow magnates—while Twain admired in Rogers the qualities he lacked in himself, qualities that were humanized by an unexpected charm in his private life. He could be "a good comrade and an affectionate friend," as *The New York Times* described him. But not even Rogers could save Webster and Company. A bank refused to renew one of its notes, and on April 18, 1894, the firm closed its doors, assigning its assets to its creditors. But the assets consisted of unsalable books, and the debt amounted to nearly $200,000. Again Rogers negotiated, and won important concessions: Livy had advanced $60,000 to the business from her own fortune, and she was recognized as a preferred creditor, with her husband's copyrights assigned to her. In that year of desperately hard times, they seemed to have little enough value, but in years to come they would make the Clemenses prosperous again. The Hartford house was saved as well, since it had been paid for with Livy's money. But the story had been front-page news, and Livy, reading the newspaper reports in Europe, had suffered deeply. To her, bankruptcy meant "ruin" and disgrace. Twain reassured her; it was "temporary defeat, but not dishonor—and we will march again." The typesetter would pay for all.

Confident of the future, he went back to Europe, for a summer in France with his family. In the fall, they rented a comfortable house in Paris, where Susy, who had always been interested in music and had a fine soprano voice, took singing lessons, while her father waited impatiently for news of the typesetter. The long-awaited test began in October, to last for sixty days, with Rogers reporting results. Problems soon developed. That marvelous machine could not stand continuous operation, it broke type, it jammed. As Rogers would explain later, "It was the nearest approach to a human being" in its capacities of any machine he had ever seen, adding that that was the problem. "It was too much of a human being and not enough of a machine. It had all the complications of the human mechanism, all the ability of getting out of repair"—but it could not be replaced as easily.

Unlike Mark Twain, Rogers had no emotional investment in the typesetter, and he was businessman enough to know when to cut his losses; a few days before Christmas, he reported failure. The news "hit me like a thunder clap," Twain exclaimed in a long and frantic reply. "It knocked every rag of sense out of my head," leaving only two thoughts: "that my dream of ten years was in desperate peril" and that "I must be there and see it die." For more than eight years his thoughts, his hopes, his anxieties and fears had centered on Paige's machine. Now all that was ended, leaving a great emptiness in his life. He had never really considered the possibility of failure.

Mark Twain did not go to America—his presence would have been useless. Nothing more could be done. His royalties were worthless, but Rogers quickly organized a new company, the Regius

Manufacturing Company, to take over whatever assets were left. The Clemenses traded their shares in the existing company for stock in the new one. Regius paid a small dividend in December of 1895, the only return that Mark Twain would ever receive for the nearly $200,000 he had spent. Ironically, that payout was apparently provided by the Mergenthaler Linotype Company, which had given $20,000 for all rights to Paige's invention. The Chicago machine was given to a college of engineering, then melted down for scrap during the Second World War. The original typesetter, built in Hartford with Mark Twain's money, can still be seen in the basement of his home in Nook Farm—a mechanical curiosity from another age.

Although the creditors of Webster and Company agreed to accept a settlement of fifty cents on the dollar, Twain decided to pay the debt in full, partly at the persuasion of Livy, who considered bankruptcy dishonorable, and partly at that of Rogers, who argued that an author's character was his most valuable asset. Ironically, the newspapers endlessly compared Twain's behavior to that of Sir Walter Scott, a writer whose work he detested. Scott had gone bankrupt and then spent the rest of his life laboring to pay off his enormous debt, but the example of Grant, dying of cancer while he wrote desperately to support his family and to repay the money he owed to Vanderbilt, probably meant more to Mark Twain.

In May of 1895, the Clemenses returned to America, staying at Nook Farm while Mark Twain considered ways of raising money. The lecture platform seemed to offer the quickest and surest return. Twain considered giving benefit performances, sponsored by millionaires, in New York, Chicago, and San Francisco, then decided on a more dramatic plan: he would go around the world, reading from his works in New Zealand, Australia, India, and South Africa, and finally write a book about the tour—a subscription book, of course, to be marketed by the American Publishing Company. It was a Tom Sawyerish scheme, barnstorming around the world to pay his debts, yet practical, too. He could earn more from a book about such a tour than he could expect from performing at home. But he could not bear the thought of making that journey alone; Livy and Clara would go with him. (Jean would remain in school, while Susy, who disliked travel at sea, chose to stay behind.)

On the evening of July 14, 1895, after Mark Twain had tested himself with a reading at the Elmira Reformatory and had a "roaring success," he and Livy and Clara set out to go around the world. There was a last glimpse of Susy, under the platform lights at Elmira, waving goodbye—father and daughter would never see each other again. After crossing the continent, with Twain performing as he went, the three travelers sailed from Vancouver. The voyages seemed nearly endless, twenty-four days across the Pacific from Vancouver to Sydney, twenty-eight from Ceylon to South Africa— days and nights of tropical peace that Mark Twain savored deeply, times when no news could reach him, when no action could be taken or needed to be taken. The tour was a success: Australia lionized him, India met all the expectations that his reading of Kipling had aroused. His earnings, beyond expenses, he sent back to America for Rogers to invest.

That journey widened his experience enormously, qualifying him, he often felt, to speak for the human race. India fascinated him, with its jungles and its mountains, its swarming population, its multiplicity of religions and cultures. He found the handful of Christian missionaries absurd, almost pathetic, with their hopes of converting a subcontinent. In South Africa, on the eve of the Boer War, he began to understand the realities behind the rhetoric of imperialism and the white man's burden. The so-called Matabele wars, he decided, had been really massacres of helpless natives by well-armed Europeans, who then stole their cows and their land. He noted the brutality of the Boers toward the blacks and saw the irony in their patriotic defense of the land they had stolen, against the English who were trying to steal it from them.

On July 14, 1896, just one year after leaving Elmira, the Clemenses sailed from Capetown to England. There they rented a house in Guildford, not far from London, where Twain could write his book. But first the family was to be reunited; Susy and Jean, escorted by Katy Leary, would join their parents. Then came a letter from a Hartford friend: Susy was ill—no details were given. A cablegram followed: she would recover, but slowly. Still her illness was not specified. Desperate with anxiety, Livy and Clara instantly sailed for America. Three days later, another cablegram: Susy was dead. It was the most terrible blow of Mark Twain's life. He could not share his grief; Livy was on the Atlantic. He knew what was waiting for her when she landed in New York, but he could do nothing to prepare her, nothing to help. The details, when he learned them, were shocking: Susy had died of cerebral meningitis, contracted while visiting friends in Hartford. She had suffered, she had been delirious for days, then blind. There was only one small comfort; she had been able to die in the family home in the care of Katy Leary.

Susy's pathetic scribblings, made in her delirium, had been carefully saved: "To me darkness must remain from everlasting to everlasting," she had written, and "the trolley cars go up and down for Mark Twain's daughter." Both mother and father were prostrated by this disaster, coming at the moment of success, with that weary journey ended and their goal in sight. It was the sort of blow from which one never entirely recovers. Mark Twain's philosophy might tell him that death was the best gift, the only true gift, ever given the human race, and he might declare that if he could, he would not bring Susy back to life, but philosophy could not comfort him. There was no comfort to be had; Howells might reassure him that unless the universe were nothing but a "crazy blunder," "that gentle creature" must still be able, somewhere, to feel his love. But for Mark Twain, "crazy blunder" exactly described the universe. This world "is Hell," he wrote to Livy, "the true one, not the lying invention of the superstitious." Father and mother felt equal grief (for Livy, with Susy dead, the poetry had gone out of life), but Mark Twain felt guilt as well. He blamed himself now, as he had blamed himself for the death of his brother Henry. He had left his daughter, and she had died.

Susy was buried in the family plot at Elmira. Mark Twain had not come home—that funeral might have been too much to bear. Then Livy went back to England with her two remaining daughters, and the Clemenses began their mourning. They did not go out, they received no one. Family rituals were suspended for the time; they exchanged no gifts on birthdays. The anniversary of Susy's death became a sacred day, reserved for solitude and meditation. All this must have been chiefly Mark Twain's invention. If he was guilty, he must pay. And he knew his own temperament, he feared his own buoyancy, he suspected his grief—its depth, its length, its sincerity. How could he prove himself worthy of the lost daughter but by grieving forever? And how could he grieve forever without continually reminding himself of his loss?

Searching for comfort, he and Livy visited two British mediums, endorsed by a well-known investigator of the Society for Psychical Research. But they did not let judgment be overruled by desire. Both mediums were "transparent frauds," Twain wrote to a friend, and the investigator "a very easily convinced man."

Luckily, he had work to occupy himself. There were still debts to pay and a book to write. He worked steadily through the fall and winter on *Following the Equator*, as he called the account of his world tour, finishing it in the spring of 1897. As he worked, he slowly recovered, and at last began to reenter the world. "We are dead people that go through the motions of life," he wrote to a friend in early May, yet in the same letter he could speak of his "comedy-fancies," and by September he could claim that he was a cheerful man again, because he could see his way to paying off his debts within a year. (Rogers had invested the lecture proceeds in stocks, with great success.) Slowly the bitterness of grief was tempered, and there were long periods when he forgot. The memory could recur at any time, but Mark Twain did not live all his life in the shadow of Susy's death.

The Clemenses stayed on in Europe, renting the Hartford house. They could not bear to live in it again. They summered that year in Switzerland, at the village of Weggis, on Lake Lucerne. There, freed from the labor of completing *Following the Equator*, Twain could write to please himself. Again his imagination carried him back to the Hannibal years. He wrote the brief "Villagers of 1840–43," a kind of biographical dictionary of the Hannibal of his childhood, with entries on 168 individuals (given fictitious names but often identifiable), besides general comments on the customs and folkways of the time. But this Hannibal is not the idyllic town of *Tom Sawyer*, for Twain describes fraud, betrayal, adultery, madness, and murder. And this time time there is no devilish outsider, like Injun Joe, to blame.

Mark Twain could make notes on Hannibal culture and characters, he could recall that vanished world in infinite detail, yet he could not make effective use of the material in a long story. At Weggis he began work on "Tom Sawyer's Conspiracy," dropping it after four chapters, when the tank must have run dry, but coming back to it during the next two years and bringing it almost to its conclusion. The king and the duke reappear, to commit a murder for which Jim is charged, with their guilt to be revealed by Tom in a climactic trial scene in the final chapters. The trial had already begun when Twain finally abandoned his story. It could have been completed within a few days, but he would never take the trouble, perhaps realizing that he had done nothing in "Tom Sawyer's Conspiracy" that he had not done better in *Tom Sawyer* and *Huckleberry Finn*.

In the fall of 1897, the Clemenses moved to Vienna, where Clara, who had become serious about her music and now wanted a career as a concert pianist, could study under the famous teacher Leschetizky. The family was thoroughly cosmopolitan by now, at home almost anywhere in Europe, and all its members had at least a working knowledge of German. By the end of January in 1898, Mark Twain was free—he had paid his debts. *Following the Equator* had been a labor to write, but while he wrote he had been able to forget his grief; and when published by the American Publishing Company in November of 1897, it had earned the last of the money that he needed. Sober, even somber in its contemplation of human injustice and cruelty, *Following the Equator* contained none of the uproarious farce that had delighted readers of *The Innocents Abroad* and *A Tramp Abroad*. Instead, it offered a new installment of Pudd'nhead Wilson's cynical maxims.

The Clemenses would never need to worry about money again. Livy's share in the Langdon family business had regained its value after the panic of 1893–94, and Twain's earlier books were bringing in a steady income. Harper & Brothers had taken over the titles published by Webster and Company, including *Huckleberry Finn, A Connecticut Yankee in King Arthur's Court*, and *Pudd'nhead Wilson*, and would issue all his future books, while, after long and intricate negotiations, a plan was finally worked out allowing the American Publishing Company to issue a collected edition of his works. That edition would bring him a continually increasing income until his death in 1910. (Harper & Brothers bought out the American Publishing Company in 1903, but that made no practical difference in his affairs.) Mark Twain would often be suspicious of Harper, would accuse the firm of incompetence or sharp dealing, but if he could never fully trust a publisher, neither would he try again to publish his own work. He had sometimes feared that he might lose his reputation, believing that all literary reputations were fragile, but his own had proved to be the most solid asset he possessed. The magnificent Hartford house, when finally sold in 1903, would bring less than a third of what it had cost.

Mark Twain was as celebrated in Vienna as he had been in Germany. Freed at last from the burden of debt and with Susy's death now more than a year in the past, he recovered his energy and enthusiasm as he had done in New York four years earlier, throwing himself into the life of the city. The spacious Clemens suite in the Hotel Metropole, a huge block of a building across the street from the Danube, drew an endless stream of visitors. He listed his callers for a typical day, May 9, 1898, in his notebook: "Visitors yesterday, Countess Wydenbruck-Esterhazy, Austrian; Nansen & his wife, Norwegians; Freiherr de Laszowski, Pole; his niece, Hungarian; Madame XXX, Hollander; 5 Americans & 3 other nationalities (French, German, English). *Certainly there is plenty of variety in Vienna.*"

New projects burgeoned in Twain's mind. He planned to translate German plays, even to collaborate with a Viennese playwright on a comedy about women in politics. He met the Austrian inventor of a carpet-weaving machine, Jan Szczepanik, was fascinated by his device, was offered the American rights for a million and a half dollars, and bought an option. Again Twain filled his notebook with calculations. Szczepanik's machine could save American manufacturers at least $18 million a year, he calculated. Rogers should "make a $2,000,000 Company" (with Twain to receive one tenth of the shares) to buy the patent and begin manufacture. Then, in a letter opening "I feel like Colonel Sellers," Twain proposed buying world rights, with a resulting profit of $50 million a year. It was the typesetter again—but this time there was a Rogers to investigate and declare that this invention had no prospects. Reluctantly, Twain accepted that judgment.

But Mark Twain was a man who *must* speculate in something. Two years later, without asking Rogers's advice, he managed to "invest" five thousand pounds in Plasmon, a health food made principally from dried milk—one pound, at least by Twain's report, contained "the nutriment of 16 pounds of the best beef"—and became a director of Plasmon, Ltd. All hospitals would feed their patients Plasmon, Twain believed, doctors would prescribe it—and the Clemenses themselves began to use it regularly, in place of meat. An American corporation would be formed later, in which Mark Twain would invest another $25,000. That investment brought no return, and the tangled affairs of American Plasmon would trouble him intermittently for the rest of his life. As Mark Twain would confess in 1906, "Whenever I have trusted Mr. Rogers to invest my savings for me I have prospered," and whenever he had "clandestinely" followed his own judgment, he had "got struck by lightning." "Immortal hopefulness, fortified by its immortal & unteachable stupidity." That had been Twain's judgment on Orion, in a letter to Howells in 1882, but it exactly describes his own disastrous career as a businessman. Unsurprisingly, he could never quite bring himself to admit that reality. That helpless dependence on another man's judgment, those recurring revelations of his own incompetence must have been deeply humiliating, spurring him on to commit new blunders in the hope of proving that he was not, after all, a complete idiot in business.

He was a favorite with journalists, of course, and with the aristocracy as well. There was even a meeting with his third emperor, the aged Franz Josef, ruler of the Austro-Hungarian Empire. He took an interest in Austrian politics, attending sessions of the Parliament. To assess Clara's professional prospects in music, the family consulted the highest possible authority, Brahms (he politely declined to pass judgment). There was a supper given to Mark Twain by the Concordia, a society of authors and journalists, at which Mahler was a guest. Yet Mark Twain remained an outsider. The culture of the twentieth century was being created in Vienna, but he could remark on "the paucity (no, the absence) of Austrian celebrities."

He luxuriated in his own celebrity, seeing himself as a kind of unofficial ambassador to the world, an embodiment of his country and culture. He wrote a brief dialogue in his notebook:

"Are you an American?

No. I am not *an* American. I am *the* American."

And he enthusiastically supported the Spanish-American War in the spring and summer of 1898, believing that it was the noblest war in history, because fought for another people's freedom. (After his return to America, he would often play a new role, that of citizen of the world.)

He wallowed in literature, as he had promised Livy he would, once freed from business. Often he seemed to write for his own pleasure, with little concern for publication. He produced competent journalism concerning Austrian affairs, but except for a long story, "The Man That Corrupted Hadleyburg," the most interesting work of the Viennese years is to be found in fragmentary manuscripts, most of them left unpublished for another sixty or seventy years. He made a serious beginning to his long-planned autobiography, going back to his Hannibal years in richly detailed, intensely evocative chapters, creating a prairie idyll that seemed to recall not only his own youth, but America's.

But except for those chapters for his autobiography, Mark Twain seemed to have lost interest in creating realistic narrative. Instead he turned to fantasy, producing two related groups of manuscripts that he would work on intermittently over the next eight years, finally leaving them all unfinished. One group concerns the arrival of a mysterious stranger, a beautiful adolescent boy, in a sleepy village—Hannibal, in one early version, later "Eseldorf" ("Jackass-ville"), in fifteenth-century Austria—where he displays miraculous powers and expresses outrageous opinions, occasionally bestowing the blessings of early death or a happy madness on villagers, and continuously demonstrating not only the hypocrisy and cowardice of human beings ("the foundation upon which all civilizations have been built," the stranger observes) and the shocking cruelty of humans to one another, but the sheer senselessness of human life and human creeds in an indifferent universe. He is infuriatingly contemptuous of the boasted Moral Sense, which allows human beings—unlike the beasts—to know right from wrong and to do wrong. "Perfectly horrible, and perfectly beautiful," Livy called "The Chronicle of Young Satan," the most coherent of the different versions. (In all but one of the versions, the stranger is identified as Satan, the traditional father of lies, but this Satan tells devastating truths, exposing the lies of official religion.)

Some of those themes he expressed more directly in a set of philosophical dialogues, entitled *What Is Man?*, begun in Vienna in 1898, arguing beliefs he had held since the early 1880s at least: that the human being is a machine and therefore entitled to neither praise nor blame for his actions, that free will is an illusion and moral judgments fatuous, that all human action is inherently selfish and the consequence of inborn "temperament" and of "training," and that no man can justly be held responsible for acting according to his temperament, or failing to act against it. Livy deeply disapproved of *What Is Man?*, but two years after her death, Mark Twain had 250 copies printed at his own expense, distributing them to selected friends and to important writers of the day, asking for their honest opinions. He made no converts. Only a few replied; one of them, H. G. Wells, pointed out the unoriginality of the book's central claim, that man is a machine. That comment disturbed Mark Twain deeply—although *What Is Man?* argues that originality is impossible.

Is life itself simply an absurd dream? In the longest of the "Mysterious Stranger" versions ("No. 44, the Mysterious Stranger"), that truth is Satan's ultimate revelation. A universe "so frankly and hysterically insane," with its all-powerful and loving God who created human suffering, who created hell—such a universe cannot exist: "there is no God, no universe, no human race, no earthly life, no heaven, no hell. It is all a Dream, a grotesque and foolish dream. Nothing exists but You. And You are but a *Thought* . . . a homeless Thought, wandering forlorn among the empty eternities!" But with that unbearable knowledge, says Satan, comes liberation: "Dream other dreams, and better!" After Mark Twain's death, his biographer, Paine, would graft that conclusion onto "The Chronicle of Young Satan." The resulting hybrid would be issued by Harper as a Christmas gift book in 1916, entitled *The Mysterious Stranger*.

The relationship between dream and reality fascinated Mark Twain, and he explored the theme in several manuscripts of this period, all left unfinished. In each, the narrator—prosperous and happy, with a family resembling the Clemenses—falls asleep at the opening of the story and dreams a succession of shattering disasters. At the conclusion he is to awake, find everything unchanged, and ask himself, "Which was the dream?" These stories take many shapes. "The Great Dark," the most successful, narrates a fantastic voyage through everlasting darkness in a sailing ship that encounters terrifying monsters, a voyage controlled by an ambiguous, ominous Superintendent of Dreams—another mysterious stranger. In "Which Was the Dream?," Twain creates a composite of himself and General Grant in the brilliant young Major General X, war hero, senator, and prospective President, who suffers ruin and disgrace thanks to his almost criminal negligence and credulity (like Grant's credulity in trusting Ward, like Mark Twain's confidence in Webster's ability, or his ruinous faith in the typesetter).

Another fragment, "Which Was It?"—finally reaching over a hundred thousand words—occupied him intermittently between 1899 and 1903. To save his family and himself, George Harrison, without quite intending it, kills a man. Someone else is arrested and charged with murder, and conviction seems sure, but Harrison does not have the courage to confess his guilt. Jasper, a mulatto, knows the truth and blackmails Harrison, treating him as his slave when they are alone. Harrison has always believed himself an honorable man, but once his honor is tested, he learns by experience that he is a coward, ready to commit any crime and bear any degradation to save himself. A similar theme is expressed in "The Man That Corrupted Hadleyburg," the most important completed work of the Vienna years—a satire on the limits of virtue, in which all of the leading citizens of a self-righteous town prove liars and cheats when tempted beyond their limits. Mark Twain had once urged Orion to write a fictional "Autobiography of a Coward." Now he himself had written the biography of one.

Vienna had welcomed the Clemenses, and there Mark Twain had enjoyed his last period of intense creativity, but Vienna could never become their home. In the spring of 1899 the family left for London, where Mark Twain learned from a friend of the "Kellgren method," developed by Heinrick Kellgren, a Swedish osteopath. For years, Jean Clemens, now nineteen, had shown inexplicable personality changes, becoming moody, irritable, and erratic, and not long after Susy's death, it became clear that she was epileptic. The Kellgren method might cure her, her father believed, and so for three months in the summer and early fall, the Clemenses endured flies, dirt, and bad food, in order that Jean could be treated at the Kellgren Clinic in the Swedish countryside. The whole family took treatments, and for several months an ever-hopeful Mark Twain believed that they had found a panacea, that the Kellgren method could cure not only epilepsy but heart disease, tuberculosis, and the common cold. (Writing to William James the next spring, he enthusiastically recommended a combination of the Kellgren treatment and Plasmon for James's ailments.) The family returned to Sweden the next summer; then the inevitable disillusionment followed. Jean's general health seemed to improve, but her epilepsy was unaffected, while Livy was left "sore & lame," full of "black thoughts & antagonisms toward the system."

The Clemenses were prosperous again, they were growing tired of exile, and there was nothing more to keep them in Europe. Mark Twain had paid his debts; he could return with honor. In October of 1900, the family sailed for America.

THIRTEEN

"Shall We Ever Laugh Again?"

M ark Twain was met at the pier by the inevitable crowd of reporters. His stature had grown enormously since he had left America in 1891. He came home a world figure, and he saw himself as somehow representing not only his country but all humanity. "I am the human race," he would declare a few years later, "compacted and crammed into a single suit of clothes." Yet he still seemed typically American, and his personal misfortunes strengthened the bond between himself and the public. For the rest of his life, he would be continually interviewed, quoted, and photographed. Everything he did was news. He enjoyed his fame and the privileges it brought; his opinions were asked on all subjects; he liked being recognized on the street and seeing the awe and surprise on the faces of strangers who confronted him.

He would never be a businessman again, that was clear, but what he might do was less clear. He needed to find a role for himself in this aggressively prosperous and self-confident America that was moving into the twentieth century. Samuel McClure, publisher of *McClure's Magazine*, suggested chartering a special train in which Twain could travel the continent "under the most luxurious conditions" and write a series of articles "reporting the United States," but Mark Twain declined. "Too circusy and too much work" was his verdict. He had been offered lucrative editorships ($10,000 a year for an hour a week of editing from *Puck*, a humorous magazine), but again he refused. He would not bind himself—he dreaded commitment of any kind. He could have lectured as often as he liked—Pond had offered him $10,000 for ten evenings—but he preferred to talk for pleasure. Without quite intending it, he created his own role: the joker-sage, the archetypal American, freely expressing his opinions on all topics, reminding his countrymen of their national ideals, denouncing injustice and oppression.

Returning to Hartford was not to be considered; that house was too full of memories. In any case, Mark Twain had become an international celebrity, and provincial Hartford was no place for him. Instead, he rented a house for his family in Manhattan, at 14 West Tenth Street, and took up his American life. Everything seemed to concern him, from the bad manners of New York cab drivers to the crimes of Western imperialism. America had joined the imperialists; American missionaries had been attacked in China, and American troops had helped to suppress the Boxer Rebellion in 1900 and, in 1901, were brutally crushing a "rebellion" in the Philippine Islands. When the New York *Sun* ran an interview with "the Rev. Mr. Ament, of the American Board of Missions," in which Ament acknowledged collecting indemnities from the Chinese amounting to thirteen times the damage done to missions, the money to be used for propagating the Gospel, Twain saw an opportunity to denounce the sins of his own country, as well as those of Europe. He immediately set to work writing "To the Person Sitting in Darkness"—the most Swiftian satire in American literature, published in the February 1901 issue of the *North American Review*. The Bible-reading audience would have recognized the ironic title taken from Matthew 4:16: "The people which sat in darkness saw great light."

The article opened with sharply contrasting quotations: first a smug New Year's paragraph from the *Tribune*, refuting the "carping grumblers" who tried to deny America's prosperity and happiness; then a shocking account of prostitution, street crime, and sexual immorality among children on New York's Lower East Side, from the *Sun*; and finally the Ament interview. The body of the essay warned against injudicious actions, such as the Boer War, which might reveal the true nature of the "Blessings-of-Civilization Trust" to "the person sitting in darkness"—the darkness of barbarism or heathenism as compared to Western enlightenment and Christianity. But while appearing to support the missionaries and the imperialists, Twain in fact discredited all hypocritical moralizing and presented imperialism as simply the robbery of the weak by the strong.

The influence of "To the Person Sitting in Darkness" reached well beyond readers of the *North American Review*; with money supplied by Andrew Carnegie (not all capitalists were imperialists), the Anti-Imperialist League distributed thousands of copies. Anti-imperialists were delighted, as no one could carry their argument to the general public as effectively as Mark Twain. The pious were outraged, the imperialists infuriated. Mark Twain began working on an answer to his critics. In the past, he had generally reserved his opinions on public matters for conversation and for private letters, but now he would not shrink from public controversy. The public response, as shown in his mail, was largely encouraging, but there were bitter denunciations: "How much money does the Devil give you for arraigning Christianity and missionaries?" asked one correspondent, and another advised him to "go back to the old world. You are not needed here, and are unfit to live under the folds of the American flag," while a few months later, President Theodore Roosevelt would exclaim that when he heard what Twain and other critics were saying about the missionaries, he felt "like skinning them alive."

Mark Twain temporarily escaped from notoriety by spending that summer with his family in a secluded cottage at Saranac Lake, interrupted by a two-week cruise in August off the Canadian coast in Rogers's yacht, the *Kanawha*, which *The New York Times* called "vastly superior" to J. P. Morgan's famed *Corsair*. In the fall, instead of returning to West Tenth Street, the family took up luxurious residence at Wave Hill in Riverdale-on-the-Hudson. There they were out of the metropolitan rush but only twenty-five minutes from Grand Central Station, living in what was almost a baronial estate, with eighteen acres of grounds and a house with a sixty-by-thirty-foot dining room, with two huge fireplaces. For economy, they kept no carriage. But there was no need for economy. Mark Twain would estimate his income for 1902 at $100,000, $60,000 from royalties.

Moving to Riverdale in no way signaled an end to Twain's extraliterary activities; he worked hard to defeat Tammany Hall and Boss Croker in the New York mayoralty campaign of 1901, even marching up Broadway in a political procession and then speaking to the crowd. "Who killed Boss Croker?" asked a paper, and answered

> Who killed Croker?
> I, said Mark Twain,
> I killed Croker,
> I, the Jolly Joker!

Exhilarated by Croker's defeat, Twain forgot his pessimism concerning human nature, and formulated a plan for a "Casting-Vote Party": it would offer no candidates of its own, but would "cast its *whole* vote for the best man put forward." To gain that vote, both major parties would nominate capable and honest men, and so good government would be ensured, whoever won. It was the Mugwump philosophy of 1884, revived.

He turned back for the last time to Huck and Tom. Harpers announced, in its prospectus for 1902, that "Mr. Clemens" was at work on a novel, set in the Middle West, which would "unquestionably rank with *Huckleberry Finn* and *Life on the Mississippi* as one of the great stories of American life." It was never completed, and the manuscript does not survive, but probably he had taken up an old plan. An entry in his notebook in 1891 proposes bringing a pathetic Huck, now sixty but believing that he is a boy again, back to St. Petersburg to search in vain for familiar faces, and to meet Tom: "Together they talk of old times; both are desolate, life has been a failure . . . They die together."

More entries in his notebook suggest topics: "Moonlight parting on the hill—the entire gang. 'Say, let's all come back in 50 years and talk over old times.' " The first part of the story would have been set in old St. Petersburg, recalling childhood memories: "Marbles. Kites—sleds—skates . . . Doughnut party. Horse-hair snakes." Howells read and enjoyed the manuscript, and Twain himself, four years later, recalled writing 38,000 words of the story, told by Huck and introducing Tom and Jim. Then, as he recalled, he decided that his characters had already done enough, and destroyed the manuscript "for fear I might someday finish it."

With his new prosperity, Twain bought a house in Tarrytown, a few miles up the Hudson, expecting to leave Riverdale when the lease expired and give his family a permanent home for the first time in eleven years. Then all such plans ended. The Clemenses passed the summer of 1902 at York Harbor, Maine, with Howells nearby, and once more the two old friends could talk and laugh and read their work to each other. Suddenly, in mid-August, Livy was taken dangerously ill, apparently with a violent attack of asthma that strained her heart. Twain described that terrifying seizure in his notebook: "She could not breathe—was likely to stifle. Also she had severe palpitation. She believed she was dying. I also believed it." Livy did not die, but neither did she recover. It was two months before she gained enough strength to return to Riverdale by train, in a special "invalid's car." There her disease was diagnosed as "nervous prostration"—a favorite, and meaningless, diagnosis—to be treated by seclusion, quiet, and total rest. She could be seen only by her doctors, her nurse, and Clara; she could receive no disturbing news; her husband was barred from the sickroom. In January, he wrote to Twichell of a "memorable episode"—"yesterday I was in Livy's presence 3 minutes and 50 seconds." He communicated with her in tender, playful notes, describing the beauty of the outside world, giving accounts of his reading, expressing his love for his "old-young sweetheart."

It was a dreadful winter. Jean fell dangerously ill with pneumonia; Livy could not be allowed to know of her condition, and so Clara lied to her mother for weeks, giving her accounts of Jean's imaginary activities each day and of Clara's own fictitious trips to the city, her shopping and visits to friends—sometimes desperately explaining away contradictions caught by the alert Livy. With spring came a slow and partial recovery, but still Livy could do nothing. To comfort her, Twain wrote a "heroic lie," as Howells termed it, asserting his belief in the immortality of the soul; Livy accepted that assurance, and was thankful for it.

The Clemenses spent the summer at Quarry Farm for the last time. Clara and Jean were grown women, Livy would never again need to rest there, and without her presence, Quarry Farm would have seemed desolate to Mark Twain. The family sailed for Italy in October, hoping desperately that a milder climate might bring health to Livy. They rented a villa outside Florence, a huge barn of a place, with sixty rooms. There Livy suffered terrifying attacks of asthma, each one leaving her weaker than before. Again Twain was barred from her presence by the doctors. A touching note from Livy survives: "youth my own precious Darling: I feel so frightfully banished. Couldn't you write in my boudoir? then I could hear you clear your throat & it would be such a joy to feel you so near." In May, he was allowed two visits a day, of two minutes each. To give his wife hope, he talked of buying a villa, subject to her approval, and even half persuaded himself that she would recover. Then, with a merciful swiftness, she died, a moment after "chatting cheerfully" with her family. A few days later, Clara collapsed; her father could see her only twice a day. "Morning and evening greeting—nothing more is allowed," he wrote to Howells, adding, "Shall we ever laugh again?" The loss of Livy could never be forgotten, at times he would be overcome by grief and loneliness—yet he did laugh again.

Clara seemed to recover, and the family went back to America. Livy was buried at Elmira, with the service performed by Joe Twichell, who had married them more than thirty-four years before. For Mark Twain, this homecoming seemed meaningless. "Wherever Livy was, that was my country," he wrote to a friend. At the end of July he answered an inquiry from Twichell as to how life and the world now looked to him by declaring "that there is no God and no universe . . . only empty space, and in it a lost and homeless and wandering and companionless and indestructible *Thought*. And that I am that thought. And God, and the Universe, and Time, and Life, and Death, and Joy and Sorrow and Pain only a grotesque and brutal *dream* . . ." That was essentially the conclusion of "No. 44, the Mysterious Stranger," the longest of the "Mysterious Stranger" versions, applied to his own situation. (Although Mark Twain could not follow his Stranger's advice—"Dream other dreams, and better!") Twichell refused to take those "automatic curses" seriously, but his answering assertions of "a steady progress from age to age . . . of righteousness" seem equally automatic and less convincing.

But troubles had not yet ended. In late July, Jean suffered a dangerous accident; on a moonlight ride with friends, her horse was frightened by a trolley, there was a collision, the horse was killed, Jean badly bruised and scraped. To her father, "the whole affair was simply another stroke of a relentless God"—a God that he alternately denied and cursed. Clara collapsed again, "ordered into retirement with the care of a trained nurse." This time it was for a year. And in September, Twain's sister, Pamela, died—the last of his family. (Orion had died seven years earlier.) It was a cataract of disaster, worse even than those terrible months of death and the expectation of death in the first year of his marriage when he had feared for the lives of both his wife and his son, and this time falling on a man almost seventy. He grieved deeply, yet he survived, and often enjoyed his life.

He had settled into a three-story brownstone, at 21 Fifth Avenue, that would be his home until 1908. He had to have a household as well, with a woman to head it. And since neither of his daughters could play that role, his secretary, Isabel Lyon, assumed it. She had come to the Clemenses in 1902, an unmarried woman of thirty-eight, as Livy's secretary. Now she became Mark Twain's hostess, companion, and confidante, directing his household affairs and expenditures, living in his home, wherever it might be, always available, ready to listen and admire when he read from his manuscripts, or to play the "Orchestrelle"—a kind of elaborate and expensive player piano—for hours at a time to soothe him on solitary evenings. All this for a salary of fifty dollars a month, plus board and room. Apparently, she never asked for more. But she had her reward, simply living in the presence of the King, as she called him, in all seriousness, in her journal. At other times he is her "master"; always, for her, his writings were inspired, his remarks witty or profound, and he himself "beautiful."

Mark Twain spent the summer and early fall of 1905 and 1906 in the mountains of New Hampshire. His important work was done, as he knew, but he was a writer, and he went on writing. He worked compulsively during that first summer in New Hampshire. He began and completed *Eve's Diary*, companion to the earlier "Adam's Diary" of 1893, publishing it in *Harper's Magazine* (December 1905), and as a small book the following year, again issued by Harper & Brothers. *Eve's Diary* was his tribute to Livy, to Susy, to young Mary Rogers, daughter-in-law of his friend ("You miraculous combination of quicksilver, watchsprings & sunshine . . . all animation & champagne & charm," he called her) or perhaps to all women, to femininity as he understood it. He took up "No. 44, the Mysterious Stranger" again, brought it close to completion, but did not finish it.

He commenced a satirical fantasy, "3,000 Years Among the Microbes," narrated by a cholera microbe named "Lemuel Gulliver," and formerly a human being, who inhabits the body of an old and diseased tramp. (Twain had known *Gulliver's Travels* since childhood, and he might easily have borrowed Swift's defense against accusations of misanthropy: that he loved the individual while detesting the human race.) "I think we are only the microscopic trichina concealed in the blood of some vast creature's veins," Twain had written in his journal in 1884, "& that it is that vast creature whom God concerns himself about." "3,000 Years Among the Microbes" makes the parallel clear—what the cholera germs are to the tramp, human beings are to the universe—but unlike Swift's Brobdingnag and Lilliput, the world of the microbes is not imagined powerfully enough to convince. He wrote short, satirical pieces as well, inspired by the news of the day and often aimed at President Theodore Roosevelt, ridiculing his "sham battle" against the trusts, his hunting exploits, so carefully reported in the press, his "insanity" on the subject of war, his vanity, demagoguery, and Caesarism. Fragment after fragment, in Mark Twain's later years, predicts the end of the American republic, corrupted by wealth, succumbing to dictatorship—"monarchy," in his political vocabulary. (This was a variation on an earlier theme. In "The Secret History of Eddypus, the World-Empire," written in 1901–2 and published seventy years later, Mark Twain had foreseen a new Dark Age for America, with liberty and enlightenment extinguished by a religious despotism, established by a religious trust, a fusion of Christian Science and Catholicism.)

Summers in New Hampshire, a few miles from Mount Monadnock, were quiet, lonely, and beautiful. The New York season was busy, with Twain in constant demand for dinners, benefits, and public gatherings. If he was not scheduled to speak at an event, he could always be called on for a few remarks, and he would always supply them. With forty years of public speaking behind him, he could respond to any audience and any situation. Whatever he said would be reported the next morning in the newspapers. The public demand was insatiable. Scheduled to speak at a theater on behalf of the YMCA, he arrived to find an enormous crowd gathered, breaking down the doors to force an entrance. Twain had to be taken to a side entrance and smuggled in. "TEN THOUSAND STAMPEDE AT A MARK TWAIN MEETING," read a newspaper headline the next morning. They had been trying to jam themselves into a theater that held seventeen hundred.

The celebration of his seventieth birthday in 1905, at a dinner arranged by George Harper, president of Harper & Brothers, and held at Delmonico's restaurant, was a national event, and Twain's speech became one of his most famous—"Threescore years and ten! It is the scriptural statute of limitations. After that you owe no active duties . . . You have served your term, well or less well, and you are mustered out." An unpublished note of the same period seems exactly opposite to that benign acceptance of age: "Old Age, white-headed, the temple empty, the idols broken, the worshipers in their graves, nothing left but You, a remnant . . . fag-end of a foolish dream, a dream that was so ingeniously dreamed that it seemed real . . . nothing left but You, center of a snowy desolation, perched on the ice-summit, gazing out over the stages of that long trek & asking Yourself, 'Would you do it again if you had the chance?' " But the Delmonico's speech could have been equally sincere—the "truth" about human life seemed a matter of mood.

In that spirit of finality, early in 1906 Twain accepted a biographer at last, a young writer named Albert Bigelow Paine. It was understood that the biography should not appear until after his death, but Twain allowed Paine access to his letters and papers and would dictate to him and to a stenographer, sometimes in answer to questions, sometimes simply commenting on whatever happened to interest him, past or present. Paine listened in fascination, feeling himself the luckiest of biographers, until he began to realize "that these marvelous reminiscences bore only an atmospheric relation to history." Instead, they were the product of "an imagination that, with age, had dominated memory," freely creating and altering details, even reversing them, all the while meaning to give the "literal and unvarnished truth," no matter how damning. Mark Twain was a writer still, and as a writer he had no use for unvarnished reality. He would tell the worst of himself, worse than the worst, exaggerating and even inventing his own crimes, but he could not tell the literal truth. As he ruefully admitted, "When I was younger I could remember anything, whether it happened or not; but now I am getting old, and soon I shall remember only the latter."

With all his fame, he was often lonely. Miss Lyon was always there, but the most devoted secretary could not replace his family. Clara, after recovering, lived her own life in a New York apartment. Jean stayed with her father, but in the late summer and fall of 1906 her epileptic seizures grew more severe. "Friday, August 21. Jean, 8:20, violent," Miss Lyon recorded in her journal. A neighbor had to be brought in, "because in Jean's present condition it isn't safe for me to be alone with her." On September 16, "Jean, 10:30—

porch. 2 weeks and 2 days"—that is, since the last seizure. Three more followed within the next two weeks. When she violently attacked Miss Lyon, she had to be institutionalized in a sanatorium at Katonah, New York.

There was still the companionship of Rogers, with journeys to the Caribbean on his yacht. But Mark Twain had begun to withdraw from the world, living more and more in his enormous bed, brought from the Hartford home—the bed he had shared with Livy for so many years. There, in a rich dressing gown, propped up on pillows, he smoked, read, dictated, wrote, often received callers. In spite of all he had suffered, he seemed younger than he was. His movements were quick, he carried his age well, with his slender figure, his ruddy complexion, his picturesque head with its mass of white and densely curling hair—the delight of caricaturists. He began to wear white suits, year round—he had always worn white in the summers at Quarry Farm. Those suits complemented his white hair, his most distinctive feature, they asserted his superiority to convention, they mockingly suggested his own lamblike innocence, and they instantly became an essential part of his public image. Living in New York, he still met distinguished visitors—Sarah Bernhardt, H. G. Wells, Maxim Gorki—and spoke, though more and more rarely, for causes he supported: Congo relief (he conferred privately with President Roosevelt on Congo affairs), aid to Russian revolutionaries, fundraising for Booker T. Washington's Tuskegee Institute, and for the Children's Theatre of the Jewish Educational Alliance, on New York's Lower East Side. He talked to Barnard students, to the Women's University Club, to the YMCA.

Instead of returning to the New Hampshire mountains for the summer of 1907, Mark Twain crossed the Atlantic for the last time, to be awarded a doctorate by Oxford University. He had already been given doctorates by Missouri and Yale, but the Oxford degree meant far more to him. He received it in distinguished company, including Kipling, Rodin, Saint-Saëns, and General William Booth (founder of the Salvation Army), as well as various diplomats, politicians, members of the royal family, and other now forgotten notables, but in the eyes of the British public, he outshone them all. Clearly, *A Connecticut Yankee* had been forgiven or forgotten. London papers were filled with interviews, photographs, caricatures—everything Mark Twain did or said was news. It was a four-week festival of self-congratulation, a celebration of Anglo-Saxon unity. He met royalty, the aristocracy, literary figures, including Bernard Shaw, who greeted him as a fellow satirist and truthteller. It was the last and greatest public triumph of his life, and he enjoyed it enormously. Tom Sawyer could have asked for no more.

After that summer, public appearances would become ever fewer. Mark Twain was beginning his final withdrawal. He had decided to build a house for himself, on land he had bought at Redding, Connecticut. It was an hour from New York by express train, and a three-mile carriage ride from the station. John Howells, architect son of his old friend, had designed the house, an Italian villa, classical and severe. Clara and Miss Lyon took care of everything else; Twain had only to move in when the house was ready. "Autobiography House," he thought of calling it, because he partly paid for it with money for chapters from the autobiography that he had allowed to be published, but "Stormfield" eventually became its name, after *Captain Stormfield's Visit to Heaven*, part of which he had finally published in the December 1907 and January 1908 issues of *Harper's Magazine*. *Captain Stormfield* paid for a loggia, a gallery open on one side, providing sweeping views of the countryside. And "Stormfield" seemed a fitting name for a solitary house on a windswept hill. There were visitors, of course, their comings recorded in the massive Stormfield Guest Book (a present from Mary Rogers, lavishly bound, the title stamped in gold, and clasped with leather straps), but their numbers declined as his strength failed. With what Mark Twain called his "tobacco heart" (angina was diagnosed in June of 1909), any exertion, any fatigue, brought pain. He had come to Stormfield to die, and he knew it, even setting the date; he had come in with Halley's comet, in 1835, he liked to say, and he would go out with it, in 1910.

Ignoring warnings against overwork, driving himself to the end, Rogers died of a stroke on May 19, 1909. The death of a Standard Oil tycoon made headlines all over America. But for Mark Twain, Rogers had not been a ruthless financier, a dominating figure in a hated trust, but a delightful companion, one of the busiest men in America, yet infinitely generous with his time and attention. The loss was irreplaceable. With Rogers gone, there seemed one less reason for Twain to live. As he waited for death, he passed the time with endless games of billiards (his guests often letting him win by a narrow margin, in order to enjoy his boyish delight), he philo-sophized ("From everlasting to everlasting, this is the law: the *sum* of wrong & misery shall always keep exact step with the *sum* of human blessedness"), shocking Miss Lyon with his heresies, denying the existence of Christ and Shakespeare's authorship of the plays. He even published a little tract, *Is Shakespeare Dead?*, and sent copies to Carnegie and the Kaiser, among others. He could never really stop writing.

And he entertained himself with the Aquarium: "a club of 12 schoolgirls," he wrote in the Stormfield Guest Book. "I am Curator (otherwise Autocrat) & the only male member." The Aquarium's device was an angelfish—"the Bermudian angel-fish," Mark Twain believed, "is easily the most beautiful fish that swims." Members generally were between the ages of ten and fifteen. Their photographs hung on the wall of the billiard room, and as much as he disliked letter writing, he spent a good part of his time writing to the Angel-Fish, as he called the club's members, and in amusing them when they visited Stormfield. They might be the daughters of friends, or he might have met them on his travels, on shipboard or in hotels, or in Bermuda, a favorite retreat in those final years, where he encountered Margaret Blackmer, a particular favorite. He could write of them with cloying sentimentality, but he could also analyze their characters with complete objectivity. Helen Allen, another Bermudian Angel-Fish, had three moods, he noted: "dreamily reposeful," "sour-hostile," "animated and winning." She was "entirely without curiosity."

He had always enjoyed the companionship of women and girls. There had been the Saturday Morning Club, which he had organized thirty years before, and the Browning class. Later, after his return to America, there was the Juggernaut Club, whose members he chose from among young women of various countries who had written to him. There were no meetings—only letters. But letters were not enough. After Livy's death, Mark Twain found himself famous, yet alone, "washing about in a forlorn sea of banquets & speechmaking." He had "reached the grandpapa stage of life," as he put it, without grandchildren. The Angel-Fish filled that void; they were the grandchildren he did not have. If sexual attraction existed, he was not aware of it. As for the girls, they might be awed by his fame, but, to judge by their letters to him, he soon came to seem a demanding but entertaining grandfather. And for the rest of their lives they could remember that Mark Twain had singled them out for friendship.

Jean came home in late April of 1909, and briefly, her coming seemed to make Stormfield a home. She had recovered, apparently; she lived an active life, helping her father, managing a little farm he had given her, riding about the countryside, and joining Clara to make a revolution at Stormfield, ousting Miss Lyon. As his indifference to life grew, Twain had put himself completely in the hands of Miss Lyon and of Ralph Ashcroft, eventually giving them power of attorney, with entire control over his affairs. Ashcroft was a seedy Englishman who had come to Twain's attention in 1904 as treasurer of the American Plasmon company, and had later sold him shares in a company manufacturing a worthless new type of hairpin. In matters of business, Twain would always remain hopeful—and credulous.

Clara grew jealous of Miss Lyon's authority, accused her of theft, of stealing clothing and jewelry, of embezzling money from the household accounts, while Twain even came to believe that she had been drinking his whiskey. It is impossible to determine the truth of those accusations. Miss Lyon of course denied everything, but for Mark Twain, her sudden, unexpected marriage to Ashcroft—a marriage that would break up within a few years—seemed to prove their joint guilt. They must have married, he reasoned, so they could not be forced to testify against each other. Bitter at this seeming betrayal, Twain began writing a history of the affair, an enormous manuscript never meant for publication. Suits were threatened on both sides, and in the end, Miss Lyon left, her devotion to her employer unshaken.

But Clara did not take over control of Stormfield; in October of 1909, she married Ossip Gabrilówitsch, a pianist she had known since they had studied together under Leschetizky in Vienna. That marriage pleased her father—one daughter's future at least was secured. Financially, Clara was already provided for. Mark Twain had made a will that summer, leaving the income from his copyrights and other property to be divided equally between Clara and Jean, "free from any control or interference of any husband." Clara sailed for Europe immediately with Gabrilówitsch, leaving her father alone with Jean.

He spent much of the fall writing *Letters from the Earth*, a satirical account of human life, morality, and religion, supposedly composed by Satan. Banished from heaven for irreverence, he passes his time in visiting earth, to "see how the Human-Race experiment was coming along," and reports his findings in confidential letters to friends still in heaven. Besides ridiculing the Old Testament's account of human history, Satan's letters contain the frankest discussion of sexuality to be found anywhere in Twain's work. The letters note that while men and women are equal in desire, they differ widely in capacity—one woman can satisfy ten men, while no man can fully satisfy any woman. Consequently, Satan points out, women, rather than men, should possess harems. The letters unceasingly point out the absurd contradictions between human nature and human morality, with the tyrannical Moral Sense condemning sexual intercourse, the pleasure that both humans and immortals value most. The immortals, says Satan, "continue the act and its supremest ecstasies unbroken and without withdrawal for centuries," while the human being "will risk even his queer heaven itself—to make good that opportunity and ride it to its overwhelming climax."

It's not surprising that Clara found *Letters from the Earth* so shocking that she would not allow it to be published until 1961, three years before her death. Twain himself would never have expected publication. He was writing for his own amusement. Witty and succinct, those letters offer the freest and most effective statement of themes that had occupied his mind for many years. The manuscript is clearly written and lightly revised—probably by the author's jotting down of second thoughts as he wrote. While Mark Twain's physical strength failed, his mind remained clear.

On doctor's orders, Mark Twain visited Bermuda in November. While there, he worked on "a delightful magazine article . . . I can fall back on it whenever time hangs heavy on my hands." It was an autobiographical essay, "The Turning-Point of My Life," which, in accord with his determinism, denied the existence of turning points. Every human life was a chain of events, equally important, each one the inevitable consequence of all that had gone before. Otherwise, he spent his time being driven about the island, enjoying the scenery and the perfect weather, refusing all invitations, reading no newspapers. "I feel no interest in news," he wrote to Clara. "I do not seem to be in the world or of it." Never in his life had he felt "such a strong sense of being *severed* from the world, and the bridges all swept away."

With Clara's marriage, only one bridge to the world was left— Jean. Then it was broken. Mark Twain had come back to Stormfield to share Christmas with his daughter. She stayed up late on the night of December 23, trimming the Christmas tree, going to bed at 1 a.m., then rose at 6:30 for her usual cold bath before riding down to the station for the mail. An hour later, she was found dead in the tub, with her head underwater, probably drowned during an epileptic seizure. Her father awoke to a confusion of noise, with a terrified Katy Leary standing in his doorway to tell him that Jean was dead. She lay in her coffin through Christmas Day, "beautiful in death," Twain wrote in the Guest Book; that evening her body was driven to the station, to be taken to Elmira for burial, "where," as he concluded his entry, "her mother, & Susy & Langdon lie buried. A snow-storm was raging [at Stormfield]. Clara is in Germany." Mark Twain did not attend the funeral—he could not have withstood the journey.

With Clara gone and Jean dead, "Stormfield was a desolation . . . I could not stay there." He went back to Bermuda, waiting for death. He expected it to come soon, and he would not be disappointed. He might tell the reporters at the dock that his chest pains came from indigestion, but he knew better. He reread the *Connecticut Yankee*, for the first time since its publication, and found himself "prodigiously pleased with it—a most gratifying surprise," but he had no thought of further work. At last his writing was done.

His daughter's death and his own failing health had been reported throughout the world; a host of admirers offered comfort and medical advice. He prepared a form letter in answer: "Dear Sir (or Madam): I try every remedy sent to me. I am now on No. 67. Yours is 2,653. I am looking forward to its beneficial results." "The Turning-Point of My Life" (the last of his works to be published during his lifetime) appeared in the February *Harper's*, and Howells, who had also received an Oxford doctorate, was moved to a final tribute: "I shall feel it honor enough if they put on my tombstone, 'He was born in the same Century and general Section of middle western Country with Dr. S. L. Clemens, Oxon., and had his Degree three years before him through a Mistake of the University.' "

When a sentimental friend offered assurances of immortality, Mark Twain answered bitingly: "You 'know there are worlds still unexplored,' do you? . . . Isn't this life enough for you? Do you wish to continue the foolishness somewhere else? Damnation, you depress me." He waited almost impatiently for death, and that "precious gift," as he called it, was about to be given him. His chest pains increased, the worn-out body was collapsing, and Paine sailed to Bermuda to bring him home to die. Clara and her husband were called back from Europe, returning just in time. Mark Twain died on April 21, a week after reaching Stormfield—going out with Halley's comet, as he had foreseen. He could not speak in the last hours, but a few scribbled requests remain:

> bring me my spectacles
> bring me my
> glasses
> pitcher

His body was displayed at the Presbyterian Brick Church in New York City, in an open coffin, and viewed by thousands. "All the quiet and dignity and beauty had come back to him," one viewer noted. "He was like a fine piece of marble." Then he was buried in the family plot at Elmira beside his wife and three of his children.

SOURCES

The most important source for this book has been Mark Twain's own writings, published and unpublished. The Mark Twain Papers (Bancroft Library, University of California at Berkeley and Los Angeles) contain a number of unpublished literary fragments, which I have examined, as well as many still-unpublished Twain letters and thousands of letters to Mark Twain, by a wide variety of correspondents. No complete edition even of the writings published during Twain's lifetime now exists. Several partial editions of Twain's writings have been published, the most nearly complete being *The Works of Mark Twain: Definitive Edition* (New York: Gabriel Wells, 1922–25). The major works have often been reprinted.

I have made use of several volumes in *The Works of Mark Twain*, an ongoing series published by the University of California Press for the Iowa Center for Textual Studies: *Tom Sawyer* (ed. John Gerber, 1980), *The Prince and the Pauper* (ed. Allison R. Ensor and others, 1982), *Huckleberry Finn* (ed. Walter Blair and Victor Fischer, 1986), and *A Connecticut Yankee in King Arthur's Court* (ed. Victor Fischer and Lin Salamo, 1979). These editions provide useful annotations and information on composition and reception and, incidentally, reprint the original illustrations.

Most of the manuscripts left unfinished by Twain, or completed but unpublished, have now appeared in the University of California Press's editions of the unpublished works, together with valuable introductions and notes. *Mark Twain's Mysterious Stranger Manuscripts* (1969, ed. William M. Gibson) includes all of Twain's versions of a story concerning a mysterious boy with miraculous powers; *Which Was the Dream?* (1965, ed. John S. Tuckey), contains "Indiantown," offering what seems almost a caricature of the Clemens marriage, and "Which Was It?" introduces Jasper, the revengeful mulatto. *Mark Twain's Satires & Burlesques* (1967, ed. Franklin R. Rogers) includes "The 1002d Arabian Night," written during the summer that Twain completed *Huckleberry Finn*, as well as the Simon Wheeler play, *Cap'n Simon Wheeler, the Amateur Detective*. *Mark Twain's Fables of Man* (1972, ed. John S. Tuckey) includes "The Secret History of Eddypus, the World-Empire," Twain's vision of a world returned to the Dark Ages. Satan's satirical letters describing human existence, written during the last year of Twain's life, are available in *Mark Twain's Letters from the Earth*, ed. Bernard De Voto (New York: Harper & Row, 1962).

The first volume of a projected complete edition of the letters has appeared—*Mark Twain's Letters: 1853–1866*, ed. Edgar Marquess Branch and others (Berkeley and Los Angeles: University of California Press, 1988)—and I have consulted it for my opening chapter. I have also used Albert Bigelow Paine's *Mark Twain's Letters* (New York: Harper & Brothers, 1917, 2 vols.). Dixon Wecter's edition of *The Love Letters of Mark Twain* (New York: Harper & Brothers, 1949) is the principal source of information for Twain's courtship of Olivia Langdon and important for several later periods of his life. *The Mark Twain–Howells Letters, 1872–1910*, ed. Henry Nash Smith and William M. Gibson (Cambridge, Mass.: Harvard University Press, 1960, 2 vols.), is a heavily annotated edition essential for Twain's literary and personal life, especially during the 1870s and '80s. *Mark Twain, Business Man*, ed. Samuel C. Webster (Boston: Little, Brown & Co., 1946), contains correspondence with Charles L. Webster, Twain's business agent during the early 1880s and manager of Webster and Company, the publishing house set up by Twain, from 1884 to 1887, as well as many family letters. A number of still-unpublished manuscripts, scrapbooks, newspaper clippings, business documents, etc., are held by the Mark Twain Papers, as well as a substantial number of unpublished letters by Twain and thousands of letters to him.

The Twain–Webster correspondence is supplemented by *Mark Twain's Letters to His Publishers*, ed. Hamlin Hill (Berkeley and Los Angeles: University of California Press, 1967), including a selection of Twain's letters to the American Publishing Company, 1867–80; to J. R. Osgood, publisher of *The Prince and the Pauper* and *Life on the Mississippi*, 1881–84; and to Charles L. Webster and Fred Hall, Twain's partners in Webster and Company, 1884–94. *Mark*

Twain's Correspondence with Henry Huttleston Rogers, 1893–1909, ed. Lewis Leary (Berkeley and Los Angeles: University of California Press, 1969), provides valuable information on Twain's finances and projects, from the time of Webster and Company's bankruptcy in 1894 to the Clemenses' return to America in 1900.

A. B. Paine's *Mark Twain: A Biography* (New York: Harper & Brothers, 1912) remains the basic biography, indispensable for all periods of Twain's life. Justin Kaplan's *Mr. Clemens and Mark Twain* (New York: Simon and Schuster, 1966) is the most recent full biography, presenting a Mark Twain split between conflicting selves, the rebellious artist and the respectable citizen. The principal source for my narrative of Twain's life up to his marriage is my own *The Making of Mark Twain* (New York: American Heritage Press, 1985), which offers the fullest account available of his early career. Dixon Wecter's *Sam Clemens of Hannibal* (Boston: Houghton Mifflin Company, 1952) contains valuable background for the early years, while, for the final decade, Hamlin Hill's unsympathetic but carefully researched *Mark Twain: God's Fool* (New York: Harper & Row, 1973) often proved useful—even when I disagreed with its interpretations. William Dean Howells's *My Mark Twain* (New York: Harper & Brothers, 1910) gives a uniquely intimate view of Twain as man and as writer. Edith Colgate Salsbury's *Susy and Mark Twain: Family Dialogues* (New York: Harper & Row, 1965) offers valuable source material on Clemens family life, 1872–96, particularly in the substantial passages quoted from Susy Clemens's "biography" of her father; and Clara Clemens's *My Father Mark Twain* (New York: Harper & Brothers, 1931) provided occasional details as well.

For Twain's career on the lecture platform, I've drawn on Fred W. Lorch's *The Trouble Begins at Eight: Mark Twain's Lecture Tours* (Ames: Iowa State University Press, 1968) and Paul Fatout's *Mark Twain on the Lecture Circuit* (Bloomington: Indiana University Press, 1960). Fatout's *Mark Twain Speaking* (Iowa City: University of Iowa Press, 1976) collects his lectures and speeches. Twain's letters to Livy, found in *The Love Letters of Mark Twain*, are the most important source for his tour with Cable in 1884–85, while Guy Cardwell's *Twins of Genius* (East Lansing: Michigan State College Press, 1953) and Louis D. Rubin's *George W. Cable: The Life and Times of a Southern Heretic* (New York: Pegasus, 1969) provide a view of the tour and of the Twain–Cable relationship as seen from Cable's side.

For the social and intellectual background of Nook Farm, I have relied especially on Kenneth R. Andrews's *Nook Farm: Mark Twain's Hartford Circle* (Cambridge, Mass.: Harvard University Press, 1950). My description of Mark Twain's Hartford home is based on my own visits and on Wilson H. Faude's detailed study, *The Renaissance of Mark Twain's House* (Larchmont, N.Y.: Queen's House, 1978). In discussing Twain's reading and literary tastes, I've drawn on Alan Gribben's *Mark Twain's Library* (Boston: G. K. Hall & Co., 1980, 2 vols.), which brings together Twain's comments on a wide variety of authors.

For information on the composition of *Huckleberry Finn*, I've relied particularly on Walter Blair's *Mark Twain & Huck Finn* (Berkeley and Los Angeles: University of California Press, 1960) and on Twain's account of its completion in his letters to Howells. The unfinished sequels, "Huck and Tom Among the Indians" and "Tom Sawyer's Conspiracy," which brings back the king and the duke, can be found in *Mark Twain's Hannibal, Huck & Tom*, ed. Walter Blair (Berkeley and Los Angeles: University of California Press, 1969).

Mark Twain's autobiographical dictations have never been published in full. I have used A. B. Paine's *Mark Twain's Autobiography* (New York: Harper & Brothers, 2 vols., 1924), Charles Neider's *The Autobiography of Mark Twain, Including Chapters Now Published for the First Time* (New York: Harper & Brothers, 1959), and Bernard De Voto's *Mark Twain in Eruption: Hitherto Unpublished Pages about Men and Events* (New York: Harper & Brothers, 1940)—valuable for its satirical comments on contemporaries, including Bret Harte, and information on Twain's methods of composition and his platform technique. I have quoted as well from unpublished dictations at the Mark Twain Papers.

Mark Twain's Notebooks & Journals, 1855–1891 (Berkeley and Los Angeles: University of California Press, 1975, 1979), ed. Frederick Anderson and others, and meticulously annotated, have proved an invaluable resource. Selections from the later notebooks can be found in A. B. Paine's *Mark Twain's Notebooks* (New York: Harper & Brothers, 1935). Merle Johnson's *A Bibliography of the Works of Mark Twain* (New York: Harper & Brothers, 1935) remains the standard bibliography of Twain's writings.

Finally, Thomas Asa Tenney's *Mark Twain: A Reference Guide* (Boston: G. K. Hall & Co, 1977) has been an essential aid, offering citations and abstracts of publications about Mark Twain, 1854–1974, continued through 1983 in annual supplements appearing in *American Literary Realism*.

Chapter One

General sources for this chapter include the first fifty-three chapters of A. B. Paine's *Mark Twain: A Biography*, for family history as well as for biographical details; Dixon Wecter's *Sam Clemens of Hannibal*; and my own *The Making of Mark Twain*, the fullest account of his early life now available. The description of his father as stern and unsmiling is found in "Villagers of 1840–43," published in *Mark Twain's Hannibal, Huck & Tom*, ed. Walter Blair. The history of the Tennessee Land and its effect on the Clemens family is recounted in *Mark Twain's Autobiography*. Notebook 1, first published in *Mark Twain's Notebooks & Journals: 1855–73*, contains Sam Clemens's diagnosis of his own character as belonging to the sanguine type, while Notebooks 2 and 3 record piloting data and experiences. Twain's own recollections of his piloting apprenticeship are recorded in the "Old Times on the Mississippi" sketches, later included in *Life on the Mississippi*. *Mark Twain's Letters: 1853–66* includes the crucial letter to Orion, previously available only in a private edition, in which he accepts his vocation as a humorist. Twain's earliest sketches have been collected in *Early Tales & Sketches*, 2 vols., ed. Edgar Marquess Branch and Robert H. Hirst (University of California Press, 1979 and 1981).

Chapter Two

Paine's biography, Wecter's *Love Letters of Mark Twain*, and in particular *Mark Twain's Notebooks & Journals* have been consulted throughout this chapter. C. W. Stoddard's reminiscences of Mark Twain in London are found on pages 61–74 of his *Exits and Entrances* (Boston: Lothrop Publishing Company, 1903). The originals of the "Expedition's the word" letters to Livy are preserved at the Mark Twain Papers, and have been published in *The Love Letters of Mark Twain*. Twain's impressions of England are also recorded in *The Love Letters of Mark Twain*. His comment that "anything but subscription publication is printing for private circulation" is quoted in Howells's *My Mark Twain*, p. 8. For the Nook Farm background, I have relied on Kenneth R. Andrews's *Nook Farm: Mark Twain's Hartford Circle*. My description of the Hartford house is drawn from my own observations and from the photographs and detailed descriptions of the interior provided in Wilson H. Faude's *The Renaissance of Mark Twain's House*. Mrs. Fields's account of her visit to the Clemenses, with her surprised comment that "he reads everything," is found in her *Memories of a Hostess*, edited by M. A. Dewolfe Howe (Boston: Atlantic Monthly Press, 1922). Howells's impressions and reminiscences of Twain are recorded in his *My Mark Twain*. "Indiantown," presenting Twain's caricature of his own marriage, has been published in *Which Was the Dream?*

Texts of Twain's speeches at the Whittier dinner and the Grant banquet are printed in Paul Fatout's *Mark Twain Speaking*. In my account of the Whittier dinner, I have used clippings from Boston newspapers held at the Mark Twain Papers, as well as Twain's letters to Howells written immediately afterward and Howells's account of the affair as an unmitigated disaster in his *My Mark Twain*. Mark Twain's account of his triumph at the Grant banquet can be found in letters to Livy, in Vol. 1 of *Mark Twain's Letters*, ed. A. B. Paine, and in Vol. 1 of *The Mark Twain–Howells Letters*.

The scandalous *1601* has not yet been included in any edition of Twain's works, but has often been reprinted in more or less private editions. The text of *Cap'n Simon Wheeler, the Amateur Detective* is available in *Mark Twain's Satires & Burlesques*. Twain reported his own experience at playing detective in the case of Lizzie the housemaid in a letter of July 17, 1877, published in *The Love Letters of Mark Twain*, and his discovery of Karl Gerhardt is recorded in a letter to Howells, February 21, 1881, in *The Mark Twain–Howells Letters, 1872–1910*.

For the composition of *Huckleberry Finn*, in this chapter and later, I have relied principally on Walter Blair's *Mark Twain & Huck Finn*. My account of the origin and writing of *The Prince and the Pauper* is derived largely from the University of California Press edition. My account of the Clemenses' journey to Europe, 1878–79, is based on Paine's *Mark Twain*, on Twain's own *A Tramp Abroad*, and most of all on Notebooks 15–18 in Vol. 2 of *Notebooks & Journals*. Twain's diatribes against French immorality and French culture in general are found in Notebook 18, principally on pages 318–25, and his speech to the Stomach Club of Paris on "Some Thoughts on the Science of Onanism" is included in Fatout's *Mark Twain Speaking*.

Chapter Three

My account of Mark Twain's journey down the Mississippi from St. Louis to New Orleans and up it to Minneapolis–St. Paul depends primarily on Notebooks 20 and 21 (in Vol. 2 of *Notebooks & Journals*), on the final two thirds of *Life on the Mississippi*, and on letters to Livy in *The Love Letters of Mark Twain*. Joel Chandler Harris's remarks on localism in American literature are quoted in R. B. Bickley's *Joel Chandler Harris* (Boston: Twayne Publishing Company, 1978). The description of Cable's *The Grandissimes* as the first modern Southern novel is found in Rubin's *George Washington Cable: The Life & Times of a Southern Heretic* (New York: Pegasus, 1968), p. 168. Twain's denunciation of Southern rhetoric and its effects is most fully expressed in Chap. 46 of *Life on the Mississippi*, "Enchantments and Enchanters," and his recommendation of a plain style is contained in "Dear Master Wattie: The Mark Twain–David Watt Bowser Letters, ed. Pascal Covici, in *The Southwest Review* (Spring 1960, 45:104–21).

Mark Twain's enthusiastic reception of Howells's *A Modern Instance* and its drunk scene, and his identification of himself with its protagonist, Bartley Hubbard, are recorded in *The Mark Twain–Howells Letters, 1872–1910*. The account of his own night in jail is reprinted in *Mark Twain's Travels with Mr. Brown*, ed. Franklin Walker and G. Ezra Dane (New York: Knopf, 1940), pp. 187–91. The *Nation* reviewed Twain's *The Stolen White Elephant* in its issue of August 19, 1882, p. 19. Besides the original edition (Boston: James R. Osgood & Company, 1882), *The Stolen White Elephant* has been issued as Vol. 19 of *The Works of Mark Twain: Definitive Edition*.

Chapter Four

Major sources for this chapter include *The Mark Twain–Howells Letters, 1872–1910*, Chap. 19 and 20 of *Mark Twain, Business Man* (especially for the history of Kaolatype), Notebook 22 in *Notebooks & Journals*, and the Mark Twain Papers for unpublished letters.

For descriptions of the Clemens home, I rely again on Wilson H. Faude's *The Renaissance of Mark Twain's House*. Twain's comment that the interiors of European homes seemed ugly in comparison is made in a letter to Livy of March 20, 1895 (*The Love Letters of Mark Twain*). Twain's description of the billiard room as the perfect study is found in a letter to Mrs. Fairbanks of April 14, 1877, in *Mark Twain to Mrs. Fairbanks*, ed. Dixon

Wecter (San Marino, Calif.: Huntington Library, 1949), and his report on his own smoking was made in a letter of March 14, 1882, to A. Arthur Reade, published in Reade's *Study and Stimulants; or, The Use of Intoxicants in Relation to Intellectual Life* (Manchester, N.H., n.d., pp. 120–22). Details of home life are drawn from Clara Clemens's *My Father Mark Twain* and (especially concerning the children) from Edith Colgate Salsbury's *Susy and Mark Twain*. Twain's observation that writers should not have children is taken from a microfilm copy of a note made a few years before his death by his secretary, Isabel Lyon (Mark Twain Papers).

Twain praised the value of solitary confinement for a writer in a letter of August 6, 1877, to Mollie Fairbanks (*Mark Twain's Letters to Mrs. Fairbanks*, p. 207), and declared his wish to escape "clear out of the world" in a letter of April 23, 1875 (*Mark Twain's Letters to Mrs. Fairbanks*, p. 191). Major Pond's and Howells's praise of Livy as the perfect lady are quoted from Pond's letter to Sam Moffett (Twain's nephew) of October 1, 1895 (Mark Twain Papers), and Howells's letter to an unidentified friend in 1874 (*The Mark Twain–Howells Letters, 1872–1910*, p. 16). Twain offered his "nugget" of advice to those about to marry in a letter to Clara Spaulding, August 29, 1886 (Mark Twain Papers).

Twain's account of his visit to the Governor-General of Canada and the Princess Louise is found in *The Love Letters of Mark Twain*. His claim that he had been talking since he was ten seconds old was made in an autobiographical dictation of February 10, 1907. His complaint that he wrote nothing at home because of social distractions is found in Paul Fatout's *Mark Twain Speaks for Himself* (West Lafayette, Ind.: Purdue University Press, 1978), p. 154. His observation that "color" and "play of feature" are lost in printed interviews is made in a letter reprinted in *The Americanization of Edward Bok* (New York, 1921), pp. 204–5. The comment that his private history is none of the public's business is taken from a letter to Orion of December 7, 1887 (*Mark Twain, Business Man*). And the reports of bogus Mark Twains in Ireland occur in a *New York Times* story of December 8, 1881, and a letter of July 3, 1882, to Andrew Chatto, his English publisher (Mark Twain Papers).

The history of Kaolatype is recorded in letters to Webster, 1880–82, in *Mark Twain, Business Man*, which also provides early comments on the Paige typesetter. Twain's complaints about his own incapacity for business—"Complexities annoy me" and "I wish I could understand *some* details of business"—are quoted from his autobiography and from an undated note in the Mark Twain Papers.

Charles F. Richardson referred to Twain's "rude and clownish 'merriment'" in his *American Literature 1607–1885* (New York, 1886), p. 396, and John Nichol accused Twain of lowering "the literary tone of English speaking people" in his *American Literature: An Historical Sketch* (Edinburgh, 1882), quoted in *Mark Twain: The Critical Heritage*, ed. Frederick Anderson (London: Routledge & Kegan Paul, 1971). Howells's comparison of a writer to a woman, in the eyes of a "real man," is quoted by Kenneth Lynn in his *Howells* (New York: Harcourt Brace Jovanovich, 1970), p. 283.

Chapter Five

Mark Twain described his completion of *Huckleberry Finn* and his invention of the history game in letters to Howells (July 20 and August 22, 1883). Further details on the history game are given in excerpts from a letter to Twichell, quoted in *Mark Twain: A Biography* (p. 752), and in an essay, "How to Make Dates Stick," found in Vol. 26 of the "Definitive Edition." "The 1002d Night" has been published in *Mark Twain's Satires & Burlesques*. Manuscripts of the unfinished tales of the prisoner beneath the castle, of the wife murderer, and of the coward's revenge are held by the Mark Twain Papers. Twain remarks that he is "grinding out manuscript" in a letter to Karl Gerhardt of July 2, 1883 (Boston Public Library), and describes himself in his study and observes that he is writing "in the midst of the hurricane" in a letter to Dr. John Brown (*Mark Twain's Letters*, 1:225).

His opinions concerning Cooper and Scott can be found in the often reprinted "Fenimore Cooper's Literary Offenses" and in Chap. 46, "Enchantments and Enchanters," of *Life on the Mississippi*, and his comment on Bret Harte's "saintly wh's and self-sacrificing sons of b's" is made in Notebook 18. His list of favorite authors, and mention of the unidentifiable "B. B.," is quoted in a dealer's catalogue of autograph letters and manuscripts from the collection of W. A. Smith, sold in 1911 (Mark Twain Papers).

Chapter Six

My principal sources for Twain's collaboration with Howells on the *Colonel Sellers* play, and for other dramatic experiments, have been Howells's *My Mark Twain* and *The Mark Twain–Howells Letters, 1872–1910*. The novel set in the Hawaiian Islands, described in letters to Howells and Mrs. Fairbanks, is now lost except for fragmentary descriptions of landscape in the Mark Twain Papers. Cable's visit to the Clemenses is described in his letters to his wife, printed in Arlin Turner's *Mark Twain and George*

Washington Cable (East Lansing: Michigan State University Press, 1960), and the letters from his collaborators in the April fool joke are filed in the Mark Twain Papers. I've also drawn on the Mark Twain Papers for the letters from Twain's public, for E. W. Howe's letter accompanying his *Story of a Country Town*, and for Augustin Daly's invitation to Twain to perform in his theater and his rejection of Twain's dramatization of *The Prince and the Pauper*. Mark Twain wrote out his own version of the plot involving "a murder, a mystery and a marriage"; it, too, is preserved at the Mark Twain Papers.

McClintock's preposterous novel *The Enemy Conquered, or Love Triumphant* was reprinted by Mark Twain in 1893, together with his own essay "A Cure for the Blues," in *The £1,000,000 Bank-Note and Other New Stories*. It is also available in Vol. 24 of *The Works of Mark Twain*. Twain's accusation that Osgood had caused the failure of *Life on the Mississippi* is in a letter of December 21, 1883, in *Mark Twain's Letters to His Publishers*, together with Osgood's denial of responsibility. The letter describing a future American empire ruled by the O'Mulligan dynasty is included in Vol. 1 of *Mark Twain's Letters*, dated "16 Nov., 1935"—actually 1874. Kenneth Lynn quotes Howell's outburst "Live all you can" in his *Howells* (New York: Harcourt Brace Jovanovich, 1970), p. 306.

Chapter Seven

The unfinished "Huck and Tom Among the Indians" has been published in *Mark Twain's Hannibal, Huck & Tom*, ed. Walter Blair. "Happy Memories of the Dental Chair" remains unpublished, in the files of the Mark Twain Papers. Details of life at Quarry Farm are drawn from Paine's *Mark Twain: A Biography*. Webster's report of the changes demanded by Raymond in the *Colonel Sellers* play is quoted in *The Mark Twain–Howells Letters, 1872–1910* (2:503). Information about the later history of "Colonel Sellers" is likewise taken from *The Mark Twain–Howells Letters*. Webster's notebook, with its comments on the selling of *Huckleberry Finn*, is held by the Mark Twain Papers. Karl Gerhardt's letters to Mark Twain are also at the Mark Twain Papers, and Twain recorded his use of bribery to win a commission for Gerhardt in a late notebook, for 1903–4.

Mark Twain's comment on the commandments violated by each Presidential candidate is recorded in Notebook 23, and his definition of a Mugwump ("pure from the marrow out"), is quoted in *Susy and Mark Twain*. The remark on the proper function of Congress—to do nothing—is by the laissez-faire philosopher William Graham Sumner, quoted in *The Gilded Age*, ed. Ari and Olive Hoogenboom (Englewood Cliffs, N.J.:

Prentice-Hall, 1967), p. 39. The manuscript of the "Mock Oration on the Dead Partisan" is held at the Mark Twain Papers, marked "probably never delivered in public" by Paine. "Consistency" is included in Paine's edition of *Mark Twain's Speeches* (New York: Harper & Brothers, 1923). Howells's comment on the election outcome, that "the rule of the best" was ended, is quoted in Kenneth Lynn's *Howells* (New York: Harcourt Brace Jovanovich, 1970), p. 279.

Twain's planning for the reading tour with Cable can be traced in his letters to Webster, in *Mark Twain, Business Man*, and to Major Pond, in letters now held at the Berg Collection, New York Public Library. Cable's responses are found in Arlin Turner's *Mark Twain and George Washington Cable* (East Lansing: Michigan State University Press, 1960). R. W. Gilder's request for permission to publish excerpts from *Huckleberry Finn* in *Century* magazine is at the Mark Twain Papers.

Chapter Eight

Major sources for this chapter include *The Love Letters of Mark Twain* and Twain's unpublished letters to Livy at the Mark Twain Papers, Arlin Turner's *Mark Twain and George Washington Cable* (East Lansing: Michigan State University Press, 1960), Guy Cardwell's *Twins of Genius*, Fred W. Lorch's *The Trouble Begins at Eight: Mark Twain's Lecture Tours*, Paul Fatout's *Mark Twain on the Lecture Circuit*, and Notebook 23 in *Mark Twain's Notebooks & Journals*, principally for Twain's travel notes and lecture plans. Twain's description of his technique in narrating "The Golden Arm" is found in "How to Tell a Story," in *How to Tell a Story & Other Essays* (New York: Harper & Brothers, 1897). His comment on the "absolute English" of Malory's *Morte d'Arthur* is from a letter to Susy of February 8, 1884. Newspaper comments are largely from clippings in Documents of the Mark Twain Papers. The diary of Ozias Pond is found in the Berg Collection of the New York Public Library, and Twain's comment that he had spent his boyhood in Hannibal in company with Huck Finn and Tom Sawyer is taken from a letter of November 11, 1884, to Major Pond, also in the Berg Collection.

He recorded his meeting with "Pet" McMurry in a letter to Livy of January 23, 1885, in *The Love Letters of Mark Twain*. His descriptions of the behavior of a bride and groom observed on the train and of such improvements as electric push buttons in hotels and electric streetlights are taken from Notebook 23. "Which Was the Dream?," which includes Twain's fantasy of black revenge, has been published in *Which Was the Dream?*, ed. John S. Tuckey (1967). My account of the surprise performance of *The Prince and the Pauper*, at Twain's return from the tour, is based on *Susy and Mark Twain*. Twain's added line, "I'll spit a dozen of ye," etc., is taken from Notebook 24, p. 138.

Chapter Nine

Victor Fischer's "Huck Finn Reviewed: The Reception of *Huckleberry Finn* in the United States," *American Literary Realism* (Spring 1983, 16:1–57) has been my source for most of the newspaper comments found in this chapter. The story of the Concord library committee's verdict was first published in the Boston *Transcript*, then widely reprinted and discussed. Twain's draft of his reply, containing Howells's suggestions and his own revisions, is reproduced in *The Mark Twain–Howells Letters, 1872–1910*. His fantasies of an unmentionable accident occurring to hostile editors were recorded in Notebook 24.

Hemingway's comment can be found on p. 22 of his *Green Hills of Africa* (New York: Scribners, 1935). The photograph of the young Hemingway outfitted as Huck Finn is reproduced in Philip Young's *Ernest Hemingway: A Reconsideration* (University Park: Pennsylvania State University Press, 1965). T. S. Eliot's praise of *Huckleberry Finn*'s innovative style is taken from his "American Literature and the American Language," first printed in *Washington University Studies in Language and Literature*, Vol. 23 (1953), and reprinted in the *Sewanee Review* (March–April 1953, 74:1–20). The letter from Thomas and Anna Fitch urging Twain to stop writing potboilers such as *Huckleberry Finn* is at the Mark Twain Papers, as is R. L. Stevenson's letter reporting that he had just read *Huck* for the fourth time.

Chapter Ten

Mark Twain, Business Man and *Notebooks & Journals* (Notebooks 23 and 24) continue to be primary sources for Twain's business affairs, *Susy and Mark Twain* for domestic life. Twain's own account of his relationship with Grant, dictated in May of 1885, became the opening chapter of his *Autobiography* in Paine's edition. Howells describes his and Twain's meeting with Grant in his Wall Street office in *My Mark Twain*, while Twain himself recorded the visit to Grant's home with Gerhardt, in which Gerhardt worked on the bust of the sleeping Grant, in Notebook 23 (pp. 106–7) and at more length in the Grant dictation. Grant's letter to his physician is quoted from William S. McFeely's *Grant: A Biography* (New York: Norton, 1981), p. 505, as are his statement of his readiness to die (p. 505) and his comment that he was a verb, not a noun (p. 516) and the description of Grant by his doctor as the "most suppressive man" (p. 512). Twain comments that with the *Memoirs* done Grant had nothing to live for in a letter to Livy of July 24 (*The Love Letters of Mark Twain*, p. 243). Newspaper clippings concerning Grant are preserved in Scrapbook 22, at the Mark Twain Papers.

Twain's declaration that "I am Webster & Co." is made in a letter to the editor of the Boston *Herald*, July 6, 1885, now at the Mark Twain Papers. H. H. Rogers's comment on Twain's business abilities is quoted in Clara Clemens's *My Father Mark Twain*, p. 82. The advice of Twain's lawyers against suing the New York *World* is quoted in Notebook 24 (*Notebooks & Journals*, 3:142), and Twain describes the *World* as "unmedicated closet-paper" in a letter to Webster (*Mark Twain, Business Man*). Webster and Company's announcement concerning the *Memoirs* is quoted in *Mark Twain's Notebooks & Journals*, 3:124, and Webster's pamphlet of advice to canvassers is found at the Mark Twain Papers. Twain's comparisons of Grant's *Memoirs* with Macaulay's *History of England* are made in Notebook 24. He characterizes Grant as "very great . . . & superlatively good" in Notebook 24 (*Notebooks & Journals*, 3:168) and describes Grant's obsequies in a letter to Livy of August 4, 1885 (*The Love Letters of Mark Twain*).

Mark Twain complains about the burden of his correspondence in a letter to Pamela dated June 12, 1885, and printed in *Mark Twain, Business Man*. His comment that "nobody who is anybody" can afford to be left out of *Century*'s war series is made in a letter of March 28, now at the Mark Twain Papers, to R. U. Johnson.

Chapter Eleven

Details of the summer routine at Quarry Farm are again taken from *Susy and Mark Twain*. Livy's diary, at the Mark Twain Papers, records her method of studying insects with Jean. The invitation to attend Buffalo Bill's Wild West Show is held by the Mark Twain Papers, and Twain's reply is published in Richard J. Walsh, *The Making of Buffalo Bill: A Study in Heroics* (Indianapolis: Bobbs-Merrill, 1928), pp. 260–61. His thank-you letter to the friends who were summering in the Catskills is given in Candace Wheeler, *Yesterdays in a Busy Life* (New York: Harper & Bros., 1918), p. 337. Twain compliments Howells—"You are really my only author"—in a letter of July 21, 1885. He reports on the progress of "A

Campaign That Failed" and calls *Century* the best magazine ever printed
in an unpublished letter to R. U. Johnson. The advertisement by the
American Publishing Company, accusing Twain of profiteering at Mrs.
Grant's expense, is found in Scrapbook 22, at the Mark Twain Papers.
The description of sales technique by a canvasser is quoted from a letter
to Mark Twain by Fred Hall, September 19, 1885 (Mark Twain Papers).
Whitford describes Fred Grant's threatening behavior and gives advice in
a letter of September 29, 1885 (Mark Twain Papers). Sherman's request
for an honest opinion on a manuscript, dated September 15, 1885, is at
the Mark Twain Papers, and Twain's reply is in the Library of Congress.

Twain's birthday note to Livy is included in *The Love Letters of Mark
Twain*, and his summing up of the birthday dinner is found in a letter to
Orion now at the Mark Twain Papers. Holmes's poetic compliment on
Twain's birthday is quoted in Paine's *Mark Twain: A Biography*, while
Rollin Daggett's letter of congratulation—"d——d if my wife don't even
think you are handsome"—is found in a letter of November 28, 1885, at
the Mark Twain Papers.

Twain calls himself a beggar outside the door of plenty in a letter to
Howells of October 18, 1885 (*The Mark Twain–Howells Letters, 1872–
1910*, 2:538–39). Susy's description of her father's reading from *A Connecticut Yankee*, and his intention of writing only one more book, are
quoted in *Susy and Mark Twain* (pp. 216 and 219), and Twain describes
the *Connecticut Yankee*'s theme as a lament for lost youth in Notebook 25
(*Mark Twain's Notebooks & Journals*). His declaration that he planned to
write two more books, one of them his autobiography, is made in a letter
to Mrs. Fairbanks, November 16, 1886 (*Mark Twain to Mrs. Fairbanks*,
ed. Dixon Wecter [San Marino, Calif.: Huntington Library, 1949], pp.
257–59). The Wanamaker controversy is described in *Publisher's Weekly*,
May 22, 1886, p. 649; Twain declares his intention of giving Wanamaker
hell in his own Sunday school in a letter to Webster, June 11, 1886 (*Mark
Twain, Business Man*, p. 361), and denounces that "sneak-thief" to Howells in a letter of July 15, 1886 (*The Mark Twain–Howells Letters, 1872–
1910*, 2:572).

Chapter Twelve

For Twain's disastrous involvement with the Paige typesetter up to
1890, I've consulted Paine's *Mark Twain: A Biography* and Justin Kaplan's
Mr. Clemens and Mark Twain, as well as typesetter contracts at the Mark
Twain Papers and Notebooks 25–30. Letters concerning the typesetter
from W. M. Laffan, F. G. Whitmore (Paige and his men were "going

right along as if there was to be no end of time or money"), and William Hamersley (that no machine could replace movable type) are held by the Mark Twain Papers. For the typesetter's later history and final failure, *Mark Twain's Correspondence with Henry Huttleston Rogers, 1893–1909*, has been the most important source. *Mark Twain's Letters to His Publishers* and the Twain–Rogers correspondence have provided information on the affairs of Webster and Company. Twain's defense of Rogers—"the only man who is lavishing his sweat & blood to save me"—is contained in a letter to Livy quoted in *Mark Twain: A Biography*, p. 973. *Susy and Mark Twain* continues to be a primary source for family affairs until Susy's death in 1896, while *The Love Letters of Mark Twain* contains Twain's reports to Livy during his trips to America to deal with the affairs of Webster and Company and the typesetter and his self-reproaching letters after Susy's death.

Twain's promise to "live in literature" is found in *Mark Twain: A Biography*, p. 978. The uncompleted manuscripts composed between 1897 and 1900 are now in print, in editions from the University of California Press: "Tom Sawyer's Conspiracy" in *Mark Twain's Hannibal, Huck & Tom*, the dream stories in *Which Was the Dream?*, the "Mysterious Stranger" fragments in *Mark Twain's Mysterious Stranger Manuscripts*. The *What Is Man?* dialogues, with related pieces, are available in *What Is Man? and Other Philosophical Writings*, ed. Paul Baender (Berkeley and Los Angeles: University of California Press, 1973).

Twain's relationship to Whitman is most fully discussed in Herbert Bergam's "The Whitman-Twain Enigma," *Mark Twain Journal*, Vol. 10, nos. 2 and 3. His remarks concerning Whitman can be found in Alan Gribben's *Mark Twain's Library*. He comments on Matthew Arnold's rebuke to America's "funny men" in a letter to the president of Yale, accepting an honorary degree, published in Paul Fatout's *Mark Twain Speaks for Himself* (West Lafayette, Ind.: Purdue University Press, 1978). The praise of *A Connecticut Yankee* as a satire on "servility and flunkeyism and tyranny" is found in a letter by E. C. Stedman, quoted in Bernard De Voto's *Mark Twain's America* (Boston: Little, Brown, 1932).

Chapter Thirteen

For the events of Twain's final decade, I have drawn primarily on A. B. Paine's *Mark Twain: A Biography*, frequently supplemented by Hamlin Hill's *Mark Twain: God's Fool*, especially for Twain's business affairs and his relationship to his secretary, Isabel Lyon, and by William R. Macnaughton's sympathetic *Mark Twain's Last Years as a Writer* (Columbia: University of Missouri Press, 1979). The quotation from Twain's last will is taken from a photocopy at the Mark Twain Papers. Unpublished letters by Twain are at the Mark Twain Papers.

"3,000 Years Among the Microbes" has been published in *Which Was the Dream?* and "The Secret History of Eddypus, the World-Empire," in *Mark Twain's Fables of Man*. The seventieth-birthday speech is available in *Mark Twain Speaking*. A. B. Paine describes the beginning of his relationship with Twain in Chaps. 88 and 89 of *Mark Twain: A Biography*.

For Twain's relationship to the Angel-Fish, I've relied on their letters to him at the Mark Twain Papers, on Dorothy Quick's *Enchantment: A Little Girl's Friendship with Mark Twain* (Norman: University of Oklahoma Press, 1961), and on an autobiographical dictation of April 7, 1908, at the Mark Twain Papers, for his description of himself as a grandfather without grandchildren. The reference to death as a "precious gift" is quoted by the editors in *The Mark Twain–Howells Letters, 1872–1910* (p. 854), from a letter to Mrs. James R. Clemens (wife of a distant cousin), and "Isn't this life enough for you?" from a letter to Elizabeth Wallace, March 12, 1910, at the Huntington Library. The final scribbled requests are held by the Mark Twain Papers.

INDEX

Adams, Henry, 214
"Adam's Diary" (Twain), 275, 298
Adventures of Huckleberry Finn, The
(Twain), 43, 79, 98, 121, 123,
190, 285; characterization in,
107–9, 114–17, 120, 189; compared with *The Prince and the
Pauper*, 50; compared with *Tom
Sawyer*, 38–39, 108, 113, 198,
204; copyright of, 176; elements
of Twain's life in, 4, 11, 42, 59–
60, 69, 101, 110–11; excerpted
in *Century*, 166, 173–75, 201;
excerpts read by Twain on tour,
168, 172, 179; illustrations in,
147–48, 152, 173–74; influence
on American literature of, 207;
language and dialect in, 62, 80,
115–18, 155; loses a chapter to
Life on the Mississippi, 81, 146;
manuscript, surviving portion of,
112, 206; publication of, 118,
124, 126, 145–48, 152, 176,
196–97; reviews of, 197–205,
252; sales campaign for, 150,
164–65; sales of, 197, 206;
Twain's distaste for Southern culture expressed in, 59–60, 83–84,
156, 243
Adventures of Tom Sawyer, The
(Twain), 11, 146; compared with
Huckleberry Finn, 38–39, 108,
113, 198, 204; dramatized by
Twain, 132, 139; as myth of
American boyhood, 37; pirated in
Canada, 37, 99; sales of, 37, 125,
180; sequel requested by readers

of, 37, 131; translated into Ger-
man, 77; Twain begins writing,
30–31
Ah Sin (Twain and Harte), 39–40,
127
Alden, William L., 205
Aldrich, Thomas Bailey, 64, 137
Alexander, Mr. (lawyer), 245
Alexander & Green, 99, 134, 190,
235
Alexander II, Czar, 18
Allen, Helen, 303
Alta California, 18–19, 71
Ament, Joseph, 5
Ament, Rev., 293
"America in 1985" (Twain), 126,
188
American Board of Missions, 293
American Claimant, The (Twain),
158, 275
American Copyright League, 229
"American on American Humor,
An" (Perry), 204
"American Press, The" (Twain), 136
American Publishing Company,
125–26, 146; contracts with
Twain, 19, 26, 45, 134, 276,
285; number of Twain's books
sold by, 50, 180; offers a book on
Grant, 246
"American Vandal Abroad, The"
(Twain), 22
Anti-Imperialist League, 294
Aquarium club, 303
Arabian Nights, The, 120–21
Army of the Tennessee grand reun-
ion (1879), 47–48, 208, 247

327

Arnold, Matthew, 135–36, 255, 268
Arthur, Chester A., 171
Ashcroft, Ralph, 304
Athenaeum, 79, 198
Atlanta *Constitution*, 265
Atlantic Monthly, 11, 31, 37, 42, 118
Austen, Jane, 118
"Awful German Language, The" (Twain), 168, 172

Badeau, Adam, 215–16, 221, 223, 246–47; *Military History of Ulysses S. Grant, A*, 215
Baton Rouge (steamboat), 65
Battles and Leaders of the Civil War (*Century*), 209, 215, 217, 241
"B. B." (Twain), 120
Beard, Daniel Carter, 270
Beecher, Thomas K., 23, 35
Belford Brothers, 99
Belford, Clark & Co., 99
Bellow, Saul: *The Adventures of Augie March*, 207
Ben Franklin Book and Job Office, 7–8
Bernhardt, Sarah, 301
Bierce, Ambrose, 260
"Billings, Josh" (humorist), 77
Bixby, Horace, 8, 65
Blackmer, Margaret, 303
blacks in American society, 6–7, 58–59, 62, 74, 108–9, 141, 158, 170–71, 187–89, 276
Blaine, James Gillespie, 158–59, 161–64
Blankenship, Tom, 110
Bliss, Elisha, 19, 26, 50, 146
"Bloody Massacre Near Carson, A" (Twain), 13
Booth, Lucia, 243
Boston *Advertiser*, 42, 202–3, 206
Boston *Herald*, 194
Boston *Transcript*, 44, 153, 168
Boswell, James: *Life of Johnson*, 120
Bowen, Will, 39
Brahms, Johannes, 287

Brooks, Van Wyck: *The Ordeal of Mark Twain*, 16, 116, 260
Brown, William, 9–10, 80
Browne, Charles Farrar, *see* Ward, Artemus
Browning, Robert, 26, 120
Buckner, Simon, 233
Buel, Clarence Clough, 241
Buffalo Bill's Wild West Show, 239
Buffalo *Express*, 23–24
Buffalo Public Library, 206
Buffalo YMCA, 206

Cable, George Washington, 82; address concerning blacks in prison, carried in *Century*, 170, 187; April Fool's joke on Twain, 142–43; concern with the experience of blacks, 62–64, 84, 141, 187–88; first appearance before an audience, 98–99; lecture tour with Twain, 153–54, 167–93, 195; literary style of, 62–64; miserliness of, 142, 185–86, 194; physical description of, 169; piety of, 63–64, 75, 140–41, 153–54, 176, 178, 185–87, 194; visits Twain home, 75, 140–42; *see also* works: *Dr. Sevier*; "Freedman's Case in Equity, The"; *Grandissimes, The*; *Madame Delphine*; "Mary's Night Ride"; *Negro Question, The*; *Old Creole Days*
Californian, 15, 18
Cap'n Simon Wheeler, the Amateur Detective (Twain), 40–42, 121, 127
Captain Stormfield's Visit to Heaven (Twain), 98, 105, 256, 302
Carlyle, Thomas: *The French Revolution*, 46, 119–20, 269
Carnegie, Andrew, 294, 303
Carpet Bag, The, 6
carpet-weaving machine, Twain's involvement with, 286
Casanova, Giovanni Giacomo, 144
"Celebrated Jumping Frog of Calaveras County, The" (Twain), 14,

184; *see also* "Jim Smiley and His Jumping Frog"

Celebrated Jumping Frog of Calaveras County and Other Sketches, The (Twain), 18–19, 26

Century, 118, 188, 235, 275; Badeau's article on Grant carried by, 223, 246; *The Bostonians* (James) serialized in, 175; Cable address on blacks in prison carried by, 170; contents of specific issues, 174–75; *Dr. Sevier* (Cable) serialized in, 170; "The Freedman's Case in Equity" (Cable) carried by, 187; Grant's contracts with, 209–10, 212–13, 215; *Huckleberry Finn* (Twain) excerpted in, 166, 174–75, 201; *Huckleberry Finn* reviewed in, 204; *A Modern Instance* (Howells) serialized in, 70; "The Private History of a Campaign That Failed" (Twain) carried in, 248; *Pudd'nhead Wilson* (Twain) serialized in, 276; *The Rise of Silas Lapham* (Howells) serialized in, 174–75, 238; Twain's contribution to Civil War series, 217, 241, 248; Twain's idea for story collection and, 142; *see also Battles and Leaders of the Civil War*

Charles Morgan (steamboat), 58

Chatto, Andrew, 177

Chatto & Windus, 77, 100, 134

"Chronicle of Young Satan, The" (Twain), 288, 289; *see also* "No. 44, the Mysterious Stranger"

Clarissa Harlowe (Richardson), 144

Clemens, Clara (daughter), 35, 281–83, 300, 302, 306–7; birth of, 36; character of, 91–92; childhood of, 49–50, 62, 74, 78, 91–96, 121–22, 143, 150, 192–93, 237–38, 251; marries, 304; memories of her father, 74–75, 90–92, 122, 193; and mother's illness and death, 296, 297; music studies of, 91, 274–75, 285, 287; opinion of *Letters from the Earth*

(Twain), 305; opinion of Saint-Simon's memoirs, 119–20

Clemens, Henry (brother), 5, 9–10, 80

Clemens, Jane Lampton (Jean; daughter), 8, 73, 283, 297; birth of, 49; childhood of, 69, 141, 150–51, 190, 237–38, 274, 281; death of, 8, 306; illnesses of, 69, 290, 296, 300–1; last year of, 304

Clemens, Jane Lampton (mother), 3–6, 128–29, 148, 180–81

Clemens, John Marshall (father), 3–5, 41, 88, 90–91

Clemens, Langdon (son), 24, 26

Clemens, Mollie (sister-in-law), 148

Clemens, Olivia (Livy; wife), 71, 74, 145, 168, 189, 220, 242, 271, 275, 277, 282, 290, 298; birthdays of, 89, 250–51; charities of, 52, 92; children born to, 24, 26, 36, 49; death of, 297; description of, 35–36, 89, 96–97; England visit (1873), 28; hostess, housewife, and mother, 68–69, 92–98, 104, 141, 143–44, 150, 190, 192, 229–30, 237–38, 258; illnesses of, 21, 24, 97, 273–74, 296; influence on Twain, 23, 36, 51, 169–70, 190, 203, 257, 281; meets and marries Twain, 21–23; religion of, 21–22, 101; and Susy's death, 283; Twain's love for, 22, 29, 90; as Twain's proofreader and critic, 22, 36, 79, 82, 99, 116–17, 198, 241, 276, 288–89; wealth of, 27, 33–34, 45, 76, 279–80, 285

Clemens, Olivia Susan (Susy; daughter), 28–29, 198, 273, 298; biography of her father, 116, 228–29, 237–38, 256–57; birth of, 26; at Bryn Mawr, 229, 267; childhood of, 49–50, 62, 69, 74, 78, 95–96, 121, 143–44, 150, 190, 192–93, 227–29, 237–38, 251; death of, 282–83; describes her father, 51, 89–90, 192–93, 228;

Clemens, Olivia Susan (*cont.*)
  description of, 91–92, 227–28, 238, 274–75, 280–81; fifteenth birthday of, 267; relations with her father, 78, 227–29, 256, 267; relations with her mother, 92
Clemens, Orion (brother), 180–81; character of, 8, 15, 131, 148; death of, 297; goes to Nevada, 11; as inventor, 88, 128; letters to Twain, 131; as printer and publisher, 5–8; religious heresies of, 131; supported by Twain, 130, 234; Twain's attitude toward, 40, 127–28, 131, 287; works on the History Game, 122
Clemens, Pamela (sister), *see* Moffett, Pamela
Clemens, Samuel Langhorne, *see* Twain, Mark
Cleveland, Grover, 250; entertains Twain and Cable, 174; in 1885 Presidential campaign, 158, 161–62; nominated for the Presidency, 159; revealed to have bastard child, 160; wins 1885 Presidential election, 163
Cody, William F., 239
Colonel Sellers (Twain), 30, 39, 52, 76, 127
Colonel Sellers as a Scientist (Twain and Howells), 127–30, 139, 157–58, 172
Concord Free Trade Club, 201–2
Concord Library Committee, 200–3, 206
Connecticut Yankee in King Arthur's Court, A, 89, 256–57, 285, 301, 306; genesis of, 180; plot of, 126, 258, 269–70; reviews of, 270
"Consistency" (Twain), 164
Cooper, James Fenimore, 156; Twain's opinion of his work, 118, 119
Corbett, James J., 278
Count of Monte Cristo, The (Dumas), 105, 106
"Coward's Revenge, The" (Twain), 106

Crandall, Prudence, 268
Crane, Stephen, 87
Crane, Susan, 30, 103–4, 238
Crane, Theodore, 30, 103–4
Critic, The, 196, 251–52, 255
"Curious Republic of Gondour, The" (Twain), 37
Custer, Elizabeth, 266

Daggett, Rollin M., 249, 252
Daily Telegraph, 270
Daly, Augustin, 127, 139
Dana, Charles A., 148
Dana, Richard Henry, Jr.: *Two Years Before the Mast*, 119
"Danbury *News* Man" (humorist), 77
"Dandy Frightening the Squatter, The" (Twain), 6
Darnell-Watson feud, 59–60
Darwin, Charles, 26
Dawson (Canadian publisher), 100
Dayton *Democrat*, 172
Death Disk, The (Twain), 139
"Desperate Encounter with an Interviewer" (Twain), 171
Detroit *Journal*, 177
Dickens, Charles, 28, 77, 101, 118, 168, 191; *Bleak House*, 110; *The Pickwick Papers*, 240
Dr. Sevier (Cable), 168, 170, 172, 187
Dodge, Richard: *Our Wild Indians*, 157; *The Plains of the Great West and Their Inhabitants*, 157
Dolby, George, 28
Don Quixote (Cervantes), 47, 83, 206, 270
Douglass, Frederick, 171
Dumas, Alexandre: *The Count of Monte Cristo*, 105
Duncan, Charles, 101–2, 143

Edison, Thomas A., 157
Eliot, George, 119, 239; *Middlemarch*, 110, 238
Eliot, T. S., 207
Emerson, Ralph Waldo, 34, 42–44

"Enchanted Sea-Wilderness, The" (Twain), 107

Enemy Conquered, The (McClintock), 142

Estes & Lauriat, 190, 202

Eve's Diary (Twain), 298

"Extracts from Adam's Diary" (Twain), *see* "Adam's Diary"

"Facts Concerning the Recent Carnival of Crime in Connecticut, The" (Twain), 37, 67, 94, 101

Faulkner, William, 276

"Fenimore Cooper's Literary Offenses" (Twain), 119

Fields, Mrs. James, 35–36

Fitch, Thomas and Anna, 201

Following the Equator (Twain), 81, 284–85

Franklin, Benjamin, 5, 7

"Freedman's Case in Equity, The" (Cable), 187, 192

French Revolution, The (Carlyle), 46, 119–20, 269

Freud, Sigmund, 273

Fulkerson, A. P., 243

Fuller, Myra, 133

Gabrilówitsch, Ossip, 304, 307

Garwood, Vashti, 133

Gauthier, Henry, 132

Gem City (steamboat), 66

"General Grant's Grammar" (Twain), 255

Gerhardt, Karl, 52, 150, 151–52, 192, 221–22, 236–37

"Ghost Story, The" (Twain), *see* "Man with the Golden Arm, The"

Gilded Age, The (Twain and Warner), 3–4, 27–30, 37, 144, 180

Gilder, Richard Watson, 142, 166, 175, 209

Gillette, Will, 52–53

Gold Dust (steamboat), 55–57

Goodman, Joe, 51, 272

Goodwin, Nat, 140

Gorki, Maxim, 301

Gould, Jay, 270

Grandissimes, The (Cable), 62–64, 170, 172

Grant, Donald, 93

Grant, Frederick, 212, 214–15, 221–22, 235, 244–46

Grant, Jesse R., 242–43

Grant, Mrs. Jesse R., 237

Grant, Julia (Mrs. Ulysses S.), 220–22, 231, 254

Grant, Ulysses S., 158, 175, 229, 281; at the Army of the Tennessee grand reunion, 47–48, 208; contracts with *Century*, 209–10, 212, 215; contracts with Webster & Company, 215; death and funeral of, 232–33; early acquaintance with Twain, 208–9; Gerhardt's bust of, 221–22, 236; Grant & Ward connection, 210–11; illness of, 212, 216, 220–22, 230–31; Twain compared with, 214; writes his memoirs, 212–23, 230–31, 235; writing ability of, 212, 215, 219, 255; *see also Personal Memoirs of U. S. Grant*

Grant, Ulysses S., Jr., 210

Grant & Ward, 210–11

Gray, Lem, 55, 57

"Great Dark, The" (Twain), 107, 289

Griffin, George, 52, 74, 91, 95, 103, 159, 193

Griswold, Sarah, 133

Gulliver's Travels (Swift), 47, 298–99

Hackett, Lem, 66

Hale, Nathan, 152

Hall, Fred, 266, 275–76

Hamersley, William, 261–63

Hamlet, Twain burlesque version of, 105

Hancock, Winfield Scott, 266

Hannibal (Missouri), 4, 6, 11, 66, 284

Hannibal *Courier*, 5, 182

Hannibal *Journal*, 5–7

"Happy Memories of the Dental Chair" (Twain), 150

Harper, George, 299
Harper & Brothers, 238, 285, 289, 295, 298–99
Harper's Illustrated Weekly, 221
Harris, Joel Chandler, 62, 205; on *Huckleberry Finn*, 252; *Uncle Remus*, 62
Harte, Bret, 76, 94, 128, 148, 197; advises Twain on writing, 19; collaborates with Twain on *Ah Sin*, 39–40; first acquaintance with Twain, 15; writing ridiculed by Twain, 119
Hartford (Connecticut), *see* Nook Farm; Twain, Mark: Hartford home of
Hartford *Courant*, 24, 34–35, 51, 122, 152, 160, 232
Hawkins, Laura, 9
Hay, John, 31–32; *Pike County Ballads*, 31
Hayes, Rutherford B., 158, 162
Hemingway, Ernest, 87; *The Green Hills of Africa*, 207
Holmes, Oliver Wendell, 42–44, 77, 182–83, 197; *The Autocrat of the Breakfast Table*, 252; tribute to Twain in *The Critic*, 251–52
"How come a Frenchman doan talk like a man?" (Twain), 168
Howe, Edgar Watson: *The Story of a Country Town*, 132–33
Howells, John, 302
Howells, William Dean, 36, 63, 75, 118, 132, 139, 197, 202, 283, 296; American consul in Venice, 95, 162; as author, 30, 87, 165, 174, 204; collaborates with Twain, 105, 127–30, 140, 157; comments on Grant's book, 255; comments on Twain, 14, 32–34, 73–74, 78, 90, 127, 168, 208, 229; complimented by Twain for *Indian Summer*, 238–39; complimented by Twain for *A Modern Instance*, 70–71; editor of the *Atlantic*, 31, 37, 204; final tribute to Twain, 306; Grant and, 209; political position of, 159, 162; reads

Twain's manuscripts, 117, 121, 139, 295; reviews *A Connecticut Yankee*, 270; reviews *The Prince and the Pauper*, 51; at the Whittier dinner, 44; *see also* works: *Colonel Sellers as a Scientist*; *Indian Summer*; *Library of Humor*; *Modern Instance, A*; *My Mark Twain*; *Rise of Silas Lapham, The*
"Huck and Tom Among the Indians" (Twain), 155–57

Indian Summer (Howells), 238–39
"Indiantown" (Twain), 36
Innocents Abroad, The (Twain), 19–20, 23, 25–26, 31, 79–80, 134, 180
"Invalid's Story, The" (Twain), 68
Irving, Henry, 27, 140
Irving, Washington, 77
Is Shakespeare Dead? (Twain), 303

James, Henry, 30, 119, 127, 148, 197, 239; *The Ambassadors*, 129; *The Author of Beltraffio*, 198; *The Bostonians*, 175; *Daisy Miller*, 76
James, William, 175, 290
James R. Osgood and Company, *see* Osgood and Company, James R.
Jefferson, Joseph, 251, 266
"Jim Baker's Bluejay Yarn" (Twain), 172
"Jim's Investments" (Twain), 175
"Jim Smiley and His Jumping Frog" (Twain), 14, 17; *see also* "Celebrated Jumping Frog of Calaveras County, The"
Johnston, Joseph, 233
Jones, John P., 272
Jowett, Benjamin, 120
Juggernaut Club, 303

Kalakaua, David, King, 249
Kaolatype process, Twain's involvement with, 85–87
Kellgren, Heinrick, 290
Kemble, Edward W., 146–47, 173, 198, 241, 248
Keokuk *Post*, 8

Kern County *Californian*, 143
"King Sollermun" (Twain), 168, 175
Kipling, Rudyard, 301; *Kim*, 206

Laffan, William M., 250, 263
Laird, James, 14
Lampton, Jim, 28
Lang, Andrew, 206, 252
Langdon, Charley, 21, 68
Langdon, Jervis, 21, 23–24
Langdon, Olivia, *see* Clemens, Olivia
Leary, Katy, 74, 91, 193, 273, 282–83, 306; *A Lifetime with Mark Twain*, 74
Leathers, Jesse, 28
Lecky, William Edward Hartpole: *A History of European Morals from Augustus to Charlemagne*, 120
Leo XIII, Pope, 249, 258
Leschetizky, Theodor, 285, 304
Letters from the Earth (Twain), 305
Library of American Literature, A (ed. Stedman), 174, 266
Library of Humor (Twain and Howells), 105
Life on the Mississippi (Twain), 134, 145, 243, 274; adapted from Twain's experiences, 56, 61, 80; based on "Old Times on the Mississippi," 11, 80; copyrighting of, in Canada, 100; *Huckleberry Finn*, borrowings from, 81, 83, 146, 179; illustrations cut from, 99; records changes in life of river, 66–67, 81, 84; records Twain's dislike of the South, 82–85, 142, 156, 188; reviewed, 125; sales campaign for, 85; sales disappoint Twain, 124–25; writing, difficulties with, 70–71, 80–83
Linotype, 262–64, 272
Loan of a Lover, The: Twain acts in, 127
Locke, David ("Petroleum V. Nasby"), 77, 178
London, Jack, 87
Longfellow, Henry Wadsworth, 42–44

Lorne, John Douglas Sutherland Campbell, Marquess of, 100
Louise, Princess, 100
"Loves of Alonzo Fitz Clarence and Rosanannah Ethelton, The" (Twain), 35
Lowell, James Russell, 17, 197
Lutheran Observer, 231
Lynchburg *Virginian*, 254
Lyon, Isabel, 298, 300–4

McAleer, Patrick, 73–74, 92
Macaulay, Thomas Babington: *History of England*, 224
McClellan, George B., 246
McClintock, G. Ragsdale: *The Enemy Conquered*, 142
McClure, Samuel, 292
McClure's Magazine, 292
McCormick, Wales, 183
McGuinn, Warner T., 189, 268
Mackay, John, 224, 261, 272, 278
McMurry, "Pet," 182
Madame Delphine (Cable), 63
Magnetic Rock Spring Company, 134
Malory, Sir Thomas, 120, 179; *see also Morte d'Arthur, Le*
"Man That Corrupted Hadleyburg, The" (Twain), 288, 290
"Man with the Golden Arm, The" ("The Ghost Story": Twain), 91, 172–73, 184, 229
Manet, Édouard, 151–52
Marion Rangers (home guard), 11, 248
"mark twain," meaning of, 13
Mark Twain (steamboat), 56
"Mary's Night Ride," from *Dr. Sevier* (Cable), 172, 177, 186
Mergenthaler, Ottmar, 262
Mergenthaler Linotype Company, 281
Military History of Ulysses S. Grant (Badeau), 215
Mississippi River, 8–10, 54–58, 65–67, 80–81
"Mock Oration on the Dead Partisan" (Twain), 163

Modern Instance, A (Howells), 70–71

Moffett, Annie, *see* Webster, Annie, 85

Moffett, Pamela, 5, 78, 130, 162, 297

Moffett, Samuel, 130, 240

Monday Evening Club (Hartford), 94, 164, 268

Montreal *Gazette*, 191

Morris, William, 206

Morte d'Arthur, Le (Malory), 120, 179–80, 232, 269

Mugwumps, and 1884 Presidential election, 161–63, 295

My Mark Twain (Howells), 44, 208

"Mysterious Chamber, The" (Twain), 105–6

Mysterious Stranger, The (Twain), 289; *see also* "No. 44, the Mysterious Stranger"

"Nasby, Petroleum V." (David Locke), 77, 178

Nast, Thomas, 154, 221

Nation, 198; comments on 1884 Presidential campaign, 160, 163; *Personal Memoirs of U. S. Grant* reviewed in, 255; speculates on reason for Grant's death, 212; *Stolen White Elephant* reviewed in, 68

Negro Question, The (Cable), 192

New Orleans, 60–61

New Orleans *Crescent*, 10

New Orleans *Times-Democrat*, 81

New York *Morning Journal*, 236

New York *Saturday Press*, 17

New York *Sun*, 148, 250, 293; Cable and Twain performance reviewed in, 173

New York Times, The, 32, 128; Cable and Twain performance reviewed in, 173; Duncan sues for libel, 101–2; on Grant's forthcoming death, 231; Rogers mentioned in, 279, 294; Twain lecture reviewed in, 25; Twain letter printed in, 137; Twain's attack on Duncan in, 101; Twain speech printed in, 158

New York *Tribune*, 262, 293; Linotypes installed at, 263–64; *Prince and the Pauper* reviewed by, 51; Twain's ire at, 51; Twain's letters from Europe in, 19

New York *World*: attributes Grant's work to Badeau, 223; Fred Grant interviewed in, 235, 245; *Huckleberry Finn* reviewed in, 199; reports altered illustration for *Huckleberry Finn*, 174

Nietzsche, Friedrich, 77

Nook Farm, Hartford (Connecticut), 24–25, 35, 75, 93, 267–68; *see also* Twain, Mark: Hartford home of

North American Review, 293

Norton, Charles Eliot, 155

"No. 44, the Mysterious Stranger" (Twain), 183, 289, 297–98

Ogilvie & Company, J. S., 99

Old Creole Days (Cable), 62, 172

"Old Times on the Mississippi" (Twain), 11, 31, 53–54, 80, 125; *see also Life on the Mississippi*

Omar Khayyám: *Rubáiyát*, 239

"£1,000,000 Bank Note, The" (Twain), 275

"1002d Night, The" (Twain), 120–21, 123

Ordeal of Mark Twain, The (Brooks), 16, 116, 260

O'Reilly, Father Bernard, 249

"Orion's Autobiography" (Twain), 40

Osgood, James R., 67, 85, 124, 250; accompanies Twain on Mississippi trip, 54; editorial suggestions for *Life on the Mississippi*, 81, 82; parts company with Twain, 125

Osgood and Company, James R., 50, 67, 70, 82, 85, 124–25

"Our Fellow Savages of the Sandwich Islands" (Twain), 28

Owsley, William, 4, 111

Oxford University: awards Twain honorary degree, 301–2

Paige, James, 260, 262, 274, 278–79; delays in development of typesetter, 225–26, 264–65, 270–71; financial arrangements with Twain, 88, 226, 261, 264–65, 272; inventions of, 242
Paine, Albert Bigelow, 228; appointed biographer by Twain, 78, 300; biography of Twain, 44, 56, 159, 176, 183, 214, 224; and death of Twain, 307; and *The Mysterious Stranger*, publication of, 289
Parker, Edwin, 49
Parkman, Francis, 120; *LaSalle and the Discovery of the Great West*, 81
Patmore, Coventry: *The Angel in the House*, 96
Paul Jones (steamboat), 8
Pennsylvania (steamboat), 9–10, 80
Pepys, Samuel, 144; *Diary*, 119
Perry, Thomas Sergeant: "An American on American Humor," 204; reviews *Huckleberry Finn*, 204
Personal Memoirs of U. S. Grant, 225, 231, 232, 245, 265; *Century* offer for, 215; excerpted in *Century*, 175; Grant dictates, 221, 222–23; literary quality of, 212, 219, 255; popularity of, 236; reviews of, 255; rumors concerning, 223, 234–36; sales and prices of, 224, 243–44; sales campaign for, 217–20; statistics of, 253–54; Wanamaker's Department Store offer of, 258–59; Webster & Co. chosen as publisher of, 213–16; writing of, 212–13, 215, 221, 222–23, 230–31, 235
Personal Recollections of Joan of Arc (Twain), 114, 207, 276
Phelps, Roswell, 54
Picturesque Incidents in History & Tradition (Twain publishing project), 240

piloting the Mississippi, 8–10, 55–58
Plasmon, Ltd., 286–87, 304
Pond, James B., 90, 186; agent and manager for Cable and Twain, 153, 169–70, 193–94; offers other tours to Twain, 154, 293; traveling companion of Cable and Twain, 176, 182, 189
Pond, Ozias, 179–80, 182, 185
Porter, Charles, 141, 189
Potter, Edward T., 27
Prince and the Pauper, The (Twain), 79, 110, 122, 146, 171, 198; compared to *Huckleberry Finn*, 50; compared to Twain's other works, 49; dramatized by Twain, 139; genesis of, 42; performed by family and friends, 192–93; popularity of, 201; publication of, 50; reviews of, 50–51; sales of, 51, 76, 78, 124–25
"Private History of a Campaign That Failed, The" (Twain), 11, 220, 241, 248
Puck, 292
Pudd'nhead Wilson (Twain), 73, 274, 276, 285

Quaker City (steamship), 18, 21, 101

Ragsdale, Bill: Twain plans work about, 138
Raymond, John, 30, 127, 138–40, 157
Regius Manufacturing Company, 280–81
Reid, Whitelaw, 51, 262–63
Richardson, Samuel: *Clarissa Harlowe*, 144
Rise of Silas Lapham, The (Howells), 174–75, 238
Robinson, Henry, 159
Robinson Crusoe (Defoe), 105, 106
Rogers, Henry Huttleston, 294, 301; character and interests of, 277–78; death of, 302; first acquaintance with Twain, 277; han-

Rogers, Henry Huttleston (*cont.*) dles Twain's affairs, 37, 278–82, 284, 286; view of Twain, 215
Rogers, Mary, 298, 302
Roosevelt, Theodore, 294, 299, 301
Roughing It (Twain), 12, 24–26, 73, 80, 180
"Roughing It on the Silver Frontier" (Twain), 28
Routledge & Sons, 25, 77
"Royalty on the Mississippi" (Twain), 175
Rubáiyát (Omar Khayyám), 239

Sacramento *Union*, 17
Saint-Gaudens, Augustus, 140
St. Nicholas, 275
Saint-Simon, Louis de Rouvroy, Duc de: *Memoirs*, 119, 144, 248
Salinger, J. D.: *The Catcher in the Rye*, 207
San Francisco *Chronicle*, 201
San Francisco *Morning Call*, 14–15
Saturday Morning Club (Hartford), 93–94, 268
Saturday Review, 198
Schiller, Friedrich von, 144; *Die Jungfrau von Orleans*, 238
Scott, Sir Walter, 84, 111, 118, 119, 281; *The Betrothed*, 238; *Ivanhoe*, 83
Scribner's Magazine, 62
"Secret History of Eddypus, the World-Empire, The" (Twain), 127, 299
Seelye, John: *The True Adventures of Huckleberry Finn*, 113–14
Sellers, Isaiah, 10
Shakespeare, William, 47, 120, 303
Shaw, George Bernard, 206, 302
Sheridan, Philip Henry, 233, 254–55
Sherman, William Tecumseh, 233, 247–48, 254–55, 266
1601, 38, 45–46, 120
Sketches: New and Old (Twain), 125, 180
slavery, 31; Cable's views on, 141,

172; Twain's views on, 3, 6–7, 11, 82, 114, 126
Slote, Dan, 86
Smarr, Sam, 111
Smith, Roswell, 215
Sneider (mechanic on Kaolatype), 86, 87
"Some Thoughts on the Science of Onanism" (Twain), 47
Southern speech, 58–59, 83, 115–16; blacks' dialect, 31, 59, 62, 115; Creole dialect, 63, 172
Southern violence noted by Twain, 59–60, 82, 113
Spaulding, Clara, 28
Spencer, Herbert, 26
Springfield *Republican*, 201, 203, 206
Stanford, Leland, 242
Stanley, Henry M., Sir, 27, 267
Stedman, Edmund Clarence, 174, 266
Stevenson, Robert Louis, 206
Stoddard, Charley, 28–29
Stolen White Elephant, The (Twain), 67–68, 121
Story of a Country Town, The (Howe), 132–33
Stowe, Harriet Beecher, 24, 50
subscription publishing: agents and sales force for, 164–65, 218–19, 234, 244; compared with trade publishing, 29–30; low status of, 30–31, 197; operation of, 50, 85, 124–25, 146, 213; readers of, 19, 61, 146; typical books produced for, 25, 152, 196, 254, 258–59
Suetonius: *Lives of the Caesars*, 119
Swift, Jonathan: *Gulliver's Travels*, 47, 298
Szczpanik, Jan, 286

Tauchnitz, Christian, Baron von, 144–45
Tennesseé Land, and Clemens family, 4–5, 15
Territorial Enterprise, 12–13, 51, 68
"Those Extraordinary Twins" (Twain), 274, 275, 276

"3,000 Years Among the Microbes" (Twain), 298–99
Tichborne Claimant, 28
Tiffany, Louis C., 72
Toledo *Blade*, 178
Tom Sawyer Abroad (Twain), 274, 275
"Tom Sawyer's Conspiracy" (Twain), 126, 284
"To the Person Sitting in Darkness" (Twain), 293
Tramp Abroad, A (Twain), 48–49, 168, 172, 180
Travelers Record, The, 32
Trollope, Anthony, 26; *Barchester Towers*, 110
"True Story, A" (Twain), 31, 103
"Turning-Point of My Life, The" (Twain), 305–6
Twain, Mark: as actor, 127, 192–93; as Anglophile, 26–27, 28; apprentice newsman, 12–14; apprentice river pilot, 8–10; apprentice typesetter, 5; April Fool's joke by Cable on, 143; Army of the Tennessee reunion and, 47–48; autobiography, projected, 4, 36; bankruptcy of, 279; bed clamp invented by, 165–66, 180; bicycle riding and, 133, 148–49, 157; birth of, 3; British reviews of, 49, 79–80, 125, 197–98, 270; Browning class taught by, 268; in Buffalo, 23–24; Cable, lecture tour with, 153–54, 167–93, 193–95, 209; Canada, visits to, 100–1, 190–91; cat lover, 73, 238; charities of, 52–53, 67, 141, 183, 189, 268, 301; childhood of, 3–4, 6, 284; Civil War experience of, 11, 14, 241, 248; collaborates with Harte, 39–40; collaborates with Howells, 105, 127–30; collaborates with Warner, 27; contracts with American Publishing Company, 19–20, 26, 45, 134, 276, 285; contracts with James R. Osgood and Company, 50, 67, 70, 85, 124–25; copyright and pirating difficulties of, 19, 25, 99–100, 176–77; copyright bill urged by, 144, 250; death of, 307; and death of Grant, 232–33; and death of Jean, 306; and death of Livy, 297; and death of Susy, 282–84; Duncan, quarrel with, 101–2; early travels of, 6, 7–8, 11–12; early writing of, 5–6, 8, 10; engagement to Livy, 22; England, visit to (1872), 26–27; England, visit to (1873), 28–29; Europe, journey through (1878), 45–47; Europe, stay in (1891–95), 273–77, 280–81; Europe, stay in (1897–1901), 284–91; family life of, 23, 29, 74, 90–93, 96–97, 103–4, 121–22, 127, 141, 143–44, 189–90, 192–93, 227–28, 237–38, 250–51, 256–57, 267, 283; fiftieth birthday of, 251–53; first love of, 9; forty-eighth birthday of, 136–37; "Forty Immortals" of American letters, voted one of, 196–97; France, views on, 46–47; Grant, friendship with, 208–9, 211–12, 214, 216, 220, 222, 231; Grant's memoirs and, 209–10, 214–25, 234, 236, 245, 253–56, 258–59; guilt and conscience in life and works of, 6, 10, 26, 37–38, 44, 66, 80, 100–1, 109, 113, 120, 283; Hartford home of, 27, 32–35, 72–74, 76, 86, 94–95, 286 (*see also* Nook Farm); Hawaiian story planned, 137–38; Hawaii (Sandwich Islands), visit to, 17; History Game invented by, 121–23, 180; honorary degrees received by, 268–69, 301; humor and wit, analyzes, 240–41; impostors, fascination with, 28–29; influence on American literature of, 207; inventions of, 89, 121–23, 134, 135, 165–66, 180, 249–50; investments in automatic typesetter, 88, 225–27, 242, 260–65, 270–72, 274, 277–81;

Twain, Mark (*cont.*)
investments, miscellaneous, 85–87, 134, 145, 165, 180, 241, 242, 286, 287, 304; investments, Webster & Company, 145–46, 197, 220, 256, 265–67, 270, 275–81; journal begun by, 7; as journeyman printer, 6–7; Kaolatype and, 85–87; in Keokuk (Iowa), 7, 8, 180, 181–82; language, use of: *see under* style and language, attention to; lectures, lecture tours, and speeches by, 16, 17–18, 22, 23, 25, 28–29, 47–48, 100, 148, 152–54, 167–93, 193–95, 209, 229, 260, 281–82, 299, 300; lecture tour "menagerie" idea, 64; lecturing style developed by, 25, 168–69; letters received by, 51, 78, 93, 130–34, 148, 158, 180, 205, 243, 247–48, 252, 255, 265, 294; marries Livy, 23; Mediterranean cruise (1867), 18–19; Mississippi trip (1882), 54–67; music and, 29, 46, 91, 141, 149, 298; in Nevada, 11–14; in New Orleans, 60–66; as newsman, 14–15, 23–24; Old South, rejection of, 14, 58–62, 82–84, 188 (*see also under* South, Southern); pen names of, 6, 8, 12–13; personality of, 7–8, 22, 36, 51–52, 60, 68–69, 75–76, 82, 86–89, 136, 183–84, 194; physical description of, 35–36, 55, 65, 104, 169, 228, 301; Plasmon health food and, 286–87, 304; as playwright, 30, 39–40, 139–40; political action by, 158–64, 294–95; popularity abroad, 28, 29, 77, 93, 132, 273–74, 286, 287; projected work left uncompleted, 126–27, 142, 149–50, 155–57, 207, 288–90, 295; at Quarry Farm, 103–7, 118, 120–23, 150–52, 155, 237–38; race, views on, 6–7, 15, 188–89 (*see also* slavery); railroads, invests in, 145, 242; reading preferences of, 118–20, 144, 239; relations with Cable after tour, 194–95; relations with *Century*, 166, 215, 217, 241; relations with Livy, 22, 23–24, 29, 36, 90; religion, thoughts on, 6, 8, 15–16, 35, 101, 137–38, 156, 191, 228, 282, 297; religious upbringing of, 6, 8, 94; reviews of *Huckleberry Finn*, reaction to, 199–203, 206; Rideau Hall (Ottawa) visit, 100–1; Salvation Army group described by, 176; Sandwich Islands (Hawaii), interest in, 17–18, 137–38; in San Francisco, 14–18, 19; self-pasting scrapbook invented by, 89, 134; servants of, 41, 73–74 (*see also under* names); seventieth birthday of, 299–300; smoking, habit of, 73, 273, 302; social life at Hartford, 93–95, 137, 250–51, 267 (*see also* Nook Farm); South, criticizes, 82–85, 142, 156–57; Southern journalism, views on, 61–62; Statue of Liberty and, 137; at Stormfield, 302–7; style and language, attention to, 19–20, 61–62, 115–16, 119, 155, 202; technology, fascination with, 34–35, 70, 84–85; telephone and, 34–35; theater, love of, 127, 192–93; Toronto and Montreal visit, 190–91; translations of, 77; typewriter, tries out, 70; unfinished work, *see under* projected work left uncompleted; Wagnerian opera, reaction to, 46; Whittier dinner speech by, 42–44; at Wild West Show, 239; world tour (1895–96), 281–82; writing method of, 30–31, 38, 41, 98, 104, 110, 112; *see also* lectures and readings: "American Vandal Abroad, The"; "Awful German Language, The"; "Celebrated Jumping Frog of Calaveras County, The"; "Desperate Encounter with an Interviewer"; "How come a Frenchman doan

talk like a man?"; "Jim Baker's Bluejay Yarn"; "King Sollermun"; "Man with the Golden Arm, The"; "Our Fellow Savages of the Sandwich Islands"; "Roughing It on the Silver Frontier"; "Some Thoughts on the Science of Onanism"; *see also* published works: "Adam's Diary"; *Adventures of Huckleberry Finn, The*; *Adventures of Tom Sawyer, The*; *Ah Sin*; *American Claimant, The*; "American Press, The"; "Bloody Massacre Near Carson, A"; *Captain Stormfield's Visit to Heaven*; *Celebrated Jumping Frog of Calaveras County and Other Sketches, The*; "Chronicle of Young Satan, The"; *Colonel Sellers*; *Colonel Sellers as a Scientist*; *Connecticut Yankee in King Arthur's Court, A*; "Coward's Revenge, The"; "Curious Republic of Gondour, The"; "Dandy Frightening the Squatter, The"; *Eve's Diary*; "Facts Concerning the Recent Carnival of Crime in Connecticut, The"; "Fenimore Cooper's Literary Offenses"; *Following the Equator*; *Gilded Age, The*; "Happy Memories of the Dental Chair"; "Indiantown"; *Innocents Abroad, The*; "Invalid's Story, The"; *Is Shakespeare Dead?*; "Jim's Investments"; "Jim Smiley and His Jumping Frog"; *Letters from the Earth*; *Library of Humor*; *Life on the Mississippi*; "Loves of Alonzo Fitz Clarence and Rosannah Ethelton, The"; "Man That Corrupted Hadleyburg, The"; "Mock Oration on the Dead Partisan"; *Mysterious Stranger, The*; "Old Times on the Mississippi"; "£1,000,000 Bank Note, The"; "1002nd Night, The"; *Personal Recollections of Joan of Arc*; *Prince and the Pauper, The*; "Private History of a Campaign That Failed, The"; *Pudd'nhead Wilson*; *Rough-*

ing It; "Royalty on the Mississippi"; *1601*; *Sketches: New and Old*; *Stolen White Elephant, The*; "Those Extraordinary Twins"; "3,000 Years Among the Microbes"; *Tom Sawyer Abroad*; "To the Person Sitting in Darkness"; *Tramp Abroad, A*; "True Story, A"; "Turning-Point of My Life, The"; "Villagers of 1840–43"; *What Is Man?*; *see also* unpublished works: "America in 1985"; "B. B."; *Cap'n Simon Wheeler, the Amateur Detective*; "Consistency"; *Death Disk, The*; "Enchanted Sea-Wilderness, The"; "General Grant's Grammar"; "Great Dark, The"; "Huck and Tom Among the Indians"; "Mysterious Chamber, The"; "No. 44, the Mysterious Stranger"; "Orion's Autobiography"; "Secret History of Eddypus, the World-Empire, The"; "Tom Sawyer's Conspiracy"; "What Is Happiness?"; "Which Was It?"; "Which Was the Dream?"

Twichell, Joseph H., 23, 136, 140, 208–9, 251, 258, 267; character and personality of, 45; ministry of, 35, 41, 75, 162, 297; political action by, 160, 162–63; Twain and, 22, 41, 45, 122–23, 148, 232, 297

Two Years Before the Mast (Dana), 119

Vanderbilt, William Henry, 211, 232

Vassar College, Twain's visit to, 229

Verne, Jules, 128, 275

"Villagers of 1840–43" (Twain), 284

Virginia City *Daily Union*, 14

Wagner, Richard, 46

Wanamaker, John, 258–59

Ward, Artemus (Charles Farrar Browne), 13–14, 76

Ward, Ferdinand, 210–11
Warner, Charles Dudley, 27, 30, 77, 160, 192, 251–52; *see also Gilded Age, The*
Warner, Lilly, 171
Washington, Booker T., 301
Webb, C. H., 18
Webster, Annie, 85
Webster, Charles L., 190, 242, 246; death of, 266; and Grant's memoirs, 213–18, 223, 234, 253, 260; and *Huckleberry Finn*, 164–65, 206; as manager of Twain's publishing house, 145–46, 155, 266; and Pope's biography, 258, 265; Twain's affairs handled by, 85, 87, 99, 124, 135, 138–40, 145, 157, 165–66, 180, 197, 260
Webster & Company (Charles L.), 190, 211, 249; *A Connecticut Yankee* published by, 270; Custer biography published by, 266; expansion of, 216–17, 266; failure and bankruptcy of, 265–67, 270, 275–81; founding of, 145–46; Fred Grant and, 245–46; Grant's memoirs published by, 207, 213–15, 219–20, 224, 231, 234, 236, 244, 254–56, 259; Harper & Brothers and, 285; *Huckleberry Finn* published by, 164–65, 197; McClellan's memoirs published by, 246–47, 255; Sheridan's memoirs published by, 255, 266; as war book publisher, 266
Wells, H. G., 289, 301
"What Is Happiness?" (Twain), 94
What Is Man? (Twain), 94, 288–89
"Which Was It?" (Twain), 188–89, 290
"Which Was the Dream?" (Twain), 211, 289
Whitford, Daniel, 226, 235–36, 244–45
Whitman, Walt, 79, 204; *Leaves of Grass*, 268
Whittier, John Greenleaf, 42
Wilhelm II, Kaiser, 75, 270, 274, 303
Woodruff, W. N., 236–37
Wright, Laura, 9

Yale University: awards Twain honorary degree, 268–69, 301
Yanks and Rebs, 266
Yung Wing, 209

PAST EGO STATES EMERGING IN HYPNOANALYSIS

PAST EGO STATES EMERGING IN HYPNOANALYSIS

By

EDITH KLEMPERER, M.D.

Consultant in Psychiatry to the Morton Prince Clinic for Hypnotherapy
Supervising Psychiatrist, Institute for Research in Hypnosis
Fellow of American Psychiatric Association
Fellow of Society for Clinical and Experimental Hypnosis
Fellow of American Society of Clinical Hypnosis
Life Fellow of American Society of Clinical Hypnosis
Education and Research Foundation
Diplomate of the American Board of Medical Hypnosis

CHARLES C THOMAS • PUBLISHER
Springfield • Illinois • U.S.A.

PREFACE

THIS volume grew out of questions which have wanted answering for a long time and which have both piqued and preoccupied me on and off for many years. The first is why patients in hypnoanalysis present their material in the different ways that they do; the second question involves the nature of these differences, and the third bears on the relation of these observed differences to known psychological phenomena and the systematization of these differences. The attempts to find answers to these questions were deferred by other interesting aspects of hypnoanalysis demanding investigation which kept cropping up continually. However, I decided a few years ago that the time was past due for me to apply myself to some resolution of the aforementioned questions, and a paper entitled "Past Ego States Emerging in Hypnoanalysis" was the result. In it, it was possible to demonstrate that the same mechanisms of defense employed by patients in psychoanalysis who fell into certain diagnostic categories could also be detected in the hypnoanalyses of patients in the same diagnostic category.

The next stage of this work must then be credited to Mr. Payne E. L. Thomas, its publisher, who not only queried me about expanding this investigation, but encouraged its growth, and concomitantly was kind enough to exercise great patience in awaiting its completion. The transformation of long and meticulous case histories and of recorded and carefully transcribed hypnoanalyses into readable book chapters demanded considerable time and manifold considerations, although a few of the case histories had to be left in their original form because the patients terminated treatment as soon as their most troublesome handicaps were overcome.

The plan of the book was conceived as a three-fold one: to explain, elucidate, and, wherever possible, collate the effects obtained in hypnoanalysis with those obtained by the use of other psychotherapies. This plan was accomplished principally with re-

gard to psychoanalytic theories. The organization of the book, therefore, took the following form: First, the methods I employ in the hypnoanalyses of patients are described; second, a brief revue of the various theories which have been published about hypnoanalysis is set down, since one finds—and probably will continue to do so for a long time to come—that hypnoanalysis is a discipline about which there are many divergent opinions, and last, the case histories are presented in the order of their diagnoses according to the Diagnostic and Statistical Manual of the American Psychiatric Association, with as many interpretations as possible without interrupting their flow too greatly. By this format with the inclusion and addition of other adventitious aspects, I have tried to make this a multipurpose work—one that would be of interest to the beginner as well as to the experienced hypnoanalyst. It is only proper at this point to indicate that the term "hypnoanalyst," as well as "hypnoanalysis" itself, as a specific entity is not subscribed to by all who, themselves, are well skilled in this technique, but who prefer to regard it as ancillary to other methods. That this is a matter of subjective preference is attested to by the absence of conclusive proof for or against its use as a major technique in psychotherapy.

What can be proven by a careful examination of the case histories presented in this book, however, is that 1) hypnosis and hypnoanalysis are effective in treating a wide variety of patients in different diagnostic categories. Most, though not all of the case histories presented in this volume, deal with patients who were regarded as seriously ill; 2) patients, after being regressed, see, as in a movie, their early lives projected into the forefront of the surrounding space. Whether these projections are reproductions of actual events or whether they are fantasies is often difficult to determine as is the case in other psychotherapies and irrelevant in terms of results. Irrespective of their veracity, the projections almost invariably help the patients understand their symptoms, abate or eliminate them, and effect cures; 3) the verbalizations patients produce of these visualizations demonstrate the same defense mechanisms operative as are revealed by free association in psychoanalyses of patients in the same diagnostic category; 4) the treatment of patients in hypnoanalysis is relatively short and the

results lasting. Patients have been checked up on many years after the termination of treatment and their gains have been found to be stable; 5) the dependency of the patient on the therapist has been found to be less in hypnoanalysis than in other therapies. This may be due to a facilitation of the transference which occurs when the patient sees his immediate family in projection and has no need to transfer the full cargo of his emotionality onto the therapist; it may also be due to the shorter duration of the treatment, and 6) there are additional and variegated methods available to the hypnotherapist to further speed up and disembarrass the therapy.

With this rationale in mind, it is but to be hoped that the body of the book adequately fulfills the commitments in the pages here.

EDITH KLEMPERER

INTRODUCTION

BOTH in its administration and its utilization, hypnosis can be performed in many different ways, and, consequently, is still in a state of change. By changing the technique, quite dissimilar results may be obtained. This is the main reason why the techniques practiced with the patients discussed in this book will be described without reference to the vast literature.

Great care was taken to first elicit a detailed anamnesis from each patient, some of whom had been sent by other physicians for the express purpose of hypnotherapy, while other patients needed some explanation as to why hypnotherapy might prove to be the best treatment for them.

If patients desired a hypnosis performed during the first interview, this was always acceded to because the cooperation of the patient is as important in this as in any other form of psychotherapy. In such cases the anamnesis was expanded and completed in subsequent interviews. A number of patients expressed doubts about their susceptibility to hypnosis; they were told that the best way to find out was to submit to a hypnotic session. No tests were made, as all tests are suggestibility tests, and the first successful hypnosis is the only real test of hypnotizability.

Every patient was hypnotized while lying on a couch, by means of eye fixation. With the patients who were hypnotized by what is called Mesmer's strokes, eye fixation was achieved by a bent Lucite® rod with a red bead at its end. In recent years an empty picture hook on the opposite wall from the couch has been used for this purpose. For many years Mesmeric stroking has been practiced on patients.

The doctor's nearness made some patients feel closed in, and in such cases hypnosis was attempted without the forehead being stroked, the doctor sitting at the patient's side at some distance from him. This method seems preferable except in hard-to-hypno-

tize cases when the stroking hand facilitates the trance because it is unconsciously reminding the patient of the mother's hand stroking the child to sleep.

Accompanying sentences were spoken clearly and rhythmically, almost like a chant or lullaby. Most of the patients discussed in this book responded immediately, in others a few repetitions of the induction were necessary before it was obvious that the patient was in a trance state. The relaxed face, the regular breathing which can be heard at such times, the thoracic rise and fall which are well discernible, soon make it clear that the patient is hypnotized. When Mesmer's strokes are used, this is often tangible to the doctor's hand.

Once the patient is hypnotized, first negative, then positive suggestions are given, each one duplicated and the positive ones punctuated with suggestive sentences such as "You feel happy, very happy and completely relaxed, and this feeling of happiness and complete relaxation will stay with you," which can be said many times. The group of duplicated negative and positive suggestions is repeated once. At the end of the hypnotic session the suggestion of sleep is undone, as well as any other suggestion which should not remain with the patient.

No patient was trained to fall asleep or be awakened on a given signal such as touching him on the shoulder or rapping a pencil on the desk. In my opinion such devices impair rapport and make the patient a kind of automaton. Such a signal can also be inadvertently given by somebody else, and the patient is then in a quandary as to what he should do. The more personal the physician's approach, the more easily will the patient accept the notion that he is being helped, and the more cooperative he will be. There are also patients who, when disturbing unconscious material starts to come up, become increasingly difficult to hypnotize. In such cases, resistance can already be recognized during the induction of the hypnosis, and the therapist should act accordingly. The patient must always have the feeling that he is treated with respect and that the physician will not behave like a strict parent or a police officer.

It is a good sign if the patient, after a time, turns his head toward the physician. Patients have later been asked why they did

this. Some answered that it made the stroking of the forehead easier, but it also occurred with patients who were not stroked. It may indeed be simply an expression of cooperation as we turn to somebody who addresses us. It means little if it happens at the very beginning of the hypnotic session but is a sign of suggestibility if it occurs after about a quarter of the suggestions have been given.

Before the combined suggestions are repeated, the patient is told that at the next session he will start to "sleep" faster and will sleep more deeply, which is really what he most desires at the beginning of his therapy; and the same information is also imparted before he is awakened. At this time the patient is also instructed that no one but a psychiatrist or a psychologist will be able to hypnotize him. The final suggestions should be a kind of high point to the session. Then it is suggested that he will feel no dizziness or headache after awakening but will be happy and relaxed.

In modern writings about hypnosis it is often stated that the word "sleep" should not be used because hypnosis is not sleep. But the association between trance and sleep is as easy for the patient as for the therapist and may therefore be practicable.

Some patients, after awakening from the hypnotic session, say that the depth of trance varied during the single hypnotic session. They are instructed that most hypnoses follow a curve-like pattern of deeper and lighter depth. Gill and Brenman claim that these fluctuations represent "shifts in defense and adaptation (regressive adaptation, linked by Hartmann to Kris's regression in the service of the ego)."

When the patient has been hypnotized several times—and it does not matter too much how deep the hypnoses have been—hypnoanalysis is begun. In the case of Anne it was started after the second hypnotic session as both hypnoses had been especially deep. In other cases, more hypnotic sessions were first performed.

Hypnoanalysis can be instituted in different ways. One cautious method is to hypnotize the patient and give only the first part of the combined suggestions. This should bring him to a state of relaxation and well-being. Regression is then immediately induced. "You dream you remember. You dream you remember. You are a very small boy (girl). You are a very small boy (girl)." The first

two sentences are repeated three times, the next one twice, so that the suggestions end with "You dream you remember. And keep it in mind. You keep it in mind." These words are enunciated slowly and intently. It is hard to describe the rhythm of this type of speech, but after some experience everybody using hypnosis finds the right cadence for himself. After a few applications of this combination of hypnosis and hypnoanalysis, the initial suggestions are dropped, and immediately after being hypnotized, the patient is regressed.

A small percentage of patients start visualizing by themselves, and this should be encouraged if they are able to remember the material in the awake state. The initial visualizations are kept short, and the patient does not talk as long as he is hypnotized. He describes his visualizations afterward; they are put on paper and then talked over. Should they be symbolical, the therapist informs the patient about symbols if he has not learned about them through having previously discussed dreams.

After a short while, if nothing too disturbing has been revealed by the patient, he is informed that next time he will talk during the hypnotic session, and after regression is induced, he is told to do so. Some talk easily; others have to be encouraged to do so. A few have repeatedly to be told to open their mouth and to describe what they see and feel. Should they recall disturbing events, protection and help must be promised by the therapist. He may assure the patient that he will go with him and guard him or do whatever the situation requires. When the recall of events is apparently too much for the patient, he is told that the session is at an end. No patient should leave the couch disturbed, but must be relaxed before he is dehypnotized. But no artificial or, as it is usually called, *posthypnotic* amnesia is induced.

Patients are usually able to tolerate what they have brought forth, and a slight spontaneous amnesia follows this kind of hypnoanalytic session in any event. The therapist must use his good judgment when to stop, and it is better to interrupt early since the same material will come up in future sessions.

Except for the first few short hypnoanalytic sessions, a tape or other recorder is used and the record transcribed, then played back to the patient, and the transcript corrected. Before recorders

were used, attempts were made to put the contents of the hypnoanalytic sessions on paper with the help of the patients in the
waking state, but this proved highly unreliable. Usually the beginning and the end of a hypnoanalysis are well remembered by
both participants, but the middle is only partly retained. In addition, the sequence of events, especially if they issue by the laws
of the primary process, is hard to retrace because logic is lacking.
A recorder is therefore valuable. When the playback is offered, the
patient's spontaneous amnesia is sometimes observed. When recordings of embarrassing or disturbing events are to be played
back, the patient usually tenders some excuse as to why he does
not desire to listen to them, at the same time stating that he has
forgotten the contents of the session. There would not be any reason for his reluctance if he were not somehow aware of what is on
the record. But as this recorded material is very important, it is
obvious that the patient must be informed about it, and only a
few calming words are needed to influence him to be open-mind-
ed. The replay also demonstrates to the patient the fact that his
inflection and tone of voice are often just as expressive as the
words he has used.

The playback of a hypnoanalytic session is, of course, only a
start. It evokes associations and memories and opens the gates to
elaboration. Old misconceptions are recognized and new insights
gained. Nocturnal dreams related to the visualized material may
then follow.

Similar to regression, but eventually deeper going, is revivification. The patient is disoriented by being told to forget the
present place, year, month, and day, and he is regressed in steps to
his childhood. With the patients discussed in this book, planned
regression was stopped at the age of four. It was left to the patients to determine the age level of their visualizations which
might be before or after the fourth year. The age at which events
occurred and the location where they took place therefore should
be ascertained in every hypoanalysis so that some firm basis be established. In this way, the patient's early life history can be re-
traced and contradictions detected. Orientation in time and place
—be it in an actual or fantasied reality—is also useful in dealing
with symbolical material because it relates to actual events which

may later come up. In this regard, questions as to what kind of clothes were worn, their color, and other details can be helpful. In this way, the patient eventually learns to spontaneously state his age, the place where the visualization occurs, his own appearance. Otherwise, he should, as far as is possible, not be interrupted by questions during his visualizations although encouraging interjections such as "Yes," "Go on," "Work it through" can be made. These also maintain and reinforce the therapist's contact with the hypnotized patient. If the patient has obviously exhausted his material, details about previous data can be sought or questions about the transference asked. In some patients, it becomes a constant dialogue between patient and physician.

There are patients who do not accept revivification. This was so with Al, who only accepted regression. In this respect, the patient is the sole judge because his cooperation is necessary for the whole treatment. Pressure has to be avoided as much as possible.

Should the patient describe a nocturnal dream or complain about some mental or bodily discomfort, it is possible to instruct him at the end of the regression to regress to the roots of his dream or to the reasons for his discomfort. It can also be suggested at the end of the revivification that he regress exactly to the age at which events occurred which have caused the dream or his mental or bodily complications. Flexibility is always possible.

As to other specialized techniques, mostly dreaming and reading were employed. Reading can be used either by telling the patient that letters forming syllables, which in turn form words, will appear, or by instructing him to read whole sentences immediately. This depends entirely on his ability to visualize. Obviously, associations and the theater technique were used.

During visualization, the patient is able to vary his images. This versatility, which is one of the great advantages and facility of a therapy that evokes pictures instead of static words, can be used to learn the meaning of symbols in a simple and direct manner. The patient is told to let the symbol, or whatever he has visualized, "change nearer to the real thing." The real thing, whatever it may be, should never be immediately asked for because this may shock the patient. But the steps to reach it are quite short and easy.

Too much prompting of the patient should be avoided, especially at the beginning of treatment. It can provoke anxiety or cause the material to be "jumbled;" a block may also occur, or the patient may awake.

I will shortly mention a technique which I have used twice with patients (Mitch, Morton) who hated one of their family members so intensely that it would have taken a long time to help them solve this conflict, let alone any others. It was obvious that these patients had harbored murderous wishes against this family member in their infancy and childhood and felt very guilty about them, with all the complicated consequences of such wishes and guilt feelings. At an appropriate occasion in the treatment, I instructed these patients to destroy this hated family member in hypnoanalysis, taking the whole guilt for the deed on myself and, at the same time, promising the patient my complete help and protection in every respect. In my estimation, this technique worked well. Al used this technique spontaneously although he only destroyed symbols of his father, except in his final hypnoanalytic session, but it was he who gave me the previously indicated idea of destroying a family member in the safe arena of the hypnoanalytic session.

The time taken by a hypnoanalytic session can vary from a few minutes to over an hour. After the session or after its replay, should the occasion warrant it, the patient may be told to draw a picture or plan of some specific material. This helps the integration of this specific content of the visualization into the personality and, at times, its identification, explanation and categorization.

How often hypnoanalysis is performed depends on the case. There are patients who, for some time, demand hypnoanalysis at each session; when they feel that their current material is exhausted, they listen to the playbacks. Others hear the replay at the next session. Or they have hypnoanalysis one session, then a few "soothing" hypnoses, as one patient called them. The playback is then heard at some time before the next hypnoanalytic session.

The hypnoanalyses discussed in this book were performed in a special room where there were the recorders. Except at sessions when hypnoses were performed, the patient sat in the office, fac-

ing the therapist. At the replay, he was also sitting, but in the room where the recorders are situated.

Gill and Brenman oppose the use of the term "hypnoanalysis" because this technique can be used in such a variety of psychotherapeutic forms. It is not standardized. This plasticity seems to prevail equally in psychoanalysis which has splintered into many different schools, only the so-called "orthodox Freudian" school still adhering rigidly to traditional procedure. Every method which regularly employs hypnosis to uncover the causes of the patient's conflicts, warrants the designation hypnoanalysis. Gill and Brenman also state, "We thought it a reasonable hypothesis that if the regressive character of the hypnotic state could keep the emotional level fairly high without obliterating ego functions, then learning in the broadest sense would occur more rapidly . . . 'working through' is in fact a learning process." This also seems to be an excellent description of what will be shown in the clinical part of this book.

The transcripts presented in this book were transcribed by myself and the recordings replayed and listened to time and again to reproduce the patients' exact wording. In the course of years, different recorders were used. First wire, then disc and, finally, tape. Since English is not my mother tongue, it is easier for me to hear and retain the lapses of speech which a person whose native language is English, might unconsciously correct. I have tried to reproduce precisely what I have heard and, in a number of cases, it has been set down verbatim in this book, while in other case histories, verbatim reportage has been omitted in order to save space. Every letter has been put down as the patient enunciated it. Endings of words which were slurred or otherwise inaudible have been indicated by an apostrophe. In those hypnonanalyses which have not been presented in direct speech, I have also tried to retain the original wording of the patients, as far as it has been possible to do so. This procedure goes far to convince that patients do not fabricate fantasies merely to please the therapist, but that visualizations originate in their own unconscious and are quite often brought forth with reluctance and timorousness.

In the reproduction of the sessions in the waking state, I have likewise tried to use the patients' own expressions. My questions

and remarks were the ones that were edited although the patients understood them as originally formulated. My frequent "yes," uttered to keep in contact with the patient, has been cut.

"S." stands for session, and the numeral following "S." represents the number of the session; "H." means hypnosis. Hypnoses and hypnoanalyses have been added together.

Coughing, borborygmi (stomach rumble), and the like are mentioned each time they were heard on the recording to show the "eloquent" interaction between mind and body. In fact, at times I would remark to a patient how much it would shorten the treatment were I able to understand the language of his stomach.

Incidentally, in psychiatry *infancy* refers to the period of life from birth to the age of five.

The diagnoses of the patients were made according to *The Diagnostic and Statistical Manual* of the American Psychiatric Association, 1955.

EDITH KLEMPERER

CONTENTS

	Page
Preface	v
Introduction	ix
I. THEORETICAL FORMULATIONS	3
II. ANXIETY, DISSOCIATIVE, CONVERSION, PHOBIC, AND DEPRESSIVE REACTIONS	21
Anne	21
Mitch	47
Ayleen	71
III. OBSESSIVE COMPULSIVE REACTION	95
Al	95
Etta	129
IV. COMPULSIVE PERSONALITY	153
Harley	153
V. PSYCHOPHYSIOLOGIC AUTONOMIC AND VISCERAL DISORDERS	184
Steven	184
Morton	228
Bibliography	257
Index	259

PAST EGO STATES EMERGING IN HYPNOANALYSIS

I

THEORETICAL FORMULATIONS

IN THIS section, I will present outlines of the theoretical foundations of a modality I have used for many years. The status of this modality, hypnoanalysis, has been discussed from a number of theoretical and clinical positions by many eminent psychotherapists, but whether it will one day grow from the adjunctive role it now plays into a special and autonomous form of treatment, is still too early to determine. Hence, we must satisfy our predictive sense with an examination of theoretical criteria of this modality. The books and articles centering on this field, written by M. V. Kline, Schneck, Wolberg, M. H. Erickson, Gill and Brenman, Meares, Gordon, Hilgard, and many others, are numerous, indeed, but the points of view from which they were handled are much too diverse; the number of patients treated is much too small; the objectives with which the patients were treated are much too disparate to permit any meaningful comparison of the respective philosophies underlying these researches on the use of hypnoanalysis.

Hypnoanalysis has undergone a development in a direction contrary to that of psychoanalysis. Psychoanalysis began in the last century with one innovator, Freud, and has since split into many branches. Hypnosis, however, is as old and widespread in its use as man himself; in its application as hypnoanalysis, it is probably much older than we think it is. It has certainly had a large number of applications. As is commonly known, Freud started with hypnosis and hypnoanalysis; he created and developed psychoanalysis for personal reasons. The theoretical framework I set down here tries to achieve a kind of structured formulation into which a number of approaches to hypnoanalysis may fit, but for the reasons stated above the actual unification and basic theory must wait.

3

Present-day psychoanalysis is chiefly concerned with transference phenomena and with interpretations of verbal and behavioral communications of the patient, be they associations, dreams, or otherwise. Without going into its more refined subdivisions, transference is defined as the displacement of affects from one object to another, more specifically, the process whereby a patient shifts affects applicable to another person onto the psychoanalyst (English and English). Since most of these affects pertain to objects from the patient's early life, a process, a modality which can reconstruct this early life, the patient's infancy—partly or completely, in actuality or in terms of fantasy or symbol—should alleviate the complications which transference invariably brings about. Consequently, counter-transference and the resolution of the transference neurosis are also unburdened of many of their various problems.

Hypnosis itself is a regressing modality, and I have already discussed the many means of intensifying regression. The value of regression as a method of treatment is not agreed to by everyone experienced in the use of hypnosis and hypnoanalysis. M. H. Erickson, who introduced quite a number of sophisticated techniques in hypnotic therapy, reports having seen many disappointing results from hypnoanalysis proper. Most of his techniques are aimed at reaching the patient's unconscious in a more direct and manipulative way than those employed in hypnoanalysis, and for each directive method discussed, the rationale is provided. However, other techniques described by Erickson, such as the "two stage" type of regression, are designed for hypnoanalysis. This method allows for a revivification of the remote past and a separate process of reporting upon those recovered memories in terms of adult understanding. I can only agree with Erickson's statement: "Since hypnosis can be induced and trance manifestations elicited by suggestions, the unwarranted assumption is made that whatever develops from hypnosis must be completely a result of suggestions and primarily an expression of it."

Wolberg, who published two valuable works on hypnosis and hypnoanalysis, in the chapter "Hypnosis in Psychoanalytic Psychotherapy" of Gordon's *Clinical and Experimental Hypnosis,* expresses the opinion that the use of regressive techniques reverts to

the early applications of Breuer and Freud, implying that the regular treatment by regression can only be temporarily effective. Incidentally, most of the follow-up reports obtained on my patients in their posttreatment periods seem to contradict this contention. Since the early researches of Breuer and Freud, altered approaches on the basis of accumulated experience and altered theoretical formulations, most of them derived from psychoanalysis, have essentially changed certain procedures in psychotherapy. Thus, a comparison of present-day hypnoanalysis with the early activities of Breuer and Freud could be invalid. The later formulations from psychoanalysis, however, may not be universally applicable to hypnoanalysis despite the prevailing fascination with the idea that the laws of one modality should apply to another modality in every respect. In many ways, hypnoanalysis does appear to be a different modality, a point of view also shared by researchers other than myself.

In psychoanalysis, interpretations of verbal and behavioral communications are made by the therapist according to his understanding of their hidden meanings and his evaluation of the patient's readiness to accept them. In hypnoanalysis, much of the intricacy of this procedure may be simplified by the patient's seeing his early life history with its conflicts, complications, and misunderstandings unfold in front of him, as in a movie. These depictions, as already indicated, can occur symbolically. But since all symbols are personal, though many are susceptible to standard interpretations, the patient can be directed to let a symbol change slowly to what it actually represents. The same applies to visualizations that are obvious fantasies and to visualizations that contradict actuality. Thus, it is possible in a great many cases to render interpretations more rapidly through hypnoanalysis and to shorten the working through process.

The archaic language of the unconscious is the image, the picture, which is plastic, flexible, changeable, two- or three-dimensional, and either sequential like a moving picture, or solitary like a photograph, or coexistent in space with other images like a kaleidoscope. By verbalizing his visualizations, the patient connects them to reality, to time and to place in the present, and in this way translates the primary process into the secondary one.

By this procedure, many resistances and defenses are quickly dissolved and much time is saved.

The language of the dream, too, is a pictorial one. By means of hypnoanalysis, dreams can be instigated, forgotten dreams remembered, partly forgotten dreams reconstructed, and recalled dreams meaningfully interpreted. Thus, archaic layers of the unconscious are quickly accessible to search.

Though it is my contention that the laws of one modality need not apply to another, I will now cite a number of investigators who have explored hypnosis and hypnoanalysis on the basis of psychoanalytic formulations, and a number of those whose concepts have been formulated without hypnosis and hypnoanalysis in mind, but whose papers seem to have some bearing on what I intend to demonstrate in these pages. These researchers do not constitute the totality of all who have done so, but have been selected because their formulations most closely apply to specific clinical aspects of hypnoanalysis exemplified by the case histories presented in this book. Whether or not principles thus analyzed will sustain the present veritability of their transposition, only time will tell; but the clinical aspects, the case histories, will always have substance, however they are later expounded.

Since I assume that most of these authors are extremely concerned about the specificity of their wording, what follows has not been abstracted, but for the most part excerpted. Gill and Brenman in *Hypnosis and Related States,* a 374 page volume, report chiefly on their researches regarding the theoretical aspects of hypnosis proper. Only eighteen of the fifty-four pages entitled "Explorations of the Use of Hypnosis in Psychotherapy" deal with hypnoanalysis. Some of their observations and conclusions on the theoretical aspects of hypnosis itself, researched from the point of view of traditional Freudian principles, appear to be profitable.

These excerpts are presented without regard for their original sequence or the headings or subheadings under which they were published. Gill and Brenman's "central proposal for the theory of hypnosis" is as follows: "In hypnosis a subsystem is set up within the ego . . . a regressed system which is in the service of the overall ego; it has control of some or all of the apparatuses. . . . It is this subsytem alone which is under the control of the hypnotist,

and it is by virtue of this control that the hypnotist can control and direct the apparatuses. The over-all ego also maintains a relationship with the hypnotist, the nonhypnotic reality-oriented relationship . . . the over-all ego can yield control of the subsystem . . . which can hallucinate, which can recall previously repressed traumatic material."

They regard hypnosis as "both an altered state (of consciousness) and a transference relationship," and suggest that " . . . hypnosis (is) a regression in the service of the ego (according to Kris) with a regressed subsystem in the persisting over-all ego structure . . . the transference underlying the hypnosis is the constellation of strivings within the subsystem, while the 'usual transferences' are, together with the current reality interaction, the manifestations of the 'persisting ego' relationship with the hypnotist." They discuss Kris's description of the metapsychology of the economics of regression in the service of the ego and summarize as follows: "Cathexes are withdrawn from defense and employed in the building of a subsystem whose maintenance requires a countercathexis of some of the cathexes retained in the over-all ego." To go further: "Unconscious energies no longer countercathected by defensive energies likewise contribute to the enhancement of preconscious thinking in the manner in which, to quote Freud, 'the unconscious becomes ego-syntonic.' "

After describing the way this subsystem is structured, and after describing its relationship to the over-all system, they state, "The superego components of the subsystem are derived not only from the subject's superego but also include incorporated apects of the hypnotist. . . . The id and superego derivatives which interact with ego structures in the subsystem are regressed, but the id and superego themselves are not regressed. . . . there may be different types of intersystemic relationships in various hypnotic subsystems." They further say, " . . . the adaptive point of view (involves) for hypnosis the assumption of both ego and superego functions by the hypnotist and in this sense the relative and partial exteriorization (reprojection) of these functions. A parallel process occurs for the id, giving rise to the realm of phenomena ordinarily called 'projection'." This may occur, for example, with aggressive impulses or homosexual urges. The authors also state

that normally "the superego never becomes completely autonomous from external objects, nor is its complete exteriorization
possible. . . . Such exteriorization may be . . . of ego functions
too." Then, as they point out, "The dynamic relationship between
the over-all ego and the intra-ego subsystem may be one of conflict
or cooperation. . . . If the relationship is one of cooperation, the
hypnosis persists and the over-all ego may progressively 'lend' its
functions to the subsystem for automatized functioning under the
aegis of the subsystem."

This is what they conclude about regression: "The ego apparatuses to which the stabilized regressed state has access differ in
both structure and function from those to which it originally had
access. The subsystem in hypnosis may in some respects resemble
early parent-child relationships, but the automatized apparatuses
which it may come to control are very different from what they
were during childhood. . . .* We believe that a hypnotic 'regression' approaches 'revivification' to the extent to which there has
been an adequate development of the subsystem with thorough-
going synthesis of its various elements, but that revivification in
the sense of the complete restoration of an earlier state is a fiction."

At the end of this section, I want to reproduce another formulation of these authors, one which more aptly supports what I
hope to clarify in these pages than does the formulation just cited.
Gill and Brenman, in their words, "advance a hypothesis for the
metapsychological description of the greater hypnotizability of
hysterics as against obsessional neurotics," and in this context state
explicitly, "We follow Freud in finding repression the major
mechanism of defense in hysterics, and isolation and undoing the
major mechanisms in obsessional neurosis. It is probable that the
forms of countercathectic energy distribution in hysteria are
different from the forms in obsessional neurosis. To speak in
terms of an analogy, in hysteria the energy distributions are
ranged along a front, with a well-defined no-man's land between
ego and id. In the obsessional neurosis the warfare is more of the
guerilla type, with deep invasions of each force into the other's
territory and islands of the enemy within each country. We are
only stating here in another form the phenomena described as the

---

* Footnote 13 in "Metapsychology of Regression and Hypnosis," loc. cit.

manifestations of the synthetic function of the ego, the erotization of thinking, and the conversion of a defense into a gratification as, in a general way, they characterize the obsessional neurosis in contradistinction to hysteria. We speculate that these different ways of deploying countercathexis make massive cathectic shifts more possible in hysteria than in the obsessional neurosis, and thus account for the greater ease of hypnotizability in hysteria." The differences observable in the structures of the hypnoanalyses of patients suffering from hysteria and of those suffering from an obsessional neurosis seem to be in accord with these hypotheses, and this book has been written to demonstrate clinically the indicated differences.

We come now to those statements most important to this research project. They concern the regressed subsystem in the hypnotic state set up within the usual ego which, according to Gill and Brenman, is "perhaps even strengthened by the development of the subsystem." They also postulate the possible existence of "different types of intersystemic relationships in various hypnotic subsystems." Such a subsystem can visualize and recall, but Gill and Brenman do not accept that revivification is ever complete because the "automatized apparatuses" of the over-all ego which the over-all ego "lends" to the regressed subsystem are different in the adult patient from those in the infant.

In J. E. Gordon's *Handbook of Clinical and Experimental Hypnosis,* Gill and Brenman reproduce their studies about "The Metapsychology of Regression and Hypnosis."

I have given more space to this research than to others because I do not otherwise present much about hypnosis per se which, after all, is the *sine qua non* of hypnoanalysis, and cite Gill and Brenman further where, in their studies about hypnoanalysis, their conclusions parallel my own. For example, there is concurrence that " 'working through' is in fact a learning process," and there is also concurrence with their hypothesis " . . . that if the regressive character of the hypnotic state could keep the emotional level fairly high without obliterating ego functions, then learning in the broadest sense would occur more rapidly." They do not lay too much stress on the depth of the hypnotic state, nor on the "standard indications and contraindications for hypnotherapy."

Other and varying formulations regarding the phenomenon of regression in hypnoanalysis now follow. M. V. Kline, in *Clinical Correlations of Experimental Hypnosis,* says this: " . . . age regression is not a unitary phenomenon, i.e. simply a chronological or ontological recapitulation. But, rather, that it represents a multiphasic alteration in the process of self awareness and self exclusion with a number of selectively determined changes in adaptive behavior. . . . In sum, there is emphatic evidence that hypnotically induced age regression may bring about varying degrees of alteration in memory, perception, general mental functioning and the more subtle mechanisms of self image and personal orientation. Psychodynamic changes in age regression are not limited to abreactive experience but appear to bring about less vigilant reality constructs and the emergence of adaptive behavior which makes greater use of prelogical operations in the organization of response mechanisms. In some instances, the degree of regression apparently influences psychophysiological functioning. . . ."

The therapeutic avenues opened by regression are, according to Kline, through the use of relationship experience. He states, ". . . there develops within the regression a reconstruction of many attitudes and values which go into the creation of the world of reality as we know it. In this rather primitive or prelogical interaction the patient makes available aspects of his own self concept and body image which may now be influenced and directed through the regressive experience, and while symbolic of earlier developmental experiences, has within it the uniqueness of the therapeutic relationship which was previously lacking. . . . The results point not to the use of regression as a *technique* in therapy but as an intense dynamic experience within which the patient's world of reality may for the first time since his own childhood be touched and influenced in a constructive manner." From extensive experience with hypnosis and hypoanalysis in its varied applications, Kline concludes that the influence of age regression on the intrapsychical processes of the patient and on the dynamics of the therapy is quite pervading.

Expressing his own views about the phenomenon of regression but concurring in many aspects with M. V. Kline on its therapeutic value, J. M. Schneck in *Principles and Practice of Hypno-*

analysis states, "The range of experience in regression and revivification is, in my opinion, much broader than is generally appreciated, and the settings, circumstances, and fine points in interpersonal relations influence the manifestations of personality expression at such times. To expect stereotyped reactions with conformity to well established patterns can blind the observer to an appreciation of the richness of hypnotic experience. One may observe considerable overlapping at times in clinical and experimental settings for the study of regression, but the diversity of possible reactions too should make one aware that differences in behavior do not necessarily invalidate the findings of others. The differences may frequently be accounted for on the basis of spontaneous behavioral participation of the subject or patient, and the special forms of attention by the subject, patient, experimenter, or hypnoanalyst." Schneck's long and intensive experience with hypnosis and hypnoanalysis has also made it obvious to him that age regression brings about varied and important changes in the dynamic balance of the mental mechanism.

I will now review some of the researches of one of the first followers of Freud, P. Federn, who, despite an old and close association with the founder of psychoanalysis, had a conception of the ego and the id which differed from Feud's.

From the introduction by E. Weiss to *Ego Psychology and the Psychoses* the following is cited because it has validity for this study: "The specific contents which are at any given time included within the ego boundary determine the specific ego state. Different ego boundaries are correlated with different ego states. . . ." Federn conceives of the ego ". . . as a dynamic entity and the ego boundary as its peripheral sense organ. . . . The boundary toward the repressed unconscious is dynamically strong enough to prevent the entrance of repressed material. . . . As sleep approaches, the ego and its boundaries lose their cathexis . . . thus hypnagogic images ensue." Of interest are the following concepts of Federn, as described by E. Weiss: "It can be experimentally proven that ego states of earlier ages do not disappear but are only repressed. In hypnosis, a former ego state containing the corresponding emotional dispositions, memories, and urges can be reawakened in the individual. In Federn's opinion, the unconscious

portion of the ego consists of the stratification of the repressed ego states."

As suggested by his son Ernst Federn, this pattern of ego states described by his father may best be compared to that which takes place inside a tree trunk where one ring forms around another, thereby repressing it. In analogous terms, psychologically one layer of ego state forms around another, repressing the earlier ego state into the unconscious.

J. G. Watkins who also uses Federn's ego concept, compares it to "the United States which is composed of common citizens but which is divided into separate states the citizens of which are bound by somewhat different laws and customs that apply within the boundaries of each given state . . . the boundaries around each would separate it from the others. As the individual lived, first one state and then another would occupy the experiential foreground and recede (be decathected) . . . " As he further explains, "Thus a state of hypnosis would represent a different ego state from one of fully conscious awareness, a dream state another, and a state during which a patient relived a childhood episode another." Whether one or the other comparison is used, the emphasis is on the dynamics and on the survival of former repressed ego states in the unconscious. Further formulations of the ego model of Federn must be studied in the original.

I come now to two other papers by Federn which are quite applicable to my findings with patients in hypnoanalysis. One is in English, "The Determination of Hysteria versus Obsessional Neurosis," the other is in German, "Hysterie und Zwang in der Neurosenwahl." I have tried to abstract and reformulate those portions from both papers which are relevant to an interpretation of patients' visualizations and verbalizations in hypnoanalysis.

Essentially, both papers discuss two psychoneurotic disorders, conversion reactions (apparently also including anxiety reactions, dissociative reactions, phobic reactions, and depressive reactions) on the one hand, and obsessive compulsive reactions on the other. The German version deals mainly with the genesis of the symptoms, the English with the ego defenses.

Two possibilities of ego defense are investigated. First, the yielding of the ego and the attempt of defense by various ego

states, as occurs in conversion reactions. There, many different ego states are represented in one symptom. Second, the maintaining of the same ego state, as happens in obsessive compulsive reactions. There, many conflicts are responded to by one and the same ego state. Whether the ego yields or maintains the same ego state is determined by the strength of the infantile ego-mechanism.

Federn indicates that an infant, who will later suffer from a conversion reaction, displays much fantasy but little psychical activity, little capacity for concentration, little independence, little criticality, and less logic.

It is normal behavior for an infant—an infantile ego—to yield, to surrender to a threatening or frightening situation. By temporarily renouncing what psychical maturation it had gained, it seeks, and finds, its defense by physical flight to the mother or a mother substitute. Through the bodily contact with the adult, the infant feels that its ability to overcome the fear and resist the threats is increased because the physical union has temporarily enlarged its bodily ego boundaries to the proportions of the adult. This kind of identification is repeated later in every other identification, normal or hysterical. The primary core of hysterical defense is physical even though the infant later attains a psychical identification as well with the mother. Those identifications with the mother, which are fearful, however, are only temporary, variable, and partial. In hysteria, fear is always felt in the bodily ego.

An infant who will, as an adult, complain of symptoms of an obsessive compulsive reaction reveals a premature psychical development, a more active intelligence, more criticality and more logical thinking than the average infant. Obsessive compulsive reactions begin later than do conversion reactions. They originate in sadistic and anal tendencies. Such sadistic cathexis involves a greater psychical activity of the ego since the anal complex is the first one which requires strong will on the part of the psychical ego to master the body and bodily needs.

The premature psychical ego of this type of infant struggles against threats and fears by thinking, not by physical contact with the parent. It dares to create active forbidden wishes against threatening ideas and prohibitions and is able to expiate these wishes by active reactions—by self-imposed thoughts. These active

reactions are not repressed. They recur and develop to the compulsions in order to keep the original forbidden thoughts repressed.

This specific pattern of self-defense is organized very early in infancy against the infant's moral conflicts generated by unacceptable thoughts aggressively directed against a strict father. It is perhaps the earliest form of sublimation. Sublimation is, according to Federn, a phenomenon by which, or through which, psychical ego substitutes for physical ego. The infant feels fear and reacts to it psychically—the primary core of its defense is psychical.

Such an infant, however, in a state of psychical tension, is able to be soothed and conciliated by the talk and explanation of the father or father substitute. Then, the infant's psychical ego identifies with the helpful father or his substitute. This identification strives to be total, is lasting, and leads to the formation of the obsessive compulsive individual's strong superego.

The ego cathexis therefore has a twofold struggle to effect, one is with the desire to gratify its repressed impulses, and the other involves expiation by self-imposed thoughts against his prohibited repressed wishes—a moral conflict. These expiations recur and develop into compulsions.

Conversion reactions have a dissimilar development. But it is known that every patient suffering from a conversion reaction shows at least some symptoms of an obsessive compulsive reaction and vice versa. The patients Anne and Al, described at length in this book, were selected because in their psychoneurotic disorders this admixture was minimal, which happens quite rarely.

Conversion reactions derive from infantile weakness and passivity of the ego—feminine passivity. These patients' egos mature later than those of the average infant and capitulate in a passive way to threats and frights. The frightening or fright inciting fantasies are repressed and with them the reacting state of the ego in which it became frightened. In conversion reactions, therefore, since a part of the ego is repressed, and with it the object representations and ego attitudes of the fragmented ego state, the ego becomes diminished and split. It is helpful in understanding the hysterical individual that in him partial ego states have been repressed.

Should a repressed psychoneurosis of infancy which started in the second, or even in the first year, reappear, it reestablishes or escalates the hysterical symptoms previously formed. This symptom formation comes about through unconscious condensation, symbolization, and conversion, and in one symptom many neurotic conflicts from different ego states originating in different periods are preserved and unified. Ego reactions are principally repressed and enter unconsciously into the symptom. But in the single neurotic outburst, in which part of the ego is always split off, varying attitudes and varying parts of the ego are involved. Since the whole ego is not implicated, the symptoms in hysteria are imposed on the individual similar to organic symptoms.

In patients suffering from an obsessive compulsive reaction, one can observe sulkiness, obstinacy, and crotchety perseverance as forms of countercathexis to the sadistic cathexis. All these converging energies fit well into the prematurely vigorous psychical ego—masculine activity. The same ego state, rigid and concentrated, is retained in its totality and full uniformity from the initial onset of the first compulsion.

Such a patient's fear is thinking fear, and it pertains to the psychical ego. He is not only unable to change his convictions, but he also elaborates them. Compulsion is doubt overcoming doubt, and doubt whether doubt was overcome.

The ego is conscious of the compulsions, but not aware that they originate from the superego. The severity of the case depends on the intensity of these demands. Defense becomes more complicated with the development of the individual and with new tasks and struggles. The symptoms change with every new conditioning object although the obsessional needs which have to be appeased by the symptoms remain the same. Every new conflicting object has given its share to the meaning of the self-defense, and any new traumatizing conflict produces some change of content. The patient who ignores the unconscious connection, believes that the previous obsession has lost its importance by a sort of automatic obsolescence and no longer appeases him. Yet, the whole ego state remains the same and the whole ego is involved, not part of it only.

In the compulsive, the connection between the causation of the

fears and the fears themselves is repressed as sometimes are the causations themselves; sometimes even their magic intensity is ignored. In the compulsive also, only the object relations are repressed, not the ego reactions. The psychical ego struggles against the unconscious conflict so that the strength of the psychical ego is more or less occupied and absorbed by the compulsions.

Patients who are afflicted with a conversion reaction have too little unification of the ego. They, in fact, lack the power of unifying their personality. Their weak ego boundaries are easily enlarged to include other persons. Some ego boundaries are overcathected with emotion, and previous ego states retain an increased cathexis through which they disturb the present ego. These patients not only identify easily, but transfer established identifications further. They are pliable, apt to build up fantasies, and are overcredulous. They are quick to accept patterns from others, quick to imitate new acquaintances, and quick to change their beliefs. With ease, they alter rationalizations, moods, and adherences. Their convictions last only as long as a positive transference is maintained. Their enmities are less important to them than their loves. Compliance alternating with obstinacy is the result of identifications, borrowed convictions, or is a residue from the split of the ego as an expression of psychical weakness. Since these patients lack a stable character with its leading goals, they often express contradictory views and attitudes.

However, inasmuch as entire and partial ego states and ego reactions, as well as object representations, can be repressed, symptoms can go on automatically without any participation of the actual ego or without a conscious awareness on the part of the hysteric that he has a split ego. The psychical ego has given way to the unconscious conflict, but through symptom formation it has absorbed and substituted some of the varying identifications and suggestion patterns so that the remaining ego does present some constancy.

A patient complaining of the symptoms of an obsessive compulsive reaction, displays an exaggerated cathexis of the unified ego and a boundary between ego and superego that is especially strongly cathected. He strives for unity but cannot achieve it because of his deep-rooted ambivalence. He preserves his large ego

boundaries, however, with great vigor; he is extremely rigid.

The etiology of this neurotic reaction resides in the fact that this patient's premature defense, by means of his psychical ego, is accompanied by an equal psychical fear of his prematurely formed superego. The sense of being guilty and the consequent fear of punishment retain their childish, magical content, even in adulthood. Because of guilt feelings, castration anxiety develops into psychical fear of punishment. In an infant, these thoughts are premature, but in an adult, they are a regressed, infantile codex of threatening consequences. Unlike the conversion reaction, the obsessive compulsive's ability to love is poor. He is a more proficient hater. But should he come to love, his love may prove stronger than that of the average person.

Furthermore, an individual possessing a compulsive personality strives always to act with a conscious superstrength of will power and concentration, with the fullest presence of mind, and with magical thoughts. He has developed an extremely strong feeling of his bodily ego and an excessive unity of his whole ego.

With respect to the enormous guilt feelings expressed by a number of patients, I offer here two excerpted sentences from Sillman's "The Analysis of Guilt and Narcissism": "Matricidal drives in both males and females cause the individual to feel and act unworthy of love and acceptance as a derivative of a powerful guiltiness about the first primordial love object. . . . The negative Oedipus complex, or the Orestes complex, leading to the rejection compulsion in adult life is, of course, facilitated if the mother has in reality been cruel or rejecting."

Before attempting a correlation between the theoretical formulations and the structural differences evidenced in the hypnoanalyses of patients suffering from conversion reactions as against patients suffering from obsessive compulsive reactions, it is necessary to mention two other cases presented in this book which are classifiable, according to the diagnostic and statistical manual, as psychophysiologic autonomic and visceral disorders. The structure of the hypnoanalyses of one of the cases follows the pattern of the conversion reaction group, whereas the structure of the hypnoanalyses of the other case follows more closely that of patients suffering from an obsessive compulsive reaction. Since the psycho-

physiologic autonomic and visceral disorders are a rather wide and somewhat loosely defined division, including, for the most part, patients whose unconscious affects are represented by visceral expressions, it is not astonishing to find variegated structures in their hypnoanalyses.

There is neither an intention nor a need to compare Federn's conceptions and conclusions to Freud's conceptions and conclusions. The application of Federn's formulations to the differing structures of the hypnoanalyses of conversion reactions and obsessive compulsive reactions should, however, be discussed.

To begin with, it is Federn's contention that the ego states of the earlier periods of life do not disappear, but are repressed. Thus, as E. Weiss puts it, "in hypnosis, a former ego state containing the corresponding emotional dispositions, memories, and urges can be reawakened in the individual." Since repression is the essential defense mechanism of conversion reactions, what is implied is that in hypnoanalysis partial and/or whole ego states accompanied by their related emotional dispositions, memories and urges are resurrected and past situations relived by the hysterical individual. This view would also correspond to Gill and Brenman's concept of the energy distributions in conversion reactions as being ranged along a front with a well-defined no-man's land between ego and id.

In conversion reactions (including all the psychoneurotic reactions stated in connection with the two previously mentioned papers of Federn) one finds a narrative structure in the hypnoanalyses. They generally possess a beginning, a middle, an end, and a recognizable background or setting. The personae in the hypnoanalyses behave in a logical manner and the action is of progressing quality. Symbols are rarely used. Most of the depicted events are plausible, regardless of whether they are actual or the products of the patient's fantasy. The acting persons have well-defined, distinctive personalities of their own which usually do not undergo changes in the course of treatment. The diverse sources of a particular symptom can be explored by the reawakening of different ego states. In a single hypnoanalysis, one event visualized in it may be worked through completely, or related events from different visualizations may be worked through to-

gether. When the working through occurs in the same hypnoanalysis, it is accomplished by the repeating of already rendered descriptions and their elaboration with additional details. Another kind of working through is trying to solve the same problem in different ways, in different hypnoanalyses which are, however, always of the above described structure. The visualizations are capable of unfolding like chapters in an autobiographical work which could be entitled, "Reawakened Former Ego States."

There is a marked difference between the structure of the aforementioned hypnoanalyses and the structural form of the hypnoanalyses of obsessive compulsive patients. These visualizations consist of shorter or longer episodes which follow one another without any logical connection, after short pauses. These same episodes may appear in different hypnoanalyses preceded and followed by other episodes unrelated to them and isolated from them by pauses. Episodes are, at times, like "happenings," utterly lacking in logical development and progressing activity of the acting persons. Furthermore, the "happenings" themselves may be contradictory or their modifying aspects may cancel each other. This undoing may also result from their nonsequential character. In addition, each individual episode has no real beginning, no middle, no end, and no recognizable background. It may even be no more than a static picture. The visualizations may be qualified as abstruse in the sense that symbols are prominent, that the acting persons are frequently unstipulated. The patient may refer to them merely as a man or a woman; or, in other episodes, they may appear to the patient as symbols without any awareness on his part that they refer to a person though the same person may be characterized by the same symbol. Instead of answering questions put to him at the end of an episode, the patient may merely pause and visualize a new episode. Somewhere in the middle of a hypnoanalysis, there may arrive a longer, coherent picture. The working through, however, is apparently achieved by the repetition of these disjoined episodes, and it is toward the end of the treatment that the episodes become longer and more coherent.

It may be tentatively assumed that these visualizations of the obsessive compulsive patient correspond rather to the expiating part than to the active forbidden wishes part of the dichronous

impulse. There also appears to be a correlation between these visualizations and what Gill and Brenman call "islands of the enemy within each country," although they use this figure in reference to the nature of the energy distribution in this type of psychological structure and relate it further to the following compulsive features known and described as ". . . the erotization of thinking and the conversion of a defense into a gratification." The contents of these episodes are quite sadistic and the visualizations principally present infants. Part of the visualizations deal with the toilet training process either as toilets literally or as water, pots, and such, all expressed in generalizations—in abstractions—in compulsive thinking, "isolated from the real world of concrete things," as Fenichel puts it. The repetition of the visualized events belongs to the compulsive category of ego defenses, and the prevalence of symbols is characteristic of archaic thinking. The description of objects as just man or woman refers to Federn's contention that the object relations are deeply repressed, though not the ego reactions. Castration anxiety developed to the psychical fear of punishment appears in both aspects of the dichronous impulse.

The mixed psychoneurotic disorders feature a combination of the structural types of conversion and obsessive compulsive reactions. Each visualization may be preponderantly one or preponderantly the other, or each visualization may be evenly divided between the two, or separate hypnoanalyses may alternately qualify in format as conversion or obsessive compulsive reaction.

The practical counterparts of these theoretical formulations are presented in the clinical portion of this book where as many illustrative hypnoanalyses have been reproduced as was possible.

II

ANXIETY, DISSOCIATIVE, CONVERSION, PHOBIC, AND DEPRESSIVE REACTIONS

ANNE

THE principal patient in this category is Anne, under thirty years of age, separated, widowed, and now the common-law wife of a man named Johnson. She looked very feminine and graceful, but apparently to accent this, she was dressed in a provocative semimilitary outfit, although she was wearing a skirt.

Some of her anamnestic data came forth in or were later changed during her hypnoanalytic sessions.

Anne complained of emotional instability which had bothered her for four years. Between the months of January and April, she was always depressed. Since meeting Johnson, she had felt more secure. Four years previously, she had been sent to a tuberculosis sanatorium for nine months, from which she was discharged at her own request. Her lungs were now in good order.

One of her difficulties was that she had never been able to finish anything. Every spring since the age of ten, the patient had had depressions. In high school, she made poor grades during the spring. Later, she was unhappily married in the spring. Three years before she came for consultation, she was promiscuous in the spring; two years previously, she drank heavily in the spring. During the last year, for five or six months, Anne had been addicted to Benzedrine® and took as many as eighteen pills daily. She stopped taking them late that spring. About four years previously, she had had thoughts of suicide although she never actually made an attempt on her own life.

At the beginning of her treatment, the patient mentioned that she had also suffered from sore throats, sinusitis, and bad breath since the age of nine, supposedly since a tonsillectomy. The real

reasons for these complaints were later uncovered in her hypnoanalyses.

Although Anne did not remember this before her hypnotherapy, it was revealed that her paternal grandmother had talked to her in German and had had a heavy accent. The patient supposed that this grandmother, who played a decisive role in Anne's early life, had emigrated from Germany around the turn of the century. She had brought money with her and had owned two houses in the community. Her husband, who had worked in a brickyard, could not have been so prosperous. This man eventually had drowned himself, and it was the patient's father who had found the body when he was eight or twelve years old.

The grandmother bore only sons, of whom Anne's father was the second. He was treated as a girl until his sixth or seventh year, and later showed great devotion to his mother. As an adult, he neither drank nor smoked, and was very religious though he did not go to church. He had such "a mania for air" that he removed doors. He shaved his body hair and insisted that his daughter shave under her arms at an early age.

"He was very sensitive about women."

He was also quite concerned about keeping his teeth in good condition. These different traits suggest exhibitionism, voyeurism, and anxiety states, including castration anxiety. The patient's father also liked to do housework. A very timid person, he was the first to be fired from his job during the Depression and, although a hard worker, he had resigned himself to remaining among the poorest in the community. Anne first described their relationship as once having been a good one.

The patient's mother had died in an accident a few years before Anne started treatment. Anne's first characterization of her was that she had been sweet, had had a good sense of humor, but little interest in the home. She was often depressed and tired. It transpired that she did not love her husband. The patient's descriptions of her mother varied throughout the therapy. Sometimes she said that the mother often worked in stores, at other times that she did nothing at all. It was probably true that she was a poor housekeeper, doing all her chores in the morning, sleeping afterwards and serving dinner at four o'clock so that everybody got

hungry again before evening. Her mother always felt cold. Quite late in her treatment, Anne said that her mother might have been "a little sadistic;" had scratched the father painfully on the head and then laughed, and had played similar tricks on the children. She seems to have been a stupid and very neurotic person.

The parents quarreled every morning. Information about the parents' sexual adjustment was contradictory in both interviews and hypnoanalytic sessions. But they slept in separate bedrooms and had no children for the eight years after the birth of their second daughter. "My parents regarded intercourse as something bad."

Anne was the oldest sibling. A married sister, Carabelle, was two years younger; a brother, Ford, ten years younger. The youngest, Barbara, was eleven years the patient's junior.

Anne's was a normal birth and she was breast-fed. Her family told her that she was a spoiled baby and cried a lot. She said that she walked and talked at eighteen months. At about two years of age, she went to her paternal grandmother, where, she said at first, she stayed for two years, though during the hypnoanalytic sessions this was reduced to apparently ten months. The patient loved her grandmother very much and tried to hide when she had to return home. She said her grandmother had been dead for a long time. The mother preferred Anne, the father, Carabelle. Both daughters wished it were the reverse. The patient did not get along with this sister.

At the age of five or six, Anne wet her bed three or four times. She had temper tantrums, but only with her mother. The patient sucked her forefinger until she was six or seven. After she returned from her grandmother's, Anne slept with her sister during the summers, but in wintertime, she had to share a bed with one or the other parent. Later, she slept with her mother until her sixth or eighth year.

The patient said that she masturbated at five, seven, or eight years of age and had guilt feelings; later she did so without guilt feelings. She had her menarche at the age of twelve, was unprepared and frightened. Her mother warned her to be careful of boys from now on. She started to lie to her parents because they both disapproved of dates.

Anne was a good student although shy in school. Thus, she was not popular with the other students. In grammar school, the teacher often scolded her for "wool gathering." She enrolled as a working student in a teachers' college. But, after the second term, she had poor grades, so she went to normal school where she met the man whom she married in April at the age of eighteen. Her first intercourse was premarital and painful; but the fourth or fifth time, she experienced a climax.

Her husband proved to be unstable and unable to support her. She bore him a son and, after a few months, left them both and returned home. She was then nineteen years old. Two years prior to the start of her treatment, her husband, who had remarried, was killed in an accident, and her son remained with his stepmother.

After the patient returned home, she tried to prepare for the same profession as her sister Carabelle, but never finished her training because she was sent to a tuberculosis sanatorium. Discharged on her own request, Anne returned home. But she left once more because her mother was now dead and she did not feel safe at home. She drifted from job to job, became a model, indulged in multifarious relations, took drugs, and was quite suicidal. At the time she came for treatment, she had accepted a night job and was living as Johnson's common-law wife. Both drank and took drugs.

Coming to Anne's hypnoanalytic sessions, I shall start with the one in which she stated the youngest age to which she regressed. Initially, I shall present hypnoanalytic sessions progressively, according to age, although the time lapse was often quite small. Later, I will submit her own evaluation of the reality and fantasy content of what she had visualized in her hypnoanalytic sessions. Still further, I shall present hypnoanalytic sessions which show the different roots of two of her symptoms, and how each of them had its sources at different age levels, from quite dissimilar ego states. As previously stated, the symptom formation came about through unconscious condensation, symbolization, and conversion.

In this connection the question of whether the patient's information about her age was accurate for the respective event, or even whether such memories are possible at all is not important

from the viewpoint of therapy. The dates have to be accepted on the basis of their subjective value. In actual fact, there were few contradictions in these accounts.

Anne's earliest information relating to her age occurred when she said that she had been nine months and then seven months old (68th H.). This hypnoanalytic session, in which revivification was induced, was performed because the patient complained of having had headaches for six days and having been tired for two days. During the hypnoanalytic session, Anne said she was lying in her crib, feeling hot, crying, and was red in the face. She had a very bad headache and felt hungry; her mother picked her up and tried to nurse her.

"And I suck very hard on the nipple. But nothing seems to come . . . And my mother keeps patting me. And she keeps rubbing my head. And I begin to cry."

After the patient reported several unsuccessful sucking attempts, she said, "And after all I begin to nurse. And I begin to suck very hard again. And my mouth is [superficial cough*] getting very tired. Because I am hungry. But I am not getting anything in my mouth or stomach . . . And my head is very hot . . . is aching me . . . But I can't stop crying. I am very hungry."

Anne went on to describe how she still got insufficient milk although her mother tried constantly to soothe her. On questioning, the patient said that she had already been on the bottle, which she preferred.

"Because something will come out of it."

Further inquiry revealed that the last bottle had been given about two days previously, but the last satiating breastfeed had been two months before that. She also said that she was coughing because the visualized situation upset her. She was very angry with her mother who knew that the infant needed milk. "She is playing tricks on me." The patient thought that her mother hated her, and the soothing was not accepted as an expression of love.

On further questioning, Anne divulged that, at the time her mother had had milk, her nipple was soft and the milk tasted better than from the bottle. It was "nice and rich." The description,

---

* This patient expressed negative and positive emotions by coughing.

"my head felt nice and warm against my mother's breast," seems important, too. There was no weaning; the mother stopped suckling suddenly, and just as suddenly tried to resume it.

Toward the end of this hypnoanalytic session, questioning brought out the fact that the infant was already able to crawl around the crib and to stand up by holding onto it. Lying on her mother's lap, she now wet her diaper.

"(Why?) Well, I just wanted to show her that she—I love her, I wish she give me some more milk. I wet my diaper to show her that—well, if she can give me milk, I can give her something too."

Anne added that her mother did not reciprocate by giving her milk and therefore must hate the baby although she did not hate her mother. "I—if she will just give me some milk, I always wet my diaper for her . . . I love her." After this hypoanalytic session, the patient no longer felt tired, and her headaches were gone.

At the next interview (152nd S.), she amplified her statements as to what she had felt in this hypnoanalytic session.

"The feelings . . . were very vivid . . . I had the nice feeling of being safe, and I was happy . . . Although at nine months when I was so unhappy I certainly had cares . . . that wonderful feeling of being happy. In hypnosis this is a wonderful feeling . . . laying on my mother's breast but the breast really was the thing that was outstanding. In the beginning . . . I saw myself very well but my mother shadowy. When she later started to nurse me . . . I could see her breast very well and the nipple. And the nipple looked different to me than at seven months . . . more protruded and rough. The color looked different . . . After a while I got a little bit milk, I could feel it. That is what it tasted to me . . . With seven months the breast and the nipple seemed more vivid than with nine months. It seemed exaggerated . . . my head was just above my mother's elbow, but I couldn't see her face. That her arm was here and my head on it gave me the feeling that I was enclosed, protected. That was . . . a wonderful feeling . . . Now when I was nine months old . . . her face was still shadowy but it was a human face and a body there. But the breast was not so large and not so vivid and outstanding. Then you asked me if I ever wetted . . . Then I could see myself on her lap and her body down to her knees and the rest was shadowy . . . I felt myself wet . . . it felt

warm . . . good. I was conscious that I was wetting . . . that I had a wet diaper on . . . A nice warm sensation almost like having a mild orgasm . . . When I wet her I was trying to show her that I loved her and in return she should give me what I wanted, which was food. I couldn't understand that I didn't get any milk, and that frustrated me . . . I think I had shoes on . . . I was sitting down and pulled myself up by the bars of the crib . . . I feel I am looking at things now through different eyes. The last two weeks . . . I am just completely happy."

This statement has been reproduced because it helps prove a number of hypotheses, especially since this patient had no knowledge of psychology. Her descriptions of her emotions in her mother's arms reveal a modified trace of what has been called "oceanic feeling," connected with the satisfaction of the infant's narcissistic and bodily needs through feeding. Such descriptions cannot be invented; they must be experienced. Anne must have regressed to a very early age level, which is also proven by her delineation of the difference in her mother's appearance when the infant was seven months and when she was nine months old. Her happiness had nothing to do, as she erroneously supposed, with her being in hypnosis.

Furthermore, there was an early oral conflict and consequently a strong oral fixation present. Psychoneurotic disorders can start in the first year. It is an accepted fact that patients suffering from conversion reactions often have unconscious fantasies about fellatio and at times a globus hystericus. Reports of fellatio occurred over and over again in this patient's therapy but apparently with some validity. Once, Anne also developed a globus hystericus during a hypnoanalytic session (40th H.) which, after its roots were explored, disappeared during the same hypnoanalytic session. Her alcoholism, drug addiction, and depressions also point to an oral fixation.

Another consequence of this oral conflict was the patient's ambivalence toward her mother. Whereas she had formerly felt herself "enclosed, protected" by her mother's arms, she later looked for help much more often to her father or to her paternal grandmother. Only after her father had shown preference for her sister, and her grandmother had died, did she return to her mother.

The next hypnoanalytic session* (69th H.) dealt with the patient's phobic reaction to high places. She had mentioned her fear of darkness and heights quite casually, and they played a minor role in her sickness. This hypnoanalytic session was performed because Anne complained about having felt depressed for two days. She described in revivification how, at the age of thirteen months, she was standing at the top of the stairs, holding a ball in her hands. Her father was at the bottom of the stairs, stretching out his arms, smiling, and encouraging her to join him; but he did not help her.

"I am trying to get down the steps to him. I want to give him the ball. I feel very afraid . . . But I hold very tight to the railing . . . My father looks too far away from me . . . And the steps look dark. It's the first time I have ever walked down these steps. And I am afraid to put my foot on the next step . . . And I love my father. (How could you reach the railing?) The railing is very low . . . (Count how many steps you have made already.) Four steps.** (Was it very hard?) It was . . . And I was so frightened at each step . . . I can't take another step. I am too afraid. I can't."

She was in fear of falling because she had fallen several times at the side of her crib. Then her father went away and left her alone. She had not thought of throwing the ball to him; she wanted to give it to him, to be close to him. She loved him. He would hold her, and she would be safe. Now, alone, she stood still for "a long time." On questioning, she revealed that the elevated railway and other high places reminded her of this incident in hypnoanalysis. Her mother could not help her as her father could because he was stronger; and Anne "loved my father best." She did not cry, she was ". . . just scared. I feel frozen." On inquiry, during the hypnoanalytic session, she stated that she could already walk "for about fifteen minutes" and that she had started to walk three and a half months previously. . . "But I am afraid of those steps. It's so dark and steep. And I am just sitting. And it's so lonesome. And my father left me . . . I just can't do anything. . . . I just wait."

On questioning, she stated that this went on "an awful long

---

* This hypnoanalytic session has been published under the title, "Symptom Removal by Revivification" in *Amer. J Clin Hypn, V*(4):277-280, 1963.

** After the hypnoanalytic session, she stated, on questioning, that she had counted the steps as a grown-up.

time;" however, she did not cry, she was "just watching those steps. (What do you suppose would happen if you cried?) . . . my father would be angry . . . He doesn't like crying at all. (What does he do then?) Well, he spanked me a couple of times."

The patient did not wet, she seemed "like paralyzed." She was just "listening for someone to come." Asked again, she stated, "After a while there is a woman that comes to the bottom of the stairs. I have never seen her before. She looks friendly . . . And she picks me up."

Questioned who this woman was, Anne replied that she was neither a neighbor nor her grandmother. The patient could not see her face well, but she was stout, with stout arms, and held the infant tightly to her putting her "in a little chair. And I feel happy in this chair . . . very happy . . . so comfortable . . . She is rocking the chair. And smiling at me."

At this point, Anne was still trying to make out the woman's face; it was not her mother. After a short while, she said in a very relieved voice, "Yes, that's my grandmother . . . she is so friendly to me. And now I feel safe. I am off those stairs. I do never want to go near them again . . . I feel so good."

After the hypnoanalytic session, she stated that her depression was now over and that she would be able to use the Elevated and go to other high places without being frightened. Her fear of heights was over.

In the previous hypnoanalytic session, the patient had lain in her mother's arms, frustrated and hungry. In this hypnoanalytic session, the contact with the grandmother's body immediately made her feel safe. At first, she did not recognize the person who picked her up, a situation which would normally frighten such a small child, but did not. The patient wanted to finish the hyp-noanalytic session at the point when she had stated that this friendly smiling woman held her tightly and carried her up the stairs. "And that's all." I intentionally had not at first asked whether it was her grandmother who rescued her because that was the most likely person to do it. Being held tightly in her grand-mother's arms enlarged Anne's ego boundaries to that of the grown-up and gave her the feelings of safety and security she needed.

Two hypnoanalytic sessions later (71st H.), the relationship be-

tween the patient, her mother, and her paternal grandmother was brought out. Anne had complained that, without any discernible reason, she had felt sick and cold that morning, had fainted and vomited.

The patient stated in revivification that she was about fourteen months old. Anne was standing at her mother's knees, her grandmother sitting just behind them. The infant tried three times to get to her grandmother, but each time her mother caught and slapped her. The fourth attempt was successful. "And it seems so good to be with my grandmother. And I feel so content now. And now I am beginning to stop crying."

When the patient was asked what connection that had to her fainting episode, she said, "I fainted this morning. Because I was upset. (About what?) . . . because my mother kept getting in my way . . . aggravating me . . . I didn't like my mother as much as I did my grandmother . . . I fainted . . . because that's how I felt . . . when my mother scared me . . . And I felt so angry toward my mother. And I felt so unhappy."

Anne's ego reactions to this upsetting situation had now repeated themselves though the reason for them was still repressed; the hypnoanalytic session had served to re-create the triangle of the infant contended for by two mothers, the bad natural mother and the good grandmother. Conscious awareness of this helped her to work the conflict through and resolve it.

The patient had had fainting spells before, which stopped when her common-law husband told her that they were "a mental symptom," and Anne did not want to have mental symptoms. Later, this patient disclosed overt death wishes against her mother which she formerly might have expressed through fainting. At other times, Anne explained her fainting spells simply as a desire to escape from the constant nagging of her family.

In her next hypnoanalytic session (72nd H.), the patient again gave her age as fourteen months. This hypnoanalysis was induced because Anne complained that that morning she had had an anxiety attack and had perspired for about an hour. During revivification she described how she was sitting in a high chair and eating with a spoon.

"And I feel very happy. My father is sitting next to me . . . smil-

ing at me. And then I see my mother coming into the room . . . smiling at me too . . . She picks me out of the high chair. And hugs me tight to her . . . And my father is standing up. And he seems to be very angry . . . my mother seems scared. I can feel her shaking. And my father . . . is scolding my mother . . . And then he pulls me out of my mother's arms. And he holds me very tight to him . . . And he feels like he is shaking. My father is scared too . . . my mother tries to pull me out of his arms . . . And I feel very upset. Because they are pulling me out of each other's arms. And they feel different to me . . . I don't like them this way. I can't understand them. My mother is holding me very tight to her now. And I can feel that a tear on her cheek. And she is trembling. And I am trembling. Because I am scared too. I don't know what's wrong with my father and mother . . . I feel confused. And I love my mother and father. I love both of them . . . I feel like I am being torn apart . . . And I feel the way they are trembling . . . My hands especially are trembling. And I feel awfully frightened. Because my father looks so mean . . . And he is raising his hand to my mother . . . He slaps her so hard that her head hits mine . . . And my mother is crying. And I am crying too . . . because I am scared . . . I feel sorry for my mother . . . And my head hurts where her head hit mine . . . And I just can feel the perspiration all over me. I feel very hot. And then I feel cold. I have this pain in my stomach . . . When they are happy they hold me not quite so hard. And their bodies feel nice and warm and happy like . . . I knew there was something wrong." In the end, the father left the room, and the weeping mother sat down with her child.

This hypnoanalytic session is interesting in several ways. It shows the excessive "somatic compliance" which could also be observed in the previous hypnoanalytic session (71st H.). Although somatic compliance is normal at this stage of development, the patient was able to reproduce these sensations. Such repeated impressions in early life must increase the later ability to effect conversion symptoms; they may function like "imprints" in young animals when experienced at the correct age. Federn stated that "the primary core of hysterical defense is already physical." Anne was not able to enlarge her ego boundaries to those of her parents, whose bodily ego and mental ego were felt to be hostile.

But this hypnoanalytic session (72nd H.) was also a transference hypnoanalysis. There was a specific reason why the patient returned to this event at this time. Anne was in conflict with her loyalties to her common-law husband and to her therapist, and in a negative transference to the latter. Shortly before this hypnoanalytic session was performed, the situation between the author and Johnson was rectified in a telephone conversation. Although there was no comment on this during the hypnoanalytic session or at any other time before or after, and, although it is questionable as to whether or not this session qualified as a transference hypnoanalysis, its contents reveal the conflict of loyalties.

Prior to her therapy, Anne's activities were heavily autoplastic. She described her vivid early fantasy life herself at the very beginning of her case history (8th S.). She reported that, at the age of ten or eleven, her father frustrated her by ordering her to do household chores when she wanted to play with her sister or to read. "Then I had daydreams in which I made myself a center of importance like a very pretty-dressed little girl going to a dance to get attention. At five years of age, I had a lot of daydreams, even when I wrote on the blackboard."

In the following hypnoanalytic sessions, I will deal with the matter of whether her father's abuses, which she recurrently described, were fact or fantasy. In the first of these sessions (38th H.), regression was induced and Anne was asked where she had spent the first years of her life, and about reciprocal visits between her parents and her grandmother. She stated that she could "see my grandmother's place again," and she was questioned about the validity of her descriptions of her relationship to her father.

"(You have often told me that things happened when you were two-and-a-half. Now, you tell me that, at that period of your life, your father had nothing to do with you.) Maybe I just thought he did. (How do you mean, you thought he did?) After the first two years. I love my father so. I could remember how pleasant it was when he did things to me sexually. And when I was at my grandmother's. I used to get lonesome for him. And for the good times that we had together. And I began to dream that he was there. And that he used to do those things to me. And then I would feel better. And I wouldn't feel so lonesome."

Anne was then questioned about a symbolical hypnoanalytic session which, when unraveled during several other hypnoanalytic sessions, showed that her father had urinated into her mouth. She asserted that this was a fact, but that she had invented the end of the occurrence described in the following transcription excerpt. "(You told me later on, this little girl had seen that you had the black spot.*) It's because some little girl came to the door. When my father was doing things to me. (She interrupted you?) Yes. (But what part about the little girl was invented?) About my father going off with her . . . (What did he do?) He went in the house. But he didn't go away with her. . . I always thought that little girl saw what was going on. But he didn't do the same things to her. (Were you jealous of her, or your mother and sister?) I have been jealous of my mother and sister. (In reality, you were not jealous of this girl at all?) I wasn't. Yes. I was jealous. (Why?) Because she came at a time when I was enjoying myself. And she stopped my father from giving me a lot of pleasure. And when I thought my father might go with her. (That was a supposition.) Yes. So I got to hate this girl. And I was very jealous of her."

Further questioning revealed that Anne was positive her father had performed all the acts mentioned in the foregoing hypnoanalytic sessions. She also connected them with their aftereffects which were some of the symptoms of her conversion reaction, such as sore throats, bad taste, bad breath, choking and coughing, which will be discussed later.

The other hypnoanalytic session (43rd H.), in which the patient mentioned her daydreaming, was induced because she had stated in an earlier hypnoanalytic session that her grandmother had called her father "Josie," a German abbreviation for the female first name Josephine. Regression was induced and she was asked to dream and to remember details of occasions when her grandmother called her father "Josie." Anne reported that her mother hated this because her father was not female, but her grandmother had hoped for a daughter. The patient enlarged on this topic. Her father tagged behind his mother, but was not her favorite.

---

* This black spot had been painted on Anne's face by her mother as a punishment.

Anne's mother made fun of this grandmother because she was German, therefore had an accent; when the grandmother combed Anne's hair, she wanted to braid it.

". . . 'like I did Josie's. Your father's.' And then she said, 'You look like him.' (What were your reactions to these incidents?) I was very happy."

Anne had realized quite suddenly that her grandmother was German and her grandfather Russian—a full recovery of repressed material which was accompanied by many conflicting emotions. She repeated with a heavy American accent the only German words she could remember at present, "Auf Wiedersehen." The patient said that she enjoyed her grandmother's way of talking at first, but was ashamed of it later, especially during the war. Actually, Anne was born after the First World War. This confusion had an emotional basis and perhaps originated in the state of war her family was constantly in.

Continuing with the hypnoanalytic session, Anne stated that she was so ashamed of her grandmother's nationality that she forgot everything about her. Now she was asked to recall more around the name Josie. "I would often think of him as Josie. (Who is Josie?) Josie was my father. (Good. But what image was presented by the name Josie? Seemingly not your father. How did you think about him?) Hm. Josie, I always thought of him as a pretty . . . [cough] blond-haired girl. . . Her hair in braids. And someone who was very cute-looking [swallows and coughs twice]. (Why do you cough?) Because I was scared about something . . . I think my father was more like a woman than a man."

After talking more about her father's abnormalities, Anne said how she had loved it when her grandmother fixed her up as she had done her father and taught her useful little domestic arts.

Of the patient's several symptoms only two should be discussed at greater length: her coughing and her depressions (her main complaint). In her anamnesis (1st S.) she had already reported having had tuberculosis. As both hospitals she had mentioned were reputable ones, there was no reason to doubt the somatic nature of this sickness.

Once she informed me that she had met her brother accidentally and that he had talked of home using some of their father's

expressions. Next day, she had a cold and said she felt as if she had pneumonia (116th S.). A few days later, she had a dream in which her father had an "awfully deep sore on his left side" in his throat which was red (117th S.). This was an identification with her father, facilitated by her earlier identification with "the girl Josie." Five days later, during a hypnoanalytic session (53rd H.), revivification was induced and Anne was regressed to exactly the age when all the trouble with her throat, the coughing and the sore throats, had started.

She reported that, when she was sixteen months old, an uncle had urinated into her mouth. She had to swallow it, wanted to throw up, but could not spit it out. "I kept gagging. And it hurt my throat . . . tickled it. And it made me cough like . . . there seemed as if something was there that shouldn't be. And I kept [coughs] cough. (Why do you cough now?) . . . There was something there that was making me cough . . . That's the reason I kept coughing . . . whatever was left . . . began to irritate my throat . . . made it sore . . . And I used to cough . . . all the time . . . And it was just because I wanted to get this thing out, that particle . . . And there was such a bad taste and such a bad smell . . . And that's what gave me that bad breath . . . And . . . the sore throats I had every morning of my life . . . But that one spot was the worst . . . almost at the end of my throat. At the left-hand side . . . It always hit at this one spot . . . it was an infected part from something foul and bad-smelling. (Is there any connection between this and the fact that people thought you had tuberculosis?) Yes . . . I was coughing all the time. And then they said there was something on my x-ray . . . And I was expectorating . . . I don't know why I coughed so much then. (Was there anything that reminded you of this incident at that time?) Well, my sister had an awful cough and she had TB . . . (There is certainly some connection.) I copy her. (Why?) . . . because she was getting a lot of attention from my father. And I thought if I got the same thing. Then I would get attention from him too. And he would be nice to me the way he was to Carabelle . . . he talked about how good Carabelle was . . . And that's the reason I began to cough."

On further questioning, the patient said that she always had a

lot of mucus which she regarded as a residue from repeated fellatio and, therefore, wanted to spit it out.

"To get it all out of my system."

During the time she was afflicted with tuberculosis, she wanted to get rid of it, but that cure of her cough proved to be only temporary. "I think I am getting rid of it now."

Her uncle only once attempted the abuse mentioned; her father did it more often, and later also performed fellatio in a manner that was painful to her physically, which added to Anne's distress.

In the next hypnoanalytic session (54th H.), revivification was induced and the patient was directed to be any specific age about which she had a feeling that she had something to tell. She described how, when she was four years old, her father had shot a puppy, a gift from her late grandmother, before her eyes. Anne said she felt very lonely then, and again felt very lonely when her sister got all of their father's attention. Asked how the spot on her chest x-ray could be explained, she pointed to the accumulation of mucus in her system. The fever she paralleled to the excitement about her father.

"I knew something pleasant was going to happen. (All right. But how did you make your temperature go up every day?) No, I didn't do anything about it. I just had a temperature . . . I don't know, I felt awfully hot . . . But I had a temperature along with it. (But why was it just at this time?) [swallows] That's because I felt so lonesome . . . because Carabelle was getting all of his attention and I wasn't getting any."

On further questioning, she replied that she had never found her father and sister in a suspicious situation. But she added, ". . . if he did it with me. He would do it with her."

On inquiry, she stated that she did not think that way at the age of four. "I just thought he was being awfully nice to her and liking her." Anne was "awfully jealous" of her sister. "And it made me hate my father at this time [swallows] . . . Because he had turned away from me [short cough] (Had it any relation to your cough?) Yes . . . Because I felt so lonesome . . . like crying but I didn't. I coughed."

The patient regarded this as the definitive summation of the reasons for her coughing.

But there were still two hypnoanalytic sessions centered around it. In one of them (55th H.), she described how, when living at her grandmother's, her mother came on a visit and washed Anne's mouth out with soap because of a fight she had had with Carabelle.

"And I am even almost gagging. And throwing up. But she doesn't care . . . And I hate her . . . My mother is making me cough . . . She wasn't my mother. I want to get her out of here, get out of the house. (She was not your mother?) No. (Who was it?) My mother was my grandmother . . . If things don't go right I don't cry, I just cough. And that's the reason I coughed this weekend. . . I was upset because I had to take that from those women. And they reminded me of my mother. And I hated them . . . the same as I did my mother."

"Those women" was a reference to a current situation, a transference of an affect she had felt in the past to a present object.

In the other hypnoanalytic session (58th H.) the patient was asked in revivification why she was still coughing. She stated that, when she was four years and three months old, her parents were quarreling one day while she was eating a piece of bread. The father hit the mother hard in the face, and the mother struck the father with a bottle.

"On the forehead, right above the eye. And his face is all blood. And I am very frightened. And a piece of bread gets stuck in my throat [swallows] . . . And I keep coughing. And I begin to choke. And then my mother said something to my father. (What?) I'm. (Listen to it.) She—she. (Yes.) Is turned blue. And my mother and father both run over to me." Her father slapped Anne's back so that the piece of bread came up.

"And I thought he was hurt badly. Because all this blood was rushing down his face. And I loved him then. I forgot that I hated him. And I wanted—I didn't want him to die . . . And I got horror-stricken . . . paralyzed . . . And then, when I saw my mother take that rag and stop that blood—Then I knew that he wouldn't die . . . And then I began to look at the blood on myself [swallows] And I thought it was his blood . . . And I couldn't stand this blood on me. And then my mother . . . wiped it off me. And I began to feel better . . . (Had he shot this puppy you told

me about before, or was it later on?) I saw this later on . . . this fight. (Was this the reason you got so frightened?) Hm, yes . . . Because I thought, he' die too. The same as the little puppy. . . (Do you have the feeling that it might be a retaliation for the puppy's death?) Yes, I felt . . . because he had killed . . . something, he was going to die. . . I still didn't want him to die. Even though I hated him. At that moment, the blood was streaming down his face. I forgot all about the dog . . . (Did you hate your mother at that moment?) Yes . . . Because she was trying to kill my father. I hated her very much . . . (What impression did blood make on you later on? Have you always been so frightened by it?) It meant something cruel. It meant like shooting the little puppy."

There is no method by which to prove or disprove whether Anne's reports of repeated fellatio by her father and urination into her mouth and the one abuse by her uncle were fantasies or the truth. The descriptions rang true, the patient believed they were true, the aftereffects were there and they disappeared after the respective hypnoanalytic sessions had demonstrated to the patient her repressed past and its connections to the present, and after they had enabled her to integrate it into her personality.

Some additional information about Anne's cough was revealed in the hypnoanalytic session (54th H.) concerning the shooting of the puppy. Asked why she did not cry when she saw the dog killed, but coughed instead, she replied, "I didn't want to cry because every time I cried my father would say, 'Ah, you little fool, crying! You should be ashamed of yourself.' And he' make fun of me . . . I never want' to cry before him. (Talk about this.) Because he'd make fun of me . . . always . . . before people. Telling them I cried. And what a little fool I was. And he called my mother's attention to it [cough] He would say [swallows] 'Look at Anne, she is a little fool. You should be ashamed of yourself, crying!' And he made me conspicuous. So that I never would cry unless I was alone. And that's the reason I coughed . . . instead of crying."

The patient stated her age at this hypnoanalytic session (54th H.) as four years. But there is no datum as to when her father started this taunting, except that in the hypnoanalytic session about the stairs (69th H.) she had also said that her father disliked her crying.

A summary of all the information about this conversion symptom would read as follows: At the time Anne was on the breast, there was an oral conflict. At the age of sixteen months, an oral trauma occurred, this time coupled with respiratory symptoms such as coughing, a sore throat (especially at the back of her throat), a bad smell, and a bad taste. Later, repeated abuses of this infant (also of a different oral kind) aggravated the symptom. In addition to this, she had been forbidden to cry and had been shamed in front of her mother and other persons when she did so. Therefore, she substituted respiratory symptoms which seemed incidental, especially the coughing. However, coughing expressed not only negative, but also strong positive emotions such as "being overjoyed." At a time when this patient suffered many negative emotions such as jealousy and loneliness, she identified with her fortunate rival, her sister, and was able to imitate the symptoms of a serious sickness, tuberculosis, supposing that would rekindle her father's affection. After the different roots of this symptom had been explored, it vanished and recurred only in a very diminished form, as in clearing her throat when she came for psychotherapy. It may be of interest to point out that it was sheer luck that Anne was not infected with tuberculosis while she was in the sanatorium.

The other symptom I would like to examine is Anne's more drawn-out depressions from which she regularly suffered from late winter until early spring, i.e. from about January until April, and which were the primary reason that she had been coming for therapy. She never made any attempts at suicide, but she had had suicidal thoughts three years before she started her treatment, and once (204th S.), toward the end of her therapy, she reported, "Just a couple of times a thought was in my mind I would like to end this all, things are getting too tough . . . The thought was not so long." This happened at a time when her common-law husband was putting strong pressure on her to stop her treatment for reasons of his own. Two weeks later, she interrupted therapy for a little over two weeks, but returned for nearly four months of further treatment. She had started her therapy during a depression on the second of March, but no long-lasting depressions were observed during her treatment.

The patient's oral frustrations have already been discussed and need no further elaboration. Aside from oral abuse, her father also abused her vaginally. When, toward the beginning of her therapy, she was asked in a hypnoanalytic session (17th H.) how old she had been when her father inserted his finger genitally, she answered: "Like I am two years old."

She felt hurt, sore, and frightened, and also depressed. One cannot be sure whether this was her first depression or whether she had just described the feelings of a hurt and frightened infant. However, she remembered that this episode occurred in spring, and that there were flowers in the garden. Discussing a much later hypnoanalytic session (65th H.), in which she related a very disturbing event, namely, that she suddenly had to leave her beloved grandmother, Anne remembered at the end of the interview (144th S.) that, at the age of about five years, she had had a suicidal impulse, a desire to jump into a nearby river. She did not give any hint at what time of the year this occurred.

In her anamnesis, she reported that she had experienced her first spring depression at the age of ten. But the events in which her depressions were rooted, had occurred long before that, previous to, or around, the patient's fourth birthday.

As already stated, Anne most probably felt happiest when she lived with her paternal grandmother, a woman who had always wanted a daughter and now saw her wish fulfilled in this granddaughter. At the end of August, when the patient came for one of her appointments (144th S.), she complained that during the week she had felt depressed for no apparent reason and could not work up any interest in food. The preceding year, during the same season, she had had similar feelings, and, in addition, had slept fitfully and had felt lonely, depressed, and apprehensive.

During this hypnoanalytic session (65th H.), in revivification, she recounted that, when she was three years and four months of age, her parents came, without warning, to the grandmother to take Anne home. The infant tried to hide behind a bush in her grandmother's garden, but her father pulled her, weeping, toward him. Her mother, looking annoyed, stood at the gate. Anne grabbed her grandmother's apron, determined not to let go. But the grandmother, herself crying, handed the infant over to her father.

"And now I am going to my father's house . . . And when we get in, it looks awfully dark on the inside . . . I feel so lonesome and I feel so sad. I have left my grandmother. And I feel so heartbroken and everything is so dingy and cold looking. And there is no bright curtains on the walls. And the walls all look grey and it's damp inside. And there is no cheerful tablecloth and there is no flowers around. And my mother—ah—won't talk to me. And I feel, well, strange, and—ahah-ah—with a strange woman. And my father I know. I—I am glad he is with me. But my mother is so—ah—cold and angry. And she is a stranger. And I—I—I feel so lonesome. I want to go back to my grandmother. And my mother is beginning to put the supper on. And e-e-everything l-l-looks so miserable. A-a-and I can't think that I have got to live here. I am just so lonesome, I can't even look at the ball. And my father is sitting down mending shoes now. And no one is talking to me. And there is no one else around but my mother and my father, and they are not talking to one another. And my mother seems so angry. And then I begin to cry all the more because I think of my grandmother and how—how dear she is and I have got to live away from her now with these strangers. And all of a sudden my mother gets very angry because I am crying so hard. And she comes over and she—ah—shakes my shoulders. (Yes.) And she tells me not to cry. There is no reason why I should cry. I am with her now. I am her mother. And I should be happy—happy to be home with her. And there is no reason why I should—ah—be acting so foolish. And after all—ah—my grandmother is just my grandmother. But she is my mother. And I should be happy. She can't understand me she said. Because I should be happy and—and not crying because I am home. And—and then I t—try not to cry so hard any more, and my mother goes on making the supper. But way down deep I am heartbroken. I am feel I just don't know what to do with myself. There is no toys around and nothing but this dull little red ball. There is no people but my-my father and my mother; and my mother is a stranger to me. And-and even though my father is familiar to me, I still, I am lonesome. I want to go back to my grandmother. And I can't think of how I am going to stay down here, and have to be home. Because it wasn't like my home. And I wanted to be with my grandmother. I was heartbroken. I wanted to be with her. And I just can't think of—

ah—living down here where there is no flowers and no sunshine coming in the windows—ah ah—nothing to play with. Nothing but to sit on but a little hard chair. And I am afraid to even walk around. I don't feel like walking around. Because I am heartbroken. And I just don't even want to play. And my mother is s-se-setting the table now. And it looks like some kind of potatoes or something. And my father—ah—takes me by the hand and he sits me down next to him. And my mother fixes my plate. But I can't eat, I just pick up but one potato, and my mother is getting angry. Because I am not eating. Then I told her, I am not hungry, that I don't feel hungry tonight. That—ah ah—I am lonesome, I want to be back with my grandmother. And then she gets angry all over again. And she said don't you mention your grandmother any more. You are home now and I am your mother. You should be happy. And she is very angry because I won't eat, and because I say that I am lonesome for my grandmother. So nothing is said at the table; it's just quiet and I try to eat a little bit more, but then I can't eat any more. Because I am heartbroken. I am down in this stingy old place and I am with strangers. I want to be with my grandmother. And I don't know how I am even going to sleep tonight in this strange house. I—I want so desperately to be, go back to my grandmother; go back where I am happy, where there is pretty toys and colored things and—ah—a sweet grandmother around. Not down here with strangers. I don't know them. I want to be back with my grandmother, to my own home. And I am just miserable and heartbroken."

This part of the hypnoanalysis has been presented unabridged to demonstrate that the nature of the patient's repetitions was elaborative, each repetition containing one or more new details, rather than compulsive. The elaborated repetitions were the heart of the working through process, for Anne as well as for other patients suffering from a conversion reaction. Then, she described her first night "home."

"I was never so sad in all my life. I was sad when my grandmother died, and after that. But that seemed to be the worst thing. When I just seemed to be taken right out of my grandmother's arms . . . to live with these strangers. And I couldn't understand why I was taken away . . . my grandmother wanted me . . .

I couldn't understand, they weren't treating me too nicely . . . And I can't understand why my grandmother didn't make them go away and keep me there with her."

This hypnoanalytic session (65th H.), which ended the current short depression, was performed at the end of August when, as Anne specified in the hypnoanalytic session, her parents took her back.

She had a bad time at home. The patient found that her father was much less interested in her than formerly, preferring her sister Carabelle more and more. Her mother decided that Anne had been poorly trained while with the grandmother, who had taught her grandchild to speak and sing in German. The infant was prohibited to do either, as well as to visit the grandmother.

Toward the end of her initial year in treatment, the patient came one day for an appointment (104th S.) stating that although she wanted to be hypnotized, for the first time in her therapy she felt afraid to be. She was hypnotized nonetheless (47th H.), and revivification was induced to the time when her parents forbade her to speak German.

"I can see my mother and she is very angry . . . scolding me very much . . . telling me never to go near my grandmother again. That it isn't right for me to love my grandmother the way I do. I am her mother. And my grandmother is—is no good for me . . . if I went near my grandmother, God would take my moth—my grandmother away."

Note the slips of the tongue Anne made at different times for different emotional reasons. She was now utterly unable to accept her mother and also in extreme conflict because of her unresolved Oedipus complex. She tried several times to run away, and once actually reached her grandmother who, despite her love for this grandchild, had the good sense to bring her back to the parents. Her mother saw them coming and took her daughter by the hand.

"She dragged me all down the hill. And when I got . . . there. My father . . . said that I could—would never see my grandmother again. That now he tell God to take her away from me . . . And I cried and cried. And I felt so miserable . . . [cries] (What happened then?) A week after that. (What?) [swallows] My grandmother died. (So soon afterwards. And you were sure you were the

reason for it. But now you know it was not so.) [cries] (Do you know it had nothing to do with your going up there? Do you know that now?) And I always felt that I was the cause of it."

This hypnoanalytic session (47th H.) was performed at the end of January, probably at about the same time of year as the patient's grandmother died, coinciding with the time when Anne's longer regular depressions had started. She stated in this hypnoanalytic session (47th H.) that she was four-and-a-half years old, but it is much more likely, in consonance with other dates she gave, that at the time of her grandmother's death the patient was not quite four. In her emotional attachment to her grandmother, Anne may, indeed, have tried to make it seem that her grandmother had lived longer than she actually did.

This hypnoanalytic session (47th H.) also demonstrates the infant's belief in her father's omnipotence. Although the mother had uttered the threat that God would take the grandmother away, the father had said, after the final visit, that he would now tell God to take the grandmother away. According to other statements, the grandmother's death just at that time was quite unexpected.

But shortly before this, at Christmastime, another grief had befallen Anne, her father had definitely turned away from her. Now, at the beginning of January, the patient came to an appointment (95th S.) complaining that she had been depressed since just before Christmas and that this depression might have to do with religion. She also felt very restless, had been drinking, and now was guilty about it. Anne was hypnotized (45th H.), regression was induced, and she was asked the reason for her recent depression. The patient reported a number of unpleasant occurrences connected with religion and Christmas.

"My father had his hands up my leg . . . And my mother came in the room. And she was very angry . . . But it's the way my father act—acted . . . And my mother was always so cold, and there was no one else, that I missed my father very very much after that. And I couldn't understand that there was such a complete change in him. He wouldn't even smile at me after that . . . It was now he —he turned to whipping me. And beating me."

Recapitulating the many losses Anne had sustained in a rela-

tively short time, I present them here in chronological order: She had to leave her grandmother in August and then had to adjust to a mother who rejected her. Visiting her beloved grandmother, speaking German and singing were all prohibited, these vetoes being later accompanied by threats. Then, her father started to loosen his ties to her, and completely broke his attachment sometime between Christmas and New Year's. The infant was unable to stop herself from trying to regain his attentions and grieving for them. Shortly afterwards, her grandmother's death occurred and she was stricken with guilt. She also blamed herself for the puppy's being shot a short while later. All these events affected Anne deeply and were the roots for her later depressions. Until her therapy, she had postponed part of her grieving and had repressed the facts connected with it.

The patient was not able to endure the many frustrations and losses of love objects she had to accept in a relatively short time. Obviously, her immature ego was still far too weak and, as she herself pointed out, "there was no one else" to whom she could turn for any kind of consolation. Only one memento of her grandmother, a slateboard, was guarded by her with great jealousy and zeal; she invested the puppy and the slate strongly with object libido, as Federn puts it in discussing emotions after an "object loss."* He also states that a feeling of "estrangement" occurs. Anne said (47th H.), "I used to think that I was wicked. Because I killed that wonderful person (her grandmother). And I was just heartbroken. And lonesome, and I—(Yes) I used to just go around dazing."

I have already mentioned that the patient started her therapy during one of her depressions. This was on February 3rd. She immediately developed a positive transference to me—which was facilitated by my accent resembling her grandmother's accent—and it was very easy to treat her despondency and her tension. I had no opportunity to observe any of her longer-lasting depressions which, according to Anne's descriptions, must have been quite severe. The next year, on her own volition, she started a business course on January 17th and consistently gained the highest marks.

---

* FEDERN, P.: *Ego Psychology and the Psychoses*. New York, Basic Books, 1952, p. 71ff.

The following year, and without discussing it much with me, she had an aptitude test on January 17th which she just reported to me over the telephone, and got a job in a field completely new to her, on February 27th. She did very well in this job, was now able to concentrate and was stable. She had stopped drinking a long time before.

It may be appropriate here to review the patient's different identifications. Despite the various stages, four in all, through which her relationship with her mother went, there was no detectable identification with her mother, except in the rejection of her own son, as Anne had been rejected by her mother after her return from her grandmother's home. However, we should not forget that the patient's acquaintance with her paternal grandmother had started quite early, at first through mutual visits, later in the course of living with her, and that there was a strong identification with this grandmother. During Anne's therapy, the good influence the grandmother had had on the infant came more and more to the fore, and it was obvious that most of the patient's positive characteristics had their roots in the grandmother's guidance despite the fact that this identification was connected with strong guilt feelings.

As to Anne's early identification with her father, "the girl Josie," it is questionable whether it was good for the patient that she identified with a father whom she regarded for a long time as a female. However, other complications might have been averted by this kind of identification. Until her treatment, she had been confused about the real role of the male and the female. Anne's identification with her sister Carabelle, as stated before, had very unhappy consequences. That the patient had a very little-unified personality is obvious.

In Anne's family, there were all the prerequisites for the development of a psychoneurotic disorder. Both parents were highly neurotic, sexually deviant, and the mother quite stupid. Constant fights between the parents which, at times, had also to do with the children's upbringing, made life bitter and difficult. The paternal grandmother had been the only dispenser of protection and affection without any sexual connotation. That the patient developed an anxiety reaction, conversion reaction, phobic reaction,

and depressive reaction was consequential to these inimical influences. During Anne's therapy, a stable, friendly, responsible, intelligent, and lovable human being came to the fore in her, one whose neurotic symptoms had diminished more and more and who was highly successful in her training for a new field of work, as well as in a new job. Her behavior was now related to reality.

Anne's hypnoanalyses showed a well-defined pattern and structure. The visualizations had a distinguishable background and pertained to plausible occurrences. Only a few hypnoanalytic sessions were symbolical, and of these many could be traced back to actual happenings. In each visualization one episode was described and worked through as a well-rounded picture with logical progression of the activity of the persons involved like a chapter in a book. The working through was often performed by duplicating or triplicating descriptions of the same spisode in similar words, each repetition yielding some additional details. This was achieved in a noncompulsive manner, and most of the elipsis points in the transcription excerpts have a bearing on this. Anne's symptoms could be traced through the various repressed ego states back to their different sources at different ages and times. Therefore, their meaning could be understood by the conscious ego of the patient, and what had formerly been warded off had been reunited with, and reintegrated into the mature personality so that a good therapeutic result was achieved.

MITCH

I will now discuss another patient who came for treatment of diverse symptoms, most of them belonging to the anxiety reaction, dissociative reaction and conversion reaction group. There were also a few traits of a compulsive personality which he only mentioned casually because they did not bother him.

Mitch's treatment being so short for financial reasons, I present it in chronological order to show how such a therapy can be conducted, and will put the theoretical part at the end. It is obvious that the case history had to be ordered to make it more intelligible though this has been done as little as possible, and it also had to be pared to its essentials. The hypnoanalytic sessions were played back each time at the next session. The theoretical part has

been restricted to these phenomena of which enough material had been developed, and not merely to those with few data forthcoming; e.g., his castration anxiety.

(1st and 2nd S.) Mitch, 38 years old, a once-divorced and twice-married hairdresser, was sent to me by one of my former patients. Two years previously, another psychiatrist had treated him but did not want to take him back.

The patient complained about general anxiety states, hot flashes, an urge to run when overcome by his own anger, nightmares, very shaky hands, and sweaty palms. However, he did not mention either his alcoholism or his coughing. At this point in his life, all his troubles had started about three months before he came to me for therapy.

Nervous symptoms had actually begun when he served in the army from 1942 to 1945. He got a medical discharge, but no treatment. From 1947 to 1948, he took vitamins because of a poor dietary condition, and his physician also recommended that he should have sexual relations. This, however, did not benefit the patient. In 1957, a chiropractor helped him to a degree but referred him to his first psychiatrist. In "analysis" it was discovered that Mitch was dominated by his mother and also by his two next-older sisters, Donna and Leila, both several years his senior. He first stated that these sisters are eight or nine years older than he is, and shortly afterwards amended this to four and five years.

His parents came from Italy where the two oldest children were born. They made "moonshine" wine, and the family "lived in the fumes." His father was a "wonderful man" who held two jobs, one of them as a shoemaker. There was "friction" with his wife, and he was a "beaten man." He hit his son only once or twice and then, apparently, at the behest of his wife who treated him "like dirt;" he had little contact with his children. Only after his mother's death was the patient able to talk to him as "a son to a father" or "man to man." Four years before Mitch's treatment, the father had died of a coronary.

Mitch's mother came from a higher social class than his father. She was very domineering, very nervous, and a spendthrift. Because of her, they had lost their house when the patient was fifteen years of age. She was obviously quite sadistic. She did not

believe in doctors or dentists and treated her children herself. The patient was her seventh child, born when she was forty-one years old. She was ashamed of him and resented this issue. She always celebrated Mitch's birthday in conjunction with the birthday of one of his sisters who was born in the same month; the sister resented this. Six years previously, Mitch's mother had died of diabetes and arteriosclerosis.

The patient's oldest sister had married at the age of sixteen. She was eighteen years old when he was born and was the only one of the siblings who had acted as a substitute good mother. Mitch's middle brother, the only one who had held a white collar job, had committed suicide seven years previously because of trouble with his wife and financial difficulties. The patient felt that his family was "going down" in every respect, and he broke away from them that year.

Mitch could report very little about his early life because nobody had talked to him about it. He said that his sisters "took it out on me with beatings" although he was told by his siblings that he had been a "spoiled child."

Before he was able to walk, he had been badly scalded with hot water. He had been informed that his rocking chair had been placed next to the stove and he had pulled a pot filled with boiling water down on himself. He sustained second degree burns on his left side. Thereafter, his next older sister Donna called him "Scarface" and "Niggerlip."

The patient had sucked his thumb. He bit his nails until his first year in the army. As a child, he wet his bed for a long time and again when he had married for the second time, a habit that had lasted until four years previous to his coming to me.

As a boy he was described as "incorrigible," he "could never take authority," he did not comply with orders, even in school, answered back, stayed out at night and smoked at thirteen or fourteen years of age. Mitch had been a liar for many years and, occasionally, stole. He always wore hand-me-downs, and because his mother refused to buy him a bicycle, he had to use one or the other of his brothers' bicycles. Since his earliest youth, the patient knew that he was "a rejected child" because his mother had to force his sisters to take him with them. Donna "smacked" him

often, and only at fourteen years of age did he dare to hit her back.

The boy was very resentful in school and was often kept back. The teachers could not handle him and they repeatedly called his mother to the school. After six months of high school, he dropped out and drifted from one job to the other.

Mitch's tonsils and adenoids had been removed when he was a child. He had had numerous accidents, one of them a fall from the school porch after which he had been unconscious. He remembered few details about these mishaps. He had never had any convulsions.

At the age of eleven, he had tried to slide down a telephone pole and had scraped his scrotum on a rusty nail. He bled badly though he had no inflammation. The patient believed this to be the reason why he was potent but sterile.

When he was small, other children had refused to play with him, and he could not figure out why. The reason may have been that Mitch pushed himself on them, though, at another session, he reported that his mother quite often did not allow him to play with other children because she wanted him to help with the household chores and sent them away. He, therefore, felt that he was "different." When he was about nine or ten years of age, his playmates tried to hang him. After this, he stayed alone.

The patient had been a bad mixer and had never "belonged;" though his feeling was that the others had not "belonged" either. This changed when he started roller skating at the age of eleven. One of his brothers gave him his first skates, but he was allowed to skate "under" the house only; however, he also skated in the streets and in Central Park, and afterwards at an indoor ring. At seventeen, his social life had started there. Mitch had later organized a club with two hundred members and had also started clubs in other communities.

In the army, he suffered from yellow fever and gonorrhea. Then, an overdose of sulfa drugs made crystals form in his kidneys. The patient had also had pneumonia, and a year-and-a-half before coming for treatment, he had an allergy to penicillin. He now took "pep" pills and various tranquilizers.

Mitch remembered some details of his abuse by his mother and

his siblings in the waking state, and others were revealed in his hypnoanalytic sessions. His sister Donna was his worst tormentor, aside from his mother. When he was an infant and his mother went shopping, she would tie him to the washtub with rags and leave him alone for a long time. "I cried and cried." At other times, she would hit him with anything she could lay hands on. Once, she injured his scalp and had not been remorseful. Both his mother and Donna scared him when he had been forced to go down into the cellar.

The patient's first marriage, which did not work out, had been entered into when he was in the army. His present wife was a hairdresser and they had a shop together. Initially, he had regarded hairdressing as "sissy." However, when he had become unemployed, his wife had sent him to a hairdressing school. At that time, he drank too much, his hands shook, and he was afraid to work on "persons." Later, Mitch had taken courses in permanent-wave and style schools. But he was unable to hold a job. Then, on his own incentive, he ran a beauty shop with his wife.

In the beginning, he had resented his wife's bossiness; she "held a club over my head" because she had a license and was experienced, and she had to be present when he worked. Later, the relationship became more equitable, and she herself asked him why he let her get away with so much previously. The patient now holds a manager-operator license.

His wife and others had told him that he not only talked and sang in his sleep but also moved his legs violently. At times, he had sleepwalked and had used the closet instead of the toilet. Once, while sleepwalking, he moved some furniture around, hurt himself, and realized this only the next morning on awakening.

(3rd and 4th S.) As to his sexual history, Mitch said that for a long time he was capable of having intercourse only in taxis and with women older than himself. He had fantasies about his sisters. There had also been some homosexual experiences. When, between the ages of eight and twelve, his mother took him to Coney Island and undressed under the boardwalk, the boy saw her naked, was aware that others did too, and was shamed by her exhibitionism.

The first attempt to hyponotize the patient (1st H.) was success-

ful. He reported afterwards that it was "not deep but relaxing" and that he had felt "enjoyable chills" through his legs, arms, and the back of his head. He also went into a trance at his second hypnotic session (2nd H.) and was aware of it.

(5th S.) He had felt relaxed after he had gone home the last time. However, he was drinking more than formerly. His wife told him that he dreamed at night and moved around. He reported two long dreams. Mitch's associations revealed that he loved dogs but was also afraid of them. He informed me that he and his wife had tried to adopt a child but that the "red tape" had been too much and they gave up. He also made a point of stating that he was very punctual, that when he agreed to be somewhere, he had somehow "bonded" himself to be at a specific place at a specific time. He said he was careful not to overbook appointments in his beauty shop.

(6th S.) At this session, the patient said he felt "not too bad."

(3rd H.) Between the two halves of the suggestions, regression was induced. Mitch visualized that he was near the washtub in the kitchen of his childhood home. He could not see his mother but felt that she was getting ready to tie him to the tub. On questioning, he stated that he might be about one year old. Then he suddenly visualized himself at ten or eleven years outside the kitchen window. He explained that his mother went to the movies three or four times a week, and she took no care to see that he was not locked out after school. If he knew in the morning that she was going, he unlocked the kitchen window before leaving for school. Now, he saw himself climbing in. In his next visualization, he found himself in the bedroom stealing money out of his mother's bank, probably on the same day. More trivial visualizations about his youth followed, among which the fact emerged that his mother was "a great party giver."

(7th S.) Mitch said that the more his wife tells him not to drink, the more he drinks. His wife had again told him that he had tried during the night to go to the closet instead of to the bathroom, and she had "steered" him to the bathroom. But he was amnestic about the incident. He complained that his wife was nervous and not as strong as he had thought her to be.

(4th H.) Mitch was again regressed after half the suggestions

had been given. He visualized himself at one year of age in the rocking chair near the stove. He was feeling very frightened of the grown-ups, choked, coughed, and moved his right leg.

(8th S.) The patient reported that he had cut down on his drinking, but he complained about intestinal trouble. This was, apparently, of a psychosomatic nature because he had the same discomfort before his hypnoanalytic sessions. He had had an argument with his wife, and a spell of uncontrollable hand shaking followed.

(5th H.) The patient was immediately regressed and visualized his mother rubbing his sister Donna's chest. The girl was coughing and the mother gave her whiskey. Donna had been suffering from bronchiectasis. Mitch said he was very afraid of her.

After this hypnoanalytic session, the patient stated that he suddenly thought that he might not have pulled the pot of hot water down on himself; he could not remember having seen his own outstretched arm. But his sister might accidentally have pushed it onto him.

(9th S.) The patient reported a rent increase. Then he coughed and said that his sister Leila had had tuberculosis. He commented that his siblings had made him feel that he was unable to express himself. They had laughed and "smirked" at him so that he felt "like a fool." A few days previously, he had visited Leila. It seemed to him that she wore the same expression on her face he remembered from twenty-five years ago which Mitch took to mean that she still regarded him as a good-for-nothing.

(6th H.) Regression was induced. Mitch talked about his running away from home as a child because he was expecting punishment for something. He had tried to time it well, but his family found out before he could get away.

(10th S.) The patient said that if he eats something hot, he loses control of his head and hands and starts to shake. He sometimes coughed when his wife tried to be affectionate to him. He added that he felt that if he coughed as loudly as his sister had, he, too, would get attention and sympathy. If he cried, it was because he had lost his temper or was sorry for himself.

(7th H.) He was told to remember the missing details of a dream he had reported during that same session, and to interpret

it. The patient then said that, in this dream, he was carrying his two younger sisters and his mother in an open pack on his back. He visualized himself in a park where he felt that his brother should have taken over this burden of relatives but the brother did not do so. This was a very good symbolical demonstration of Mitch's interaction with the members of his family.

(11th S.) On questioning, the patient said he understood from this dream that his family was trying to shove responsibilities upon him, but he had wanted to hand them over to his brother, who had refused to accept them. This hypnoanalysis (7th H.) was visualized in color, he had seen himself as a teen-ager, and the brother was not as clear as the others.

In his childhood, Mitch said, he had often been accused of exaggerating and not knowing what he was talking about.

(8th H.) In regression the patient was asked about possible reasons for his hands shaking. He stated that it had originated from having been beaten so often. His sister Donna had frequently tried to choke him, and he was twelve or thirteen years old before he had dared to hit back. When he was an adolescent, his mother had either turned him over for punishment to his more grown-up siblings or she shut him out of the house. A neighbor boy also beat him.

(12th S.) The patient stated that he felt very well, that his hands have been steady. "I use liquor as a crutch," he said. He had again walked into the closet during the night. He also said that when he thought of his sister, he put his own hand around his throat.

(13th S.) Mitch reported that his wife had hurt her back in a fall and was in the hospital.

He described a dream in which dark brown eyes were staring directly at him.

(9th H.) Asked about this dream, the patient told that these eyes belonged to Donna. She had always knotted his tie too tight [cough]. She had put his sweater on underneath his "chemise," which made him very hot. She had buttoned his "chemise" too high [cough]. All this had happened when he was about seven years of age. Then he remembered that, at the age of four, he had had a cold and the brother in whose bed Mitch was sleeping had

complained about his cough. This brother had also spat at him.

(14th S.) The patient reported that he had trembled, perspired, and had increased his drinking. He revealed that, although he was hungry, he was unable to eat because of the feeling that something was stuck in his throat. This condition had just now disappeared. Apparently, he had suffered from a globus hystericus.

(15th S.) Mitch said that he felt very well. He had been quite busy in his beauty parlor, and his wife now realized that he was competent to manage the shop alone. She was at home although in and out of bed.

(16th S.) Mitch said that his wife was now out of bed but had to wear a brace. Business was very good when he worked alone. Aside from his nervous cough, he was now suffering from a cold.

(10th H.) Revivification and later regression were both induced. The patient reported that, at two years of age, his mother had sat him too close to the stove and he had felt too hot. She had also "packed" him too tightly into bed. Then came visualizations of events already mentioned. Later he recalled that when, at the age of thirteen, he was hit by his father, he reacted by becoming a bad boy because it made him feel as if he were different from the others. He ran away and also stayed out too late at night.

After awakening, the patient stated that he could see the world much more clearly now and observe things he formerly had not realized were there. His relations with other people had improved.

(17th S.) Mitch reported that he could now handle the shop quite well by himself. He had brooded a good deal over Donna's eyes in the dream. "To me it's a terrible picture." As a boy, when he had to enter the cellar, he was always afraid that this sister would jump out on him and scare him, although he had not been afraid of the darkness itself.

(18th S.) The patient said that he felt worse; he had drunk too much, and his wife had told him that he had fallen out of bed twice though he could not remember it. Only next morning did he realize that he had bruised his right eyelid. He stated that his wife—"No, my sister"—was jealous that he was getting along so well. Such slips of the tongue, he observed, occurred quite often, e.g. when calling his mother-in-law by his wife's first name, or

calling his wife "Mame." In any case, he did not feel like a small boy anymore. He had been amazed that his wife's family "listens now to what I say, and they digest it." People in the shop also paid attention to his words. They were "human beings like myself." Only the members of his own family never answered more than "yes." He was still coughing.

(11th H.) Revivification was induced and he was questioned again about the reasons for his coughing. He described yet again how his mother had sat him too near to the stove, at two years of age. When he had tried to move farther away, she had tied him around the stomach and the chest. But the bond around his chest had slipped upwards around his neck. Mitch also said that she gave him scalding foot baths. At twelve years of age, he had fallen from the porch in school, and at home had been given a scalding bath and a shower. There had been so much steam that he had fainted, whereupon his mother had pulled his tongue forward. His mother and Donna had also pulled his tongue forward when he was using "bad words." Once, he had bitten his sister because she did this and she had slapped and choked him.

When the patient was leaving after this hypnoanalytic session, he remarked that, when buttoning his shirt up, he no longer had the feeling that his throat was so tight and did not feel the urge to cough.

(19th S.) Mitch felt worse again. He had been coughing since the night before when he had been "deep thinking." He had also been drinking, and he had "dry retches." On arriving home, he had vomited and perspired. Coming for his appointment made him feel relaxed, but his genitals and his back were paining him badly. "Sex is on my mind," he said; he had not been able to have relations with his ailing wife.

Talking over his last hypnoanalytic session, he stated that the mistreatment of his tongue had stopped only when he was eight or nine years of age, but beatings went on "well into my teens."

(12th H.) In revivification, he was asked about further reasons for the pains in his genitals. He said that Donna had hurt his genitals intentionally when she washed him at the age of four. The pains in his back were due to the fact that he had almost fallen over in the rocking chair, tried vainly to keep his balance and, in

so doing, had hurt his back. He said that his sister had also tipped up the baby carriage quite often and he had fallen on his head.

The patient was questioned whether his hypnotic trance was now less deep because of his new awareness that his therapist was female, which might be reminding him of his sisters. He stated that he saw many eyes during the induction of this hypnosis without knowing to whom they belonged.

(20th S.) Mitch reported again that he had been coughing badly though the cough had eventually eased. His dog had jumped on him, putting its paws on his stomach. Subsequently, he had the feeling that "something shot up and closed up my throat. I could not breathe." His wife told him that his color had changed "to blue and purple." For about a quarter of an hour, phlegm was discharged from his nose and mouth. Because of his inability to control it, it reminded him of an epileptic fit. He had coughed continuously until the day before. On renewed questioning, he admitted that the reason that he was at times hard to hypnotize might be because the doctor was a female. At the beginning of his treatment, he regarded me as just "a person." When he coughed, he suffered pains in his genitals, abdomen, and back. He had erections at night and his genitalia looked red as though inflamed.

Mitch reported two dreams. In the first one, he hosed the soap from his middle sister's back in the bathtub, and Donna watched, disapprovingly. In the other dream, the patient had gone into an enormous haunted house. One of his brothers was there, and a brother-in-law, and both had given him very "mean" looks. He lay down in a bed in a large room guarding his genitals with his left hand. Strange hands were reaching toward him and he was trying to fend them off with his right hand, holding on to his genitals with his left. Although he tried to call for help, he was unable to do so. Mitch coughed while relating this dream.

(13th H.) Regression was induced and he was asked why he coughed so much and about the meaning of the dreams. The patient talked about the second dream only, coughing considerably. He reported essentially the same visualization as in his dream. He was lying in bed and hands came from the right side reaching at him. He guarded his genitals with his left hand. Between him and the person to whom the hands belonged was a headboard. "(Let it

change.)" The headboard changed into a flower. Then he described his sister's eyes as two cesspools because she hated him and had often scared him. He was questioned as to when he had started to cough, and he stated that it was when he was six or seven years of age because his coughing sister had gotten all the attention. Recalling this, Mitch coughed badly.

(21st S.) He reported that his cough was "dwindling" although the previous night he had awakened his wife with it, also by raising his legs. At this point, he cleared his throat frequently.

When the thirteenth hypnoanalytic session was played back to him, he coughed shortly after hearing the first cough in the record, then coughed no more.

(14th H.) This hypnoanalysis and the following one are presented in a transcribed form; the ellipsis points in them usually mean that parts were not intelligible.

"(You dream and remember what your sister has done to you. You feel protected. Please talk.) (What happened?) Nothing comes. (Why not?) I don't know. I seem choked up. (You moved your right leg again.) Yes. (Why did you do it) I don't know. (You are moving it again.) I did it all last night when I was sleeping. (What choked you up?) Just thinking about her. (Can you see her?) I can feel her. (Where?) At my throat. (Does she have her hands at your throat, or what?) Yes. (How about pushing her away?) I tried but she was too strong. (You tried with your right leg? No. (Do it. Push her away.) [moves his right leg] (Good. You are moving the other leg.) No. I did that later on. (How old were you?) I was about fourteen. I kicked her. And I stepped on her feet. Until she let me alone . . . That was the only way she would let me alone. (Has she still got her hands around your throat?) Yes. (Push her away with your hands. You are much stronger now. She is a sick woman. Just push her away, then you will be able to talk. Push her with your feet.) [moves his feet] (Good. You pushed. Has she moved away?) (Sure, she is away.) Oh. Ah, yes. (Do it once more. Make fists and push her away.) [moves his arms] (That was good. Now she is away and you can talk. Is it better?) Much better. (Talk about why, and get rid of her completely.) She threatened me with all bad things. With all the bad things. They don't come to my mind right now, but I

know they were bad. Because she frightened me something terrible. (They come to your mind. Just let them come. One after another. They must not come all together. Just start with the easiest thing. What was the easiest thing she did to you?) Well, she used to grab me around—around the throat. And she always—when she grabbed me this way, my—my—my jacket came apart. She ripped my jacket. So then I would say to her, 'I will tell Mama.' And then she realized, well, when she ripped my shirt or ripped the button, my mother want' to know what happened. Then she tried a different grip and she gripped me around the throat. She gripped my clothes and just pull' like that . . . (Why are you so frightened?) Not frightened, I—I—I just feel relieved. (That is very good.) . . . (Why do you breathe so deeply?) Because I got rid of her . . . [cough] (Did you get frightened again?) Yes. (Why?) That she could do that. (What?) Frighten me. (Talk about it.) . . . When I think of her, my stomach jumps . . . (Do you feel better?) Yes. (Should we stop?) Yes."

There was another part. He also visualized as many hands as the Indian gods possess, choking him with one hand and slapping him with the other. He said he was "scared" when his sister called him "Niggerlip" and "Scarface" and, for years afterwards, felt himself to be "nothing." On these occasions, Mitch had always had the feeling that his lip thickened and that the scar was quite visible. Now he knew that it was not so. He was unable to let the flower he had described the last time, change further. The patient saw his sister's eyes full of mud and dirt. [cough] Mitch moved his legs, especially his right leg. He did not know why he wanted to protect his genitalia.

(22nd S.) The patient reported that he felt good although he had been drinking and was shaky. He was asked about his feelings when he pushed his sister away, and he answered, "very good, very comforting." To the question whether he felt stronger as a consequence, he replied: "In a way I felt stronger, very relaxed." When he was told to specify whether this was while he was pushing her, or after she had been pushed. Mitch stated that it was ". . . after. While I did it, I felt very uncomfortable." He admitted that he had also been afraid.

At the playback of the fourteenth hypnoanalytic session, he

coughed at the beginning and said that this was his "first cough in five days." When about one third of the record had been played back, he started to cough superficially and continued to do so. The flower which he had visualized in the thirteenth hypnoanalysis, he described as quite broad. He was told to draw it, and he now called the headboard a "backboard."

(15th H.) Regression was induced. "(Why do you cough? What is the matter with your throat?) My throat, as you were taking me back—my throat seemed to get larger and larger. (Larger? That must be quite agreeable. Then you get more air.) No. (Talk it out. Don't cough it out.) It's swelling. (How does it swell?) (What is making it swell?) I don't know. I—I—it—it just started to swell and—and—and—and—and my shirt seemed to get tighter and tighter around my throat. And I get coughing. (Who is at your throat?) I don't know. (Look at the person. Who is it?) My sister. (Which one?) The younger one. (She has her hand on your throat, or what?) Sometimes. (What did you feel just now? What did she do to you?) Nothing. But the thing that—my—my throat was getting larger. That my—my shirt didn't quite fit around it. And I now—I remember that a lot of times she used to [cough] (What?) When—when she had to, dressed me. She used to take my shirt and just throw it across . . . and it used to close off my throat. (That would make the throat smaller, not larger.) No. But act as she would put me to sleep, i-it seemed like a-all the veins and my nerves and everything, my glands would just get larger and larger. And my shirt was getting smaller and smaller and smaller. (Was that not a substitute for another part of your body? Which, at times, gets larger?) I don't know [cough] I don't know. (Don't you suppose?) Well. (There is only one part of the male body that can get larger. What is it?) The gum makes it. (Go on.) [cough] Possible. I mean, not that you brought the thought up. I never thought about it in my conscious mind. (Want a hanky?) Thank you. [cough] (Is your sister still there?) Yes. (What is she doing?) She kept pulling the shirt over and—and buttoning up tight. And I like the way my—my—my shirt tight. I like them making look neat my towels and my ties. I like them to make—to make them look neat. But when I think of her I—I—I feel all choked up. (Is she very near you?) Standing alongside of

me. Looking down at me. (Looking [cough] down at you. I will completely protect you and help you. I will completely protect you and help you. Now put your hands to your sister's throat and choke her back. Just do it well.) (Put your hands to your sister's throat and choke her back, exactly as she did it to you. Just do it.) I can't. (Sure you can. I am helping you, I am protecting you. You are strong enough. Just do it.) I can't. (Last time you could push her away. Isn't that true?) Yes. (O. K. [cough] Now grab her. Grab her throat.) I can't. (Why not?) My arms. They feel like lead. (I am helping you and you are strong enough. Lift your arms. Your left arm first. Lift it up.) (Lift your left arm. Lift it up.) (More up. Farther, farther up. O. K.) (And now the right arm. Let the hanky drop. Drop the hanky. Lift the right arm. Lift it up. Now, grab her. Grab her by the throat.) I can't. (Grab her; you can do it. Just do it. I am helping you. I am helping you. I protect you. I protect and help you. Do the same thing she did to you. Just do it. You will feel much better. Do you have her by the throat?) No. (You wanted to do it many times. You wished it. Now wish for it very strongly and you will be able to do it.) (Good.) [cough] (Courage. Good.) Ah, ah, I can't. [laugh] (What happened?) I don't know. I have a strange feeling. (Let me hear about it. Is it a good or a bad feeling?) Now it's good. But when I did it, it was a bad feeling. I felt very bad. (Are you rid of her?) I think so. I think so. (Do you know now that you are stronger than she is?) Maybe that's what frightens me. (Why does it frighten you?) Because she was always stronger than me. (Now you know you are a grown man and strong. Yes?) Yes. I am, I am starting to realize it. (What do you see now? Is she still there?) No."

The patient now felt that he had actually hurt somebody and felt that, in his own way, he had hurt his sister before. . . . "I am afraid of her," he reiterated. (But you just choked her.) Then he said as follows: "I can hurt her by as bad as she is, I be better than her. I be good. And that hurts her more." Asked how it was that he could now talk so well, he answered, "I don't know. I—I—I think you helped me. Maybe I am trusting you a little more." Mitch declared that he was not even able to trust his own wife, that he was "cagey" because he had been hurt so often.

The patient went on to talk about his sister's eyes—the "cess-pools." He said he did what was right, did his chores, wanted to be in people's good graces. He felt well now because he could trust.

(23rd S.) Mitch brought what he called "very bad news." His whole body had been shaking for the last few days. "As if my whole nervous system was falling apart." He had been drinking, but he did not know why. He had to hold the razor in both hands to steady it. Neither tranquilizers nor alcohol had always helped. The right side of his upper right arm had been shaking more than the left although about an hour and a half before he came for his appointment, "I settled down."

After the playback of the previous hypnoanalytic session, he stated that he coughed when he felt aggravated or when his wife pressured him. But the patient was annoyed when his wife coughed because he put it down to "her nerves. Maybe that makes me angry." He meant because his wife was not as strong as he had believed her to be. The sister who suffered from bronchiectasis had been the first one in the family to cough though he cannot remember that the sister who had tuberculosis had coughed.

(16th H.) Mitch was asked why his right arm was shaking. He answered that he had often fought the sister who "tore" his right arm to the left. Then his left arm dropped to the side of the couch, and he stated that he now felt relaxed. But his right arm seemed to be very heavy and leaden to him, and he felt rather cold on the left side of his face. He had experienced the same sensations when his sister had bathed him at three or four years of age in the kitchen sink. She had been rough with him, had doused him with cold water and had washed his genitals, which he had tried to protect, especially roughly, with a resultant erection. His sister then told their mother that he was enjoying himself, whereas, in reality, she had hurt him. During the bath, he urinated into the kitchen sink. Despite the protests of his family, he also did this on later occasions when the bathroom was not available. He had come to regard the sink as his personal urinal.

After the hypnoanalytic session, he reported that he had visualized the house where the family had lived although there were no people in it.

(24th S.) Asked whether his sister was left-handed, the patient answered in the negative. He reported that he felt well now but that he had been very nervous during business hours. He had felt as if his body was going to fall apart. He had also been drinking. At night, he awakened and lay with his legs up, bent at the knees. Mitch thought he had not slept, but his wife assured him that he had. Nevertheless, he felt tired in the morning. Pills did not help him, though he did not take any "pep pills." He had not had a backache for two weeks, but that morning it returned. He had also felt a cramp coming on in his left calf for three or four days and had actually got it yesterday. The patient was less able to control his right upper arm than his left one. His nervous cough was better but had returned sporadically. Five or six hours before coming for his appointment, he had felt better and had drunk less.

(17th H.) The patient wanted only relaxation induced. Afterwards he reported that he had nevertheless had visualizations although he could not remember them. He had slept very deeply.

(25th S.) Mitch said that he had felt relaxed for a few days, then his tension had recurred. His sister Leila had come into his shop, and the patient realized that his relatives visited him only when they needed something. Leila was not feeling well, and although he was very busy, he offered her a choice of drinks. She informed him that their oldest sister was quite ill; then she started an argument with him. He told her not to fight in front of the customers and asked her to sweep the floor—not as a favor to him, but because he had done enough for his family. His sister complied.

After the playback of the sixteenth hypnoanalytic session, Mitch said, "I almost have a burden off me." This statement may have been connected with his expectation of punishment. "I need to trust you," he then added. But he did not know what I could do to protect him, and did not really comprehend how he could be protected. However, he declared himself as "almost through" with his sisters.

(18th H.) Much protection was promised and he was regressed. The patient visualized the family house with its yard, his mother, and himself, nine or ten years of age, cutting grass with some sort of "scissors," a poor instrument to use. He hated having to do it

because he had to go down on his knees, and they hurt him. His middle brother came out and "looked nastily" at him. [The muscles in his right arm started to jump] The patient stated that he was afraid his brother might punish him for some unknown reason. He put his right hand on his thigh because he was tired out by the muscular twitches. Although he had not remembered this at first, he now recalled that he had played immediately after school and only later cut the grass. His brother saw that the boy had cut less grass than he should have. Mitch did not recollect his punishment for this. Everybody in the family had ordered him around, and he had few friends because he was rarely permitted to leave the yard. The patient also had to help with chores in the house and had to scrub the floors. His middle brother inspected them and ordered him to scrub the hall and stairs over again. Mitch wanted to hit his brother with the brush but did not dare to do so because of the punishment he would have received. He was hit all over with anything—a cold poker, a "noodle wood," a knife—whatever his mother happened to pick up; he protected his face and head with his right arm. [The twitching of the arm muscles abated a little.] The boy would have liked to hit his mother back. When he was older, he took the tools out of her hands; but when she grabbed others, he ran. Therefore his mother "steamed up" his siblings against him. On questioning, the patient denied any connection between his middle brother and the "quivering" in his right arm. [It was better] This was the brother who did not want any responsibilities. Mitch said that he was not frightened now but that his heart was beating fast. He was told to dream before the next session.

Afterwards he stated that his arm felt better. "I feel easier." But he had a recurrence of his postnasal drip which he had not had for some time past.

(26th S.) The patient reported that he had cleaned his shop last night but had been wearing the wrong shoes, without rippled soles. For this reason, his right foot hurt in the morning. However, today he had been able to shave with his right hand alone although his muscles had "jumped." That morning, and one other morning, he had felt good, but apart from this "I felt like I slipped back." The previous night, he had slept very well, had

even overslept and not heard his alarm clock. Immediately after awakening, he had taken pills.

Later, two customers came in who had been in a state hospital, and this had upset Mitch's intestinal tract badly. Since then, he had been drinking. He could not understand why he drank because it now made him vomit; whereas formerly he could stand it. The drinks "hit right on top of my throat." Thereafter, the patient reported that only his right foot hurt today, from ankle to heel and from calf to thigh. Saturday, when he had slept at his sister-in-law's, he had a cramp in his left calf. This had happened once before when he had slept there, but he did not have it at home.

After the playback of the eighteenth hypnoanalytic session, the patient was asked whether he had meant "head" or hedge" scissors. He stated that he meant "hedge" scissors but had pronounced the word as "head" scissors because he had much to do with "head scissors." At this time, Mitch limped on his right leg.

(19th H.) Regression was induced and protection promised. The patient described how he had cut the grass with the "scissors." Afterwards, his right arm and right leg gave him pain. He would have liked to cut his mother's throat because she had "looked dirty" at him when he paused in his work. She did not permit him to cut the hedge, saying that he did not understand how to do it, although he did know. When he was twelve or thirteen years of age, he once was at a movie but for some reason ran out, clambered over a gate and got "a point" embedded in his thigh. He treated it himself because he did not dare to inform the family about it for fear that he would be beaten. At an even younger age, he had "wrenched" his ankle, and another time, trying to repair his toy carriage with a bent nail, he had accidentally "opened" his foot above and behind the ankle. He said the wound looked like "marble," and he was very curious about it "because I had never before seen the inside of my leg." He said he know nothing about medication and that the injury was probably treated by his family.

Mitch remarked when leaving that he no longer coughed when he closed his uppermost shirt button.

(27th S.) He came limping to his last session and told me that

he was suffering from sciatica. For this reason, his wife was now helping in the shop again. That morning, his hands shook badly and his teeth "rattled." But he took two pills and was able to shave with one hand. He was also drinking more than before. The patient related a dream. In it, he was supposed to be in his own shop but, in actuality, was in his father's shoemaker shop. A woman was waiting to be served and he attended to her. As in his own shop, everything was painted blue. There were two foot pedals like those on a sewing machine, but he felt that they were very strange. He set the woman's hair, but there were no dryers. He added that his father had had a regular sewing machine pedal in his shop, but in the dream, the pedals were shaped like feet.

(20th H.) Regression was induced. He again reported that he was going through the house where he grew up, but nobody was there. Revivification was then induced, and Mitch visualized his mother having tied him to the leg of the bathtub. He freed himself just at the moment when his mother entered the bathroom.

This patient terminated his treatment because of financial difficulties which arose because both his wife's and his own sickness had incurred heavy expenses. When I telephoned Mitch a few months later, he told me that he still was very nervous but that he was rid of his sisters. In a letter nine months afterwards, subsequent to a telephone call from me, he reported that he was feeling well.

This patient, by the unhappy accident of his birth late in the life of his mother, and being felt by his siblings as an inimical intruder, was not only rejected by his family, but was used by most of his nearest relatives as an outlet for their hostilities and sadism. He could be called "a beaten child," and it is a wonder that he survived at all. The mother's sadistic and uncontrolled behavior certainly influenced her children's actions toward the weakest member of the family.

Although Anne and Mitch came from about the same socioeconomic background, Anne had always striven "to rise above my family," whereas Mitch was glad not to sink deeper, as he felt that the rest of his family did (1st and 2nd S.). His endowment also, in most respects, was much more limited than Anne's.

Due to rejection by his family, his infantile ego must have been

quite weak and remained so for a long time. The only two protective members of his family, his oldest sister and his father, were hardly mentioned in his case history and never in his hypnoanalytic sessions; they played a minor role in his life. Therefore, he had rarely had an opportunity to identify physically or mentally with a loving object, and his narcissistic needs were largely unsatisfied. The patient mentioned that he felt "different" at an early age and gave diverse reasons for this, which all seem valid. One of the first was the unwillingness of his sisters to "take me with them," which may also have had to do with his bodily disfigurement and was a repeated early narcissistic hurt. To the same category pertains his feeling of "not belonging" (1st and 2nd S.). He felt also that all others "did not belong" either, but still felt them to be his mutual enemies. Mitch identified mostly with "aggressors," and he behaved accordingly by being "incorrigible" (1st and 2nd S.). As he was not able to distinguish which of the demands of his family was in his interest and which opposed his interests, he disregarded all. "I could never take authority" (1st and 2nd S.), and he was "cagey" (15th H.). Interesting in this respect is the dream he related in his last session (27th S.) when he had already improved, which shows an identification with his father. The scene reveals a shop, a condensation of his own and his father's, with equipment used in both types of shops. Although in his dream the patient was dressing a woman's hair, the inclusion of a cobbler's implements indicates that he was now able to accept a loving authority.

Going back to Mitch's early infancy, there was rarely a chance to display any independence, psychical activity, or logic. Although he never reported any fantasies, it must be assumed that he had many, but deeply repressed ones.

The patient's many accidents speak for a strong masochism quite early in life, concomitant with many guilt feelings. His nineteenth hypnoanalytic session supports this view. It is more usual for a child to cry when he injures himself than to examine the injury, as Mitch did. However, through the many mistreatments he had sustained, he might easily have developed a hysterical analgesia. On the other hand, his curiosity bespeaks some psychical activity, somewhat later in life it is true, although he did not give any exact age information in this connection.

His emphasis on punctuality (stressed in his fifth session) and neatness belongs to his compulsive personality traits. One would expect a child brought up under such trying circumstances to be little concerned about his appearance and, as punctuality is demanded by authority, not to care about it. In the middle of his fifteenth hypnoanalysis, he remarked that he liked "them" making his ties and towels neat, though the former gave him some discomfort. Also his concern with "being good" expressed at the end of the same hypnoanalytic session points in this direction. He also felt burdened by his responsibilities toward his family (7th H., 25th S.). There was a strict superego present but, apparently, only in certain areas.

The conversion symptom which could be interpreted and, to some degree, influenced in this short treatment, was his coughing. His dependency on his sister Donna was broken and his relationships to other persons improved. The patient's hyperkineses also changed, but not always for the better. A longer therapy would most probably have produced more gratifying results.

In his anamnesis, he did not even mention his coughing. As to chronological information Mitch gave about the genesis of his cough, he visualized himself at one year of age in the rocking chair near the stove, feeling very afraid of the grown-ups and choking, coughing and moving his right leg (4th H.). Also, at two years of age, he was placed too near the stove by his mother and she had him tucked too tightly into bed (10th H.). Again at two years of age, she put the infant too near the stove and, when he tried to move away, she bound him around the stomach and chest. But the tie around his chest slipped up to his neck, and this may be one of the implications of his cough (11th H.). Whether the scalding baths and showers and the pulling forward of his tongue, mentioned in the same hypnoanalytic session, had started at the same time, he did not say. However, on one occasion, when his sister pulled his tongue forward, he bit her and she choked him in revenge. At four years of age, the brother whose bed the infant shared, complained about his cough which was the result of a current cold (9th H.). Asked directly when he started to cough, he reported that it was at the age of six or seven when his sister had gotten all the family's attention (13th H.). Apparently relevant to

this statement is the visualization, although no age was given, in which the patient recalled his mother rubbing the chest of his sister and giving her whiskey for a cough. He had been very afraid of this sister (5th H.). When he was about seven years of age, his next older sister, Donna, always knotted his tie too tight [cough]. She put his sweater under his shirt making him very hot, and she buttoned his shirt too high [cough] (9th H.). Another similar description, but regarding his shirt only and without any age indication, occurred in his fifteenth hypnoanalytic session. This sister finally stopped choking him when he was twelve or thirteen (8th H.) or fourteen years old (14th H.). At that age, he began defending himself. But when thinking of her, he put his own hand around his throat (12th S.). Being "almost through with my sisters," Mitch gave up the symptom which he had shared with them (25th S.). At the completion of his eighteenth session, and again when leaving at the end of his twenty-sixth, he remarked that he no longer coughed when closing his topmost shirt button. His identification with the aggressor had diminished more and more and finally stopped.

There were a few instances in which the patient suffered from a globus hystericus. He reported once that he had been hungry for some time but was unable to eat because something had been stuck in his throat (14th S.). At another interview (20th S.), he related how his dog had jumped on him putting its paws on Mitch's stomach, which the patient apparently felt as an aggression. He had the feeling that "something shot up and closed up my throat. I could not breathe." The following hypersecretion does not belong to a typical globus hystericus, but it was another of his conversion symptoms related to his coughing. However, there was a displacement upward from his genitalia to his throat, as one can perceive from the same interview. The genitalization of his throat was still more clearly expressed when, in his fifteenth hypnoanalytic session, he described feeling how his throat was getting larger and how he had to cough when his sister had thrown his shirt "across" and "it used to close off my throat." Sexual excitement by means of choking is known and, in some cases, has led to death. Mitch did not accept this interpretation immediately, but that might have come later. He had, after all, had sexual fantasies

about his sisters (3rd and 4th S.) though he did not describe of what kind. His information that he coughed when his wife tried to be affectionate (10th S.) points in the same direction. He also coughed when pressured by his wife (23rd S.) or when aggravated.

Whether some of his more latterly mentioned symptoms were substitute symptoms is hard to say. I have never seen substitute symptoms, and I believe that they are a theoretical hypothesis, not a proven fact. They presuppose a logical behavior of emotional reactions although we know that emotions do not behave logically. When a patient starts out with many symptoms and later on complains about some not previously reported, it is no matter for surprise. However, this topic is open to discussion.

Mitch's social relations with his wife's family as well as with his customers also improved. This betterment started apparently when his tension lessened and it was helped by his wife's accident. Her "bossiness" (1st and 2nd S.) must have reminded him of the situation at home. Now, operating the shop alone, he had an opportunity to prove his competence in his field of work and he was making the most of it, having always been regarded by his own family as "good-for-nothing" (9th S.). As early as his fifteenth session, the patient reported that he was very busy at work, and in the following session (16th S.), that his relations to people had improved. He had also been realizing aspects of life of which he was formerly not aware. In his eighteenth interview, he related that he no longer felt like a small boy and that his wife's family had been listening to him and digesting what he said. People in the shop were also doing so, and they "are human beings like myself," thus projecting his own emotions into them and indicating a reduction of his inferiority feelings. In his twenty-fifth session, he reported that he had even been able to stand up to his middle sister although the relations with his own family were generally still quite ambivalent.

Mitch's hypnoanalytic sessions all had a recognizable background and logically progressing activity of the persons involved. However, there was usually more than one episode described in a single hypnoanalytic session. Whether this was a consequence of the admixture of compulsive traits in his psychoneurotic disorder or simply of the pressure of his financial situation, which had al-

ways been precarious, it is impossible to decide. There is no question that such reality demands can influence visualizations. He brought forth very few symbolical distortions. At least one of the patient's symptoms could be traced through various repressed ego states back to its different roots.

When I tried to rid Mitch of his sister Donna in the fourteenth and fifteenth hypnoanalytic sessions, his reactions and replies were quite similar to those of the two other cases which will follow. At first, he answered that he was unable to do anything, his arms were "leaden." (15th H.) He was told to lift his arms slowly, which he did, but he was still incapable of following my suggestions. Only when I suggested that he himself desire to do this, was he able to fulfil his task. Not only my promised help and protection, but also his own repressed desires, now stimulated and allowable, seemed to be the motivating force. Mitch's feelings both during his act of emancipation and afterwards were "strange," at first "frightening" and subsequently "liberating." The results so far seem to be beneficial.

AYLEEN*

Ayleen is a Southern girl, presently living in New England, who visits me when she comes to New York, which is one to three times yearly. When she began psychotherapy, she was thirty years of age and single, and although the patient has been in treatment, in compressed terms, for a much shorter period of time, we have had a doctor-patient relationship for over twenty years.

At her initial interview, she complained of suffering from intense timidity when in groups, a shyness felt since her eighteenth year. Prior to that, it had been the very reverse, she said, although she tended to blush easily during her high-school stage. She injected the statement that somewhere in her development, she had felt that she should behave "more humbly." As an infant, she heard for the first time violin playing on a phonograph record and decided to become a concert violinist. At the age of six, she received piano instruction; at eight, she took violin lessons, but from an earlier age onwards, she had been cutting violins out of cardboard. The patient has perfect pitch, had always enjoyed per-

---

* This case was discussed briefly in the *J Nerv Ment Dis, 106*:176-185, 1947.

forming for an audience, and had frequently played in church. However, at twenty-one years of age, she was stricken with stage fright. This occurred during a radio performance, when she started to tremble and was almost unable to finish. One to one-and-a-half years prior to that event, there had been minor complications. Now, Ayleen was suffering from such anxiety that she could no longer play. She said that her fingers felt as though they were paralyzed. She claimed that teaching was easier, but when she came to me, she was holding a modest job with the Federal Government. The patient never completed her musical education and her enjoyment of music had diminished. Also, since her eighteenth year, she had been suffering from short depressions, without suicidal thoughts however.

She grew extremely frightened when taking the Sacrament. While talking, even to friends, she sometimes felt as though her face and arms were numb. There were other symptoms. Ayleen trembled during such acts as picking up small objects and eating soup, though there might be no more than one or two persons present. At times, she spilled fluids, especially when she had to balance a shallow container. She grew tense before leaving a subway car out of fear that she might become paralyzed. She grew tense in the mere anticipation of a "sudden" noise, as from a firecracker or fat spitting in the pan. This had started in her sixth year. She grew tense during electrical storms, and she became tense when swimming. She dreaded anesthesia and, therefore, the dentist. She also dreaded having to run downstairs or step out on a high pier. She was afraid of being alone in the dark in the country or in her own apartment, but was not afraid in a hotel. The patient was nervous about small buttons, especially white ones near her mouth, and she feared fishes' eyes. She was unable to eat a chicken's neck. Ayleen was "morbidly fascinated" by electrocutions she read about, although she found them terrifying. She regarded beheading as the most terrible way to die. Her diagnosis was anxiety reaction, phobic reaction, and conversion reaction.

Her paternal grandmother, described as strict but "jolly," had lived intermittently with the patient's family. She was of a generation that still talked about the Indian attacks and often related how she had run into the bush and held her hand over the baby's

mouth, taking the risk of smothering it rather than letting it cry. She was an earthy woman who bound the legs of chickens and turkeys before decapitating them. There was a period when she confessed to ill feelings toward her grandchildren, so that Ayleen's parents were constrained to hide knives and other sharp instruments where she could not find them. At times, the woman suffered from depressions.

The patient's paternal grandfather, a "psychopath," was unable to support the family and was penniless when he died. It was Ayleen's father who provided for them all. One of her father's brothers was a dope addict who would disappear for long periods and otherwise lived in fear of going blind. One of her father's sisters, as well as her father himself, were afflicted by the "shakes." In addition, the father suffered four depressions, one of them when the patient was sick as an infant, another when she left home. He and his brothers had all been such excellent swimmers they were called "ducks." Ayleen had preferred him to her mother and to her grandmother. He was still alive during the patient's treatment but died a number of years afterwards of chronic brain syndrome associated with cerebral arteriosclerosis.

Ayleen's maternal grandmother died during the patient's psychotherapy. Ayleen had been very fond of her, but her maternal grandfather was an alcoholic, extremely tense, and he and a sister of his died of tuberculosis.

Before marriage, the patient's mother had contracted tuberculosis and had to spend a year in Arizona to be cured. The disease recurred during her first pregnancy, which turned out to be a miscarriage. When she became pregnant again, the parents moved to the South where Ayleen's oldest sister was born. Two years later, they moved to another, less southern location. The parents had always been very much in love with one another, and her husband's wishes had always come first with Ayleen's mother.

The mother was very thrifty and bought plain garments without frills, usually heavy and thick. The gifts she gave at Christmas were small. On train trips, she never used the dining car. If it can be said that she was overly prudent, it can also be said that she was overly cautious, even to the point of fear. She was afraid of the dentist, of swimming, and of water, warning the patient as a

child not to go too near to it. When there was lightning, she forbade Ayleen to play the piano, to sew, or to use the telephone. The mother's ostensible derivation for these apprehensions was witnessing in her childhood the damage of a house by lightning. The patient stated that the mother preferred her older daughter and kissed the younger one later in life only. The closest the mother came to talking about the "facts of life" was telling her girls that childbirth was "like having an arm cut off." To quote the patient, "She had a way of making you feel so small and guilty just for nothing." The mother is still alive, a vivacious, self-sufficient woman, and now on excellent terms with her daughter.

Ayleen always felt that she was an unwanted child because she was a third daughter. Her oldest sister died at the age of eight, when the patient was roughly three-and-a-half years old, about a year after two operations had been performed on Ayleen. The patient had been forced to kiss her dead sister. She remembered the cemetery, and in a hypnoanalytic session recalled part of the burial. The patient's second sister developed eczema between her toes when she was a week old and has suffered from eczema all her life. This sister Ayleen described as "shaking" before playing the piano.

Six years after the patient's birth, a brother was born. During this pregnancy, around the time of Easter, the mother cut out of a magazine a picture of a blond boy with a rabbit in his arms, framed it, and remarked that that was what she wanted—a blond boy. Everybody in the family was brown-haired. The brother had endocrine stigmata, was complicated for some time, but is now married and self-supporting.

Ayleen had learned to walk at nine months. She had stopped using baby talk at eight years of age and had sucked her thumb for an unknown amount of time. During a hypnoanalytic session, she had a visualization in which her arms were bound by bandages so that she could not put her finger into her mouth after masturbation; she could not verify this. At two-and-a-half or three years of age, she had pneumonia and a pyothorax. Two operations were necessary, and she was sick for many months. During this time, she also suffered from "convulsions." She said that one of her nurses had "fits," was "a dope fiend," and may have given her

dope. In consequence of this illness, Ayleen had become very weak and insecure, had forgotten how to walk and had to relearn it.

The role this sickness played in the symptoms about which she complained, will become extremely evident. In one of the hypnoanalytic sessions, she recalled a cat seated on her bed, staring at her until she began to cry. At another, Ayleen remembered sitting on the pot trying to grab the cat's tail, whereupon the cat scratched her. Then she visualized learning to walk again, a cat under her arm, trying to "place" her foot on a narrow step descending from the porch, and being paralyzed with fear when the cat suddenly jumped in front of her.

The summer following her illness, when the family went to another state for recuperation, Ayleen had terrible temper tantrums. She would grab her mother's long hair and pull her down by it. She also tore the tablecloth and other objects.

During and after her sickness, the patient experienced a number of exposures of boys and girls. At about four or five years of age, she believed that sex was located in the anal region, and she and a neighbor's little girl exposed this part to one another. Whipping or spanking in school was associated with sexual feelings and therefore regarded as quite humiliating. The patient played at spanking with this neighbor girl. Ayleen's parents often gave her enemas, which she felt as sexual manipulations. Her idea was that they were pleasant but prohibited. She also believed that childbirth occurred in this part of the body. Despite these many anal fantasies and activities, however, there were only few symptoms of an obsessive compulsive reaction detectable in her psychoneurotic disorder.

At ten years of age, Ayleen had a tonsillectomy and was frightened by the mask. At about the same time, her mother told her that her nose was too long, and this made the patient quite self-conscious. For a long time, she cut out paper dolls and stopped this activity at eleven years of age only. Ayleen still cuts her own bangs. Her mother told her that she was complicated in her adolescence and hard to educate, "sassy" was the description.

She had her menarche at eleven and felt "superior" because of it. When she was about twelve, a cousin told her where babies

come from, but she did not believe it. There was no recollection of ever having masturbated. Ayleen started dating at fifteen. Later, she had, and enjoyed, many sexual relations. There were several engagements to be married, but all were broken. Occasionally she went to bed with a man because she was afraid to be alone at night when her roommate was out.

In her first year of treatment, Ayleen had thirty-seven sessions, including twenty-three hypnoses. The next year, there were one hundred and nineteen sessions, including thirty-three hypnoses and hypnoanalyses. The following year, Ayleen came only four times. Then, against my advice, she married a man who had been divorced three times. During this year, there were seven appointments, including two hypnoanalyses. The following year, she had twenty-three sessions, including ten hypnoses and hypnoanalyses. The next year, there were nineteen interviews. Most of the hypnoanalytic sessions that I present were undergone toward the end of the following year when the patient came quite often and regularly. That year there were twenty-one sessions, including five hypnoanalyses. After that, she did not come for three months, but later in the year had ninety interviews, including forty-five hypnoses, most of which were hypnoanalytic sessions. The year after that, there were six more appointments, including five hypnoanalyses. Then, Ayleen left for New England. During her therapy, she rejected every psychoanalytic interpretation.

At the time of her seventy-second hypnoanalytic session, the patient complained of attacks of vasomotor rhinitis and was under treatment by a dentist. I had given her a prescription for Amytal® Sodium (0.1 gr). When the trance state was induced, as had happened many times previously and thereafter, she immediately moved her right hand to the right side of her neck. When she started to cry, she put this hand at her right eye. A trance was very quickly achieved; no suggestions were given, and regression was induced.

"I am just thi-thinking about that I was small. And I can see the way my hair was fixed. And there was a big hair ribbon on top of my head. And I have on a wool dress . . . checked wool, and dark stockings like they are black and a sweater. I feel like I am holding something in my arm. And that I am listening to people

talking and that I am lying down and it seems like I am just been examined or something and I feel very sorry for myself. (Do you have pains somewhere?) No, not particularly. (In what part of your body did you feel that you had the examination?) Well, I don't know yet. I can hear people talking and discussing what should be done. (Do you distinguish their voices? Do you hear words or sentences?) No, not yet. I just know they are talking about me. (Are they in the same room or elsewhere?) Oh, I felt they said a few things while they were around me. It seems as if there were a doctor there. And then he called them out into another room or something. And I heard enough to be very anxious, you know, and terribly sorry for myself. I mean that sounds silly, but just while I was thinking about how sorry I was for myself I felt like I could almost cry. And I—I felt so helpless, you know, being so small and knowing what they were saying. (How old do you suppose you are?) Oh, I should say about—ah. (What is the matter with you?) [cries] (Why are you crying? Why do you put your right hand to your right eye?) I don't know why I—I feel that I am so [cries again] (Just bring it out. Let everything come.) Too young to run away or to defend myself, that I just sort of have to lie there and wait for them to decide what's to be done for me . . . (What is it? Just [cries] talk it out, then you will feel better.) It's funny I don't feel any pain at all. (What is it then?) [cries louder] . . . I just feel it's so unfair . . . Talking or going to do something to a child and they [cries] and. And I can't do anything about it. I don't know. (Do you feel yourself a child?) Yes. (How old do you suppose you could be?) Well, I don't know. I—I shall imagine. (A baby?) No, about three or four years old. The way I—I feel that I looked at that time [sniffle] And I—I keep gripping something in my left arm like a doll or something and [makes unspecific movements with her arms in front of her body] . . . (Just bring [sigh] your feelings and emotions out.) [sigh] (It's much better for you.) I—I—I don't like the feeling that I am feeling sorry for myself. But [whining voice] that's the way I feel. [several sighs] (If you want to feel sorry for yourself, that is your right.) [sighs] . . . . feeling awfully sorry for myself . . . [sighs] (Do you feel that on the right [sniffle] side of your neck?) No, I—I don't feel any twitching there now that. (But you

felt it in the beginning?) Yes, I did. I always feel that just as I am being hypnotized . . . After a while sometimes it leaves me . . . (What do you feel?) [sigh] (Bring it out.) But it seems silly. But I can see it seems like in this dream or whatever it is that my stockings are all baggy. And that I have some sort of a supporter belt with my stockings being held up. And it seems like I feel that I am just ugly as a child . . . And that I wanted to have something more you—I might say frivolous. That here I was in this ugly old wool dress [sigh] . . . And stockings were [sniffle] dark and I thought they should have been white [sniffle]. (Why are you starting to cry again?) . . . I just start to feeling sorry for myself [whining voice]. (The reason for it will come with time. Just talk it out.) Oh, I haven't cried like this in I don't know when. (There is certainly a reason for it, that most probably [sniffles the whole time] you are not yet able to detect. But it will come sooner or later.) Well, I don't know. (What don't you know?) [sniffles] Whatever I was thinking I don't know, it must have kind of left me. (Did the grown-ups frighten you very much?) [sniffle] I thought they were discussing things in front of me that sort of gave me an inkling of something and then they went into another room and . . . (Do you still see them?) . . . I don't see them at all. I—I never have. I just see myself lying there and waiting and thinking how horrible it is to be so, you know, little and . . . they were talking about it I need an operation or—or— (Or what?) Or what they were talking about. (What do you suspect?) I don't know. I—I just feel kind of like I was in an office of some kind. [sniffle] (Do you feel unprotected?) Yes. And I . . . don't know, I get the idea that they were saying that I was going to have to be operated on again. And I was just thinking how horrible it was. But if they were saying that, I would have felt some pain or something and [sighs] I don't. [swallows] (Why did you swallow just now?) I—I don't know . . . And I am just waiting for them to come back and kind of give me the—verdict or whatever it is. [whining voice] I think there are three of them. [sniffle] (Three of them?) Aha. (Who do you suppose they are?) I think it's Mother and Dad and the doctor. [cries] . . . (Do you have the feeling the same thing has happened to you before?) [sniffles] Well, I don't know whether it's that or whether I just

know there is something awful is coming. [sniffles] (Should we stop now?) I don't care. [whining voice] (Or do you want to wait until they come back?) [cries] Oh, I don't know . . . I am just a victim of circumstances and [cries]. (What do you feel?) [sniffles] Nothing more, it's just the same thing. (I believe then we'd better stop.) All right."

The patient woke immediately. On questioning, she stated that she had felt like a small child and now was instantly grown-up. She apparently had the feeling that her behavior had been silly and was reassured by being told that she had stated just the right thing. At the next two interviews, this hypnoanalytic session was played back to her, and her comments on it were set down.

"All of a sudden I was overwhelmed with self-pity. I hate self-pity, they say it is a feeling of weakness . . ."

On being questioned, she stated that she saw her visualizations outside of herself. "I was just looking at my size when you asked me my age. (Did you see yourself in technicolor?) Yes." She described the big hair ribbon attached to a golden clip which her mother had put in her parted hair.

After the playback was finished, Ayleen stated, "I had the feeling I was in a doctor's office. I believe I had a tube in my side, and it did not heal properly, and they brought another surgeon down."

The first operation had been performed by the family doctor. She must have been between two-and-a-half and three-and-a-half years of age. "I cried more than other children. I just always cried."

At the next session, the patient told me that her maternal grandmother had died. Because it happened so shortly after the last hypnoanalytic session, she felt very upset. She had been very fond of this grandmother. Then she revealed that she had had a dream. In it she was under the ground, as though in a coffin. She felt that she could not get out and earth was being thrown over her. Her associations to this dream were that she must have seen earth thrown over her dead sister's coffin. Then she thought of Snow White and the "twelve dwarfs." During the last hypnoanalysis, she had already thought of this movie, about sleep, and about death. The girl was lying there in the dream like the girl in the

movie. Ayleen had been told that her sister's dead body lay at home for several days. However, she only remembered the cemetery and that she pulled at her mother's skirt and asked why everybody was crying. The associations to the dream also refer to the equation of the hypnotic state with death, first described by Schneck.*

This seventy-second hypnoanalytic session dealing with her wait in the doctor's office seems to be an example of a genuine recall of a former ego state, containing the corresponding emotional dispositions, memories, and urges. The patient's indication of her age can be disregarded in this case because she knew how old she was when she was operated upon. Otherwise, there are only four expressions in it that a child would hardly use. These are "unfair," "frivolous," "verdict," and "victim of circumstances." The word "unfair" she might easily have heard and have understood its meaning. This is not likely in the case of the word "frivolous." The sentence was, "And that I [pause] wanted to have something more you—I might say frivolous." Before the word "verdict" there was also a pause in the sentence. "Victim of circumstances" came out without any complications. However, Ayleen stated, on questioning right after the hypnoanalysis, that she had felt like a small child. She never returned to this incident.

The emotions described were appropriate to the occasion. Ayleen felt alone, defenseless, and at the mercy, or rather unmercifulness, of the grown-ups, deeply afraid of what they would decide about her. These emotions returned later in many of her hypnoanalytic sessions. She stated that she would "go into fits" and would cry whenever she heard the doctor's footsteps on the porch the times he came to change her bandages. The infant had regressed, which was only natural as her sickness had bound her to her bed for many months. That she later hated self-pity, is very understandable because each occasion for it reminded her of the time she had been so sick, the generating circumstance for her self-pity.

It is interesting that during the hypnoanalytic session she mentioned her appearance but not the drain in her side. This drain

---

* Schneck, J. M.: The unconscious relationship between hypnosis and death. *Psychoanal Rev, 38*:271, 1951.

she must have carried for many months but either regarded it as part of herself, had incorporated it into her body image, or did not want to be reminded of this sensitive spot. Infants, especially girls, may place more importance on their clothes than their parents suspect because descriptions of poor exterior appearances have been rendered by other patients when they were in distressing situations, apparently as visible expressions of their emotions. Anne's dresses were blue when she was at home and unhappy, red when she was with her grandmother and happy, therefore her color choice had a symbolical significance. Another patient, when asked about the color of her dress, answered "blue" and added spontaneously "checked." In another hypnoanalytic session, this same patient complained that her mother, who apparently was pregnant, wore a black cape and hat. In the next hypnoanalytic session, she again complained about this cape, but also about what she herself was wearing, "That stupid white dress with the white stockings. Why the hell didn't she put a decent pair of socks on me. (Who?) My mother. White, thick stockings. I hated them! And I didn't like white stockings. I wanted silk stockings." She said, on questioning, that she was three or four years of age. Her younger sister had white silk socks, but she was regarded as too big for them. She hated the dress because it was loose, therefore sloppy. Ayleen also felt "ugly"—deserted by all; unable to defend herself.

I may add that, for a long time, the second physician involved had not been mentioned by the patient, and I had been under the impression that both operations were performed by the same doctor. Ayleen gave me the idea that the original doctor had not much understanding for the feelings and the emotions of a small child and that she retaliated. She said in a subsequent interview that her parents later changed to another family physician, apparently under the influence of her contention.

The seventy-fourth hypnoanalytic session was performed because the patient complained that when she was waiting in line for some sort of test, she started to "shake" although she had taken Amytal Sodium beforehand. She became very tense, excused herself, and went home. Tension and anxiety were still present the next day. She had "a splitting headache," felt nauseated, and could not eat. The day afterwards, she was well.

Even before the hypnosis was induced, Ayleen put her right hand on the right side of her neck and stated that she felt twitching there. Here is the transcript:

"(You dream you remember why you were so frightened and tense and what the real reason was for your tension when you were about to take the test. Please talk.) Well, I was thinking about waiting in line. And it would be my time to move or to act and that I wouldn't be able to move when my turn came . . . And I couldn't explain that to them why I couldn't move. That was my whole reason; what if I felt kind of paralyzed . . . ? (You dream you [soft sob] remember why you should feel paralyzed when you are waiting in line. [cries softly] Please sleep as deeply as possible. [louder crying] Why are you crying? Please talk. [sobs] Why do you move your right hand to your right eye?) I don't know . . . As—as if I were trying to move my legs and I couldn't move them. [loud sobbing] (When did this happen?) I —I was in bed or something and I [loud sniffle] tried to lift them up and I—I couldn't move. [sniffle] I knew I was supposed to move them but . . . (How did you know and who made you think you had to move them?) [sob] . . . . I—I must have been in bed. [sniffle] I don't—I didn't have anything, my legs in splints or anything but I—I was trying to get up and [sob] I couldn't move [last three words with a desperate inflection] . . . (Quiet down. [sniffling] Sleep very deep. Deeper, ever deeper. And you remember [sniffles] when it happened that you should have moved your legs and were not able to do so.) I can't even remember moving my arms. (Why not?) I don't know—know. But I—I felt so weak that I [sniffle]—I couldn't even sit up. I couldn't even move to get up. (How old do you suppose you were?) Oh, I don't know. I—I would say about two or three years old. [sniffle] (You are sleeping very deeply. Deeper and deeper. And you dream and you remember more [louder sniffles] about this happening. Please, just remember.) I—I was so weak I—I just couldn't even get the energy to—to—to raise myself up. I knew I should be able to move . . . my arms up and my legs . . . I couldn't even raise them up like that [raises her legs less than an inch from the couch] . . . (You mean [sniffle] you could not even raise them one or two inches?) No. (As you raise them now?) No,

no! [very emphatic] . . . I was just too weak . . . I—I knew I should have the strength to get up and I couldn't. (Any connection with your operation?) I—I must have been sick in bed and I was lying there. [sniffle] (Was your mother or somebody else in the room?) No, I don't think anybody was in the room . . . (Why did you try to get out of bed?) Because I felt I should be able to get up like anybody else. And . . . I was flat on my back and I—I felt so [sigh] sort of frightened that I couldn't move. (You dream [sobbing starts again] you remember. You dream you remember more about this occasion. What happened then? Please talk.) I—I just felt helpless and afraid . . . I just had to lie there, perfectly still . . . (Had something frightened you?) No. I just felt that I couldn't move. . . . (Were you able to move before today?) I couldn't remember that I—that I had moved at all. I just knew that all of a sudden I was too weak to move. [sniffle] (Sleep deeper, always deeper. Remember other details in connection with this event. Please talk.) Well, I was trying to figure out how I could move the back of my neck to get up and down my backbone. If I shouldn't be able to get the strength in the back to how you first get up from a lying down position how you. Where the strength starts to get you going and why you can't get the strength in the back of your neck and down your back to—to once get up off the bed and off the pillow and then how you get up from there. . . . (You dream you remember what happened before that made [sigh] you so weak. Please tell me.) I had the feeling that I had . . . bandages and splints all on both arms and I don't guess I ever did that. I don't know why. And I had the feeling my legs were in splints and bandages all over—all over. My arms and legs I felt were in stiff splints the way I could move them. [sniffle] When I put my arm out, I couldn't get my thumb into my mouth . . . I was just stiff as a bone. . . . my legs were . . . the way I couldn't even bend them. Then I—I was so tied down the way I was so helpless to move. (Do you know [sniffle] who put all those splints on you?) No. But there were a lot of light gauze and bandages all over . . . I guess that isn't true. I don't know why that should be but that's the way I had the feeling. (There is most probably [sigh] a reason for that feeling.) . . . It's just as if I were a mummy all wrapped up in this gauze. (You dream you remember the reason

for this feeling that you are in splints, or maybe you were really in splints. Which is it?) Well, I just had the feeling that I am lying there by myself [sniffle]. And wondering why I was all wrapped up . . . and just so bewildered . . . (Why didn't you cry?) I don't know. I guess I did. (Did you call [starts sobbing] for your mother?) No. . . . (Why didn't you call [cries] for your mother? Do you know?) No . . . I was just supposed to keep lying there by myself [sobs]. (Sleep very deep. [cries] You still remember a few more details about what happened at that particular moment or what happened before.) Well, I–I can kind of see myself in . . . a little sort of a flannel nightgown. [sniffle] I was so weak that I could just turn my head this way and that way. Somewhere that is where my neck comes in, I think I just turned that way and my head hit back and forth. (You tossed your head back and forth.) Yes, like this. That's all I could move. [sobs, moves her head] (That is, to the right and to the left.) Aha, that's all I could move. (But how did it come about that just the [sniffle] right side always gives you this twitching and not the left side?) I don't know. I just keep putting my hand up like that all the time. (That is what I see. You started even before the hypnosis.) . . . It seems like it's something that runs up all the time. [moves her right hand from shoulder to ear] (From your shoulder to your ear?) Yes. Right in here. Up that vein or something in there and I just keep my head this way and turn right and left. (Why are you starting to cry again?) I just feel sorry for myself all the time. [sob] . . . (Just talk it out. Get rid of it.) . . . I am just wondering if I was ever going to be able to move or if I ever am. [sobbing] And I am always by myself . . . (Your mother never comes?) No. Nor my sisters. Just-I just always lie there by myself. . . . (Why is she always with your sisters?) Well, it isn't that she is with them, but they are supposed to stay out of the room . . . [sniffle] (Why are they supposed to stay out of the room?) Because I am supposed to be quiet. (Why?) Not to be disturbed. [sob] (Are you so sick?) No. I–I am not in pain. (What is the reason then?) I don't know. . . . I am [sigh] lying there just trying to recuperate . . . (You can still dream and remember more details regarding what really happened and why you felt so weak.) I couldn't remember having been up before that. And I was wondering if– if I could move if I was sure I could move. (Yes.) If I did try if I

weren't so weak and wondering why I was so tied down and so weak that I couldn't get up and just trying from the back all the time to move. [sniffle] (Is this all or do you suppose you could remember something more?) I don't think I can any more. (You mean that's all?) Yes. (Shall we stop?) . . . I guess so. I think I have gone as far as I could go."

After the hypnoanalytic session, the patient stated, on questioning, that she felt perfectly well. However, she did not want to hear an excerpt played back and left the room as fast as she could.

She stated in the next interview that she did not believe that we had "hit the real cause" in the hypnoanalytic session. She said that when she had to wait in line to get off a train, she was afraid of whether she would be able to coordinate as in a performance. "It is like a puppet. What comes first, arms or legs?" During the hypnoanalytic session, she had had the feeling she could move only her head and was not supposed to move any other part of her body because of the tube in her side. She believed that she had really always been left alone. At the test, she said somebody in uniform should have taken her down; this might also have increased her tension. The Amytal Sodium she had taken before the examination had only made her dizzy.

At the following session, she was sure that she had been tied down in some way. After the hypnoanalytic session was played back to her, Ayleen stated that she had already forgotten saying at its beginning that she had no splints on.

However, in the session after the next, she complained that "one foot suddenly stops, one leg, just for a second sometimes when I go down the stairs as if I couldn't move it. . . . A block comes down as if I were suddenly paralyzed . . . If I had splints on or not, something was on me to prevent me to move, I am sure about."

The question of whether or not the patient had had splints, bandages, and gauze on her in the amount she described, was never completely solved. There may have been splints to prevent the development of a pes equinus, but they would not have extended to the knees. It is also possible that the physician put splints on her arms to keep her from disarranging the bandages and touching the wound. On the other hand, one wonders how

much damage so weak a child really could have wrought, even if she were able to move her arms.

Ayleen presented another interesting piece of information during this hypnoanalytic session. She did not feel like a child, but was looking down at herself. For instance, she observed that her little nightgown was split on both sides. She also judged her age according to her height.

Comparing Ayleen's hypnoanalytic visualizations to Anne's, I find Ayleen regularly used much longer sentences to describe them. Both patients stated that they visualized occurrences as in a color movie. However, in observing each I had the feeling that Anne always *was* an infant and Ayleen often *saw* an infant despite her strong emotional reactions and expressive movements, although there were other hypnoanalytic sessions after which Ayleen stated clearly that she had felt like an infant in addition to seeing herself as an infant. On other occasions, she only felt herself an infant.

Three expressions in the last hypnoanalytic session which would hardly be used by such an infant are "paralyzed," "energy," and "recuperate." The word "paralyzed" she stated at the beginning when she described her inability to move before the test. For the other two expressions I have no explanation.

The feelings of loneliness, helplessness and utter isolation returned very often. It should not be forgotten that time passes for a child much more slowly than it does for a grown-up. There were also a few hypnoanalytic sessions in which the patient stated that her mother was in the room. Once, the mother prayed and cried (96th H.) which upset the sick girl very much. Her father's room was next to hers and he was there suffering from one of his depressions. It is quite improbable that the mother, a devoted and tender person, did not quite often look into the room and that even the father watched over his invalid daughter. Whether the parents did not want to disturb their desperately sick child or had been told not to do so by the physician is impossible to decide. However, despite what will be stated in the next paragraph, there must have been sufficient occasions to identify with the members of her devoted family because Ayleen is a very considerate and lovable person.

Her opportunity to develop a strong and mature ego was very slim, however. Weak and sick for many months, she had regressed, the illness eliminating, as it did, opportunities for psychical activity, for independence, for criticism, for logic, for concentration. But she had plenty of time to spin fantasies and most of the time experienced people as aggressors, also projecting her own aggressions onto them. For the principal part, she identified physically and psychically with inimical objects and was as constantly afraid of grown-ups as of pain or other bodily discomforts. Her inability to move, her incapacity for flight contributed to her capitulation to fears and frustration. The development of a somewhat mature ego came later, by repressing a good part of her illness and the fantasies connected with it. Ayleen's current symptoms represented—mostly by derivatives—many of the emotions she had felt during and shortly after her ailment. The patient's motor disturbances were identifications with a past ego state when her weakness and immobilization prevented coordinated movements.

In many hypnoanalytic sessions, Ayleen provided different explanations for the sensations in her neck. Once she mentioned that she had been given an injection in the right side of her neck. Another time she said that she had stabbed herself there with a knife, adding in the same hypnoanalysis that this was fantasy. On other occasions she said the doctor had pressed his nails into this spot, cut her there, was preparing to decapitate her, and do other harm.

It is known that irritations of the pleura give rise to pains in the shoulder region of the same side. A few years ago, Ayleen's mother, when questioned, replied that her daughter had never had an injection in the neck.

Later, the patient even compared herself to Jesus Christ nailed to the cross, his head hanging limply to the side, and his blood running down. Thus, she used in a double sense the word "nail." She demonstrated the position of crucifixion by bending both arms and putting both hands on the lateral ends of her collarbones. When she was reminded after this hypnoanalytic session that Christ had his arms outstretched, she answered that she had only now realized this. I may add that Ayleen is a Methodist, had had an excellent religious education, and not only went to church

regularly as a child and as an adolescent, but often played there as a musician.

At the following interview she said she was sure that blood was "streaking" down from Christ's shoulder. She also had no recollection of the spear in Christ's side. She was told that blood had run from his palms, feet and side. In the hypnoanalysis in the same session, she lamented the unbearable pain she had experienced at the change of her dressings, and was asked whether she could remember that the previous day she had forgotten about the spear in Christ's side. She answered that she could not recall but "I didn't like the sight of blood. And ah, the sight of blood was very upsetting to me when I even saw it on my bandages. And ah, I have forgotten the flashes before that they tried to keep that away from me. Anything with blood on it. But I would see it. And every time I saw the sight of blood, it was a very horrible thing."

It may be of interest here to set forth a later hypnoanalytic session which had more bearing on Ayleen's reactions to the changing of her bandages than that which has been previously mentioned. This is the one-hundred-and-second hypnoanalytic session following the one during which she had described Jesus Christ. Ayleen started with her hands at her waistline. During the induction of hypnosis, she began to jerk. Later, she placed her right hand laterally below the collarbone. I did not induce regression.

"(A while ago, you started to jerk both your hands at your waistline. Did you see or feel anything?) Oh, I feel at the verge of crying. And on the back, the tears are coming out, but I can't quite—ah . . . I don't—ah, quite know what it was. I had a quick flash of a . . . holding my arms down. Holding me some way to where I couldn't—ah—move and that's why I—I was jerking so, because they took off the bandage and lay the bandage open like that. And—(Was the bandage on your side?) Yes. That was a wide bandage and they took it off and laid it back to where my side was exposed. And I couldn't even stand the thought of my side being exposed, because . . . [slurred] I would yell. And I needed to do something to it because the fact that they had gotten the bandage off. (Yes?) And I was all exposed meant they were going to touch it. . . . [cries] (Talk it out.) [sniffle] And I—I didn't know what when they had gotten the bandage off, they were going to

do something [sniffle]. And I was completely helpless to do anything, I had just to lay there. And wait for them to start. And the anxiety of that knowing it was going to be painful and so tender, it just almost used to drive me crazy. And I was—start jerking before. It just. When they just started to . . . take off the bandage, I—I—I—I would begin to just get wild. And the—(What?) . . . And when they got there into the last layer . . . I got the idea that my side was exposed. Between that moment and the moment when they did touch it, I was just I can't tell you how wild . . . just every second they were going to start. And then—(Bring it out.) And ah, I always get that wild when they get . . . the electric light bulb and ah—they get that on the—this long extension and bring it over, and put it down at the side of the bed so they could look in better. And when they start all that procedure, I was just, I get—I just thought oh, I just can't bear it again, I—I just go' to go crazy. . . . (You just stopped jerking.) And ah, I don't know where they held me down [sniffle] or whether they tied me sometime so I could not move and turn and twist . . . to where I was completely helpless to move. And ah—ah, sometime just a moment ago I got the flash of that light when they turned the light on . . . And the flash of the light made me think of lightning and I wonder if there is any connection between my awful anxiety, about faint [slurred] the that light is going to flash and the feeling of lightning. (Talk it out.) And to me that was the first indication . . . That was just the signal that I needed that they were going to start looking and probing and—and doing that bandage . . . my side was exposed and how awful—awful anxiety at that moment and waiting for them to start touching it. Just—just at that moment I just had to jerk. Because it was so horrible. (Is this the same feeling as when you expect something to explode?) No . . . They I think trying to keep me from knowing what they were going to do until they had to let me know. (That is not what I asked [sniffle]. I mean, until you expect some sudden noise to come.) No. Aha. No. I don't think it's related to that at all . . . (Did you see the flash of light at the same time as they exposed your side?) Yes. . . . when they begin working that—that light would go on . . . And when they started just going inside the incision I just get wild. And, just talking about it now is making both

my legs jerking in back of my knees. And tremble terrible because when they were working around my side, I would just lay and just tremble . . . In both legs and my arms. . . . I would—would shake just like this and shake constantly. And even my—the—ne—back of my neck would pull on in the back all the muscles down my back, they pull always on such tenterhooks waiting for that pain to strike. And, ah—I was just like this trying to hold my breath and just praying they would hurry and get over with. And ah, i-i-it was—it was an unbearable moment that I can't tell you [soft sobbing] (Can you remember, and tell me the prayer?) No, I was, I don't know what I prayed about but I mean that's my way of expressing it now. I just would hope every second would be the last. And when they were doing that I just be shaking just like this . . . I—I don't know they must have had the, to get my arm back like this someway . . . (The right one?) [sniffle] I guess they had to, to get in there and look at it. I guess they had to hold me back. And—(Your trembling is in reality a little less than in the beginning.) Oh, the knees, my knees i-it's all jerking inside the way you can't see it. . . . And ah, sometimes I feel that ah, they may must have been holding my arm back like this, they—ah—must have had my head maybe like this, you see so that. (Onto your collarbone.) Like, like that. So when they pulled my arm back and held my arm like this, oh, my hand must have rested right there. And ah—(On the side of the chest.) . . . But I was so-o-o nervous that I—I just shook constantly inside. I can't even describe it to you. . . . They were doing the dressing and I don't think they probed very often, but they had to change the dressing . . . I couldn't even stand it. (That's obvious.) And ah, I get my head over like this. Oh, I was so tense and I would shake. (That I can see.) . . . all over. And to tremble constantly until they got through. And recently nervous and tremble now just to recall that —that this awful feeling that I had. (Can you remember [sniffle] the reason why you forgot yesterday about the spear in Christ's side?) No. I don't, except that I didn't like the sight of blood. And ah, the sight of blood was very upsetting to me when I even saw it on my bandages. And ah, I have gotten the flashes before that they tried to keep that away from me, the, anything with blood on it. (That's clear. They would always do that.) And ah,

but I would see it. And every time I saw the sight of blood it was a very horrible thing . . . it gives me a very weak, sick feeling . . . I get a very funny feeling when I—I can't stand it when I look at the blood . . . Christ clung with his hand [sniffle] and the blood streaming down to the hand. But I don't recall it from there in the side. Because, I guess, having seen the blood on the bandages giving me such a—a feeling of distaste and fear that I didn't want t-to have any connection with blood around. (Out of Christ's side came not only blood, but water too. Don't you remember?) No . . . I don't remember any part of the story there. (Why are you trembling more now?) Oh, my legs have never stopped and I am quivering inside. (I can see it.) Ever since I—ah, get up down in deep into the hypnosis I started and I just haven't stopped. And it is inside more than you can see. I think the reason I get that sudden jerk is that they would do something that was particularly painful you know . . . (I can now see it strongly on the right side.) I guess sometimes they touch me and they finally get out. I guess it has been in for a long time. (Talk it out. Get rid [sniffle] of it.) I feel it all the way down in my back. And down in my spine and all those nerve centers. I was so tense, you see, and so nervous that ah, it was both in and out, so far as expression was concerned. . . . And ah, it's ah, too horrible to try and tell. (You have had your entire right hand for some time on the end of your collarbone.) Yes. (But at the beginning, for quite some time, you did not have it there.) No, i-it changes. I don't know how to explain the change. But it—it changes very often . . . And the tender spot. And ah, it's funny when I get deep in hypnosis, I just start trembling inside now like this and I—I don't know how to explain it or how to stop it and that, it just trembles out that way. (It doesn't matter.) If I am terribly too long, you can stop it. (Just talk.) I don't know if I have anything more to say. (Are you sure?) I don't feel I do." Ayleen then awakened very quickly, without trembling or jerking.

In the next session, the patient was shown John 19:34 in the Bible, where Jesus's side was described as being opened with a spear. Saying that she did not have any recollection of this, she remarked that menstruation, blood, and cramps might have some related meaning for her. Also that light was like lightning. It was

a signal that something would happen to her. Already the long extension cord of the lamp brought in alarmed her that her incision would again be examined.

As I have already stated, Ayleen was never as deep in hypnosis as Anne and most of the other patients were. Despite this and the fact that she even told me spontaneously at times to induce a deeper trance or used the word "hypnosis" in different connections, she not only had very vivid visualizations but also brought out the accompanying emotions very well. Appropriately, her motor reactions to recalled events were such as an infant would have. It could be asked why the doctor had not made things easier for her. He may not have fully realized how painful his manipulations were or may have been afraid that any not absolutely essential drug would be harmful to the sick infant. Apparently, he did the best he could under the circumstances and did, in any event, save her life. But through associations, everything connected with the original highly traumatic occurrences brought back the jerking, trembling, and other complications about which Ayleen complained in her anamnesis and later on.

This may also be an explanation for Mitch's various muscular phenomena. By coming in direct contact with his many relatives in the small community where he lived, or indirectly through associations, he was often reminded of what they had been able to inflict on him. As an infant and child, when he trembled in fear of them, he had had aggressive impulses which he had to suppress and/or to repress. The trembling he experienced when shaving himself, might be interpreted as representing envy of his older brothers, or fear that one of them might harm him with the razor, or that he himself might harm some member of the family with it, or all of these emotions together.

Ayleen never spoke of any vengeful fantasy against the grownups though she did report in hypnoanalytic sessions that she had bitten the physician, had pulled his hair, and so on. Her temper tantrums during the summer following her sickness and her aggression against her mother are indicators of her suppressed and/or repressed intentions, wishes, and fantasies; her prolonged cutting out of paper dolls is also suspicious in this respect, as is the fact that she still cut her own bangs.

Her amnesia for the wounding of Christ is interesting, repressing, as it did, an incident that must surely have reminded her of her own ailment although, in her own case, not blood and water, but blood and pus came out after her side had been "lanced." In one hypnoanalytic session, she remembered the bad smell of pus. Her description of "blood streaming down to the hands" of Christ was also inaccurate.

In another hypnoanalytic session, the patient stated that she was afraid that her insides would be taken out, or had already been taken out, through the opening in her side, as is done with a chicken. In this same hypnoanalysis, she wondered whether "they" would cut off her head the way a chicken or a turkey is beheaded. This was not simply castration anxiety, but annihilation anxiety which, in her case, had a very real basis. The fantasy of the decapitated and eviscerated chickens emerged very early in her therapy and returned time and again. She had often seen her paternal grandmother bind the feet of a chicken, decapitate it and clean it out, the remembrance of which probably being a symbol for her fears for her bodily intactness.

After her one-hundred-and-second hypnoanalytical session, Ayleen came for about twenty-one further interviews, the last six of them some months apart. When she was asked thirteen years later about her hypnoanalytic sessions, she told me that she remembered them quite well although, after the seventy-second hypnoanalytic session, very few had been played back to her. This was occasioned by lack of time. The patient was on the verge of moving to New England. She also stated in 1965, that the right side of her neck and her right arm had bothered her very little for the last ten or twelve years, which would put the date somewhere between 1953 and 1955, or from one to three years after the termination of her regular psychotherapy. This is not to say that she had no symptoms in between. Her husband proved to be very difficult; later he became unreasonable and sick and lost his business. There were, indeed, many unpleasant occurrences which, for short periods, brought back some of her complications. However, she was able to bear up very well under these different strains. For a number of years, she has been back in the musical field, is self-supporting, runs her own home in another community in New

England, has boy friends, and is very content with her way of life.

When the patient visited me in 1966, I gave her this chapter to read. She told me that she was sure that what she had recalled during hypnoanalytic sessions, had actually happened. She felt well and was successful and satisfied. Her chronically ailing husband had obtained financial help from other sources and was no burden on her though she still provided tender care for him.

I have intentionally written up Ayleen's family history very carefully. Heredity has for many years played a minor role in the theoretical formulations about the genesis of psychophysiological autonomic and visceral disorders, pyschoneurotic disorders, and personality disorders whereas, in former times, it may have been overrated. An approach in which heredity is taken into some account, would seem preferable to me. Whether such complications are inherited, or a disposition to them is inherited, or whether the exposure of an infant to its "nervous" relatives and the accompanying family disturbances make such individuals more prone to later complications or provide a pattern of reactions during breakdowns is impossible to decide. However, this patient's family history showed so much disturbance in its different members that some hereditary influence on her cannot be excluded. In many cases, a family history is not available for any number of reasons; but where it exists, I feel it should be taken into consideration.

Each of Ayleen's hypnoanalytic sessions presented a well-rounded picture with recognizable background and logically progressing activity on the part of the persons involved. But at times associations arose which switched the theme to other areas. The patient reported quite a number of recurring symbols, mainly of her own body. She used much longer sentences than Anne did. She did not speak like a child or an infant. This made the reproduction of the patient's speech in hypnoanalyses easier than in other cases. She not only reiterated the same description in a particular hypnoanalytic session, but brought it up in her hypnoanalyses over and over again—although with some changes—and, in this way, worked through her problems.

III

OBSESSIVE COMPULSIVE REACTION

AL*

A L, who had a serious problem with alcohol, had been referred to me from a reputable hospital, where one psychiatrist had made the diagnosis of a mild schizophrenia and the chief of the service had set him down as a schizoid personality with superimposed psychoneurosis. During the course of treatment, I changed this diagnosis for reasons which will become apparent during the presentation of the case. His complaints, expressed during our initial interviews, were that he was run down, nervous, upset, "blue," and that he had a poor appetite and slept badly. More often than not, he suffered from feelings of guilt with the impression, at times, that others could read on his face how "bad" he was. He rarely felt that he was as good as the next person, and although his symptoms abated somewhat during his stay in the hospital, it was generally mornings and nights only, in the absence of people. So great was his self-consciousness that to relax he drank on a daily basis some twenty whiskeys chased with beer. For a long time, his explanation for this condition was a simple, "I am just born shy."

It should also be mentioned that, at the hospital, Al had received eight electroshock treatments and two Pentothal® Sodium interviews, after one of which he had been hypnotized. He com-

---

* This patient was discussed in Social anxiety, early sexual and aggressive theories as revealed through hypnoanalysis. *Psychoanal Rev, 87*:44-81, 1957, was referred to briefly in Past ego states emerging in hypnoanalysis. *Int J Clin Exp Hypno, 13*: 132-143, 1965, and still more briefly in other papers. It was always necessary to curtail the number and the length of the hypnoanalytic sessions in these articles, however, and so most of those herein presented have never been published.

plained about a faulty memory for many months afterwards—probably due to the electroshocks.

When he came to me for treatment, the patient was twenty-eight years of age, single and by occupation a truck driver on the night run. He could be described as good-looking. His hair was dark and his skin was light. In later sessions, he revealed that he was the only one in his family who was fair-skinned. This fact may have given him at an early age, a sense of being "different" or "separate" from others. As a young adult, he underwent a rhino-plasty after having obsessively abused his nose for many years. He offered for this operation the explanation that when he was a child he lived in a Jewish neighborhood, was frequently thought to be a Jew, and was scolded for not keeping the Sabbath. He claimed to prefer Irish people to Italians and Jews because "they ask fewer questions." The patient manifested a tendency towards over-cleanliness and, for many months, blushed constantly during his interviews.

Aside from this, he was punctual, cooperative, and intelligent, but almost unable to associate. He doubted his recollections; he doubted every explanation and interpretation; he almost doubted his own doubts. For a long period of time as well, he was unable to comprehend symbols or the transference. What helped him greatly in the therapy was his mother's and older sister's substantiation of certain of his early memories regarding his father's "dirty habits."

The patient had two sisters, one three years his senior, whom he described as a "show-off;" the other, three years his junior, referred to as "the baby." He also had a younger brother, whose arm had been crippled by osteomyelitis, and a still younger brother, who died at the age of seven.

During his childhood and early adolescence, Al slept in a small room and in a small bed with his sisters, even long after the older sister had had her menarche. He lay against the wall, his older sister next to him, and the younger one on the outside. He could never remember what took place between supper and breakfast, or whether he and his siblings had put on their nightclothes. But from his bed he was able to observe his parents' sexual life and felt very guilty about it. He did display scoptophilic tendencies.

His parents were Italian in origin. His mother married his father to escape from a spinster aunt, who had taken over her rearing after she had been orphaned. Her husband had been her social inferior, and she once told Al that she should have left him immediately after their marriage. Instead, both parents emigrated to the United States and settled on the Lower East Side of Manhattan. Many of Al's statements, and much of his behavior which appeared to be schizophrenic or schizoid, were nothing but repetitions, elaborations and consequences of his parents' superstitions, ignorance, and fear. Because he had been incapacitated by rickets for a good part of his infancy and had had little contact with anyone but his parents, the opportunities to correct these early impressions were denied him. "I had no choice," he said, "if my parents condemn me continually. They were my whole world." There may also have been a language barrier because he was told in school that he had a foreign accent and also because the few times he heard his parents talk in his hypnoanalytic sessions, it was in an Italian dialect. He expressed a dislike for the Italian tongue.

The patient described his mother as good-looking, with a somewhat lighter complexion than that of other members of the family. Her schooling consisted of the first two grades of elementary school; her household and kitchen habits were unclean and sloppy. He recalled that, during his infancy, his mother made artificial flowers at home and did other types of work to add to the family income. Apparently devout, the woman avoided eating certain foods on weekends because of a religious vow she had taken, and, in addition, spent several hours a day in church. Their early quarters were invariably infested with rats and mice, and even now Al avoided eating in the house which the family had owned and lived in for the past several years, purchased with the patient's savings, because of the "filthy" kitchen.

The patient's father was a furrier and tailor, and possessed sufficient literacy to read American newspapers. It is apparent from the patient's descriptions and recollections of him that the man had a sociopathic personality with sexual deviation and that he suffered from a psychoneurotic hypochondriacal reaction, and from alcoholism as well. In his youth, for a time, Al felt sorry for

his father and would accompany him on his numerous visits to hospital outpatient departments, probably as a kind of reaction formation. His father never took the drugs prescribed, and the patient, in relating this array of symptomatology to his own disturbances, said, "It all adds up to an extreme fear of death. Maybe, all I have seen from my father, all this display of anxiety."

The patient had also seen his father brought home by friends dead drunk after being absent from home for several days. He had, in addition, seen his father experience several attacks of delirium tremens which terrified Al since, in his own words, his father ". . . appeared dying or out of his mind."

His father had other traits which made a deep impression on Al —what the patient referred to as his father's "dirty habits." These included never taking a bath, masturbating visibly and frequently, with his hands in his trousers, manipulating both the genital and rectal areas, and evacuating into a pot. The patient mentioned his father's "dirty-smelling" fingers and revealed that only a few years ago did his father begin to improve in this respect.

The patient remembered well his father's violent behavior and his threats of violence. Time and again, even in the presence of neighbors, the father had threatened to cut off Al's penis. He also threatened to chop off his hands, especially when he thought the boy was masturbating. Then, expressed in an Italian term that combined both the genitalia and the anus, was the threat to kick Al in the rectum. That these threats were regarded seriously is demonstrated by an early fear the patient had of being crippled for the rest of his life, of never becoming "whole" again. Whether the threats materialized or not, the father did nearly kill his older daughter in the course of smashing her baby carriage. However, whether the father, as a rule, abused this daughter and the patient equally, is difficult to say, but many of the patient's hypnoanalytic sessions bespeak the fact that he did. The girl was very cold to the father, though close to the mother. Nor were other sources of fear scant in the patient's early life. Both parents, in ghost stories, tales of the "Black Hand" and of a "dangerous black dog," provided them liberally. Quite late in his treatment, Al stated that his parents still talked about such things.

Together with neighbors, Al's mother and father made wine

illegally in the back yard. The grapes were crushed under boots, then taken into the apartment where the entire family inhaled the fumes. The effervescing of the wine frightened the patient. He had the feeling that something in the liquid was alive but never received an "intelligent answer" to his questions about what was taking place. The children were served a share of wine in water, and if they became unruly as a result of drinking, were told that they had "worms" inside their bodies. Also ascribed to worms "coming out from drinking," was the vomiting the father did when he overindulged. There is more said about these "worms" later on. What is interesting here is that the patient himself could never throw up and that, later in life, he could not drink wine. "I knew it was not made sanitary," was the reason given.

Other data about the patient's early period are that he was a normal birth, that the mother was extremely proud of the fact that all of her children were "dry" by seven months of age, that Al was so rigid in this respect that, as early as 18 months of age, he could urinate at home only. His mother told him that as an infant he already felt "ashamed."

The patient was weaned at twelve months of age and afterwards was largely fed black coffee or caraway seeds in water. He was able to walk at eleven months of age, but at about eighteen months, had both the measles and a bad case of rickets, and his legs became so bowed he was able to do no more than crawl inside the apartment and when he was outside he had to be carried by his mother.

Successful operations were performed on both legs when he was three-and-one-half or four years of age, and he had to learn to walk again. He said in one hypnoanalytic session that, when he saw his legs after the removal of the casts, he felt castrated. There were other situations which contributed to sexual confusion. Up to his fifth year, his mother dressed him in skirts, and he resented being taken for a girl. On the other hand, he had often wished to be a girl, he said, because they were treated "more tenderly," and while in the hospital, he had been shamed because he played with dolls.

In the area of further early development, there is other information concerning the mother's methods of training her offspring.

And here, too, we can say that fear was the principal parental device in the patient's early existence—an instrument for protection as well as oppression. To avert the possibility of drowning, the mother warned Al never to go near the East River because children were cut up and thrown into its waters. She also told him not to walk close to the houses as some mysterious "they" might pull him down into the cellar. His mother never kissed him, caressed him, or put him on her lap. In this regard, he was not worse off than his siblings. He was beaten often, however. Once, she had forgotten that she had sent him on an errand, and when he returned, whipped him so hard that his ear went "bad," his gums bled, and his head was full of "bumps." She often gave him laxatives and soap enemas; the latter frightened him very much. She told him that she gave them to him "to get the worms out." At other times, she indicated that they were a punishment. At a later age, the patient would feel the urge to have a bowel movement when he felt very happy. Often, his mother dumped him out into the hallway of the apartment, and he felt lost. Before he was two, he had to use the dirty hall toilet of which he was very much afraid.

Al's mother had still other educational gambits. When he once asked her about the holes in Christ's hands, she answered that, if he was naughty, he would be nailed in the same way. She also told him that little dwarfs would come and carry him away, or that the Devil would appear out of the sink. When he complained about his chilblains' itching, she said it was caused by lying, which he always did. Imitating his sisters, he occasionally stole from his mother's purse and felt quite guilty. Another time, his mother cautioned him to be good, otherwise the Lord would pass a wand over him and make his penis disappear so he would not be able to urinate. When she saw him playing with his navel, she said that it would open and he would die. She also threatened to put him under an older woman's skirts, apparently to suffocate him. On the other hand, in his infancy, he experienced erections when he looked under the skirt of an older woman, and had had fantasies about intercourse a tergo.

When his parents made sausages and used the "meatmasher" to mince the meat, they threatened to grind him up in the same way if he misbehaved. Should the boy ask what these sausages were

made of, he was told that "cats and dogs" were in them. For each sausage they filled "the gut of a pig" and tied it up at both ends. These sausages also had some connection with the "worms" already mentioned.

Worms played an important role in this boy's rearing. When his mother spoke of worms, for instance, it was of a kind quite different from the one a neighbor first talked to him about. This neighbor, whom Al described as a sadist, told the patient that he had a worm in his rectum. Al was never sure whether it was in his rectum or in his genitalia; he only felt it was something "unmentionable." On another occasion, he stated. "The minute I got an erection, I thought the worm takes over. He was a symbol for the Devil." It would enter through the rectum and make him "mischievous." Al went on "It takes possession of me . . . would have pleasure at my expense . . . Then it faded away." Asked whether it had anything to do with homosexuality, he answered, "I guess, yes, but I was never a homosexual."

The patient, however, reported fantasies, dreams, and had hypnoanalytic sessions which indicated a latent homosexuality. As a boy, he had had daydreams about other boys, which he called "crushes." He fantasized hugging and kissing them although he did not get an erection at the time. On the one hand, he stated that he wished for companionship; on the other hand, he thought about active anal intercourse and felt very guilty about it. At about fifteen years of age, these fantasies diminished. There were a few passive homosexual experiences at ten, twelve, or thirteen years of age, which he found unpleasant. Until he was treated, he refused to frequent the YMCA because he believed that the place was full of homosexuals. At other times, he told me that people could see on his face that he was a homosexual. These feelings disappeared during his treatment, and he began spontaneously to visit the "Y" regularly because he liked the activities.

Before describing the other kinds of "worms" in Al's case, it may be well to enlarge on his sexual history. Al must have seen all members of his family in the nude from infancy onward. Even as an infant, he had been afraid that his erections would be detected. Most probably, the sexual manipulations by his older sister, which he described in his hypnoanalytic sessions, did take place and

frightened him. Especially in puberty, he had fantasies about his mother and older sister, but he regarded sex as evil. Another day-dream involved a neighbor's daughter; she was "angel-like;" he made love to her and felt ashamed.

From about eight until fifteen years of age, he had fantasies about having intercourse with a horse. "My feelings toward the horse were like for a woman." He admitted the horse could have been a symbol for his mother since, as an infant, he had been ter-ribly afraid of horses also. When he came for treatment, he was able to have intercourse with a married woman or a divorcee only, and only in an automobile; even then, he was often impotent. He felt that his penis was somehow malformed, insecurely at-tached to him, that it might remain in the female. This was a con-sequence of having seen his father's erections before, but not the flaccid state after intercourse.

The patient believed that the reason he developed late, as dem-onstrated by the fact that he did not need to shave fully until he was nineteen or twenty, was a fear he had of adult responsibility.

Returning to the subject of "worms," I asked Al once, in some context, whether he felt that there are worms in water. His an-swer was "I had the feeling plenty of water produces something internally, worms. Neighbors and parents said it so often, I be-lieved it. (Did you really feel it was true?) Yes, but I was skeptical. They never gave us any explanation . . . Every time I get wild, they threaten to cut off my penis and had me in doubt. Probably, it goes back to my second year. At that age, we got a lot of water with seeds in it. (Caraway?) Yes. I thought it was to sterilize the water. . . (Does plain water breed worms?) One or two, definitely."

Al was a good pupil at first, but became increasingly self-con-scious and dropped out of school at the age of fourteen or fifteen to take various mechanical jobs. Outside of the human element, he was most afraid of the school toilet, which he was unable to use. When not in school, the patient mostly played alone on the roof, which was forbidden.

Not only did the water tanks of toilets generally frighten Al, but also the water tanks on the roof, and even the holy water in church. He felt there was some monster below the water's surface; on the other hand, he expected somebody "familiar" to emerge. A

little dark man would come down the chain from the water tank of the toilet. But at the same time, frightened though he was, the boy was also curious and looked into the water tank. Being ambivalent in every respect, he was both afraid of water and its containers, as symbols, and interested in them, too.

Talking over the playback of his one-hundred-and-thirteenth hypnoanalytic session, at a time when he was greatly improved, Al told me, "Well, as far back as I can remember, those were really the feelings I have . . . that there is a man nearby watching me; he would jump out of the shadows and torture me . . . (Do you still feel it?) No. (How long is it since you have felt it?) I would say the last year. (Has it entirely disappeared?) I don't think so. (When do you still feel it?) My dreams now and then are still disturbed. And at certain periods, from time to time, I still feel it. (When?) When it comes up. I don't know. It has no special time. (Can you remember how old you were when it started as a child?) Yes, I think it was after being operated on for my legs. I must have been about four years old. Being left day and night in the crib with very little attention. Nights began to scare me. From there on, I began to use only my imagination in my own way. There was nothing else I could do. That was about the earliest recollection I have. Of course, I remember I would imagine all kinds of terrible things with the coming of night."

The traumatic impact of operations on children has often been discussed. In Al's case, there were several hypnoanalytic sessions on this theme. That the unloved and unprotected infants would be more affected than those who are not, is obvious. The insight Al displayed was always remarkable.

I will now present Al's eighty-ninth hypnoanalytic session. Regression was induced, and he was asked, "(Of what are you frightened?) The toilet bowl leads a long pipe right into the river. (What frightens you?) I am afraid of falling it it. (How?) I am pushed in by somebody. (Do you see somebody?) Yes, he is walking to me. (An Italian?) I see his feet. They are walking away. (Away? Then there is no danger.) Some man's feet. (Look at his face. Is he your father?) He is familiar. I don't recognize him, and he is spying on me. (What could he find out about you? *Parlate.**)

---

* Italian for *talk*

He don't want me to talking; he beat me up afterwards. (I will protect you. He can't beat you up. *Parlate.*) [pause] He gets a big, big tower and I just want evade him. I just want. (How can he become as big as a big tower?) He is growing. (What part of his body?) Whole, whole body is getting—is getting big and—and. (Then he will burst like bubble gum. Does he burst?) He can always overpower me. (You are stronger. I will protect you. *Parlate.*) [pause] Hands around my neck and between—between his— his legs on the toilet, he is choking me. (Did he really do this when you were a small child?) Yes. (Why?) I refused to do something. (What did he want?) Big penis. (Did he want to put it into your mouth or into your rectum?) In the mouth, in the mouth. (In the mouth?) Yes. (What happened?) Tried to put me in the toilet bowl. (Did he really do it when you were a little boy? *Parlate.*) Yes, and—(And?) Nothing threatened me, but I am scared that he is going to put me in the toilet bowl. (Are you afraid you will flush into the river?) Yes. (It is impossible.) No, I have seen the pipe leading right through the whole building down into the ground. (It is much too narrow.) No. (How do you suppose you could pass through?) The pipe leading from—from the toilet bowl directly into the—down to the building, into the wa—into the ground. (I believe you, but did you not think about its width?) It is wide, two feet wide. (That is impossible, that is your imagination. Is it a symbol for your father's penis?) Yes. It don't look real. (What frightens you?) The pipe stands alongside the stairway the whole length of the building. (*Parlate.*) All—all the toilets are opened. (And?) I don't see nothing in there. (Look inside.) Yes, the doors are all opened. (How many?) I see them all, all five stories. (Five stories?) Yes. (Why are you so interested in toilets?) There is somebody hiding in there. (Your father?) [pause] Going down in and afraid of going down along with it. (How is that possible? Could you flow down along with the water in the drain?) My father is walking away. (You father is walking away? Talk.) All the feces and—and the water is backing up and getting closer to me. (Did your father defecate on you?) No, it is coming right out of the pipe, it is coming right out of the—it is just rising. (How did you get this feeling?) [groan] (Does it enter your body?) No, I am standing in the tub. (And?) It is rising

higher and higher. I can't get out. (Of the tub?) Yes. (In the bathroom?) Yes. (Did you defecate in the bathtub?) No. (What happened? How can the water rise by itself?) It is backing up and—(And?) It is backing out—(And?) The water is going—going to overflow and I can't get out, it is going to following me, the water. (How can it follow you?) Dripping over and—(And?) And still—(What?) And still cover me. [pause] (The water is coming, and?) Down in the pipe and through—through his penis. (Is the pipe his penis?) Connected with his penis. (What important things are inside?) [pause] From the water tank into his penis. (What comes down?) All the water is gathered up in the tank. (Dirty or clean water?) Urine, urine. (And?) It comes out of a penis. (To you? Or where does it go?) He urinates in the sink; it goes in the bathtub. (And?) Where I am standing. (Your age?) A year and a half. (A year and a half?) Yes. (He urinates into the sink. From there it goes into the bathtub where you stand?) Yes. (Do you get dirty?) Yes, I put my hands in it. (Is it pleasurable?) Yes. (Has it a nice smell?) No, my mother comes over and hits me. (Why?) Playing in the water. (Is it urine?) Yes. (Children do not find anything wrong with such play.) [two groans] [pause] My father comes and urinates. (And?) All the time, the water fills up. (Where?) In the bathtub. (And?) I am afraid I won't be able to get out. (How far does it reach up on you?) On my chest. (Talk.) In the penis. (Yes?) There was no pipe from the water tank and a lot of water in it. I take him out of the water. (That is your father's penis? Yes. (That is the same thing as the pipe on the water tank?) Yes. (Was this the reason that you always looked into the water tank?) Yes, a big supply of water, a big supply. (Do you suppose your father has a water tank inside him?) Yes. (Talk it out.) Yes. [pause] I am in the bathtub. (Does it scare you when he urinates near you and you are in the bathtub?) Yes. (How often did he do it? Many times?) Yes, time and time again. (Do you smell it?) No. (Was he drunk?) I don't know. (Were you frightened by his big penis?) Yes. [pause] Ducking me in the water. (Why?) My father. (Talk.) Just shaking. He looks—(And?) He does not look right; he is shaking and—(And?) And is—(Is he drunk?) Yes. (Does he have the d.t.'s?) No. (What does he want to do to you?) He is just teasing me and—(And?) And has a lot of pleasure. (Who?)

My father. (What does he do?) Dipping me up in and out of the water and holding me. (Is it water or urine?) I don't know. It looks clear. (He plays with you?) Yes. (Are you frightened?) Yes. (Do you have a bad conscience?) No, I am just scared. [pause] He is coming over and—(What does your mother do?) Picks me up. Telling me not to be afraid. (Was this before or after you had the rickets?) Yes, yes, before. (Before?) Yes. (What does your mother do?) Just holding me and—(Do you feel better? Do you feel protected?) Yes. (And?) My mother says he is bad. My father is bad. She points to my father and—(Does she talk Italian?) Yes. (Did she say, *Padre non e bene?*) She point him, push him, she point him, pushing him away and—(Is he drunk?) I think so, he is in a corner. (Your mother protects you now?) Yes. (What happens now?) My father is trying to stand up. (Can he stand up?) No, he is trying to stand up, he is sitting on the bed. (Is he shaking?) Yes, his hands are going all over. (Talk it out.) Just stand there, my mother just stands there watching him. She is holding me. (Do you feel better?) Yes. (What frightens you so much now?) He comes over and wants—(What does he want?) I think he wants to make a grab, a grab at us. (Does he want you or your mother?) My mother is laughing now. (Talk it out.) My mother is running in the toilet, running to hide. I am with her. (Talk it out.) They put me on the floor. (And?) And—and I think they are doing something dirty. (Do they have intercourse?) Yes. (In the normal way?) Yes. (In the toilet or the bathroom?) In the toilet. (Does your mother sit down?) Partly sit down. (Does he take up her skirt?) Yes. (Describe it.) Standing, standing in the corner, and am all—ah—ah—(And?) Wrapped up. (With what?) With bandages. (How?) All wrapped up. (Are you sick?) No, just diapers and bandages. (You are still in diapers?) Yes. (Do you see them having intercourse?) Yes. (Describe it.)"

At this point, the recording spool ran out, but Al finished, "I don't see anything, they are dressed again."

Before I start describing the way in which this patient brought out material in his hypnoanalytic sessions, which is so different from all the cases I have presented before, I must explain that, when this hypnoanalysis was performed, I already knew much about the patient, and my questions were geared to that material.

At the beginning of many hypnoanalytic sessions, the reprojected introject of his father worked to prevent Al from talking. At other times, he saw this reprojected introject of his father more clearly than in this visualization, The patient had not only psychically, but also physically, identified with his hated and feared father —in other words, with the aggressor.

Al's parents used to tell him that they could read his thoughts by looking at his forehead. Thus, his father always knew what his son was going to do. When Al grew up, he projected his capability onto others, still feeling as he did when a child vis-à-vis the omnipotent adults. In addition to his awe of their powers, a deep sense of shame of his parents' behavior, especially his father's, made it very difficult for the patient to talk about events at home. Before Al, I never had a patient who used a "strong" father as a kind of resistance in hypnoanalysis to avoid communication. Al talked anyhow, although a dialogue, considerable coaxing, extensive questioning, and repeated reassurances of protection were always required. Despite the reassurances, however, he informed me, when questioned, that he did not feel protected, that I had no influence on what he reported, and that my voice seemed to come from the other end of a long hall.

Patients suffering from an obsessive compulsive reaction are supposed to identify with their fathers only psychically. But Al was dependent for a much longer time than other children because, from the time he had had the measles until after he had learned to walk again, he had regressed and was forced into passivity. The protection he got from his mother was quite unreliable as the end of the foregoing hypnoanalytic session proves. There were few episodes in his hypnoanalytic sessions when he went to his mother for protection, or felt protected by her, even for a short time.

These visualizations in which his father tried to prevent the patient from talking could also be a projection of the "internalized parental prohibitions, the forerunners of the superego." However, the punishments his father threatened to inflict on the patient were not worse than what actually happened to him. A visualization of some components of his superego will be presented when this hypnoanalytic session has been discussed.

Al's phobias must also have developed at that period. Castration fear being especially marked in phobic reactions, the patient told me that at times, as a child, he was not even sure that it had not already happened to him. There were also many reasons for his erythrophobia and general shyness. He was always told that he was a good-for-nothing, and obviously a heavy burden on his mother.

Talking over another subject, Al once said, "I could not express myself, so I had to be satisfied just by watching." This may be the best interpretation of his scoptophilia. He was forced to live in an inimical environment and was not able to move except by crawling; he was incapable of walking for several years. These conditions may have laid the foundation for his later claustrophobia. The stay in the hospital, with casts on both legs, utterly unable to understand what had happened to him, can only have reinforced his tendency to a fear of being closed in.

According to Federn, patients suffering from obsessive compulsive reactions, are expected to have only a scattering of fantasies in their infancy. At that period of his life, however, Al's opportunity to test reality was very limited. What little opportunity he could grasp he utilized to achieve some coherence in all the nonsense he had heard from his parents and neighbors. This forced him to a greater mental activity and criticality on the one hand; on the other hand, if he was unable to find a reasonable solution, he had to create fantasies which he later partly repressed. That his active, forbidden wishes against the threatening prohibitions which he had started to create at a still earlier age and which he was able to expiate by self-imposed thoughts were now amplified is obvious. Later in his treatment, he once admitted that he might have "felt" death wishes towards his father, but "I never dared to think such a thing." He had a superabundance of time for all such deliberations, with the frequent result of contradictory solutions, even later in childhood when he played alone for the most part, and this also contributed to his apparent confusion.

Returning to this hypnoanalytic session, I should explain that his father was the "big tower." The family lived near the Williamsburg Bridge, and from the windows of their railroad flat, the patient could see the bridge towers which he developed in his fan-

tasies as a symbol for his father. There was also a connection between his father's being "bad" and the East River having been described to him as dangerous. His father was as strong, unassailable, and dangerous as a bridge tower. This bridge tower sucked children in, ground them to pieces, "tortured them," and spat them out again. There is also a connection between the "meat masher" his parents used and their threats that he would be "mashed up" the same way as the meat was.

The descriptions of attempted or actual fellatio and other abuses at different age levels and in different locations repeated themselves so often that I had to assume that they may have actually occurred. At times, Al believed they did. Whether or not they were merely visualizations of his fear of his homosexual desire for his father is impossible to decide. The patient reported only shame, disgust, and fear at these occasions.

His father's "dirty habits" played an important role in Al's visualizations. When this part of the hypnoanalytic session was played back to him, he remarked, "It all started with my father's dirty habits." The threat to throw him into the toilet bowl and flush him into the terrifying East River might quite easily have really been made to him although he never mentioned it. The patient told me that the toilet bowl was often clogged, and added that he himself might at times have thrown too much paper into it to keep the Devil from jumping out. Then, of course, the water would back up in the bowl. The visualization of his father urinating into the sink and the bathtub is probably the reawakening of a repressed memory of an actual occurrence. The prospect of being spattered by his father's urine Al reported dreading ". . . as a terrible punishment." This hypnoanalytic session involved still another fantasy, namely, that water was in some way alive, a notion that stemmed from the fermenting wine Al had seen in his infancy. It was able to follow him—as his father's urine actually did at times.

My question as to what "important things" were inside the penis referred to a statement formerly made by the patient that all of his important belongings were in there. However, this query was not answered. He mentioned that, at the age of five or six, he had tried to wreck a water pipe in order to see what was inside it.

Evidently, his father derived a great deal of pleasure from frightening the boy and often behaved sadistically. Occasionally, he would put the infant into a filled sink. "If my father is against me, the whole world is against me," Al said. All these manipulations strengthened the patient's impression that his parents wanted to get rid of him because he was no good. During the incident in question, his mother came to his rescue but provided protection for only a short while. Al's first impression that his mother was running into the toilet in order to hide with him, proved to be fallacious and, as previously stated, her protection was short-lived. Once inside the toilet, his father apparently seduced her from her original purpose. To avoid having to describe his parents' conduct, the patient stated that he was still in diapers and in bandages of an unknown kind and, by implication, too young to detail the proceedings.

The difference between the visualizations of this case and those previously presented is obvious. The former had one logically developing occurrence, few or no symbolical distortions, and a clearly defined background. However, even in the case of Mitch, who, unlike the rest, recalled in one hypnoanalytic session several episodes in which no symbols appeared, further treatment might have disclosed some compulsive features.

Al as a rule, however, spoke in short, abrupt sentences. His visualizations were disconnected; there was no logical development, no defined background, and symbols were frequently used. The same symbols and episodes recurred in other visualizations, in other connections; they were repeated. The continuity of an entire visualization was maintained only by one emotion—fear—and over and over again it was the same ego state. The episodes in every visualization were separated by pauses; they were isolated. Not one single episode had a real beginning or an end. Often the patient did not even answer a final question; he would pause, and then another part of the visualization would begin. Between the short spurts of visualizations, however, there was at times a longer sequence. No actual, specifically designated background was described; it was always just the toilet bowl, the toilet, the pipe, the tub, and so forth.

These spurts of visualizations may correspond to, or may even

be the result of, the "islands" which are discussed in the theoretical part of this book. There is also a possible connection to the "self-imposed thoughts" mentioned by Federn. Al "struggled against threats and fears by thinking."

As to the early age to which Al stated he had regressed, this occurred quite frequently, and the particular hypnoanalytic session quoted was not selected for this reason. On questioning, he told me once that he judged his age according to his height and his feeling about it.

I will now present his sixty-fourth hypnoanalytic session in which he visualized his superego or, more accurately, some aspects of it. This and the following hypnoanalysis were not recorded mechanically, but put down on paper by me immediately after the session and later corrected by the patient.

Al was regressed and told to remember his childhood fantasies about sex. "I close a box; I turn the chairs upside down; I nail a box . . . I am on the roof afraid somebody would open the water tank. (Who?) A stranger, a middle-aged Italian man. (Your father?) No. (The neighbor?) No . . . (Is he the landlord?) He acts like the boss. He opens the skylight and hides in the hall toilet in a pipe. (What does he want to do?) To cut the children up, to crush them, and to throw them in the river. [long pause] My sister told me a man was hiding in the toilet, there I was scared. Suddenly I found myself in the toilet, and a boy seemed to have me covered. [very tense, breathing deeply, awakens, protection is promised, he is rehypnotized] The boy seemed at the same time to be a monster as far as strength. A man tried to push, to force me into the bowl. [very tense, breathing deeply] Then I dreaded suffocation. (Is it sex he wants from you?) I did not see any sex. [awakens very tense]."

The patient told me that he often awakens from such "dreams" and "a lot of it is true." His mother told him that, at about three years of age, he frequently turned chairs around and used a hammer and nails. "(Did the boy in the toilet forbid you to talk?)" Al stated that he was a strong, foreign boy and that he himself had been informed that a former playmate had recently been put in an asylum. "(Did he tell you he would do something to you if you talked?) He walked in on me, had me cornered, and I felt

trapped. (Were your trousers open or closed?) I believe I moved my bowels." The patient said that he had not felt protected by me and that his only concern was that he could not run away fast enough.

At his next session, there was an elaboration of this part of the hypnoanalytic session. "(Who was the boy?) He looked familiar, a very small child, about three or four years old. What I wondered about was how I became so terrified in my dream [visualization] of such a small child. (Was he a monster?) I feared him like a monster. He looked innocent, but it was my feeling that I will be tortured. (By being pushed into the bowl?) Yes, that was part of it. Being forced into the bowl was the second part. The first part was being frightened by a small boy. The suction of the water, not exactly the water, forced me into the bowl. (A "force" did it?) Yes. (Where did you feel it?) I started to be stuffed in. I was condensed, I was being stuffed into the bowl. (In which part of your body did you feel it?) Right up to my shoulders, I was into the bowl. (Did they force you from above or pull you from below?) From above. (The suction of the water would be from below?) It was not exactly the suction. (Did somebody push down on your shoulders?) Yes. And yet I did not see anybody. On leaving here, I tried to figure out who the small boy was. He was so familiar. Could he be myself? (What did you do in the toilet?) My feeling was I was completely alone on the toilet. (Did you masturbate?) No. I felt on this toilet I was away from everybody, and I was surprised to see this door opened and the boy suddenly in the door. He surprised me. (You were double?) Yes. Sometimes, but I can't be sure. (Do you have this feeling at other times, too?) No. He was a young, innocent child, just like myself in appearance. (Was it your bad conscience?) My guess is yes. He just stared at me as if I had done something, although I did not do anything. I felt I was caught red-handed. For what reason I don't know. I was doing something dirty; my guess is a bowel movement. (Did you have sexual feelings?) No. I just felt that was no place anybody prey or spy on you. (Did you play with your bowel movement?) No, and yet I feel I was up to something when I was discovered. I was from a place I thought was completely secluded, spied on, and that

frightened me out of my wits. My mind was practically blind at that time." He denied that homosexuality was involved, that he had had an erection or that he had played with his rectum. "(Do you wash your hands after using the toilet?) Yes, but I have no phobia about it. (What happens if you cannot wash them?) It does not bother me too much . . . I do remember playing with my penis, but never with my rectum. (This boy's bowel movement looked like a penis?) Yes. (You had an internal penis?) I had some kind of wild worm in me. (Did you try to bring it out?) Maybe. As a small child I was overcurious about this worm the olders told me about. I would try to jump around and then to hide." Another time, he told me he jumped on the roof so much that the people on the top floor complained.

In the following hypnoanalytic session, Al was told to dream and to remember what had really happened in the hall toilet. He became very tense several times, and then was told that he was being protected. I will summarize his statements only partially but adhere to the sequence of events. He visualized a staircase and many roofs. When asked about the hall toilet, the patient recalled being below gound in a dirty cellar and trying to peer out onto the street, trying to get out to where "the public were," and, at the same time, feeling ashamed because he was unclean from "associating with the cellar." He grew more and more tense, but could not provide a reason for it. "There is a fire burning. People with pokers. They had somebody over red-hot coal. I was watching the operation. . . They were drawing the intestines from underneath the person, and that is the way they were getting the Devil out of him. It is a skin." He explained afterwards that it was the gut of a pig which Al, as a small boy, had often seen Italian people use in cooking. "After I saw what went on, a woman with the 'evil eye' appeared. She just stared at me in such a way as to dare me to tell —not to tell, rather, and I was afraid of horror . . . she could do me harm." It was not his mother, but she looked like a neighbor. "(Who is the Devil?) It seems my father said that I was getting away with something. I am getting out of his clutches. He told it to someone standing by the fire." His father was a member of the party, and the people his friends, perhaps. "Priests do such things,

but they were no priests. (Did they take it out of you?) No. (Who was the person?) It seems I was watching it. (Who was it who had the Devil in him?) I could not see; all was fire."

This was not a feeling he had about purgatives; purgatives he simply felt afraid to take. His mother said of the long animal intestines they used at home, that they came from something dead. "I wonder if I did not equalize all the long bowel movements with all those dead matter my mother would cook." It was "dirty stuff," and Al said he never could eat the soup she prepared from it.

About six months later, I discussed several of his symbols with the patient. "(What is a sneak wire?) An identical thing to an intestine. (What is all this about a woman with the 'evil eye'?) I was always told there were witches in circulation. (Do you remember the hypnosis in which they took the intestines out with a hot poker?) That is removing the Devil. (What is the Devil inside of you?) The wrong acts I committed. (Which ones?) At times, my mother said if we did not take laxatives, we would get worms inside. (Did you have sexual feelings on the toilet?) I can't recall. I can honestly say I have never played with my rectum. In one hypnosis, it stands very clear in my mind. I was sitting on the toilet. The door opens and somebody is spying on me. The funny part is, it was me that scared myself. I felt myself with the water, some human force with the water pressed me down. It appeared by vision; the little boy was my image, but the personality behind was a monster. (Did you feel yourself a monster?) No. Certainly it terrified me."

Again a little more than a year later, when Al disclosed that his troubles had started at the time of his operation, he said, too, that, at that time, he also "became fearful of all hiding places," meaning toilets. He had the feeling that somebody was "after" him.

Digesting what the patient told me, it seems that an innocent facsimile of himself—an infant of about four, but strong as a monster—spied him out in some secluded place—the toilet. As punishment for some unknown bad deed, the facsimile tried to push Al down the toilet bowl, and Al was in it up to his shoulders —the "filthy," the "bad," the unacceptable part of his body was in the sewer. Had not the double looked at him as if he had done something wrong? Had not the patient felt apprehended? This

wrong act, since he disclaimed everything else, could only have been an evacuation of the bowels. The reasons the patient regarded his acts of defecation as "bad" may be numerous. The frequent expressions of disapproval that must have accompanied his early toilet training may be one source; his father's uninhibited behavior another. It is doubtful that the patient's parents showed solicitude over his defecatory exercises. In the area in which he lived, however, he may have observed among some of the neighbors parental concern about the evacuating functions of their children. This his own mother was undoubtedly constrained to feel on occasion, judging from the purgatives and enemas she administered to the patient, and thus, ambivalent as he was, it supplied a further reason for regarding evacuation as evil.

As far as the burning coals and the exorcisings in the cellar are concerned, multitudinous sources for these visualizations lie in the patient's upbringing. First, there is the violence and the threats of violence made by his father. Then, there are the worms his mother talked about. There was a worm in the patient, the "Devil," of which his father's friends tried to purge him by means of a poker, red-hot coals, and evisceration. The boy himself felt very unclean because he had been in a dirty *cellar,* a symbolical projection of his own abdomen. That the people performing the operation were friends of his father may be due to the fact that his father often made public exposures of his son's bad deeds and public threats. The father himself was watching the proceedings, a reprojection of his introjected father and a multiplication. The woman who he said was not his mother, but a neighbor, was really his mother because the neighbor often substituted for her. Thus, both parents were looking on as the bad son who, because he had or had not done his duty, was being operated upon in an especially painful way, with a poker (a penis) over red hot coals, and what was removed from the boy was not only the evil part of both his parents, the Devil and the witch, but the boy himself for, while he was being operated upon, he, too, was watching the proceedings. It would take too long to enumerate all the connections and ramifications of these visualizations, but the relationship between "watching" to his scoptophilia and of the "evil eye" to another of his symbolizations "turning into stone," should be mentioned

here. Add to this his statement that he was on the roof initially and immediately afterwards in the cellar, that he was punished first by water, then by fire, and we have ramifications and interconnections in these visualizations that are theological, environmental and, at the same time, uniquely personal to this patient.

Following this hypnoanalytic session, Al still came for regular treatment for over a year. Then there was a lapse of six months succeeded by a few sporadic interviews and hypnoanalytic sessions, and six months later, he again returned for regular therapy.

At this juncture, the patient was considerably improved. For some time, he had been keeping company with a woman of experience whom he did not intend to marry. He was usually potent, but not invariably. A long time ago, he had given up drinking spontaneously, and his social anxiety, the greatest hindrance in his life, as well as his constant blushing and perspiring had greatly abated.

He was also working during the day, in an occupation different from the one he had before, and, as always, carried two union cards. The new job was that of a presser, which was closer to the sort of work his father did. He still lived at home.

A few weeks before the next hypnoanalytic session which I present took place, the patient had met a girl with whom he was slowly falling in love and whom he later married. She had a background similar to his, an Italian background, and was, in his words, "a good working girl."

After the one-hundred-twenty-first hypnoanalytic session, I was told by the patient that he had taken four Dexamyl® Spansules® No. 1 beforehand, the last one about two hours prior to the start of the hypnoanalysis. In the presentation of this session, I have shortened a good part of my prompting, especially during the pauses.

Regression was induced. "(Why do you breathe so deeply?) I am in a big place and I am all closed in. (Are you frightened?) Yes. (Of what? Of whom?) I am all along trapped, and in a trapped place. And it's—it's a large place. (Describe it. Please.) [pause] (Why did you swallow just now?) I am afraid I fall down. (Where can you fall down?) Down the black. (What is black?) Top of the ground. (Are you up?) There is something all around me and—

and—(And?) It will torture me. (Are there clouds or what?) They are big. They are big. Steel pipe. (Is there a big steel pipe around you?) Yes. (You are in a big steel pipe?) Yes. They are around me. (Are you crawling through?) I am just staying there. I am just lying there. And it is all—(Yes?) It's a very, very big place. (Is the steel pipe very big, or is it situated in a very big place?) In a big place. (You are in a big place and the steel pipe is in a big place. Is that right?) Yes. (The steel pipe is near you. Is that right?) Yes. (You are afraid you will fall in?) I am; it's suspended from the ceiling, from the ceiling. (Is there an opening in this steel pipe?) Slide down in the pipe. [pause] (Please talk.) Somebody will push me in there. (Somebody will push you in?) Yes. (Can you walk around it?) No. (Why not?) Nn, too small. I am stuck in it. (You are in it?) Yes. (You just told me you are outside. Now you are inside?) Yes. (How did you get in?) It's—it's all around me. (The steel pipe is around you?) Yes. (Was it around you all this time?) Yes. (What are your feet resting on?) On one side. On—on —on the bottom of the pipe. (The pipe also has a bottom?) Yes. (How can you fall deeper then?) [pause] (How old are you?) Two. (Two years of age?) Yes, yes. [swallows] (Why did you swallow again?) I am afraid of the water, of the water in the pipe. (Is it clean or dirty water?) I don't know, but it's there. (How high up does it come on you?) I didn't reach me yet. It didn't reach. (It's below you?) Yes. (At the bottom of the pipe?) Yes. (And where do you stand?) I—I am—I am higher up. (There are two bottoms?) [pause] (Please talk.) The water is splashing all around, and—[swallows] (What's the end of this sentence?) I am afraid. I am—I might get covered up with the water. (What is the splashing like?) Like the end of a—the end of a—(The end of what?) Oh, a small tower. (Is it a bridge tower?) I don't know; it's dark. (Do you hear the water or do you see it?) I see it. (What color is it?) Clean and dirty, everything. All kinds. All kinds of water. (Where does it come from?) I don't know. From the ground. (From the ground?) Yes. (How did you get into this pipe?) I am stuck there. Hiding. (Hiding? From what? From whom?) There is more than a tower. (Talk it out.) They are going to find [slurred] for me. Yes. [swallows] (Why do you swallow?) I am stuck in there. [pause] (Please talk.) I shouldn't be

there. I shou—(Why not?) I don't—(What?) I don't know. (What is wrong?) I am stuck and I am lost. And I am—I don't—I don't know. (What don't you know?) Nn—nn—what to do. And how I got there. And—[swallows] (Why do you swallow again?) I am —[swallows] (*Na.*) I am—I am climbing higher away from them. And—and—(And what?) I am—I am climbing over it. I am cov—I am covered all over. (And you are climbing.) I am. [pause] (Talk.) And as a result but instead of—instead of being higher, I am coming always lower. All the time. All along. And— (And what?) Here I come all the way down. Into the ground now. Oh. (Talk it out.) Oh, all the way down. Into—into a big—It's a ditch. It's a big ditch. (Talk, please.) It's a big—ah. (What?) It's a big black ditch and it has no bottom. It's long. (Where are the men?) I don't see anybody. [swallows] (There are no more men around?) No. (What about the water?) There is nothing around me. (There is no water any more?) No. But there seems to be two walls. [short cough] (Two walls?) Yes. And a deep ditch. And— (You are between the two walls?) Yes. (How do they look?) Like the side of a—ah, excavation. (How did you get there? Just by trying to climb the pipe you came down into the ditch?) I drifted away from the pipe. And—(Please finish the sentence.) I am coming out by the—by the bridge. (You are coming out by the bridge?) Yes. (Which one? Williamsburg?) It has a tower. Near the tower. (Near the tower of the bridge?) Yes. (Is it the Williamsburg Bridge?) Yes. (In the neighborhood where you were born?) Yes. (You know this neighborhood. Please describe it.) There is— there is people going up. But I can't get out from the bottom of the tower. (Talk about it.) I can't—I can't get out. (Why don't you yell to the people so they can help you?) They are far away. (They are far away?) Yes. (How far away are they?) Very high up. Very high. (They are very high up and you are low?) Yes. (Down?) Yes. [pause] (Please talk.) Inside a giant. (Inside a giant?) A giant. (What?) Ah. (What is the giant?) A brick. It's a brick. (One brick only?) Bricks all around. The wall is all around me. (Is it your father?) I don't know. (What?) I don't know. (What do you think?) There is a man over my head. There is a—(Somebody is over your head?) A big man. (Yes.) He is climbing away, and—(Is he a dark man?) Yes. (Is he an Italian?) I am not sure. (Are you

still asleep?) Yes. (Is the man still near you or has he gone away?) He is around somewhere. (How do you know?) Near me. (How do you know this?) I—I feel he is near me. (What do you feel?) Being near me. A man, a man. But I don't know who he is. (Is he your father?) I don't know. He'll whip me. (What?) He'll whip me. (Can you go nearer to him?) I am. (What?) No. I am stuck. (You are stuck?) Yes. (Is it tension that makes you stuck?) Nn—nn— (What?) There—there is a big ledge, and I can't reach him. A big ledge of bricks. (Is he sitting on the ledge?) [swallows] He is standing there. (He stands there?) Yes. (Can you throw a brick at him?) No. (How can you get rid of him?) Climb out there. (Are you climbing out now?) No. [pause] (What is happening? Please tell me.) There is a big—a big shoe, and a—a leg. They don't follow me and—hm, I am not [jumbled] I can't pass. [pause] (Reach for this leg and shoe with both your hands and grasp them. Just dare. Can you?) N—no, I slip, I—(You slip?) I can't hold it. (Hold it. Do you have them?) No. (No?) No. (Move your hands. Just grasp it.) [small movement of right hand] [pause] (You moved your right hand a little bit. Now really move it. Do you have it?) Yes. [clears his throat abruptly] (Okay.) [small movement of right thumb] (You moved your right thumb a little.) It's—(What?) It's—it's not an old man. (What is it?) It's only—it's—(What is it?) It's a big— (What?) It's a big boot. [pause] (What happens now with the big boot? Do you see it?) Yes. They are big and it's standing there. But I don't know how to get out. I don't know how to get—to get away from there and to get home. (Is the big boot before you?) Yes. (Do you have to walk around the boot, or what?) It's in, ah— (What?) It's in a square and there is over all g-girders and steel all around me and I am under. I don't know how to get out of it. (Do you suppose it will be easier for you if I walk with you?) No. (Hm?) Yes. (Let us walk together. I am sure all this rubbish will then disappear. Has the boot disappeared?) Yes. (Has the steel disappeared?) Yes. It's—(It's what?) There is a tunnel and it comes out in the car [jumbled] in the street. (Are you in the street now?) Yes. (Can you see the sun?) I see the—(What?) Horses and trolleys and—(Do you feel free now?) Yes. (Are you still asleep?) Yes. (Do you want to go home?) Yes. (Do you think you are able to go home alone or do you need me?) No, I—(What?) I don't

know what street this is. (First Avenue and Twelfth Street. Will you find your way home now?) Yes. (Do you think you can go home alone without being tense?) Yes. (Shall we stop now?) Yes. (Okay.)"

When Al was awakened, he appeared to come out of a deep trance. He stated immediately that it was like coming out of a barrel.

The pauses in this hypnoanalytic session were filled largely with my promptings; therefore, isolation used as a defense was more difficult to detect. The mechanism was there, however. Another ego defense was also well documented here. The patient discussed "climbing and coming down at the same time" and expressed the opinion that something was wrong with his "sense of balance." In this he was correct because as often before, he had visualized something called "biphasic," having contradictory qualities consequent to his contradictory impulses. My various interpretations that the situation might pertain to dizziness, or sex, or the fact that his parents may have swung him up and down as an infant were rejected by the patient who also told me that sometimes he felt afraid of being "inside" although he would have liked to be inside because he felt alone outside—one of his claustrophobic features.

What Al had really experienced in a visual manner was the defense mechanism of "undoing." He did this by changing the modifying aspects of his visualizations, for instance, clear water and dirty water were both present in the same place, which is actually impossible. He climbed, "rather rising to the clouds," as he explained later, but "came to the ground." To an extent, he was even undoing his father's projected introject. After the part about the boots had been played back to him, he stated, "I believed there was a man lying in wait for me. That was a big surprise when there was nothing more than a boot." But in the hypnoanalytic session itself, he stated that he saw a "big shoe and a leg," though how far up the leg was visible he never said.

It is impossible to present the full explanation Al brought to this hypnoanalytic session when it was played back to him. The gist of it was: "I felt myself stuck in a huge steel tubing, and I felt there was no way out of it. The steel pipe was gigantic; it seems

like the ground floor of a big factory." He accepted the fact that, in his childhood fantasies, the pipe was a symbol for his father's genitalia.

I do not believe that it is necessary to interpret the many symbols the patient used in this visualization for his father and his father's genitalia. What may be significant is that in this hypoanalysis what he described as a "small tower" had in former visualizations always appeared very solid and very tall. His father's main symbol was decreasing. In this visualization also, the patient mentioned "girders" indicating that the wall was no longer solid. It may be interesting to explore further the symbol of the tower. After the ninety-ninth hypnoanalytic session, the patient revealed that he remembers visualizing his father variously as part of the bridge tower and as replacing the bridge tower. The foundations of the tower that he saw were right in the water.

The patient's father actually was only of medium build, but he had what the patient described as a "fierce look." He was able to scare people other than the patient, for example, a tough union delegate. After this hypnoanalytic session, Al also revealed that he formerly had the image of a man atop the tower waiting to torture children by squeezing and smashing them and tearing them apart and then throwing them into the river.

Nevertheless, the brick wall was still a "giant" though, at the end, Al found only a big boot. Except for this boot, these symbols were repetitious, but repetitions occurred in his visualizations only, and he had no complaints about repetitions as a complicating factor in his life. One had the distinct impression, however, that in his visualizations, Al was repeatedly and unconsciously testing to determine which of his visualizations or combination of episodes would appease, even expiate, the incomprehensible guilt which resulted from his unconscious conflict, at the same time that he was exploring the conflict's causation. However, aided by therapy, and with the passing of time, Al's understanding and acceptance of his difficulties increased. He was able to work them through so that he became less and less preoccupied with "thinking fear." His next hypnoanalytic session will show the great improvement that had taken place by this time.

I will now present the one-hundred-and-twenty-second hyp-

noanalytic session, the patient's last, which followed the session just described. I have already indicated that the idea of allowing a patient in hypnoanalysis to destroy the most hated member of his family came to me while listening to a patient. This patient was Al. Originally, he was told to push his father away, and he accepted the suggestion. Since the patient, at that time, was deeply in love with the girl he later married, it was imperative to demonstrate to him that he was stronger than his father and that he could overpower his reprojected introject. This is what transpired.

Regression was induced. Al swallowed. "(Why do you swallow?) I am getting smaller. (What is going on?) I am moving on a— (Moving. Yes?) In a carriage and [swallows] somebody is walking alongside of me. (Are you a baby?) Yes. (How old are you, approximately?) Four. Four years old. (You could not walk at that time?) Yes, I walk. (Then why are you in a carriage?) Somebody wa—(What do you see?) There is a man standing near me and he is—ah—blocking me. (What is he doing?) Leaning over and—ah —hiding me. (Is he leaning over the carriage, or what?) Yes. And I can see nothing. (What can you not see? The street, the room, or what?) I am—I am in the street. (How do you know?) Ah—ah, there is people and a dog and—(What color is the dog?) It's a brown dog. (A brown dog?) Yes. (What kind of dog?) I don't know. (A big or a little dog?) A small dog. (Is the man still leaning over you?) Yes. (A dark man?) Yes. (An Italian?) I don't see his face. (Your father?) Ahhh, I think he is. (Can't you push him away?) H—he is stronger than I am. (What? I didn't get it.) He is stronger. (Is he very near you, or is he far away?) Near. (Can you reach him with your hand?) N—n—no. (Why not?) I am stuck. (Can't you move your hands?) They are stuck. (How are they stuck?) Are they—(What?) I can't lift them. [swallows] (Why not?) They won't move. (Try it. Move the right hand up, please.) [starts to elevate his right hand and forearm] (Good, You moved your right hand and forearm up a little. You see, they move. Move them up more. Still more. A little more.) [moves his right hand and forearm slowly to a vertical position] (So. Now they are up. Look how they go up. How about the left one? Move the left arm up.) [elevates the left forearm and hand slowly, in two

or three stages, in the same way he did the right one. His palms are turned away from him] (As high as the right one. Now push him away. Both forearms are straight up now. Push forward.) [some small, weak forward movements of both his hands take place, scarcely any of the forearms] (Good. Once more. Push him away. A little more. What is it? Can you push him away?) He fell on the floor. (He fell on the floor?) He was sitting on the—he was sitting on the edge and he fell on the floor. (You see how strong you are. And you moved your forearms so little. You have moved them again. Good.) [same small movements] (Just do it once more. Good. Very good. You are doing it. And now you put them down. You see how strong you are. It's true.) Yes. (Do you know it now?) Yes. (What do you feel?) I am better now than in years. Ah. (Are you still asleep?) Yes. (What do you feel, and what do you think now?) I can climb out now. (What can you do? Crawl out?) Climb out and—(Yes, climb out. And?) He—(He?) He is very small now and on the ground. (He is very small and on the ground?) Yes. (Very good. Are you out of the carriage?) Yes. (Where did you climb to?) At the sidewalk. (You are on the side-walk?) Sidewalk. (Very good. What are you doing on the side-walk?) I am watching. (What?) On the man. (You are watching the man?) Yes. (The man you have just pushed down?) Yes. (De-scribe everything about him that you see.) He gets smaller and smaller and now he—he is so small I don't see him no more. He—(Describe it.) He—(Very good. What?) Is getting smaller to noth-ing. (That's very good. Did you see his face?) No. (Was it your fa-ther? What do you suppose?) Yes. (You know it was your father?) Yes. (How did you know?) Hmm. (What?) I—(*Na.* Come on.) I felt it was my father. (You felt it. So you know now that you are stronger than your father. Do you know it?) Yes. (Will you keep it in mind?) Yes. (I am not so sure. Your 'yes' is very soft.) Ah. (Will you keep it in mind?) Yes. (Good. Will you always know it?) I will remember. Yes. (I didn't get it entirely.) I will; I will remember. (Good. Talk a little louder, please. Why do you breathe so deeply? Are you afraid of somebody or something?) The carriage rolled away into the water. (Very good. The East River, or where?) It's—it's by the street. (By the street?) Yes. (How old are you?) Three. (You are now three. You have become smaller,

younger?) Yes. (What's going on?) Ah. Ah. I am standing all alone
and—and there is people walking all—ah—all around. (What
kind of people?) All kinds of people, and, ah, ah—(What?) Walking. [pause] (Talk, please.) I am. I don't recognize anybody and
I feel I am lost. (You are feeling lost?) Yes. (But you are so strong
that you are stronger than your father. How can such a strong boy
be lost? Just talk.) There are people that are bigger than I am.
(Do you know that you are stronger than they are?) Yes. (You just
overpowered your own father, so you must be very strong. Is that
true?) Yes. (Are you walking along the street or what?) I am
standing on the sidewalk. (What's going on? Is the dog still there?)
No, I am—I can see, I can see my house now. (Good. Describe the
house.) I am on the street by the house where I live. (Where you
live now or where you lived as a child?) Where I lived as a—as a
boy. (On the Lower East Side?) Yes. (What street?) Willett. (What
do you see?) I recognize a house and—and—(And?) Sit on the
stoop. (Good. What do you see from the stoop?) Thh—there are
people and the pushcarts and—And the buildings. (Do you see
women walking up the stoop?) I don't know. (How old are you?)
Four. (Four years old again. What's going on?) There is a—there
is a man calling me from the house. (Who?) Hmm. (Do you recognize the voice?) Yes. (Who is it?) My father. (What does he say?)
He wants me to come upstairs. (In English or Italian?) Italian.
(Can you repeat it?) *Sali** . . . (Do you intend to do it?) I don't
like to go up. (Why not? Are you frightened of him?) It's dark and
I might ah—I don't like to go up. (Tell me why.) I am afraid he
might do something to me and would beat me up and—(What are
you really frightened of?) [pause] Ah. There is a—(What is he?)
He is a—[pause] [swallows] (Why did you swallow just now?)
There is a long pipe that goes down and down and—and—ah, it's
a—it's like a penis. (Where is this pipe?) Oh, up in the hall. I
know it's there. In the hallway and—(And?) It goes down. (Just
talk it out.) Just. (It's like a penis, you mean?) Yes. (In what respect?) It looks like it. And the same size and it—it gets longer
and longer and—(And?) And—(Are you frightened of it?) Yes.
(Why?) Of course. (Yes.) It's so much—it's, ah—ah—ah—very
higher than I am. Very big. And—(And?)— On the end of it there

---

* *Sali* may be *sali su,* meaning *come up.*

is a man. (Talk it out, please.) There is—(Yes?) There is—
[swallows] (What is happening with the man with the long
penis?) He is just ah, high up over me. (Yes?) And he is. (Does he
threaten you with his penis?) Yes. (In what respect?) It—(Yes?) It
comes. I am afraid it comes close to me. (To what part of your
body?) I think my face, my head. (What will he do with your face
and with your head?) He might choke me. (Put it in your mouth,
or what?) Yes. (Has he ever done it before?) I don't know. (Why
are you afraid of it then?) It's scares me. Or I—and—(And what?)
I—I am afraid I might get stuck. (How?) Get cornered, ah, by the
pipe and—and the penis. And—(Talk it out, please.) There is—
(Where is the danger?) I got crushed and—and—(And what?) I
don't—(What?) I—I can't move away. (Talk it out, please.) By the
ground, and—Th-this pipe is over my head. Over my face and—
(And?) It's bigger than I am. There is—(And?) There is somebody
there. H-high up, and he doesn't move away from me. [pause]
(Please talk.) There is—[pause] (Please talk.) I—(What?) I
don't know everything that's, ah—that they are doing. (Who?) Oh,
the men. (There are several men or one man?) One man. One.
(What do you think he might do?) Oh, take something—ah—out
of his pants. (What can he take out of his penis?) Out of his pants.
(What do you suppose he will take out of his pants?) His penis.
(What do you expect he will do with it?) He might—wet me, or—
(Wet you?) Yes. (Urinate on you?) Yes. (Has he done it before?)
[swallows] I saw him. (How do you come to have this idea?) He
is near me. (Yes?) And—[pause] (What is going on? Please talk.)
There is—(What?) [swallows] (Why did you swallow?) There is
something at the other side of the wall. But I ain't—I don't see it
no more. I don't see what's going on. (What do you mean? The
man has disappeared?) He is on the other side of the wall. (Left
side or right side, outside or what?) On the—(What?) It's on the—
on my left—my left-hand side. (Before he was on your right-hand
side?) Before it was directly over me. (Also the man is now on
your left-hand side? On the wall?) On the other side of the wall.
(What does it mean, on the other side?) There is—(Outside?) No.
There is, ah, ah—on the—ah, on the—ah, on the half of the wall,
and I know he is there. And—(Just talk.) He is watching me. (Are
his pants open or closed?) There is the wall and I don't—I don't

see him. (Ah, you can't see him. How do you know he is there?) I can see his head. (Is he a dark man?) Yes. (Your father?) I am not sure. (Are you still asleep?) Yes. (Okay.)"

Immediately after awakening, Al was told to describe what he had felt. Although he pointed to his hips, he stated that the "change" took place above his "waistline." The following elaboration was also recorded and transcribed: "(What did you see and feel?) I remember being in a carriage and a man sitting at the side of the carriage crowding me in." Another time, he described the carriage as large, and felt himself "completely blocked in." Asked whether he felt that the man was very tall, he stated, "Very tall and strong. Like a giant compared to me. In other words, I was afraid of him." Further in the transcript, the patient said, "Then I seemed to have the strength to push him off and he fell to the sidewalk. As I did, I grew large from the hips up, as I am now, even as I was a baby. And the man seemed to get smaller and smaller and disappeared in nothing. (How were your legs?) That of a child, and from the hips up I was a man. And when I climbed out of the carriage down to the walk I became a child again. (How were your arms?) They felt very heavy, leaden from my tips of my fingers to the forearms, the whole forearm. And when I touched my open hands and pushed the man off the carriage, I had to do it with some effort. (Did you wish it?) Yes. And I was greatly surprised when I succeeded in moving my arms and pushing him off the side of the carriage. (Did you have the feeling that your arms had grown at the time when the whole upper part of your body had been growing?) Yes. My arms had grown and the upper part of my body had grown and I felt I had the strength. But it seemed for a little while too much effort to move them. But I finally did. First part-way, and then I had full power to move them. (When did you feel the growing?) When he fell, was pushed off the side of the carriage to the sidewalk, I stood up and felt very strong from the waist up. I had suddenly matured as I am now. (You grew before or after you pushed him off?) I grew afterwards. But I felt the strength coming as I pushed him . . . I felt a great relief when I saw him fall to the floor and I felt I became strong. (What about your wish that he would go away?) I did wish that he was completely destroyed or something."

In this hypnoanalytic session, the patient dared, for the first time, to permit his aggressive wishes against his father to break through and immediately translated them into action. My prompting helped although I had never suspected that he would do what he did. It was acting-out; nevertheless, occurring as it did in hypnoanalysis, it related to the past, not to the present, thus freeing him from the shackling influences of this past and proving to him that he could overcome them. The words, "I am better now than in years," signified a high level of relief for the patient. What occurred, in a way, was an actual "undoing," and when the carriage, the symbol of his helplessness, of his infancy, rolled "into the water," meaning that it was destroyed, it was also a measure of the greatest single advance the patient had yet made in therapy. It is interesting, however, that the patient fought the reprojected introject of his father and not one of his symbolizations. These were still dangerous, though much less so than before.

Despite all this progress, Al was still only greatly improved, not cured. At the final playback, he mentioned that, at times, he felt small and, at times, grown-up. "I believe when I felt frightened I was small and when I was grown, I felt myself." He added that fear was no longer so much a part of him. He also was sure that, in the hypnoanalytic session, he had not seen people in the street, but again felt lost. He did not elaborate on his expression, "I am lost," however, a certain element of that feeling was still present. The patient did not recall, during the playback, that he had visualized his former home, but, at least in the hypnoanalytic session, he had not heeded his father; he did not go to him when he called.

His father's sexual organ was still a cause of great concern to Al, and he visualized on that occasion his father "high up . . ." and, still unyielding, expressed in his words as, ". . . and he doesn't move away from me." However, the patient had been potent for quite some time. The feeling he had formerly had that his own genitalia were not in proper condition rarely returned.

Further signs of Al's improvement were revealed when he changed one of his other symbolizations for his father, the wall. In the hypnoanalytic session, it was apparent that this wall, unlike the way it appeared before, was no longer confining, no longer circumscribing, and evidently not too high since he could see his father's

head on the other side. His father was still watching him. Al had not entirely gotten rid of him, but in this last visualization, he was on a level with the patient, no longer above him.

I saw Al nine times after this last hypnoanalytic session. About two weeks after this session, he informed me that he had broken a wall at home when repairing something and, as he put it, had "got anxiety and perspired." He had postponed doing this work for some time, but was able to perform it eventually. On one occasion, he said to me, "I am interested in people although I don't get too much experience." On another occasion, he stated, "One thing, I still hate to be with people . . . Sometimes I feel one-hundred-percent self-confidence."

At his final visit which took place about eight months after his last hypnoanalytic session, Al asked me for drugs to help him feel relaxed during the marriage ceremony. A few weeks later, he married and impregnated his wife. Thereafter, he refused further treatment, but there were long telephone calls and an exchange of Christmas greetings. Seven years after he had terminated his therapy, he wrote me that a tumor at the apex of his lung had been detected. He died of lung cancer two years later. Obviously, the marriage had been a good one because his widow wrote me a touching letter.

Since this case has been presented for the structure of the hypnoanalytic visualizations in patients suffering from an obsessive compulsive reaction, I should like to mention here the opportunity which arose during the latter part of Al's treatment to confirm or disconfirm the diagnosis I had made of him. Al had expressed a desire, at that time, to be hypnotized by another doctor. I sent him to an experienced psychiatrist who told me, after careful examination, that the patient was suffering from an obsessive compulsive reaction and that he could not detect any basis for the diagnosis of a schizophrenic reaction or of a schizoid personality.

It is regrettable that this patient, who had endured so much before he found a measure of relief, should have had a premature termination of his existence. It would have been even more regrettable had psychotherapy not allowed at least a few of these years to be fulfilling to him.

ETTA

Etta, thirty-three years old and married, a clothes cutter by trade, was born in one of the larger European cities. She came to this country after having spent several years in South Africa where she said she had felt less tense than previously or since. This case history probably leaves one with a kind of "scattered feeling," the same feeling I got while treating the patient.

Etta had always suffered from persistent and recurrent anxieties and doubts, although until somewhat prior to coming to me, she had been able to cope with them. She stated that she did not know what it was that frightened her and that this insecurity was affecting her husband, who, from her descriptions, was an already inhibited person. It had been hard for her to tell him that, despite her anxieties, she wanted a child. It was not the pain of childbirth the patient had feared, but the responsibilities a child would entail. When she did conceive, she felt very well during her pregnancy and worked almost up to the time of delivery. There had been shorter periods of increased tension, but a few months after her confinement, the heightened tension became constant. This tension was always worse in the morning, though her sleep was generally undisturbed. At times, she awoke feeling panicky. Etta had to stop nursing the baby because this tension had diminished her supply of milk. She was no longer able to eat regularly and had lost five or six pounds of weight over a short period of time.

Everything the patient did was a huge problem for her; she had conflicts over whether to bathe the baby or whether to do something else. She tried to keep busy the entire day, but when she had a visitor, or when she herself had to pay a visit, her tension increased. Previously, she would feel tense only before starting a new activity, and her tension would ease the moment she would finish. This was no longer the case.

The patient's background was middle-class, her father having been a wholesale merchant. However, there were money problems at home, principally because her father helped his sister financially. Etta resented this aunt not only because she thought that the money problems caused differences between her parents and the

tension her mother exhibited at times, but also because this aunt was a meddling person.

Etta's mother was a native of a smaller city a few hours away from where the patient was born. Etta had been afraid of her maternal grandmother, in whose house everything seemed to have been prohibited. This grandmother disliked kissing or hugging for health reasons. She regarded food as extremely important and hoarded apples and candy. She also hoarded boxes and newspapers. During one hypnoanalytic session, a cockchafer, which disgusted and frightened Etta, changed into this woman. Her paternal grandmother the patient described as a nice, but distant person.

Etta's uncle, her mother's brother, lived in the same city. She liked both him and his wife and always felt very much at home when visiting them. The patient was under the impression that her maternal relatives had better values than her paternal relatives, possibly because the latter looked down on Etta's immediate family.

The patient heard her mother described as much more energetic and self-reliant before her marriage than afterwards. She had been a teacher, and people in trouble had come to her for advice. She once liked to swim, but later was afraid to do so. She was also afraid of jumping from low heights, of being in a crowd; she could not stand smoke, and in addition, had been a poor traveler. She was always trying to put things in a "sweeter" light; could not bring herself to say anything "bad." Her attitude was one of pushing things off. Her interest in social functions was small. She disliked visiting her husband's family because she felt they did not care for her. She was obviously prudish and had never allowed her daughter to see her in the nude. She also disliked off-color jokes, and though Etta herself enjoyed them, she would never have admitted it.

When the patient was about two or three years of age, her mother had to go to a hospital because of an infection, and the infant told everybody that her mother had run away. Etta could never remember whether she had been told this or whether she had invented it.

Etta's mother always expected her to perform, but never backed her up when she did. The mother seems to have withdrawn in most situations, including those involving her daughter's need for her support. At the same time, she would admonish her daughter not to be "forward," as she herself had been. When the child expressed an intention to undertake something, her mother would criticize her, and if she actually ventured on some activity, the mother would either be obstructive or show indifference. When the daughter received a gift, the mother would question its usefulness or necessity. Because of the mother's passivity, the patient became unable to engage in anything whole-heartedly, or to assert herself. Nevertheless, Etta could not remember any specific incident in this connection and had identified with her mother to a large extent.

In her own way, the mother had been protective. She had always encouraged her daughter to study or to learn skills that would be useful in the future. She had sent the girl to dancing schools of various kinds and to classes in rhythmic gymnastics. The patient had liked to dance socially and had been a good dancer, but she was usually a wallflower, for which her mother comforted her with assurances that she would eventually get everything she wished for, only a little later than others did. She had beaten the patient only once. This occurred when the child, who had a compulsion to take valueless articles from other youngsters and often felt that she should take something from the place she was visiting, had brought home a dirty, torn picture of an angel. Other data about the mother were that she had suffered from migraine headaches and, at other times felt ill, but refused to consult a physician. This behavior confused the girl.

Etta said that if they came upon an accident, mother and daughter would look away while the father would go to investigate. The mother liked taking her daughter to the outskirts of the city to pick flowers. From about eight to twelve years of age, however, Etta preferred to accompany her father to a coffeehouse where she enjoyed thumbing through magazines, or to attend the races with him.

The mother would have liked to spend vacation time in the

mountains, but the family usually went to the seashore. She was interested in music, the arts, and in education, and brought up her children almost single-handedly.

The father did not share any of his wife's interests. He liked the sea, and early remembrances of the Mediterranean and the North Sea often appeared in the patient's hypnoanalytic sessions. The father had been a heavy smoker and experienced several nicotine intoxications. If he was unable to go out on a weekend, he suffered some kind of intestinal trouble. Because he liked to spend his evenings in a coffeehouse and was not home when Etta felt she needed him, she did not feel secure with him. She said he had spoiled her, but that they had not been close. The father would have enjoyed displaying his daughter, but she was too obese. He was also quite quick-tempered and once told her in a pique that she would not succeed in life.

Etta's father used to travel on business. Much English had been spoken in the house. When the patient was twelve or fourteen years of age, the father had suffered a stroke and started to age quickly. Always afraid of other children, Etta drew closer to her mother.

The patient had one brother, her senior by eight years. They slept in the same room, and only when she was fifteen years of age, a folding screen was placed between the beds. At first, she stated that she had never seen her brother in the nude, that he had not dressed or undressed in the same room. Elaborating during her fifty-seventh hypnoanalytic session, she told me that she often visualized "a man's underwear," but she did not know to whom it belonged, except that it belonged to somebody in her family. She knew she had seen her father's underwear, but said she could not even imagine her brother's. However, she did remember now that she had seen her brother dress, but said she had always looked away. Another time, she reported that, as a child, she had seen "a boy urinating" and she "had looked away mentally"—a screen memory.

Sometimes, when her brother had friends home to study with him, the infant would sit under the table, and give way to a compulsion to pinch the boys' legs or pull hairs out of them. Some of

the boys regarded her as a little nuisance, others as her brother's "sweet kid sister." Only once had one of them punished her, but this did not prevent her from continuing to annoy them. It was an excellent opportunity not only for bodily contact and direct aggression, but also for studying the boys from below—a kind of scoptophilia.

Etta's brother had also suffered from social anxiety, though he had many friends. He was very intelligent, and successful in his profession. Etta followed him to the United States and, when en route, a letter came telling her that he had married, it upset her badly.

Brother and sister often played a game called "wheelbarrow." He held the girl's feet while she walked on her hands and fell down constantly. Though she was covered, enough was visible to suggest voyeurism on the part of the brother, and some exhibitionism on the part of the infant—both traits connected with social anxiety. More details of the sister-brother relationship are given in the reported hypnoanalytic sessions and their subsequent discussions.

The patient, a seven-month baby whom the mother nursed for some time, was small and thin until her third year. At that time, a maidservant who had played an important role in her and her brother's life, suddenly was dismissed without the infant having been told about it. Etta was quite frightened about this. She could not remember whether she actively began to overeat thereafter or whether she was given too much food, but she became very heavy. Even her swimsuits had to be made to order, and their delivery was often delayed because the manufacturers, incredulous over the size, would check the measurements before proceeding. The many jokes about her weight had humiliated Etta both as infant and child. At fifteen years of age, she had her menarche, grew more tense than she had been and simultaneously lost weight.

Etta had been very frightened by her toilet training. She was constipated most of her childhood and had been given enemas every second or third day and many laxatives. The tendency towards increased dependency was subsequently overtly expressed in the patient's history. Her father once told her that the constipa-

tion would cause accumulated fecal matter to emerge orally. At another occasion, he said that the enemas would do the same. Both these remarks had alarmed her greatly.

The patient often suffered from large hives. She also experienced gastrointestinal disorders, including repeated vomiting in her infancy, which would force her mother to stay home. This stopped when Etta entered school, although she reported that she had always felt fearful and uneasy before going to school; she vomited only once or twice in school.

As an infant, she liked to dance and sing for her parents but felt frightened at the prospect of having to recite English nursery rhymes when her father's English speaking business friends were invited.

The patient had entered kindergarten at an early age and was already in school at five years of age. At the age of six or seven, she had a strange nightmare each night for many months, in which "scrolls and figures," abstract designs in different colors plunged in on her. She awoke in panic and would try not to go back to sleep.

The primary school and the technical high school she attended were the same schools her brother had been to, and she was either spoiled as her brother's sister or was expected to be just as good a student as he had been. Both had been hard to bear.

In grammar school, she was afraid of the principal, the teachers, and the other children. There was only one teacher whom Etta liked, and she had written fairy tales for her in the style of Hans Andersen, had bound them carefully in book form, and presented them to her. Unfortunately, this teacher died.

While at technical high school, Etta had an "accident" in class. She had not dared to ask for permission to leave the room, not only because that particular teacher did not like it, but also because she was afraid of the toilet. The teacher had taunted her because of the accident, as had the other pupils. Also while in this school, she said she intentionally tried not to look at anybody—a derivative of her previous scoptophilia—and had been mocked for this by the more successful girls.

In dealing with this patient's fear of toilets, I will not discuss the many similarities in Etta's and Al's cases. Etta's mother always

had to accompany her when the girl had to use an unknown toilet. In school, she tried to go to the toilet only when other children were "out;" or she would ask the school janitress to escort her, although there were features possessed by the janitress, such as yellowish hands, which had disgusted her. These hands had also been discussed by other pupils, but Etta felt anything was better than having to go alone. The toilet flush still gave the patient "the creeps;" she always tried to flush just before leaving the toilet, and there were added difficulties when the toilet was too small or the door would not open outwards. When the toilet was raised on a step, Etta said she was not able to "keep the distance." For a long time, she also had the fear that something, such as a mouse, could emerge from the bowl, and she had often looked in to see whether one had. At other times, she had been afraid of falling in. She had had many dreams about toilets, mostly multiple ones with various hazards, as for instance, "frightening pipes."

In the same way as she had been disgusted by the janitress's yellowish hands, Etta had been easily sickened, for instance, when certain persons prepared food for her, especially the paternal aunt whom she disliked, and had been unable to eat. This fastidiousness had, however, stopped some time ago.

There was still another feature in the bathroom at home that had frightened Etta very much. The metal bathtub had leaked, and when the plumber soldered it, yellowish patches resulted which had to be hidden under a sheet when the child used it.

Other symptoms which Etta reported at various times included the fact that, as a child, she had felt compelled to step on paving stones in such a way as to avoid the clefts between them. She revealed that learning to swim had been difficult for her; that, at one time, she had been frightened of green water and of what might lie on the bottom of a lake, and of the green pillars of the bathhouses. Earlier as an infant, though, she used to run into the ocean, and enjoyed strolling in the rain. As a child, she had not been able to learn skiing, but delighted in it now, though she was still afraid of steep slopes, with or without snow. The patient had first also been afraid to mount a horse, but now loved to ride and had her own horse in South Africa.

Her worst handicap, however, had been her social anxiety. She

had been afraid to voice an opinion even when she had one. She had always felt outside of things, that she had never been fully accepted.

As to her sexual history, she said only that she had learned about sex from books and her girl friends.

I will now present her more significant hypnoanalytic sessions in the sequence in which they happened.

At her fourth hypnosis, regression was induced. She reported afterwards that, as a child of nine, she remembered being in a train in Denmark, but in a different compartment from the one of the other members of her family. This was a good demonstration of her feelings of loneliness, even within her own family.

After her fifteenth hypnoanalytic session, in which regression had been induced, the patient said that she had twice been to Denmark and, between visits there, had gone abroad somewhere else. She was then seven or eight years old, at the age when her father liked to take her out. She was very clothes conscious, and used to wear special hats. Once, on the beach, she discovered a cuttlefish (she used the German word, *Tintenfisch*), and she and her brother were both disgusted by it. Then she said that, at three years of age, she had been to Switzerland and remembered the hotel where they had "a wonderful sausage for breakfast." After talking about another vacation spot, she remarked that her father usually missed trains because he would linger too long on the platform when the train stopped at stations.

In this hypnoanalytic session, Etta visualized former ego states accompanied by their respective emotions, and she also described symbolizations. She stated several times how she had tried to overcome her social anxiety by wearing an especially nice dress and how bitterly disappointed she was that this charm never worked. The importance she attached to wearing a hat showed that it was a symbol, displaced upwards.

Another episode was described in which the patient and her brother had both been readily disgusted. And we will hear later also of various "seafood" sickening and frightening Etta—all being sexual symbols. Then came information about a particular sausage with a wonderful taste; in another hypnoanalytic session, she was even able to smell it. I need hardly mention the uncon-

scious equation of penis, sausage, and feces, and the importance of smell for patients suffering from obsessive compulsive reactions.

In her next, the sixteenth, hypnoanalytic session, Etta was again regressed and told to talk during the hypnoanalysis. Here is what she saw.* "My father is taking me to school. The chestnut trees are blooming. There are caterpillars (she used the German word, *Raupen*) on the ground. I am disgusted (in German, *Es graust mich*)." After the hypnoanalytic session, she stated that she not only saw the chestnut trees, but also smelled them. She had always been afraid of caterpillars and had tried to avoid them. The symbol is obvious. It is interesting that this particular visualization, combined with a smell sensation, occurred when Etta was told now to express herself and report on what she had seen *during* the hypnoanalytic session, not afterwards.

In the seventeenth hypnoanalytic session, I first gave her relaxing suggestions, then regression was induced. She reported that she was in school, although she saw neither the teacher nor the other pupils; she felt afraid. The patient was now told to let the visualization change more closely to resemble what she was afraid of, and she saw a toilet with an overhead flush. She was directed to let it change yet again, and she said, "Male part."

In the eighteenth hypnoanalytic session, regression was also induced, and Etta stated that she was in Denmark. She saw her father eating pastry with *"crevettes,"* and felt disgusted. Told to let the image change nearer to what it really meant, she said, "Many male parts."

In the nineteenth hypnosis, the patient first received relaxing suggestions. Then she was directed to visualize a movie and to describe what she saw. She related that, when she was about eight years of age, a teacher who had been on friendly terms with her mother berated Etta because she had been impertinent to her mother. The patient stated that her reason for being rude was that she had always resented her brother's having more freedom than she had. Next, she described how she sat under the table and pinched his friends' legs. This was a recurring visualization. Talking over this hypnoanalytic session at her subsequent appoint-

---

* In this case, the records have not been transcribed, but the wording has been retained as much as possible.

ment, she told me that she was not able to visualize her brother when he was fifteen or sixteen years of age—a repression.

At the following hypnosis, she received relaxing suggestions before and after she was supposed to visualize. Between the relaxing suggestions, she was told to imagine the stage of a theater. Etta could see nothing. Then it was suggested that she let an actor appear from the right wing and an actress from the left wing of the stage. Both should perform. The actor appeared, bent down to an approximately four-year-old "actress," took her around the waist and lifted her up to himself. The patient felt tension. After the hypnoanalytic session, she reported that she not only could not see the actor's face, but that he also had a mask over it. Obviously, it was her brother whose face in early adolescence she had been unable to remember, raising his little sister up to him.

Very interesting was the symbolical content of her twenty-second hypnoanalytic session. She received relaxing suggestions at the beginning, then was told to visualize a theater. Etta spontaneously pictured a few undiversified people, then her mother on the left side from the audience, isolated. More to the right were her father, one of his friends, and the paternal aunt, who wore a disapproving expression on her face. The patient, six years old, stood a little farther away. She and her mother were both frightened.

At her next appointment, the patient informed me that outside the family circle, her father was more charming than at home, whereas her brother had behaved in the opposite manner. In the hypnoanalytic session, Etta skipped over her brother, but introduced the father's unlikable sister into the immediate family. The differing interests of the patient's parents have already been mentioned, also that her mother was shy and retiring, apparently just as much afraid of this sister-in-law as was her daughter. The strong emotional interaction between Etta and her mother and the "egotization" of her mother the patient demonstrated clearly in this visualization since she made herself stand quite apart from her mother. The absence of the brother might have had different reasons. Either Etta's quite ambivalent feelings with regard to the two males in her family caused it, or he might have been represented by one of the indistinguishable persons around her mother.

The patient, at times, was very jealous of the relationship between her mother and her brother, for instance, when both went out to play tennis. She may, therefore, have relegated him to the status of one of these incidental males. A third possibility would be that she had so strongly identified with her brother that she herself presented the two of them.

The twenty-third hypnoanalytic session demonstrates very well Etta's constant state of doubt and her inability to make up her mind about anything. She first received relaxing suggestions, then was told to visualize the stage of a theater with an actor and an actress appearing on it and performing. She described how her favorite maternal uncle had wanted to buy her a birthday gift when she was about twelve years old and, walking around a shopping center with her, asked her repeatedly whether she wanted a book or a practical gift. She was unable to make up her mind and received a book which she never read. The girl had felt very uneasy the whole time. She then remembered this uncle's two boys and how the younger one had embraced and kissed her on the stomach when she was six years old. She always had the impression that this family had been much closer knit than her own, and also that her uncle and aunt knew much more than she herself. This may have been the reason why she chose a book in the end. There had also been family talk about these relatives having brought their children up more liberally than the patient had been. The cousins were allowed to spend the summers at a camp, and Etta had once visited this place, accompanied by her mother, and, although she knew everybody, did not dare to leave her mother's side. The further visualization dealt with this aunt's and her family's philosophy of life.

This hypnoanalytic session disclosed several isolated episodes and former ego states related to different age levels of the patient, connected only by the appearance of the same persons and by Etta's emotions with regard to them. The patient's distress about her shyness and restricting education, and some revolt against it, are clearly indicated.

At the beginning of the twenty-fifth hypnosis, Etta received relaxing suggestions, then was regressed, but without success. She was therefore told to visualize a theater for the interpretation of a

dream. This suggestion also failed. But when she was told to let an actor and an actress appear, she informed me that she saw herself, at about five or six years of age appear on the stage. She then lifted her arms pleadingly to one of her brother's friends, on whom she had had a "crush," begging him to understand her. But to the boy she was only his friend's little sister.

At her next appointment, Etta told me that she had always fantasized that this boy would marry her, without having the slightest foundation for the daydream which continued from her sixth year until she left Europe. She had preserved all his letters, relating their contents solely to herself. However, the patient had not seen him again, although he was now in the United States but a married man. On the other hand, she had not reciprocated when another boy in junior high school had made it obvious to her that he liked her. The first youngster, who had entered her life much earlier than the second one, was, as her brother's friend, apparently a substitute for him. This conjecture is strengthened by Etta's admission that she never told her mother about this boy although she had speculated with one of their maids whether, when she was married to him, they would have children. The maid, a mother substitute, had answered in the affirmative.

At the same appointment, the patient told me an interesting fact which had a connection with her hypnoanalytic sessions only in so far as it had occurred when she was showing improvement because of them. I had given her a prescription for Carbrital,® half strength, for her tension, and Ritalin®, 10 mg, to put her in a better frame of mind. Her need to take drugs had already decreased considerably, but when she did take any, Etta informed me that she took two Carbritals along with the Ritalin. Anne, the first patient discussed in this book, once told me that she always took two drugs at the same time, or broke one tablet in half and took both halves, one against her father, the other against her mother. In Etta's family, there were three consequential members, which meant that she required three tablets.

In the twenty-seventh hypnosis, Etta received relaxing suggestions and was again told to visualize the stage of a theater. She visualized both her parents in the dining room. During this hypnoanalytic session, Etta made one use of the word Mama. The

patient and her brother were listening to an opera on the radio. Then, she made a bed for herself of two chairs, and felt very protected by her brother's presence. She had often "curled up" to him. Her father then left the room. The parents had nothing to do with the occurrences in the visualization. This hypnoanalytic session, which demonstrates a reawakening of a former ego state, makes previous conjectures that the patient behaved towards her brother and felt about him as she would towards a husband, still more believable. However, she stopped short of accepting this and, in her fantasies, often substituted her brother's friend for him. The parents, in this hypnoanalytic session, were present as "chaperons" only and not involved in the events. At her next appointment, Etta told me, "I feel wonderful. I don't know what happened." The patient was now able to do small chores at home.

In her forty-first hypnoanalytic session, Etta received relaxing suggestions, then regression was induced, but she did not visualize anything. She was therefore told that she was again in a theater, that an actor would appear from the right side of the stage, an actress from the left, and that they would perform. She reported that she saw herself as a very small girl, three or four years of age, looking up to two tall persons. Afterwards, she was crawling around in the foyer at home. At the end of this foyer was a toilet which had a darkened window, from which the infant had often looked down into the courtyard and had felt afraid. Etta said that this toilet had been remodeled and had a new seat. Her brother was leaving the house, and she went to a pantry off the foyer and ate a cookie there to console herself for the brother's departure. She then rearranged the cookies so that it would not be detected that she had eaten one.

At her next session, the patient told me that she felt in this hypnoanalysis as if she were at home, looking for something, running around restlessly without knowing why. She said this is still occurring. Although Etta did not visualize anything when regression was induced, the contents of this hypnoanalytic session clearly show a regression, a reawakened former ego state, and not a performance on the stage of a theater. The leaving of her parents affected the infant much less than the departure of her brother, prompting her to seek consolation in an oral manner. She did not

specify what it was in the courtyard that frightened her, but her behavior once again demonstrates her ambivalence because there had apparently been no overt cause to look down into the courtyard that she found frightening. Whether the departure of her brother had also had a symbolical meaning is hard to determine. He was, after all, now married, and through psychotherapy she was weaned from him.

In the fifty-fourth hypnoanalytic session, Etta was told to let the different symbols in a dream change to their real meaning. To begin with, a flower on a suitcase turned into some kind of material. Then she visualized the steps of a fountain in her native city, a spot at which she had always felt uneasy. Next came a longer dissertation on an arts-and-crafts school she had attended before her emigration. She was directed to let the images change once more. The patient now visualized a stove in a corner, then a railroad station with wooden benches, an unfriendly waiting room. Nearby was the door of the ladies' room, but she could not open it; she had no need to do so, and she was also afraid to do so. Borborygmi were audible, and Etta was asked why she was experiencing them. She said that she was in a train going to Boston and was enjoying the sleeper. However, she felt very uncomfortable because she was afraid of the peculiar train toilet which had a raised step. The toilet was black, and she was not able to use it. Then, the patient saw a mirror in the powder room, also the curtains there. She felt quite uneasy although she likes the idea of traveling. For some reason, she had to dress in this room, and was very happy to leave it.

Etta later added to this hypnoanalytic session only that she had disliked European trains, but had always enjoyed traveling because it gave her a feeling of importance.

At her next appointment, the patient outlined a dream in which she was eating noodle soup, but the noodles were toothpicks. She associated to it tension and sex and felt as if she had swallowed the toothpicks which hurt her.

In her fifty-fifth hypnoanalytic session she received relaxing suggestions, then was asked the meaning of this dream. She said, "I was in the street, but I didn't see anything. (Look well.) We were on a vacation in Helgoland. I was six or seven years old and

I was eating fish. I see the family sitting around the table and I thought I had swallowed a bone. I do not know whether I imagined it because everybody told me it was impossible. I might not have done it, but the bone pricked me. (Were you frightened?) Yes. And it took me years until I was able to eat fish again. However, recently I have not thought about it. (How can a noodle prick?) When I ate it at first, I thought that the soup was not cooked. (Why?) The noodles were not soft. They tasted like straw and wood. I had a whole bunch of them in my mouth."

Only when she went to South Africa, had Etta been able to eat fish again. Nevertheless, this trouble had its root in another episode which she described shortly afterwards, in her fifty-seventh hypnoanalytic session. In kindergarten, she had difficulty with some apple peelings and had had the feeling that they were stuck in her throat. The most probable explanation of these episodes is that they were nothing but a globus hystericus. The patient's psychoneurotic disorder was a mixed one, and even though her main diagnosis was obsessive compulsive reaction, there was still detectable a considerable admixture of the symptoms of a conversion reaction and of a phobic reaction.

In her sixty-fifth hypnoanalytic session, Etta was told to interpret two dreams and to elaborate on them. Her boss had called her into the office to show some kind of a gown to a physician. He had asked her to bring it with her in order to sell it. The patient took her child in with her. The doctor was not particularly interested. Also present were one of Etta's girl friends and a bookkeeper. The patient had waited until the physician was in the office and then tried to persuade him to buy the gown. They did not leave the office until two hours later, and it was late. Etta would have liked to take the subway home, but it was now five o'clock, and she was aware that the rush hour was on. She told the bookkeeper that she expected to be paid for the extra time. Her girl friend then advised her not to charge overtime because Etta had previously gotten other things gratis. It became very late and the patient decided to go home. Then they were in the cutting room, standing at the cutting table. She realized there were two ways to reach the subway. One was to leap down because the subway was somehow situated below them. The other was to go back over the

cutting table, which was very long and now looked like a street. Not being able to jump, Etta had to return the whole length of the table and awoke very tense and annoyed.

In the next dream, she was in one of the larger cities of South Africa and had to catch a ferry, but she was unable to remember to what place she had to go and had forgotten the name of that locality. She walked around with a girl friend who also could not remember which ferry the patient had to take. One ferry departed from ground level; another, from the first floor. Etta again awoke feeling very tense because she had not been able to think of the name of the place she wanted to go to.

"(Talk about the second dream.) There is a building upstairs, and downstairs it is like a passage. (Letters will appear forming syllables, and the syllables will form words. Please read what you see.) Father. (Read the names of both ferries.) Ferries have no names. (Please read.) It is funny because I can see both printed. (What is the name of the first ferry?) I see the first ferry, it looks like the swan in *Lohengrin*. Nothing is written on it. (Let it change nearer to what it really represents.) I am trying to get on it, but it is backing away. I am very small. (What is your age?) I don't know. Three."

She then saw and felt herself as very tiny, smaller than before. The swan was also very small and was wearing a sailor suit. It came back and tried to bite the patient. She felt annoyed and would have liked to pinch its neck.

"(Pinch him.) I have my hands stretched out. (Do it.) I try to pinch him, but I feel sorry. Maybe he is my brother. He stands there, and he is my brother. He has his head in his hands. I try to climb on his lap. I fall on my behind; I do not cry, but I feel furious. (What does the second ferry look like?) It has a blond head . . . it sails away. I cannot make it. (Yell.) I cannot. It is just out of reach. I stand there, and I do not know what to do because I am afraid to yell. (What is your age?) School age . . . A figure turns around and beckons me to come. I cannot make it, I cannot reach him. (In both dreams there were two courses of action open to you.) Maybe it had something to do with it that as a child I was not able to jump, only when somebody held one of my fingers. I do not know why. I was annoyed that I could not jump, but I

could not take the other way either. I wished I could have jumped. (What could have happened if you had jumped?) I don't know. My mother could not do either—any of these things. We also were both afraid to learn swimming. I tried to be like my mother, but I resented it too. (By the next time you will remember the meaning of the other part of the dream, or present another one.)"

After this hypnoanalytic session, Etta was asked which bird customarily bites females. She was unable to remember its name although there is no question that she must have known it. She had just repressed it—a secondary repression.

There were no associations to the first dream; however, with the help of the material known about the patient up to this time, and the hypnoanalytic session, it may be possible partly to interpret it. Etta's social anxiety would have made her a poor saleswoman. It would have taken her a long time to persuade a customer to buy anything. Then, vacillating because of her ambivalence, she intended to try to overcome her inhibitions by asking for overtime pay. But her girl friend (actually herself) convinced her that it would be wiser not to do so. Her inability to jump may also have symbolized her incapability of jumping to a conclusion or making a decision, which inability she shared with her mother.

Whether the two ways of reaching the subway represented her brother and her father is hard to decide. The subway was the way home to her "husband;" should she jump down to her brother or walk back to her father? She chose the longer way.

The beginning of the second dream also symbolized her indecisiveness as well as her inability to remember what it was important to know. However, the hypnoanalytic session went much further. When I told the patient to read during visualization, the word "father" appeared. Then the first ferry changed into the swan in *Lohengrin* (to her brother) which tried to bite her leg. She would have liked to pinch its neck as she had pinched the legs of her brother's friends and, eventually, her brother's when she was an infant—an occasion for bodily contact and exploration and, at the same time, for aggression. The symbols are obvious. Let us remember "Leda and the Swan." Everybody was beyond her reach; the father belonged to the mother, and her brother let

her fall on her buttocks—a regressively quite sexualized part of her body—without helping her up onto his lap, where she felt she belonged—a miserable situation into which she had been born and into which she was fixed by the inability of her family to rear her sensibly.

At her next appointment, Etta related a dream which I will present in the way she told it at her sixty-sixth hypnoanalytic session and which includes a few additions from her first account. She dreamed of a ballet which had two circles of girls. Instructions as to how the dancing should go were given by somebody who looked like Etta's primary school teacher, a man of whom the child had been greatly afraid. In the hypnoanalytic session, she called this teacher "the judge," and his appearance changed later. The patient felt she was about six years of age. She was unable to pay attention to the instructions because her mind was wandering. She, therefore, had to ask her girl friend what had been said. There was a chorus line in the middle of the ballet of which only the heads of the dancers were visible. As these girls turned, their bodies looked gray, but their heads yellowish. This was a "trick" which was effected by means of yellow or orange drapes. In the outer circle were the "rebels" who were dancing, too. The "judge" was suspended in air and was closer to the girls whose heads were turning. One of these looked like an embryo. New dancers came in continuously and passed out of the ballet which was a constant twirling of heads, like balls "kept moving." Etta said there was "no limitation, no number."

"(What is happening with the embryo?) It is getting longer and does not look like a ball any more. (Is it yellow, too?) It is bending down on top like a hook and it becomes very tall. I feel very small, about three years of age, with a large hat . . . In the room— with only one leg—with a round head like a mushroom—with a big foot in the center. It gives me the feeling that I am sitting below something. (A foot?) It is very tall and it keeps getting thinner and thinner . . . (What is the connection between this tall thing and the small girl?) I don't know."

As Etta looked up, she said, this thing moved lower, bent down, and became a person.

"(Look the person in the face.) I don't know. (What kind of clothes is the person wearing?) A jacket and pants."

It was her brother, about twelve years of age. He held a spoon to feed his infant sister who was sitting on the floor, as was he.

"(What does he give you to eat?) I don't know. My brother taps the spoon on an egg. The egg is gone; my brother gets up. I am sitting there alone, and I feel helpless. My brother wanted to give me something to eat, and he went away. (What did he want to give you to eat?) I don't know."

The other girls, the rebels, were shadowy and kept moving. They were not identifiable, just a background. At this point, the patient said both her eyes itched.

"(Who are the girls?) They are my school friends who run away, they keep leaving. (Who is the 'judge'?) He is suspended in air, he sits on a rope. He is either balancing or there is a seat attached to it. He is bald. (Who was bald?) I cannot think of anybody who was bald, middle-aged, and heavy. I am not at ease with the 'judge'. (Why not?) He judged the ballet. I was in it, and I could not follow the instructions. I don't know who he is. (Why could you not follow the instructions?) I was always sidetracked, thinking about something else. (About what? Letters will appear forming syllables, and the syllables will form words.) I am reminded of school when I was about six years old. I was ordered to do nothing for one minute and was afterwards asked what I had thought. I could remember nothing, and I was told that that is not possible. (Why did your mind wander? Letters will appear . . .) My mother does not know why. I cannot reach her."

It is interesting to note here the color in which Etta saw letters. When asked about this, she described them as red, two to three feet tall.

Reverting to Etta's dream and hypnoanalytic session, I should remind the reader that she had had very good training in rhythmic gymnastics, dancing, including tap dancing; the latter she liked very much. The "judge" in this dream was some part of her superego, reprojected. It was a strict, rigid part of it, yet somehow balancing in air, whereas she had been unable to balance herself even on solid ground. She (her ego) was incapable of listening to "the judge" because around that age she had been what she later in her treatment labeled a "disgusting misfit," torn between her instinctual conflicts.

The "rebels" outside were just a background, just what the pa-

tient would have preferred to be but had never been, unable to have her own wishes fulfilled or, to be more precise, unable even to formulate wishes, except indistinctly in her many daydreams. Etta stated several times that she had always had a rich fantasy life. In her own opinion, when she was about six years old, she had been a nuisance at home. Whether the itching of her eyes had any connection to her scoptophilia or bore another significance such as looking for the girls who constantly moved away like her indistinguishable schoolmates, it is not possible to say. The reason for all her frustrations had been her inability to reach her mother, who also did not know the cause of these disturbances.

The inner circle to which the patient belonged, consisted of her school friends or, as I have just called them, schoolmates, a more accurate description because Etta had seemingly had no real friends as a child. They appeared gray and amorphous, their heads the color of the hands of the janitress in primary school who had disgusted them—the color of cowardice. One of them took the form of an embryo which then became elongated, whereas the patient, at the same time, shrank to a three-year old infant with a large hat, recognized from her other hypnoanalytic sessions. Out of this elongated form—a sexual symbol—her brother developed, he being the purpose and goal of her emotions, at whose feet—below the table—Etta had sat as an infant. But he also had been moving away. The symbolical meaning of the other parts of this hypnoanalytical session is too overdetermined to need further discussion.

In Etta's eighty-first hypnoanalytic session, regression was induced. The patient said, "I am sitting on my bed. (Your age?) I am still in a crib (in German *Gitterbett*). I can't get out. It is night. There is a chair in front of the bed. I see myself sitting there with steam kettles, my mother, some umbrellas and sheets. My mother is sitting with me below the sheets. There is a lot of steam. (For what purpose?) I am sick. I see an umbrella against the wind. A wind shelter (in German, *Windfaenger*) in the hotel in Helgoland. There are crabs walking on the beach. (Your age?) Five. They seem to march in a row. I am afraid to jump over them. I don't know, they might get up under my skirt. Now, I just see the beach with mud. Now, I see nothing. (Look well.) I am at

home at night. I am in bed with my mother. (Your age?) Five or six, maybe younger. My father has left his bed and is looking out the window. It is still dark. I have seen this once before. I ask him what he is doing. He has used the pot, and he tells me that he does it only to stay upright. I remember this had happened quite often. He would say that he was looking out the window to see whether his secretary has gone to work yet. When I asked him what the pot is for, he said it is to keep his balance. That has bothered me for some time."

Etta did not like to sleep alone. On Sundays, she and her brother went into their parents' empty beds.

"Now I see these things in the bathtub, and I think they look like crabs. I believe the crabs were there before because I had to have a sheet in the bathtub." She went on to say that her father had fixed the elbow of the sink and had burned his fingers on an overhead pipe.

In this hypnoanalytic session, the patient again brought up a number of short episodes or former ego states. In the first, she was simply in her crib. Then followed an episode when Etta had apparently had some respiratory ailment, and her mother provided steam from a steam kettle and also protection—umbrellas which did not belong to this equipment. Etta remembered an umbrella for the wind in a hotel in Helgoland where crabs on the beach "marched in a row"—a sexual symbol—and there was mud; they were dirty. Now she described a longer episode about which she had already had some knowledge before hypnosis. The father's answers to certain questions were, to say the least, peculiar. Her difficulty in keeping her balance has already been mentioned, and her father's statement about his reason for using the pot may well have contributed to it. Then, she and her brother were in the parental beds playing what she would have very much liked to be reality. Thereafter, she went back to her sexual symbols, the yellow patches in the bathtub mentioned in her anamnesis. Her father's working on a pipe and burning himself on other hot ones, also sexual symbols, concluded this easily analyzable recital.

There had been another occurrence connected with her father which the patient had partially recalled without the aid of hypnosis and which had returned in several of her hypnoanalytic ses-

sions. Again she was in her parents' bedroom, looking onto her father's night table. There were two rings, one of which had always looked mysterious to her. Etta had often wished to know why the father did not want to talk about this ring. It had a dull red or brown stone with a foreign inscription. Her father had warned her not to touch this ring. The other ring had been like a snake with a blue or a red eye. When she had later asked her brother about these, he had remembered only one ring with a blue stone, and nothing special about it.

In Etta's eighty-third hypnoanalytic session, regression was again induced. The patient said, "I am sitting on the beach. I am squatting near a cabana. (Your age?) I must be very small, three, because I recall a photograph. But it is not the picture I am seeing now. My mother looks thin and tired [borborygmi]. I am sitting on her lap. I am looking at my father's night table. I am so small I cannot even see the top. I have to get up on my toes. I see a small girl, but I feel quite detached from her. I see my parents' bedroom. Now I see my mother holding this enema, and I do not want to have one. She says I must have it until the water is halfway down the glass. (Do you feel it?) No. [borborygmi] My stomach hurts me. I feel hot water. Now I am afraid it will go too high up. (What would happen if it did?) I do not know. It stopped in time. I remember every Friday night having supper in bed." Her description of a peaceful Friday evening followed, and then that of another time when the infant was in one of her parents' beds. The visualization continued.

Here again we have a string of past ego states. Etta's squatting near the ocean and her getting an enema apparently have an associative connection. She was emotionally enough involved to feel stomach pains, to feel the hot water, and to have borborygmi.

Another description of a similar incident appeared in her eighty-fifth hypnoanalytic session where, toward the end, she described a wobbling night pot which smiled maliciously at her and walked away. She then talked about a clock whose ticking had made it sound like a man coming nearer and nearer to her bed and then walking away again; she had always been afraid of this clock. Her mother had entered the room and had looked annoyed; Etta's bed was wet. The child expected a complete change

of sheets. She had felt constipated and had wanted to hold back, describing herself as being "tied in knots," and had sat very defiantly on the pot. She had insisted on having an enema as the only way to get rid of her uncomfortable feeling. She said it was like a routine. Afterwards she saw herself in another bed with her parents.

Here, the situation was different from the one formerly described, even to the extent of being partially reversed. She never explained what she meant by "feeling constipated," but clearly indicated that she had intended to hold back, an active dependency, as was her insistence that her mother help her by administering an enema. What she did by herself, holding back, was for the purpose of making herself dependent on her mother—to relieve her of the fecal matter and, at the same time, of her tension: a passive-aggressive kind of behavior expressing ambivalent emotions. The episode also demonstrates her tendency to want others to do things for her. It is obvious that this experience, as well as the incident formerly described must have excited Etta very much, simultaneously aggravating her anxiety.

With reference to the eighty-fifth hypnoanalytic session, I want to remark that, at the beginning of her therapy, the patient complained that she had had great difficulties in keeping her balance, especially when engaging in certain sports such as skiing down a steep incline. She would anticipate the predicament but enjoy performing the sport until the point at which balance was involved. At the playback of the hypnoanalytic session, Etta herself felt that the problem she had in balancing related to her early annoyance with the "wobbling pot" and to her father's peculiar explanation for his use of the pot de chambre. There seems to have been a sexualization of her infantile sensations of equilibrium and of bodily movements in space. These are considered as masturbatory equivalents. The patient's apprehension and fantasy about the ticking clock go back to the same root—a rhythmic sound regarded as a projection of the patient's genital pulsations emanating from repressed sexual excitement. The equilibrium phobia* not only related but also contributed to her neurotic in-

---

* FENICHEL, OTTO: *The Psychoanalytic Theory of Neurosis.* New York, Norton, 1945.

decisiveness which, essentially, was generated by identification with her psychoneurotic mother and by Etta's special upbringing by this mother. She also suffered from neurotic indecisiveness on a claustrophobic level, that is to say, a definite decision excluding the possibility of escape. In the same way, a choice between her father and her brother was impossible for her to make.

Three months after this hypnoanalytic session had been performed, Etta stopped her treatment. She felt well enough not to want to clear everything up. In the meantime, she has had another child without any complications, and is feeling well and content.

An examination of Etta's hypnoanalytic sessions revealed the existence of many more factual reawakened past ego states than existed in Al's hypnoanalyses. Many of her visualizations not only seemed isolated one from the other, but also undid the previous part. However, there was very little undoing of the modifying aspects of the visualizations. Much more background material was described than in Al's case. The same short spurts of episodes repeated themselves in different combinations in various hypnoanalytic sessions. A lot of symbolization was apparent, less than in Al's case, but more than with the patients of the former group described in this book. Etta displayed a strong admixture of the symptoms of a phobic reaction and of a conversion reaction to her obsessive compulsive reaction.

I would like to add that the patient's upbringing was not typical of Europe as, for instance, a shared bedroom for two children of different sexes shows. This must have been obvious to Etta when she visited in other homes. Her brother's friends may also have made remarks about it, possibly disapproving, though Etta reported nothing to this effect. However, it must have influenced her impression that she and her brother belonged together, strongly coloring her complicated Oedipus complex.

IV

COMPULSIVE PERSONALITY

HARLEY

HARLEY was a mechanical engineer, twice married, once divorced, who came to me for treatment at the age of fifty-two because of the difficulty he experienced expressing himself effectively with his superiors. Despite the fact that he was a very diligent worker, he was often discharged or constrained to leave positions voluntarily, his last dismissal having been quite disagreeable. He also made poor showings at job interviews. When talking to a superior, he would find himself unable to think and afterwards felt a "deep sense of guilt" because his answers seemed to himself to be stupid. They were appropriate to the questions put to him, but he was conscious of adding, embellishing and expatiating too much. To repair the effects of these excesses, he would explain further. When he was dismissed the last time, it was due to the fact that he did not reveal that an error that had been made was not made by himself but by his immediate superior.

For a few years, he had been concerned about himself and had consequently been reading books about psychology and psychiatry.

The patient was highly intelligent and extremely conscientious. He possessed a good sense of humor, was gentle in manner, and clean in habit and person. He disliked hurting people. Early in life, he learned to control his anger to so great a degree that he himself thought he could not hate. He enumerated a perfect list of reaction formation character traits. He was very well read on a variety of topics, cultural as well as scientific. He held a number of patents, but never made money with them. Several of his pa-

153

pers had been published in Navy magazines and in journals that paid for his contributions, and he had been working on a novel, chiefly autobiographical in nature.

He had always felt more relaxed in female company and desired to be treated by a female psychiatrist.

He had been in treatment at a reputable hospital for two-and-a-half years because of an ulcer of his vocal cords, and was regularly taking Compazine,® 5 mg, which the hospital had prescribed.

Originally, Harley was a Southerner. Both his father and his paternal grandfather had been employed as public officials by a small community in the South and both generations had resided in the city hall.

Harley had been a breach birth, was nursed for an unknown period of time, his mother having so much milk that he suckled just a little on the other breast. In his thirty-eighth hypnoanalytic session, he made the claim, based on hearsay, that a puppy was used to finish his feeding. He professed ignorance about his weaning, but in his thirty-third hypnoanalytic session he seemed to recall that his paternal grandmother was responsible for it, and in his thirty-fourth hypnoanalytic session, he expressed the opinion that it occurred too early. In other hypnoanalytic sessions, he indicated that he may have been toilet trained by the age of eighteen months, since he no longer needed to wear diapers then. He remembered that he could not talk but was walking at that time. It was to that extent that his earliest infantile development was known to him.

When he was about two years and two-and-a-half months of age, his mother died while giving birth to his brother, and his father left for points unknown. The patient was taken to live with his paternal grandparents; his brother, with his maternal relatives, where there were other children.

The patient stated at the beginning of his treatment that his only recollection before his third year was that he had found a dollar bill and that his father had taken it from him. For a long time he was under the impression that it was a dream, but his grandfather told him that it had actually occurred.

Both his grandparents were in their late forties when he joined

them. They left the place where he had been born but returned to it shortly before he entered school.

He described his grandfather as barely literate but intelligent, shrewd in business, good at mental arithmetic, and possessed of a sense of humor. Grandfather and grandson were fond of each other, but quite early Harley felt intellectually superior to him. The grandfather used to tell him fairy tales of a sort, for example, that at the bottom of a hole in the ground the bones of a burned elephant could be seen, and although the boy did not see them, he indicated that he did to spare his grandfather's feelings. In the evenings, he would sit on his grandfather's lap and listen to invented stories in which the youngster was the central character. He had never questioned his grandfather about "real things," however.

Harley's grandmother came from an "aristocratic" family. She scorned her husband's background and liked to say so. She also spoke about her beauty as a young girl, though her nose, the patient said, was flat. She was partly deaf and, despite the fact that she was literate, stupid. She lacked a sense of humor. The boy used to call her Lala and had the feeling that she had encouraged him to use this appellation. Keeping the house and her grandson clean had been her whole life. She regarded other people and their offspring as nuisances who dirtied everything up. She, apparently, possessed rigid compulsive traits. The patient's paternal aunt, who was ten years his father's senior, told him much later that his grandmother was the most innocent woman to have ever had two children. His grandparents slept in separate rooms.

Harley sucked his thumb, but did not know for how long. He started to bite his nails at three-and-a-half years of age and stopped when he came to New York, only three years before he started psychotherapy.

The patient always believed that there had been no other family members living with them in the three different places where they stayed before he entered school. However, in the hypnoanalyses he found out that, at some time, a great-grandfather and a great-uncle had lived with them. He was under the impression that the great-grandfather had passed away shortly after coming to

live with them but did not know more about him. The great-uncle died when the patient was twelve years of age. Unlike the way the other family members reacted, the boy had not been able to feel any grief about his passing, and felt very guilty about this. He was also always under the impression that, for four years, his only companions had been about five hundred chickens, and he even remembered talking to them.

One of his grandmother's most potent methods of educating him was the "silent treatment," which he came to resent strongly while he was still quite young. He had already known before his third year that he was expected to be spotlessly clean at all occasions, and he was. He was educated generally according to the principle that children should be seen, but not heard. He was not supposed to "talk back" to his elders and did not dare to do so. He addressed his grandfather as "Sir." Until his fourth year, he did not ask any questions, but later on became deliberately insolent. Despite their mutual fondness, he and his grandfather had no actual communication. Harley had already some "concepts" before his fourth year, but knew his grandparents would not understand them. He had also had a limited vocabulary and was therefore unable to express them.

Because his grandmother regarded the boy as having a "delicate constitution," he slept in her bed until his sixth or seventh year. He did not like the odor of her body. Later, he slept with his grandfather. Although he had been well trained, he wet his bed three or four times a month. His grandmother took him frequently to various physicians. One of them recommended poached eggs with salt crackers. As a teenager, he was able to eat one dozen poached eggs for breakfast, and when he was in the Navy, he ate five or six dozen eggs in the evening.

Once, in his grandmother's presence, the patient sang and she told him he was unable to carry a tune. Since that time, he had been able to sing only when alone or drunk, and then quite well. Towards the end of his treatment, he also related his verbal difficulties to this incident.

At about four years of age, his grandparents took him to a family gathering. There he joined a twelve-year-old cousin in a rowboat, which floated away on a lake. The two boys enjoyed the fun,

but Harley's grandmother saw them, screamed, and frightened them, so they returned and disembarked. On the same day, a similar incident took place.

When he was about three-and-a-half years old, his grandparents gave him two small Bantam chickens. He was fond of them because they were pretty. Shortly afterwards, he was taken to a country baptism and subsequently tried to baptize the rooster, which drowned as a result. He hid the body and, when the odor of its decay called attention to it, he denied the deed to his angry grandmother but confessed it later to his grandfather who did not make a fuss.

The grandfather beat him just a few times, but the patient did not resent it. He liked it when his grandfather praised him, but disliked it when his grandmother did. When he was older, he often lied to his grandmother. Later, he got disgusted with himself and stopped the practice.

Though he also remembered a pair of overalls, his grandmother dressed him in girl's clothes until his sixth year and kept his hair long. When she bathed him, she made it obvious to him that she disapproved of his genitals by washing them in a rude way and referring to them as ugly and rough. It might be significant at this juncture to point out that the grandmother had preferred her daughter-in-law to her own son, Harley's father.

In childhood, Harley had had a bad case of chicken pox, a bad case of measles, and the whooping cough. Occasionally, when he walked, he would get severe leg cramps. This occurred until his sixth or seventh year. In his fifty-third hypnoanalytic session, he reported that his grandmother used a liniment which burned on his legs to ease the pain. "When I cried, she got angry and careless, and it splashed around, at times on my genitals and into my rectum." He often suffered earaches. The grandmother, who regarded being sick a "crime," either scolded him or gave him the "silent treatment." For this reason, he once played baseball for an entire day, despite bad earaches. Later, several colds aggravated his ear condition. His left eardrum was perforated, and his right ear was not quite normal.

In his one hundred and second hypnoanalytic session in which revivification had been induced, he gave a good description of his

grandmother's unsympathetic care of his constipation which also comprised daily dosages of Castoria®. ". . . even in intense strain I would try to—I would try . . . so that—ah—so that she wouldn't be giving me salts . . . And—ah—the—the ah—the anguish, that agony that I suffered due to the burning of the rectum that due to the raw . . . would be just like fire . . . I think that sometimes she gave me salts as—as a kind of punishment . . . a certain amount of hatred that accompanied it . . . at least dislike of me . . . The frequent bowel movements that occurred from salts and that, in turn, would be something she would disapprove of . . . although I was very small why ah—ah I went to the privy by myself."

Only in very cold weather did he use a low chair with a pot underneath which his grandmother, of course, had to clean.

When the use of salts ceased, a treatment equally distressing followed: ". . . maybe a doctor told her that to stop that salts business . . . it was harmful . . . he told her to use an enema instead."

The soapy water which his grandmother so inexpertly administered, frightened the patient and caused "excruciating pains." It was done, in his words, ". . . until my abdomen was distended and almost burst." He developed hemorrhoids, and he had his first operation on them at sixteen and another one three years before he came for psychotherapy. The second one was performed in an excellent hospital and though the surgeon had taken great care not to shrink the rectum too much, it was somehow small.

As to his sexual history, Harley stated that, before his sixth year, he had often had erections which his grandmother apparently did not detect. He has had a morning erection as far back as he can think. In his fifteenth hypnoanalytic session, the patient mentioned for the first time that, at about three years of age, while playing on the floor, he had looked accidentally under the dress of an eleven-year-old girl and was not astonished at what he saw. In his twenty-ninth hypnoanalytic session, he brought more details about that occurrence. This girl's mother, his grandmother, and other relatives were in the same room when Harley giggled and remarked that this girl had another mouth down there, that she should kiss him with it. "I think they were all very shocked," and nobody said a word. Afterwards, his grandmother gave him the "silent treatment" for some time. In the same hypnoanalytic session, he remembered a boy, around this girl's age, who fascinated

him because he had a gyroscope. This boy was crippled, and he was generally in a wheelchair or on crutches. When I asked the patient whether the connection between these two children was that he had had the impression that the girl was also crippled, sort of "cracked," he answered, "This does not register." There had been some link between these two children, but he could not remember what it was.

He recalled in his eighty-first hypnoanalytic session that, also about his third year, he had seen a mother nursing her baby, then diapering it and, while doing so, kissing the baby's penis a few times. The baby "chortled" and Harley was fascinated. He felt a "sort of loneliness, sort of being left out of things, that my grandmother never did that to me." This recollection was new. Talking over that hypnoanalytic session, he stated that he believed his alienation from his grandmother might have started on that occasion. He often reverted to the complaint that his narcissistic needs had never been met.

In his eighty-second hypnoanalytic session, he reported that he remembered during the week that once, as a very small boy, he looked under the dress of a grown-up. He could not see much because of the genital hair. However, the woman remarked jokingly, "Did you see something green?" The patient felt astonished and fascinated.

Here we might report on a peculiarity of his prudish grandmother. At every one of the three locations where they had lived, she requested of her husband that he build a platform behind the kitchen. From this platform she used to urinate to the ground. Harley could never remember trying to peep. When the grandfather took the little boy with him, the child saw the grandfather's penis when he urinated, but no more than that.

In his one hundred and fourth hypnoanalytic session, he expressed the impression that, before his fourth or fifth year, he had not been aware of his testicles. His recollection of his penis was only in connection with the times his grandmother bathed him and expressed hostility towards this organ. He did not masturbate until he entered school.

I shall describe his sexual experiences during his first years in school.

His grandparents returned to the patient's birthplace shortly

before he started school at six years of age. His grandfather became community sexton. All of Harley's schoolmates were one year older than he. They talked freely about their "nuts" and "balls," and about other sexual matters. Since his grandparents had never used any sexual expressions, he had to feign more knowledge than he actually had. The other boys were not too well informed, either. In the second grade, a playmate told him how babies are made, and the patient got the notion that some sort of "gizm" was squirted out of the testicles, as through a syringe. Harley was deeply impressed, but he was not shocked. As sex had never been mentioned at home, he thought that this was the reason he had neither a very strong inhibition about, nor aversion to it. He learned about masturbation from the other children.

At about six years of age, he started to sleep with his grandfather. When he was seven, eight or older, he peeked when his grandmother took a bath, but he was not astonished about what he saw. He had already had information from his schoolmates. At about the same time, his grandmother caught him once with another boy of the same age under the house in homosexual practices. She made a big thing out of it, and he felt very guilty, but only because he had been caught.

Going back to the patient's life history where I have left it, at his first year in school, all the other children had either lived in this community all their lives, or they had close relatives living there, or both. He began to feel very lonely.

Harley was an excellent pupil and skipped half grades. He learned to read very rapidly. The first Christmas after their return, the weather was very bad and his grandmother kept him home for a fortnight. He read his first book, *Black Rock* by Ralph O'Connor.

When the patient was about eight years old, he visited his maternal relatives and found that in this home, there were much fewer restrictions than in his own. The house was quite dirty.

About one year later, when Harley was about nine years old, his grandfather took some money out of the boy's bank to pay for Harley's father and stepmother's trip home. The patient described his father as dumb, vain, and poorly controlled. His grandmother tore her new daughter-in-law down. The father got his old job for

the community back. Harley could have lived with his father and stepmother but preferred to stay with his grandparents.

His brother came home to live with them when the patient was eleven years old and the brother was nine. The boys had very little in common, as Harley was already a voracious reader and his brother was hardly able to read. But the boys got along fairly well. At first, they slept together. Then, the grandmother demanded that her husband build two extra rooms with separate entrances for the "two filthy boys."

The report about his first emission came in his seventy-third hypnoanalytic session, in which revivification was induced.* "I see myself this time as the observer. . . ." He was twelve years old.

"It was a warm summer night and I don't know what time it was I woke up. But there was faint moonlight outside . . . I was sleeping alone . . . and all the windows were open . . . to the south there was a porch . . . The screen door was hooked and the door that let in through the parlor of the house . . . was open. And as I always did, as I was sleeping naked . . . I woke up with the . . . realization of what was happening. And I could feel this warm sticky stuff landing in gushes on my—all around my stomach and all way up above my waist, toward my waist . . . And I knew exactly—I knew somehow—I knew exactly what it was that. And I lay there on my back until it was finished. . . . And then I was quite excited about it. I jumped out of bed and I tried not to make any noise. I closed the door that led into the parlor to make sure that nowhere would I get caught. I locked the door . . . Then I drew the shades . . . I turned the light on and moved back into the corner well clear of the window . . . and started to examine what had happened . . . I was very excited . . . I started to masturbate and I can remember . . . in some very vivid that the pubic hair, the black hair was only—only was very sparse . . . it was small. But nevertheless the whole thing was a tremendously exciting experience . . . I had to go through all the rest of the house . . . to get to the bathroom. But there was a typewriter . . . and so I used that paper to wipe clean with . . . because I was lying on the bed and it all landed on me. And just as I am telling you . . . I

---

* Harley's hypoanalyses had to be cleared of constant repetitions of words and syllables to save space.

was standing in the south-east corner of the room . . . My point of view is that I am watching this—that I am watching this young boy. (Go on.) And although I am standing away and watching it, I can feel all of his excitement and all of his sensations. And the sensation when he first, after the wet dream he was awakening from that, and then the masturbation that immediately followed, the moment of reaching a climax. The sensation was so great that was although I wanted—I wanted to continue the motion . . . it was just impossible. Well, it was at the same time—it was—it was —it felt so good that it was painful. . . ."

Before going further with the patient's history, I would like to put down a few words about this "observer." He described it as a point of view, comparing it to nondimensional time, and stating that he had had this "observer" in night dreams and day dreams, as well as in the hypnoanalyses, always, in fact, except in sexual dreams where he is active. This had been the first time he experienced the "observer" in a hypnoanalytic session dealing with sex. There is a connection between the "observer" and the "watcher," and other projective phenomena occurring in hypnoanalyses which I have described in previous research papers.*

Much earlier in his treatment, in his twenty-second hypnoanalytic session, Harley had been told to look at a movie. He described himself and his brother locking themselves in the bathroom when he was about thirteen years of age. Seated on the toilet, he demonstrated masturbation to his brother and was able to ejaculate. The patient experienced intense pains and gripped the window sill. The window fell on two of his finger tips. His brother yelled for the grandmother and opened the door to admit her. When the grandmother saw what had happened, she sent the brother away and slapped Harley before releasing his fingers.

Around this time, several of his sexual fantasies started in which no other men figured. The first one he related to his brother who regarded him as insane. The patient imagined himself as very tiny. He was variously between his mother's breasts or wandering in and out of her genitalia having vaginal intercourse with her from the rear so that she would not be able to observe him.

---

* Projective Phenomena in Hypnoanalysis. *Int J Clin Exp Hypn, 10*:127-134, 1962. Dissociation and Projection in Hypnotic States. *Amer J Clin Hypn, 9*:114-117, 1966.

When he had visited his maternal relatives, he had seen his mother's picture just in passing. He was sure, however, that she had been very beautiful, especially since his grandmother had told him so, too.

At that time, he regarded all women, except his grandmother, as lily-white, gentle creatures who had no need to urinate or to defecate. He was quite disillusioned if they proved to be less ethereal. Still another fantasy represented distorted derivatives of his Oedipus complex. As an infant, he had seen hogs slaughtered. Their heads were severed, their hindlegs elevated and the blood allowed to run out. The day dream was that Harley would kill a very beautiful woman and eat her—an oral incorporation wish. He was not able to produce the fantasy of killing her, but the anticipation was a great pleasure. The relation of this fantasy to his mother was that he had the feeling of not having sufficiently devoured her when he was an infant. How to eat this beautiful woman always proved a dilemma. Should he raise her legs and drain the blood, the woman would be dead and, therefore, he only contemplated this prospect and had an erection at the same time. He started having this dream in prepuberty and knew that it was a sexual one involving his mother. He had never fully realized the sadistic component of the distortion of his Oedipus fantasy, so contrary to his code of ethics. In the theoretical part of this book, I cited a paper which states that destructive fantasies concerning persons for whom attachment and dependency are felt, create deep guilt feelings. Although this day dream was reported by the patient to have begun at a later age, it is very easily possible that it had started quite early, had been repressed and returned later. Whatever the course of events might have been, it is sure that this patient had cannibalistic fantasies regarding his mother, and with them a deeply felt sense of guilt.

After he had ejaculated for the first time, as he described it in his seventy-third hypnoanalytic session, he examined the fluid and found that it was not "dirty." At the same time, he experienced that the head of his penis was quite sensitive, whereas when he had formerly masturbated, it was without any sensation. He masturbated again with the intention of catching the seminal fluid in his hand and tasting it. When he had it in his hand, how-

ever, he lost the desire to put it in his mouth; the excitement had abated. Afterwards he often put it into his mouth without feeling excitement. He felt that the seminal fluid of other males would be dirty, but not his own. Harley had not thought about that in a long time. He had shown great ingenuity in the matter of bringing the fluid to his mouth, had had a glass tube prepared to make the transport a direct one. But essentially he was disappointed because he was not able to perform self-fellatio. Only his own penis would have been satisfactory.

When Harley was twelve or thirteen years of age, he and his brother were both circumcised because never having been instructed in genital cleanliness, they had developed adhesions. At the age of thirteen, Harley contracted typhoid pneumonia, and since that time grew one inch each month until his fourteenth year.

At that time, also, the patient was quite shy and awkward with girls. He first became aware of breasts when looking at pictures of Grecian goddesses, although breasts had later been quite important for him. He regarded them as "the source of all love of which I later was deprived." In high school, he had a crush on a teacher, but at night only did he dare to fantasy about how she would look naked and about having sex with her. His grandmother never mentioned his nocturnal emissions; nevertheless, she had changed his bedsheets.

In high school, he had but one friend, an only child. There had been some attempt to accompany a girl he knew from school, but she sent him for a glass of water and when he returned, she was gone. When he was thirteen years of age, his grandmother, for the first time, invited other teenagers to the house. Nobody came.

He started writing early. He wrote for the school newspaper and later for the local town daily. Thereafter, he was a newspaper boy, worked in an ice factory, and helped his grandfather dig graves, for which he was paid.

Harley lost his interest in school, grew more and more bored and restless. To prove to himself that he had enough courage, and also because the girls would admire him, he ran away at the age of fifteen and joined the Navy as a member of the deck crew.

At that time, he was still a "virgin" and did not quite get the older men's talks, nor their homosexual advances.

After about a year, his father took him out. He went back to school where, as he remembered, an English teacher praised him a great deal.

This time home, he visited a prostitute. He was so inexperienced that she had to tell him not to spread his legs. She was gentle with him and, from then on, he liked such women.

However, his restlessness recurred and he felt that he did not fit in. The patient even started shop-lifting in the five-and-ten-cent-stores. When his grandfather confronted him with this fact, he ran away again. He lived in the South in a shelter for the destitute; then, from another city, telegraphed for money and returned home.

His grandmother refused to talk to him, and his grandfather kidded him. The grandfather told him that, since he was seventeen years of age, it was time he decided what he wanted to do.

Harley again joined the Navy. His grandfather told him that he would not get a penny from him anymore. Now, the patient enlisted in the engineering department as a fireman. He also studied for the Asian fleet. In every class, he was the youngest and best. He went to the Orient where he stayed for three years.

In the Navy, he had a few paid homosexual experiences. He was often drunk and only then was able to talk to his superiors in an adequate manner. When intoxicated, he often went with his shipmates to prostitutes from whom he contracted syphilis and gonorrhea. For half a year, he stayed in a naval hospital where he was operated on because of an epididymitis. As a consequence, he has been sterile since his twenty-first year. However, both his venereal diseases have been adequately treated, except that, at times, his prostatitis tends to flare up.

After he was in the Navy for three years, his paternal aunt wrote him that his grandparents were destitute but did not want to inform him about their plight. The patient had his allotment sent to them. He got thirty days shore leave and visited them.

When he returned home, he learned that his father had run away with another woman and had taken all the money with him. His grandfather was nearly eighty years old and suffering from an illness from which, according to the physician, he would not recover. On this visit, the patient was able to talk to his grandfather

as man to man. He provided good whiskey for his grandfather and returned to the Navy.

He enlisted immediately for the submariners' school. He preferred submarines because the food was better, discipline was less formal, and inspections less frequent than in other branches of the Navy. He remained in the submarines for four years.

When Harley received a telegram that his grandfather had died and left him all of his money, he was unable to grieve too much and he felt considerable guilt about it. His brother was so sorrow-stricken that he deserted from the Navy.

During his period of enlistment as a submariner, the patient married. He did not love his first wife, and, although she tried to convince him that he was the father of her two children, he, knowing that he was sterile, divorced her.

Later on, Harley served on aircraft carriers. On the whole, he had been in the Navy for fourteen years. After his discharge, he remained in the Orient and held various jobs there.

At the age of thirty-one, he married for the second time. His second and still present wife is the same age as the patient, and he has never been unfaithful to her. Even when he elucidated a positive transference dream in a hypnoanalytic session, he was careful not to go too far. He does his best to please her in all things. During the first years of their marriage, he still had a sense of loneliness, but they came to a good understanding. When he started treatment, Harley felt very guilty about his wife's having to work. He felt that he should be able to support her. She is frigid but, as he told me, gets her satisfaction by participating in his release. In addition, though she has strict moral standards, she adapted to his desire to walk around the house nude—his exhibitionism. The patient has always found female genitalia "alluring" to the point of preferring them shaved so as to have a better view of them. He liked vaginal intercourse a tergo because he could better observe what was happening—voyeurism—and, at the same time, fondle the clitoris. His preference for sex a tergo might also be connected with his interest in the female buttocks—anal regression. He always wanted the woman to have as much pleasure as possible—reaction formation.

Harley was easily hypnotizable. At his fourth hypnosis, regres-

sion was induced. The patient stated afterwards that there was more light in the hypnotic visualization than in an ordinary dream. He recalled the first place where they had lived in the Midwest. There, he had been in the outhouse and had had an impulse to exhibit himself. He opened the door, took off all his clothes and stood stark naked in the door. On that rural road, however, nobody passed by. He dressed again and went back to the house. His grandmother was very angry because he had put his clothes on inside out. Harley was not yet four years of age. He told me that he had always known about this event, but had not thought about it for many years. The other event about which he had always had conscious awareness, was about the two Bantam chickens. Both occurrences returned several times in his hypnoanalytic sessions.

In his eighth hypnoanalytic session, revivification was induced, and he was told that something important had occurred in his fourth year. At first, he recalled something nonconsequential. Then, he reported having the impression that he was in a jungle and that something emerged from it which he could not recognize. Afterwards, he remembered that, at the age of four, while living in the Midwest, his grandmother wanted to show him off. He had to recite a short poem in a school. "And when you don't come and kiss my sweet little lips, I run like a turkey." His recitation was good. He had no recollection, however, of his emotions at this occasion. He could see himself, but did not feel anything. He seemed to be standing about twenty or thirty feet away from this little boy. "Everything connected with me seems to be visual." The visualization was in black and white, but the "sweet little lips" he saw in red, and they were wet. His grandmother was standing beside him.

After his twelfth hypnoanalytic session, there was a hiatus of two months in his therapy because he was not employed.

The patient brought part of a dream. He saw the stern of a ship which was round and sloped down to the water. Harley did not know its name although the letters on the hull were red and the color of the ship was light gray. It was not fully loaded since it showed a little above the water line. His associations to this dream can be omitted.

In his sixteenth hypnoanalytic session, he was told that this dream should change closer to its real meaning. The patient visualized the lower side of a woman's breast, the red of the name changed to the nipple, but the dock did not alter.

He talked this visualization over at his next appointment. Much of his fantasy life involved sex with nude, beautiful, older women. Harley idealized them; as formerly stated, all these fantasies were constructed around, and connected with, his mother.

From here on, I will present especially the hypnoanalytic sessions which pertain to his feelings of inadequacy as a man, of cowardice, and to his castration anxiety.

In his twenty-fourth hypnoanalytic session, revivification was induced. He visualized the same scene as in his fourth hypnoanalytic session, himself at four years of age, standing stripped in the door of the outside privy and hoping somebody on the road would see him. When he dressed himself again, some of his clothes were inside out. His grandmother noticed this and suspected that something terrible had happened. She was also furious. The patient saw the small boy at the door of the privy, but he did not know why he had undressed. He had hoped that some passer-by would see him naked. I told him twice to allow letters to appear, and put him into a deeper hypnotic state, but it did not help. He reported seeing the whitewashed privy, dark inside. Through the three holes in the seat—one for each of the grandparents and one for the boy—stream three beams of light, symbolizing, I may add, genitalia. Fifty yards away is the dirt road. The sun is hot; the grass, dry, and he hears the katydids. The small boy envies the horses and the cows because they do not need clothes. The door of the privy faces east. He sees the observer, who is stationed somehow to the right, about one-third the distance from the road, but not between the boy and the road. The small boy hears the noises and he feels the heat directly on his body. He is interested in his small penis and its foreskin.

"(Let the observer go to the small boy.) The observer is in space and a tremendous distance away in time; he cannot walk to the small boy, there are millions of miles of time between them. Something is between the observer and the small boy." . . . Harley now named the place where this all happened. The small boy is

fascinated by the fact that horses can defecate without dirtying themselves; he once tried; he shed his clothes but soiled himself. He is spellbound by the beetle which takes horse manure into its burrow, and he watches it. He envies animals. "(By the time of your next hypnosis, you will remember why you took off your clothes and why you wanted to be seen by somebody.)"

I will omit the patient's theory about the "observer" given in the ensuing session. He did add, though, that a chief engineer on one of his former jobs had had the same kind of an "observer." Harley realized that some details in this hypnoanalysis were new, as, for example, the little boy's awareness of the foreskin. He had never before known of his attempt to imitate a "defecating horse." After the replay of this hypnoanalytic session, he observed that he had felt all the heat and had heard the katydids. I told him that he might have envied the animals because they had no grandmother.

In his twenty-fifth hypnoanalytic session, revivification was induced and he was asked why the boy of four stood naked in the door of the privy. The patient has the feeling that this morning there had been an especially unpleasant session when he was dressed. This might have been a consequence of my telling him that he envied the animals because they had no grandmothers. "(Sleep deeper.)" His grandmother might have said that his sex organs are especially ugly. "(What did the small boy feel on this occasion?)" He does not know. "(Sleep deeper.)" Whenever his grandmother bathed him, she washed his genitals, especially his testicles very roughly and hurt him. For this reason, he did not like his grandmother to touch his body. Later, he also did not come to her to have his fingernails cut. Whenever his grandmother was angry, he had the feeling that he had done something terribly wrong and felt guilty. Especially outstanding to the observer were the boy's genitals and the three holes in the privy seat out of which the sunbeams streamed. In this scene also the light diverges upwards and is too bright. He was then told to remember by the next hypnosis the reason why the small boy stood naked in the door of the privy hoping for someone from the road to look at him.

After the twenty-fifth hypnoanalysis had been played back, Harley was hypnotized, revivification was induced and he was

asked the same questions. He sees the small boy and the observer
standing in the same places as before. "(Sleep deeper. Why did the
boy want somebody from the road to see him? Why were his genitals and the three beams of light important to him?)" He noticed
that, although the privy is dark inside and has a roof, there is no
limit to the height of these three beams of light. The patient
standing outside can see the roof as the observer. The small boy is
not especially conscious of his genitals, but the observer is. He is
conscious of them and of their details as, for example, that the
foreskin is longer than the penis. But the small boy is conscious of
the "whole unit of his naked body" and he is convinced that somebody from the road will see him.

"(Let somebody see him.) That would be fiction (But we would
find out what the small boy really wants.)" He has the strong feeling that somebody should pass by. "(A man or a woman?) It makes
no difference. (Who passes by?) My grandfather with the horse
and buggy."

The observer shifts now from the boy's genitals to the horse's
genitals. The grandfather is in the buggy holding the reins. The
horse is a gelding with a partial erection; his genitals are black
with red patches.

"(Why is the observer so interested in the horse's genitals?) I
don't know. The horse has not been bathed and his testicles have
not been hurt."

The observer is aware that the horse is a gelding. The horse is
trotting, but always on the same spot. The small boy and his
grandfather cannot see one another, nor are they aware of one another, but the observer can see them both.

"The small boy looks there, but the road is empty for him.
(Why can't the small boy see it?) He did not know anybody. It
might be a complete stranger. (Let a stranger pass by.)"

In the patient's mind, a stranger would not consider the genitals ugly. In his mind, male genitals were ugly, female were not.
That was before he had seen the little girl's genitals. . . . Some
stranger would approve of the small boy's naked body, feel that he
was not ugly. The genitals of this one small girl were different,
but the small boy makes no comparison. He had the feeling that
"just the small boy has this ugly equipment." Even the indifference

of a stranger would have been reassuring. "(Why does the small boy stand in the door of the privy?) It is the only private place." The small boy wears small pants and a small dress. He puts the pants on wrong side out and the dress as well, the buttons are "cockeyed." "(Between now and the next session, you will remember more about the small boy's ideas and feelings.)"

The patient made it evident that his grandmother's expressed disapproval of his sexual organs created a craving in him for approval of his sexual organs. He added details, spoke about how he envied the animals, and described the beams of light. Despite his vivid fantasy life, however, he stuck principally to real occurrences. The development about his grandfather was static. There was also no explanation as to why the statement in the twenty-fourth hypnoanalysis that the small boy was interested in his penis and foreskin was contradicted in the following hypnoanalytic sessions when this function was ascribed to the observer.

In the four preceding associated hypnoanalytic sessions, Harley attributed to his grandmother—the highest authority of his infanthood—a complete rejection of his masculinity. His original strong desire to be acceptable to "somebody, even a stranger," was, at the end, reduced to a willingness to be satisfied with the indifference of a stranger—anything but rejection. That this almost daily repeated objection to his genitalia must have deeply influenced the patient's psychosexual development is obvious.

At his next session, Harley reported that he had forgotten about his appointment and had gone home first—a resistance. He had been a little hoarse, but his physician told him that his condition was much improved and gave him some drug.

The twenty-sixth hypnoanalytic session was played back to the patient, and he remarked that he wore overalls on the farm; therefore this act must have occurred either shortly before or shortly after a visit to town. In the twenty-seventh hypnoanalytic session, he was asked about more details concerning the scene in the privy, but he reported on the episode when he observed the little girl's genitals.

In the thirtieth hypnoanalytic session, revivification was induced, and Harley was asked to remember more about the small boy, the small girl, and their interconnection. At first, he did not

recall anything new. He was rehypnotized twice. Then, he related that, at about the age of three, he was playing on the front porch. A woman visitor and his grandmother were sitting in the front room. The boy "broke wind quite noisily," felt utterly ashamed, ran immediately and hid behind the house. "(Why were you embarrassed?)" He can see himself playing, and through a screen door, he can see the two women . . . He does not know and cannot understand why he was so embarrassed. He remembers it at times. But he was not embarrassed when he told me about the girl. "(Your grandmother's toilet training must have been quite strict.)" In this connection, the patient recalls a small porcelain pot only. He cannot remember any time when he soiled himself, except when he imitated the horse, for which he was severely punished. He often wondered why he was so embarrassed since he had frequently observed other children being "quite innocent" about it. . . . He also reports that the clothing he had gotten in the morning was still clean at "nightfall," something he never before recalled . . . "I cannot remember any particular pressure to stay clean." His grandfather had nothing to do with it, "that was all in the grandmother's jurisdiction. Just staying clean was taken for granted. . . ." At the age of eight or ten, he had grass stains on his clothes, but at that age, he no longer felt guilty, and his grandmother's "silent treatment" bothered him only when he thought he was guilty.

In his forty-second hypnoanalytic session, revivification was induced and the patient was asked about the events that brought about his compulsive talking. He paused many times in this hypnoanalysis. "There is somewhere, I think, has something to do with buttercups. A buttercup is a small yellow flower. A yellow flower which would make . . . of blond hair. (Just go on.) I reached a dead end. (Can you see the buttercup?) No. I just think of it. . . . (What passes through your mind when you think of a buttercup, aside from blond hair?) Another cup, a tea cup. And a saucer . . . And I don't recall, I don't recall anybody with blond hair. (Go on. Please talk.) A woman's blond hair. I just don't know. All in my family had black hair . . . Something else is yellow. (What?) A dress—a dress is yellow. (Whose dress?) I don't know yet . . . I said I see a yellow dress, but no identifying person

. . . I think it's a small girl. I am not sure about the blond hair . . . No, the blond hair is a woman's hair. It's long . . . (Should I put you into a deeper sleep?) . . . (What about the yellow?) Now I think of butter. Butter derives of milk. And we turn to the matter of the breast again. (But butter is not made from women's milk.) No. But butter suggested milk . . . (But we want to find out why you talk compulsively at times.) . . . That little girl is here. She got a pretty face with yellow hair . . . I think is, I am not sure of this but I think it's probably because I wanted to be a little girl with yellow hair. (What did you do to become one?) . . . is trying to put a pan of biscuits in the oven. On the base flat kitchen stove. And I see my grandmother. She is putting wood in the fire on the stove and through the top of it. She takes the lid off and puts a piece of stovewood in . . . I am getting—getting in her way . . . But before I get through with it; it took too long or something; she got annoyed with it, got impatient. And I was chased out of the kitchen. And that's—that's when I suddenly saw the little girl. She was out sitting on the porch. Ah because—because I felt she should be, she was just chased out of the kitchen . . . The buttercup still suggests two things. Both butter and a cup. The cup there is a milk in it. It was the milk that was supposed to go into the biscuits. (Go on.) Nothing happens . . . (Could you not visualize the complication that hinders you today?) No. (What do you see just now?) Just a little girl sitting on the edge of the porch. (Let her change slowly to the real thing or person.) No, she is me, just me . . . I am in the yellow dress. I have been chased out of the kitchen. (Are you happy or unhappy?) I am not happy about it. (Why?) Well, the thing I was made to feel that I was—I was stupid and annoying. (Go on.) And I am telling, I am sitting on the porch and I am talking to one of the chickens. I am telling the chicken about it . . . that I am not being permitted to let—to go ahead with what I was doing in there . . . my grandmother said I could. And now she is saying I can't and so just words of that sort and I am telling the chicken. . . . But I don't have the words of that type to express all that . . ."

Harley had no comments when the forty-second hypnoanalytic session was replayed to him. Later, I will discuss these hypnoanalytic sessions together although they are self-explanatory.

In the forty-third hypnoanalytic session, the patient was told to dream and to remember the entire dream which he had related to me about a popular singer. In the dream, she was sitting on a stool near him and a cat was rubbing her right cheek on his left cheek. He was also told to recall the missing parts of this dream. In the hypnoanalysis, he wonders what he thought when she sat on the stool near him, and says he does not know what he felt because he was the observer in the rear, ten or fifteen feet behind them. He could not see his own face. The visualization now is the same. She has her arm around him, and he has his arm around her. He looks straight ahead and does not see the audience, but somehow knows that it is there. He does not know what she is talking about, but her manner and her voice are the same as when she is in front of an audience. Her dress is canary yellow and her hair is blond.

"(What are the missing parts?) They do not come." He sees it very vividly, over and over again.

"(What about the cat?)" That he also sees over and over again. He is alone on the stool and the cat is there. He believes it must be in the star's home, but he does not see the house. Now, he thinks he must be sitting on the floor. The cat faces him from the sofa, then comes over to be petted and rubs her cheek on his right cheek. "(Who is the cat?) . . . this is a Persian cat with a long bushy tail and long hair. She sits in front of the sofa." He feels that he has petted the cat before [rehypnotized].

"(What are the missing parts?) Nothing comes." He thinks that a cat is a pussy, and that is also slang for a woman's genitals. He wonders whether the singer has blond pubic hair also and feels guilty about this thought. . . . As far back as he can remember, he has felt guilty. He should not think in this way about a nice woman. She is sexless. He does not know why. And she does not evacuate. He knows, intellectually, that she does; but he feels it should not be, because of his grandmother whom he had often seen urinating the manner of which, when he imitated it, wet his clothes. This girl's personality is nice and she is sincere. He does not see them, but he wanted to touch her genitals, her pussy, and then the cat came. He does not know for whom she stands . . .

"(Let her change.)" Nothing happens. But he thinks in many ways

that the singer's personality is the kind he would have liked his mother's to be. "(Therefore you cannot touch her.) Yes." He thought of touching her in fantasy. His mother's hair was auburn. But something about yellow is there.

"(In you?)" A tremendous anxiety when he was thinking that he is a coward. Cowardice is yellow, and that is the reason he joined the Navy and went into the submarines. "(Girls do not have to be brave.) Possibly." In recent years, he felt that he was effeminate. Also the fact that he cannot talk up to a superior is yellow.

The patient reported at his next interview that his job had been confirmed. The concern where he had worked had been taken over by an international organization, and Harley with it. "The singer has a very nice personality, and she is sincere. There is nothing off-color in her show." Even in his hypnoanalyses he talks reluctantly about certain things because I (the therapist) am a female. His language would be different with a man. His forty-third hypnoanalytic session was played back to him.

In the forty-fourth hypnoanalytic session, he was told to see in a movie or on the stage his dream reenacted in which a horse, whose foreleg was swollen, had been relieved by having it skinned. The flesh of the foreleg was yellowish. Harley visualizes the stage and is very conscious of the heavy velvet curtains which are yellow. He also sees besides the stage, the proscenium, the footlights, and the heavy folds hanging in front of the screen. He describes the curve of the stage where the footlights are. "(Let the horse appear somewhere.)" He does not visualize the horse, but the yellow bothers him. He is unable to find any explanation. "(Let that change.) It is in folds, like the pleats of a yellow skirt of a gigantic woman, with the bottom very close to the floor, like the old-fashioned ones which dragged on the ground." He sees it up to the waistband from which it flares. The hips are broad and the waist narrow. Above the waist, there is nothing. "(Who is the woman?)" He does not know, but she must have had something to do with him when he was very small because she is so gigantic. His line of vision is a little above her knee. "(Approximately how old are you?)" He feels himself about three years old. "(Do you see or do you feel it?) It is just a feeling . . . The skirt clears the floor one inch." He is very conscious of its getting much smaller above

the hips. He does not see any background, but the yellow sticks out sharply. The waistband is one to one and a half inches wide. The flaring hips and narrow waist are due to a corset restraint. It is an old type corset, with strings in the back to pull it up tight. But there is nothing beyond. "(Let letters appear.)" Nothing appears, only the skirt is there. "(What do you have to do with it?)" It is very intense what the yellow means. The connection of the skirt is to female and yellow.

"(Go nearer to it.) It is very near, but I cannot touch it. (Why not?) I do not know but I may make the skirt dirty. (Do you have dirty hands?) My hands are clean, but I could dirty the skirt. My hands were never clean enough because of my grandmother. But the yellow is important. (Let it change to what it really means.) It is still always the skirt. I think of the horse and yellow flesh, the yellow hair, the yellow genital hair, the buttercup. (By the next time, the real meaning of the yellow will come.)"

I should remark here that the absence of the upper part of this woman pertained to Harley's feeling that his grandmother was a poor mother—breastless, and that she was quite stupid—headless.

At his next session, Harley complained about a backache because of an awkward position in which he had to work. He reported that he came off well in a somewhat antagonistic conference. Aside from that, he had a discussion about religion with his wife, who goes to mass three times a week. She does not talk much about religion though. The forty-fourth hypnoanalytic session was replayed to the patient.

In the forty-fifth hypnoanalytic session, he was told to visualize all the yellow things, not as they appeared in the hypnoanalyses, but what they really stand for. He visualized something like a formal evening jacket with a yellow ribbon across one shoulder, and somewhere a yellow tassel. There is no sword. There is no face; just the clothes. He sees the shirt front, white, but the ribbon yellow. They are static. He knows that there must be coattails, but he does not see them. He pictures the shirt front and the dark jacket. He does not know where the yellow tassel is. It is a slender man, and the ribbon goes from the left shoulder to the right waist. It may be a minister. "(Are you in church?) Yellow, and the person is like a pope with a high hat and yellow trimmings, a

white robe, a statue; the altar is yellow and white, and a yellow tapestry; much yellow is around. A priest conducts some sort of a service, there is much motion." The patient is very close to him, and others stand behind the patient. Harley is ten to twelve feet from the railing. The person is the church dignitary. The patient is not there in person but as a point of view in front of the center aisle. The priest is not aware of him. He is swinging a "gadget" (described by the patient as a yellow metal bowl suspended from three chains in which there was some kind of light or flame.*) "A ceremony is going on, and he crosses at times, but mostly he swings it around without making a sound. Much yellow is there, and it is important that it is yellow, not that it is gold. The insignia on a naval officer are also yellow." We had spoken before about the church and about religion. His grandmother was a Protestant and belonged to the First Christian Church. The patient had seen total immersion and, as was previously mentioned, drowned a chicken by baptizing it. The Protestant religion repels Harley. The Catholics, he feels, have more dignity. Now, the evening coat has disappeared. The hat of the priest resembles, front and back, the doors of a restaurant† seen in a former hypnoanalysis, with a skull cap situated between the two. "Everything is in filigree, with yellow like a cardinal or the Pope. A great profusion of yellow is in the robes, in the decorations, and in the background. (What should it be?)" He does not know. The Eternal Light is also yellow, but it is not especially important in this connection. The priest is behind the rail where there are three steps covered by a carpet. The carpet should be red, but this one is yellow. The patient thinks the yellow is a stain of baby feces. "(Is that the real meaning of yellow and dirty hands?)" The patient has a revulsion against getting his hands dirty. "(That is your education.)" That the red carpet is stained, is only a feeling. "(By the time of your next session, you will have more information about this baby and its feces.)"

After the playback of this hypnoanalysis, the patient said that he has often had fantasies of being a dignitary.

Harley repeated in the next interview that he was never able to

---

* Probably a censer.
† These doors were rounded like Roman arches.

hold his own amongst men. However, he got along well with his shipmates, except for a few fist fights. After talking about his wife, he reported a dream about surgery performed on his testicles. I will present here only briefly his associations to this dream which is repeated in his hypnoanalytic session. He stated that he had never had this kind of a dream before. As previously reported, in his teens when he masturbated, he intended to swallow his own seminal fluid. After ejaculation, the desire to do so vanished. He also had cannibalistic dreams about females, which were not nightmares. He had neither guilt feelings nor feelings of hostility or disgust about them. Every evening, he ate two dozen poached eggs, and should he be hungry again, he ate another dozen. In the dream in question, one testicle was sliced first. When he discovered that its contents were lost in this manner, he decided not to slice the other one. He asked whether that had anything to do with homosexuality. Other men's seminal fluid did not attract him, and he was not troubled by homosexual dreams.

In the forty-sixth hypnoanalytic session, revivification was induced and the patient was told he was now the age when the event or events occurred that interrelate to the dream about the surgery of his genitals. "Nothing particular seems to come. (What age do you feel you are?)" He does not know, he does not feel anything particular. "(Repeat your dream.) I was in the kitchen somewhere and I knew that my genitals, although they were healthy, had been removed by surgery because of some other trouble." At the same time, Harley was aware that he still had them and he had told the surgeon to save the ones which had been removed. They had been frozen and he now prepared them for cooking. He sliced one testicle lengthwise, but not the other. He had decided to let it remain whole. The problem was how to cook them. The one that was sliced was fried in butter. The pan was very shiny, and the butter bubbled. The other one got roasted, and the dream ended before he ate them. [rehypnotized] "(Do you see the dream?) Yes, I see the dream. (Look well and let it slowly change nearer to what it really means.)" The visualization did not change. But he suspected that part of the meaning is that he sliced one but not the other because the contents of the first testis had been lost. He has eaten his own testicles because to eat

the testicles of others would be horrid. He needed them for the manhood he lacks, virility and courage. Slicing caused the contents to spill, but the whole one held all its contents. Since they were male, they were unclean and had to be purified by cooking. They would give him courage, strength and ability to stand up to members of his own sex, like other men. "(You still have your own.)" What he cooked would give him an increase, but they must be his own . . . "(Why do you want to eat them?) To acquire the essence of manhood which they have. (People ate their enemies to acquire strength. Are you your own enemy?)" Perhaps he is because he cannot hold his own and he is not tough enough when he should be. He is too kind when he knows that it is not justified, and his kindness is weakness.

"(Are you weak?) Yes, because I have not the ruthlessness to look after my own interest if others take advantage of me." He is foolish. "(Sleep deeper.) Yes. (Now let it change.) It is unchanged. (What?) I need some help in interpreting it. (Did you do it because you do not yet have enough self-confidence?) I am in trouble. (There appear letters . . .)."

He is in the kitchen. "(Where is the point of view?)" His position is different from what is was on other occasions because sex has no objective point of view. He seems to watch it from his own rear. He stands at the sink and at the stove and is frying the slices.

"(Where is your grandmother?) She is not here, but she may be the reason why they have to be cooked to be clean. (Who took your self-confidence away?) My grandmother. (Is it her kitchen?)" It is not grandmother's kitchen; this is more modern.

"(Let it change.)" Frying changes the color of the slices. When they cook, they look like mushrooms. "(How do they look?) A greenish-brown dotty texture. (Let it change further.)" They remain unchanged. It reminds him of mushrooms when they are partially cooked . . . "(Do you sleep deeply?)" He does.

"Male flesh is supposed to be filthy, but the female flesh is clean. (Clean female flesh gave you two ailments in China.) That was before China. (Your grandmother's flesh had a bad odor.) Yes. (That is contradictory.) Yes. (Whether flesh is clean or dirty depends upon the circumstances.) But that does not work. (Let your grandmother appear.)"

Females may be clean because of his idealized mother, but not his grandmother. "(She was a female, too.) My grandmother had an offensive odor, but my mother was clean. I did not like to think of my grandmother as a woman. The male was filthy and ugly, and my grandmother was too. She was equally equipped."

But he needed testicles, uneaten, because cooking destroyed one and the other was in the oven.

"(You did not become the man you wanted to be.) No. (You depreciate yourself.) I do not understand you. (You regard your manhood as bad.) Because of my difference from other men or because my relationships with men were not satisfying. (You are not satisfied with yourself.) I was fired a couple of times. (That can always happen.) Others can debate with the boss and disagree forcefully. I do not know when to stop. When I stopped, I got enraged, and I went too far. (No boss likes to be talked back to.) It depends on how you do it. (Is there still anything else?) Stalemate."

I will only comment on the patient's statement that his nonobjective—because of the sexual content of this hypnoanalysis—point of view was from his own rear. He was looking from the posterior portion of his body at his attempt to incorporate his own lost genitalia. But since they had been destroyed by the process of purification, his effort had been unsuccessful. Yet, his reality orientation was sufficiently firm so that, even in the dream condition, he knew he still had his genitalia.

A man's genitals were essential, but unacceptable to Harley. His grandmother had been right. There is additional material for this contention. His seventy-sixth hypoanalytic session was performed because of a slip of his tongue, which was that the operation on his scrotum had had an effect on the size of his "intestines" —instead of on the size of his testicles. On the one hand, when he had an operation on his protruding hemorrhoids in his teens, he had sexual fantasies about his nurse. On the other hand, when his scrotum was operated upon, "there was a lot of pus and filthy stuff that ran out with the opening . . . what was—ah—subconsciously confirmed what my grandmother thought." These operations were very close in location also. It was another, quite real proof that his grandmother had been right.

The hypnoanalytic sessions about the buttercups produced

much new material. As he told me once, he was "greedy" for all milk products. His desire to please his grandmother in every way —though all his endeavors were futile—brought about his attempt to perform female chores. Already as an infant, he had created the blond fantasy girl in the yellow dress, in the color of cowardice. His talking to the chickens was what he regularly did, lacking any companion. In the next development, the dream about the singer and the cat—the pussy—his strict, but corruptible superego, comes fully to the foreground. The star symbolizes his mother; therefore he should not think about her in a sexual way. But he did constantly. At the end of this hypnoanalysis, his panic about being yellow burst forth, somehow out of context. He just had continuously to prove to himself that he was not a coward.

There was no connection between the content of his next hypnoanalytic session and my instruction to let the dream about the horse be reenacted in a movie. Under the skin, the horse's color was yellowish, most probably symbolizing his grandmother, and its swollen leg her genitalia which he regarded as male. The skinning might have been a castration to return her to her natural sex. However, in the hypnoanalytic session, the movie was visualized and the curtains were like the yellow skirt of a giant woman —his grandmother. The thought which he did not express, apparently, was, why does not this giantess fight somebody her own size instead of a defenseless little boy, which also signifies cowardice— on her part. Although the patient did not state so, the fact that he had not touched the garment at all may signify some trepidation that her cowardice might, in a magical way, further infect him.

In the last development, he turned his grandmother into a man, at first without a sword—without genitals—then into one who does not function as a man sexually—a pope—despite the sexual symbol of the swinging gadget. She made the final decisions in everything; she knew how to perform complicated ceremonies. There is certainly again the intimation that one so lofty should leave one so small alone. At the end, the suggestion that the red carpet might be stained with baby feces, which is not actual but only a feeling in the patient, is nearly a joke, a retribution for his enforced and unobtainable cleanliness.

In the last hypnoanalytic session I reproduced, the patient's fear

that he was not man enough emerged. Harley was regressively very orally oriented. At the time he was in treatment, he ate six eggs daily for breakfast, two to three pounds of lean steak for dinner, accompanied by three to four sweet potatoes, ten biscuits and a quarter of a pound of butter. I have to reveal that he was not at all obese. The desire to swallow his own seminal fluid also points to a high degree of orality. There is some intimation that nothing would be lost; on the contrary, something would be regained by swallowing it. In the forty-sixth hypnoanalytic session, he stated that the contents of one of his testicles had been lost, his manhood reduced although he still had his genitalia at their anatomical location. This anxiety may be one of the results of his operations. The greenish-brown dotty texture he ascribed to the fried testicle he compared to the appearance of mushrooms—another edible. They should be eaten—an oral regression, but before that, cleaned—by fire—because of his grandmother's views. Here, he expressed the feeling that his grandmother was not a woman but a man and, therefore, dirty like a man.

Evaluating Harley's hypnoanalytic sessions, their most important characteristic is the slowness of their development in every respect, their rigidity, their stickiness, the infrequency of his ability to let them change. Before the story of the naked boy in the door of the privy was unfolded, as far as the patient was able to develop it at all, four hypnoanalytic sessions were required, and it took the same number of hypnoanalyses to bring out the meaning of the buttercups. One can also find in them repetition compulsion and doubting. This stickiness deprived the hypnoanalyses of the dramatic impact their content would otherwise have provided.

All of his hypnoanalytic sessions had a recognizable background and a logically progressing activity of the involved persons. There was much symbolism, and for the most part, only one episode was described in each hypnoanalytic session.

Harley fits very well Federn's definition of the compulsive personality. The patient was always striving to act with a conscious superstrength of will, attention, and the fullest presence of mind. There were magical thoughts. He had an extremely strong feeling of his bodily ego, and he had developed too much unity of his ego.

No attempt was made to influence his sexual perversions. He was fifty-two years of age when he started his psychotherapy and was not bothered by them at all. He reported during the treatment that his wife had the impression that in intercourse he now behaved as he did in his younger years.

I want to add that Harley's treatment has been very successful. He not only kept his position, but advanced rapidly in it. During his therapy, he was promoted several times and his salary increased with these promotions.

V

PSYCHOPHYSIOLOGIC AUTONOMIC
AND
VISCERAL DISORDERS

STEVEN*

STEVEN, sent by his general practitioner for hypnotherapy, was thirty-four years of age, married, the father of three children, and a designer by profession. Because his case history is relatively short, I will present it unabridged, but somewhat reorganized and cleared of inconsequential statements.

Steven complained of a feeling of distress around the heart region. At times, he was quite disturbed by pulsations to his fingertips. In fact, for the previous three or four weeks he had suffered from them continuously, experiencing relief from this symptom only during the two days preceding his appointment. He frequently took his own pulse rate, and indicated that his heart felt more disturbed when he attempted some activity. During intercourse, he felt this disturbance only once, but he always felt it when he was in water. His electrocardiogram was normal. However, he had heart palpitations when he visited his mother in the hospital, and occasionally when he was looking at a wrestling match on television. He said that drinking six to seven ounces of liquor daily relieved him. He was also taking small amounts of phenobarbital, but did not know the dosage. The patient complained, too, of becoming breathless when singing and revealed that he had given up smoking nine months ago.

Other data given by the patient include a urination pattern of every seven or eight hours; always eating very rapidly with belching a source of relief, and having recently cut down on his food

---

* This Case was discussed in brief by the author in "Shortest Distance" Therapy in Hypnoanalysis. *Int J Clin Exp Hypn, 9*:63-77, 1961.

intake. He had fainted twice in a barber shop, the last time six months ago. He was a sound sleeper and needed a great deal of sleep, but for the last month had been awakening suddenly. His sex life was very satisfactory; both he and his wife experienced orgasm. At the start of their marriage, intercourse took place daily. Now, it occurred three or four times a week.

Steven told me that he had always been a "stickler for details by sight." But his father had often charged him with being sloppy and awkward, about which they argued. His father would also reproach him for being both negligent and stubborn. In fact, Steven invariably liked to do things quickly, on the spur of the moment, so that he could view the results, which haste his father thought unnecessary. The father also urged his son to avoid physical exercise, and, for his part, Steven regarded him as a very intelligent person.

Steven's father rarely praised him but never whipped him; however, he "often raised his hand or his fingers to his mouth." When Steven was an adolescent, his father seemed to him "like a buddy;" he seemed to like Steven's friends, too, although in this connection he engaged in "a lot of double talk."

The father ran a business in partnership with an uncle with whom he frequently quarreled. The father was regarded as nervous and irritable, suffered from colitis, for which he had been placed on a rigid diet, and, eighteen months before Steven began treatment, died suddenly of vascular failure, following an appendectomy. Because his father was known to be nervous and highstrung, the doctor had not taken seriously his complaints of feeling weak. Steven was bothered by a statement made by his general practitioner that his troubles began shortly after his father's death.

Before describing the mother, about whom more information is available than about the father, mention should be made of Steven's brother, his junior by two years. The siblings were not close, but the patient felt that his brother had been "kept back," though this was probably a consequence of his encephalitis. The brother was often "down in the dumps," and Steven's further description of him was "he does not go out, sits and mopes." Heavy at birth, the brother later often "pretended to be tired" so that he would be carried by the mother, as Steven had been.

As far back as the patient could remember, he worried constantly about his mother and felt guilty because of her. For years, she had been in and out of hospitals, having undergone twelve or thirteen operations, all performed "just in time." At thirty-four years of age, she had a hysterectomy because of tumors of the uterus, and an appendectomy as well. When Steven was still quite small, his mother had had all her teeth extracted, and at that same age a tonsillectomy. On both occasions, she bled profusely and, in addition, hemorrhaged from the mouth and nose at other times. A sufferer from sinusitis, she had headaches very frequently and Steven often remembered seeing her with her head bandaged. He said she also had "dropped kidneys and dropped tubes," and several "nervous breakdowns," and, for some time, had been taking Demerol.®

Though "sickly," his mother "always did her best." She was compulsively clean and took three showers a day. She fainted at the sight of an earthworm; could not bear to see a fly or mouse killed, and exhorted her children not to "step on an ant." No one in the family dared inform her of a demise. Thus, an awareness of death had frequently and forcibly been impressed on the patient.

Steven had been his mother's favorite child, and even before he was six, she had tried, he said, "to create animosity against my father in me." When he was five years of age, she called him "my confidant" and "my kaddish." She referred to herself as a very good person, and to her husband as mean, but at about the age of eight or nine, the boy began to doubt her statements.

In his childhood, when Steven asked his mother a question, she would push him away and say, "Don't bother me." Because she was "a sick woman," she demanded that he be good to her. Whatever Mama did was right; rarely did she feel rewarded by her children. "Everything I did was wrong," Steven said, confessing also that he never dared to laugh at anything concerning his mother because she took herself so seriously.

Steven recalled being greatly impressed when he was a child by the statement he overheard his mother make to a neighbor woman that her husband had never seen her in the nude. He had also overheard her say that she was not "conscious of sex." When his father died, the patient thought that his mother was surely the cause of it.

While she was pregnant with Steven, the mother became ill. Steven was a seven-month baby. The labor was severe and lasted five days, with no instruments used to facilitate the delivery. The circumcision was poorly performed; the infant bled a great deal, and Steven had always been under the impression that his penis was too small. He had often been told that it was red.

His mother suckled the infant for a short period of time, then underwent surgery. His mother's oldest sister, however, whom Steven called Grandmother because she had married his grandfather as her second husband, was simultaneous to Steven's birth delivered of a baby girl and had sufficient milk to suckle the boy, too. Both families had lived in adjoining houses, and the two children were later very competitive with, and hostile towards, one another.

Until his seventh year, the patient openly drank from a bottle. Then he did so surreptitiously under the bed because he had been shamed. His crib was in the dining room. He did not sleep with his parents, and he said there were no toys about.

At the age of six months, eighteen months, and again at the age of two or two-and-one-half, Steven underwent mastoid surgery. He remembered that, on the first occasion, his mother had put a blanket around him and had run with him into the street to find a doctor. He claimed that he could still feel the blanket. Regarded as delicate, Steven was carried by his mother when she went shopping. Despite this, he was an active child.

The patient had always suffered from constipation. When he was two or three years old, the doctor prescribed oil enemas after, as Steven said, "my large intestines came out." He recalled sitting on a pot in a dimly lit kitchen, his mother crying and his aunt and other female neighbors entering the room. He disliked this experience. Later in his treatment, Steven compared the sensation of swelling in his hands during some of his hypnoanalytic sessions to the feeling of distention in his lower bowels when he was a child and sitting on the pot. He had always been affected by odors, and the patient himself connected this sensitivity to his constipation. The odor of a movement was pleasurable to him, but he also felt guilty about enjoying it. His mother had given him many enemas and had consulted the doctor about his constipation even when the boy was as old as ten or eleven, which he

did not like. The father was concerned about this condition in the patient up to his fifteenth year. Steven did not recall much about his toilet training, except that he was considered a clean child. Some of the consequences of his mother's obsessive compulsive reaction were still discernible in the patient; other troubles originated in his own anal conflicts.

Steven had been a late walker; he talked at the age of thirteen or fourteen months. He did not suck his thumb, but was a nail biter, and used to eat dirt from the sidewalk. When he was four, he contracted influenza, and at the same time his brother contracted encephalitis. The patient had also suffered from a sinus infection and hence from headaches. At the preschool period of his life, he had to wear eyeglasses for about six months, and when another boy called him "cockeyed," Steven chased him for many blocks. He also had the whooping cough and, at the age of six, diphtheria. At six years of age also, he stopped addressing his father by his given name and called him Papa.

The patient had been the center of affection of his family and, indeed, of the entire neighborhood. He enjoyed this attention, but was also somehow ashamed of it. He was ashamed, too, of the fact that he was unable to do what other children did. Because, until his seventh year, his hair was cut in a Buster-Brown style, he was called Sissy. He cried often and easily, and his mother would tell him that his tears would turn to icicles.

Steven could not recall having had nightmares. However, he did remember that, before the age of five, he had had a dream about a big truck with barrels on it. Beside the barrels lay somebody's head and inside the barrels other parts of the corpse. Once, before his sixth year, his mother had gotten out of bed to fetch something for him; she fell over a mop, and he was extremely frightened.

The patient had always been very superstitious and had never entirely gotten over it.

He started to study the violin at the age of six. At the first lesson, he was afraid and cried. Later, he found himself liking it and continued to study for ten years. This instrument played an important part in Steven's symbolizations and, at various times, he made the following remarks about it: "The violin scared me."

"The piano is something definite and solid." "Maybe the violin is a mistrust in somebody." "Something slipshod is attached to the violin." "I always realized that the violin is very delicate, and the line between life and death is very thin, and a wrong note is death."

His mother expected her children to be at their best at all times, but never let Steven go to school when his forehead was warm. He also was never late to school. "I was so frightened in school," he said. He always felt his heart beating heavily before tests. In elementary school, he had studied little and had been at the top of his class, but in high school, his grades were not as good. He remembered that his mother once forced him to talk to the teacher about skipping a grade. Steven attended college for three and a half years, then dropped out because of lack of money.

Steven had always been afraid of suffocating. He was told in school to breathe through his nose, but had not been able to do so. Later, his nose was operated on, and he had two postoperative hemorrhages. He was also invariably afraid of rats, mice, and snakes.

The patient described himself as having been a "regular guy;" he was popular, and he "always had a group of ballplayers." He learned to dance quite early. An older boy once told him "how girls look" sexually, but he already knew. At fourteen years of age, he masturbated, occasionally with feelings of guilt about it. The patient had been told "quite early" that he would grow hair in the public area; this did not disturb him. He never talked much about sex. At the age of seventeen or eighteen, he joined a "fast crowd." All the other members were much older than he, but they never discovered this fact. At that time, he visited a prostitute who repelled him a little. At the age of nineteen, he had a satisfactory intercourse with a girl. Beginning at the age of twenty and continuing for several years, he had "a kind of an affair" with a singer. He never had any homosexual experience.

The patient knew his wife for some time before he paid much attention to her. Then he took her out, and they "had a lot of fun together." He proposed to her the following week, and, when he was twenty-six years of age, married her. His honeymoon im-

pressed him deeply; the couple had their first intercourse at that time. His wife was orthodox, which his mother liked, but which his father did not care for. However, she was a "clear-thinking person" and, in a short time, had a good understanding with his father. She always advised Steven not to worry about his mother, but for a long time he thought that she felt "an animosity" towards his mother. After his father's death, his mother had lived with them for one year, but at the time of his treatment she was living with strangers.

Steven was very easy to hypnotize and felt quite relaxed by it. At his following appointment, he related a night dream about his hypnosis and about me. He told me that, in the dream, I had been very excited and demanded that others help me take notes very fast, and that I gave my commands in German. He added that his mother spoke German, too—it had been a transference dream. The patient also stated that during his first hypnosis his feet immediately started to sleep; then this sensation spread upwards; he had felt his heartbeat, but from his neck downward he had a good, relaxed feeling.

After his second hypnosis, Steven informed me that he imagined at first that he was lying in the hay or on the beach. When he was told to sleep, he pictured himself "playing in two baseball fields, being the catcher." He always fell asleep by imagining a baseball game in which he was a famous player.

In his fourth hypnosis, his second hypnoanalysis, the patient was asked the meaning of a dream, but the main part of his visualization concerned his business. Steven reported afterwards that he had visualized his boss and some other men in a conference. One of them, a man with whom Steven intended to go into partnership, turned spontaneously into a snake. Then the man who had introduced this presumed partner to the patient changed into a rat. Another man, heavy-set, with a short neck and dark complexion, changed first into a buffalo, then into a polar bear; a fourth man became a fox or jackal. All these animals had been the size of people, and resembled the persons mentioned. The presumed partner was big, tall and handsome, but Steven described him as too slippery, a little like an eel, perhaps more like a snake. The man who turned into a fox was "cute and smart,"

but the patient did not like him. All these men had more experience, more money, and were on a higher level socially than Steven. The spontaneous use of the symbolic process to express his emotional response to these different persons so early in his treatment was a rare ability which facilitated this patient's therapy considerably.

Before his fifth hypnoanalytic session, Steven was told that he would be able to talk in his trance. It was very difficult for him to do so; he opened his mouth several times without result and had to be told repeatedly that he was able to speak. Regression was induced. His voice was small, soft, and frightened. He said: ". . . a small boy. (Why are you frightened?) I am not. (Yes?) In the hall. (What happens?) Before the hall mirror. I hurt my arm. (Did you break it?) No. My mother did not want that I do it. (What?) Climb on the mirror. (You fell down?) Yes. (Your age?) I don't know. (Five or ten years?) Four years." The patient appeared to be so frightened that he was awakened. This was difficult for him. Steven stated then that the episode had occurred at his aunt's and that, until this hypnosis, he only knew that he had scratched the mirror. Whereas the former hypnoanalytic session brought forth a spontaneous symbolization of the patient's emotional reactions with regard to his business associates, this hypnoanalytic session was the reliving of a former ego state, which had been partly repressed.

At his next appointment, Steven informed me that his mother screamed when he fell, but his aunt was only worried about the furniture. Questioned, he stated that his left arm had been involved.

The patient then reported a partly forgotten dream in which the ratty man played a role. Steven had to appear in front of a board, was asked unfair questions, and was helped by me. Later, Steven informed me that he is now playing basketball and running up the stairs.

Then ensued the sixth hypnoanalysis which was taken down with the recorder. The patient was told to recall his dream completely and to explain it. He again had difficulty with talking, breathed heavily during the whole hypnoanalytic session, and was pale.

Excerpts of what he said now follow. He had to answer questions put to him by examiners for a position as a doctor on Staten Island. Another doctor was laughing at him. "(How did it happen that they asked you questions which you could not answer?) Because I didn't study those questions. (Why not?) They had nothing to do with being a doctor . . . (How did it come to pass that in this dream you were a doctor?) I always wanted to be a doctor. (Why?) Mother always wanted me— (Why? You can talk very well.) Prestige, I suppose . . . I didn't become a doctor because we had no money for me to continue studying. (Were you very sorry about it?) I was sorry in the beginning. But not now. (What is it?) Something stopped me. (What did?) I don't know. (What did you feel?) I couldn't answer the questions . . . And somebody helped me. (Who?) . . . (A man or a woman?) It's a woman. (What does she look like?) Clean . . . And honest. But it didn't help . . . (What do you think this whole dream means?) . . . I had to go to work . . . (You apparently had the feeling you didn't get a fair deal.) That's right. (Who didn't give you the fair deal?) Maybe my mother. (What's your feeling about her? Dare to talk.) She was sick. They needed the money for the doctors. And I knew it would be no use. (What?) That when I graduated from college, I wouldn't have the means to go further . . . (Can you repeat any of the questions put to you by the examiner?) Who is the health commissioner under . . . Mayor O'Toole. I don't know that . . . (Do you know his name?) No. I was a little boy when Mayor O'Toole was mayor. (Just talk it out.) He was a very corrupt mayor . . ."

It was hard for the patient to come out of the trance, and for some time afterwards, he was rubbing his arms. Immediately after the hypnoanalytic session, he stated that he remembered the tonsillectomy he had when he was five years old. The man with the ratlike face resembled the man who had thrown Steven over his shoulder and carried him into the room where the ether was administered. Then he reported another visual recollection of when he was two years of age and his father had had a fight on the stairs.

Steven also stated that, while I was repeating the suggestions to help him remember his dream, he had the sensation that his forearms, his fingers especially, and his face had gotten bigger and

bigger, and that only his nose remained small. He could not understand how so small a nose "could support enough breath" for so large a face. Initially, he thought that he first had such feelings at the time of his tonsillectomy; then he recalled that, as a small boy, before going to sleep, he very often had such sensations. The directing in the hypnoanalytic session to remember a half-forgotten dream and to explain it, not only produced this dream and its interpretation, but also other associatively connected former ego states. The dream as well as the hypnoanalytic session exposed his mother's frustrating demands that her son bolster her own prestige when she knew very well that the money needed to achieve his further education would have to be used for herself. She did not give him—she never gave him—a fair deal.

At his next appointment, Steven reported that he had "played baseball like a young boy" and climbed a mountain.

Because the patient complained at the following session about having been tense for several days, his next hypnosis was only a "soothing" one. However, he reported afterwards that he remembered that before his second year, he was once stung by a mosquito in the park, and his face became very swollen. The sensation had been the same as he had had at other hypnoanalyses. The tenement whence he was taken to the park was the same building on the stairs of which his father had had the aforementioned fight.

At his ensuing appointment, Steven was suffering from a bad cold. He told me that, several nights back, he had a terrific pain in his heart and had to go to the bathroom. Notwithstanding, he climbed the highest peak in the mountains on his recent short vacation. He also said that he did not feel as well after his last hypnosis as he did before it. "I find myself waiting for something," he remarked.

At his eighth hypnoanalytic session, the patient received relaxing suggestions after which regression was induced. The recorder could not be used because of interference, but immediately afterwards, Steven was told to report into the microphone what he had visualized, and this was transcribed. "(Please tell me what you saw during the hypnosis.) I saw myself as a little boy standing at the curb, urinating . . . (Please start at the beginning. You told me a boy was running after you, and that there was a second boy

who was four years of age, just as you were.) Yes. But— (Talk.)
The second part was—took place previous. (How?) The way it appeared in the dream . . . This other friend of mine . . . we were
playing in the street. This little boy, even at that young age,
played the violin. And I liked to hear him play and we became
very good friends . . . I think—ah, we were riding on the sidewalk
when this other boy came over with a stick and started to run
after me. And this little friend of mine ran with me. He traced us
into an alley which led to a backyard. Before we actually got to
the backyard, he tripped and fell and both of us ran to our respective houses . . . He dropped as he fell, he dropped the stick. I ran
up to my mother . . . I cried, I remember. I don't remember what
my mother said to me . . . (After I directed you to again remember
what happened, you told me you complained to that older boy,
your cousin.) Yes. I told an older cousin of mine about this and he
whipped this other boy . . . I don't know whether you were watching me, but I felt that I had a grin on my face because I felt very
happy at the prospect of seeing this other bully beaten up. But
the thing that seemed to me to be more important was when I
first saw this bully. I was standing at the curb urinating as all little
boys did then . . . And he came at me. Told me to stop . . . or
something. I wasn't sure whether he held a stick in his hand . . . or
something sharp. I immediately started to run before I could button up my trousers. And since then . . . he continuously chased
me . . . his face was so very clear while I was dreaming. (You told
me that he had green teeth?) Yes, he was an ugly child, high
cheekbones, and his teeth . . . looked very bad . . . They looked
green. As a child I thought the worst thing that can happen to
anybody was to have green teeth because that was a sign that . . .
you never brushed your teeth. And the sign that if you didn't
brush your teeth . . . you didn't keep the rest of you clean. Probably impressed on me by my mother. (What did you feel during
the hypnosis? Your breathing was very heavy.) After the questioning stopped, I felt that there was a constriction right across my
chest as if I had to burst . . . a chain around my chest. And my
hands again felt extremely numb. As a matter of fact I tried . . .
and I couldn't move them. It was only toward the end of the hypnosis that I could move the last two smaller fingers. (What caused

this heavy breathing at the beginning? You were almost unable to talk.) That was just that I was getting myself ready to talk. Because you impressed on me before the hypnosis that I spoke very low and that it was difficult for me to speak. As a matter of fact, this one was much easier for me. I think I spoke louder. (Yes.)"

The foregoing hypnoanalytic session was again the reawakening of a former ego state. At the session following the next (Steven's ninth), he was told to remember the events of the last hypnoanalysis, including its missing parts. As far as possible, the later sequences will be reproduced.

"I can see again myself . . . standing at the curb, urinating. (How old are you, about?) About four years old. (What is happening?) I am interrupted. A bigger boy . . . told me he would cut my penis off and I ran. (Did you believe he would do it?) I don't know but I was frightened that he might. (Had it ever occurred to you that anybody could cut it off?) Perhaps I thought that the rabbi might have been able to do something like that, at circumcision. But it was never important. (Did you compare the penises of other little boys?) No. I don't think I ever saw the other little boys'. I imagine I was just frightened by the . . . penknife with a white handle. And the larger blade was open. (He put it near you?) No, I didn't give him a chance to. He must have been about four or five feet away from me when I started to run. (Did he yell at you?) He—he didn't yell. Maybe he did . . . (You remember very well what he said.) He said, watch out or I cut. And don't do it here any more. If you do, I will cut it off . . . (Had you done it before at that spot?) No. (Had you seen him then for the first time?) I think so. (Remember the other occasions.) I remember another occasion . . . before. This little friend and myself were skating and he wanted to take one of the skates away from us. But he didn't take them away. But I can't remember if this happened before this episode or afterwards. (Why did this boy always come after you?) It seems as if he did come only for me . . . (Did you believe he would really cut it off?) I must have. (Had you been frightened on some previous occasion that it would be cut off? Did your heart pound?) . . . I think I must have been. That somebody perhaps would cut it off. (Were you urinating on the other occasions, too?) No . . . (What did he have in his hands on these

occasions?) Just a stick. (Larger than the knife?) Yes . . . He hit me with the club. (What did you complain to your cousin about?) Only about the club. (Why not the other occasion?) I didn't want to discuss it. (Why not?) I was always told that was something private. (But you did it in the street.) Yes. But my parents sanctioned my urinating in the street . . . But my parents always told me not to discuss anything about . . . (Something must have happened before between you and this boy. You dream, and remember what happened between you and this boy.) I may have beat that boy. (You dream, you remember.) We are on the sidewalk . . . The first time I saw him, I had a hammer in my hand and I was banging on the sidewalk. He wanted it but I didn't give it to him. He said he might get even with me . . . He was waiting for me. Every time I came downstairs. He used to run after me, but I always eluded him. (Where did this hammer come from?) . . . I just broke up the sidewalk with it a little, and he wanted to do the same. It was my father's, and I did not want to give it to him. (What else frightened you?) There was another occasion . . . He had a kitchen knife. It was not the same as he did with the penknife. But he threatened to stick me with it or cut me . . ."

At the playback of this record, the patient stated, on questioning, that he had seen the colors black, white, gray, and brown during visualization, and that the teeth of this boy were greenish-gray. It was a continuous picture, like a movie. He said he also saw the background because when he saw the street in front of the basement, he visualized the trolley rails there.

This hypnoanalytic session by which the former session was supplemented, worked through, and completed was, of course, again the reawakening of a former ego state and, as a consequence to my questioning, the reawakening of other ego states. When answering my questions, Steven spoke, for the most part, in short sentences, but not when describing occurrences. There were very few words (for example, the word "elude") which such an infant would not use. But the episodes are all quite likely to have happened. That they were an expression of the patient's castration anxiety was obvious from his having recalled these particular incidents out of the reservoir of thousands of others.

At his next session, Steven reported that he did not feel well

and was anticipating a visit to the cemetery, where he had refused to go until his fifteenth or sixteenth year, when he had been forced to do so. He had twice suffered from palpitations; he had had headaches and had slept restlessly. He stated that he resented and feared being hypnotized and having to remember past events. My questioning in the hypnoanalyses annoyed him because he does not keep anything back. Here again is the unconscious equating of the hypnotic sleep with death, first described by Schneck.

At the following interview, the patient again did not care to be hypnotized and complained of a severe headache—a resistance. He also reported that he had once been afraid of the local butcher. He had believed that this man was a giant.

At the ensuing session, Steven changed his mind and asked for a hypnosis. He first received "soothing" suggestions, then regression was induced and he was told to talk. "(You open your mouth.) Yes. (What do you see?) [deep breathing] I see myself. And my little friend. We are walking in the street . . . And we are trying to guess . . . the names of all the automobiles. And we are having a lot of fun. (How old are you?) I am five years old. [deep breathing] And my friend invited me to his house to hear him play the violin. He played very nicely. And his mother was very proud of him. And I thought I might like to play, too. (What happened?) [deep breathing] (Is it hard for you to talk?) I am trying to remember what happened. (You dream, you remember. You dream and remember. What passes through your mind? Everything is all right. Talk.) . . . And his mother, I think, teased me. (About what?) About the fact that he could play and I couldn't. And that if I would be a good boy, I might be able to play like him some day. (Did you feel you were a good boy?) Yes. [repeated deep breathing] (What is it? Why do you move your mouth without talking?) My arms are very heavy . . . My hands, yes. (Your hands? What's going on?) My hands are heavy and lying on my stomach. (Talk it out.) And I can't lift them off. (Is it very disagreeable?) Nn. Yes. (You are now able to lift your right arm. Your right arm goes up. Just lift it.) [slowly lifts his right hand and forearm] (Your hand is going up and you see it's possible.) [description of what the patient does] (You are now clenching

your fist.) [places his right arm and hand on the right side of his body] (Now your left arm goes up. You are now spreading your fingers. You are moving them, and you see it's possible.) [places his left arm on the side of his body and keeps the hand on his abdomen so that the arm does not fall down] (Do you feel better?) Yes. [expression of relief] (What do you feel now?) I feel a good deal more comfortable. (Why did you spread the fingers of your left hand again?) Just flexing. Now my hands started to get very big. (Talk it out.) I don't know why. (What passes through your mind?) And it seemed that all that bigness started to creep right up to my chest. It feels better now. I felt it difficult breathing before. (Talk everything out.) I was thinking about playing the violin. He sounded very good to me . . . And I told my mother I wanted to take lessons. She told me I might later. And I remember once I couldn't play so well. (Why not?) I just couldn't play. (What kept you from playing?) I didn't have enough experience playing. (How old were you?) Not much older. (You told me once that at that time you did not have enough lessons.) No. (You just tried to play?) Nn. (What?) No, after I had started lessons. I was about six years old. I tried to play and then I couldn't. And I was disappointed. (What hindered you?) The fact that I didn't know how to play. (The teacher had not yet shown you how?) That's right. (Tell me.) I was disappointed because . . . even after having taken lessons for six months, I couldn't play as well as my little friend. But he had been taking lessons for a long time. And I think that his mother made fun of me . . . I was upset. (You were disappointed.) Greatly. (Is there anything else?) No."

After this hypnoanalytic session, Steven stated spontaneously that he had experienced this sensation of having enlarged hands as a child before starting to sleep and in dreams. Federn has described such variations in the bodily ego feeling in gradually falling asleep, but without any emotional accompaniment, certainly not with anxiety attacks.* He also states that the "erotically significant zones or parts are more resistant than the others." We will later see that in this patient for whom odors were quite significant, the nose and, at times, the mouth were excluded from this "swelling" with rather disagreeable consequences.

---

* Federn, P.: *Ego Psychology and the Psychoses.* New York, Basic Books, 1961, pp. 29-31.

This hypnoanalytic session had some relation to the patient's sixth hypoanalysis, the first one in which Steven talked, which might have been partly a symbolization of this event. He pointed out that in both hypnoanalyses he had done his part; he had studied, but failed to reach his goals, in the one to obtain a job as a doctor, in the other to play the violin well. But he was also laughed at in one endeavor and teased in the other. The deleterious effect on his emotional development is obvious. In this hypnoanalytic session Steven again spoke in short sentences.

At his next appointment, the patient was told that the sensation of having swelled hands pertained to his inability to play the violin, and that this instrument might also have some other meaning for him. He stated that during the hypnoanalytic session he had had the feeling that I was bending down to look at his face. He did not attempt to move his arms. That morning, he "awoke semi-paralyzed, like after a hypnosis." The last hypnoanalytic session was then played back to him.

At the following session, Steven stated that he feels well and that he now understands much better what was disturbing him. He had been impressed by my remark that the violin probably had some symbolical value for him. At some time, when he was not yet five years of age, he had seen a man's genitals. The testicles looked as though they were swollen. Steven was horrified and thereafter avoided this man. It may be that the man had cancer of the genitals because he died of cancer shortly afterwards. Steven said he had the appearance of an ape, beat his children, and was "wild." The patient thought he could remember that this man's daughter had given him piano lessons, and that was the reason Steven renounced his interest in the piano in favor of the violin.

At the ensuing interview, the patient felt well, but did not want a hypnosis performed. He told me that once, when he had seen his father shave, he experienced an erection, which he reexperienced the first time he shaved himself. He stated that body odor nauseates him. At four years of age, he had smelled freshly cut hay and liked its odor, as well as the scents of lilacs and roses.

At his next session, Steven reported several upsetting occurrences at his job and said that because of them he had been drinking. While dozing, he had had a dream in which he finished working on his basement. This entailed restyling, not construction. His

associations were that, when he had actually done this about a year ago, it constituted a release for him, just as it was in this dream.

In his eleventh hypnoanalytic session, the patient was told to recall this dream and was asked its real meaning. "I remember finishing up my basement and making it into a beautiful room . . . everything was almost perfect . . . it was very eye-appealing . . . You could actually smell the colors. And the color combinations. And it made me feel very good. (Just talk about everything [deep breathing] that passes through your mind.) I think I understand what it all meant, too. There was nobody criticizing. And everything I did, I did because I wanted to do it that way . . . And making any comparisons. At least there was nobody there to tell me this is better and this is nicer . . . The colors were very—very striking and they blended beautifully. (What kinds of colors?) Reds, green. (Just talk it out.) And a shellacked pine, let's say, that's a light shade, tan-brown. The floor had black and red with just a little yellow through it. And also some white. Everything was smooth and finely polished. And I saw myself rubbing my hands over a couple of the walls. It was very clean and smelled beautifully down there. It smelled as if there were flowers a-a-a-against all the walls. Not perfume . . . (What kind of flowers?) Roses, sweet-smelling flowers. Not too sweet, but just enough to be stimulating. (Can you smell it now?) Yes. (Of what does the odor remind you?) It reminds me of the outdoors and a—of a place that's not too—that's not too large, but of a small garden. Not very small, but it doesn't remind me of fields. It does not remind me of tall grass. It reminds me of neatness and comfort. It seemed that—ah—the cellar was just the same way, it wasn't too large, but it had a coziness about it that was very gratifying, very satisfying, where I could sit down and really relax. (Where did you experience this kind of coziness the first time in your life?) I don't know if I ever saw anything like it. But I do know that I must have read about it or imagined it. It was something that I always wanted to be part of or to be surrounded by. There were no obnoxious smells, there was all s—s—s clean. (What kinds of smells are obnoxious?) The smells that I don't like . . . (Which ones don't you like?) I don't like the smell of a perspiration. I don't like an unclean smell or a musty smell . . . the exhaust of an

automobile. (What is so disagreeable about it?) I just don't like it.
(There must be a reason.) Maybe it's the color that I don't like
about it. It's dense . . . it's just unclean-looking. And perhaps I associate the look with the odor . . . I feel like vomiting . . . (What
other odors do you dislike?) . . . I guess it's all associated with—
with being clean or not clean. Ahah—I don't like the smell of
dirty clothes. That is the worst smell. . . I don't like the smell of
rotting animal matter. That makes me sick . . ."

After being awakened, the patient stated that he feels comfortable because nobody had criticized or interfered with his work; he
had done it all by himself.

At his next interview, he spoke at length about his constipation. Then he told me how, when he saw his wife for the first
time, "she was so clean-looking, and she smelled so nice."

The following time, Steven informed me that he had had a lot
of fun over the weekend. But the previous day, he had seen his
mother and she had given him "the creeps."

He explained in connection with his eleventh hypnoanalytic
session that the colors red, green, and yellow have no odor, only
cleanliness. Pastels did have smells, depending on the circumstances. "I am a bug, a stickler for smells, and I detest many per-
fumes. I can tell a clean person by the perfume she uses. The perfume a woman uses will give me an idea why she uses it. There
are certain odors I like, probably because the person who wears it
is clean." The patient himself sometimes had the feeling that he
was smelly, therefore would take a shower, and feel better afterwards, although his wife often told him on these occasions that
she did not notice any odor at all.

At his next session, Steven reported that, shortly before arriving, he had drunk about one-and-a-half ounces of whiskey. He related he had had a dream about himself as a small boy in which
his mother may have figured, but he could not describe it. "Maybe
the side of a mountain sliding and something white." His associations were that he had painted white furniture the day before.
Perhaps it had some connection with sex. He had a Chinese-red
wall and something green in the room, then "a Chinese-red table
to it," and now he wanted to add some yellow. This was just as he
had seen it in his recent hypnoanalytic session.

The following is a transcript of the patient's twelfth hypnoana-

lytic session:* "(You dream, you remember the dream you had last
night about yourself as a little boy, with all the details, and you
know what the real meaning of this dream was. Please talk.) . . . I
remember the dream quite clearly. I was on a large white horse . . .
and my mother was walking alongside. And I wanted the horse
to gallop faster. My mother warned me not to. She was afraid that
the horse would fall. We were—ah—on a narrow path on the side
of a mountain . . . the horse . . . might slip and fall off. I galloped
the horse anyway; the horse did fall. And instead of falling down,
the horse all of a sudden had wings and we glided—glided down.
That was the entire dream. (What passes through your mind on
thinking about this dream? Just talk.) N-n-n-nothing much except that—that when I did disobey my mother, when I would,
nothing drastic ever happened anyway. Except that I had a little
fun. And this gliding down to earth was very—very exhilarating.
(What did you feel?) I felt as if I were flying, not soaring, but
gliding. It was a good . . . clean feeling. (What is the meaning of
this white horse? What passes through your mind?) Ordinarily the
animals frighten me. And this horse was—was white. I felt as if it
were n-nothing to be frightened of. That it was clean and we rode
very smoothly. But I didn't enjoy the ride until I started to descend. (Just talk.) Then I enjoyed it very much. (What do you
think is the real meaning? What's your idea about it? What passes
through your mind?) My idea about it is simply that if I did anything I enjoyed, everything works out all right, anything. (What
did you enjoy?) I enjoyed the ride on gliding down the horse, ah
—galloping . . . It was exciting. It was thrilling despite that my
mother said not to gallop . . . (In what way could you have hurt
yourself?) In falling off the horse or—or toppling or—off the side
of the mountain. Ah, it was actually—ah—a—a—a precipice in
the path where we—where I was on the horse. (How did the horse
look?) A—a—a big, a tall horse, but white as a—white as snow
. . . It was a clean-looking animal with, I don't know, with eyes
that looked pink or red. (What does this horse represent?) I don't
know. (Of what did this feeling remind you?) A—a—a feeling of

* Part of this hypnoanalytic session has been published under the heading,
" 'Shortest Distance' Therapy in Hypnoanalysis" in the *Int J Clin Exp Hypn, 9:*
63-77, 1961.

f-floating, of—of being free. Of being unfettered. A feeling of doing what I want to do. (What do you want to do?) I didn't know. I meant what I wanted to do. (Yes. What did you want to do?) Oh, very often I wanted to play ball. My mother said not to; she had other things for me to do. Because she was ah, sickly. I—I should help her with the floors. Then the woodwork. The washing. When I much rather would have been out playing. There was a feeling riding that horse of complete—complete freedom. Freedom from anxiety. Despite the fact that I did—was—I wasn't supposed to do. (Yes.) It made me feel very good; the—the consequences weren't as dire as my mother had predicted. All I did was enjoy my ride down. (Do you still see this horse? Can you see it?) Yes. (Okay. Now look very closely at it. This horse will now change and you will see the real meaning of this dream. This horse will now change and you will see what the real meaning of this dream was. You see how the horse changes? It is changed now, and now I want you to tell me what you see. Just talk.) A—now I see myself on a bicycle. But I—I—I am having the same sort of difficulty . . . (Yes.) Mother thought I am too small to ride a bicycle. (Yes.) But I insisted I am getting one, so my dad bought me one. I learned how to ride by myself. At least as a little boy. I used to ride it when we lived out in Lewistown. (Do you believe that is the real meaning of the dream? No, now look closely at the bicycle. Yes. Look closely at it, and now the bicycle will change. The bicycle will change to the real meaning of this dream. I am sure there is still something behind it. Just look carefully at it. It is changing more and more. At first it was a horse, then a bicycle, and now it changes to the real thing, to what you meant when you had this dream. It changes to the real thing. Why do you breathe so deeply?) My arms are getting very heavy. (What is the real thing?) And my face. (Yes. What is the matter with your face?) Is getting very, very big. (Just now?) Yes. [inhalation and exhalation become deeper, like sighing] (What is it? What is it? Talk it out.) My face is getting very big and my mouth and nose [inhalation] are small. (Yes.) [inhalation and exhalation sound like sighing, slow] I find it difficult to breathe. (Just talk it out. Talk about all your feelings. Then you will be more comfortable.) [exhalation like sighing] (Your forehead is perspiring?) Yes, and

my heart is beating very rapidly. [inhalation] (Do you have anxiety?) I don't know what—what. It's all [breathing is slow and sounds like sighing] (Should we stop?) Yes, please. (Okay.) [inhalation like sighing, slow] (You feel more comfortable.)" Actually, Steven's inhalations could be heard from the beginning of the hypnoanalysis and his exhalation was audible from the time of the change to the bicycle.

The patient was rather pale, his breathing slow, and deep like a sigh. Except for the pallor, all returned to normal during the very slow awakening which was accompanied by repeated suggestions that he would feel very comfortable and that his body would return to its proper size. Immediately after awakening, Steven stated that the last thing he had visualized was a violin. "The bicycle changed to a violin." Asked whether the hypnoanalysis was disagreeable, he said, "I don't know if it was disagreeable. I started to feel so very uncomfortable." His face remained numb for some time. He informed me that in the hypnoanalysis only his legs had retained their normal proportions. Otherwise he felt the same sensations he usually experienced just before fainting. It was like dying, he said, he had experienced it in the anesthesia administered before his tonsillectomy, and a few other times as a child when he was running a temperature. He repeated that his father's vascular failure might have felt like the attack he had just had. He was told that if an attack can be brought about and then stopped by hypnosis, it must be mental. He then added that the legs of the horse changed to the wheels of the bicycle, the forelegs to the front wheel, the hindlegs to the back wheel. This back wheel then turned into the curved back of a violin. He also added, in contrast to his other hypnoanalyses, that, during the anxiety attack, it was of comfort to him to hear my voice. The theoretical implications of this will follow.

At the next session, Steven complained of a bad cold despite a good time he had had that very day. His nose was congested and felt uncomfortable. The pictures he drew of what he had visualized during his hypnoanalysis were poorly executed for a designer. First, he drew a horse, then a tricycle instead of the bicycle. About a string instrument he remarked, "And it was not a cello either, a cello has its neck up." He also commented anent this visualiza-

tion that his mother most often walked behind him, though, at times, she went alongside. On questioning, he said, "I must have been a grown-up. It never occurred to me. I don't remember." After the record was played back to Steven, he stated that he could break the picture down further. At first, he made two connecting vertical lines, on the one hand linking the anterior part of the horse's body, the front wheel of the tricycle and the part of the violin near its neck, on the other hand the rear part of the horse's body, one of the rear wheels of the tricycle, and the lower part of the violin's body. Then he pointed to the horse's neck, the seat of the tricycle (he called it bicycle) and the neck of the violin, and asked me whether I knew what he was getting at.

Hence, he drew another picture, also quite poorly executed. This was of a horse, below it an image that looked somewhat like a bicycle, then the violin, an animal he called a rodent, eyeglasses, and, far down, very poorly and faintly sketched, male genitals. He then told me for the first time that he wore eyeglasses because of his sinus trouble although he had perfect eyesight. He also remembered that, in a dream the previous night, he had seen his father, but that was all he could recall.

Both these last hypnoanalytic sessions also picture former ego states, only in a symbolical way expressing emotions. In his tenth hypnoanalytic session, Steven pinpointed an old wish, to be free of criticism, to be able to do exactly what he wanted, and to have his Garden of Eden all to himself. The eleventh hypnoanalytic session went further. Despite the fact that he disregarded his mother's warnings, no harm had come to him, he had even enjoyed what he did; sex and its consequences were very agreeable. The horse, as the patient had already told me on another occasion, was his father "carrying the load of the family," but also carrying the patient to where he was himself: mature sex—gliding to earth. He was white, not black as the mother painted him, and red might either be the natural eye color for a white animal, or have been symbolic of the tears his father may have shed because of his marriage, which Steven now started to view more realistically. The bicycle-tricycle had been bought by his father against the mother's wishes. It symbolized freedom from her; his father had proven he could have his own way. The violin was an overdetermined sym-

bol. Steven was looking for praise, which he rarely got, and was also teased when he played prematurely for his friend's mother. But it was still an achievement of which he could be proud. In a later dream interpretation, it also represented money which his father was often short of. The rodent was also his father when he behaved with authority like the patient's former boss, or symbolized the mother's opinion of the father. The eyeglasses might also symbolize authority, or they might stand for shortsightedness, or for being "cockeyed," as he had been about his own emotions. The small, faintly sketched genitalia may have symbolized the father under the mother's domination, or the patient's impression of his own genitalia. Steven's bad cold at his next session was most probably consequential to his still very ambivalent emotions.

Two sessions later, the patient was again hypnotized, and regression was induced. It was his thirteenth hypnoanalytic session: "I am riding a little . . . blue bicycle. Which I have got from my cousin. (Your age?) I am four years old . . . And I make believe I am a policeman on a motorcycle . . . I see my cousin. Trotting alongside. (How old is he?) He is about a nine-year-old. And he is as happy as I am . . . And he feels grown-up because he has given his little cousin his own bicycle . . . (Why are you coughing?) It tickled my throat. (What comes to your mind?) I really enjoyed the bicycle. I seem to remember somebody threatening to take it away from me. Just about a block from my house . . . And he looked like the butcher my mother . . . bought the meat from. A tremendous man. I was very frightened, but my cousin . . . told me not to be frightened because the man was not serious . . . But I ran away very quickly . . . To me he seemed . . . ruddy-faced with a red-blond moustache. White apron covered with blood. He always intimidated all the little children . . . Once my mother took me in there . . . he picked me up. And sort of threw me in the air . . . I started to cry. I was . . . about three years old . . . And I always tried thereafter to avoid passing the store . . . I think he spoke . . . a foreign language anyway . . . (What makes it hard for you to breathe?) It's not hard. It just felt good to take a deep breath from talking. (What is so hard about talking?) It's nothing hard to talk except that it's a— (What?) . . . I don't—I hold my breath actually when I talk . . . (Do you do it also when you are

not hypnotized?) I probably do it always. (Why?) I don't know, just stupid that way. (No. Things have reasons.) As a matter of fact, when I talk over an extended period of time, I find myself breathless. Perhaps I try to say too much in one phrase without breathing. (Why don't you breathe correctly?) . . . In school, in the speech class . . . and the teacher remarked about it too . . . I always thought it to be because I was frightened . . . Not frightened of anything serious. But because it was school and it was a lesson . . . Even if I were correct and I don't know all the answers. But every time I went reciting in a class on anything, any quiz, I would find myself speaking—ah—ah—the same way. I remember the same thing happening . . . just as I started to go to school . . . (Of whom did the teacher remind you?) Of nobody in particular . . . The teacher I had in the first year . . . seemed all right, except . . . to be too strict. And I would watch my step. (What passes through your mind?) My hands are getting heavy again. (Is this very disagreeable?) Yes. (Of what does this remind you?) I am trying to think . . . I remember having had these feelings of numbness in school . . . when I was a little bit older . . . (Should we stop?) Please."

Duplications of letters and words have been cut out of the transcript of this hypnoanalysis, and elliptical points put in their place. In this hypnoanalytic session, a number of former ego states were reawakened. Steven was again riding a bicycle, now the symbol of a policeman, an authority figure. It is much more probable that such an infant rode a tricycle which this time was given to him not by his father, but by his nine-year-old cousin. (Would the patient's over-cautious mother have permitted him to ride even a children's bicycle?) Be this as it may, it was more important that Steven stated after the hypnoanalytic session that he had seen colors this time. He was frightened by the butcher because this man had once threatened the children with a meat cleaver when they were "too noisy." The patient could very well visualize his cousin's face, although the cousin died thirteen years ago. He added that before this hypnoanalysis, he did not remember that he had had the heavy feeling in his arms in school.

Steven tried very hard to recall the pictures he had drawn at his previous session, and I told him that they had some connection

with his anxiety attacks. He stated on questioning that he had a cough.

At his next appointment, the patient reported that he felt very well, but that after having seen a technicolor movie one evening, he felt tense. His father had once had an anxiety attack while watching such a movie, and Steven and his wife had been present. When the patient fell asleep that night, he had the sensation that his right hand was becoming bigger, and he awakened himself. Also, on turning his head to the left in bed, he became dizzy; his father, too, had had attacks of dizziness. Steven's identification with his father, and especially with his father's bodily complaints, repeated itself time and again, as his mother had very early put him in his father's place, strengthening his Oedipus complex by calling him her *kaddish* and other grandiose names. At the same time, she was as frustrating, demeaning, and demanding to the son as to the father.

At his following session, Steven reported that he felt well and had no longer been thinking about heart attacks. The last hypnoanalytic session was read to him. He said, "To me the butcher is the coldest-looking person in the world." He remembered that he had mentioned him in a former hypnoanalytic session. The patient also stated that he is not afraid of blood because his mother had hemorrhaged so often.

Pondering why it was that he became shortwinded when he was not able to answer a question in hypnoanalysis, Steven recalled being unable to talk at his first violin lesson. "Why have I been so frightened?" he asked. The answer is that everybody in authority was identified by him with his mother; but we did not have the time to discuss the influence of this fact on his transference situation.

At the ensuing interview, the patient reported that since he last saw me, both before and after having had some kind of fun, he had been with his mother, had become depressed, breathed heavily, and had the feeling that he had "dropped," as if his heart had skipped a beat, like the sensation he experienced in hypnosis. He had the same feeling the following day and again today. "I hate her nearly, but I should not."

At the next visit, Steven read the transcript of the hypnoanaly-

tic session and remarked, "Bicycle is recurring." He said that the cousin mentioned was not intelligent, but the patient had been proud to be accepted by an older boy.

Steven said he had ridden a horse for the first time after a party, was the only one who had not been taught to ride and had, therefore, had a hard time. He added that he had had other disagreeable experiences with horses, but did not specify.

At his following appointment, Steven reported trouble with his mother. He had visited her in the hospital where he had had a bad coughing spell. The people with whom she lived now refused to take her back. Telephoning his brother about this situation made the patient cry for two hours, and later he vomited. "Today I am just dead."

At the next session, the patient related a dream in which there was an explosion, and, emanating from his father who looked down from heaven, streamed a brightness like daylight which shone in Steven's left eye, then passed over to his right eye as he lay on his belly. His association and interpretation were that the light was like a searchlight, and his father might have been trying to illuminate a problem for him, most probably related to the mother about whom he knew so much more than their son. The patient thought one of the beams of light might have been for his wife, who sleeps to the left of him, and that the whole dream might mean that he was on the right track regarding his mother.

At his ensuing session, the patient related another "light dream." In this, a straight shaft of clear, white, artificial light was passing from his left eye to his right eye, shining across. His association to this dream was that the light had something to do with his coughing. He complained again about a cold, a tickling in his throat, and a chill he had had. This light also pertained to his mother, and he recalled that in the former light dream, both his parents had been present and that suddenly his father was in heaven.

At his following appointment, the fourteenth hypnoanalytic session, Steven wanted to examine his light dreams under hypnosis.

"(What passes through your mind as far as the first dream is concerned?) I think it was an indication that no matter what I will do as far as my mother is concerned I will do the right thing.

Not to worry about it because from all directions, everybody thinks that I was doing the right thing. (What has this to do with the light shining into your eyes?) I think the light was a direction. If it hadn't been shining in my eyes, it would have been misdirected if it had passed me on either side. (Why?) . . . In other words, if I were doing the wrong thing, the light would be pointed or directed at another object which shows me perhaps in what way to proceed . . . I seemed to feel that it was a sort of an okay . . . (Your father had something to do with it?) . . . I feel that he was in full approval. Perhaps that I am now in full agreement with him . . . about the whole situation . . . finally I understand what he understood. (The light went from one eye to the other?) No. There were actually two shafts of light. The first one is directed at one eye. (Which one?) The left. And the other was directed to the right eye. They started out as one shaft . . . as they reached me, they split up into two. It seemed that they went directly into both eyes. (Why did they start with the left one?) Well, the only reason I can think of is that previous to this I have always worried about my heart and everything being on the left side . . . Perhaps because . . . it was all about my mother and she is still my mother; I still love her, on one side. On the other side, I don't love her too much because of what I think she is doing, what she has done to me. (Are you sleeping deeply?) No. [rehypnotized] (What passes through your mind now?) That I wanted to cough before. And I didn't . . . (Has it to do with the light?) No. I think I felt good, and thinking about that dream, I didn't cough. (Are you sleeping deeper?) Yes . . . I am thinking about the following dream . . . with the one light. It passed across the other way. (What was there?) More confusion because the light passed in front of me, as if to direct my attention somewhat. I don't think it has anything to do with my mother, though. It seemed something to do with my place of business. Actually, it was a revolutionary thing as far as I was concerned. I think the following day I made up my mind not to cover up for anybody, not to take—to do things the way I really think they are right. The light coming from left to right is a little confusing. Because ordinarily to make a change like that you change towards the left. But perhaps it went from left to right to indicate that I only did

it the other way because I thought it would be easier for myself to bow instead of to assert myself . . . (Do you have any other ideas about these dreams?) I think they were only directional dreams. In other words, backing me up in what I was doing. My arms are getting heavy. (Should we stop?) Not yet. (What do you still want to tell me?) Those two dreams evidently made me feel good. At least they gave me action . . . I think I might have overcome any fears I have had on this subject. (Should we stop?) Please."

The patient drew a picture illustrating how he felt his body expanding and stated that he feels very good.

This hypnoanalytic session did not represent a former ego state, but the "enlightenment" he was experiencing regarding his emotions and his behavior as a result of his treatment. The lights in both dreams were a symbolization of parts of his superego relieved of his mother's unreasonable demands. In the second dream, he demonstrated that his ego strength had increased "to do things the way I really think they are right." It is interesting that the patient spoke during this hypnoanalytic session not in the short sentences he mostly used in the regressed state, but like an adult, in full sentences.

At his next session, Steven reported that he had been awakened at four o'clock in the morning by the sensation that his head and his arms from the forearms down were swelling. Instead of becoming frightened, however, he laughed. This sensation of swelling pertained to a speech he was to deliver to a critical audience. He commented that the last hypnoanalytic session had eased his conscience, especially as far as his mother was concerned. During the hypnoanalysis "I felt so wonderful to have found the answers."

He said that, while at his place of business putting a dress on a dummy, he felt dizzy, had palpitations, and "a disagreeable sensation" which lasted for about five hours. Next day, when putting another dress on the dummy, he again started to get the same feelings. Then he realized that both dresses had "the same back treatment," and his discomfort ceased. He drew pictures of the styling of the back of these dresses, a U-shape reaching below the waistline and immediately beneath that a shirring. He associated the U-shape with the female breast. The shirring below was important for him; it might signify hair or buttocks. He said he might

have seen his mother exposed; he certainly had seen her breasts. But he found no connection between this and his sensation of swelling. The first time he had palpitations was shortly after his father's death when he had put a dress on a dummy; for a long time afterwards, he had avoided doing this.

It is interesting that in this patient's case there was an immediate conversion of a symbol into a bodily symptom, into the body language, and that it disappeared just as fast when he was intellectually able to grasp the connection between them. According to Steven, "The left side is the heart side, the right one the mind side. Left to right means don't let your heart be your guide, let your mind be your guide." The previous night, he had coughed after not having done so for three or four days. The record was played back to him.

At his following appointment, Steven still had his cough. But he told me that his speech had been a huge success. This day, a model tried on a dress, and for a moment he again felt tension. He went on to say that the first time this very model had tried on a dress, she had been pregnant; an hour-glass figure was the sexiest for him; a fountain pen, being round, was a female symbol for Steven. He had formerly cheered the underdog, now he cheered the winner. It can be pointed out here that he was now identifying with the winner. He added that the heavy feeling in his last hypnoanalytic session was different from the feeling on other occasions, but he did not specify in what respect.

At the next meeting, the patient complained about having felt miserable. He had been tense, and he expected trouble. He reported a dream about a woman in a white dress who was run over by a car and who warned him not to get run over himself. He telephoned his mother who was at the back of his mind. "As long as trouble is attached to her, it couldn't be anybody but my mother," Steven said. He had been drinking too much and had switched to beer. Shortly before his father died, he had some pimples. The patient recently discovered a pimple on his leg and said, "Maybe I die, too."

The fifteenth hypnosis was purely "soothing." Steven coughed once, and stated afterwards that every time the word "anxiety" was mentioned, he felt it for as long as it took to say the word.

Questioned why he coughed when the expression "healthy and strong" was suggested to him, he related that while this was being said, he felt that the "mask" of his face (eyes, nose, mouth) had become a little swollen. Afterwards, he was very relaxed.

At the ensuing session, Steven felt much better. He stated that the reason he felt bad the last time was that he had expected snow and that there was a connection between this and the dream about the woman in white. In his childhood, several accidents had occurred when it snowed. Between his last session and the current one, he had been upset by a telephone conversation with his mother during which he told her that because of her he needed psychotherapy, and at that moment he hated her.

The sixteenth hypnosis was also just "soothing." At the mention of the word *tense,* the patient coughed. Afterwards he said that he had visualized an old man with glasses, a long, skinny neck, and a funny red complexion, like a "shicker.*) Maybe the drinking made him so." This could very well be a symbolization of how Steven himself had once expected to look after years of drinking. Although quite relaxed at the end of this hypnosis, the patient felt as if his hands had been turned back to front on his forearms—a consequence of his slowly awakening realization of his aggressive emotions towards his mother and, at the same time, his attempt to master them.

At the following interview, Steven reported that he had drunk too much because of a phone call from his mother, whom he had not seen for two weeks, which bothered him. He related another dream: A different woman, probably in white, too, but whom he did not recognize, asked him who he thought would die immediately. He answered, "Al Jolson." His associations to this dream were that Jolson was "an old guy" in theater who had had several young women. Steven did not believe that this woman in white had any connection with the white clad woman in the other dream. The one in the earlier dream had been so clean-looking, and the one in this dream was so dirty. She was wearing a hood and a tattered dress, she was old, and had had wicked experiences. Under the hood there was little hair and a wrinkled face. The head was tremendously large, the jaw very long. The body was

---

* Yiddish term for *drunkard.*

misshapen and without hips. One of the hands rested on a yellow bicycle seat. Then there was a green automobile which looked as if it had been in an accident. The radiator cap resembled bicycle handlebars. Behind the automobile lay a human being, whether dead or alive, Steven was not sure. "It could not have been my automobile, I saw two doors, mine has only one." He made a drawing of his dream. "I completely sobered up while I was drawing it . . . What would the 'horns' on the radiator represent? And the bicycle? Green and yellow are my colors. . . . What would bicycle 'horns' represent?" He made another drawing, the front of a woman, with handlebars closely identifying her breasts. "Why I said horns instead of handlebars I don't know. That could be a very voluptuous woman. No question that's my wife. I am thrilled by her breasts anyway . . . On the automobile, the radiator cap may be my daughter; she is developing quite a bit . . . The old witch, let us place no question, is my mother, fear . . . The circles under the eyes I made three times. I do not know why it is my mother . . . Al Jolson? . . . my father's first name was Joe . . . I feel my mother was one of the prime reasons my father died . . . The whole thing is a threat from my mother . . . The human being on the floor is my father, the corpse . . . Right after I awoke, I knew 'Al Jolson' was my father." The patient stated that he likes to undress his wife, and, while making this statement, he coughed. When his wife menstruates, she gets into bed looking like the second drawing. After having completed these two drawings, Steven told me that he feels good. He had made a valid interpretation of his dream with the help of the drawings.

At the ensuing session, the patient reported that he had continued to feel very well until a "dress upset me. The top does not upset me any more." He drew a picture of the front of this dress; the skirt was set in at the waist in a **V** which ended just above the mons veneris; at the back, the **V** rounded into a **U**, which is what was upsetting him. He told me that, in his first successful design, the dress had had this **V** line. "It is the height of sensuousness. It builds up the bustline and drapes the hips." I reminded him that this was where his mother had had most of her operations.

At his following appointment, Steven admitted to drinking too much. However, he had appeared in an amateur show and felt

good while performing. He had met his mother at a party, but she did not bother him. Later, he felt a pounding of his heart without being upset. The patient had coughed at night and in the morning, his nose was "stuffed." From time to time, he felt a tingling in the four fingers on the ulnar side of his left hand. He added that lately, he had been more productive in the firm.

When Steven came the time after next, he related another dream. He was motoring with his family, and they stopped for the night somewhere in the Middle West, or "near California." They all had to sleep in the same room and were ready to go to bed when they heard dogs barking. "So, Daddy had to be brave;" he had to go out to see what the trouble was. He opened the door and saw three creatures that looked like fish, but were barking like dogs and "sticking their schnauzes through." Two of them were above the ground; the third lay flat on the floor. This one was Chinese-red in color and had feelers on its nose like a cat. The creature in the middle was white, and the uppermost was greenish. When Steven opened the door, they bounded in like dogs, half in flight because of an absence of legs. To him they appeared to move high above the floor. Among his associations to this dream, was the film *Lost Weekend* which, after he saw it, made him abstain from drinking until the early afternoon of the next day. Steven drew a picture of this dream. The creatures looked "more like cat fish than dog fish," and the feelers were in the center of their faces instead of at each side of their noses; they looked "funny." The patient had the feeling that they represented something he feared; he was afraid of dogs. He now said that he disliked green, contrary to his former declaration that it was "his color," he also disliked this particular blood-red shade, as well as the white, although this was "not bad."

Steven then described another dream he had the same night. It seemed that someone had cut off, with an ax, the entire lower section of a woman's body, and blood was streaming out of the vagina. He associated to it his wife's menstruation. He felt that both dreams belonged together, then he associated violins to them, and drew other pictures showing feelers that looked like the strings of one violin and an ax that looked like the bow of another.

At his following session, the patient said that he had taken his

children to the Museum of Natural History. At first, he had a "bad reaction" to the snakes; he then was able to smile and became interested in snakebites and their treatment. He related the snakes to the rodents his mother was unable to look at. "I think my mother was a very cold character . . . I try to look for depth where there is none." A teacher had told him once that he was "not able to see the forest for the trees."

He stated that I reminded him of a dark, very attractive lady who was one of his teachers in college when he was nineteen years of age. Once, when he had gotten drunk, she had him ejected from the course, but he had harbored no ill feelings towards her. This was a quite ambivalent transference.

Steven said he thought the dream about the three fish had a reference to sex and to his family. He had trepidations that his children would discover that he was afraid of dogs. I was involved, too, because I had tried to help him overcome his fear. He had played the violin before starting treatment, although not since, but played the guitar in the summer, and still played the piano.

At Steven's next appointment, hypnosis was induced. It was his seventeenth hypnoanalysis and centered on his dream with the three dogs that looked like fish. "I was about four years old, maybe younger. My brother was in the carriage. And I was sitting at the front . . . My mother was wheeling us . . . And they were digging . . . building a subway . . . They hadn't put up the steel yet, and there were holes in the ground. And all three of us toppled into the very deep holes. And the three fish sort of remind me of what the people looked like, as they looked down on us . . . (Work it through.) They were strangers . . . and their eyes seemed to be . . . the scales of the fish. I wonder if *phosphorescent* would be the word for it. But they glistened in the dark. Of course, my mother screamed. (Were you frightened?) I must have been . . . it was dark, and we fell into a deep hole. (Do you remember your feelings?) I remember trying not to cry because I was the big brother. And it was difficult for me . . . (Your little brother cried?) Yes. (You dream and remember all the feelings and emotions you had then.) I must have been hurt . . . also being upset because somehow or other I must have been forced to feel sorry for my mother. (Which part of your body hurts?) My left arm. (Why do

you breathe so deeply?) I was trying to recollect my feelings. My mother is the one who is supposed to have had all the trouble with—well, with me. I was a sickly child, and my brother was a naughty child . . . I was hurt and I still had to feel sorry for her because she was upset [at] what my father would say if she came home late . . . instead of getting a little sympathy for myself . . . I had to show my mother sympathy. (How did you do that?) I put my arms around her and told her not to worry and not to cry. Everything would be all right. Nobody would be angry . . . Several people that looked down at us helped us out . . . (What happened first?) . . . The entire carriage toppled over. Both my brother and I were underneath it. Actually, now I don't see how my mother could have gotten in there . . . Because the carriage was pushed ahead of her. So the only thing that could have happened was that the carriage went down and she came on after us. And momentarily . . . she started to scream so that the people came around. (Did you have to urinate?) I may even have wet myself . . . I wasn't so much concerned about my brother . . . The entire episode was unnecessary. And I think my mother knew it. It seemed that there were public baths that she insisted to go to . . . I was outside watching the carriage and my brother in it. And my mother . . . made me feel that what she was doing my father would not approve of. And, of course, she may have said also that she was punished by God because she did something that my father didn't want her to do. And I think I was frightened at the prospect of further punishment. If God could do what he did. I had left the carriage alone for a few minutes, too . . . I don't think that my physical hurts were what upset me at that time . . . I was afraid and all this was a punishment . . . And when we did get home that night, I was put to bed immediately. And I remember overhearing my mother and father discuss it. I attempted to keep awake . . . evidently I fell asleep. I was very frightened at the prospect of being punished even the following day. (Why do you breathe so deeply? Do you feel something?) No. My left arm is numb a little bit. I think that the people that looked down at us . . . they may have frightened me, too. They looked awfully weird, and distorted, and shiny. It was very dark, but still I could see them. And I felt . . . it was the eyes of God that were looking at me . . . (Describe them.) First of

all, no bodies, only eyes. They were black with white around them like for the—around the pupil. And long eyelashes that didn't look like eyelashes, of course. They looked like brushes . . . like wire . . . The eyes were focused without blinking. Seemingly only on me. They were in a funny sort of a position. They were on the left side as I looked up—seemed to be not in line with the others. It was above the others. The eyes seemed to form a triangle. The left one on the top, the one in the middle and the one on the right in one eye. And each eye starts to get red. And the eye begins to get a little bloodshot. And then they get bigger, and then they get smaller. But always they shine. (Whose eyes are they?) Somebody who is—was watching me. (Were the eyes real?) Well, they looked like eyes. They must have been the people around the pit. (Is there anything else?) No."

Immediately after the hypnoanalytic session, Steven drew a picture of these eyes, which showed two eyes in one face, and then, a little above, another half-face with only one eye. The eyes were relatively large, with dark pupils and long eyelashes. This dream interpretation evoked a quite frightening, repressed former ego state, and there was also evidence of a symbolization of part of his superego. The sentences in this hypnoanalytic session were generally long, and the patient sounded more like a spectator describing the episode than a participant.

At the ensuing appointment, Steven reported three dreams in each of which the number three was present in some way, and he talked of different combinations of his family members, which also resulted in this number. He said that in each of the pictures he had previously drawn he could point out the three most important features. The patient asked why three eyes should represent God for him when he had grown up exclusively among Jews. The three eyes in the last hypnoanalysis were steady; they did not move or blink; stiff, frightening eyes that scared him. He said that in the episode mentioned he had fallen on the upper part of his left arm. The last of the dreams he reported that day was a positive transference dream although he was astonished at the young age of the psychiatrist. It does not seem necessary to elaborate here upon the universal meaning of the number three.

At the patient's next appointment, the recording of the hypnoanalysis was played back to him.

At his following interview, Steven again returned to this hypnoanalytic session. "The first thing that occurred to me was it was God looking at me. The eyelashes were like steel needles, very close and pointed together in a row. That is also a sex impression of the vagina. Why did my mother go to the bath where women paraded in the nude? When I was six, she took me to the bath. But when this occurred, I must have been three . . . The position of the eyes is the same as the position of the fish in the dream. We could make out of an eye or a fish, female genitals. I was certainly frightened by the eyes and upset by the fish." His pictures of the fish and of the eyes were suggestive of a vagina dentata despite his assertions of a good sexual relationship with his wife. Of course, the eyes could have related to his mother. According to this dream, he would have to defend his family against her intrusion.

At the following session, Steven complained that he had felt disturbed the previous weekend. In his eighteenth hypnoanalytic session, he was told to dream and to remember the actual reason he had felt this way. "I seem to see my mother and I walking down the stairs in front of the house we lived in. (Your age?) . . . At least under four, I think. My mother has me by the hand . . . It was icy and slippery. And my mother lost her footing and fell. (What happened?) And I got frightened. (Are you now afraid?) No, I am seeing this thing again . . . (How did she fall?) About four steps down. (Was it a stoop?) Yes . . . I fell after her . . . (She dragged you with her?) Yes, I didn't hurt myself, except I think she blamed me for her falling. Because she said that . . . if I had walked nicely, she wouldn't have to hold my hand so tight, and she wouldn't have lost her balance. (In what respect did you not walk nicely?) I wanted to stretch over to the other side of the stoop. (Why?) So that I could hold onto the railing . . . As it was, she was the one that held the rail on the right side. I had my hand . . . in her left hand and I tried to reach the other side . . . I must have pulled a little bit . . . Actually, she slipped down the stairs. It wasn't too far. The feeling I have now is that I wanted to laugh at the time. But mother said it's not a laughing matter. And that it

was my fault that she got hurt. I don't really believe she got hurt. (Did she lie there or get up immediately?) No, she kept sitting . . . Now it seems to me that a few people came over to help her up. I must have started to cry for being berated thusly. It wasn't really my fault . . . (Were you angry?) I must have been angry . . . But I couldn't show it. (You didn't get hurt at all?) I? No. (She was sitting on the last step?) No, on the sidewalk, practically. And it struck me very funny. Seeing a grown-up in this position. (Squatting?) Yes. Sitting with her feet extended in front of her . . . should it happen now, I probably would laugh right out loud . . . I had to . . . tell her I was very sorry, I didn't mean it. (Why are you breathing deeply?) My arms are getting big. (What part of them?) From the elbows down. (Should I stop?) Not yet. As soon as the people came over, she stopped berating me. Started to smile as if she realized it was a joke. But I could see through it. (Why do you breathe so deeply?) My chest is getting big, too. (Should I stop now?) Yes. Please."

The patient felt unhappy that he could not finish the hypnoanalytic session. On questioning, he stated that he saw his mother wearing pink bloomers and a gray coat. She was toothless. He also saw blood along the stoop, and I gave him several interpretations of this. He recalled that he had also visualized the cellar entrance. Steven was reminded that his mother had frequently warned him of unknown dangers, and he replied that his father was more likely to do this. I mentioned also that a horse might be a father symbol, and the patient recalled his twelfth hypnoanalysis in which he was on a horse, probably symbolizing his father, and his mother was giving the directions.

At the ensuing interview, Steven reported that he had felt better and had had two dreams about his mother. The recording was played back to him. He said that, at about the time when he saw the blood in the hypnoanalysis, his arms started to get heavy. The blood was probably a visualization of what his mother warned could have happened to her.

At the session after the next one, he informed me that he had discussed his money situation with his wife and had gotten upset. Recently, he had been drinking less, but he now became hung over, which had never occurred before.

He recalled his mother standing on the stoop, in an old bathrobe, a bathtowel around her head, her hair streaming down, and yelling: "You will be the death of me. I am so deadly sick, and you are playing downstairs." Instead of taking a hot-water bottle to his mother, he continued to play, then tripped while running, and cut his chin.

At this interview and at the next one, Steven was bothered by an old memory of a time when he may have been sick, and his father came home late. His mother had kept the infant awake by talking about herself and telling him that his father did not care enough about her. The father arrived with some records, probably operatic, and a fight ensued between the parents, his mother complaining that while she was home working hard, he was out spending money foolishly. The boy felt that his father was right.

In the nineteenth hypnoanalytic session, regression was induced, and the patient was told to remember what had happened the noon, the evening, and the night of the day his father came home late with records. "I remember that I was the one who was sick that day . . . I was constipated. My mother was very upset by it. And she called the doctor during the day . . . what to do. (What was it?) Make me the oil enemas. And she put me to bed in her own bed . . . (How many days have you been constipated?) Three or four days. (Why did you not go to the toilet?) I imagine . . . I wanted to do other things. (Wasn't there any emotional reason? You dream and remember the real reason for your constipation.) [deep breathing] I believe that it was because my mother was never quite satisfied that it was normal and that I must—I should have moved my bowels to a greater extent . . . (Did she look into the toilet bowl?) Yes . . . it was one of these pots . . . (Your age?) About four years old. And I was probably worried. That I wouldn't satisfy her. And I think for that reason that I didn't want . . . to move my bowels . . . During that particular day, one of the neighbors came in and felt very sorry for my mother. To all the troubles that she had with herself . . . and a sick child, her husband doesn't come home nights. God knows if he works when he says he works. Maybe . . . he . . . is having fun. (You heard all this?) Yes. Because I was in my mother's room . . . next to the kitchen . . . I felt sorry for my father because he wasn't there to

defend himself . . . When he came back at night . . . I was awake
. . . My mother didn't greet him as nicely as I—as she should have.
And then he brought out the records, and then she started to ha-
rangue him, browbeat him . . . that instead of the records, he should
have come home . . . when other men come home. For a while, my
father was at a loss for words because he did work very hard, and
actually, he brought the records for her enjoyment . . . records by
cantors. (Why do you breathe so deeply?) I am getting very heavy.
(Where?) My chest, my left arm. (Should we stop?) My right hand.
Let's just a little bit further . . . My aunt was involved, my father's
sister . . . my mother had called her . . . during the afternoon . . .
talked to her about my father . . . she waited also . . . and my father had nobody to take his side . . . And I felt very sorry for him
. . . He looked very tired. And it was one of the few times that he
ever made a gesture of bringing home records . . . and she didn't
approve of it. And they had a terrific argument. The fact that . . .
however hard he worked, it didn't show . . . That we all didn't
have what we should have. Then my father started to cry. And he
argued while he was crying. I was very, very moved . . . I felt as if
I wanted to put my arms around him and tell him that I loved
him and that I thought that he was doing the right thing. But I
was afraid to get out of bed. (What is it?) The same thing. (Should
we stop?) Yes. Please."

At the following session, the patient reported that he had
drunk much less. The record of his last hypnoanalytic session was
played back to him, and he said, "The first time I felt that I just
kept talking whether it made sense or not. I had no idea what
happened on this particular day until my father came home, until
this hypnosis." I may add that this hypnoanalytic session, the reawakening of a former ego state, shows the mother in an especially bad light, seducing her neighbors, and even her husband's own
sister, into suspecting her husband of wrongdoing and later berating him for the gift he had bought for her.

At his next interview, Steven complained of having had palpitations several times, each attack brought about by some form of
stress, for example, by overwork.

The ensuing time, the patient felt well again despite having
had a very disagreeable dream about his boss, which had made

him quite tense. In this dream, both his uncle and his boss disliked a dress which Steven had made.

At his following interview, Steven reported an anxiety-producing dream which, in his opinion, had left him with a "heart attack," worse than the ones he had supposedly had in my office. It was a negative transference dream: He felt himself hypnotized, and three female psychiatrists were being very skeptical about his treatment. Only a young doctor, who had long hair and was very sexily dressed, was sympathetic. Then, he dreamed that he was in my waiting room being shamed by a big, husky man who told him that he was taking too much time. Steven "banged him on the ceiling." In his associations, Steven indicated that the young psychiatrist was his wife, and one of the older ones, his mother.

This appointment was his last one, most likely for financial reasons. A short time before, he had given me a kind of veiled warning of this when he said that he had talked over his financial situation with his wife and had become upset. The negative transference dream, which he related in his last session, was either a result of his decision to stop therapy or made the resolve firmer. Ten months later, however, his general practitioner advised me that the patient no longer complained about his heart and that he was feeling well. Steven also intended to open his own business and sent me his best regards.

In the discussion of the case, different features must be distinguished. Although Steven's diagnosis was psychophysiologic cardiovascular reaction and he came for treatment because of cardiac trouble based on emotional disturbance, he also had long-standing complications of an emotional nature with his respiratory system, including colds and coughing, so that an additional diagnosis of psychophysiologic respiratory reaction had to be made. Both afflictions existed in this orally and anally regressed patient, plus alcoholism, and it is impossible to hold these separate disorders apart. Therefore, I will discuss them without putting any artificial cleavage between them. Steven's case is also interesting for two other reasons. One is that a number of his symptoms were known and can be described and discussed as typical or standard. The others are unusual, and about their origin, meaning, and importance I can make only hypotheses.

Both of the patient's parents were highly neurotic, long before his birth. His mother had an unknown ailment throughout her pregnancy with him, and whether it had any influence on the infant is hard to say. However, she had a premature and complicated delivery and, shortly afterwards, one of her many operations. She constantly complained about her many illnesses and demanded that her son be good to her. Nobody ever was good enough to her. These maternal sicknesses and her filial demands were each of them sufficient reason to have made Steven feel guilty about his mother since infancy.

The change from his mother's to his aunt's breast must have constituted an acute oral trauma for the infant. The use of the nursing bottle for so many years may be evidence that he was orally regressed, and his alcoholism may be further testimony to that.

The infant's mastoid operations so early in life also accounted for his regression. Whether the recollection of his mother putting a blanket around him, which he could still feel, and running out on the street with him in search of a doctor is a screen memory is hard to say. There were other depositions which were also not ascertainable.

The patient's constipation started very early; in fact, he once dated it long before his second year. When I asked him in his nineteenth hypnoanalytic session about its real causes, he admitted that he postponed evacuation not only because he wanted to play, but principally because his mother had never been satisfied with the quantity of his movements. As he stated that he was four years of age at that time, and experience must have taught him that the results of this delay were enemas, he must have had positive feelings towards enemas since he did not try to avoid them. At least, he did not complain about them. What he complained about was that his evacuation was made a public display and that his parents were concerned so long about this problem that they consulted a doctor about it as late as his adolescence. However, he was consciously aware that his interest in odors was connected with his constipation—in other words, with his anal retention pleasure.

Returning to the patient's mother, it is plain she was not only strongly depending on her firstborn, but tried to make the "weak" and often sickly infant strongly dependent upon her, thus turning the relationship into a nearly symbiotic one. The boy, both enjoying and resenting the too close affinity, was also filled with guilt about this ambivalence. These emotions he transferred to me. Despite his mother's demeaning remarks about the father, Steven had had a considerable desire to identify with him, as evidenced in his nineteenth hypnoanalytic session. A great part of the symptomatology of his neurosis was an identification with his late father's last illness, namely, vascular failure. The patient had, therefore, felt quite ambivalent to both his parents.

As Steven stated in his anamnesis, death was often and deeply impressed on him, and he suffered from annihilation anxiety, which was connected to his fainting. On the other hand, in several of his hypnoanalyses, his castration anxiety came to the fore, and he stated, on being questioned, in his ninth hypnoanalytic session when he said he was four years old, that such an operation could be performed by a rabbi, a father substitute. His overly close relationship with his mother generated strong guilt feelings on this score also, starting in the preoedipal stage; the butcher figuring in the thirteenth hypnoanalytic session, when Steven was "about three years old," as a threatening and feared father figure. On the other hand, the poor execution of his circumcision gave this fear a reality base.

The patient's colds and/or coughing always occurred at times of emotional stress, except on two occasions. One occasion was the time that he associated to the dream about Al Jolson and remarked that he (the patient) liked to undress his wife; the other was during his fourteenth hypnoanalytic session which centered around his light dreams. As was the case with Anne and Mitch, Steven mostly expressed negative emotions by coughing, but also some positive ones. I have mentioned that the patient stated very early in his treatment that he was quite superstitious, although he never specified what these superstitions were. In the session before his fifteenth hypnosis, after he had reported his first dream about the woman in white, he said that his father had had a pimple

shortly before he died, and that he himself had seen a pimple on his own leg. "Maybe I die, too." Superstition is one of the obsessive-compulsive features.

Steven's difficulties with breathing went far back in his infancy. In his thirteenth hypnoanalytic session, he called them "breath holding,"* and stated that he had had them before he entered school. He himself was well aware that they were the consequence of fear, but he was unable to control them. He had always been afraid of suffocation—annihilation anxiety—and already in school had been told that his way of breathing was incorrect. This part of his respiratory trouble was to a great extent the hyperventilation syndrome. During his hypnoanalytic sessions, forced inspirations were first manifest, then forced expirations. He also suffered from paresthesias, asymmetrically in his fingers and around his mouth, once with pallor and perspiration, another time with the feeling of chains binding his chest. Even his palpitations and fainting are explainable in terms of the hyperventilation syndrome. What is not obvious is why all these symptoms stopped when the hypnoanalytic session was ended, and how they ceased when he had them on other occasions. Also, he did not show signs of the hyperventilation syndrome during "soothing hypnoses," but this may have been a consequence of the calming effect of this kind of hypnosis despite the visualizations he had several times during these sessions. What does not fit in at all are the changes of his body image in the hypnoanalytic sessions, and his contention that he was a good singer, which requires disciplined breathing.

Before discussing the changes of his body image in the hypnoanalytic sessions, I will treat the significance for Steven of his left side because all these complications originated on this side. When he described his fall from the mirror in the fifth hypnoanalytic session, and also when he reported that the baby carriage fell into the hole in his seventeenth hypnoanalytic session, it was his left arm that was hurt. Both light dreams started from the left eye. Having seen him draw, I know the patient was right-handed. But as he himself stated after describing his disagreeable sensations when dressing a dummy, his "heart side" played a great role in his neurosis.

I have already compared the changes of Steven's body image to

those Federn describes as occurring when gradually falling asleep, the erotically significant zones or parts being excluded. Steven made two drawings of these changes. In the first one, after his fourteenth hypnoanalytic session about the light dreams, there was only a circle to indicate his face, but a tremendously enlarged left arm, left half of the body, and right forearm and hand. Even more interesting is the second drawing made after the nineteenth hypnoanalytic session which dealt with the fight between his parents. This time, he called the sensation during the change of his body image "heaviness," and marked it with heavy pencil strokes. It started at his left hand, then went to the medial side of his left arm, then to the left side of his body, thence "around the genitals" to the right hand, whence it "traveled" up to his face and around the mouth, by which time he had to stop talking. In the picture, however, the nose is also included, with pencil strokes over the mouth and nose that look like a guard. An arrow points from his right hand to the right side of his face. This time, the genitalia themselves were excluded from these sensations, not just the erotically related zones or parts. In the interview after his eleventh hypnoanalytic session in which he compared his finished basement to a garden, he stated that this swelling of his hands is the same sensation he had had when he was not quite two years of age and was sitting on the pot, his lower bowels "swollen." He also made other comparisons with later occurrences, but this comparison to early evacuation difficulties seems to be the most important.

Fenichel says it is presumed that "in the act of smelling, a particle of the exterior world is actually taken into the body."* Steven stated that he could smell certain colors, especially pastels. There is no doubt that he had scoptophilic tendencies, but one can only hypothesize as to this combination of higher and lower special sense perceptions, in his case, the adding to specified colors of certain smell modalities. One hypothesis would be that his mother not only judged the quantity of his movements but also made other evaluations of them, perhaps in regard to color. Identifying with his mother, the infant received at the same moment a smell and color impression and applied it later to other

---

* FENICHEL, OTTO: *The Psychoanalytic Theory of Neurosis.* New York, Norton, 1945, p. 322.

areas. Another possibility would be that assisting his mother during some of her frequent hemorrhages acquainted him with the distinctive smell of blood. He stated after the dream about the "dog fish" that he disliked "this blood-red shade of red." However, more cases of this sort are needed before these hypotheses (and possibly others) can be affirmed.

Odors revive old memories which can go back as far as symbol formation. One might well consider whether Steven's ease of symbolization, his facility in interpreting the symbols, and his ability to trace them back step by step to their repressed meaning were manifestations of this pregenital trait.

The structure of this patient's hypnoanalytic sessions was of the type discussed in cases of patients suffering from conversion reactions. All had a recognizable background and a logically and uniformly developing activity of the persons involved. Symbols were not frequently used. The patient expressed his unconscious attitudes through specific organs, innervated by the autonomic nervous system.

MORTON

Thirty-two years of age, married, and the father of two children, Morton came to me right after five years of psychoanalysis by a lay analyst. He held a job in which every breath of air and every movement he made brought him in contact with material that was irritating to his allergies, which expressed themselves in asthma, in a pruritus, and in a weeping skin. These allergies had started when he was still quite young. The patient was in constant pain and in persistent discomfort and hence extremely eager to have his condition alleviated. It was impossible to procure a regular, continuous anamnesis from him, but much information was gained in his interviews and from remarks he made when his hypnoanalytic sessions were played back. Morton was the third patient who was able mentally to rid himself in a hypnoanalysis of the member of his family he hated most. Although this chapter will be presented as a case history, emphasis will be put on a few selected hypnoanalyses and the patient's reactions to them. I will omit details of his many asthmatic attacks and his complaints about his allergic skin manifestations. Their alleviation by hyp-

notherapy was temporary only. But these symptoms disappeared when the patient, of his own volition, changed his job and went into a business in which he was quite successful.

Morton's diagnosis was psychophysiologic respiratory reaction and psychophysiologic skin reaction.

All the patient's presentations, as well as his hypnoanalytic sessions, were heavily influenced by his preceding psychoanalysis despite his deep resentment of it. He described his parents and siblings, including himself, as very selfish and old-fashioned. The family was opposed to taking action; therefore, he had evaded success all his life.

He regarded his mother as a "slob," unattractive and undesirable; she did not even know how to use make-up properly. Her taste was "horrible." However, as a boy of about five or six years, he felt that she was "the best-looking woman." His mother had been the boss of the family and was also shrewd. She had done all the work although she constantly complained about this and nagged her husband. She also had suffered from allergies. After the patient's birth, people told his mother that they wondered how she could have born "such a monkey," and his father asserted that Morton had been his "greatest mistake."

The father had come to this country at twelve years of age. Together with his wife, he worked in the restaurant and delicatessen business. The patient, as a child, had the impression that his father was "great." But the father did not like the store, although it was a good source of income. He had been unfaithful to his wife and had associated with politicians and prizefighters. At times, Morton said, he would sit in the back of the store eating so much that the son believed his father would "fall apart" from the amount of food he ingested. When Morton was five or six years of age, the money disappeared and the father moved to Pittsburgh to evade family responsibilities. Only after the father had made some good connections, did the rest of the family join him there. Later, they had all returned to New York.

The patient often complained bitterly about his father who had shown no interest in his son, would neither protect him nor stick up for him, and had never taken him anywhere. Morton claimed that his father could have helped him to become a sales-

man, but did not lift a finger to do so. There had been times when he felt sorry for his father, but he no longer did so. Morton stated, however, that until a few weeks before he came for hypnotherapy, he had identified with his father. Although the father was now daily quite close to where the patient lived, he had visited his son's family only once. When his mother told him that his father was sick, he did not believe it.

The patient had two older sisters, Catherine and Lynn, and an older brother, David. The family apparently had the idea that after one son was born, they should have stopped having children, and the patient always felt that he had been an unwanted child.

Morton described his brother as the "big shot." According to the patient, their Rorschach tests showed that he, Morton, had constantly competed with his brother who had, however, welcomed Morton's birth. David always made "his own rules;" for instance, though the patient claimed that he himself was the better card player, he always lost. Supposedly, David had no integrity, but was very talented and creative and held a good, steady job. Once, by chance, I met David's psychoanalyst who informed me that his patient was completely different from the human being Morton had described to me. I am unable to judge how large a part countertransference played in this opinion.

The patient did not know any details about his birth, only that his mother had required an operation afterwards. She had not nursed him.

His sister Lynn who was apparently the only member of his family who consistently cared about Morton, had stated that a maidservant had performed fellatio on him when he was about one year old. At the age of two, a draught from an open window caused an abscess in his neck.

Statements about his toilet training were contradictory. Lynn said that he had been toilet trained late and that the mother had taken a week off from the store to train him. She either let him smell a wet diaper or put it over his face. He himself merely had the impression that he had been trained too early.

Of the very few occasions the father had taken any interest in him or guided him in anything. Morton recalled one when he

was four or five years old. His father had put him on the toilet seat next to the sink in the bathroom so that he could look into the mirror. The father had then shown him how to wash his face. Around this time, the father had also demonstrated to his son how to tie his shoe laces in a bow, and Morton said nobody else had ever tied them so clumsily. Also at the age of five or six years, Morton had once slept in his mother's bed because he had been sick. The next morning, he did not want to go to school, but his mother accused him of faking and did not allow him to stay home. He had liked the warmth of her bed, and it was on this occasion that he regarded her as "the best-looking woman."

Shortly before the family moved to Pittsburgh, when the patient was about six years old, he was with his mother in the kitchen one day when an aunt and uncle paid a visit. They decided that the boy looked as if he needed some decent food, and he had gone to stay with them for a few days and had felt good there.

The patient said he had never had any toys, and when his mother promised him a train, his brother got it.

Morton had always been afraid of coercion and of stronger kids who he felt "blackmailed" him. At school, the patient had gotten attention by being "a dunce" and had become "the laughing stock" of the class. His schoolmates thought him conceited, and he said nobody ever understood that he had really felt inferior. On one occasion, a teacher marched the boy to another teacher and presented him as the "bold kid." At first, Morton had been proud of this, not knowing the meaning of the word "bold," but he cried when he found out. The school principal had often called his mother to the school because the boy talked too much, which may well have been the case because nobody at home ever listened to him. One time when he was in the fifth or sixth grade, his mother was supposed to have gone to the school for an interview, but the older brother went instead and "bawled out the principal." Then, he encouraged the younger boy to play truant for two days. Morton reiterated that his father had not been interested and that his mother could not spare the time to go to the school.

Around the age of four, the patient had a friend who was better adjusted than he was, and once, after his brother had taken the two of them out, he told Morton that this friend could do every-

thing better than he could. Probably as a consequence of the patient's psychoanalysis, he told me that his older brother took care of him like a woman; that he managed him the way a woman would do.

Morton reported that, as a boy, he had only one pair of short pants, but he had been told that he was hard on clothes. When relatives bought him long pants, he was never permitted to wear them and this made him quite angry.

He related that, as a youngster, he had often stolen money from his father in the morning and had used it to buy crackers, which he ate in the afternoon. He had wandered the streets, had sold newspapers, and said he had felt like an orphan. In the evening, he feared going home from the restaurant because of a fantasy that a group he called the "Purple Gang" would kidnap him. This last statement was made in a hypnoanalytic session.

Before the age of six, seven, or eight, Catherine had slept in the bed next to the patient's and had kissed his face many times. Later, he had kissed her legs and thighs, and, thereafter, had washed her stockings and been a "good kid brother." However, he felt now that sex was involved because he had fantasies about the region where the stockings ended. Once, when he was nine years of age, he had not taken a shower before going to bed, which made his mother so angry that she awoke him later that night and threw him into the shower, and this had made him cry. He remembered that, at about this time, he had once been chased out of a store and did not want to go home.

Also at the age of nine, Morton had gotten an ear infection, and his father had been angry because he had to call a doctor. Since that time, the patient had felt guilty whenever he was sick.

Morton stated that he was not interested in homosexuality. Only in puberty, he once put his penis at a friend's, but the other boy did not react because he was already going out with girls.

The patient related that, when he was quite young, he was already "preoccupied with sex." When masturbating, he had had a feeling that the blood vessels in his penis were swelling. He also thought that too much masturbating would make him age early and that too much sex would use him up.

Morton said he had married his wife because she was "latent

like a spore," because he wanted to prove that he was a man, not a homosexual, and because he wanted to acquire a "real" mother and father in the person of his wife. However, his marriage was "a flop." His wife was very sweet and talented, but, as he put it, "stands in the corner." At times, he was "also allergic" to her, especially when she gave him foods to which he was allergic. At other times, he complained that she was not cooperative in sexual foreplay and during intercourse. She "lies there like a rock," were the words he used. He thought his wife might be afraid to grow up (she had also undergone psychoanalysis); she was afraid of certain animals. Morton also felt that his sister Lynn was trying to disrupt the marriage. Sometimes, he had the feeling that Lynn was a Lesbian.

Morton was so eager to get relief from his symptoms that he was very easy to hypnotize, and, after a few words of the induction were spoken, he was already in a trance. At his third hypnosis, subsequent to a few suggestions to alleviate his asthma, he was regressed.

After the hypnoanalytic session, he started his statement by saying that when I had instructed him to be in a happy mood, he told himself that he had laughed during his former hypnosis, "but not this time." He fell asleep even faster than on previous occasions, and felt well because he sensed that something good would happen to him. When he was told to regress to a small boy, he immediately started to cry, then restrained himself although he had tears under his eyelids. He felt as if he were moving down on the couch, and thought of himself "as a kid." He recalled that when he was in first grade, the second day of school the teacher told him not to talk so much and sealed his mouth with a bluish gummed paper. Morton had felt himself choking and wanted to kill the teacher. His feet were moving on the couch as he spoke because he said he wanted to go out; his asthma cleared up. He added that he thought now that this incident with the teacher must have been the beginning of his "idiotic days," because he had felt that everybody in school was watching him. He had been thinking back; in reality, he had been looking at himself as a boy while he himself was "right here." He had the feeling that I was helping him, and no longer listened to my voice. The patient

thought that everybody had ignored him in Pittsburgh because he wore short pants. They had taken his picture at some fountain; it was a "cockeyed" photo. His pants were always dirty, and he started to cry. Then, he saw himself suffering from measles at the age of four or five, standing at the window of the family apartment in Brooklyn. He was told that this was bad for his eyes. Later, he visualized an evening at a resort hotel where the sky looked like lattice work, with clouds like small boxes and striped in gorgeous colors. At that time, his mother had just returned from an operation. Then he recalled having fallen from a swing onto a box "busting" his lip and feeling inferior and a "cry baby." The next visualization was of a miserable Sunday afternoon when Morton was nine, ten, or eleven years of age; his parents were sleeping, and his sister Lynn was recuperating from tuberculosis. He had nobody to play with because the other kids were away; there was little money in the house, and the room in which he felt he was, was dark and morbid. His whole family was sleeping while music played, and he was angry. Next, at the age of five or six, he saw himself at his parents' restaurant during the rush hour. He was washing dishes, and his family accused him of doing so to get attention. No more glasses needed to be done, so he had washed cups. Afterwards, he was late for school. He had also left his books behind at the restaurant, was frightened, and did not want to go to class.

Talking over this hypnoanalytic session, Morton stated that aside from the information already supplied, he had known, from his psychoanalysis, about the teacher who had pasted up his mouth, but felt the incident had not been sufficiently discussed there. The photo taken at the fountain had been "cockeyed, and my head, too." He was now "looking differently at things." He said, "Formerly I was seeking sympathy," but at present he felt more cooperative because he was working out his frustrations. The whole visualization was in black, white, and grey although the sky was in colors.

The patient was indeed working through his frustrations; except when he talked about the beautiful colors of the sky (a rare experience for a city-bred infant), he had reported only unhappy incidents. Some episodes were shorter than others, some were pro-

vided with a background, others not, and all were connected by the thread of Morton's defeats. Only the logic of the patient's emotions could be discerned, not any logic inherent in the activities of the persons involved. In this hypnoanalytic session, Morton did not visualize any symbols although in many others he did.

In his fifth hypnoanalytic session, Morton was immediately regressed. During the trance, he made many movements, and some of his sentences were slurred. Here is the transcript: "My father took me to the park. He brought me a pair of gloves. And I waved one of the gloves. [moves his right arm] (Oh, you waved with your right arm?) Yes. And they took a picture of me with my head to the side. (To which side?) My right side . . . (Your age?) Four. He and I were the only ones that went. That's the only time he took me for a ride. He did me a big favor. (Why are you laughing?) . . . He always does you a big favor by paying a little attention to you . . . If you come to visit him, he plays cards or any . . . (Do you feel like a little boy?) I just remember it back. (Do you see yourself?) Not alive. In a picture. (You saw that photo they made of you?) Yes. A little boy. And my brother saved the gloves. And he is so proud to show me the little tiny glove that I had. This is some kind of an affection. Like an infection. [laughs] I don't know why he is—be—doing me such a big favor by saving the glove. As a matter of fact, it doesn't belong to him. It should be mine. Like everything else."

When he was eight years old, his uncle had asked Morton whether he wanted some kind of a filing box, and he said he did, but his brother came home and got it instead.

"My brother is a big shot. Everybody—nobody looks at me, they all look at my brother . . . I saw this. I am sitting with him . . . in a dark, dim light in that lousy house in Pittsburgh. Oh, what a brutal place that was! Ah, we moved to Pittsburgh, and though my father—mo—went out there first, something like he deserted us really. My mother was working for my uncle downtown. (Where?) In New York. He went away after the Crash. And I had a dream that we were going to move to Pittsburgh before my father even went out there. I always had the idea that I foresaw it. But I didn't. Because I must have heard them say something. Because now I realize how children hear parents talking . . . I went

with my mother. And we went on a train into Harristown. We got off, and some distant relative met us there. And I felt so small next to that big steam engine. Puffing the steam out. Like asthma. [laughs] It sounds funny, doesn't it? (Do you see the steam eng—?) Oh, yes, I see the steam engine on that station. I saw it so many times. And my mother like—a—like a little orphan child. My brother was a big shot. I see him going with the moving-van people in the front seat. And I was laughing, more like crying, left alone with my mother. And there was a kind of a feeling of a relative, meaning that she is doing you a favor, you know. You felt always very poor. And that we were of a lower class. (Talk it out.) Yes. We always felt we were very superior culturally. I think that's a lot of crap. Oh, that we always thought that we had money. We spent it even though we didn't have it . . . (Why are you coughing?) I don't know why I did it, because I felt it. (What?) It did. It's irritating. (What?) What's in my chest. It's like there is something there to get out. [coughs twice] (Make words out of the irritation.) Sort of, my brother used to sit up until two o'clock, three o'clock in the morning making designs. He was going to high school, art school . . . he used to make me sit up and watch him so he has some company . . . And I used to have to keep telling him how good he was."

There followed a description of the table the two brothers sat at. Then, Morton reported how his brother and the brother's friend made a fool of him by promising him money for some chores and never paying him. . . . "I had to memorize the forty-eight states and the forty-eight capitals. (What did you think about him? That he should drop dead?) N-no. I think he should drop dead now. Which is, I feel—although I feel good about it when I say it . . . now he is—acts sick, I suppose, I—I have to feel sorry for him. He will always get mad at you and then, he was very mean. Everybody is afraid when he got mad because he yelled. He was so spoiled. And my sister, the older sister, was afraid of that, too, and they used to fight." The hypnoanalytic session continued.

When this session was played back to Morton, he remarked that he had known about the glove and the filing box without hypnoanalysis: however, he had never realized that the experience

with the box had impressed him so deeply. There were many other occasions when David got things promised to Morton. His mother also paid no attention to him because "she was a better man than my father." She had made him "feel poor" with other people; she and her son had been poor together. His opinion as to the difference between psychoanalysis and hypnoanalysis was "My direct feeling is I am the kind of person who always wanted to express himself in analysis, but there was something too formal, like being watched. I am more uninhibited in hypnosis. I find that much easier . . . I feel today I can learn things I could not before. I read up two books today, I could not formerly."

The structure of this hypnoanalytic session is very similar to the foregoing one. There were again long and short spurts of visualizations, partly connected by one dominant emotion, in this case hatred of his older brother. At other times, no apparent link was discernible; there was no rounded picture. Morton jumped from one visualization to the next, without much background, little logically progressing activity of the functioning persons, few symbols.

The transcript of his twelfth hypnoanalytic session follows: "(You will see written in some way the reason why you have to scratch. Letters will appear, [cough] the letters will form syllables, and the syllables words.The words will tell why you itch and why you have to scratch. Just look carefully. [cough] A letter is now slowly appearing in front of you. What letter is it?) Weird. (Go on.) Gold. (What else?) I don't see any more. (What kind of writing was it?) [cough] Gothic letters. (What color?) Red and white. (What is it?) Skin and blood. (Just talk.) Red and white is skin and blood . . . I nearly went to sleep just now. Because I felt myself really going off to sleep, because I am so tired. (What do you see?) A church inside. Very high. And the letters come from across into the . . . The church is far away. [coughs twice] And the letters come across inside the church. Like on a screen. Letters don't come on a screen, but it's like a moving picture screen where you see the church and the letters come across. (Let me–) And . . . (–hear. And?) We have gone. (Who?) A long way . . . (Go on.) That's all it says. We have gone a long way. (What does it mean?) [wheezing] I don't know. (Who should know but you?) I know

what it means. I am mad. (At whom?) [cough] Everything. I am so painful. I am always in such pain. It isn't worth . . . (What?) My job [wheezing, coughs twice] to be in such pain, to work at this thing. Fingers, asthma. (Why do you come to be in such pain?) [wheezing] Why I come in such pain? [cough] (Read it from the screen.) We have gone a long way. (Go on.) [cough] Not far enough. (Go on.) [wheezing] No, isn't that silly. (No.) Because that always says just what I could say if I was awake . . . (Just talk.) That means that I have gone to analysis. I have come here. But there is something to be discovered. But nothing comes across the screen after that, nothing helps after that. [wheezing, cough] And I have only discussed it with myself, because I can't find the way to make money in another way. What do I need it for, to suffer like this? Who do I need it for? Why do I have to be so unhappy and in such pain? . . . (How do you come to be in pain? Just read it from the screen [coughs twice]. Letters, syllables, and words appear on the screen.) This sort of letters looks like letters on Christmas cards. Christmastime. Happy New Year. Merry Christmas. All that. (What does it mean?) Christ. (Go on.) Is my troubles. Crucified. (Go on.) Red and white. White flesh, red blood, nails. Driven through. Driven through just like my hands. (Do you see it or do you read it?) I see Him. (You see Him?) The cause of all my troubles. Christ. (Go on.) I never thought about this before. He is the cause of all my troubles. (Let me hear.) They had not killed Him, there wouldn't be no anti-Semitism. (Go on.) Troubles, my brother, another Christ. (What is behind this itching? You were just scratching again.) It itches because I am allergic to animals. (What have animals to do with Christ? Read.) The screen. The Radio City theater. The Music Hall screen. No, it doesn't look like the Music Hall screen . . . (Just read it.) Christ. Christ's sakes, that's what he always used to say. When he gets mad. For Christ's sakes. That's what he says. And I used to get so scared—I—I—I get so scared of that guy. (What's his name?) David Field, prick number one. Big shit. How one can store up so much resentment and then feel so guilty afterwards! It's beyond my imagination. (Do you still see this screen?) Yes, Christ. He is still hanging there. But the dogs around His feet . . . around His feet those dogs. (Go on.) Who are these people? That are standing around Him, looking. Were all these peo-

ple right about Christ? Their theory that He couldn't have gone such a place, couldn't have arisen from some ashes or shit, because somebody was—stand there, for *x* person or *y* person in the *n*th degree. Who gives? Nobody cares. The intellectuals. The cultured people. (Care about what?) How all this happened and what. But the person with the sword doesn't care. They go on, they kill. They don't care, you can't explain anything to them. Hitler, McCarthy, Stalin, Mussolini, they don't care. Those people who have nothing don't care. They would just want what they want. And they don't care. (Why do—) S-s-s (—you care? Look at the screen.) Christ bending over. (What is He doing?) Spitting. (Where?) On the ground. (What happens to his spit?) The soil is too dry and dusty. It doesn't go through. It stays on the top. Because it's too dusty. And it's only—dries up on top, and the dust rolls over it. And you can roll it away. Nobody is though there. (Where are the dogs?) They are not there. He spit. There was nobody around. Nobody watching him . . . (What else?) Everybody talks about all this. (Who is everybody?) Social workers, psychiatric-social workers like my sister-in-law. She is strictly full of baloney. They talk very glibly. That man must have a castration complex. Or this one has—ah—something-else complex. And everybody talks. Who the hell? They don't know what they are talking about. And—oh, I took that Rorschach test. My psychoanalyst's friend Mrs. Cohen says to me, 'What does it look like?' I said it looks like legs that are bloody. Because it was colored red. It looked like somebody sitting there and without the rest of their limbs or standing. Red and bloody. So she says I got a castration complex. My brother has got a castration complex. A friend of mine has got a castration complex. Everybody has got a castration complex. Doesn't anybody—has a castration. (What did you see in front of your eyes?) Light. (Describe everything you see.) What? (In front of you.) I am thinking of my asthma, and I nearly opened my eyes and saw the light in the room. I think so. (Are you asleep?) I don't know. I don't feel so good by the sleep. I don't feel so groovy. (Should we stop?) No. This is too good. (You see letters again in front of your eyes . . .) Did He do it? (Who? What?) Christ. He is bending over. Like out of a barn door. Like a half door. And the door is open on top. Just like a stable. And

He has got goats' horns and looks like a jerk. And it says, 'Did He do it?' (Did He do what?) I must be crazy talking so. I don't know, did He do it? Does He stink like a goat? Or did He do it? (What?) I don't know. (What does a goat do?) He is a billy goat. He has intercourse with the goats. (Did He have intercourse?) Christ? Did He have intercourse? I don't know what they say about it. I am very ignorant. I never read the Bible. But they think about Christ very much. I don't know. I always kept away from that. (I am only interested in what you believe.) I don't know what to believe. They believe He was just—oh-h, a Communist factually. (What should He have done?) He should have stopped trying to be such a hero. Stopped trying to save the world. Nobody asked Him. Why didn't He leave the people suffer and let the other ones persecute? They won't come out by themselves. (Do you still see Him?) No. I see a skeleton. With a black scarf around his head. Dead. A dead skeleton. (Skeletons are usually dead.) That's the skeleton in the closet. My brother. (Could the skeleton very slowly change to the real thing?) It's my brother. (Do you see him?) Yes. Very fast he changed . . . (He makes you scratch your hands?) Yes. He makes me scratch—I get. My hands are so painful from all the holes. And from everything in it. And so painful I can't bend just —just so far. (What has he to do with your hands?) Everything has eaten up my hands. Eroding me. No. He didn't eat them up. Why do I have to be so sensitive? They say I am sensitive to chemicals. Why do I have to be so sensitive? I got the same skin as everybody else. (What has he to do with your skin?) I don't know. I wish I knew. (Should we stop?) Yes."

In order to save space, I indicated only at the beginning the many attacks of coughing and wheezing the patient had during this hypnoanalytic session.

At his next appointment, Morton made the following remarks: His allergies were quite bad. Gothic script was like the writing on Christmas cards, and he was able to read this because he had studied German. The church was in the background. The other visualizations, projected as though on a screen, came back several times. His brother was a martyr, like Christ, and he stank like a goat. When the patient reported that "He spit" and that the saliva did not sink into the ground, he said it showed that he had no

confidence that what he told was true. During the hypnoanalysis, he had thought that he himself was Christ, and that nails had been driven through him. Red and white were life and death. White is death, surrender, cowardice—white feathers. Red is aggression and Communism; and this confused him now because he thought it a marvelous color. People said that Christ was radical; Morton's brother was too, and so was he himself.

The patient said he had several times fallen into real sleep and had "told more." The morning after the hypnoanalysis, he said, his blisters had been better, but they were better no longer, and he had scratched his nose bloody. Scratching made the skin red and white; in the middle, it was white and around it was redness. Morton said he believed that "the words came from my arm, not my mind." The mongrels at Christ's feet, a pack of stray dogs, were part of the crowd, like "everybody kicks you when you are down." He himself may be Jesus Christ because "they" tortured him. Christ did not care for the dogs because he suffered martyrdom. The patient equated spittle with ejaculation and with asthma. However, it was not ejaculation because saliva does not have to be raised, whereas this jelly-like spit that rolls onto the floor is a relief.

At the playback, Morton made the following comments: He was in very bad pain during the hypnoanalytic session and was wheezing because of his asthma. "I really was trying to fall asleep." He said that the Gothic letters are "to enable you to read the words more easily." People were nicer around Christmas, and that made life a bit more optimistic. A church to him was a foreign place; it was also "sanctimonious," and had much to do with anti-Semitism. "What do I need it for?" By this he meant his job. He was like Judas Iscariot because he wanted to sell (the job) out for money. The cracks in his hands sometimes felt like nails. He had to pay for the sins of his people. By making money he was betraying something, although he did not know what. His brother had a big bar mitzvah, and consequently was a "big shot," but Morton was quite small at the time, and when they walked from their grandmother's house to the synagogue, the patient did not even have a hat. They bought him a sailor hat in a candy store. He himself was not bar mitzvahed because the Depression was on. He was

glad of it because he was sure he would not have been as good as his brother had been, but he had also felt ashamed. The synagogue may be this church because he had believed before his psychoanalysis that he was only half-Jewish. He once tried to mimic a parson, in ridicule, and had confused everything that had been told him by different people about Christ. Einstein had been another Christ. Morton remarked that he had pronounced the word "sword" like "sore." He had always been afraid of force. He was allergic to dust, which brought on asthma attacks, but dust was always present, even when he spat a lot; everything was dry. The patient did not understand what he had meant by the term "sink in." His spittle was like catarrh, and naturally it could not sink in; it made no impression, no sense, "no money." It was like the Holy Rollers. He did not know why he had been so concerned about the castration complex, except that he had lost one testicle.* Maybe, by scratching his nose, he wanted to castrate himself. Christ had been a salesman for the Gospels. His father had once bought a farm with male goats. Their shed stank even after the goats were no longer there. A cousin who visited them at this farm had had more appeal for women than Morton had. People took out their "hostilities" through humanitarian causes, as his brother, his sister, and he himself had done. "The skeleton of the radicals in the closet." The black scarf looked like a funeral. Here he stated his intention to change his job.

There is not much to add to the patient's own interpretations. He was extremely ambivalent, competitive, and envious of both his brother and younger sister. Morton was afraid to cut his ties to his family and resentful because he was not able to do so. He identified strongly with his hated brother, much less with his sister. Christ was for him at the same time the originator of anti-Semitism and the prototype of the sufferer. The patient was to some degree aware that the Socialist Party to which he had belonged in his youth, had been mostly an outlet for his neurotic conflicts. The symbolization of the common people by mongrel dogs may be a consequence of this. The martyr's changing into a goat is not so surprising if one remembers that Satan has often

---

* When he had undergone a hernia operation, an undescended testis had been removed.

been represented as having goats' horns and, at times, hooves. The strong masculinity of a male goat is a popular assumption, especially effective for a man who has lost a testicle and makes fun of the castration complex, indicating that he has much castration anxiety. The significance of the goat in different religions is substantiated by Frazer in *The Golden Bough*,* in Michelet's *Satanism and Witchcraft*,† and in other books. It would take much too much space to go into this subject in detail.

It is even more interesting that this patient brought forward such relations in a hypnoanalytic session which was entered upon to uncover the reasons for his pruritus. I did not ask Morton, but I am sure that he never had read *The Golden Bough* or any other such book. The patient regarded himself as the scapegoat of the family. The importance of phlegm to a person suffering from asthma is obvious. Morton was never able to cough enough of it up to get rid of the all-pervasive dust.

The structure of this hypnoanalytic session is different from any other I have presented. However, I doubt that the reason for this was that I did not use regression but word visualization. With other patients, this did not change the structure of the hypnoanalytic session. It may be that reading had a special significance for Morton which I did not have time to go into because his treatment was too short.

Whatever the reason, though this hypnoanalytic session consisted of different episodes, these were connected by the re-use of the same symbols and/or persons. Activity was logical in an emotional sense only, but on the whole, there was little activity because each episode was interrupted by changing pictures. Very little background was detectable.

In Morton's fifteenth hypnoanalytic session, regression was induced. Here is the transcript: "My nose is wet, snotty, and running. And I always wipe it with my hand. The back of my hand. And I never seem to be able to be comfortable with a handkerchief. Just like sometimes when I get allergic . . . Seems like a lint of the handkerchief goes in my nose or like Kleenex; all that stuff

---

* FRAZER, SIR JAMES G.: *The Golden Bough*. Imperial Ed., New York, Macmillan, 1958.

† MICHELET, JULES: *Satanism and Witchcraft*. New York, Citadel, 1946.

that is fluttering in the air, that lint that comes off. And the baby can't keep this stuff from over its hands. (Which baby? Which stuff?) Me. The . . . (How—) . . . stuff. (—old are you?) A year. (Do you see yourself?) Ah. (Or do you feel yourself?) I see myself. (What do you see?) Banging on top of the crib. With a stick. Like a bow and arrow. Like the bow. (Which is the bow?) From a bow and arrow. (You mean the stick is like the—) Yes, yes. (—the bow?) There is something like a string attached. Like a bow has. Banging. Making noise. (On the bar of the crib?) Yes. Over the top. (Do you hear or do you feel it?) I feel the idea of it. The feeling of the baby doing it. I don't actually hear it now. (Just now, you made movements with your arm.) Yes, like I was banging on the crib. (With the right arm?) Yes. The baby seems younger here than before.* And happier. And this baby has a—like a pushed-up nose. Not a nose like mine. And it looks entirely different. Not too much as—like I look . . . (How near to you is the baby?) Years away. (No, I mean where do you see it?) I see it in that same crib. (Where does the crib stand?) In the same place like before. (Is it near you?) I am not there. The baby is there. (How many yards away?) I am not in that room. (You are looking at that room?) Yes. But i-it seems like it's—like an inset in the corner of the picture. (An inset in the corner of the picture?) Yes. Say, like a picture in the newspaper, of somebody. Who is—I don't know how old. Thirty years old. And in the corner is a picture of how the same person was when he was a baby. It's not like I was there. I don't feel like I was there. It doesn't even seem to be like me . . . (Maybe it's another baby.) I don't know who it can be. (Your brother?) I never saw him that way. He was older. It doesn't look like even the picture I saw of my brother when he was a baby. Oh, when he was three or four years old, anyway . . . And this baby makes a lot of noise . . . (What does the baby want?) Nothing. He is playing. (Is he alone?) Yes. (Is he happy to be alone?) He seems to be. He doesn't quite know, I guess . . . Or maybe he is trying to make himself happy because he is alone. So he is getting himself interested in these different things. Or maybe the noise; it's very possible; the noise is made to try and track—attract

---

* He had spoken of another baby in the preceding hypnoanalytic session.

attention . . . (Now, what is the connection to the lint and the hanky or the paper you cannot stand?) Well, repeat that question. (You told me you are unable to stand the lint of a hanky or of a paper hanky?) Yes. (How did you come from this to the baby? Where is the connection?) Well, I don't know. Maybe the baby is allergic to these things. Maybe when he bangs, he makes a lot of dust. And that makes him unhappy because he is alone. And he has nothing to do but to bang. So he makes dust and the dust makes him sick. (Do you see the baby being sick? Do you see the dust?) I can see that black window shade. (Where?) It's drawn down next to the crib. (Is it dusty?) Yes. (Which side of the crib? Left or right side?) Left side. (It's dusty?) It's clean. It's on the wall. Yes. It's very dusty. (It's on the wall?) Yes, the crib is up against the wall. And the window was right there* . . . Before, I never saw this window. Just now I see this window which has a black shade. Maybe this is a different place. It's very possible. Because I was born in a different place. Then the place is that I were talking about. And maybe the shade is not torn. But the shade is dusty and you can see the dust when the sunlight comes through . . . if the shade, I mean, is turned to the side or pulled up, then the sunlight comes through. (Is sunlight now coming through, or is it evening?) No, it's the sunlight outside but no ones comes in. It's almost a dark room. (The room is dark?) . . . Well, like a black window shade and everything is fitted to keep light out. (Haven't you been feeling a little asthma for a few minutes?) No, I had it before I came here; I took a pill on the way here . . . The pill didn't do me too much good. Anyway . . . (What happens with this dusty window shade?) Nothing. That window shade stays there for years and years with no worries. No worries at all. It doesn't have to eat, to sleep, to talk too much. (What does?) Eats. (What does the baby think about the window shade?) It's a way to get into the outside world . . . (Is the baby once in a while permitted to look through the window?) Yes. The baby can look through the window. And nobody is there anyway. They don't give a darn. So I guess he can look through the window all he wants to. (But you tell me the shade is drawn.) Yes. Well, he pushes it at the

---

* Here was some poorly phrased information about a "torn shade."

side, like. (Oh, he can push it to one side? Does it make dust then?) But the windows are dirty too. When the sunlight comes in. It's very hard to look through them anyhow. (Does the dust come down on the baby when he pushes the window shade away?) Not necessarily. I really don't know. (What do you feel?) There is a dust. (Flying around?) Yes. Only when he pushes th—the—(I mean when he pushes—) Yes. (—it away, the dust may fall onto the baby.) Right. That's right. So . . . (What do you suppose?) The baby gets choked up with a lot of stuff. (Did you see the baby choked up?) No. (What do you see now?) I see a goat. (A goat?) Yes, a goat. (A billy goat?) I don't know what kind of goat it is. (What does the goat do?) It's a white goat. (What does it do?) . . . It doesn't do anything, just stands. (Let it change. What does it change to?) The goat? (Yes.) A cannon. (Go on.) And now the cannon looks like a long bottle of liquor. (Let it change.) The bottle of liquor? (Yes.) It's broken about and it's thrown away. (By whom?) Somebody who found her. (And what happens now? What happens to the pieces of the liquor bottle?) People may cut themselves. (Let them change. What are they?) What—what, the—the —the pieces? (Yes. Let them change.) I was thinking just when you asked me that question of a place called Mandard, Pennsylvania. In Mandard, Pennsylvania, they have a company called the Pennsy Traprock Company. And there they have mounds of stone which they shovel out, or anyway they can get it out. (What do they get out?) The stone, they break it off . . . And they carve out a whole side of a mountain. When you drive by there . . . (Yes?) . . . there is a—sometimes they are cutting rock or loading it. There is a big mist of pieces of rock. Very small. I believe they call that condition of people work on the rocks chalicosis. (That's right.) And I hate to be around there when they start there. I close my mouth and my nose right away. And now I breathe, but . . . (But?) I can't stand that—that junk around. (What's the matter with your nose? Does it itch?) It itches. Yes. (Let me hear about it.) And I can't stand that handkerchief. Or any—that dust around, I can't stand the dust. (Why? On account of the baby and the window shade?) That's part of the reason. (What is the other part?) Oh, my mother is a big part. The mother of the dancer. (Which dancer?) I just saw a dancer dancing around on a dance floor.

(How did she look?) That was a male. (How did he look?) Society. (You itch behind your left ear?) Yes. That's a very itchy place for me. All over here on this side of the face. My ears hurt me. My throat is very sore. And there must be some inflammation of my eustachian tube. (I believe we should stop now.) Yes. (Okay.) I hate."

Morton made his next appointment for three weeks later. He told me that, for one and one-half weeks, he had been working in a business and that his itching and asthma had ceased.

The playback of the last hypnoanalytic session elicited the following information from the patient: When he was younger, he was happier. He had always tried to get attention, thus the banging of the stick. However, that time, he had been alone—Morton was now identifying with the visualized baby. The wiping of his nose was as uncomfortable as the wiping of his penis. The baby got a bang out of life and created a lot of asthma-producing dust. He said that when he made the slip of the tongue and said "track" instead of "attract," he may have meant that the baby wanted to learn how to become allergic. He believed that the baby was learning how to attract attention by making himself sick. The baby opened the shade a bit to let the sunlight in. When he asked me to repeat the question about the lint and the paper hanky, he was nearly asleep and later tried to stay awake. About his statement that the baby could push the shade to one side, Morton commented, "It doesn't sound realistic to me," adding that, maybe when he "saw" dust, he became allergic. He was always allergic to house dust. A goat meant sex, e.g., "my wife gets my goat," or "I will be an old goat before I really enjoy myself." The cannon meant that he would get tough and go out. Mandard is a very desolate place where the patient and his wife once lived. Toward the end of this hypnoanalytic session, Morton felt better though he was still not getting enough attention and said he had to resort to exhibitionism and "dancing around." He had always blamed his wife for his allergies. Although the patient's description of the baby and the banging on the top of the crib seemed more to be a fantasy than a factual remembrance, he said his sister Lynn told him that he had described the position of the crib and of the window shade correctly.

Structurally, this hypnoanalytic session was the same as the majority of his hypnoanalytic sessions, little background, episodes both long and short, no logically developing activity of the involved persons; the whole tied together by an emotion, specifically a desire for attention. As for the concept of the inset photograph, I have no interpretation, except that it may have been brought about by his inferiority feelings.

In the seventeenth hypnoanalytic session, regression was induced. Transcript: "I see very far away a very tiny looking crib. And the baby in it is very small. (How old, about?) That's a peculiar thing. The baby is dressed up like it's older. And it puts its leg over the bar, the top bar of the crib. And then, as it does that, and it has this funny, smiling expression on its face, like it's raising the devil, having a mischievous time, the leg looks larger like a big leg, like a grown-up leg. It seems like fantasy. It doesn't look real. Although he is standing far away, it really is that everything is been made smaller. Like in a model size—(How far a—) Scale. (How far away is it?) About a—ab—a third of a city block. (Oh, so far.) But still, it looks smaller. It almost looks like a picture in a television set. (Could you not let it come nearer? Then you can look at it better.) I don't want to look at it nearer. (Why not?) I am scared. (Of what?) I—I am afraid. (Of what?) Of this child. (Why?) It doesn't seem real. Like as if it were me, that was a baby that had gone a little crazy. In the way not crazy altogether, but like it didn't care about anything. And it was silly and impish-looking. And it has dressed in a peculiar way. (How?) Like the little stockings are long black. Cotton stockings going over the knee. With a funny collar, like here, like round. (A large collar?) Yes . . . Large in comparison to regular collars. Like a Lord Fauntainroi, Fauntleroy.* (Eton?) Collar. And it doesn't quite look like me. (Just talk.) Ohh, ohh. (What is it?) There is a picture taken of my brother when he was four years old with a collar like that. With a haircut across the forehead. [demonstrates with his hands] (You are showing it?) Yes, this way. Almost like bangs. And then straight down. (Isn't that Buster Brown?) Yes, Buster Brown. And it's something like that style, that collar. Maybe I am scared of

---

* Different pronunciations for Fauntleroy.

that picture of my brother. (I expect you have admired it.) Every-body used to look at that picture. I didn't have any picture like that; I was jealous of it. But I had one very clear association with that picture. And that was the time they told me he had had an operation. And since I had an undescended testicle, I never knew whether that was the operation that he had; they took the testicle down, or whether he had a hernia. They told me it was a hernia operation. But I don't know which it was. Because later he had that testicle taken out. So I don't know why I am scared of that picture. S-s-s. (What is it?) I don't know. Tears started to come into my eyes when I get scared about that thing coming closer. (When I protect you, will you be able to let it come closer?) How are you going to protect me? (I am protecting you. Certainly, I protect you.) How? (Sure, I protect you.) I—(Let it come closer.) How I am afraid! (I will protect you. Let it come closer.) How I am afraid! (I will protect you. Nothing can happen to you.) I know nothing will happen to me. I am scared of—(So, better let it come nearer; then we will know why you are scared.) Oh, it's going to crash into me! It will get too big for me! (You lifted your hand. Are you so frightened?) I don't want it to come near me. I am afraid. (It will not crash into you. It will crash into me.) Ohh, it won't! (Nothing will happen to you. What is it?) It gets very giant —big, that's. (You are lifting your hand.) Now it looks like that picture. It is him. But when I see it far away, it isn't him. It looks different. It doesn't look like anybody I know. But now when it gets closer, if I let it come closer, it's him. (It will crash into me. Not into you.) Ah—I don't want to see him that close! (What's wrong with him?) I don't know. The last few days, the weeks, he has been calling me and acting very nice. He gave me a new customer and another one possibly. (But it's long ago that you were frightened by him. That's not from the last days or weeks. What is behind it?) I don't know. (You are crossing your hands in front of your chest as if to guard yourself. What is it? Let him change. What frightens you? Look at it.) He gets too big. [scared voice] (He is a big shot. That's an old story.) Yes. He— (He changes, he gets big and small.) He—if I let him come close, he gets big. But he is over me. Up there! (Above you?) I—he is looking down at me, menacing me. But I wasn't around when he

was that age. I wasn't there. But I have a feeling like I don't want
to go back when he was there. Because he makes such a complaint
all the time. (About what?) He is spoiled. He wants his own way
all the time . . . (What is it?) And now I am afraid of him getting
nasty. (He can't do anything to you. I will protect you.) Ha—ha!
(Just talk it out.) I don't know what to talk about this. (Let it
come nearer and talk about what you feel.) I am obligated to
know him again. Because he is so nice now. (Not now. What happened before?) But I am afraid. I wanted to get rid of him entirely. I was hoping that he would be the same way. That he is bad.
So that I have a good excuse. Now, if he acts nice, I have trouble.
(What did he do to you?) I don't know. He wants to stifle me. He
wants to push me into a small box. (What kind of box?) Any kind.
A small box like that. (And you would have to be as small as that?
That is not even two or three inches.) Yes, I should be this big.
(Three inches?) He wants to do something to me. When he is . . .
(What?) Like that. When he is four years old. (What did he want
to do to you?) He wants to scare me and suppress me. (What did
he do in—) He is . . . (—reality?) Jealous. (Remember. What did
he do?) He did it indirectly to me. I ran errands for him. He was
going to pay me half a cent. (You told me.) And so he paid me
nothing. Then he always was—made fun of me in front of my
friends. (But how did he make you so small that you would fit
into a two-inch box?) And if I said something or if I used—ah—to
tell a joke and—or a saying that had a dialect like a—like a J-J-
Jewish dialect and he had some gentile friend there, he would
make a face at me to stop. I always had to watch what I say. He'
always criticizing me. I don't read enough. I don't know enough. I
should read about the heroes that jumped into the darkness. They
don't know what they' going to—ah—. They are not afraid to go
forward into strange places and—and find out about themselves.
(Why do you gesticulate so much with your hands today? You do
not usually do that.) I don't know. I feel better when I do it that
way. (Are you trying to keep him away by moving your hands?)
Yes, I push him away. (Tell me about the babies you have been
seeing at other times. Who were they? Were they you or he?) I
don't know who it is. (This time it's apparently he.) Yes. (But the
other times?) He becomes closer. But if he is small . . . (Let him

come very close so that we can see what happens.) Ooohh. (Let us try.) Oh. (How near is he now?) I don't want him to come so close. (How close is he now?) Close to the room. (In the room?) Yes. (He is in the room now?) Yes. Across the room. (What is he doing to you?) He stays like a little chimpanzee. Like a gorilla. (How tall are you?) I don't know. (Did you feel yourself shrinking?) No. (You see, nothing can happen to you! He can't do anything to you.) Huh. (He is unable to harm you.) He bothers me, though. He makes me feel bad. He . . . (Come on.) He has bad motives. (What are his motives? How do you know?) I don't know. But that's the way everything turns out that he . . . (What?) Wants. He projects his own crazy neurosis onto everybody else. (Come on.) In. (You didn't think that way as a kid. What did you think about that when you were small?) He is going to take things away from me. (What?) The things that were promised me. That I never got. That he already took. (The long pants?) Everything. (What?) The trains they promised me to . . . (What else?) The bigger portions at the table. Although I never ate at the table. I don't know. Anything worth while having I couldn't hold. He would get it from me. That's why I want to keep him away. (How near is he now?) At the same place. (Let him come closer. Nothing will happen to you. Let him come near, quite near. Then tell me what's happening.) I see his way; he is in the picture. And there is—it's like a little Chinese decoration in the—on the picture frame. And it's red. And I see that red. Maybe it got something to do with penises. (Let me hear.) Maybe he is trying to make mine smaller. He used to say to me there, in front of the mirror, look at your physique. You are getting a good physique. When I was very young. I—made me feel good. But whom was he kidding? I don't have a good physique. (Why not?) I am thin. I am skinny. I don't have any frame. (So what?) You see them at the beaches. They are very well put together. (They get high blood pressure.) That I know. That's the only consolation. (How near is your brother now?) He is sitting now on the crib. Then he is playing. (Did you compare your penis with his?) Not at that age. I just thought about it during the years. I always felt his is bigger than mine. (He was older anyway.) Aahh. Maybe it's too big. It probably is too bigger than mine. (Come on.) May—I don't know. He used to play with

two little sticks . . . (What did he do with the two sticks?) He had one stick here and one stick here. And he used to make—I could never do that. (Between the fingers of the—?) Yes. (Right hand? Between?) Yes. (The second and the third, and the third and the fourth.) Yes. Right here. And he used to get quicker and quicker, click-click. (So he could click them.) Yes. (So what?) And so he used to do that. I think he used to fool around with a knife all the time. And when he lost his testicle—I felt very guilty. Maybe he is trying to castrate me. (What are you doing with your right arm?) Operate him. [laughs] (You cut it off?) I didn't cut anything off. He—I made the wrong kind of incision. Crazy. So it's not real. (Is there anything else? Hm?) He—(Where is he now?) I want to get rid of him. He is still in the room and I can't get rid of him now. (Let him come quite near. Then kill him.) I can't kill him. (Sure, you can.) What am I going to kill him with? I haven't got a thing to kill him with. (How near is he now?) In the middle of the room here. (Let him come quite close to you.) I don't know. (And then wring his neck.) Why I am—why am I so mad? (Then wring his neck.) Oh, I couldn't do that. (Sure. Sure, you can do it. I am protecting you. I will help you. Just let him come quite near to you. How near is he now?) Oh, I wa—I was going to do it, I . . . (You see, you are doing it.) I couldn't quite do it. Oh. (You are doing it. Now you are covering your eyes.) Oohhh, I wring his neck. (You wring his neck. Good.) Oohhh. [grinds his teeth] (What is?) It was good. [satisfied voice] (And nothing happened. Nothing happened.) Oohh, I am scared. (Don't be scared.) [cries] (What happened to him?) I killed him. (Did he drop dead?) Yes, he is dead. Separated . . . There is a string between—(Between his head and the body there is a thin string?) Yes. Nothing. (Good, good, excellent.) Oh. (Did anything happen to you?) Yes. I started to get an erection. (What else?) That's all. (That will quiet down. What else?) Nothing. (Is he dead?) H—he is in pieces. (Are you rid of him?) I—I hope so. (You feel better?) Y-y-y-yes. (Are you quieted down?) Yes. (Should we stop?) Yes. (Okay.) I won't feel bad when I wake up? (What?) I am going to feel bad when I wake up? (Why should you feel bad when you wake up?) Because I feel funny about it. Oh. (Don't feel funny about it. Was he a piece of you?) No. (Then it's okay. Then you are whole and you are rid of him. Yes?) Yes. (Okay.)"

When the patient was awakened, he had to dry his eyes. He stated that he had had no erection for the last month. Morton believed it would be hard for him to hear the playback. He said, "For what is analysis good?"

At his next appointment, Morton remarked, "That experience matched all my other psychological experiences altogether. I enjoyed it, being frightened—any reaction I got. It was totally unexpected." He said he had forgotten everything until he got home. When he told his sister Lynn about it, she felt much better. Since his last hypnoanalytic session, he had felt stronger and talked louder. During the session, the patient had the feeling that he would act because he could not accept the extent of his fear. Morton thought my promise of protection foolish, but did feel protected in the sense that, if he did act, I would defend him, and he would not be prosecuted. Morton was also astonished that it was so easy to kill his brother. The patient said he had always been "bad" with his hands. For instance, when he cut meat, he was never able to separate it cleanly; there was still always a "string" remaining. Nevertheless, in the end, his brother had been in pieces. Morton believed that the string between the body and the head had been a nerve, and that he himself had acquired the "nerve." On the one hand, he did not know whether he was still too frightened to hear the playback; on the other hand, he was anxious to hear it.

The patient's remarks at the replay were as follows: His brother had had a Peter Pan collar. Morton had never been able to spell "Fauntleroy" and had given two different versions of it. He believed that his brother was "a little crazy." The patient, as a boy, had worn Buster Brown shoes. He had wanted to "throttle" the picture because his brother looked so innocent in it, like Little Lord Fauntleroy. They never took a picture of Morton as a boy (which was contradicted in his fifth hypnoanalytic session). He did not like his brother near him because he had always been "crushing" to the patient. His brother used to claim that Morton became angry with him when he offered to help him. The patient felt that his brother did not really intend to help, but that what he really wanted was to suppress him. The brother had never gone to a doctor with Morton, but he had gone to a doctor with his brother, specifically when he was operated upon for a tumor of the testicle.

Morton himself could have died from his undescended testicle if a tumor had developed. When the brother was closer in visualization than Morton cared to admit, he really looked like a giant, his face, neck, and feet puffed up with fat. What Morton found interesting was the awareness of having tears in his eyes when he did not want his brother to come close to him, that he was really scared of him. The photo he described had most probably been taken shortly after his brother's operation. His brother had been cured, but the patient always worried about his own operation. Morton may have had the idea that he would have to do everything alone. He had been afraid of being hypnotized. The patient could not explain how his brother could crash into him. "Something is obliterated when I do anything to him. He will come back at me." As long as the visualization was far away, it looked less like the photo; when it was close, it looked more like it. Morton had been told in his psychoanalysis that he had played a female role in relation to his brother, like the power behind the throne. Then, the patient expressed his dislike of the fact that his brother was very feminine. Morton always ridiculed homosexuals and pointed them out. He did not notice that the two foregoing statements were partly contradictory. "Actually, my brother appeared for a while on my right side. There is a wall (where the couch for the hypnoses stands), but he was there." The brother had been enlarged to a height of six or seven feet, his arms and legs distended, as if by a terrific edema. The patient himself did not feel any change of his own body image. He plainly visualized the box as being six inches square. "He is really trying to make me smaller." Morton believed that there was antagonism among his sister Lynn, his brother, and himself, each one trying to push the other down. His brother was "a pain in the ass," and always laid down all kinds of restrictions, arranging everything for his own comfort. "I had the feeling that I was smacking my lips. Because I knew that something big was going to happen. That's the reason I was gesticulating. In this record I knew I would get rid of him." Despite this, however, the patient only listened to the playback of this record until the point at which he compared his brother to a chimpanzee; he never listened to the actual attack on his brother.

Before discussing this hypnoanalytic session and Morton's reactions to it, I will finish his case history. I saw him four more times during the following three years, and even on the first of these occasions, which was about one year after his seventeenth hypnoanalytic session, his exterior was very much changed. His skin was perfectly clear; he looked much better, had put on weight, and was much more elegantly dressed. He still had problems, but was able to cope with them. He liked his new field of work and was successful in it. Morton has since been the source of many referrals to me, the first one being his own sister Lynn.

Comment upon this final hypnoanalytic session first leads to the baby's "grown-up leg" in the visualization. This change in the body image (the patient's projected affects into his brother's body image) of the patient's brother—he was obviously aware from the beginning that it was his brother—most probably symbolized the brother's genitals. There is, however, a second possible interpretation, although related to the first: The legs being covered with black stockings may have constituted some peculiar symbolization of the cloven hoof of the devil, for whom his brother stood in the patient's unconscious. The other oddities of appearance made me suspect that they had something to do with the Buster Brown outfits about which many of my patients have complained.

It is interesting that the brother's body image was subject to change, whereas the patient's sensations with regard to his own body did not vary. Although his brother planned to compress him into a small box, Morton's ego was now strong enough to resist. Immediately after wanting to compress the patient into a small box, the brother, supposedly, wanted to enlarge him to a hero. Both fantasies were very frightening for Morton and expressive of his ambivalent feelings towards his brother. The patient was extremely suspicious of his brother's "motives," and his castration anxiety increased his animosity towards his brother, whom he himself wanted to get rid of.

There is not a very accurate description, either during the hypnoanalytic session or afterwards, of how the patient felt when he first tried to wring his brother's neck and how he felt when he succeeded in doing so. Only when he was "mad" enough, when his

constant wish to get rid of his brother was powerful enough, did he triumph. Although he was immediately afraid of the aftereffects of his deed, the results were positive. Morton had proven to himself that he was strong enough to stand up to his old adversary—as he had always regarded his brother—and, in so doing, had gained the ego strength to cope with the problems of life.

BIBLIOGRAPHY

AMERICAN PSYCHIATRIC ASSOCIATION: Mental disorders. *Diagnostic and Statistical Manual. Washington*, Mental Hospital Service, 1955.

ENGLISH, HORACE B., and ENGLISH, AVA CHAMPNEY: *A Comprehensive Dictionary of Psychological and Psychoanalytical Terms.* New York, Longmans, 1958.

ERICKSON, MILTON H.: Experiential knowledge of hypnotic phenomena employed for hypnotherapy. *Amer J Clin Hypn, 8*:299-309, 1966.

FEDERN, PAUL: The determination of hysteria versus obsessional neurosis. *Psychoanal Rev, 27*:265-276, 1940.

FEDERN, PAUL: Hysterie und Zwang in der Neurosenwahl. *Int Z Psychoanal, 25*:245-263, 1940.

FEDERN, PAUL: *Ego Psychology and the Psychoses.* Basic Books, New York, 1952.

FENICHEL, OTTO: *The Psychoanalytic Theory of Neurosis.* New York, Norton, 1945.

FREUD, SIGMUND: *The Problem of Anxiety.* New York, Norton, 1936.

GILL, MERTON M., and BRENMAN, MARGARET: *Hypnosis and Related States.* New York, Int. Univ., 1959.

GORDON, JESSE E.: *Clinical and Experimental Hypnosis.* New York, Macmillan, 1967.

KLINE, MILTON V.: *Clinical Correlations of Experimental Hypnosis.* Springfield, Ill., Thomas, 1963.

SCHNECK, JEROME M.: *Principles and Practice of Hypnoanalysis.* Springfield, Ill., Thomas, 1965.

SILLMAN, L.: The analysis of guilt and narcissism. *J Nerv Ment Dis, 133(4)*: 293-302, 1961.

WATKINS, JOHN G.: Symposium on posthypnotic amnesia: Discussion. *Int J Clin Exp. Hypn, 14*:139-149, 1966.

WOLBERG, LEWIS R.: *Medical Hypnosis.* Vols. I and II. New York, Grune, 1948.

WOLBERG, LEWIS R.: *Hypnoanalysis.* New York, Grune, 1964.

INDEX

A

Abdomen, 115, 158
Abreaction, 10
Abuse, 49 ff., 55, 56, 59 f., 62, 64, 66, 68, 98, 233, 234. *See also* specific acts.
sexual, 32 f., 35 f., 38, 39, 40, 44, 98, 101 f., 109, 125. *See also* specific acts.
Accidents, 50, 53, 56, 57, 65, 67, 131, 191, 193, 213 f., 216, 219 f., 221, 226
Acrophobia, 28, 72
Acting out. *See* family-member destruction.
Affects
in transference, 4
visceral expression of, 18. *See also* psychophysiologic disorders
Age of patient
in regression, xiii, xiv, 24 f., 27, 28, 30, 32, 35, 36, 37, 38, 40, 44, 52, 53, 54, 55, 56, 58, 62, 63, 65, 68 f., 77, 79, 80, 82, 86, 105, 112, 114, 117, 122, 123, 124, 136, 137, 138, 139, 140, 141, 142, 144, 146, 147, 148, 149, 150, 154, 156 f., 161, 162, 167, 168, 172, 175, 191, 194, 195, 197, 198, 206, 216, 219, 221, 233, 234, 235, 244, 248
at start of psychoneurosis, 27
Aggression, 7, 14, 51, 87, 92, 127, 133, 145, 181, 213, 241
Aggressor
identification with, 67, 69, 87, 107, 242
Alcoholism, 21, 24, 27, 44, 46 48, 52, 55, 56, 62 f., 65 f., 95, 97 ff., 116, 156, 165, 184, 199, 201, 212 ff., 223 f.
Allergy, 228, 233, 240. *See also* specific conditions.
Ambition, 45 f., 66, 71, 165, 189, 190, 192 f., 198 f. *See also* frustration.
Ambivalence, 16, 27, 103, 138, 142, 151, 206, 225, 242
American Psychiatric Association, 257
Amnesia, xii, xiii, 93

Amytal sodium, 76, 81, 85
Anal complex, 13
Anal conflict, 188
Anal fantasy, 75
Anal intercourse, 101. *See also* homosexuality.
Anal regression, 166, 223
Anal retention, 151, 224
Anamnesis, ix, 21, 228
Anesthesia, 72, 75, 192, 204
Animal symbolism, 190 f. *See also* specific species.
Annihilation anxiety, 93, 225, 226
Anti-Semitism, 238, 241, 242
Anxiety, 12, 21 ff., 30, 46, 47 ff., 72, 74, 81, 89, 129, 151, 182
bodily ego and, 198
from prompting, xv
Asthma, 228, 233, 238, 241, 242, 243, 245, 247
Attention, 36, 68 f., 103, 182, 188, 206, 234, 245, 247, 248
Authority, 67, 207, 208
Autonomic (psychophysiologic and visceral) disorders, 184 ff.

B

Baby carriage, 122 f., 126 f., 216 f.
Balance. *See* equilibrium.
Ballet, 146, 147. *See also* dancing.
Ballplaying, 157, 189, 190, 191, 193, 203
Baptizing, 157, 177
Bar mitzvah, 241
Bathing, 56, 62, 68, 157, 159, 169, 170, 217, 219, 232
Bathroom 135. *See also* toilet.
Bathtub, 57, 104, 105, 110, 135, 149
Beating, 44, 48, 49, 51, 54, 56, 64, 100, 104, 131, 194, 196. *See also* spanking; whipping.
Bedroom, sharing of. *See* sleep.
Bicycle, 49, 203 ff., 206 f., 209, 214
Birth, 23, 49, 99, 133, 154, 187, 224, 230

Black, 81, 116, 142, 170, 172, 196, 200, 205, 218, 234, 240, 242, 255
Blocking, xv
Blood, 37, 38, 88, 90, 91, 93, 163, 220, 228, 237, 238
Blue, 66, 81, 150, 206
Blushing. *See* erythrophobia.
Body contact, 13
Body ego. *See* ego.
Body image, 10, 81, 126, 226, 227, 254, 255
Body odor, 156, 179, 180, 199, 200, 201
Boot, 99, 119, 120, 121
Borborygmi, xvii, 142, 150
Bottle feeding, 25, 187, 224
Bowel
  Distention, 158, 187, 227
  movement, 112 ff., 187, 221, 224, 227.
  See also feces; toilet training.
Breast, 211, 214
  feeding, 23, 25 ff., 39, 133, 154, 187, 230
Breath, bad, 33, 35, 39
Breathing, 184, 194 f., 197, 198, 203 f., 206, 207, 208, 217, 220, 222, 226
Brenman, xi, xvi, 3, 6, 7, 8, 9, 18, 20, 257
Breuer, 5
Brother
  -brother relationship, 161, 185, 230, 231 f., 235 ff., 241 f., 250 ff., 253 ff., 255 f.
  -sister relationship, 132 ff., 137 ff., 140, 144 ff., 230, 233, 242
  See also sibling
Brown, 122, 150, 179, 182, 196, 200
Buster Brown, 188, 248, 253, 255
Butcher, 197, 206, 207, 208, 225
Buttercup, 172 ff., 180

C

Cannon, 246, 247
Carbrital®, 140
Cardiovascular reaction, 184 ff., 223
Castration complex, 17, 20, 22, 48, 93, 98, 99, 100, 102, 108, 168, 195, 196, 225, 239, 242, 243, 252, 255
Cat, 75, 174
Caterpillar, 137
Cathexis, 7, 20. *See also* countercathexis.
Cellar, 55, 113, 115 f., 199 f., 220
Chamber pot, 20, 98, 149, 150, 151, 158, 172, 187, 221

Chestnut trees, 137
Chickens, 73, 93, 156, 157, 167, 173, 181
Child
  rearing, 99 f., 131, 139, 145 f., 152, 155, 156, 157, 185, 230 f.
  unwanted, 49, 66, 74, 229, 230
Childhood illness. *See* illness.
Childhood surgery. *See* surgery.
Choking, 33, 37, 54, 56, 58, 59, 60, 68, 69, 104
  sexual excitement from, 69
Christ, 87, 88, 90, 91, 93, 100, 238 ff., 241
Christmas, 44 f., 73, 160, 238, 240, 241
Church, 22, 87, 176, 177, 237, 240, 241, 242
Circumcision, 164, 187, 195, 225
Claustrophobia, 108, 120, 152
Cleanliness, 96, 155, 156, 172, 176, 177, 179, 181, 186, 194, 200, 201, 202, 213
Climbing, 191, 193
Clothing, xiv, 32, 40, 49, 76, 78, 79, 81, 99, 133, 136, 146, 157 ff., 167 ff., 171 ff., 174, 175 f., 177, 181, 194, 220, 232, 234 ff., 248, 251
  of opposite sex, 99, 157, 172, 173
Colds, 55, 193, 204, 206, 209, 223, 225
Color, xiv, 26, 41 f., 54, 66, 78 f., 81, 86, 146 ff., 167, 170, 172, 175, 179, 196, 201, 205, 207, 213 ff., 220, 227, 234, 237 ff., 241, 251
  odor of, 200, 201, 227
  See also specific colors.
Communism, 240, 241
Compazine®, 154
Compulsion, 14, 15, 16, 20, 131, 135. *See also* obsessive compulsive reaction.
Compulsive eating, 133, 156, 178, 182
Compulsive personality, 68, 153 ff., 182
Compulsive talking, 153, 172, 231
Condensation, 15, 67
Conflict, triangular, 30, 31 f., 37, 40 ff.
Constipation, 133 f., 151, 158, 187 f., 201, 221, 224
Conversion reaction, 8, 9, 12 ff., 21 ff., 39, 46, 47 ff., 68, 72, 143, 152
  analgesia in, 67
  countercathexis in, 8 f.
  defense in, 8, 12 f., 18, 31
  ego in, 8, 12 f., 14, 16, 45

infantile mechanism, 13, 14
ego states in, 12 ff.
fantasy in, 16, 18, 32 ff.
fear and, 13
hypnoanalysis of, 18 f.
hypnotizability and, 8, 9
identification in, 13, 16, 35, 46, 67, 86 f.
obsessive compulsive reaction and, 14, 70
personality in, 16
repression in, 14 f., 16, 18
somatic compliance and, 31
symbolization in, 18, 47, 71, 94
symptom formation in, 15, 16, 18, 24, 33 f., 39, 75
transference in, 16, 32
visualizations in, 18 f., 47, 70 f., 79, 86, 94, 228
working through in, 18 f., 42, 47, 94
Coughing, xvii, 25 *n.*, 33 ff., 35 ff., 38 f., 48, 53 ff., 56 ff., 59, 60 ff., 68 ff., 208 ff., 212 f., 214, 215, 223, 225, 236 ff., 243
Countercathexis, 7, 8 f.
Countertransference, 4, 230
Cowardice, 148, 168, 175, 181, 241
Crab, 137, 148, 149
Crib, 103, 187, 244, 245, 247, 248, 251
Criticism, 13, 108, 200 f., 205, 211, 250
"Crushes," 101, 140, 164
Crying
  repression of, 28, 29, 36, 37, 38, 39
Cutting, 63, 64, 65, 71, 75, 92, 98, 129, 195 f., 252

D

Dancing, 131, 146, 147, 246 f.
Danger. *See* warning.
Daydreaming, 32, 148. *See also* fantasy.
Death, 79, 186, 204, 225
  depression and, 44
  of father, 48, 73, 185, 186, 204, 212
  of grandmother, 43 ff., 73, 79
  guilt and, 156
  hypnosis as, 80, 197
  of mother, 22, 49, 154
  of sibling, 74, 79 f., 96
Death wishes. *See* murderous wishes.
Defecation. *See* bowel movement; feces; toilet training.

Defense, 6, 7
  conversion of, 20
  in conversion reaction, 8, 12 f., 18, 31
  hypnosis fluctuation and, xi
  isolation as, 120
  in obsessive compulsive reaction, 8, 13 f., 15, 17, 20
  undoing as, 8, 120
Dehypnotization, x, xi, xii
Dependency, 99, 133, 151, 187, 225
Depressive reaction, 12, 21 ff., 27, 28, 34, 39 ff., 44, 45, 47, 72
  seasonal, 21
Dermatitis, 228 ff.
Devil, 100, 101, 109, 113, 114, 115
Dexamyl® Spansules®, 116
Dirt eating, 188
"Dirty habits," 96, 98, 109, 115
Disfigurement, 49, 59, 67
Dissociative reaction, 12, 21 ff., 47 ff.
Dog, 52, 57, 69, 215, 216, 238, 239, 241, 242
Doubting, 15, 96, 102, 139, 182, 186
Drawings, xv, 60, 204 f., 207, 211, 214, 215, 218, 226, 227
Dream, xiii, xiv, 6, 33, 52, 66
  interpretation of, 53 ff., 57 f., 142 ff., 167 f., 174 ff., 178, 190 ff., 199 ff., 209 ff., 212 ff., 215 ff., 218 ff.
Dress, 211 ff., 214
Dressing, 54, 56, 60, 168, 223, 248
Drinking. *See* alcoholism.
Drug
  addiction, 21, 24, 27, 50
  -taking ritual, 140
Dust, 239, 242, 243, 245 ff.

E

Eating, compulsive. *See* compulsive eating.
Ego
  activity, 15
  bodily, 13, 17, 29, 31, 182, 198, 226 f.
  boundaries, 11, 13, 16 f., 18, 29, 31
  in conversion reaction, 8, 12 f., 14 f., 16, 87
  fear and, 13 ff., 28
  in hypnosis, xvi, 9, 18
  infantile mechanism of
    in conversion reaction, 13, 14
    in obsessive compulsive reaction, 13 f.

in obsessive compulsive reaction, 9, 13, 14, 15, 16 f., 147
passivity, 14
patient-therapist relationship and, 7
psychical, 13, 14, 15, 16 f.
reactions, 30
  repression of, 14 f., 16, 18, 30
regression and, xi, 7, 8, 9
reprojection of, 7 f.
splitting of, 14, 15, 16
state. *See* ego state.
strength, 66 f., 211, 255, 256
subsystem, 6 ff.
unification of, 46
Ego state, 11 ff.
  identification with a past, 87
  reawakening of a past, 11 f., 18, 27, 29 ff., 33 ff., 36 ff., 40 ff., 43 f., 80, 150, 195, 196, 205, 207, 222
  repressed, 14 f., 16, 18, 34, 38, 47, 191, 193, 218
  visualization of a past, 110, 136, 139, 141, 149, 150, 152
  See also ego.
Electroshock therapy, 95
Embryo, 146, 148
Emission, 161 f., 164
Emotions
  logic of, 70, 235, 237, 243, 248
  symbolization of, 191, 205
Enemas, 75, 100, 115, 133 f., 150, 151, 158, 187, 221, 224
English, A. C., 4, 257
English, H. B., 4, 257
Equilibrium, 149, 151
Erection, 101, 158, 252, 253
  shaving and, 199
Erickson, 3, 4, 257
Erotic zones
  bodily ego feeling and, 198, 227
Erythrophobia, 71, 96, 108, 116
Evil eye, 113, 114, 115
Exhibitionism, 22, 51, 133, 166, 167, 168, 169, 170, 247
Expiation, 14, 19, 121
Eye fixation, ix
Eyeglasses, 188, 205, 206
Eye itching, 147, 148
Eyelashes, 218, 219

Eyes, 54, 55, 57, 58, 59, 62, 209 f., 216, 217, 218, 219

F
Fainting, 30, 185, 204, 225, 226
Falling, 28, 56 f., 144, 146, 188, 191, 202, 216 f., 219 f., 221, 226
Family
  emotional illness in, 22, 23, 46, 73, 86, 94, 185, 186, 224
  fights, 31, 37, 46, 221, 222
  See also specific members.
Family-member destruction, xv, 58, 59, 61, 71, 122, 123, 126, 127, 228, 252, 253, 255
Fantasy, 5, 14, 16, 18, 32, 67, 75, 108, 148, 163, 178, 179, 180, 182. *See also* specific symbolizations; daydreaming; sexual fantasy.
Father
  -child relationship 22, 27 ff., 35 ff., 40 ff., 44 ff., 48, 55, 67, 98, 103 ff., **107**, 109 f., 115, 131 f., 149 f., 185, 229 ff., 235
  death of, 48, 73, 185, 186, 204, 212
  "dirty habits" of, 96, 98, 109, 115
  emotional illness of, 73, 86
  genitalia of, 121, 127
  identification with, 14, 34, 35, 46, 66, 67, 107, 208, 212, 225, 230
  illness of, 132, 185, 204
    identification with, 208, 225
  omnipotence of, 44, 107
  personality structure of, 22, 33, 34, 46, 48, 97, 110, 185, 229
  sexual abuse by, 32 f., 36, 38, 40, 44, 109, 125
  See also grandfather.
Fear, 13 f., 15 f., 17, 20, 59, 61, 73, 75, 80, 83, 85, 93, 98, 100 102 f., 110, 111, 127, 226
  thinking, 13, 15, 121
Feces, 104, 137, 177, 181. *See also* bowel movement.
Federn, E., 12
Federn, P., 11, 12, 13, 14, 18, 20, 31, 45, 198, 227, 257
Fellatio, 27, 36, 38, 104, 109, 125, 164, **230**
Female genitalia. *See* genitalia.

Fenichel, 20, 151, 227, 257
Ferry, 144, 145
Fever, 36
Fighting. *See* family fights.
Financial problems, 47, 53, 61, 66, 220, 223
Fingernail cutting, 169
Finger sucking, 23, 49, 74, 155, 188
Fire, 113, 114, 115, 116, 158
Fish, 215, 216, 219
  bones, 143
Flight, 13. *See also* running away.
Frazer, 243
Freedom, 203, 205
Freud, 3, 5, 7, 8, 11, 18, 257
Frustration, 45, 159, 192, 193, 198, 199, 208, 234

G

Gelding, 170
Genitalia
  abuse of, 56, 62
  disease of, 199. *See also* testicles.
  doubt about, 98, 99, 102, 127
  of father, 121, 127
  female, 158, 159, 166, 170, 174, 181, 215, 219
  male, 137. *See also* penis; testicles.
  pulsations in, 151
  rejection of, 157, 159, 169, 170, 171, 180
  surgery of, 165, 178 ff., 182, 242, 243, 249, 252, 253 f.
  symbolization of, 121, 181, 205, 206, 255.
    See also specific symbols.
Genitalization
  of throat, 60, 69
Giant, 118, 121, 175, 181, 197, 249, 254
Gill, xi, xvi, 3, 6, 7, 8, 9 18, 20, 257
Globus hystericus, 27, 55, 69, 143
Goat, 240, 242, 243, 246, 247
God, 217, 218, 219
Gold, 79, 177, 237. *See also* yellow.
Gordon, 3, 4, 9, 257
Grandfather
  -child relationship, 155, 156, 157, 165 f.
Grandmother
  -child relationship, 23, 27, 29 f., 33 f., 40 ff., 44 ff., 155 ff., 167 ff., 171 ff., 176, 179 ff.

death of, 43 ff., 73, 79
identification with, 46
Gratification, 14, 20
Gray, 146, 148, 167, 196, 220, 234
Green, 135, 159, 179, 182, 196, 200, 201, 214, 215
Grieving, 45
Guilt, 17, 95, 121, 153, 160, 166, 169, 174, 186, 224, 225, 252
  cannibalistic fantasy and, 163
  death and, 45, 156
  drinking and, 44
  hatred and, 238
  identification and, 46
  illness and, 232
  loss of love object and, 45
  masochism and, 67
  masturbation and, 23, 189
  matricidal fantasy and, 163
  murderous wishes and, xv

H

Haircut, 188, 248
Hammer, 111, 196
Handkerchief, 243, 245, 246, 247
Hands, 57, 240, 250
  dirty, 176, 177
  enlarged, 198 f.
  washing of, 113
"Happenings," 19
Hartmann, xi
Hat, 136, 146, 148, 177, 241
Headache, 25, 81, 197
Head turning, x, xi
Heart, 184, 210, 215, 226. *See also* palpitations.
Hemorrhoids, 158, 180
Heredity, 94
Hilgard, 3
Hives, 134
Homosexuality, 7, 51, 101, 109, 113, 160, 164, 165, 178, 232, 233, 254
Horse, 102, 170, 175, 176, 181, 202, 204, 205, 209, 220
Hostility
  and ego boundaries, 31
  See also abuse; family fights.
Hyperkinesis, 68
Hyperventilation syndrome, 226

Hypnoanalysis, xvi, 4, 5, 6
  of conversion reaction, 18 f. *See also*
    conversion reaction.
  family-member destruction during, xv,
    58, 59, 61, 71, 122, 123, 126, 127, 228,
    252, 253, 255
  follow-up, 5
  multiple episodes in, 70 f.
  of obsessive compulsive reaction, 19 f.
    See also obsessive compulsive reac-
    tion.
  physical environment of, xv, xvi
  technique of, ix, x, xi, xii, xiii, xiv, xv
  theory of, 3 ff.
  transcribed, xii, xvi, 193
  transference in, 7, 32
  See also visualizations.
Hypnosis, 3, 4, 6
  awakening from, x, xi
  as death, 80, 197
  depth of, 92
  ego function in, xvi, 9, 18
  ego state reawakening in, 11 f., 18
  ego subsystem in, 6 ff.
  in first interview, ix
  fluctuations in depth of, xi
  regressive character of, xvi
  as "sleep," xi
  speaking during, x, xii, 191
  technique of, ix
  theory of, 6 ff.
Hypnotizability, ix, 8, 9
  and disturbing unconscious material, x
Hysteria. *See* conversion reaction.

I

Id, 7, 8
Identification, 67, 86
  with aggressor, 67, 69, 87, 107, 242
  in conversion reaction, 13, 16
  with father, 14, 34, 35, 46, 66, 67, 107,
    208, 212, 225, 230
  with grandmother, 46
  with mother, 13, 46, 131, 145, 152, 227
  in obsessive compulsive reaction, 14
  sexual, 46, 99
  with sibling, 35, 39, 46, 139
  with winner, 212
Illness
  childhood, 74, 75, 77, 78, 80, 81, 82 ff.,

86, 87, 88 ff., 99, 107, 134, 157, 164,
  188, 204, 217, 221, 230, 232, 234.
  See also surgery.
Images, 5
  hypnagogie, 11
  variety of, xiv
  See also visualizations.
Impotence, 102, 127
Impulses, 14, 19 f., 120
Inability to associate, 96
Indecisiveness, 129, 139, 145, 151 f.
Infancy, xvii, 4, 5
Inferiority, 53, 70, 231, 235, 236, 237,
  242, 248
Infirmity
  symbolization of, 82 ff., 85, 87, 89
Intercourse
  anal, 101
  a tergo, 100, 162, 166
  See also homosexuality; marital rela-
    tions.
Interpretation, 4, 5. *See also* dream in-
  terpretation.
Intestines, 113, 114, 180, 184
Introject
  reprojected, 107, 115, 120, 122, 127
Isolation, 8, 120
Itching. *See* pruritus.

J

Jealousy, 33, 36, 39, 249, 250. *See also*
  sibling rivalry.
Jerking, 88, 89, 90, 91, 92
"Judge," 146, 147
Jumping, 144 f.

K

Kicking, 58
Klemperer, 28, 70, 95, 162, 184, 202
Kline, 3, 10, 257
Knife, 195, 196, 252
Kris, xi, 7

L

Language, 22, 34, 43, 45, 97. *See also*
  vocabulary.
Laxatives, 100, 114, 133, 158
Learning, xvi, 9
Left side, 209 f., 212, 216, 218, 226
Leg, 248, 255

Light beams, 168, 169, 170, 171, 209, 210, 226, 227
Lightning, 74, 89, 91
Lint, 243, 244, 245, 247
Literature, 3 ff., 6 ff.
Loneliness, 32, 36, 40, 42, 45, 80, 86, 127, 136, 159 f., 166
Lord Fauntleroy, 248, 253
Love, 16, 17
  object, 40 ff., 45
Loyalty, 31 f., 186, 221, 222, 225
Lucite® rod, ix
Lying, 23, 49, 100, 157

M

Magic, 16, 17, 182
Manhood, 179, 180, 182
Marital relations, 24, 51, 52, 53, 55, 56, 62, 70, 166, 185, 189 f., 233
Masculinity
  rejection of, 171
Masochism, 67 *See also* accidents: falling.
Masturbation, 23, 74, 75, 98, 112, 151, 159, 160, 161, 162, 163, 178, 189, 232
Matricidal impulse, 17, 163
Meares, 3
Medication, 50, 62, 63, 65, 66, 76, 81, 85, 116, 140, 154, 184
Menstruation, 23, 75, 91, 133, 214, 215
Mesmer's strokes, ix, x
Mice, 97, 189
Michelet, 243
Milk products, 173, 181
Money, 154, 160, 192, 193, 206, 220, 221, 223, 238, 241, 242
Moral conflict, 14
Mosquito sting, 193
Mother
  -child relationship, 23, 25 ff., 29 ff., 37 f., 40 ff., 44 f., 46, 48, 52, 54 ff., 64 ff., 68, 74, 99 f., 106 f., 110, 115, 131 f., 134, 138 ff., 145, 147 f,, 186 ff., 191 ff., 198, 202 f., 205, 208, 211, 216 f., 232, 237
  death of, 22, 49, 154
  deprecation of father, 186, 221, 222, 225
  dominance of, 229
  egotization (identification) of, 138
  identification with, 13, 46, 131, 145, 152, 227
  illness of, 73, 130, 131, 186, 187, 221, 224, 229, 230
  operations on, 186, 187, 214, 224, 234
  personality structure of, 22 f., 46, 48 f., 73 f., 130, 131, 132, 188, 229
  pity for, 216, 217
  sexual fantasies about, 102, 162 f., 168
  substitute, 30, 37, 40 ff., 133, 140, 187, 224
  See also matricidal impulse; grandmother.
Motor reaction, 92
Mouth
  urination into, 33, 35, 38
  washing with soap, 37
Movie technique. *See* theater technique.
Mushrooms, 179

N

Nail biting, 49, 155, 188
Nails, 111, 238, 241
Neck twitching, 76, 77 f., 82, 84, 87, 93
Needs
  narcissistic, 27, 67, 159
Nervousness, 90 f., 95
Neurosis. *See* specific reactions.
Nightmares, 134
Noodles, 142, 143
Nose, 241, 242, 243 f., 246
  abuse of, 96
  wiping, 243, 247
Number three, 218
Numbness. *See* paresthesia.
Nursing. *See* bottle feeding; breast feeding.

O

Obesity, 29, 132, 133
Object libido, 45
Object relations, 15, 16, 20
Observer, 86, 161, 162, 167, 168, 169, 170, 171, 174, 179, 180, 218, 233
Obsessive compulsive reaction, 12 f., 15, 75, 95 ff., 107
  aggression in, 14
  ambivalence in, 16
  and conversion reaction, 14, 70, 152
  countercathexis in, 8 f.
  defense in, 8, 13 f., 15, 17, 20

diagnosis of, 128
ego in, 9, 13, 14, 15 f., 16 f., 147
  infantile mechanism in, 13 f.
expiation in, 14, 19, 121
fear and, 13 f., 15 f., 17, 110, 111, 121
guilt and, 17, 95, 112, 114 f.
"happenings" in, 19
hypnoanalysis of, 19 f.
hypnotizability and, 8, 9
identification in, 14
mixed, 143, 152
object relations in, 15, 16, 20
personality in, 15, 16, 17
repression in, 14, 16
superego in, 14, 16 f., 112, 147
superstition in, 226
symbolizations in, 19, 20, 110
symptom formation in, 15
undoing in, 19, 120
visualizations in, 19 f., 110 f., 128, 152
working through in, 19, 121
Oceanic feeling, 27
Odor, 93, 136 f., 187, 198, 199 ff., 224, 227
  and color, 200, 201, 227
  and symbolization, 228
  See also body odor; breath, bad.
Oedipus complex, 17, 43, 152, 162 f., 168, 208 ff.
Omnipotence, 44, 107
Operation. *See* surgery.
Oral conflict, 25, 27, 39
Oral consolation, 141, 181
Oral fixation, 27, 182
Oral frustration, 40, 154
Oral incorporation wish, 163
Oral regression, 181, 182, 223, 224
Oral trauma, 39, 187, 224. *See also* fellatio.
Orestes complex, 17
Orientation in
  place, xiii, xiv
  time, xiii

P

Palpitations, 184, 197, 211, 212, 222, 226
Pants, 146, 232, 234, 251
Parents
  hostility between. *See* family fights.

sexual activity of, 23, 96, 106, 186
  See also family; father; mother.
Paresthesia, 184, 194, 204, 207, 215, 217, 226
Passive-aggressive behavior, 151
Peer relationships, 24, 50, 148, 164, 231
Penis, 104 f., 109, 113, 124, 125, 137, 159, 187
  inferiority, 102, 251
  wiping, 247
Perfume, 201
Personality
  in conversion reaction, 16
  expression in regression, 11
  in obsessive compulsive reaction, 15, 16, 17
  See also father; mother; specific features.
Perspiring, 30, 116
Pet loss, 36, 37 f., 45
Phenobarbital, 184
Phlegm, 57, 243. *See also* spittle.
Phobic reaction, 12, 21 ff., 28, 46, 72, 108, 143, 151, 152. *See also* specific phobias.
Photograph, 150, 234, 235, 248, 249, 253, 254
Physique, 251
Picture. *See* images; visualizations.
Picture hook, ix
Pinching, 132, 137, 144, 145
Pink, 220
Pipe, 103 ff., 109, 111, 117, 120 f., 124, 125, 135, 149
Policeman, 206, 207
Politics, 242
Pope, 176 f., 181
Possessions appropriated, 235, 251
Prelogic, 10
Privy, 158, 167, 168, 169, 170, 171
Projection, 7, 87, 162
Promises broken, 235, 236, 237, 238, 250, 251
Prompting, xv, 120
Pruritus, 228, 237, 238, 243, 246, 247
Psychical ego, 13 ff.
Psychoanalysis, xvi, 3 f., 5, 6, 228, 229, 237, 253
Psychoneurosis. *See* specific reactions.
Psychophysiologic reactions, 17 f., 184 ff.

cardiovascular, 184, 223
respiratory, 223, 228 ff.
skin, 228 ff.
visualizations in, 196, 199, 234 f., 237, 243, 248
Psychotherapy, xvi

Q

Questioning, xiv

R

Rabbi, 195, 225
Radicalism, 241, 242
Rats, 97, 189, 190, 191, 192
Reaction formation, 98, 153, 166
Reading, 160, 161, 243
Reading technique, xiv, 144, 145, 147, 168, 176, 237 ff.
Reality, 10, 71, 108
Recall, xii, xiii
Recitation, 167
Recordings, xii, xiii, xiv
playback of, xiii, xv, 47
Rectum, 113, 114, 158
Red, 41, 81, 113, 115, 147, 150, 167, 168, 170, 177, 181, 200, 201, 202, 205, 206, 213, 215, 218, 228, 237, 238, 239, 241, 251
Regression, xiv, 4, 5, 6, 7, 8, 10 f., 87, 111, 166
age in. *See* age.
behavior alteration in, 10, 11
discomfort during, xiv
ego and, xi, 7, 8, 9
in hypnosis, xvi, 9, 18
fluctuation in depth of and, xi
induction of, xi, xii
planned, xiii
psychophysiologic functioning in, 10
"two stage," 4
Rejection, 45, 49, 66, 229
compulsion, 17
of genitalia, 157, 159, 169, 170, 171, 180
of masculinity, 171
Religion, 44, 87, 116, 176, 177, 190
Repetition, 121, 182
Repression, 8, 11, 14 f., 16, 18, 138, 145
Reprojection, 7 f., 115, 120, 122, 127, 147

Resistance, x, 6, 107, 171, 197
Respiratory symptoms, 21, 33 ff., 39, 64, 193, 204, 209, 223, 228 ff.
See also colds; coughing; etc.
Responsibility, 54, 64, 68, 102, 129
Revivification, xiii, xiv, 4, 5, 8, 9, 11
Rhinoplasty, 96
Ridicule, 38, 39, 105, 198, 206, 231, 235, 238, 241, 249, 250
Ring, 150
Ritalin,®, 140
Rodent, 186, 205, 206, 216
Roof, 102, 111, 113, 116
Running away, 43, 53, 55, 164 f.

S

Sadism, 48, 66, 110
countercathexis to, 15
in distorted Oedipus complex, 163
in obsessive compulsive reaction, 13, 20
Satan, 242, 255. *See also* Devil.
Sausage, 100 f., 136 f.
Sealding, 49, 53, 56, 69
Scapegoat, 243
Schizophrenia, 95, 128
Schneck, 3, 10, 11, 80, 257
School experience, 24, 49 f., 102, 134, 135, 137, 146, 147, 160, 164, 165, 189, 207, 231, 233, 234
Scoptophilia, 96, 108, 115, 133, 134, 148, 227
Scratching, 237, 238, 240, 241. *See also* pruritus.
Seafood, 136. *See also* crab.
Self concept, 10
Self-consciousness, 95, 102
Self image, 10
Seminal fluid, 161, 163 f., 178, 182
Sentence length, 94, 196, 199, 211, 218
Sexual abuse. *See* abuse.
Sexual excitement
from choking, 69
Sexual fantasy, 51, 69 f., 102, 162 f., 168, 232
Sexual history, 23, 24, 51, 74, 75 f., 101 f., 136, 139, 158, 159, 160, 164, 165, 189
Sexual identification, 46, 99

Sexual inadequacy, 102, 168, 179, 182
Sexualization
  of equilibrium, 151
Sexual symbols, 137, 145 f., 148, 149. *See also* specific symbols.
Shaking, 53, 54, 55, 59, 62, 64, 66, 72, 81
Shame, 34, 107
Shaving, 62, 64, 102, 199
Shyness, 24, 50, 71, 95, 108, 130, 133, 139
Sibling
  death of, 74, 79 f., 96
  identification with, 35, 39, 46, 139
  illness of, 35, 39, 53, 62, 63, 69, 74, 96, 185, 234
  operation on, 249, 252, 253 f.
  relationships, 53, 54 f., 57, 64
  rivalry, 23, 33, 35, 36, 37, 39, 49, 139, 230, 231, 235, 236, 237, 242, 254
  Sexual fantasies about, 51, 69 f., 102, 232
  See also brother; sister.
Sillman, 17, 257
Sister
  -child relationship, 48 f., 51, 53 ff., 59 ff., 68 f., 101
  See also brother-sister relationship.
Skin, 237, 238, 240
Skin reaction, 228 ff.
Skirt, 175 f., 181
Sleep
  arrangements for, 23, 96, 132, 149, 150, 151, 152, 156, 160, 161, 187, 231, 232
  bodily ego and, 193, 198, 226 f.
  ego cathexis and, 11
  hypnosis as, xi
  talking in, 51
  walking in, 51, 52, 54
Slip of tongue, 55 f., 180
Smell. *See* odor.
Snakes, 189, 190, 216
Snow, 213
Social anxiety, 24, 50, 70 f., 95, 116, 135 f., 145
Somatic compliance, 31
Sore throat, 33, 35, 39
Spanking, 75. *See also* beating; whipping.
Spittle, 239, 240, 241, 242
Stage fright, 72

Stealing, 49, 52, 100, 131, 165, 232
Stick, 194, 196, 252
Stockings, 78, 81, 232, 255
Stomach language, xvii
Stress, 222, 225
Sublimation, 14
Subway, 143, 145
Suffocation, 111, 189, 226
Suggestion, 4, 52, 58, 71, 119, 122 ff.
Suicide, 21, 24, 39, 40, 49
Superego, 7 f., 14, 15, 16 f., 68, 107, 111, 112, 147, 181, 211, 218
Superstition, 97, 188, 225, 226
Surgery
  in childhood, 21, 50, 74, 75, 79, 81, 99, 103, 108, 114, 187, 189, 192, 193, 204, 224
  of genitalia, 165, 178 ff., 182, 242, 243, 249, 252, 253 f.
  of mother, 186, 187, 214, 224, 234
  of sibling, 249, 252, 253 f.
Swan, 144, 145
Swelling, 60, 187, 192, 193, 198, 199, 203, 204, 208, 211, 212, 213, 220, **227**
Swimming, 73, 130, 135, 145
Symbol
  conversion to body symptom, 212
  understanding of, 96
Symbolization, xii, xiii, 15, 94, 136, 152, 182
  change in, xiv, 5, 57 f., 59, 127, 137, 142, 168, 173, 174, 175, 178, 179, 203, 237 ff., 246
  in conversion reaction, 18, 47, 71, 94
  of emotion, 191, 205
  of infirmity, 82 ff., 85, 87, 89
  in obsessive compulsive reaction, 19, 20, 110
  odor and, 228
  reading technique, 144, 145, 147, 168, 176, 237 ff.
Symptom
  formation, 24, 212
    in conversion reaction, 15, 16, 18, 24, 33
    in obsessive compulsive reaction, 15
  substitute, 70
Synagogue, 242

T

Talking
compulsive, 153, 172, 231
difficulty in, 191, 195, 197, 206, 207, 208
Taste, bad, 33, 35, 39
Taunting. *See* ridicule.
Teasing. *See* ridicule.
Temper tantrums, 23, 75, 92
Testicles, 178 ff.
surgery of, 165, 178 ff., 182, 242, 243, 249, 252, 253 f.
Test taking, 81, 85
Theater technique, xiv, 137, 138, 139, 140 f., 162, 175
Thinking, 13, 15, 20, 111, 121
Throat
genitalization of, 60, 69
Thumb sucking. *See* finger sucking.
Ticking clock, 150, 151
Toilet, 20, 100, 102, 103, 104, 106, 109, 110, 111, 112, 113, 114, 134, 135, 137, 141, 142
training, 20, 99, 115, 133 f., 154, 172, 188, 221, 224, 230
Tongue pulling, 56, 68
Toothpicks, 142
Tower, 104, 108 f., 117, 118, 121
Trains, 136, 142
Trance, x, xi
Tranquilizers, 50, 62, 63, 65, 66
Transference, xiv, 4, 7, 16, 32, 37, 45, 57, 96, 166, 190, 208, 216, 218, 223
Treatment, silent, 156 ff.
Trembling. *See* jerking; shaking.
Tricycle. *See* bicycle.
Tuberculosis, 21, 24, 34, 35, 36, 39, 53, 62, 234
Turning into stone, 115

U

Unconscious, 12
archaic layers of, 5, 6
disturbing material from, xii, xiii
and hypnotizability, x
and visualizations, xvi
Underwear, 132
Undoing, 8, 19, 120, 127, 152
Urination, 35, 38, 51, 52, 54, 62, 105 f., 109, 125, 159, 163, 193, 194, 195, 196

V

Vagina. *See* genitalia.
Vagina dentata, 219
Vasomotor rhinitis, 76
Violin, 71, 188 f., 194, 197, 198, 199, 204, 205, 208, 215, 216
Viscera
affect expression of, 18
disorders of, 184 ff.
Visualizations, xii
age of patient. *See* age.
biphasic, 120
change in, 5, 137, 203, 240
modifying aspects of, 120
color in, *See* color.
in compulsive personality, 182
in conversion reaction, 18 f., 47, 70 f., 79, 86, 94, 228
episodic, 152
hypnosis depth and, 92
image variation during, xiv
isolation in, 152
letter symbols in. *See* reading technique.
in mixed psychoneurotic disorders, 20
movie technique in. *See* theater technique.
in obsessive compulsive reaction, 19 f., 110 f., 121, 128, 152
of past ego states, 110, 136, 139, 141, 149, 150, 152
in psychophysiologic reaction, 196, 199, 234 f., 237, 243, 248
reality demands and, 71
repetitions in, 121
of superego, 111, 112, 147, 211
symbolization in. *See* symbolization.
theater technique in. *See* theater technique.
of words. *See* reading technique.
Vocabulary, 80, 86, 94, 156, 196
Vocal cord ulcer, 154
Vomiting, 30, 65, 134
Voyeurism, 22, 133, 166

W

Wall, 118, 119, 121, 125, 127, 128
Warning, 23, 73, 100, 131, 202, 203, 205, 207, 220

Washing, 113, 232, 234

Watcher, 162

Water, 20, 100, 102 ff., 109, 111, 112, 114, 116, 117, 118, 121, 123, 135, 184
tanks, 102, 103, 105, 111

Watkins, 12, 257

Weaning, 26, 99, 142, 154

Weiss, E., 11, 18

Wet dream. *See* emission.

Wetting, 23, 26 f., 27, 29, 49, 150 f., 156, 217

Wheezing, 237 ff., 241

Whipping, 44, 75, 194. *See also* beating; spanking.

White, 78, 81, 177, 195, 196, 200, 201, 202, 205, 206, 212, 213, 215, 218, 234, 237, 238, 241, 246

Wife-mother relationship, 190

Will, 17, 182

Wine making, 48, 98 f., 109

Winner
identification with, 212

Wishes
forbidden, 108, 127
formulation of, 148
murderous, xv, 30, 65, 71, 108, 250. *See also* family-member destruction.

Witch, 213 f.

Wolberg, 3, 4, 257

Woman
idealization of, 163, 164, 168, 174, 175, 180, 181
phallic, 181, 182

Word visualization. *See* reading technique.

Working through, xvi, 5
in conversion reaction, 18 f., 42, 47, 94
and learning, xvi, 9
in obsessive compulsive reaction, 19, 121

Worms, 99, 100, 101, 102, 114, 115, 186

Y

Yellow, 135, 146, 148, 172 ff., 175, 181, 200, 201, 214

Many different color morphs exist within the species *Pseudotropheus zebra* of Lake Malawi. Photo by G. Marcuse.

· In these African lakes the cichlids also reach the peak of their diversity in regard to coloration, with a chromatic array approaching the brilliance of some of the tropical coral reef fishes. There is, however, no paucity of color among the cichlids of other aquatic systems of Africa or the waterways of Central and South America. Even the lake cichlids of Africa would be hard pressed to outshine a magnificent male Jack Dempsey, a mature Heckel discus, or a spawning pair of jewel fish.

By far the most intriguing aspect of the cichlid family after all things are considered is their breeding behavior. It would be difficult to describe the parental care displayed by cichlids without using adjectives which lend a certain personification to the creatures by characterizing their actions as motivated by human qualities such as anger or concern— which such creatures are supposedly incapable of feeling or expressing. The almost unbelievable displays of spouse selection, spawning site preparation, care of eggs and babies, and diverse manners in which they approach the business of pro-

7

Fry returning to the protection of a parent's mouth (*Geophagus juru-pari*). Mouthbrooding is only one of the diverse methods of parental care practiced by cichlids. Photo by Dr. O. Klee.

creation could hardly help but warm the coldest and most scientific of hearts.

Because cichlids are generally larger than most tropicals, are often territorial or even aggressive, and show more individualism than most other freshwater tropicals, it is not surprising that keeping and breeding them effectively requires certain techniques and considerations. This book ventures into the basic care and quartering of these fascinating fishes as well as the various refinements of their reproduction.

II. WHERE CICHLIDS COME FROM

The family Cichlidae is a large and widespread group of fishes found in South and Central America (with one species, *Cichlasoma cyanoguttatum*, occuring northward into Texas), throughout most of Africa and Madagascar, and one genus occurring in India and Sri Lanka.

While many of today's aquarists think primarily of Africa when cichlids come to mind, with the exception of a few species most of the aquarium cichlids which have been available until a relatively few years ago have been from South and Central America. One of the first tropical fishes kept in America was the chanchito, *Cichlasoma facetum*, of Argentina. A number of other American cichlids arrived on the scene and stuck, such as the Jack Dempsey, *C. octofasciatum*, the port cichlid, *Aequidens portalegrensis*, and of course the magnificent fish which ruled as "King of the Aquarium" for half a century, the angelfish, *Pterophyllum scalare*. Through these and a number of other cichlids which were to become "standards" the aquarium world was introduced to the fascination of such intense parental care and such close family relationships that it was almost unbelievable to the uninitiated. As a matter of fact it still is!

A few Africans such as the jewel fish, *Hemichromis bimaculatus*, the Egyptian mouthbrooder, *Pseudocrenilabrus multicolor*, and the Mozambique mouthbrooder, *Sarotherodon mossambica*, drifted in over the years. It was not until the mid-1950's, however, that Africa began to relinquish the almost overwhelming array of piscine treasures encompassed in her waters in numbers which put them in reach of the

9

aquarium hobbyist. Among them were not only fantastic creatures such as elephant-noses and butterfly-fish, which until then had remained almost legendary as far as the aquarist was concerned, but there were also large and small cichlids so varied as to make any cichlid lover's mouth water. These first shipments, which subsequently became known in the aquarium world as "the Congo bonanza," were only the beginning. Fishes like *Nanochromis, Haplochromis* and *Pelvicachromis* (including the beautiful "kribensis," *P. pulcher*) had whetted the appetite of aquarists who were seeing literally dozens of new species imported weekly. Collectors expanded into other parts of the Dark Continent, partially as a natural progression and partially because in a few years political problems in the Congo made collecting increasingly difficult.

It was at this point that Africa's Great Lakes or Rift Lakes, especially Lakes Malawi and Tanganyika began to contribute their unique resources, which amounted to an unimaginably rich and unique assortment of jewel-like cichlids. These strange, varied and often almost gaudy creatures had managed to speciate in some of the lakes so intensely that they had, within this single family, filled almost every available ecological niche.

Pelvicachromis pulcher ("kribensis") was among the beautiful fishes imported during the "Congo bonanza." Photo by R. Zukal.

The orange chromide, *Etroplus maculatus,* occurs in India and Sri Lanka. It and the green chromide, *E. suratensis,* form a faunal link between the freshwater fishes of India and those of Africa. Photo by K. Nilsson.

It would be unfair not to mention the royalty of the cichlid world. The discus species, *Symphysodon discus* and *Symphysodon aequifasciata*, are unquestionably among the most majestic of fishes and are native to the Amazon Basin and surrounding areas. Although less fantastic in its proliferation of desirable cichlids than the Rift Lakes, the Amazon does have a wealth of spectacular and intriguing cichlids.

Represented by only two species, the orange chromide (*Etroplus maculatus*) and the green chromide (*Etroplus suratensis*), the Asian branch of the cichlid family inhabits Sri Lanka and India. The orange chromide lives as much as sixty miles inland while the green or striped chromide, as it is sometimes called, is found only in brackish and salt waters along the coast. The chromides are significant in that they form a faunal link between the freshwater fishes of India and those of Africa.

The island of Madagascar, which is now known as the Malagasy Republic, also has its endemic population of cichlids mostly in the genus *Paretroplus*.

III. THE CICHLID AQUARIUM

Although some of the so-called "dwarf" cichlids will do well and even reproduce in small aquariums of five gallons or less, generally the cichlid aquarium should be as large and roomy as possible. Since many species express their territorialism by staking out a corner, a rock or a particular plant or other object, any tendency toward quarrelsomeness or aggression is minimized by allowing each fish enough room to feel comfortable. Only a few years ago large aquariums were prohibitively expensive and were rather rare in anything above the three-foot length and thirty- to fifty-gallon size. Today larger, sturdier and less expensive aquariums are available, and they come in a much wider assortment of shapes and sizes so as to fit the needs of the decorator as well as the builder. These changes from conventional forms benefit the breeder and fishkeeper, especially in the case of cichlids since the form and shape, as well as the gallon capacity, can play a definite role in the temperament and behavior of many cichlids.

Water is heavy, something near 8.3 lbs. per gallon. A long, narrow tank which is perhaps four feet long and twelve inches wide not only has better weight distribution, it has a decided advantage over the earlier and chunkier types, which were perhaps three feet in length and eighteen inches thick, when one is concerned with fishes which are disposed to taking an occasional whack at each other. The longer tank, although its gallon capacity and weight may be the same as the stockier model, in effect presents a larger territory of sorts. There are, of course, exceptions and some of the very tall aquariums which are popular today can be quite appropriate for cichlids such as angelfish and discus because of their extreme vertical development. Tall aquariums can also be adapted to some of the extremely colorful lake cichlids of Africa by building a tall labyrinth of caves up a side or back wall to function as retreats if one or another of them becomes overly aggressive. Such a network of caves also lends an air of security to the entire cichlid population of such an aquarium, resulting in not only a maximum color display but in overcoming any initial shyness the fish might have toward their surroundings.

Territories are three dimensional: they can often be laid out vertically as well as horizontally. If large rocks or pieces

Large rocks properly arranged form caves and shelves which become defended territories. A *Melanochromis auratus* male patrols the perimeter of his rocky home territory. Photo by Dr. Herbert R. Axelrod.

of driftwood are spaced so that the aquarium is divided into well-defined "sections" of suitable size to allow the proprietors plenty of "elbow room," additional territories may often be designated by shelves, ledges or other overhead or vertically definable objects.

While natural plants have little chance in the presence of most cichlids because of their landscaping tendencies and the fondness of many for vegetable fare, some of the more realistic plastic plants can be used to tasteful advantage. If such plastic plants are to be used in an aquarium with large cichlids it is wise to anchor them to the bottom glass or slate of the aquarium by cementing the anchor "cups" in place with silicone rubber sealant. This must be done, of course, while the aquarium is dry, adding sand and water after the sealant has cured. Some plastic plants are equipped with small plastic "pins" which are inserted through a center hole in the anchor cup and pushed into the bottom of the plant "stem." Alternately the pin itself may be glued to the aquarium floor rather than the entire cup.

Silicone sealant is also excellent for use in forming permanent cave structures out of rocks, pieces of shale, etc. A very useful structural form for beginning a cave is a flower pot cut in half vertically and placed on its side so that a basic cave-like structure is formed. This can then be covered with pieces of rock or shale which are glued in place with the silicone. It is important to use only the silicone rubber sealant which is made specifically for aquarium use since bathtub sealant or other special purpose types may contain toxic chemicals designed to retard the growth of fungus, etc.

IV. LIGHTING THE CICHLID AQUARIUM

Aquarium lighting primarily has two functions. First and most obvious is to allow the aquarist to observe his charges going about the daily business of living and in general to illuminate the underwater scene. The other is to provide the light necessary to promote photosynthesis if plants are to be grown in the aquarium. Photosynthesis is the process by which plants, when exposed to the sun's energy (or suitable light) convert it, if supplied with the proper nutrients, into carbohydrates and other useful food substances while at the same time producing oxygen. Remember, however, that plants respire and in the absence of enough light will utilize more oxygen. For bringing out colors and growing fine plants, natural sunlight is unbeatable at its best and uncontrollable at its worst. Although natural sunlight can be a blessing, it can also be a scourge.

While over-the-shoulder sunlight can illuminate fishes producing radiances which the aquarist never even knew were there, unfortunately in many cases it is difficult to find a location which leaves enough room for the viewer to get between the aquarium and the light source since the place most likely to be available is in front of a window. This light from the window illuminates the tank, but from the wrong direction since the fish are silhouetted. For those with the good fortune to have picture windows and glass doors capable of effusing bright, natural light across the room or to a center-placed aquarium in mid-room, terrific! Even this, however, does not solve the problem of having the correct amount of light where you want it when you want it. The sun simply refuses to stay over and beyond one's shoulder twenty-four hours a day.

Aquarium hoods equipped with fluorescent tubes are the answer. Fluorescent lighting is cool in operation and uses relatively little energy. The tubes are also available in certain models which were designed to promote the growth of living plants. Certain frequencies of the color spectrum which are favorable to plants are emphasized. As it happens the colors of many fishes and other objects are dramatized by these same wave lengths. While it is futile to try to keep plants with many of the larger species, such as *Cichlasoma* and *Tilapia*, many cichlids are at least partially vegetarian, especially some from the African lakes. However, the plant growing tubes also promote the growth of algae which are eaten with relish by a number of species.

Many cichlid keepers prefer full-hood lighting fixtures on their aquariums. These can be decorative in themselves, often being finished in walnut-grained vinyl or some similar "furniture" finish which is easily kept clean by wiping periodically with a damp cloth. There are no openings for the

It is futile to try to keep live plants in with many of the cichlids. This *Aequidens pulcher* has made short work of these plants. Photo by R. Zukal.

Many aquarists prefer to keep their tanks fully covered. It would be a shame to lose fish such as this *Apistogramma agassizi* by having them jump out of the tank. Photo by C. Milan.

fish to jump out of and the full cover cuts down considerably on evaporation and heat loss. There are generally "punch-out" or "cut-out" openings at the back to provide entrance for filtration, aeration and heating equipment and some models even have an enclosed "tray" in the hood for keeping food, thermometer, net and any other items which come into constant use.

Fluorescent strip lights are also popular. They cover only a portion of the aquarium, sliding backward or forward leaving either the front or back few inches open. This is hardly a problem, since sliding aquarium glass covers are available for almost every tank size. In one type two sheets of glass ride in "tracks" so that the front glass easily slides back and forth for feeding, etc. The rear glass has a plastic fitting on the edge which can be cut out for filters, heaters, etc.

While strip lights are perhaps a bit less "customized" in appearance than some of the full hoods, they are also available with the "walnut look." Combined with the sliding glass cover, the strip light has a good appearance and offers most advantages of the full hood. The glass cover also has the advantage of keeping the light fixture from getting wet. For the latter purpose, cover glasses should also be used even with full hoods, not only to keep parts of the light from prematurely corroding but also for safety.

V. WATER REQUIREMENTS

Most of the larger and more robust cichlids are not too particular about their water quality as far as pH and DH are concerned. These are the terms used to indicate the relative acidity or alkalinity (pH) and the relative hardness (DH) of aquarium water. The pH is determined by a number of factors including various solubles in the water, while DH or "degrees hardness" refers to the amount of dissolved calcium and magnesium salts present. The more of these compounds present, the more difficult it is for soap to sud. One of the oldest and still extensively used tests for determining water hardness is called the "soap test" since a standard liquid soap solution is added, drop by drop, to a given amount of water until it can be shaken to form a "permanent" lather, i.e. one which will stand for a number of minutes.

Pure water is neutral in pH, or pH 7.0 based on a scale from 1-14, the lower numbers being extremely acid and the higher numbers extremely alkaline. Aquarium water usually ranges between 6.0 and 8.0. A pH of 6.6 to 6.8 is considered mildly acid; pH 7.2 to 7.4 is considered mildly alkaline.

It is easily understood how heavy tropical rainfall, which washes over the jungle floor of the rainforest composed of over hundreds of years of decaying vegetation, can leach sizable amounts of tannic and humic acids from the forrest floor as it runs off into the rivers and streams. In some areas the resulting dissolved acids and other materials become so concentrated that the water in the rivers, even where they are otherwise quite clear and transparent, become the color of tea. As the waters of rivers and tributaries intermingle there is sometimes, depending on the terrain which has fed the streams, a deep contrast in color where the waters well together.

Besides the rainforest streams, which take their chemical qualities from the expired forest growths, other waterways have their pathways through limestone and other calcium or magnesium deposits which become dissolved in the water along with other minerals. In contrast to the tea-colored waters which remain relatively free of mineral content and often result in water which is not only rather acid but also extremely soft, water which flows over limestone deposits is quite likely to be both hard and alkaline. Between these two extremes are all sorts of variations. There are also the highly alkaline lakes in East and Central Africa which have water which is very salty and quite hard. Many of our

Many of the African lake cichlids such as this *Lamprologus brichardi* from Lake Tanganyika require very hard and alkaline water. Photo by H.J. Richter.

most gorgeous cichlids come from African lakes which seem almost to have been sculpted from chalky rock.

Obviously, fishes from such widely opposing environments cannot be tossed immediately into an aquarium together and thrive. Cichlids are, for the most part, sturdy and adaptable creatures which, through several aquarium generations, will sooner or later adapt to most situations. It is safe to say that the majority of cichlid species will do quite well in most water conditions which occur locally. There are, of course, exceptions such as discus and angelfish which require reasonably soft water for breeding and some of the Lake cichlids of Africa which require hard, alkaline water to be at their best. There are even some which are found in brackish water and prefer an addition of marine salt to their aquarium.

One thing which cichlids have in common is that frequent partial changes of water are important. There was a time when "aged" water or "old" water was considered a must when keeping and breeding so-called "Problem-fische" or problem fishes such as neons, discus, *Aphyosemion*, etc. Some expert aquarists, especially in Europe, carried this to such an extreme that they considered water less than two or three months old to be "new water" taking a full measure of pride in water which was yellowed with the age of many months. This theory has been reversed in more modern aquariology and fishkeepers today remove and replace as much as a quarter or a third of their aquarium water weekly or biweekly. This removes urine and other soluble wastes from the water which otherwise would build up to the detriment of the fish involved. Reaction to water change is immediate and rather striking in the increased activity, intensified coloration and overall improved "looks" of the fish.

VI. TEMPERATURE

Since cichlids are restricted for the most part to tropical waters in nature, in the aquarium they prefer warm water. Generally, a temperature range of 70-80°F. is preferable, although lower temperatures of 65° or even 60° will be tolerated for short times by most. At low temperatures, however, they become quite lethargic. Large specimens withstand chill much better than smaller ones, returning to their normal state as soon as the correct temperature is restored.

While many authorities recommend gradual temperature change to bring fish out of a chilled state, in the author's experience there is less danger of losing cichlids which have suffered extreme chill by adding warm water slowly but steadily over a ten minute or even less period of time until a more normal temperature, perhaps in the lower or mid-70's, is reached. Most fishes, including cichlids, are more susceptible to diseases and parasites after being subjected to extreme chill and should be observed closely.

Breeding temperatures for most cichlids are in the 78-82° range, although cichlids will spawn at considerably lower temperatures upon occasion. Hatching time and growth will be slower at lower temperatures.

High temperatures of 82-85°F. are useful in the treatment of many of the more common fish maladies such as ich or "ick" and velvet (*Oodinium*) since the high temperatures make the diseases cycle more rapidly, allowing medication to work more effectively.

There is a rather remarkable phenomenon occurring in certain areas of North America which illustrates not so much the temperature tolerance of certain cichlids as their adaptability to temperature situations. One of the first occurrences of such an unusual temperature situation, as far as I am aware, happened just a few miles from my own home in Texas.

One morning several years ago some friends of mine who work for the Texas Parks and Wildlife Department called saying that they had been seining that morning in an area lake and had an unusual fish which they hoped I might help identify. About an hour later they showed up with a very large perch-like fish in a bucket of water cold enough to make their teeth rattle. It was mid-winter and a miserable wet, cold and generally nasty day with a temperature in the 30's. The fish, still alive, was stiff with the cold and seemed destined for that big oceanarium in the sky. Since drastic measures seemed to be called for, he was placed in an aquarium where the water was about 70°F.

The fish appeared to be a *Tilapia* at first glance. Subsequent checking revealed it to be *Tilapia aurea*, obviously not a native Texan. I recalled that during the previous summer a local ichthyologist had discovered a nearby bait dealer selling *Tilapia* for catfish bait. As it happened, someone had apparently bought *Tilapia* for bait and released those which were unused into the lake. This was a happy situation for the *Tilapia*, for in warm weather this particular lake is loaded with vegetation and other organisms which they thrive upon. Winters, however, are colder in Texas than in the areas of Africa where *Tilapia* abound, and the winter water temperatures would surely have killed them if it had not been for what was quite a remarkable shot at survival.

The lake involved had been constructed by a power company to furnish electrical power. There is a canal which runs to the lake from the generating equipment and as the water passes over the turbines it becomes heated. As winter approached and the water became chilled, the *Tilapia*, which had reproduced in the meantime, had the "foresight" to move into the man-made, warm water effluent to spend the winter. The fish that had been brought to me was seined from this canal along with a number of others which I was

Some cichlids are extremely hardy and tolerant of adverse conditions. *Tilapia aurea* is one of the more resistant species. Photo by G. Timmerman.

given later. The reason for the fish becoming so chilled was that water was taken from another part of the lake instead of from the heated waters of the canal where the fish was captured.

This was several years ago. Each winter, when the water begins to become intolerably cold, the *Tilapia* (at least some of them) return to the warm water canal. In spring when waters warm sufficiently, they disperse once more throughout the lake to forage and reproduce.

At the time of this writing the large male fish, which incidentally survived his chilly ordeal, is still a show specimen in a very large aquarium containing assorted large fishes.

23

VII. FILTRATION

Nowhere has there been more progress made toward the evolution of fish keeping to its present degree of refinement than in the area of aquarium filtration. Filtration is the process through which the aquarium water goes through continual cleaning. This can consist of physical removal of waste, debris, uneaten food etc. or the conversion of these products into harmless and inoffensive substances. It may even be a combination of both.

Most aquarists who have taken even a partial interest in the family Cichlidae are familiar with the more commonly used aquarium filter types such as the inside or bottom filter, the outside filter, the several types of motor driven power filters and the undergravel or biological filter. It should not be necessary to rehash in this book what each does except in the very briefest terms since this has been done quite adequately in other volumes.

Mechanical filtration is simply the removal of solid waste and other materials by passing the water through a "bed" of synthetic wool, charcoal or some other substance which removes the undesirable material from it and returns the water to the tank in a state of comparative clarity. When the wool or other medium becomes dirty or clogged, it is removed and replaced.

Biological filtration, on the other hand, utilizes a system in which the filter medium through which water is drawn contains harmless bacteria. The bacteria feed upon the unwanted substances until they are converted into harmless by-products which are no longer noticeable *as long as the filter system isn't overworked.* Such biological filter systems usually employ a gravel-covered perforated "wall-to-wall" (or glass-to-glass) plate which is set just above the aquarium floor, with airlift tubes at the two back corners. As water is "lifted" by a stream of air bubbles through these tubes, it is drawn from beneath the plate, causing replacement water to flow downward through the gravel, through the plate and back out the bubbling airlift. This action traps the waste in the gravel where it is attacked by bacteria which convert it to ammonia, nitrites and finally nitrates, each progressively less harmful than the foregoing. The last byproduct is useful in nourishing plants.

A similar system is employed when using "sponge" type filters, which are nothing more than a piece of polyurethane (or other) sponge into which an airlift has been incorporated so that water is drawn through the *sponge* instead of a separate bed of gravel. The bacterial colony builds up in the sponge, converting wastes which the flow of water brings in into nitrates. The filtered water is returned through the airlift to the tank. These "sponge" filters are excellent when a temporary aquarium with filtration needs to be set up quickly for newly received fish, or when an "outlaw" needs to be isolated.

Where sponge-type filters really shine, however, is in an aquarium where baby fish are present since the tiny openings in the sponge will neither trap baby fish or tiny live food such as baby brine shrimp. Performing the dual function of both aeration and filtration, they are ideal for a bare tank situation where eggs have been placed to hatch separately from the parents. Until hatching or perhaps the free-swimming stage at least an air stone should also be used to insure adequate circulation near the eggs since the air stone can be more accurately placed. Also, if acriflavine, methylene blue or other dyes have been added to the water for the protection of the eggs it is best not to start the filter until the eggs have hatched since the dyes will be removed.

Sponge filters are also quite useful in the larger and more established breeding tank. Other filtration can be stopped while two or three sponge filters do an admirable job of

A bare tank with an airstone is best for raising baby fishes. The addition of a sponge-type filter will make this tank complete.

interim filtration until more ordinary procedures can be resumed. The sponge filter works biologically but there are occasions when it may become overworked and obviously loaded with waste and detritus. A couple of good squeezes and rinses under running water will put it back in top operating condition.

The more familiar undergravel filtration system, while it is invaluable in marine aquaria and many other applications, is not recommended as a top choice for most cichlid aquariums. To operate at maximum efficiency the aquarium gravel should be about three-sixteenths of an inch (2-5 mm) in size. This is too large if babies are present since it will not only suck the tiny morsels of food provided for the youngsters beneath the gravel, it may also trap the babies themselves on occasion if they try to follow living shrimp or microworms into the gravel or if they become frightened and dive into the medium just far enough to get stuck. Finer sand is an alternative, but the efficiency is much less and the chance to establish a healthy bacterial colony, which is the heart of the system, will be diminished. This offers a greater chance for contamination of the gravel, which has possibly led to the demise of more healthy aquarium fish in the past twenty years than any other factor.

A primary reason against undergravel filtration in most cichlid aquariums is that the majority of cichlids are diggers and excavators of the first order. Not only do many of them continually rearrange the landscape but their pits and holes are diligently dug all the way to what seems bedrock, which is the perforated filter plate. This obviously destroys the whole filtration procedure.

A combination of aeration (air stones) and power filtration is recommended for cichlid aquariums because of the high rate of water flow available in power filters and the supplemental gas exchange and additional circulation created by the aeration. The fast flow of a power filter removes

Because of the digging habits of cichlids, undergravel filters are not recommmended. The fishes would soon uncover the filter, making it useless. Photo of *Tilapia* sp. by C. Milan.

large quantities of waste which might otherwise accumulate. This waste removal is actually enhanced by the air stone which creates water currents which aid in keeping particles in circulation until they are filtered out. Power filters come in many shapes and forms. Most familiar, perhaps, is the outside power filter which is similar to the classic air driven outside filter. Others have hoses for intake and output leading from the aquarium to a pump-driven canister containing the filter material which is usually synthetic fiber (floss) or a combination of this and charcoal.

Other filters are useful in cichlid keeping, but mostly in a supplementary capacity. For general house cleaning, which is a good idea to undertake every few weeks at least in an aquarium of large cichlids or one which is relatively crowded, the diatom filter will do a superb job. It scours the sand and washes sediment and detritus out of cracks and corners as its fast flow and rather concentrated output stir the aquarium well while the tiny pores presented by the diatomaceous earth coating on the filter bag will remove micronsized particles leaving the water sparkling clear. Its usefulness is perhaps limited to major cleaning jobs of this sort by its great efficiency since its effective removal of the tiniest particles soon leaves the filtering surface clogged and laden with waste. Cleaning requires disassembly of the filter, washing it and replacing the diatom powder, reassembly and restarting, which is a somewhat less convenient procedure than cleaning less efficient filters but which last longer between floss changes.

VIII. FEEDING REQUIREMENTS

Cichlids are quite diverse in their feeding habits, one species or another utilizing almost every conceivable food source which might be available. Some feed primarily on other fishes, others prey upon insects and insect larvae. Still others are almost exclusively vegetarian in nature, feeding on algae and other aquatic vegetation. There are even those so specialized as to feed upon the eyes which they bite from other fishes or eat the scales which they pluck from the sides of others. Fortunately, feeding cichlids in the aquarium does not necessarily encompass all their specialties and the aquarist can keep most species in excellent condition by utilizing a few foods to which almost all respond.

Most cichlids will accept meat, whether they are vegetarian by nature or not. Beef heart is excellent, not only because of its excellent nutritive qualities, but because even when finely ground it is a relatively "clean" food which does not tend to cloud the water. Liver is also excellent, although it should be combined with some sort of "binder" if it is blended or finely ground for small fish; otherwise it causes definite clouding and pollution problems. A reasonable "binder" is oatmeal. Pureed liver can be mixed with oatmeal and the two cooked together. There are those who wish to carry this binding process even further, adding cooked spinach, raw fish and numerous other ingredients which add various nutritive qualities to the resulting mixture. After combining ingredients and cooking them, adding enough water to end up with a product of regular oatmeal-type consistency, the mixture should be chilled and packaged in containers which will last for several days' feeding. Keep one container in the refrigerator for immediate use and freeze the others so that they can be pulled out as needed.

Beef heart can also be "stretched," not only adding a note of economy but actually somewhat supplementing its food quality which is already excellent. Two cups of blended beef heart can be mixed with one or even two packages of plain gelatin (prepared according to directions on the package). While still warm, this mixture can be spread rather thinly (¼") on a cookie sheet or similar receptacle, chilled until jelled, and then sliced with a butter knife into strips or even "worms." These "worms" are quite appealing to large cichlids as they appear to flutter and wiggle on their way to the bottom. Or the warm mixture may be allowed to cool enough to lose most of its "sticky" qualities and then rolled into individual balls about the right size for one feeding. Gelatin is practically pure protein, adding its own value to the heart.

Many cichlids at maturity are able to ingest large live foods such as mealworms and earthworms, both of which are excellent live foods which can be easily cultured. Mealworms are actually not worms, but the larvae of a beetle. They are kept in and feed on wheat bran, which is available from dealers in livestock feed, where they grow rapidly at room temperature. They soon turn into pupae, an intermediate stage which looks almost like a light-colored, legless beetle, and finally into the beetle stage. When beetles are seen crawling around in the culture production has started since they lay eggs every day. Each egg becomes a mealworm, tiny at first but later reaching perhaps an inch in length. They are dry and perfectly clean and can be picked right from the bran. When gathering large quantities put a double handful of the bran containing worms on a piece of newspaper and flatten it out a bit. After letting it settle for a couple of minutes, the meal can be gently dumped back into the culture container, leaving a great number of mealworms clinging to the paper. These can be picked up in whatever sizes needed. Culture containers for mealworms must have smooth, sloping sides to keep the worms and beetles from climbing out.

Mealworms (larvae of a beetle) are one of the recommended foods for cichlids. Shown are two adult beetles, three pupae, and assorted larvae (mealworms). Photo by R. Gannon.

An enamel dishpan is good. Moisture for the beetle and worm population can be provided by periodically quartering a small potato or piece of fruit (not citrus).

Earthworms are excellent for larger cichlids and can also easily be cultured. An old styrofoam fish shipping box, half filled with peat moss and half with good garden soil, is an ideal culture box for earthworms. They can be fed on coffee grounds, starchy table scraps, occasional oatmeal and bread crusts, etc. The lid, which usually fits fairly well, is used to keep the worms from climbing out and to retain moisture. It also keeps predators such as mice and ants out of the box. Punch two or three holes in the bottom to keep water from collecting. Soil should be moist but not wet and the box is best kept in a fairly cool location.

While earthworms to use as "seed" stock can easily be collected at certain times of year, perhaps the best way to get a "start" is to check the classified ad section of any leading hunting and fishing or outdoors magazine under the heading "Live Bait." Gardening magazines also carry such ads and fine, hybrid red wiggler earthworms which are just bite size for large cichlids can be often be purchased for about $4-8/1,000 postpaid. This is enough to begin using and still have plenty for breeding since they are very prolific. Breeding instructions are often included.

Cichlids are fond of all live foods which are commonly available, including tubifex worms, live brine shrimp, and such collectable types as daphnia, *Gammarus* (the little freshwater shrimp which is often found in plants) and mosquito larvae. Small fishes such as baby guppies are a true delicacy, especially to angelfish which put on a real show in pursuit of such a treat.

Frozen foods are excellent and are used as staple food by some aquarists, but with cichlids of medium and larger sizes this can become rather expensive. Frozen brine shrimp, blood worms, etc. can be quite adequately supplemented with high quality flake foods, pellet-type food, chopped or scraped frozen fish, and all manner of tantalizing tidbits. One of the more recent introductions which seems to be an almost perfect answer to cichlid feeding is freeze dried plankton such as euphausiids. These bite-size shrimps are tremendously abundant in the marine waters of the Pacific Northwest and are a primary food item for salmon and other game fish. In the aquarium, there could hardly be a more choice morsel for medium and larger fishes.

Some of the king-size cichlids such as oscars, *Astronotus ocellatus*, appreciate really large living food such as live goldfish, minnows, or crayfish. Not only is such fare expensive on a regular basis (unless one seines his own minnows or traps his own crayfish) but there is the risk of introducing disease any time wild fish are placed in an aquarium and crayfish are known to be the intermediate host of certain types of parasitic copepods. Somehow, except for an occasional treat, pieces of fresh or frozen fish, pieces of liver or pieces of beef heart seem more practical and sensible.

For the vegetarian section of the clan, such as many of the Malawi cichlids, many *Tilapia*, etc., few things could be more suitable than the algae which grows   prolifically, often undesirably, in outdoor ponds. Some cichlids are very fond of duckweed. Cooked spinach, either canned or fresh,

Oscars, *Astronotus ocellatus,* appreciate live foods such as goldfish, minnows or crayfish. Photo by Dr. Herbert R. Axelrod.

Freeze-dried foods are as popular among cichlids as they are among other aquarium species. Photo by Dr. Herbert R. Axelrod.

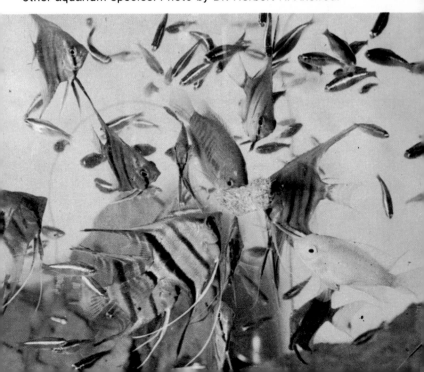

Many of the Malawi cichlids are vegetarians or partially so in their native habitat. Fishes such as *Labeotropheus fuelleborni* should receive some vegetable matter in their diet. Photo by G. Marcuse.

are eaten by many vegetarian cichlids. Some are fond of celery tops and fresh leaf lettuce. Both of these may be "softened" somewhat by freezing and thawing, making them easier to tear apart.

Feeding cichlids, as with other aquarium fishes, is perhaps the most enjoyable part of the avocation. To feed fishes, especially the large and deliberate fishes such as these and the small and retiring members of the family, is an acquired skill. After some time one can tell by the "expression" of a given fish whether it is hungry or merely seeking attention. Feeding is better accomplished at least two or three times per day in smaller amounts than once a day in a larger amount. Give the fish enough, but always leave them just short of being fully satisfied. Above all, don't leave uneaten food in the tank.

IX. BREEDING CICHLIDS

To witness the nuptial activities of "typical" cichlids is an experience which will never be forgotten. While several approaches to the proliferation of their kind are employed by cichlids, such as rock and substrate spawning, mouthbrooding, cave spawning and spawning on the leaves of sturdy plants, cichlids almost invariably seem to show a degree of "concern" for their progeny. This seems almost out of place in the cold-blooded world of fishes and it seldom fails to make the heart of a romantic beat a little faster. Scientists tell us that such "concern" is instinctive, a mere reflex, and yet, it hardly seems so superficial.

While there are intricacies separating spawning procedures of even very closely related and similar species, cichlids generally can be placed in one of several typical groups according to basic similarities and basic differences. To give an idea of how these spawning groups differ, typical representatives of the various approaches are described separately.

THE "BASIC" CICHLID

There is not a better beginner's cichlid than *Aequidens portalegrensis*, commonly known as the "port" or "port cichlid." Also called the brown acara, lace cichlid and black acara, a more steadfast, exemplary parental guardian of their offspring could not be found.

For many years this was perhaps the most popular cichlid, with the exception of the angelfish, although it is not as often seen as it once was. It has, however, introduced a mul-

Substrate spawners like this *Aequidens curviceps* first meticulously clean a suitable spawning site (above). After several false starts the female begins depositing eggs on the rock and is immediately followed by the male, which fertilizes them. They often follow each other in circles over the rock surface (below). Photos by H.J. Richter.

After hatching the fry are often moved to "safer" grounds, usually a pit dug by one or both of the parents in another part of the tank. Photo by H.J. Richter.

titude of aquarists to the fascination of cichlid breeding and a description of its activities during selection, courtship and spawning will always seem to many of us a prime example of "typical" cichlid breeding procedure.

Ports are among the "medium-large" to "large" cichlids. They are robust of build and hardy in nature. They live for years and become more handsome with age, as do many cichlids. In large quarters with good care ports may reach six or seven inches, although most remain smaller. They have a wide tolerance for water conditions, temperature and feeding requirements and in general are an excellent representative of its far-flung family.

Male and female ports are rather similar in appearance with the male being perhaps a bit more ornate. He has a handsome, lace-like pattern formed by dark-edged scales and a delicate pattern which carries the lace-like effect onto the dorsal, caudal and anal fins. The main sexual differences, as with most larger cichlids, such as *Cichlasoma* and *Aequidens*, two of South America's common genera, are the longer, more elaborate and more pointed dorsal and anal fin tips. The basic color for both sexes is normally a rather golden brown which at times can turn quite dark ("black" acara). The typical midside "cichlid spot" is present, although at times it may fade into the lacy, golden brown pattern.

An interesting legendary account of how cichlids in general came to have this "cichlid spot" is derived from Luke's New Testament documentation of the Miraculous Draught. Jesus had gone to the shore of the Sea of Galilee and found two ships which had returned after a night of fruitless fishing. As the fishermen were drying their nets. He went aboard one of the ships and asked the fisherman, Simon, to take the ship back out and try again. The big, rough fisherman undoubtedly was somewhat less then elated over the prospect of putting out again after just having spent a sleepless night without any luck, but the stranger must have impressed him and he did as he was asked. No sooner were the nets out than they began to fill and soon they were bulging. The nets even were beginning to break and they called for the aid of the

The *Tilapia* spot is located at the base of the dorsal fin. In this *Tilapia galilaea* it is ocellated with white. Photo by G. Marcuse.

other ship. When finally the fish were all aboard they were so heavy that the vessels started to sink. According to the legend, many of the fish were *Tilapia*, which are common in the lake. Simon started picking up fish and throwing them overboard to lighten the load. Where his thumb on one side and his forefinger on the other touched these cichlids as he picked them up, a black ocellus or spot was formed and to this day many of the world's cichlids bear this mark.

Ports will usually breed at about three inches length. When two prospective mates find each other there is often a test of strength to determine their fitness for each other. If both are in breeding condition, they will challenge each other face to face, circle each other with fins flared while "tail slapping" and otherwise attempting to bluff each other into retreating. If they are well matched they eventually will lock jaws, roll over, shaking and twisting, and perhaps losing their grip so that they have to re-lock their jaws. In well-matched pairs the amount of physical thrust with which each faces the other can be remarkably equal, neither giving an inch as they slug it out toe-to-toe. This ritual may last only

There is no better beginner's cichlid than the ever-popular *Aequidens portalegrensis*. The spawning site is first cleared of all debris (upper photo, opposite page). Spawning itself typically occurs with the male following the female and fertilizing the eggs as they are laid (lower photo, opposite page). Once spawning is completed the eggs are fiercely guarded (above). Photos by R. Zukal.

a few minutes or extend even up to an hour or more, often resulting in rather bruised and bloody lips. Once satisfied with the physical prowess and determination of each other, they begin to hunt for a suitable depository for their precious spawn.

Ports prefer a hard, smooth surface such as a large, flat rock. Once selected, the site is literally "scrubbed" with their teeth, biting, scraping and polishing every inch. Often one partner will alternate with the other in digging several pits around the rock and removing any plants in the immediate area which might obstruct their view, while the other polishes the spawning site, then vice versa.

Usually within a day or two the pair have developed little nipple-like protuberances at the vent or anal opening; the female's is called an ovipositor, meaning "egg placer." When spawning is imminent, the female, easily distinguished by her larger and quite blunt ovipositor, will begin trial runs, scooting over the surface of the rock. The male follows and after a few runs the eggs are placed, one by one, with a touch of this breeding tube. A row of eggs is laid and she steps aside so that the male can fertilize the eggs behind her. The fish spell each other until all the eggs, which may be 100-1,000 depending on the size and condition of the fish, have been deposited.

When spawning has been completed the fish continue to scoot over the eggs, fanning them vigorously with their pectoral fins to aerate them and keep debris from settling on them.

At 80-82°F. fanned and guarded by the steadfast parents who carefully remove any eggs which prove infertile by turning white, the amber colored eggs hatch in a couple of days. After hatching the eggs appear almost to be a wriggling mass of jelly. The babies, which are still adhered to the rock by adhesive organs on the head, flail their tails vigorously in celebration of their new-found life. If one should become so vigorous as to become unstuck and fall off the rock or go sailing off in its burst of uncoordinated effort, one or the other of the parents will quickly seize the youngster and spit it back to its place on the rock with the others.

Once the ports form a pair they begin to hunt for a suitable spawning site. Photo by L.E. Perkins.

At some time after hatching the helpless babies are usually transferred either to one of the pits which has been previously dug or perhaps even to another rock which has been cleaned. The transfer itself is a rather remarkable lesson in coordinated effort one parent guarding while the other picks up a mouthful of babies and moves them. Some pairs periodically exchange these duties, sharing equally in playing watchdog and hauling babies.

Once removed to the pit or other new location the babies are periodically picked up in the mouths of the parents, "chewed" vigorously to clean them, and spit back into the pit. Just before they become free-swimming they begin to "bounce" higher and higher out of the nest sometimes creating quite a chore for the parents to keep track of each and every one. Finally, however, the yolk sac is absorbed and almost miraculously the babies will rise in a cloud almost as one. The proud parents soon take the fry for an excursion around the tank to familiarize them with their surroundings. It is at this period of free swimming that they must first be

For more advanced hobbyists the very colorful *Hemichromis bimac-ulatus* II is a challenge. They are generally rougher in their spawning activities; mating sometimes results in the death of one of the pair. Spawning proceeds in the typical manner of the substrate spawners (opposite page). Once free-swimming, the fry will take newly hatched brine shrimp until their bellies buige (above). Photos by H.J. Richter.

fed. A combination of microworms and freshly hatched brine shrimp is excellent and will carry them rapidly to the size when other frozen or prepared foods are accepted.

This "typical" form of hard substrate spawning is used by many of the cichlids such as *Cichlasoma, Aequidens, Astronotus*, and such Africans as *Tilapia sparrmanii* and jewel fish, *Hemichromis bimaculatus*. The last-mentioned sometimes show a preference for spawning in a clay flower pot which has had the bottom knocked out. Otherwise the spawning procedure is the same.

ANGELFISH

The angelfish, *Pterophyllum scalare*, once called "King of the Aquarium," has perhaps been deposed in recent years by the discus, *Symphysodon discus* and *S. aequifasciata*. But there is still an air of regal dignity about a magnificent, mature angelfish which for sheer grace and form cannot be surpassed in the aquatic realm. Delicate of appearance they may be but they are cichlids at heart, and although continued interference from the outside can make them eat their spawn or babies through frustration, initial intrusions by the keeper's hand will be assailed with all the fury of a tigress in defense of her cubs. Almost everyone dreams of raising a tankful of fledgling angels and the feat is less difficult than might be expected. Six or eight young, healthy fish kept together and well fed in a spacious aquarium will, at maturity (at the end of a year more or less), begin to pair off. The "paired" fish begin to accompany each other and will be seen mutually investigating for a spawning site. The spawning site selected may be a broad, stiff plant leaf, a piece of slate leaned against the side of the aquarium or a piece of green tubing, to be used as a depository for their spawn.

Other fishes will be kept away as the site is prepared by biting, chewing and scraping the surface clean. Eventually, in reasonably warm water, the breeding tubes, or papillae, will appear. The female's tube is rather short and blunt, the male's longer and more narrow. Spawning from

Angelfishes select a more vertical spawning site, such as a piece of slate leaned against the side of a tank or, as in this instance, a broad leaf. Photo by R. Zukal.

here on is in rather conventional cichlid-style; egg-laying, fanning, removal of dead or infertile eggs, guarding, etc.

Angelfish are a bit more nervous than some cichlid species and upon too much provocation may make a meal of their eggs or progeny. While some cichlids are difficult to dispose of in the quantities that a good pair can produce even in one successful spawning, there is almost always a market for baby angelfish. So to circumvent the possibility of parental cannibalism of an almost sure-fire cash crop, most breeders who are serious about production remove the slate or leaf upon which the spawn was deposited to a gallon jar or other small container for separate hatching. An air stone is bubbled near the eggs for better circulation and many breeders add methylene blue until the eggs are barely visible in good light for fungus protection. Prolonged exposure to strong light is best avoided, but eggs should be periodically inspected so that any which turn white can be quickly removed so as not to endanger the others. A basting syringe is excellent for this purpose. After hatching, the babies will, in a day or two,

Like the flat surface of the stones, the leaf must also be thoroughly cleaned. Photo by H.J. Richter.

Egg deposition by the female proceeds as the male waits close by. Photo by H.J. Richter.

Fertilization by the male proceeds even as the female continues depositing more eggs. Photo by H.J. Richter.

Some hobbyists prefer to remove the parents immediately after spawning to prevent their eating the eggs. Care must be taken to prevent the eggs from fungusing, however. Photo by H.J. Richter.

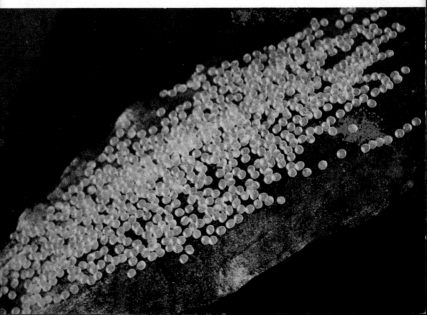

have fallen to the floor where they will stick together in a ball. This ball of youngsters may be "blown" apart periodically with a gentle, steady stream from the basting syringe. Depending upon temperature, *which should be kept from fluctuating as much as possible*, about a week or a bit less should see them to the free-swimming stage, at which time they can easily eat newly hatched brine shrimp. Microworms are also good during the first few days although they are best used in a bare aquarium.

Angelfish babies are ready to sell when their bodies have reached the size of a dime or slightly larger and when they are eagerly accepting high quality flake or other prepared food as well as frozen brine shrimp, finely ground beef heart or finely scraped fish or shrimp.

DISCUS

While discus, *Symphysodon discus* and *S. aequifasciata*, are seen in many pet shops and aquarium shops today a full treatise on their breeding, with the exception of an outline of the procedure, is beyond the scope of this book. They are, however, being spawned on a more regular basis as equipment and technique improves and as more aquarium-bred fish reach the market.

For years discus were considered next to impossible to breed successfully. Occasionally someone would raise a few babies almost as if by accident, but while spawning reports were not so infrequent as to be considered "rare," the babies almost invariably died soon after they became free-swimming. Finally Mrs. Lois Saphian of St. Louis, Missouri was able to successfully raise babies, getting them to feed successfully before they starved.

Because discus were very expensive and in most instances were possessed by experienced breeders of angelfish, the eggs were usually removed from the parents in order to prevent their being eaten. They spawned in rather typical angelfish style on plant leaves, strips of slate or other vertical objects, but since serious breeders of angels usually remove their eggs for separate hatching the precious discus eggs were

Parent discus take turns "feeding" the babies. Through a complex behavioral maneuver the young are shifted from one parent to the other. Photo by G. Budich.

treated in the same manner. Eggs hatched, babies became free-swimming, refused to eat and starved.

Then it was discovered by Gene Wolfsheimer of California and others that the natural first food of the babies was a special high protein slime which was secreted by the parents at breeding time. When babies were left with their parents, as soon as they were swimming they would flock to the sides of the adult fish, "plugging in" on this custom food supply and covering the sides of their providers almost like flies on a honey pie. A few days of this feeding and the baby discus are large enough to eat newly hatched brine shrimp and will begin to find them acceptable. From here on growth is rapid and the youngsters soon look like discus.

There are recent reports of other, more common cichlids such as *Aequidens portalegrensis*, the port cichlid, practicing this method of "body feeding" as a source of first food. It is not unknown in nature, since certain members of the catfish family Bagridae around India and surrounding areas practice "body feeding" to such a degree that the skin of the parent fish becomes extremely rough and reddened in brooding fish in the areas where their offspring have been feeding.

After some courtship and strength-testing, a male and female discus form a pair which will cooperate in further spawning activities. Photo by A.L. Pieter.

Once the egg-laying is completed both parents share the burden of guarding the eggs. At this time they should be left alone as much as possible. Photo by Dr. D. Terver, Nancy Aquarium, France.

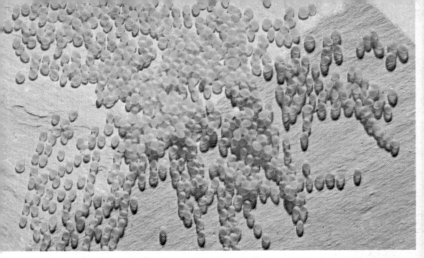

Eggs are usually placed on a vertical surface. They can be hatched artificially, but a special diet must be available for the fry. Photo by Dr. D. Terver, Nancy Aquarium, France.

If left with the parents the young take nourishment from the secretions of the parents' sides. Until recently the formula for a substitute diet was unknown. Photo by Dr. E. Schmidt-Focke.

DWARF CICHLIDS

The so-called "dwarf" cichlids belong for the most part to the two genera, *Nannacara* and *Apistogramma*, of South America. As with their larger brethren dwarf cichlids are quite deliberate in their actions. In some ways they are reminiscent of miniature game fish seeming quite sure of what they are doing as they go about their business.

The sexes of most dwarf cichlids are quite distinguishable when mature. The male is in most cases larger, more colorful and has longer and more pointed fins. Females, on the other hand, especially in the case of *Apistogramma* species, are usually rather plain in comparison and as a matter of fact are difficult to recognize as to species since many are quite similar in appearance. For this reason it is better for a would-be breeder to purchase stock from aquarium raised fish in order to be sure that the fish are the same species rather than to buy "mixed" dwarf cichlids which often represent a substantial savings per fish, but some of which might be of questionable heritage. As with other cichlids six or eight young fish purchased from a breeder will almost certainly assure the presence of at least one pair.

Dwarf cichlids in most cases follow rather standard cichlid breeding procedures for typical substrate spawners but with a few modifications. They enjoy access to caves and flower pots or other sheltered areas such as under rocks. Territories are established and choice spots are jealously guarded.

Spawning takes place in these sheltered sites with both mates, which are usually less violent in their mutual acceptance of each other than some of their larger relatives, participating in the pre-nuptial site preparation. The increased activity of the pair indicates their plans and in some cases their apparent attempts to look like they are not really "up to anything" can be quite comical. Surprisingly, the first sure sign of spawning, if the cave or other location is hidden from view, may be the banishment of the male from the scene. Despite her being vastly overmatched as far as weight is concerned, the onslaught of the female is too much. At times,

Two male *Nannacara anomala* lock jaws in a battle over the female waiting below. This behavior is also seen in pre-spawning sequences between males and females. Photo by R. Zukal.

unless the male is removed, he may be injured by his infuriated mate. From this point on she assumes brood care similar to that practiced by blue acaras, firemouths, etc., but with only one parent at the helm.

When the fry emerge they are cared for as with other cichlid fry. Generally they are large enough to accept the tiniest of brine shrimp nauplii or microworms.

A pair of dwarf cichlids can easily be kept and spawned in an aquarium of five gallons or so. In larger aquariums with plenty of rocks, pots, plants, etc., several pairs can be kept providing they are able to define precise territories.

For those who have a large aquarium available and are able to obtain "mixed" dwarf cichlids, a very interesting cichlid "community" can be set up. While females are difficult to distinguish as to species because of the similarity of one to another, the fishes themselves have no such problem and will select each other. In uncrowded, heavily furnished aquariums of this type with a mixed dwarf cichlid population, broods can actually be raised in the presence of others. Many aquarists, however, would prefer to remove the spawn when breeding occurs, hatching the eggs in a separate container or aquarium as described for other cichlids.

With a tank housing several pairs of the same species (here *Apistogramma cacatuoides*) there are often encounters between males such as this one. Photo by R. Zukal.

The extension of all fins and some vibrations of the body and tail fin serve as a threat to a neighboring fish. Photo by R. Zukal.

Guarding of the eggs and fry is shared by both parents. Here the male is at his post while the female is off in the background. Photo by R. Zukal.

At a signal, the male and female change places, the female taking over the duties of tending the eggs while the male remains in the background. Photo by R. Zukal.

MBUNAS

Seldom has such a splash hit the fishkeeping world than that caused by the sudden influx a number of years back of fantastic and spectacular cichlids from the African lake which at that time was commonly known as Lake Nyasa. The name has since been officially changed from "Lake Nyasa" to Lake Malawi since its waters rest mostly upon the shores of that country. The name "Lake Nyasa" was redundant to begin with, "Nyasa" means "lake" in Swahili, so there's really no need to say it twice despite the size of the monstrous 360 miles long body of water. In this vast impoundment cichlids have diversified almost beyond belief and fill almost every available role of specialization. To the aquarist, however, leading the group in most brilliant fashion and flaunting the colors of the rainbow are the mostly small, inshore-dwelling fishes collectively known as "Mbuna." While they have from time to time been designated by such labels as "Nyasa nasties" and simply "Malawis," the accepted name at this point is Mbuna (pronounced UM BOO' NAH) which is the Swahili word for the group.

The Mbunas live along the rocky shores of the lake, among and around the rocks where they can feed on the abundance of algae and invertebrate life found there. The various species have for the most part specialized toward one or the other (or even both) of these sources of nutrition, having developed a remarkable variety of structural adaptations of their teeth to fit their specialties.

The waters of Lake Malawi are hard and alkaline, the pH ranging from 7.6 to 8.6. As the marine aquarist is well aware it is difficult to maintain such high readings unless a few basic procedures are followed. First, the substrate or "gravel" is best composed of such saltwater standbys as dolomite (a kind of limestone often used in gardening because of its calcium and magnesium content), crushed oyster shells, or crushed coral. Also, it is recommended that about a tablespoon per gallon of good quality marine salt be added. A number of *Pseudotropheus* species have been spawned in soft, acid water in the aquarium, but it would seem best to

Large amounts of rockwork are essential to Mbuna tanks. The caves formed provide shelter for the fishes and are often used as spawning sites. Photo of *Labeotropheus fuelleborni* by R. Zukal.

match natural conditions where possible.

Large amounts of rockwork are essential in the Mbuna aquarium in order to provide plenty of caves and other retreats. The attempts to keep a single pair of, for instance, *Pseudotropheus elongatus*, together in an aquarium can be a disaster, with the dominant fish relentlessly persecuting the other until it may be either killed or injured. Several pairs, however, can create a more harmonious situation or more of a "standoff."

During spawning the ovipositor of the female may not be as noticeable as in the case of other cichlids, a factor which is even further emphasized by the comparatively small size of most Mbunas. Often, in a well set-up Mbuna aquarium, a spawning may go completely unnoticed without constant observation and the first indication something happened may be the somewhat expanded mouth of the female. Usually she will refuse food until her charges are released and free-swimming although there have been reports of the brood fish actually setting its precious cargo temporarily aside in order to take a snack. When the female is noticed to be carrying eggs she should be removed to another aquarium. Most Mbunas will hang relentlessly onto the eggs as

It is safer to include a number of pairs of Mbuna in a tank rather than a single pair. Aggressiveness is then spread around rather than directed at a single individual. Photo of albino *Pseudotropheus zebra* by Dr. Herbert R. Axelrod.

A flat surface generally is selected as the spawning site, but after the eggs are laid and fertilized they are picked up and held in the mouth of the female. Photo by L. Weiner.

Upturned flower pots may also serve as suitable "caves" for most cichlids. They provide the privacy often required before spawning will take place. Photo by L. Weiner.

Often spawning is not observed, and only when the female appears with a lowered gular region, as seen here, and refuses to eat does the aquarist know that it has taken place. Photo by L. Weiner.

they are being moved, and there is little danger of eggs or babies being eaten.

The typical courtship and spawning of most Mbuna species is much less involved socially between male and female than with most other cichlids. There is no "pair bond" as such, simply a rather brief courtship in which the female allows the male to approach, followed by side-by-side tail-slapping, mutual nudging and biting at the flanks, followed perhaps by brief pit-digging by the male. The pair circles each other, after which the female deposits a very few, surprizingly large, eggs each time in the nest. The male circles oppositely as his sperm is released. The eggs are picked up as they are deposited by the female, who continues to follow and "bite" at the so-called "dummy egg spots" found on the anal fins of many African cichlids. This allows her to "inhale" sperm-charged water, passing it over the eggs already in her mouth to insure their fertilization. Depending on the size and species involved the spawns may number from a very few eggs to about 25 or as many as 40 for very large females. Incubation time varies with temperature and species, but may run for 15-20 days at a temperature of 76-80F. (25-27C.).

For some reason some females break off relations with their offspring sooner than others. At times, as soon as the fry are released for the first time, the female will ignore them and leave them to forage on their own. Other females will sometimes even "dump" her eggs for one reason or another. If the eggs are found abandoned it is often worthwhile to try incubating them artificially. This is accomplished by scooping them up in a net and placing the net in another aquarium with equal water quality and temperature and allowing an airstone to bubble gently under it. Treat the water with acriflavine and give the eggs a mild "shake" once or twice daily to turn them. Remove any dead eggs immediately. When fry reach the free-swimming stage they can be raised as any others. Another successful method is to place the eggs in a narrow-neck bottle which is completely submerged. Bubble an air stone in the bottom just enough to keep the eggs in slight motion.

OTHER MOUTHBROODERS

Africa's mouthbrooders encompass a vast number of cichlids aside from the Mbunas. They include the *Sarotherodon* group, the *Haplochromis*-group and the *Pelmatochromis*-group, although not all have forsaken the more traditional parental guardianship roles. There are variations in their mouthbrooding procedures which seem to show evolutionary trends from the former "guarding" of a rock or open pit to more and more sophisticated oral incubation as refinements become incorporated.

In the majority of cases the female takes on brooding duties, in some instances only after the eggs have hatched. In other cases (for example *Sarotherodon*) both parents participate in brooding both eggs and young. In *Chromidotilapia guentheri* (formerly called *Pelmatochromis guentheri*) the eggs are brooded by the male while both parents brood the hatched young in their mouths. *Sarotherodon heudelotii*, the black-chin mouthbrooder (formerly called "*T. macrocephala*"), assigns brood duty of both eggs and babies to the male.

As if the mouthbrooding procedure itself were not enough to fascinate, to assure fertilization of the eggs a number of species have the anal fin of the male adorned with "dummy egg spots." These spots resemble eggs in size and color and as the female attempts to pick these false "eggs" up, she "inhales" sperm-laden water which passes over eggs already gathered, assuring fertilization.

Most of us familiar with cichlids of various sorts rather automatically equate "mouthbrooding" cichlids with Africa, while rock-spawning would seem to be more "typical" of South American cichlids. There are exceptions, however, and one of the more interesting South American cichlids, *Geophagus jurupari*, has combined the best of both worlds. Appearing in profile almost more like a toucan, or other tropical bird which never quite caught up proportionally to the size of its beak, than a fish, *Geophagus jurupari* is a strangely handsome, mild-mannered fish which continuously picks up mouthfuls of sand, chews it up and spits it back out after sift-

Male cichlids like this *Geophagus balzanii* male often develop an enlarged hump or bump over the eye as they grow older. Photo by H.J. Richter.

In delayed mouthbrooders the eggs are deposited on the spawning site in the normal fashion. Here the female is guarding the spawn. Photo by H.J. Richter.

After a day or two the eggs are picked up by the parent (usually the female) and brooded in typical mouthbrooder fashion (left). After the eggs have hatched the brooding continues, the fry being let out from time to time (right). Photos by H.J. Richter.

If danger approaches the fry are taken back into the mouth for protection (left). As the babies grow they are released more often, until eventually they remain out all the time (right). Photos by H.J. Richter.

ing out any nourishment which might be contained (as might be expected from the generic name *Geophagus* = earth-eater).

The "devil fish," as it is also known, spawns first on a rock or other object which has been thoroughly cleaned in typical cichlid fashion. The eggs are laid and fertilized textbook style. Some while later, however, the eggs have disappeared and the fish act a bit jittery and nervous and appearing for all the world like the household feline which had just successfully converted the family goldfish into groceries. Actually, closer observance shows the eggs merely to be covered with a layer of sand. The fish seem to have a most innocent expression on their "faces" as if they have no idea where the eggs could have gone.

A bit later the newly hatched babies actually do disappear, and the "expression" of incredible innocence on the countenances of the parents seems even more convincing. Closer observation will show the female to have a slightly "swollen" jaw where she has taken up the young for mouth brooding. The male should be removed although there are cases of both parents assuming normal cichlid duties after the fourteen day (more or less) brooding period. The devil fish is one of several cichlid species which have been observed taking adult brine shrimp or other food such as earthworms or white worms apparently "chewing it up" into tiny, almost microscopic particles and expelling the food into the midst of the swarming offspring.

Oddly enough another close relative, *Geophagus brasiliensis*, which is also called the pearl cichlid or mother-of-pearl cichlid because of the beautiful pearl-like spangles adorning the sides and fins of the fish, follows the textbook on "typical" cichlid breeding. There is the test of strength, site selection and preparation, spawning, guarding of young and generally doing what good cichlids do in parenthood.

X. BRINGING UP CICHLID BABIES

Breeding techniques of most cichlids have enough similarities that the babies of most species can be raised using, for the most part, a few similar procedures once eggs have been produced. Many breeders prefer to remove eggs from the parents in order to avoid the possibility of the eggs being eaten; others prefer the more natural technique of letting the parents raise their own offspring.

For "typical" spawners such as ports, *A. portalegrensis*, or congos, *C. nigrofasciatum*, it is a bit traumatic for fish and fishkeeper alike to rob them of their precious spawn. They will fly at the attacking hand with the determination of the last trusted defender of the king's jewels and look for all the world as if they intend to rip the invader apart, piece by piece. While more eggs can possibly be saved this way, certainly the natural way of leaving eggs with the parents is the more rewarding way from an esthetic viewpoint.

While few things could delight the heart of a true aquarist more than to peer into his own tank full of youthful cichlids being escorted by their parents, this turns out to be more practical with some of the stockier, more perch-like species. Angels and other more "delicate" species, seem more inclined to eat their eggs or spawn before the babies ever get to the free-swimming stage. For most, but not all, this is perhaps the most crucial point of all.

Without hesitation many breeders remove their eggs as soon as spawning is completed to insure against losses. The leaf, slate or other egg depository is removed to another, small aquarium or even a wide-mouth gallon jar containing water from the original aquarium. Methylene blue or acriflavine can be used to protect the eggs and an airstone should

Cichlasoma nigrofasciatum will fly at an intruding hand with the determination of the last trusted defender of the king's jewels. Photo by R. Zukal.

If the eggs are not fertilized they may eventually fungus. Here an *Apistogramma wickleri* female still guards a lost spawn, perhaps out of inexperience. Photo by H.J. Richter.

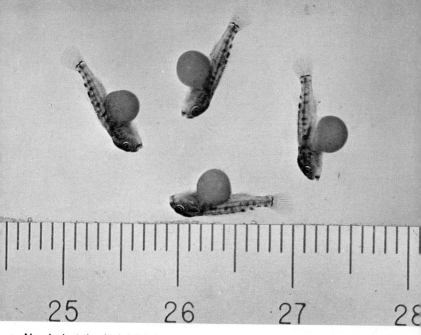

Newly hatched cichlid fry (like these Mbuna) have a yolk sac. Until this is absorbed and the fry become free-swimming they need not be fed. Photo by Dr. D. Terver, Nancy Aquarium, France.

In about three weeks female *Melanochromis auratus* release the babies for short feeding excursions. The females are able to take nourishment at this time also. Photo by A.F. Orsini.

Eggs are carefully tended by the cichlid parents. Fungused eggs are removed and the remaining eggs are fanned, causing fresh water to pass over them, keeping them clean and allowing better gaseous exchange. Photo of *Aequidens curviceps* by R. Zukal.

be bubbled just with enough force to keep the water in good circulation but not disturb the eggs. It is MOST important that temperature remain constantly within plus or minus two degrees of a base temperature. It is the lack of variation here, not the exact temperature, which is important. Example: with a base temperature of 27°C. fluctuations should not go above 28°C. or below 26°C.; with a base temperature of 26°C., fluctuation should go above 27°C. or below 24.5°C.

During the hatching period eggs which turn white or show signs of fungus should be removed. Some breeders prefer to do this with a needle, others with an eye dropper or a basting syringe. In a couple of days, depending on the temperature, the eggs become a wriggling mass of "jelly," each baby vibrating its tail violently in unison with the others.

At this point baby angels and other cichlids are hardly more than a yolk sac and a tail. For a few days the yolk sac is the source of nourishment for the baby fish and as this food source is absorbed the youngster gains in strength. As this happens, in their uncoordinated efforts to swim they may dislodge themselves and fall to the bottom. No harm is done and soon they all will probably have broken free and congested on the floor. More and more they make "leaps" out of the mass only to tumble downward again until finally, in a few days, they become free-swimming, often within such a short time of each other than it's as if a magic word had been said.

They should not be fed until this time. Free-swimming cichlid babies can in almost every instance eat freshly hatched brine shrimp and/or microworms. When bellies turn pink from shrimp and eyes turn black, they are obviously feeding. Some breeders, especially of smaller cichlids, supplement first feeding with "green water" or other sources of microscopic food such as infusoria. This is hardly necessary with most species, although it may help some of the slow starters develop more quickly.

Free-swimming babies can almost always be started on freshly hatched brine shrimp and/or microworms. Photo *Cichlasoma cyanoguttatum* by G. Marcuse.

As the yolk sac is absorbed the wriggling mass of "jelly" breaks up, with individual babies dislodging themselves and falling to the bottom. Photo of *Herotilapia multispinosa* fry by H.J. Richter.

In a few months angelfish fry will start to take on the characteristic vertically elongate shape as the dorsal and anal fins grow. Photo by H.J. Richter.

Like the discus, orange chromide *(Etroplus maculatus)* parents provide early nourishment to the fry through secretions from their sides.
Feeding by the fry from their parents' sides is known as "glancing"
or "contacting. Photo by H.J. Richter.

Cichlasoma nigrofasciatum is another cichlid that has been found to
engage in contacting, but to a much lesser degree; *C. nigrofasciatum*
fry can be more easily raised than discus fry, which are more dependent on the parental secretions. Photo by H.J. Richter.

One of the most astounding techniques used by cichlids is the process of feeding the babies through "glancing" or "contracting." Here the babies' first food is a high-protein slime secretion which they pick from the sides of their parents. This is mentioned in the section on "Breeding Discus" since it was the discovery of "glancing" in 1959-1960 which led to the first really consistently successful results in breeding discus. For years it was considered a "unique" procedure, the sole use of which was granted to this monarch of aquarium fishes.

Orange chromides (*Etroplus maculatus*) have been rather mysterious for years in that some of the most skilled breeders have never quite succeeded in spawning them, even employing the best technique they could muster. On the other hand, there have been occasions where the rankest of amateurs have spawned this handsome little cichlid again and again. I recall many years ago being told by an exceptionally skilled breeder who did his fishkeeping "by the seat of his pants" instead of through literary endeavor, that the reason he was flooding the local market with orange chromides while no one else could seem to breed them was because he let the parents raise the babies. He didn't know the reason, but he knew the rhyme. It is known now that the orange chromides participate in "glancing" or "contacting," although babies have occasionally been raised successfully while removed from their parents.

The list grows longer, *Cichlasoma labiatum*, *C. nigrofasciatum* (rarely), *C. beani*, *C. managuense* and *C. spilurum* (among others) have been observed to glance or contact as a normal part of their behavior. These, for the most part, seem certainly less dependent on the procedure than *Symphysodon*, but at least it makes an excellent back-up system should the supply of bite-size baby food become scarce.

XI. CICHLIDS IN COMMUNITY AQUARIUMS

Despite the notoriety of some of the larger *Cichlasoma* and other similar cichlids, they often fit perfectly into certain community aquarium situations. Many of these larger cichlids never have the opportunity to achieve their full magnificence when kept in their own aquariums. While spawning cichlids usually display their most beautiful colors, they can in some cases become rather drab between times. Fish kept in pairs tend to quarrel from time to time resulting in less-than-perfect fins, occasionally missing scales and other signs of physical disagreement. At times the disputes become so serious that it may be necessary to separate the pair in order to avoid injury to one or the other of the pair.

For those who have very large community aquariums containing large fishes, this can be an excellent place to "rest" large breeding pairs of cichlids. Suddenly, faced with the presence of other fishes the "pair bond" often becomes strengthened, the fish presenting themselves as such as a competitive, but usually not overly aggressive, unit. Colors often intensify to the point that the pair is in semi-breeding garb for the greater part of the time. Fins become more elongated and more contrastingly patterned and the fish generally present their best appearance, growth and often most harmonious behavior.

Among the most magnificent individual cichlids which have been observed by the author have been "loners," single individuals of species such as blue acara, Jack Dempsey, port

Some individual cichlids, for example the Jack Dempsey *(Cichlasoma octofasciatum),* have been observed by the author to develop into magnificent specimens as "loners." Photo by Dr. Herbert R. Axelrod.

Large cichlids are best kept with other large cichlids. Here *Cichlasoma managuense* shares a tank with, among others, an oscar, *Astronotus ocellatus.* Photo by Dr. R.J. Goldstein.

Most cichlid aquaria should be provided with many rocks and few plants. Included in this tank are angelfish *(Pterophyllum scalare)* and flag cichlids *(Cichlasoma festivum).* Photo by Dr. Herbert R. Axelrod.

Cichlasoma severum when young is a relatively peaceful fish. As it grows older it becomes more quarrelsome and less suitable for a community tank. Photo by Aaron Norman.

cichlid, severum, *Sarotherodon mossambica*, convicts and others. These were not "zoo" specimens or inhabitants of a public aquarium which could allow them larger quarters and better facilities than most aquarists could provide; they were fishes owned by individuals who simply enjoyed keeping larger fishes together. Strangely, the fishes involved seemed invariably to mellow with age and increasing size. Even notorious species are often content to live harmoniously in an aquarium with other fishes of comparable size when kept singly.

Among the better community tank companions for larger cichlids are large tinfoil barbs, large gouramies, *Mylossoma* species of "silver dollars," (not *Metynnis*, which may nip the fins of large cichlids), large sucker catfish (Loricariidae) and numerous other larger and more mild-mannered species. Not recommended are *Leporinus* spp., *Anostomus* spp., *Abramites* and other anostomids (Family Anostomidae) which are among the worst offenders in nipping fins of slower, more deliberate fishes such as cichlids. These fishes can relieve a beautiful show cichlid of a magnificent, trailing dorsal extension while maintaining a "look" of almost incredible "innocence" and "surprise" when the molested fish leap half way across the tank and perhaps crashes into the glass. Most *Metynnis* and other "silver dollars," with the exception of *Mylossoma*, can hardly resist taking a nip at long, trailing fins. Certain barbs present the same problem although tinfoils (*B. schwanenfeldii*) are among the gentlest and least offensive of large aquarium fishes in regard to compatibility with others.

One memorable "community" I recall was in a public aquarium in which a huge tank containing several thousand gallons of water, several large stumps and logs and a number of extremely large fishes such as shovelnose cats (*Sorubim lima*), tiger cats (*Pseudoplatystoma fasciatum*), various other large, predatory catfishes, a couple of huge arowanas (*Osteoglossum*) and assorted other great and predatory fishes including several species of huge cichlids. Swimming apparently without concern among this assemblage of hungry mouths was a tremendous, unblemished pair of "red devil" cichlids,

Parent fishes work as a team in caring for the young. They have signals which are interpreted by the young as "change direction," "tighten the formation," etc. Photo of *Cichlasoma meeki* with young by R. Zukal.

herding rather loosely between them several thousand babies about one-half inch long. The huge cloud of youngsters and their response to parental suggestion such as "change direction" or "tighten the formation" or whatever other message might be offered was a thrilling glimpse at the family life and discipline of these creatures under conditions approaching those in nature, where the game is survival. I was told that the pair had actually raised young in this situation successfully.

Deliberately "mixing" species can be advantageous when this is used as a device to stimulate spawning or simply to invigorate listless fish which seem to have lost their zest for life and possibly their appetites with no apparent reason. Discus at times seem to lose interest and become not only

Substitutes for rockwork can be used in cichlid tanks. This red zebra *(Pseudotropheus zebra)* adapted well to the plastic arches. Photo by A. Kochetov.

A community tank housing only Mbunas from Lake Malawi. Driftwood can often be used to good advantage in combination with rocks. Photo by Dr. Herbert R. Axelrod.

Single-species tanks are often necessary with more quarrelsome species. *Hemichromis bimaculatus* is one of these species. Photo by Dr. D. Terver, Nancy Aquarium, France.

African lake cichlids do best in a tank set up with only rocks. If live plants are desired, be ready to replant them often. Photo by Dr. Herbert R. Axelrod.

very shy but also "picky" about food which previously would have been gobbled up with greed. The introduction of half a dozen or so ravenous young angelfish will often bring about a total change almost immediately. As with almost any cichlid, discus have a certain amount of territorialism and competition built into them, and the arrival of a set of new upstarts of reasonably similar form which would appear not only to lack respect for their elders but would also attempt to usurp grazing rights, can raise the adrenalin level of the original homesteaders to a point of throwing themselves back into the competition with all flags flying! No harm is done, since angels can "take it."

There are a number of species such as "kribs" or "kribensis" (*Pelvicachromis pulcher*), several of the mbunas, as well as *Cichlasoma* and *Aequidens* spp. which for one reason or another seem content to swim about the breeding aquarium day after day without doing the business intended. At times this may go so far as to change what had been a compatible pair to almost impossibly quarrelsome. By introducing other fishes which they consider competitive, spawning may very well be triggered rather quickly. Since fighting could break out between the old and the new, this is easily averted by putting a partition between the two groups. Introduction of a single "competitor" such as a common goldfish may be all it takes, although the goldfish could take a bit of a beating if the pair becomes really outraged.

Several of the Mbunas, for example *Pseudotropheus elongatus*, can seem almost impossibly aggressive, the male pursuing the female relentlessly and unmercifully. Oddly enough, one of the more practical and workable answers here is to add more fish of the same species; as one Mbuna expert put it, "The more the merrier!" If enough retreats are available the aggressiveness of an individual will at least be spread among several others instead of only one. There is also the possibility that a reasonably harmonious "standoff" may occur in which each would-be yard-boss is too busy looking over his own shoulder in defense to head up a good offense.

XII. DISEASES AND PARASITES OF CICHLIDS

Cichlids are subject to a number of maladies including most of the "common" tropical fish diseases such as "ich," velvet disease, various bacterial infections, flukes, etc. Fortunately, they are less susceptible to certain diseases than many fishes and because of the robust nature of many species seem to suffer less ill effects than less sturdy fishes.

One of the oldest and most recommended rules of fish-keeping which is routinely broken by even the most experienced aquarists is that of isolating or quarantining every new fish for a few days before introducing it to an established aquarium. For some reason, even the most learned piscophile cannot, at times, resist putting new fishes into old situations. If such a gamble works, OK, but if it doesn't there can be a major epidemic within a few days which may cause the loss of irreplaceable fishes. Many fishes which appear completely disease-free have been either pond-raised or imported and may carry parasites or diseases which are not immediately apparent. A few days in isolation will generally allow any symptoms to develop and treatment is generally easier in an unfurnished quarantine tank than in an established aquarium.

When moving fish into a new situation, no matter if they have just been purchased or just been shipped, the use of one of the recently available "water conditioning preparations" can do wonders in preventing the occurrence of problems. It is not exactly a "medication," but has its effectiveness in helping avoid the shock and trauma of moving which often may weaken fish enough to make them susceptible to infection. This is very important because many times a fish which seems "clean" but which in reality may have a

Avoid a fish that appears lethargic and keeps its fins tightly closed. Even healthy-looking fishes may carry disease and should be quarantined before being placed with other fishes. Photo of *Tilapia shirana* by M. Oliver.

Oodinium disease is caused by a dinoflagellate with a free-swimming stage. Shown here are numerous daughter cells produced by cell division. Infected fish have a "velvety" appearance. Photo by Dr. H.-H. Reichenbach-Klinke.

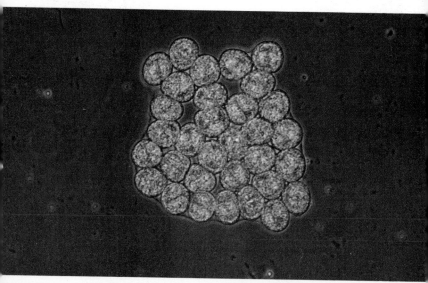

This *Tilapia* is infected with a mild case of *Ichthyophthirius multifilis,* or "ich." If detected early enough it is curable.

Close-up of cells of *Ichthyophthirius multifilis* imbedded in the fins. Photo by Frickhinger.

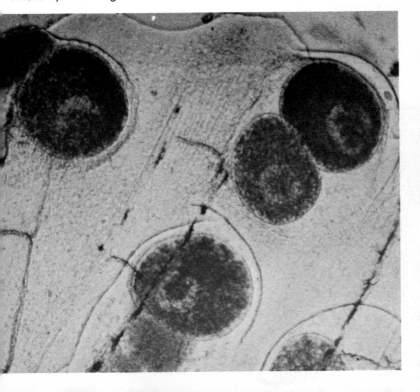

parasite or two present but not noticeably active, may suddenly through stress become subject to a veritable explosion of parasites.

Look very carefully at new cichlids to be purchased. Make sure their fins are free of blemishes, red spots or "worn" looking ends which might indicate bacterial disease. Their eyes should be clear and their body free of spots or cloudiness. Fishes should act alert and hungry. If possible get the dealer to feed them so you make sure there is no problem here.

OODINIUM. . . "VELVET" OR "RUST" DISEASE

Oodinium is similar to ich but the spots are much smaller and less distinct. It is caused by a dinoflagellate with a free-swimming stage. Infected fish have a "velvety" appearance to their skin and look as if they had been sprinkled with tan or rust-colored powder. Treatment is easily accomplished by adding 4 drops of formalin per gallon to the aquarium. Temperature may be raised to 80°F (26°C) to hasten the cure.

Texas cichlid *(Cichlasoma cyanoguttatum)* with early stages of tail rot. Antibiotics can be used in the treatment. Photo by R. Zukal.

ICHTHYOPHTHIRIUS MULTIFILIS OR "ICH"

"Ich" is the most common aquarium disease and almost every species of freshwater fish is susceptible to it, especially young or debilitated fish. It is caused by a protozoan parasite which as a free-swimming parasite attaches itself to a host fish, usually within twenty-four hours of its becoming free-swimming. It imbeds in the skin of the fish, feeding on its hosts' body juices and forms a cyst which eventually falls to the bottom of the aquarium where it matures and releases up to one thousand or more free-swimming tomites.

It is during this free-swimming stage that most controls for ich are effective, although some of the ich medications on the market, of which there is an ever-expanding proliferation, claim to kill all stages of ich.

Aside from the "store-bought" medications, many of which are quite good, formaldehyde, or more correctly, formalin which is about 37% formaldehyde, is a reasonably effective cure. Four drops per gallon can be added to the aquarium and if the temperature is raised to 80-82°F (26-28°C), treatment time is shortened.

Symptoms of *Ichthyophthirius* are well known to most aquarists. In early stages "scratching" against rocks, plants and other objects often occurs and there is a loss of appetite. White spots, almost like grains of salt sprinkled on the fish, appear on the fins and body of the fish, while the fins become clamped and the fish just generally does not "look" good.

Ich is very contagious and great care must be taken not to pass it from one aquarium to the next.

BACTERIAL DISEASES

The breakdown of fin or skin tissue, often accompanied by folded fins, listlessness, convulsions, malformation, dropsy or discoloration is often indicative of bacterial infection. Virulent bacterial diseases can cause rapid die-off, while non-virulent types are slower to cause large-scale mortality and allow at least some time for treatment if recognized early enough.

Head-on view of a discus which is suffering from hole-in-the-head disease possibly caused by the flagellate *Hexamita*. Photo by Frickhinger.

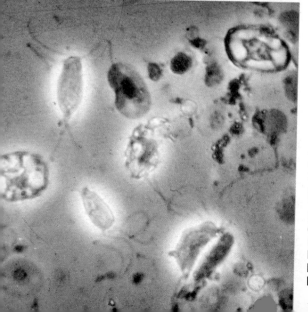

A microscopic study of the flagellate *Hexamita*. Treatment includes preparations containing Metronidazol. Photo by Dr. H.-H. Reichenbach-Klinke.

A plasmodium of *Oodinoides* (another organism suspected in causing hole-in-the-head disease) producing a sporangium Photo by Dr. H.-H. Reichenbach-Klinke.

Hole-in-the-head disease can attack many species of cichlids, such as this *Haplochromis polystigma*, although it is most often thought of as a disease peculiar to the discus. Photo by Dr. H.-H. Reichenbach-Klinke.

The "hole-in-the-head" disease of discus and similar infections which have been reported in oscars (*Astronotus*) and angelfish is quite possibly caused by a bacterial infection and in a number of cases seems to be circumstantially linked to the feeding of tubifex worms. This, as well as other bacterial diseases, can be difficult to cure.

Antibiotics seem most effective and work best when given internally, adding it to the food. Terramycin® (oxytetracycline) is less expensive than tetracycline and can be added to food in a proportion of about 200 mg. to 4 ounces of fish food. This should be fed for ten days and then discontinued. Tetracycline or nitrofurazone can also be used, and a commercially available "one-drop" to a pinch of food which contains Chloromycetin® seems to have merit with bacterial infections.

While internal medication for bacterial infection is by far preferred, in cases where this is not possible for one or another reasons, water soluble antibiotics are useful in treating the aquarium water. Dosages should be administered in a proportion of 50 mg. of the active ingredient to 10 gallons of water and may be repeated every other day. My first choice is again Terramycin® . Tetracycline has been successful in a number of instances, but with heavy aeration it tends to "foam" out of solution and become deposited on the glass above the water line.

PARASITIC COPEPODS. . . *ARGULUS, LERNAEA*, ETC.

Several species of copepods, which are crustaceans and are related to *Cyclops* and *Daphnia*, are parasitic to fishes. They usually attack scaled fishes and attach themselves to an area where there is a good blood supply. Small abscessed lesions (sometimes resembling a pimple) appear and the fish involved often brushes against objects or "scratches" itself on the bottom in an effort to relieve itself of its unwanted guest.

Lernaea or anchor worms sometimes become rather deeply imbedded, but close examination will usually show the creature "dangling" in the water from its toe-hold posi-

Lernaea cyprinacea deeply imbedded in a fish's skin tissue. Anchor worms usually succumb to treatment with salt. Photo by W.A. Tomey.

tion. It has been suggested that scissors be used to simply cut the exposed part off of deeply seated *Lernaea*. Most cichlids can stand a considerable amount of salt and *Lernaea* will usually succumb to about 3 teaspoons added to the aquarium water. Dylox (obtainable at veterinary supply stores) is effective used once per week for four weeks with a strength of .25ppm (parts per million).

Grubs, larval worms of various kinds, may show up on fins or skin as little black, yellow or white spots in the skin. These usually disappear after a time since they ordinarily need an intermediate host after reaching maturity and leave the fish before more can be produced.

A green terror, *Aequidens rivulatus,* covered with lymphocystis disease. Although there is no known treatment for this viral disease, infected fishes may recover by themselves. Be sure to isolate the diseased fishes. Photo by Dr. H.W. Huizinga.

A close-up view of the fish louse *Argulus.* These parasites do not usually survive long in warm water. Photo by Dr. E. Elkan.

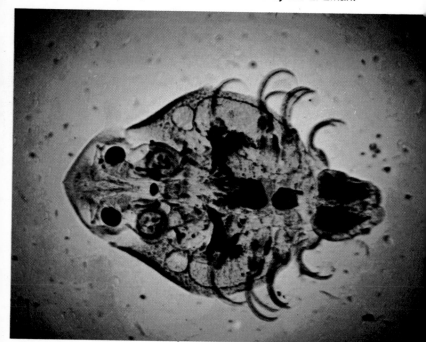

The yellow grub trematode *(Clinostomum)* over the eye of a kribensis *(Pelvicachromis pulcher)*. Grubs usually disappear after a time because of the lack of an intermediate host. Photo by R. Zukal.

A view of the entire anchor worm *(Lernaea)*. This parasite can sometimes be removed by snipping off the small portion of the fin in which it has become imbedded. Photo by Dr. F. Meyer.

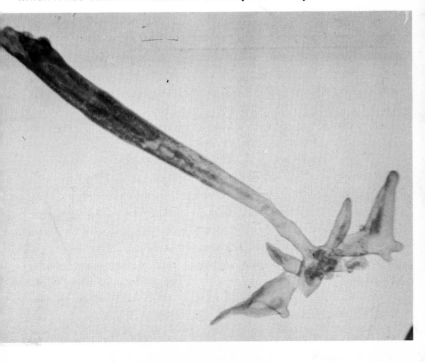

XIII. CONCLUSION

The family Cichlidae seems to offer something to every fishkeeper no matter what his taste, purpose or facilities might be. From delicate dwarfs like *Apistogramma reitzigi* to streamlined voracious predators like *Crenicichla*, the pike cichlid, keeping and breeding one or another can be accommodated in aquariums from 2½ gallons up to hundreds of gallons. From the incredible beauty and grace of mature discus to the downright homeliness of the bizarre bumphead, *Steatocranus*, cichlids seem to have decided somewhere in their evolutionary past to try nearly everything at least once.

They have become favorite tools of the behaviorist because of the remarkable relationships between parents and young as well as between adults in their interactions with each other. There is a vast amount of knowledge to be gained through cichlids in the field of animal communication since they definitely attribute certain meanings to certain fin movements, body actions and even color changes. More research needs to be done on the possibility of sonic communication since some cichlids definitely produce sound.

Fish and game departments have shown interest in several species, including *Cichla ocellaris*, the so-called "peacock bass" for possible introduction into southern regions as a game fish. Some cichlids have accidentally become established already in Florida.

Cichlids are adaptable creatures in many cases and they may one day play a very important role in feeding the protein poor countries of the world because of their adaptability to pond culture. Several *Tilapia* species have been experimentally cultured in China, southeast Asia and even some of the islands in the Carribbean, since they are capable of converting non-useful vegetable waste such as rice hulls into usable protein. Their quality as food is excellent, similar to our North American sunfishes, and they are becoming of increasing interest to fish farmers in the United States.

INDEX

Page numbers printed in **bold** refer to photographs.

Aequidens, 38, 46
  curviceps, **36, 37, 70**
  portalegrensis, 35, **40,** 51, 67
  pulcher, **16**
  rivulatus, 92
Anchor worm, 91, **93**
Angelfish, 5, 20, 46, **47, 48,**   **77,** 90
Apistogramma, 5, 54
  agassizi, **17**
  cacatuoides, **56, 57**
  reitzigi, 94
  wickleri, **68**
Argulus, 90, **92**
Astronotus, 46
  ocellatus, 32, **33, 76**

Bacterial diseases, 87, 90
Biological filtration, 24
Black acara, 38
Breeding
  angelfish, 46-47, 50
  discus, 50-51
  dwarf cichlids, 54-55
  Mbunas, 58-59
  other mouthbrooders, 63, 66
  port cichlid, 35,   42-43

Centrarchidae, 5
Chanchito, 9
Chloromycetin, 90
Chromidotilapia guentheri, 63
Cichla ocellaris, 94
Cichlasoma, 16, 38, 75
  beani, 74
  cyanoguttatum, 9, **71, 86**
  facetum, 9
  festivum, **77**
  labiatum, 74
  managuense, 74
  meeki, **79**

  nigrofasciatum, 67, **68, 73,** 74
  octofasciatum, 9
  severum, **77**
  spilurum, 74
Cichlid aquarium, 10-14
Cichlid spot, 38
Cichlidae, 9
Clinostomum, **93**
Community aquarium, 75, 78-79, 82
Community tank fishes, 78
Congo bonanza, 10
Congos, 67
Contacting, 74

DH (degrees hardness), 18
Diatom filter, 28
Discusfish, **4,** 5,   46, 50, **51, 52, 53**
Diseases of cichlids, 83, 86-87, 90
Dwarf cichlids, 5, 54
Dylox, 91

Earthworm, 31
Egg spots, 62, 63
Egyptian mouthbrooder, 9
Etroplus maculatus, 11, **73,** 74
  suratensis, 11

Feeding,   29-32, 34
Filtration, 24-28
Fish louse, **92**
Flag cichlid, **77**
Fluorescent lighting, 16-17
Formalin, 86, 87
Frozen foods, 32

Gammarus, 32
Geophagus
  balzanii, **64, 65**
  braziliensis, 66
  jurupari, **8,** 63
Glancing, 74
Green terror, **92**

Green water, 71

Heckel discus, 7
Hemichromis bimaculatus, 9, **81**
Hemichromis bimaculatus II, **44, 45,** 46
Herotilapia multispinosa, **72**
Hexamita, 89
Hole-in-the-head, **88, 89,** 90
Hoods, 16

Ich, 21, **85,** 87
Ichthyophthirius multifilis, **85,** 87
Jack Dempsey, 7, 9
Jewelfish, 7, 9

Kribensis, **10,** 82, **93**

Labeotropheus fuelleborni,   **59**
Lamprologus brichardi, **19**
Lake Malawi, 10, 58
Lake Nyasa, 58
Lake Tanganyika, 10
Lernaea, 90, 91, **93**
  cyprinacea, **91**
Lighting, 15-17
Live foods, 30-32
Lobochilotes labiatus, **6**

Mbuna, 58-59, **69, 80,** 82
Mealworms, 30, **31**
Mechanical filtration, 24
Melanochromis auratus, **13, 69**
Methylene blue, 70
Miraculous Draught, 38
Mouthbrooding, 62, 63, 66
Mozambique mouthbrooder, 9

Nannacara anomala, **55**

Oodinoides, **89**
Oodinium, 21, 86
Oodinium disease, **84**
Orange chromide, **11,** 74
Oscars, **33, 76,** 90

Parasitic copepods, 90-91
Paretroplus, 11
Peacock bass, 94
Pearl cichlid, 66
Pelmatochromis guentheri, 63

Pelvicachromis pulcher, **10,** 82, **93**
pH, 18
Photosynthesis, 15
Pike cichlid, 94
Plants, 14
Port cichlid, 9, 35
Ports, **43,** 67
Power filter, 27
Pseudocrenilabrus multicolor, 9
Pseudotropheus elongatus, 59, 82
Pseudotropheus zebra, **7, 60, 61, 81**
Pterophyllum scalare, **1,** 9, 46, **77**

Red zebra, **80**
Rift lakes, 11
Rust disease, 86

Sarotherodon heudolotii, 63
Sarotherodon mossambica, 9, 78
Soap test, 18
Sponge-type filtration, 25-26
Symphysodon, **4,** 5, 74
  aequifasciata, 11, 46, 50
  discus, 11, 46, 50

Tail rot, **86**
Temperature, 21-23, 70
Terramycin, 90
Territories, 13
Tetracycline, 90
Texas cichlid, **86**
Tilapia, 16, 22, 23, 32, **85**
  aurea, 22, **23**
  galilaea, **39**
  macrocephala, 63
  shirana, **84**
  sparrmanii, 46
  species, **27**
Tomites, 87

Undergravel filtration, 26-27

Vegetable food, 32, 34
Velvet, 21, 86

Water, 12, 18-20

Yellow grub trematode, **93**
Yolk sac, **69,** 70

Zebra angelfish, **1**